**Association for
Computing Machinery**

Advancing Computing as a Science & Profession

WiSec'12

Proceedings of the Fifth ACM Conference on

Security and Privacy in Wireless and Mobile Networks

Sponsored by:
ACM SIGSAC

Supported by:
AT&T, Ephibian, and University of Arizona - College of Engineering

**Association for
Computing Machinery**

Advancing Computing as a Science & Profession

The Association for Computing Machinery
2 Penn Plaza, Suite 701
New York, New York 10121-0701

Notice to Past Authors of ACM-Published Articles
ACM intends to create a complete electronic archive of all articles and/or other material previously published by ACM. If you have written a work that has been previously published by ACM in any journal or conference proceedings prior to 1978, or any SIG Newsletter at any time, and you do NOT want this work to appear in the ACM Digital Library, please inform permissions@acm.org, stating the title of the work, the author(s), and where and when published.

ISBN: 978-1-4503-1265-3 (Digital)

ISBN: 978-1-4503-1724-5 (Print)

Additional copies may be ordered prepaid from:

ACM Order Department
PO Box 30777
New York, NY 10087-0777, USA

Phone: 1-800-342-6626 (USA and Canada)
+1-212-626-0500 (Global)
Fax: +1-212-944-1318
E-mail: acmhelp@acm.org
Hours of Operation: 8:30 am – 4:30 pm ET

Printed in the USA

ACM WiSec 2012 Welcome Message

Wireless technologies have had significant impact on how society views computing and communication. Ubiquitous wireless network access has caused a dramatic shift in how we apply network services, moving us ever closer towards the "anytime anywhere" promise of the mobile Internet. However, the same affordability and availability of wireless technologies that make them so attractive also make them an enticing target for security threats.

As a community, we are asked to continuously adapt and expand our definition of "wireless security." Achieving security and privacy over an open broadcast medium using affordable and increasingly programmable wireless devices in an environment where new mobile and social applications are continuously deployed (often without accounting for security into their design) is fraught with challenges. Compounded by the fact that security associations must be made without prior trust relationships, these challenges call for new techniques to address the emergence of new types of threats.

The ACM Conference on Security and Privacy in Wireless and Mobile Networks has been a premier venue for researchers in wireless security and privacy to present the latest research in the field. It has also served as a forum for fostering international collaboration to address eminent security threats faced by our society. Over the years, we have seen an evolution in research, from traditional network security to complex, multi-faceted security problems that cannot be effectively addressed using conventional techniques. In particular, we have witnessed the emergence of new wireless systems (e.g., cognitive radios, RFID, vehicular networks, 4G/WiMax), the widespread deployment of new communication platforms (e.g., smartphones) and of their applications (e.g., social media), as well as an increased awareness of privacy issues associated with these emerging technologies.

The WiSec'12 call-for-papers attracted 63 submissions from Asia, Australia, Europe, and the United States. We saw many exciting papers cross our (virtual) desks, and after a thorough review process (many thanks to the reviewers for their diligence), we arrived at a collection of 17 papers that we felt are mature and ready to be presented to the security community and to be included in the conference proceedings. The 17 accepted papers can be broadly classified into the following themes:

- Physical-layer security for wireless systems
- Privacy in wireless systems
- Mobile device and application security
- Supply chain and manufacturing security
- Foundations of wireless network security

We have chosen to arrange the talks according to these rough topical areas, realizing that such a classification is never perfect and hoping that the authors and the audience appreciate all the talks for their individual and collective merit.

In addition to the research papers being presented at the conference, we also have two exciting keynotes, to be delivered by Dr. Ed Felten, Princeton University and the Federal Trade Commission ("Toward a Healthy Wireless Privacy Ecosystem") and Dr. Tadayoshi Kohno, University of Washington ("Security for Cyber-physical Systems: Case Studies with Medical Devices, Robots, and Automobiles"). We are fortunate to have both speakers, who have made significant contributions to security research at various levels, ranging from foundational contributions in cryptography, to system implementations and hacks, to guiding public policy. In addition to the two keynotes, the program includes two exciting panels, which aim at engaging industry, government, and academia in defining the problem space for security and privacy in wireless and mobile networks. Finally, we have included a poster session, with the goal of encouraging researchers to share their work-in-progress. We sincerely hope that you will take the opportunity to visit these posters and interact with their presenters.

Putting together ACM WiSec'12 was a team effort. We first would like to thank all authors for supporting the conference by submitting their manuscripts and providing the technical content of the program. We are grateful to all technical program committee members for their valuable reviews and their efforts in shepherding conditionally accepted papers. Special thanks go to Patrick Tague (Publicity Chair), Reza Curtmola (Proceedings Chair), Cristina Nita-Rotaru (Poster/Demo Chair), and Alejandro Proaño (Web Chair) for their efforts in making WiSec'12 a success. We also thank April Mosqus, Maritza Nichols, Adrienne Criscti, and Stephanie Sabal from ACM for their timely assistance and organizational support. We gratefully acknowledge the support of our host the University of Arizona, ACM SIGSAC, and our generous corporate supporters, AT&T Security Research Center and Ephibian. Last, but not least, we appreciate the trust and guidance of the WiSec Steering Committee.

We hope that you find this year's program interesting and thought-provoking. Enjoy the conference and the beautiful Tucson.

General Chairs
Marwan Krunz and Loukas Lazos

Technical Program Chairs
Roberto Di Pietro and Wade Trappe

Table of Contents

Session 4: Supply Chain and Manufacturing Security

Session 5: Foundations of Wireless Network Security

Author Index

2012 WiSec Conference Organization

General Chairs: Marwan Krunz *(University of Arizona, USA)*
Loukas Lazos *(University of Arizona, USA)*

Program Chairs: Roberto Di Pietro *(Università di Roma Tre, Italy)*
Wade Trappe *(Rutgers University, USA)*

Publicity Chair: Patrick Tague *(Carnegie Mellon University, USA)*

Proceedings Chair: Reza Curtmola *(New Jersey Institute of Technology, USA)*

Poster/Demo Chair: Cristina Nita-Rotaru *(Purdue University, USA)*

Web Chair: Alejandro Proaño *(University of Arizona, USA)*

Steering Committee Chair: Gene Tsudik *(University of California, Irvine, USA)*

Steering Committee: Levente Buttyan *(BME, Hungary)*
Claude Castelluccia *(INRIA, France)*
Virgil Gligor *(Carnegie Mellon University, USA)*
Jean-Pierre Hubaux *(EPFL, Switzerland)*
Douglas Maughan *(DHS/HSARPA, USA)*
Peng Ning *(North Carolina State University, USA)*
Adrian Perrig *(Carnegie Mellon University, USA)*
Radha Poovendran *(University of Washington, USA)*
Nitin Vaidya *(University of Illinois, USA)*
Cliff Wang *(Army Research Office, USA)*
Dirk Westhoff *(NEC Europe Network Lab, Germany)*

Program Committee: Jaime C. Acosta *(U.S. Army Research Laboratory, USA)*
Giuseppe Ateniese *(University of Rome "La Sapienza", Italy)*
Gildas Avoine *(UC Louvain, Belgium)*
Arati Baliga *(AT&T, USA)*
Sonja Buchegger *(Royal Institute of Technology, Sweden)*
Mike Burmester *(Florida State University, USA)*
Levente Buttyan *(BME, Hungary)*
Srdjan Čapkun *(ETH Zurich, Switzerland)*
Claude Castelluccia *(INRIA, France)*
Yingying Chen *(Stevens Institute of Technology, USA)*
Mauro Conti *(University of Padua, Italy)*
Sajal K. Das *(University Texas at Arlington, USA)*
Emiliano De Cristofaro *(PARC, USA)*

Program Committee (continued):

Robert Deng *(Singapore Management University, Singapore)*
Tassos Dimitriou *(Athens Information Technology, Greece)*
Xuhua Ding *(Singapore Management University, Singapore)*
Karim Eldefrawy *(Hughes Research Laboratory, USA)*
Stephen Farrell *(Trinity College Dublin, Ireland)*
Philip Ginzboorg *(Nokia Research Center, Finland)*
Virgil Gligor *(Carnegie Mellon University, USA)*
Urs Hengartner *(University of Waterloo, Canada)*
Yih-Chun Hu *(University of Illinois at Urbana-Champaign, USA)*
Frank Kargl *(University of Twente, The Netherlands)*
Javir Lopez *(University of Malaga, Spain)*
Wenjing Lou *(Virginia Tech, USA)*
Di Ma *(University of Michigan, USA)*
Ivan Martinovic *(University of California Berkeley, USA)*
Suhas Mathur *(AT&T, USA)*
Rene Mayrhofer *(Upper Austria University of Applied Sciences, Austria)*
Refik Molva *(Institut Eurecom, France)*
Yi Mu *(University of Wollongong, Australia)*
Cristina Nita-Rotaru *(Purdue University, USA)*
Guevara Noubir *(Northeastern University, USA)*
Kaisa Nyberg *(Aalto University, Finland)*
Gabriele Oligeri *(University of Trento, Italy)*
Melek Önen *(Institut Eurecom, France)*
Radha Poovendran *(University of Washington, USA)*
Kasper Bonne Rasmussen *(University of California Irvine, USA)*
Ahmad-Reza Sadeghi *(TU Darmstad, Germany)*
Nitesh Saxena *(Polytechnic Institute of New York University, USA)*
Jean-Pierre Seifert *(TU Berlin, Germany)*
Elaine Shi *(University of California, Berkeley, USA)*
Abdullatif Shikfa *(Alcatel-Lucent Lab, France)*
Tao Shu *(Oakland University, USA)*
Claudio Soriente *(ETH Zurich, Switzerland)*
Alessandro Sorniotti *(IBM Research Zurich, Switzerland)*
Angelo Spognardi *(University of Rome "La Sapienza", Italy)*
Michael Steiner *(IBM Research, USA)*
Ersin Uzun *(Palo Alto Research Center, USA)*
Wenyuan Xu *(University of South Carolina, USA)*
Shouhuai Xu *(University of Texas at San Antonio, USA)*
Xinwen Zhang *(Samsung, USA)*
Nan Zhang *(George Washington University, USA)*
Yanchao Zhang *(Arizona State University, USA)*
Haitao Zheng *(University of California, Santa Barbara, USA)*
Sencun Zhu *(Pennsylvania State University, USA)*

Plenary Talk

Toward a Healthy Wireless Privacy Ecosystem

Edward W. Felten
U.S. Federal Trade Commission and Princeton University
Princeton, NJ, USA
felten@CS.Princeton.EDU

Abstract

Privacy can be a fraught topic even on traditional desktop systems, and mobility only complicates the issue. Consumers, companies, researchers, and government all want an outcome in which consumers feel safe entrusting their data to mobile technologies, rapid innovation continues, and researchers create the technologies of the future. What does this healthy outcome look like, and how can we get there? What can we do now to make it more likely? How can researchers contribute?

Categories & Subject Descriptors: C.2.1 [Computer-Communication Networks]: Network Architecture and Design - Wireless Communication; C.2.m [Computer-Communication Networks]: Miscellaneous - Security

General Terms: Security

Keywords: Security, Privacy, Mobile technologies, Wireless privacy

Bio

Edward W. Felten is a Professor of Computer Science and Public Affairs at Princeton University, and the Director of Princeton's Center for Information Technology Policy (CITP), a cross-disciplinary effort studying digital technologies in public life. His research interests include computer security and privacy, and public policy issues relating to information technology. Specific topics include software security, Internet security, electronic voting, cybersecurity policy, technology for government transparency, network neutrality and Internet policy.

On the Capacity of Rate-Adaptive Packetized Wireless Communication Links under Jamming *

Koorosh Firouzbakht
Electrical and Computer
Engineering Department
Northeastern University
Boston, Massachusetts
firouzbakht.k
@husky.neu.edu

Guevara Noubir
College of Computer and
Information Science
Northeastern University
Boston, Massachusetts
noubir@ccs.neu.edu

Masoud Salehi
Electrical and Computer
Engineering Department
Northeastern University
Boston, Massachusetts
salehi@ece.neu.edu

ABSTRACT

We formulate the interaction between the communicating nodes and an adversary within a game-theoretic context. We show that earlier information-theoretic capacity results for a jammed channel correspond to a pure Nash Equilibrium (NE). However, when both players are allowed to randomize their actions (i.e., coding rate and jamming power) new mixed Nash equilibria appear with surprising properties. We show the existence of a threshold (J_{TH}) such that if the jammer average power exceeds J_{TH}, the channel capacity at the NE is the same as if the jammer was using its maximum allowable power, J_{Max}, all the time. This indicates that randomization significantly advantages powerful jammers. We also show how the NE strategies can be derived, and we provide very simple (e.g., semi-uniform) approximations to the optimal communication and jamming strategies. Such strategies are very simple to implement in current hardware and software.

Categories and Subject Descriptors

C.2.0 [**Computer-Communication Networks**]: General —*Security and protection (e.g., firewalls)*

General Terms

Security

Keywords

Jamming, rate adaptation, capacity, game-theory.

1. INTRODUCTION

Over the last decades, wireless communication proved to be an enabling technology to an increasingly large number

*Research partially supported by NSF Award CNS-0915985.

of applications. The convenience of wireless and its support of mobility has revolutionized the way we access data, information services, and interact with the physical world. Beyond enabling mobile devices to access information and data services ubiquitously, wireless technology is widely used in cyber-physical systems such as air-traffic control, power plants synchronization, transportation systems, and human body implantable devices. This pervasiveness elevated wireless communication systems to the level of critical infrastructure. Radio-Frequency wireless communications occur over a broadcast medium, that is not only shared between the communicating nodes but is also exposed to adversaries. Jamming is one of the most prominent security threats as it not only can lead to denial of service attacks, but can also be the prelude to spoofing attacks.

Anti - jamming has been an active area of research for decades. Various techniques for combating jamming have been developed at the physical layer [36] which include directional antennas, spread spectrum communication, power / modulation / coding control. At the time, most of the wireless communication were not packetized nor networked. Reliable communication in the presence of adversaries regained significant interest in the last few years, as new jamming attacks and the need for more complex applications and deployment environments have emerged. Several specifically crafted attacks and counter-attacks were proposed for packetized wireless data networks [28, 23, 22, 44], multiple access resolution [5, 14, 4, 2], multi-hop networks [46, 41, 22], broadcast and control communication [19, 10, 9, 40, 21, 26, 25], cross-layer resiliency [24], wireless sensor networks [47, 48, 49], spread-spectrum without shared secrets [39, 37, 38, 16], and navigation information broadcast systems [35].

Nevertheless, very little work has been done on protecting rate adaptation algorithms against adversarial attacks. Rate adaptation plays an important role in widely used wireless communication systems such as IEEE802.11 standard as the link quality in a WLAN is often highly dynamic. In recent years, a number of algorithms for rate adaptation have been proposed in literature [15, 17, 42, 33, 34, 8, 18, 45], and some are widely deployed [6, 20]. Recently, rate adaptation for the widely used IEEE 802.11 protocol was investigated in [31, 7, 29]. Experimental and theoretical analysis of optimal jamming strategies against currently deployed rate adaptation algorithms indicate that IEEE 802.11 can be significantly degraded with very few interfering pulses. The commoditization of software radios makes these attacks very practical and calls for investigation of the capacity of packetized communication under adaptive jamming.

In this work, we focus on the problem of determining the optimal rate control and adaptation mechanisms for a channel subject to a power constrained jammer. We consider a setup where a pair of nodes (transmitter and receiver) communicate using data packets. An adversary (jammer) can interfere with the communication but is constrained by an instantaneous maximum power per packet (J_{Max}) and a long-run average power (J_{Ave}). Appropriately coded packets can overcome interference and are lost otherwise. Overcoding (coding at low rates) reduces the throughput, while under-coding (coding at high rates) increases the chances of loosing a packet. An important question is to understand the interaction between the communicating nodes and the adversary, determine the long-term achievable maximum throughput and the optimal strategy to achieve it, as well as the optimal strategy for the adversary. While, the capacity of a channel under a fixed-power jammer, and the optimal strategies for communication and jamming, derive from fundamental information theoretic results (See Section 5), these questions are still open for a packetized communication system.

Our contribution can be summarized as follows:

- We formulate the interaction between the communicating nodes and an adversary within a game-theoretic context. We show the existence of the Nash Equilibrium for this non-typical game. We also show that the Nash Equilibrium strategies can be computed using Linear Programming.

- We show that earlier information-theoretic capacity results for a jammed channel correspond to a pure Nash Equilibrium (NE).

- We further characterize the game by showing that, when both players are allowed to randomize their actions (i.e., coding rate and jamming power) new mixed Nash equilibria appear with surprising properties. We show the existence of a threshold (J_{TH}) such that if the jammer average power exceeds J_{TH}, the channel capacity at the NE is the same as if the jammer was using J_{Max} all the time.

- We also show that the optimal NE strategies can be approximated by very simple (e.g., semi-uniform) distributions. Such strategies are very simple to implement in current hardware and software.

The rest of the paper is structured as follows. In Section 2, we present our model for the communication link, communicating nodes and the adversary. In Section 3, we introduce the players, the *transmitter* and the *jammer*, and their respective strategies and payoffs. We discuss how additional constraint on jammer's mixed strategy space makes our game model different from a typical zero-sum game. In Section 4, we show that the Nash equilibrium indeed exists. We also prove the existence of a threshold, J_{TH}, for the jammer and its effect on the game outcome. In Section 5, we study two particular cases. The case of a *powerful jammer*, when jammer's average power is greater than the threshold, and the case of a *weak jammer*, when jammer's average

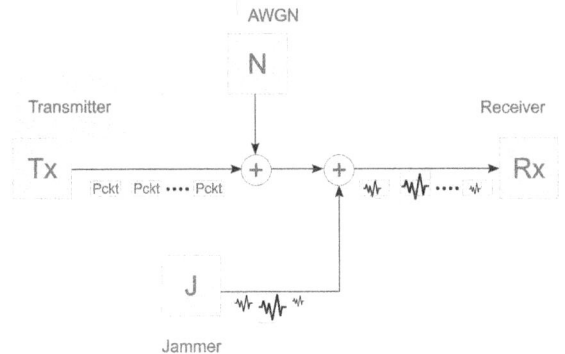

Figure 1: System model

power is less than the threshold. We will also provide transmitter's optimal strategies in these two cases. In Section 6, we study the case where players have infinite number of pure strategies (the continuous zero-sum game) and finally, we conclude the paper in Section 7.

2. SYSTEM MODEL

In this section we introduce and define our system model. The overall system model is shown in Figure 1. The communication link between the transmitter and the receiver is an AWGN channel with a fixed noise variance. Beside the channel noise, transmitted packets are being disrupted by an additive jammer. Jammer's peak and average power are assumed to be limited to produce a more realistic model.

2.1 Channel Model

The overall system model is shown in Figure 1. The communication link between the transmitter and the receiver is assumed to be a single-hop, additive white Gaussian noise (AWGN) channel with a fixed and known noise variance, N, referred to the receiver's front end. Furthermore, the communication link is being disrupted by an additive adversary, the *jammer*. The jammer transmits radio signals to degrade the capacity between the transmitter and the receiver. We assume transmissions are *packet-based*, i.e., transmissions take place in disjoint time intervals during which transmitter's and jammer's state (parameters) remain unchanged. We assume packets are long enough that channel capacity theorem could be applied to each packet being transmitted, this is justified by today's Internet protocols that use packet sizes of up to $1,500$ bytes[1].

In section 3 we introduce and study a two-player zero-sum game in which transmitter-receiver goal is to achieve highest possible rate while jammer tries to minimize the achievable rate.

2.2 Jammer Model

Radio jamming or simply *jamming* is deliberate transmission of radio signals with the intention of degrading a

---

[1]IEEE 802.3 and IEEE 802.11x protocols allow MAC frame sizes of up to 1,642 and 2304 bytes respectively.

Table 1: Table of Notations and Parameters

Parameter	Description
P_T	Transmitter's power
N	Noise power spectral density
J_{Max}	Jammer's maximum power per packet
J_{Ave}	Jammer's average power
J_{TH}	Jamming power threshold
J	Variable denoting jammer's power
J_T	Jamming power corresponding to the transmitter's rate
$\boldsymbol{J}^T = \begin{bmatrix} J_0 & \dots & J_j & \dots & J_{N_J} \end{bmatrix}_{1 \times (N_J+1)}$ $J_j = \frac{j}{N_J} J_{Max}$	Jamming power vector
$\boldsymbol{R}^T = \begin{bmatrix} R_0 & \dots & R_i & \dots & R_{N_T} \end{bmatrix}_{1 \times (N_T+1)}$ $R_i = \frac{1}{2} \log \left(1 + \frac{P_T}{N + \frac{i}{N_T} J_{Max}} \right)$	Vector corresponding to transmitter's rates
$\boldsymbol{x}^T = \begin{bmatrix} x_0 & \dots & x_i & \dots & x_{N_T} \end{bmatrix}_{1 \times (N_T+1)} \in \mathbb{X}$ $\boldsymbol{y}^T = \begin{bmatrix} y_0 & \dots & y_j & \dots & y_{N_J} \end{bmatrix}_{1 \times (N_J+1)} \in \mathbb{Y}$	Transmitter's mixed-strategy vector Jammer's mixed strategy vector
$\mathbb{X}, \mathbb{Y}$	Mixed-strategy space, transmitter's and jammer's respectively
$C_{(N_T+1) \times (N_J+1)}$ or $C(\boldsymbol{x}, \boldsymbol{y})$ or $C(J_{Ave})$	Game matrix and expected game payoffs

communication link. The effect of jammer on the communication link is reduction of the effective signal to noise ratio (SNR) at the receiver and hence decreasing the channel capacity. As long as reduction in effective signal to noise ratio is concerned, the jammer can use arbitrary random signals for transmission but, it can be shown [11] that in the AWGN channel with a fixed and known noise variance, a Gaussian jammer with a flat power spectral density is the most effective in minimizing the the capacity between the transmitter and the receiver. In other words, in the communication game described above, the optimal strategy for the transmitter is to use a zero-mean white Gaussian input with variance equal to P, the transmitter power, and the best strategy for the jammer is is to use a similar distribution with variance J, the jammer power.

A fairly large number of jamming models have been proposed in the literature [32]. The most benign jammer is the *barrage noise jammer*. The barrage noise jammer transmits bandlimited white Gaussian noise with power spectral density (psd) of J. It is usually assumed that the barrage noise jammer power spectrum covers exactly the same frequency range as the communicating system. This kind of jammer simply increases the Gaussian noise level from N to $(N+J)$ at the receiver's front end. Another frequently used jamming model is the *pulse-noise jammer*. The pulse noise jammer transmits pulses of bandlimited white Gaussian noise having total average power of J_{Ave} referred to the receiver's front end. It is usually assumed that the jammer chooses the center frequency and bandwidth of the noise to be the same as the transmitter's center frequency and bandwidth. The jammer chooses its pulse duty factor to cause maximum degradation to the communication link while maintaining the average jamming power J_{Ave}. For a more realistic model, the pulse-noise jammer could be subject to a maximum peak power constraint. Other jamming models, to name a few, are the *partial-band jammer* and *single/multiple-tune jammer*.

However, we study a more sophisticated jamming model. The jammer in study is a reactive and additive jammer, i.e., he is only active when a packet is being transmitted and silent otherwise. We assume that the jammer has a set of discrete jamming power levels uniformly distributed between $J = 0$ and $J = J_{Max}$. The jammer can choose any jamming power level given that he maintains an overall average jamming power, J_{Ave}. The jammer uses his available power levels according to a distribution (his strategy), he chooses an optimal distribution to minimize the achievable capacity of the communication link while maintaining his maximum and average power constraints, i.e., J_{Max} and J_{Ave}, respectively.

For reasons given in section 2.3, burst jamming (transmitting a burst of white noise to disrupt a few bits in a packet) is not an optimal jamming scheme. Hence, we assume the jammer remains active during the entire packet transmission, i.e., the jammer transmits a continuous Gaussian noise with a fixed variance $J \in [0, J_{Max}]$ for each transmitting packet.

2.3 Transmitter Model

Transmitter has a rate adaptation block which enables him to transmit at different rates. Popular techniques to increase or decrease the rate of a code are puncturing or extending. Puncturing and extending increase the flexibility of the system without significantly increasing its complexity. Considering jammer's activity, the transmitter changes his rate according to a distribution (his strategy). Changing the rate can be accomplished using techniques like rate-

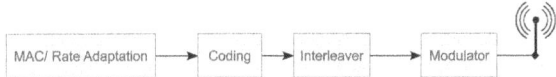

Figure 2: Transmitter Model

compatible puncturing. The transmitter chooses an optimal distribution to achieve the best possible average rate (payoff). Same as before, we assume transmissions are *packet-based*, i.e., transmissions are taken place in disjoint time intervals during which, transmitter's rate remain unchanged. Transmitter's model is shown in Figure 2.

The interleaver block in transmitter's model is a countermeasure to burst errors and burst jamming. Interleaving is frequently used in digital communications and storage devices to improve the burst error correcting capabilities of a code. Burst errors are specially troublesome in short length codes as they have very limited error correcting capabilities. In such codes, a few number of errors could result in a decoding failure or an incorrect decoding. A few incorrectly decoded codewords within a larger frame could make the entire frame corrupted.

Fortunately, combining effective interleaving schemes such as cryptographic interleaving and capacity-achieving codes such as turbo codes and LDPC codes results in transmission schemes that have good burst error correcting properties (see [23]) which make burst jamming ineffective. Therefore, in our study we do not consider burst jamming and instead assume that the jammer remains active during the entire packet transmission.

3. GAME MODEL

In this section we discuss the game setup in detail; we introduce and define the players, their respective strategies and the constraints in the game. We present the game model and define and formulate the payoff function in a game theoretic frame work. As discussed in section 2.2, in the AWGN channel, the additive white Gaussian jammer is the optimal jammer, in the sense that the white Gaussian jammer minimizes the channel capacity. Henceforward, we will only consider the additive Gaussian jammer.

We present the jammer's strategy set and introduce the jammer's average power constraint and its impact on the mixed strategy space. The additional constraint makes our game model different from a typical two-player zero-sum game. We also introduce transmitter's strategy set and define the game utility function and the payoff matrix.

We begin by introducing a discrete version of the game to prove basic concepts and conclusions. Generalization to the continuous case is given in Section 6

3.1 *The Jammer's Strategy Set*

The jammer has the option to select discrete values of jamming power, uniformly distributed over $[0, J_{Max}]$. We assume there are $(N_J + 1)$ pure strategies available to the jammer. Hence, the jammer's strategy set (set of jamming powers), $\mathcal{J}$, is given by

$$\mathcal{J} = \left\{ J_j; 0 \leq j \leq N_J \right\} \tag{1}$$

where

$$J_j = \frac{j}{N_J} J_{Max} \tag{2}$$

We can write the possible jammer power levels in vector form, hence the jammer's pure strategies vector, $\boldsymbol{J}$, is

$$\boldsymbol{J}^T = \begin{bmatrix} J_0 & \dots & J_j & \dots & J_{N_J} \end{bmatrix}_{1 \times (N_J + 1)} \tag{3}$$

where ^{T} indicates transposition and J_j is defined in (2). Unlike typical zero-sum games in which there are no other constraints on the mixed-strategies, in our model, the jammer's mixed-strategy must satisfy the additional average power constraint, $J_{Ave} \leq J_{Max}$. Hence, in this model, not all mixed-strategies (and not even the pure strategies that are greater than J_{Ave}) are feasible strategies [30, Sec. III.7]. If we let $\boldsymbol{y}$ be the jammer's mixed-strategy vector and $\mathbb{Y}$ be the $(N_J + 1)$-simplex, we have the following relations:

$$\boldsymbol{y}^T = \begin{bmatrix} y_0 & \dots & y_j & \dots & y_{N_J} \end{bmatrix}_{1 \times (N_J + 1)} \in \mathbb{Y} \tag{4}$$

$$\sum_{j=0}^{N_J} y_j = 1; \quad y_j \geq 0, \quad 0 \leq j \leq N_J$$

By using the jammer's pure strategy vector we define the constrained mixed strategy space $\mathbb{Y}_E$ as

$$\mathbb{Y}_E = \{ \boldsymbol{y} \in \mathbb{Y} | \; \boldsymbol{y}^T \cdot \boldsymbol{J} = J_{Ave} \} \tag{5}$$

which is a subset of the $(N_J + 1)$-simplex that satisfies the average power constraint. By substituting the equality constraint in (5) with the less than or equal sign, we define a new mixed-strategy space which consists of all mixed-strategies that result in an average power less than or equal to J_{Ave}. The new mixed-strategy space, $\mathbb{Y}_{LE}$, is

$$\mathbb{Y}_{LE} = \{ \boldsymbol{y} \in \mathbb{Y} | \; \boldsymbol{y}^T \cdot \boldsymbol{J} \leq J_{Ave} \} \tag{6}$$

It is obvious that

$$\mathbb{Y}_E \subset \mathbb{Y}_{LE} \subset \mathbb{Y}$$

A typical mixed strategy space with equality constraint, as defined in (5), is shown in Figure 3 where $N_J = N_T = 3$. In this case jammer's mixed and pure strategy vectors are $\begin{bmatrix} y_0 & y_1 & y_2 & y_3 \end{bmatrix}_{1 \times 4}$ and $\begin{bmatrix} 0 & \frac{1}{3}J_{Max} & \frac{2}{3}J_{Max} & J_{Max} \end{bmatrix}_{1 \times 4}$.

Since by introducing the new mixed strategy spaces of (5) and (6) we are eliminating some mixed strategies that could have been otherwise selected, the existence of the Nash equilibrium for this case must be first established. This is unlike a typical zero-sum game with a finite number of pure strategies in which the existence of the Nash Equilibrium is assured. In section 4.1, we provide an outline of the proof of the existence of the Nash Equilibrium in our game where the jammer's mixed strategy space is limited to $\mathbb{Y}_E$ or $\mathbb{Y}_{LE}$.

3.2 *The Transmitter's Strategy Set*

The transmitter strategy set is a set of discrete transmission rates corresponding to different assumed jamming power levels, i.e, the transmitter chooses his rate, R, from the set

$$\mathcal{R} = \left\{ R_i, 0 \leq i \leq N_T \right\} \tag{7}$$

where

$$R_i = \frac{1}{2} \log \left(1 + \frac{P_T}{N + \frac{i}{N_T} J_{Max}} \right) \tag{8}$$

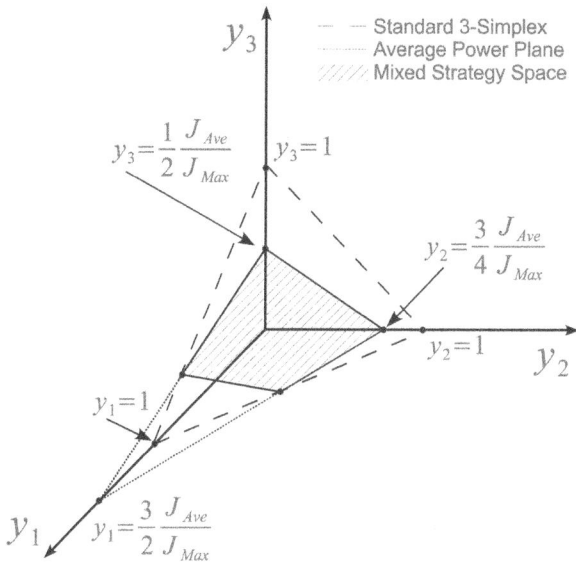

Figure 3: A typical mixed-strategy space for average power constrained jammer ($J_{Ave} < J_{Max}$).

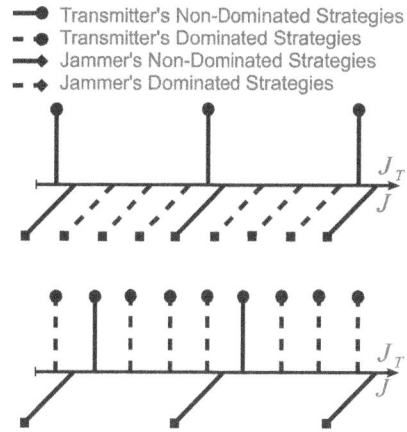

Figure 4: Uniformly distributed pure strategies; $N_J > N_T$ (top) and $N_J < N_T$ (bottom)

and $\frac{i}{N_T} J_{Max}$ denotes the jammer's power level assumed by the transmitter. If the actual jammer's power level is less than or equal to the assumed value of $\frac{i}{N_T} J_{Max}$, then transmission at rate R_i is possible, otherwise reliable transmission is not possible, the packet is lost, and the actual transmission rate drops to zero. Same as the case with the jammer, we define the vector of mixed-strategies for the transmitter, $\boldsymbol{x}$, as

$$\boldsymbol{x}^T = \begin{bmatrix} x_0 & \dots & x_i & \dots & x_{N_T} \end{bmatrix}_{1 \times (N_T+1)} \in \mathbb{X} \quad (9)$$

where $\mathbb{X}$ is the $(N_T + 1)$-simplex with no additional constraints.

3.3 The Payoff Function

The *payoff* to the transmitter is defined assuming transmissions at the channel capacity. Defining the payoff based on channel capacity (or other variations of channel capacity) is a common practice in the games involving a transmitter-receiver pair and an adversary [43, 13, 1].

Because transmissions occur in the presence of an adversary, recovery of the transmitted information at the receiver is not always guaranteed. The information can only be recovered when the actual jamming power, J, is less than or equal to the jamming power level assumed by the transmitter, J_T, i.e., if and only if $J \leq J_T$. If $J_T < J$, the corresponding transmission rate would exceed the channel capacity and the information would be lost. Therefore, the transmitter's payoff function is given by

$$C(J_T, J) = \begin{cases} R(J_T) = \frac{1}{2} \log \left(1 + \frac{P_T}{N + J_T} \right) & J_T \geq J \\ 0 & J_T < J \end{cases} \quad (10)$$

Since the game in study is a zero-sum game, the payoff to the jammer is the negative of the transmitter's payoff. We can formulate the payoffs in a payoff matrix where the transmitter and the jammer would be the row and column players

respectively. The resulting payoff matrix, C, is

$$C = \begin{bmatrix} R_0 & 0 & 0 & \dots & 0 \\ \vdots & \ddots & 0 & 0 & \vdots \\ R_i & \dots & R_i & 0 & \vdots \\ \vdots & & & \ddots & \vdots \\ R_{N_T} & R_{N_T} & \dots & R_{N_T} & R_{N_T} \end{bmatrix}_{(N_T+1) \times (N_T+1)} \quad (11)$$

where R_i is defined in (8). The expected payoff (or the game value) of the game is

$$C(\boldsymbol{x}, \boldsymbol{y}) = \boldsymbol{x}^T \cdot C \cdot \boldsymbol{y}, \qquad \boldsymbol{y} \in \mathbb{Y}_E \text{ or } \mathbb{Y}_{LE} \quad (12)$$

In defining (11) we have assumed $N_J = N_T$. As discussed below, without loss of generality, we can always assume that $N_T = N_J$.

LEMMA 1. *Let C be the payoff matrix in the two-player zero-sum game defined by the utility function (10). The payoff matrix resulted by removing the dominated strategies is a square lower triangular matrix with size less than or equal to $\min [N_T, N_J]$. Furthermore, if the power levels were uniformly distributed over $[0, J_{Max}]$, the size of the non-dominated payoff matrix would be the minimum of N_T and N_J.*

PROOF. Assume the jammer's power levels are arbitrary distributed over some range, $[0, J_{Max}]$, and $N_T < N_J$. A typical case where $N_T < N_J$ is depicted in Figure 4 (top). In Figure 4, the transmitter's pure strategies are mapped to the jammer's power levels for better visualization. Between some of the transmitter's pure strategies there might be a pure strategy of the jammer but since $N_T < N_J$, according to the *Pigeonhole* principle, between at least two of the transmitter's pure strategies (not necessarily any two pure strategy as sketched) there must be more than one jamming power level (shown as dashed or solid lines ending in squares). Any of these jamming power levels (or pure strategies) could be used to terminate the information transmitted by the rate corresponding to the power level immediately to the left of them (shown as solid line ending in circles). From these pure strategies, a rational jammer would choose the one with the lowest power level (the solid line) and hence, it would dominate the rest (dashed lines). therefore, the number of non-dominated pure strategies for the jammer is at most equal to the the number of the transmitter's pure strategies (first part of the lemma).

If the pure strategies were uniformly distributed over $[0, J_{Max}]$, as sketched, for every transmitter's pure strategy there would be exactly one non-dominated strategy for the jammer and hence, there would be no intention for the jammer to use more pure strategies than the transmitter. The same discussion can be given for the number of pure strategies a rational transmitter should use for the case $N_T > N_J$ (see Figure 4(bottom)). Henceforward, without loss of generality, we assume $N_T = N_J$. □

As a consequence of Lemma 1, in our study, we need to consider only square matrices which simplifies further studies and assumptions. In the section that follows, we will study the outcome of the game when jammer's average power assumes different values.

4. GAME CHARACTERIZATION

In this section, we study the basic properties of the game. We will show that although we have put an additional constraint on the jammer's mixed strategy space, the existence of the Nash equilibrium is still guaranteed.

Furthermore, we will show that by randomizing his strategy, the jammer can force the transmitter to operate at his lowest rate, given that he uses an average jamming power, J_{Ave}, that is more than a certain threshold, $J_{TH} < J_{Max}$. We also provide an upper bound for J_{TH} in this section.

4.1 Existence of the Nash Equilibrium

We begin this section by the following lemma that shows existence of the Nash equilibrium under the additional average power constraint is guaranteed.

LEMMA 2. *For the two-player zero-sum game defined by the utility function $C(J_T, J)$, given in (10) and the payoff matrix C, given by (11) and the transmitter's mixed strategy, $\boldsymbol{x} \in \mathbb{X}$, and the jammer's mixed strategy, $\boldsymbol{y} \in \mathbb{Y}_E$ or $\mathbb{Y}_{LE}$ (defined in (5) and (6), respectively), at least one Nash equilibrium exists.*

Nash in his 1951 seminal paper, "Non Cooperative Games" [27], proved that for any game with finite set of pure strategies, there exists at least one (pure or mixed) equilibrium such that no player can do better by unilaterally deviating from his strategy. In the proof of the existence of the Nash equilibrium, no additional constraints were assumed on the mixed strategy spaces. But, in our game model, we are assuming an additional constraint on the jammer's mixed strategy space; the jammer must maintain a fixed or maximum average jamming power (corresponding to (5) and (6), respectively). These additional assumptions change the jammer's mixed strategy space from the n-simplex to a subset of it. Therefore, the Nash equilibrium theorem cannot be applied to our model directly and the existence of the Nash equilibrium must be established.

PROOF (OUTLINE). The proof of the existence of Nash equilibrium hinges on the *Sperner's lemma* and *Brouwer's*

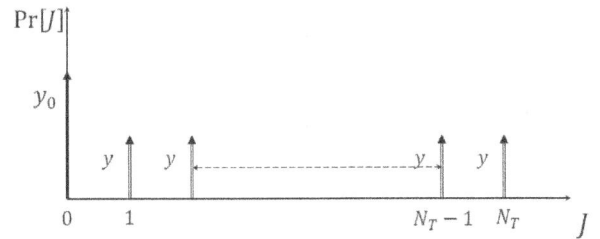

Pr[J], y_0, y, y, y, y, 0, 1, $N_T - 1$, N_T, J

Figure 5: Semi-Uniform Distribution

fixed point theorem and a corollary of this theorem on simplotopes [2]. Sperner's lemma applies to simplicially subdivided n-simplexes. It can easily be shown that by using a *radial projection*, the mixed strategy space in our model, which is a result of additional constraint of maintaining an average jamming power (or maintaining a maximum average power), can be projected to an appropriate lower dimension m-simplex where $m < n$. A similar argument can be used to generalize the Brouwer's fixed point theorem to any arbitrary convex and compact set. Since the additional average power constraint does not effect the convexity or compactness of the mixed strategy space, we can conclude that all the conditions and requirements assumed by the Sperner's lemma and the Brouwer's fixed point theorem are satisfied [3] and the existence of the Nash equilibrium for our problem is guaranteed. □

4.2 Existence of Jamming Power Threshold

The following theorem proves the existence of a threshold jammer power that plays an important role in our further development.

THEOREM 1. *For the two-player zero-sum game defined with the utility function $C(J_T, J)$, given in (10), and the payoff matrix C, given in (11), and the transmitter's mixed strategy, $\boldsymbol{x} \in \mathbb{X}$, and the jammer's mixed strategy $\boldsymbol{y} \in \mathbb{Y}_{LE}$, given in (6) and for all $P_T, N, J_{Max} > 0$*

$$\exists J_{TH}; \quad 0 < J_{TH} < J_{Max}$$

such that, if $J_{Ave} \geq J_{TH}$ then, $\exists \boldsymbol{y}^* \in \mathbb{Y}_{LE}$ for which we have

$$\boldsymbol{x}^{*T} = \begin{bmatrix} \boldsymbol{0}_{1 \times N_T} & 1 \end{bmatrix}_{1 \times (N_T+1)} \quad (13)$$
$$C(\boldsymbol{x}^*, \boldsymbol{y}^*) = R_{N_T}$$

where $\boldsymbol{x}^*, \boldsymbol{y}^*$ are transmitter's and jammer's optimal mixed-strategies, respectively and $C(\boldsymbol{x}^*, \boldsymbol{y}^*)$ represents the value of the game.

Theorem 1 states that there exists a jamming threshold (J_{TH}) such that if the jammer's average power exceeds J_{TH} then the transmitter's optimal mixed-strategy is to use the lowest rate.

PROOF. Assume the jammer is using a mixed strategy with the pmf given in Figure 5 (*semi-uniform*)[3] which is

---

[2]There are alternative proofs for the existence of the Nash equilibrium, i.e., using *Kakutani fixed point theorem* [30].
[3]We will refer to this class of pmf/pdf as the *semi-uniform*

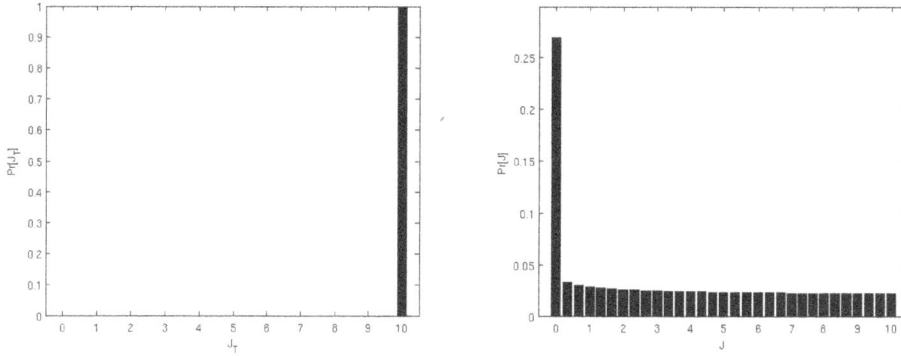

Figure 6: Typical optimal mixed-strategies for the transmitter (left) and the jammer (right) for $J_{Ave} \geq J_{TH}$

not necessarily an optimal mixed strategy. The parameters of this pmf are

$$
\begin{aligned}
y_0 &= 1 - \frac{2N_T}{N_T + 1} \cdot \frac{J_{Ave}}{J_{Max}} \\
y &= \frac{2}{N_T + 1} \cdot \frac{J_{Ave}}{J_{Max}}
\end{aligned}
\tag{14}
$$

It can be easily verified that the semi-uniform pmf satisfies the average power constraint

$$
\begin{aligned}
&\sum_{j=0}^{N_T} J \cdot \Pr[J] \\
&= \sum_{j=0}^{N_T} \left(\frac{j}{N_T} J_{Max} \right) \cdot \Pr\left[J = \left(\frac{j}{N_T} J_{Max} \right) \right] \\
&= J_{Ave}
\end{aligned}
$$

We assume the transmitter is using an arbitrary mixed strategy in which rates R_{N_T} (the lowest rate corresponding to $J_T = J_{Max}$) and R_i (an arbitrary rate corresponding to $J_T = \frac{i}{N_T} J_{Max}$, $0 \leq i < N_T$) have probabilities x_{N_T} and x_i respectively. Define C to be the expected payoff for the jammer's semi-uniform mixed strategy against the transmitter's arbitrary mixed-strategy:

$$
\begin{aligned}
C &= C_{-i,N_T} + R_{N_T} x_{N_T} \times 1 + R_i x_i \times \Pr\left[J \leq J_T = J_i \right] \\
&= C_{-i,N_T} R_{N_T} x_{N_T} + R_i x_i (y_0 + iy)
\end{aligned}
\tag{15}
$$

where C_{-i,N_T} is the partial expected payoff resulting from all pure strategies except for the i'th and N_T'th strategies. In order to improve his payoff, the transmitter, deviates from his current strategy to $x'_{N_T} = x_{N_T} + \delta$ and $x'_j = x_j - \delta$ where $\delta > 0$. Defining C' to be the expected payoff for the new strategy, we have

$$
\begin{aligned}
C' &= C_{-i,N_T} + R_{N_T} (x_{N_T} + \delta) \\
&\quad + R_i (x_i - \delta) \times \Pr\left[J \leq J_T = J_i \right] \\
&= C + \delta\left[R_{N_T} - R_i (y_0 + iy) \right]
\end{aligned}
\tag{16}
$$

Let ΔC be the difference in the expected payoff caused by

deviating to the new strategy

$$
\begin{aligned}
\Delta C &= C' - C \\
&= \delta \left(R_{N_T} - 2R_i \frac{N_T - i}{N_T + 1} \cdot \frac{J_{Ave}}{J_{Max}} \right)
\end{aligned}
\tag{17}
$$

where $\delta > 0$ and $0 \leq i < N_T$. We show that there exists a jammer power threshold, denoted by J_{TH}, such that if $J_{Ave} \geq J_{TH}$, then for all $\delta > 0$ and for all $i \in [0, J_{Max})$, we have

$$
\Delta C > 0
\tag{18}
$$

Assuming (for now) that $\Delta C > 0$ we can rewrite (17) as

$$
\begin{aligned}
J_{Ave} &\geq \frac{1}{2} J_{Max} \frac{N_T + 1}{N_T - i} \cdot \left(1 - \frac{R_{N_T}}{R_i} \right) \\
&= Z_i, \qquad 0 \leq i < N_T
\end{aligned}
\tag{19}
$$

where Z_i's, for $i = 0, \ldots, N_T - 1$, are a set of N_T finite values. Let us define $J_{TH} = \max Z_i$, then for

$$
J_{Ave} \geq J_{TH}
\tag{20}
$$

and for all $\delta > 0$ and $i \in [0, N_T)$ the inequalities in (19) and (18) are satisfied.

We showed that for $J_{Ave} \geq J_{TH}$, the transmitter can improve his expected payoff by dropping probability from any arbitrary rate (except for the lowest rate) and adding this probability to the lowest rate. We can continue this process until all other probabilities are added to the lowest rate probability and no further improvement to the expected payoff is possible. This shows that the low rate is indeed an optimal strategy for the transmitter against the jammer's semi uniform mixed strategy.

By using the semi-uniform pmf and $J_{Ave} \geq J_{TH}$, the jammer can force the transmitter to operate at the lowest rate and given that the expected payoff is bounded between the transmitter's lowest and highest rates, we can conclude that the semi-uniform distribution is indeed an optimal mixed strategy for the jammer when (6) is the mixed strategy space[4]. $\square$

It is interesting to note that the packetized transmission model employed here and the transmitter's lack of knowledge of the actual jammer power level benefits the jammer.

---

[4] The J_{TH} given by (20) is not necessarily the lowest possible threshold since we have limited jammer's strategies to semi-uniform distributions. However, it is an upper bound for the lowest J_{TH}.

In fact, the jammer uses a power level less than J_{Max} but forces the transmitter to transmit at a rate corresponding to J_{Max}. This is similar to the situation in fading channels where although the ergodic capacity can be large, the outage capacity is considerably lower.

It can be shown that Z_i in (19) is maximized for $i = 0$ [12]. Therefore an upper bound for J_{TH} is

$$J_{TH,U} = \frac{1}{2} \frac{N_T + 1}{N_T} \left(1 - \frac{R_{N_T}}{R_0}\right) J_{Max} \qquad (21)$$

In section 5.1 we show that by using an optimal mixed strategy, the jammer can achieve a lower threshold than (21).

5. GAME ANALYSIS

In this section we study the optimal mixed strategies for the jammer and the transmitter. We provide analytic and computer simulated results and a comparison between power thresholds resulted from computer simulation and the upper bound derived in section 4.

Based on relative values of J_{Ave} and J_{TH}, we study two cases, the *powerful jammer* where $J_{Ave} \geq J_{TH}$ and the *weak Jammer* where $J_{Ave} < J_{TH}$.

5.1 Powerful Jammer

As a result of the Theorem 1, there exists a jamming threshold (J_{TH}), such that if the jammer's average power exceeds J_{TH}, then the transmitter's optimal mixed strategy (or more accurately, the optimal pure strategy in this case) is to use the lowest rate. We formulate this fact in the following theorem.

THEOREM 2. *There exists a threshold J_{TH} such that if $J_{Ave} \geq J_{TH}$, the expected payoff of the game is*

$$C\left(J_{Ave}\right) = R_{N_T} = \frac{1}{2} \log\left(1 + \frac{P_T}{N + J_{Max}}\right)$$

The value of J_{TH} is given by

$$J_{TH} = \left(1 - \frac{1}{N_T} \alpha^{-1} R_{N_T}\right) J_{Max} \qquad (22)$$

where R_i is defined in (8) and

$$\alpha^{-1} = \sum_{i=0}^{N_T - 1} (R_i)^{-1} \qquad (23)$$

In other words, if the average jamming power exceeds J_{TH} given in (22), by randomizing his strategy, the jammer forces the transmitter to operate at his lowest rate as if the jammer was using J_{Max} all the time (Barrage noise jammer). If we define the effective jamming power, J_{Eff}, to be the jamming power a Barrage noise jammer needs to force the transmitter to operate at the same rate (R_{N_T} in this case) then, for the powerful jammer the effective jamming power becomes

$$J_{Eff} = J_{Max} \qquad (24)$$

Typical optimal mixed strategies for the transmitter and the jammer in a powerful jammer case are given in Figure 6. Proof of Theorem 2 is similar to the proof of Theorem 1. Details of deriving relation (22) are given in Section 5.2.

Unfortunately, jammer's optimal mixed strategy cannot be formulated in a closed form relation and the optimal distribution has to be calculated numerically. As we showed

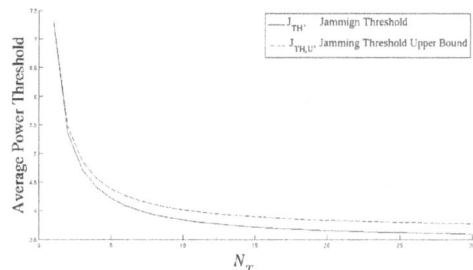

Figure 7: Comparison between the average power threshold and its upper bound

in section 4.2, the simple semi-uniform pmf, shown in Figure 5, could be used to derive an upper bound for the jamming threshold and as an approximation to the jammers optimal mixed strategy (see Figure 6 (right)). The price paid by deviating from the optimal mixed strategy to the simple semi-uniform distribution is that the jammer has to use more average power to force the transmitter to operate at the lowest rate. A comparison between the jammer's average power threshold given in (22) and the upper derived in (21) is given in Figure 7.

5.2 Weak Jammer

A weak jammer has an average jamming power less than the threshold, $J_{Ave} < J_{TH}$. Typical optimal mixed strategies for the weak jammer case are given in Figure 8.

In this case the expected payoff, $C\left(J_{Ave}\right) \in \left(R_{N_T}, R_0\right]$. Although a useful closed form relation between the expected payoff and the jammer's average power where $J_{Ave} \in \left[0, J_{TH}\right)$ cannot be derived, for specific values of the average jamming power the relation reduces to a simple form. For these specific values, the expected payoff of the game, $C\left(J_{Ave}\right)$, corresponds to one of the transmitter's rates R_i, $i = 0, \ldots, N_T - 1$. We present this fact in the following theorem without providing the full proof. The interested reader is referred to [12] for the proof.

THEOREM 3. *Assuming $J_{Ave} < J_{TH}$*

1. *The expected payoff of the game is*

$$\begin{aligned} C\left(J_{Ave}\right) &= R_{m+1} \\ &= \frac{1}{2} \log\left(1 + \frac{P_T}{N + \frac{m+1}{N_T} J_{Max}}\right) \end{aligned} \qquad (25)$$

where m is the solution of

$$J_{Ave} = \left(m + 1 - \alpha^{-1} R_{m+1}\right) \frac{J_{Max}}{N_T} \qquad (26)$$

2. *The transmitter's optimal mixed strategy is*

$$\boldsymbol{x}_m^{*T} = \begin{bmatrix} x_0 & x_1 & \ldots & x_m & 0 & \ldots & 0 \end{bmatrix}_{1 \times (N_T + 1)}$$

where

$$x_i = Pr\left[J_T = \left(\frac{i}{N_T}\right) J_{Max}\right] = \alpha_m R_i^{-1}, \quad 0 \leq i \leq m \qquad (27)$$

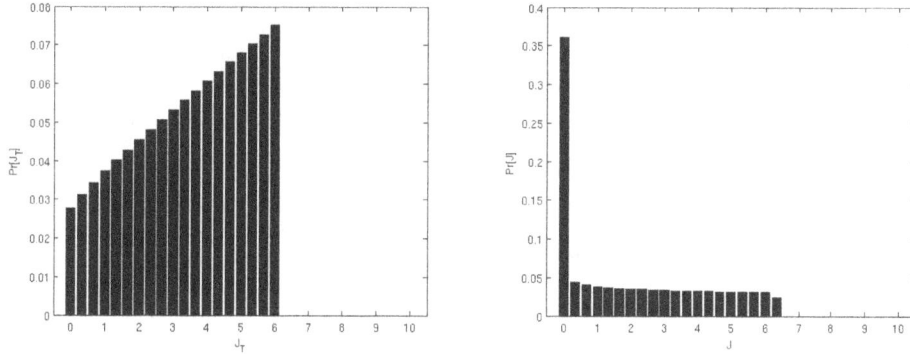

Figure 8: Typical optimal mixed-strategies for the transmitter (left) and the jammer (right) for $J_{Ave} < J_{TH}$

and

$$\alpha_m^{-1} = \sum_{i=0}^{m} (R_i)^{-1} \qquad (28)$$

The optimal mixed strategies for a typical zero-sum two-player game could be calculated by *linear programming*. Our game model differs from a typical zero-sum game however, linear programming could still be used to calculate the optimal mixed strategies by making the proper modifications [30] and even though we do not provide the full proof for the transmitter's optimal mixed-strategy, the consistency of (27) can be verified by computer simulation. Numerical calculations verify that results achieved by using (27) as the transmitter's optimal mixed strategies are accurate to the order of 10^{-15}.

In order to prove (26), we first introduce the following lemma without a proof.

LEMMA 3. *The semi-uniform distribution and the jammer's optimal mixed strategy (see Figure 8 (left)) result in the same expected payoff against the transmitter mixed strategy given in (27), if they have the same support and average jamming power.*

The outline of the proof for (26) will be given next.

PROOF (OUTLINE). Assume J_{Ave} is such that the transmitter is using $(m+1)$ of his pure strategies, i.e.,

$$\boldsymbol{x}_m^{*T} = \begin{bmatrix} x_0 & x_1 & \dots & x_m & 0 & \dots & 0 \end{bmatrix}_{1 \times (N_T+1)}$$

where $\boldsymbol{x}_m^{*T}$ is given in (27). Using Lemma 1, the jammer only needs to use the strategies J_j where $j = 0, \dots, (m+1)$ and the expected payoff of the game would be at least R_{m+1} (otherwise the jammer had to use more strategies). Lemma 3 suggests that the following semi-uniform distribution which has the same support and average power as the jammer's optimal mixed strategy could be used instead to compute the expected payoff of the game.

$$\boldsymbol{y}_{SU}^{T} = \begin{bmatrix} y_0 & y_1 & \dots & y_{m+1} & 0 & \dots & 0 \end{bmatrix}_{1 \times (N_T+1)}$$

$$y_j = \begin{cases} 1 - \frac{2N_T}{(m+2)} \cdot \frac{J_{Ave}}{J_{Max}} & j = 0 \\ \frac{2N_T}{(m+1)(m+2)} \cdot \frac{J_{Ave}}{J_{Max}} & j = 1, \dots, m+1 \end{cases} \qquad (29)$$

If we let the expected payoff of the transmitter be exactly R_{m+1}, then

$$\boldsymbol{x}_m^{*T} C \boldsymbol{y}_{SU} = R_{m+1} \qquad (30)$$

Substituting (27) and (29) in (30) and solving for J_{Ave} results in (26).

Finally, letting $R_m = R_{N_T}$ or equivalently letting $m = (N_T - 1)$ in (26) we obtain the desired relation in (22). $\square$

For a weak jammer, the effective jamming power, J_{Eff} is

$$J_{Eff} = \left(\frac{m+1}{N_T} \right) J_{Max} \qquad (31)$$

If we define the effectiveness factor E to be the ratio of the effective jamming power to the actual average jamming power, we have

$$\begin{aligned} E^{-1} &= \frac{J_{Ave}}{J_{Eff}} \\ &= \frac{\left(m + 1 - \alpha_m^{-1} R_{m+1} \right) \cdot \left(\frac{J_{Max}}{N_T} \right)}{\left(\frac{m+1}{N_T} \right) J_{Max}} \\ &= 1 - \frac{1}{m+1} \alpha_m^{-1} R_{m+1} < 1 \end{aligned} \qquad (32)$$

Similar to the case of the powerful jammer, the weak jammer can cause more damage to the communication link than a Barrage noise jammer with an average power J_{Ave}.

6. CONTINUOUS CASE

In this section we study the case where the jammer and the transmitter have infinite pure strategies. In this case, instead of finite number of pure strategies, the transmitter and the jammer have a continuum of pure strategies that could be represented as points in intervals $R \in \left[R(J_{Max}), R(0) \right]$ and $J \in \left[0, J_{Max} \right]$ respectively.

By letting $N_T \to \infty$ in (22), we can find the jamming power threshold for the continuous case to be

$$\begin{aligned} J_{TH,Lim} &= \lim_{N_T \to \infty} J_{TH} \\ &= J_{Max} - \frac{1}{2} \log \left(1 + \frac{P_T}{N + J_{Max}} \right) \\ &\quad \times \int_0^{J_{Max}} \left[\frac{1}{2} \log \left(1 + \frac{P_T}{N + J} \right) \right]^{-1} \cdot dJ \end{aligned} \qquad (33)$$

Similar to the discrete case, we can use a continuous semi-uniform distribution to approximate the jammer's optimal mixed strategy and find an upper bound for $J_{TH,\text{Lim}}$.

$$J_{TH,\text{Lim,UB}} = \frac{1}{2}\left[1 - \frac{R(J_{Max})}{R(0)}\right]J_{Max} \qquad (34)$$

7. CONCLUSIONS

We formulated the interaction between rate-adaptive communicating nodes and a smart power-limited jammer in a game-theoretic context. We show that packetization and adaptivity advantage the jammer. While, previous stationary information-theoretic capacity results correspond to a pure Nash-Equilibrium, packetized adaptive communication leads to lower game values. We show the existence of a mixed Nash Equilibrium and how to compute it. More importantly and surprisingly, we show the existence of a threshold on the average power of the jammer, above which the transmitter is forced to use a rate that corresponds to the maximum power of the jammer (and not the average power). We finally show how the optimal strategies can be computed and also derive a very simple (semi-uniform) jamming strategies that forces the transmitter to operate at the lowest rate (as if the jammer was continuously using its maximum power and not its average power).

8. REFERENCES

[1] E. Altman, K. Avrachenkov, and A. Garnaev. A jamming game in wireless networks with transmission cost. *Proc. The International Conference on Network Control and Optimization (NET-COOP 2007)*, 4465:1–12, 2007.

[2] B. Awerbuch, A. Richa, and C. Scheideler. A jamming-resistant mac protocol for single-hop wireless networks. In *ACM PODC*, 2008.

[3] T. Basar and G. J. Olsder. *Dynamic Noncooperative Game Theory*. Academic Press, 1999.

[4] E. Bayraktaroglu, C. King, X. Liu, G. Noubir, R. Rajaraman, and B. Thapa. On the performance of ieee 802.11 under jamming. In *Proceedings of IEEE INFOCOM*, 2008.

[5] M. A. Bender, M. Farach-Colton, S. He, B. C. Kuszmaul, and C. E. Leiserson. Adversarial contention resolution for simple channels. In *SPAA*, 2005.

[6] J. Bicket. Bit-rate selection in wireless networks. *MIT Master's Thesis*, 2005.

[7] I. Broustis, K. Pelechrinis, D. Syrivelis, S. V. Krishnamurthy, and L. Tassiulas. Fiji: Fighting implicit jamming in 802.11 wlans. *SecureComm*, 2009.

[8] J. Camp and E. Knightly. Modulation rate adaptation in urban and vehicular environments: Cross-layer implementation and experimental evaluation. *MobiCom*, 2008.

[9] A. Chan, X. Liu, G. Noubir, and B. Thapa. Control channel jamming: Resilience and identification of traitors. In *IEEE ISIT*, 2007.

[10] J. Chiang and Y.-C. Hu. Cross-layer jamming detection and mitigation in wireless broadcast networks. In *MobiCom*, 2007.

[11] T. M. Cover and J. A. Thomas. *Elements of Information Theory*. Wiley, 2006.

[12] K. Firouzbakht, G. Noubir and M. Salehi. *Notes On the Capacity of Rate-Adaptive Packetized Wireless Communication Links under Jamming Power Constraint*, 2012. Available On-line: http://myfiles.neu.edu/ firouzbakht.k/Notes/TechnicalManual.pdf?uniq=-s4dgc0.

[13] K. Firouzbakht, G. Noubir, and M. Salehi. Superposition coding in an adversarial environment. *45th Annual Conference on Information Sciences and Systems (CISS)*, May 2011.

[14] S. Gilbert, R. Guerraoui, and C. Newport. Of malicious motes and suspicious sensors: On the efficiency of malicious interference in wireless networks. In *OPODIS*, 2006.

[15] G. Holland, N. Vaidya, and V. Bahl. A rate-adaptive mac protocol for multihop wireless networks. *ACM MOBICOM*, 2001.

[16] T. Jin, G. Noubir, and B. Thapa. Zero pre-shared secret key establishment in the presence of jammers. In *Proceedings of the tenth ACM international symposium on Mobile ad hoc networking and computing, MobiHoc'09*, pages 219–228, New York, NY, USA, 2009. ACM.

[17] G. Judd, X. Wang, and P. Steenkiste. Efficient channel-aware rate adaptation in dynamic environments. *MobiSys*, 2008.

[18] J. Kim, S. Kim, S. Choi, and D. Qiao. Cara: Collision-aware rate adaptation for ieee 802.11 wlans. *INFOCOM*, 2006.

[19] C. Koo, V. Bhandari, J. Katz, and N. Vaidya. Reliable broadcast in radio networks: The bounded collision case. In *ACM PODC*, 2006.

[20] M. Lacage, M. H. Manshaei, and T. Turletti. Ieee 802.11 rate adaptation: A practical approach. *ACM MSWiM*, 2004.

[21] L. Lazos, S. Liu, and M. Krunz. Mitigating control-channel jamming attacks in multi-channel ad hoc networks. In *Proceedings of the second ACM conference on Wireless network security*, WiSec '09, pages 169–180, New York, NY, USA, 2009. ACM.

[22] M. Li, I. Koutsopoulos, and R. Poovendran. Optimal jamming attacks and network defense policies in wireless sensor networks. In *INFOCOM*, 2007.

[23] G. Lin and G. Noubir. On link layer denial of service in data wireless lans. *Wiley Journal on Wireless Communications and Mobile Computing*, 5, 2004.

[24] G. Lin and G. Noubir. On link layer denial of service in data wireless lans. *Wirel. Commun. Mob. Comput.*, 5(3):273–284, 2005.

[25] S. Liu, L. Lazos, and M. Krunz. Thwarting inside jamming attacks on wireless broadcast communications. In *Proceedings of the fourth ACM conference on Wireless network security*, WiSec '11, pages 29–40, New York, NY, USA, 2011. ACM.

[26] Y. Liu, P. Ning, H. Dai, and A. Liu. Randomized differential dsss: jamming-resistant wireless broadcast communication. In *Proceedings of the 29th conference on Information communications*, INFOCOM'10, pages 695–703, Piscataway, NJ, USA, 2010. IEEE Press.

[27] J. Nash. Non-cooperative games. *Annuals of Mathematics*, pages 286–295, 1951.

[28] R. Negi and A. Perrig. Jamming analysis of MAC protocols. Technical report, Carnegie Mellon University, 2003.

[29] G. Noubir, R. Rajaraman, B. Sheng, and B. Thapa. On the robustness of ieee 802.11 rate adaptation algorithms against smart jamming. In *Proceedings of the fourth ACM conference on Wireless network security*, WiSec '11, pages 97–108, New York, NY, USA, 2011. ACM.

[30] G. Owen. *Game Theory*. Academic Press, 1995.

[31] K. Pelechrinis, I. Broustis, S. V. Krishnamurthy, and C. Gkantsidis. Ares: an anti-jamming reinforcement system for 802.11 networks. In *Proceedings of the 5th international conference on Emerging networking experiments and technologies*, CoNEXT '09, pages 181–192, New York, NY, USA, 2009. ACM.

[32] R. K. Peterson, R. E. Ziemer, and D. E. Borth. *Introduction to Spread-Spectrum Communications*. Prentice-Hall, 1995.

[33] H. Rahul, F. Edalat, D. Katabi, and C. Sodini. Frequency-aware rate adaptation and mac protocols. *MobiCom*, 2009.

[34] K. Ramachandran, R. Kokku, H. Zhang, and M. Gruteser. Symphony: Synchronous two-phase rate power control in 802.11 wlans. *MobiSys*, 2008.

[35] K. B. Rasmussen, S. Capkun, and M. Cagalj. Secnav: secure broadcast localization and time synchronization in wireless networks. In *MobiCom*, 2007.

[36] M. K. Simon, J. K. Omura, R. A. Scholtz, and B. K. Levitt. *Spread Spectrum Communications Handbook*. McGraw-Hill, 2001.

[37] D. Slater, P. Tague, R. Poovendran, and B. Matt. A coding-theoretic approach for efficient message verification over insecure channels. In *2nd ACM Conference on Wireless Network Security (WiSec)*, 2009.

[38] M. Strasser, C. Popper, and S. Capkun. Efficient uncoordinated fhss anti-jamming communication. In *MobiHoc*, 2009.

[39] M. Strasser, C. Popper, S. Capkun, and M. Cagalj. Jamming-resistant key establishment using uncoordinated frequency hopping. In *ISSP*, 2008.

[40] P. Tague, M. Li, and R. Poovendran. Probabilistic mitigation of control channel jamming via random key distribution. In *Proceedings of International Symposium on Personal, Indoor and Mobile Radio Communications*, 2007.

[41] P. Tague, D. Slater, G. Noubir, and R. Poovendran. Linear programming models for jamming attacks on network traffic flows. In *WiOpt*, 2008.

[42] M. Vutukuru, H. Balakrishnan, and K. Jamieson. Cross-layer wireless bit rate adaptation. *SIGCOMM*, 2009.

[43] T. Wang and G. B. Giannakis. Mutual information jammer-relay games. *IEEE Transactions on Information Forensics and Security*, 3(2):290–303, June 2008.

[44] M. Wilhelm, I. Martinovic, J. B. Schmitt, and V. Lenders. Short paper: reactive jamming in wireless networks: how realistic is the threat? In *Proceedings of the fourth ACM conference on Wireless network security*, WiSec '11, pages 47–52, New York, NY, USA, 2011. ACM.

[45] S. H. Wong, H. Yang, S. Lu, and V. Bharghavan. Robust rate adaptation for 802.11 wireless networks. *MobiCom*, 2006.

[46] W. Xu, K. Ma, W. Trappe, and Y. Zhang. Jamming sensor networks: attack and defense strategies. *IEEE Network*, 2006.

[47] W. Xu, K. Ma, W. Trappe, and Y. Zhang. Jamming sensor networks: attack and defense strategies. *IEEE Network*, 20(3):41–47, 2006.

[48] W. Xu, W. Trappe, and Y. Zhang. Channel surfing: defending wireless sensor networks from interference. In *Proceedings of the 6th international conference on Information processing in sensor networks*, IPSN '07, pages 499–508, New York, NY, USA, 2007. ACM.

[49] W. Xu, W. Trappe, and Y. Zhang. Defending wireless sensor networks from radio interference through channel adaptation. *ACM Transactions on Sensor Networks*, 4:18:1–18:34, September 2008.

Physical-Layer Attacks on Chirp-based Ranging Systems

Aanjhan Ranganathan*
aanjhan.ranganathan@inf.ethz.ch

Boris Danev*
boris.danev@inf.ethz.ch

Aurélien Francillon†
aurelien.francillon@eurecom.fr

Srdjan Capkun*
srdjan.capkun@inf.ethz.ch

* ETH Zurich
Department of Computer Science
8092 Zurich, Switzerland

† Eurecom
2229 Route des Cretes
F-06560 Sophia-Antipolis

ABSTRACT

Chirp signals have been extensively used in radar and sonar systems to determine distance, velocity and angular position of objects and in wireless communications as a spread spectrum technique to provide robustness and high processing gain. Recently, several standards have adopted chirp spread spectrum (CSS) as an underlying physical-layer scheme for precise, low-power and low-complexity real-time localization. While CSS-based ranging and localization solutions have been implemented and deployed, their security has so far not been analyzed.

In this work, we analyze CSS-based ranging and localization systems. We focus on distance decreasing relay attacks that have proven detrimental for the security of proximity-based access control systems (e.g., passive vehicle keyless entry and start systems). We describe a set of distance decreasing attacks realizations and verify their feasibility by simulations and experiments on a commercial ranging system. Our results demonstrate that an attacker is able to effectively reduce the distance measured by chirp-based ranging systems from 150 m to 600 m depending on chirp configuration. Finally, we discuss possible countermeasures against these attacks.

Categories and Subject Descriptors

C.2.0 [**General**]: Security and protection

Keywords

Chirp, Ranging Systems, Physical-layer attacks

1. INTRODUCTION

The rapid deployment of wireless systems has driven an increasing interest in the use of radio communication technologies for ranging and localization. The combination of data communication and location determination enables a broad application space of location-aware services [19]. Examples include people localization and tracking, asset management as well as safety and security applications such as emergency support [11] and access control [16, 33].

Numerous ranging and localization technologies were developed in the last decade [24]; they differ in communication channels (e.g., radio frequency, optical), position-related parameters (e.g., received signal strength (RSS), time-of-arrival (TOA), time-difference-of-arrival (TDOA)), target operating environment (e.g., indoor, outdoor), precision and reliability. Prominent examples include GPS [26] for outdoor localization and systems based on RSS [6, 44], TDOA [41, 46] and round-trip time-of-flight (RTOF) [42, 3] operating both outdoors and indoors. Most of these distance measurement techniques are inherently insecure. For example, an attacker can fake the signal strength in an RSS based distance measurement system. Similarly, in an ultrasonic ranging system, an attacker can gain advantage by relaying messages over the faster RF channel [37]. For short and medium-distance precision ranging and localisation, ultra-wide band (UWB) and chirp spread spectrum (CSS) emerged as the most prominent techniques and were standardized in IEEE 802.15.4a [21] and ISO/IEC 24730-5 [22]. Their ranging resolution and reliability makes them suitable for numerous applications including indoor asset tracking and guidance [36], loss protection [3], etc. While UWB provides robust and precise distance measurements, the difficulties of building small-size, low-power receivers has currently limited its use. However, the properties of CSS [7, 39] allow low-complexity and low-power implementations of both the transmitter and receiver on a single integrated hardware [28]. This enables the realization of two-way distance-ranging solutions using RTOF with relatively high distance resolution (1 m) [3].

In this work, we study the security of CSS-based ranging systems. Although CSS-based ranging solutions have already been commercialized (e.g., for child-monitoring, mine safety, warehouse monitoring systems), their security, and therefore their appropriateness of use in security- and safety-critical applications has so far not been evaluated. The implications of distance modification attacks in scenarios where these systems are deployed in security-critical applications like access control to automobiles, buildings and medical devices are significant. Recent examples of attacks on the physical distance (e.g., on near-field communication (NFC) payment systems [14], passive vehicle keyless entry

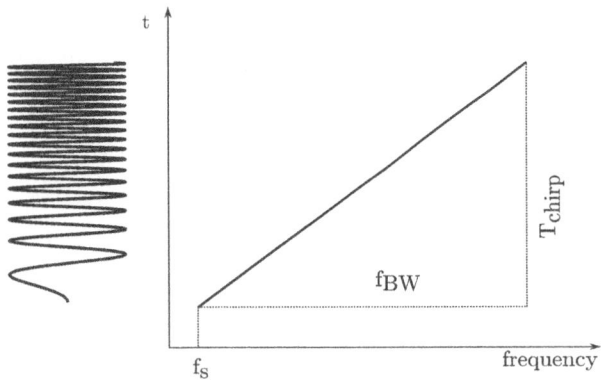

(a) Frequency vs Time representation of chirp signal.

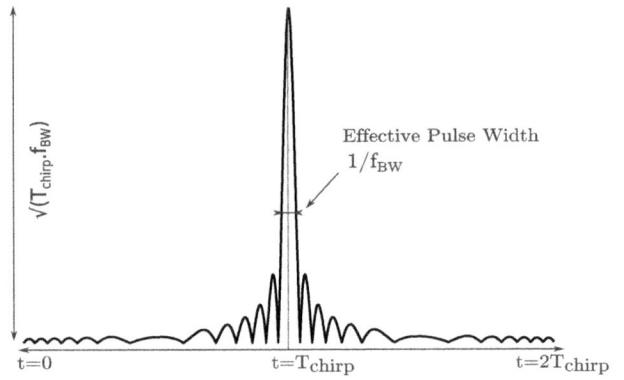

(b) Result of pulse compression.

Figure 1: Chirp signals: (a) The linear variation of chirp signal frequency with time. (b) Compressed pulse output of the matched filter.

systems [13]) further motivate the need of investigating and understanding the security implications of physical-layer distance measurement mechanisms. Such understanding enables us to evaluate their use in security-critical applications.

The contributions of this work are as follows. We analyze the security of CSS-based ranging systems, focusing on standardized schemes adopted in the ISO/IEC 24730-5 standard for real-time localization (RTLS) and used in a commercial-of-the-shelf (COTS) ranging system [29]. We show that distance modification attacks on CSS-based ranging systems are feasible by exploiting the inherent physical properties of chirp signals; we focus on attacks which result in a decrease of the measured distance since these have been shown to be most relevant in majority of security applications. We validate our findings by simulations and measurements from COTS CSS transceivers in several indoor locations to account for real-world channels. Our distance decreasing attacks account for the attacker's hardware delays and thus are close to practical conditions. Our results demonstrate that an attacker would be able to effectively reduce the distance estimated by a trusted distance-ranging system by more than 150 m for typical short chirp durations and more than 600 m for longer chirps. Since the attacks exploit physical-layer characteristics of CSS communication, we show that higher layer cryptographic mechanisms cannot prevent these attacks. Finally, we discuss possible countermeasures against these attacks.

The remainder of this paper is organized as follows. In Section 2, we provide CSS background. In Section 3, we define and discuss the attacks that can be mounted on chirp-based ranging systems. In Section 4, we describe our experimental setup and evaluate the feasibility of the proposed attacks through simulations and experiments. We also discuss the implication of our findings. In Section 5, we enumerate possible countermeasures. We provide the related work in Section 7 and conclude the paper in Section 8.

2. BACKGROUND: CHIRP SPREAD SPECTRUM

In this section we provide an overview of chirp signals and pulse compression commonly used by radar systems for distance measurement. We then describe typical chirp-based

ranging and discuss the existing CSS standards and commercially available chirp-based ranging solutions.

2.1 Chirp Signals

Chirps are sinusoidal signals whose frequency varies with time. Depending on the type of chirp, the frequency variation is linear or exponential. Chirp signals [7] have been extensively used in radar and sonar systems [9, 30] to determine, among other characteristics, range, velocity, and angular position of a target object. The representation of a linear chirp signal $y(t)$ is shown in Equation 1 where f_s is the starting sweep frequency and θ_0 represents the initial phase of the signal. Figure 1(a) shows how the chirp signal changes in frequency with time. Equation 2 gives the sweep rate α of the signal in terms of the chirp duration T_{chirp} and chirp bandwidth ω_{BW}.

$$y(t) = sin[2\pi(f_s + \alpha \cdot t)t] \qquad (1)$$

$$\alpha = \frac{\omega_{BW}}{2 \cdot T_{chirp}} \qquad (2)$$

$$f(t) = f_s + \alpha \cdot t \qquad (3)$$

Due to the linear frequency sweep, chirp signals can be efficiently compressed to pulses referred to as **pulse compression**. This is achieved by correlating the received chirp signal with its matched filter. The matched filter output with a chirp input is a short pulse as shown in Figure 1(b). The pulse width of the chirp T_{chirp} is compressed to an effective width of $1/\omega_{BW}$. The effective output of the matched filter is the combined energy of the chirp pulse over its entire duration. This results in a processing gain that increases the signal-to-noise ratio at the receiver, thus reducing the bit error rate. Chirp pulse compression combines high processing gain with the improved distance resolution of short pulses.

The use of chirp signals for communication provides several advantages. Chirp signals exhibit high effective bandwidth as they sweep through the entire frequency space. Due to the larger bandwidth, they are less susceptible to multi-path and other channel disturbances. Another advantage is that chirps can be processed only using analog signal processing blocks e.g., SAW filters [38]. This allows low-complexity and low-power realization of both communication and ranging. The strong auto-correlation properties

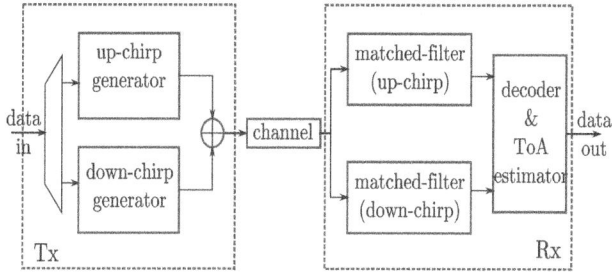

Figure 2: Building blocks of a CSS system: Data is modulated using BOK scheme at the transmitter. The receiver decodes and estimates time-of-arrival based on the matched filter outputs.

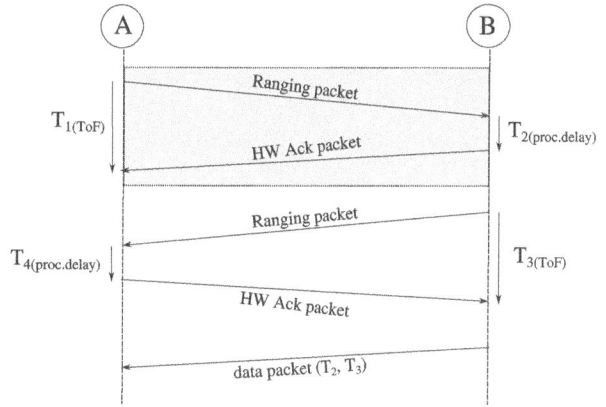

Figure 3: SDS-TWR ranging scheme: RTOF measurements $(T_{1(ToF)}, T_{3(ToF)})$ are calculated by both nodes A and B. In the final step node B exchanges its time measurements with A. In a single sided two way ranging (highlighted), the RTOF measurement is calculated by node A only.

of the chirp signals add more robustness to distance measurements in multipath environments.

2.2 Chirp-based Ranging System

In this section we describe the modulation and demodulation blocks of a generic chirp-based ranging system. We further explain how the time-of-arrival (TOA) of chirp signals is estimated to provide ranging information.

2.2.1 Data modulation and demodulation

There are typically two ways of modulating data in a chirp-based communication system: Binary Orthogonal Keying (BOK) and Chirp Direct Modulation (CDM). In the BOK scheme [43], '1' is represented by a chirp with increasing frequency sweep and '0' is represented by a decreasing frequency sweep. Monotonically increasing frequency sweep signals are referred to as "up-chirps" and decreasing frequency sweeps – "down-chirps". Since the up- and down-chirps are mutually orthogonal, their cross-correlation is zero. This simplifies the receiver's decision making about which data bit is being transmitted. In the CDM scheme [15, 20], the data bits are modulated using a conventional modulation technique, such as *m-ary PSK*. The data is first modulated and then spread with a pre-configured chirp signal. Here, the chirps are primarily used for spreading and are independent of the underlying modulation technique. We focus the remainder of this paper on the *BOK* modulation scheme. Figure 2 illustrates the key blocks of a CSS-based communication system using BOK modulation. At the receiver, the signal is processed through two matched filters for up- and down-chirps respectively. The decision making block compares the outputs of the matched filters to decode the data bit. It should be noted that for the extraction of ranging information, additional signal processing is required.

2.2.2 TOA estimation and ranging

Distance ranging with CSS-based systems relies on time-of-flight (TOF) measurements obtained by accurate time-of-arrival (TOA) estimation. There are two possible approaches to obtain the TOA of the chirp signal at the receiver. One uses dispersive delay lines to perform pulse compression. Different frequency components in a signal experience different delays in the delay line which results in a compressed pulse containing the summed energy of the entire chirp signal. The maximum peak of the delay line time response indicates the time of arrival. The TOA precision depends on the sampling rate of the time response. This

approach distinguishes itself by low-power consumption as the dispersive delay lines are passive analog components.

A second approach consists of generating the compressed pulse by cross-correlating the received signal with a template chirp signal using a digital signal processor (DSP). The incoming chirp signals are sampled and fed to the DSP. The DSP correlator's output is also a compressed pulse as in the previous approach. The peak output indicates the signal TOA. This design would typically consume more power, but offers high flexibility as most of the signal processing is done in the digital domain.

Further processing techniques such as spectral estimation and sample interpolation could be used to increase TOA estimate precision. It should be noted that TOF measurements also depend on tight clock synchronization between the transmitter and receiver. Given that local clocks may not exhibit sufficient long-term stability, ranging systems work by round-trip time-of-flight measurements. In such case, the distance between two nodes A and B is given by $d = \frac{c \cdot (t_{RTOF} - t_p)}{2}$, where c is the speed of light $(3 \cdot 10^8 \, \text{m/s})$, t_{RTOF} is the round-trip time elapsed and t_p is the processing delay at B before responding to the ranging signal. This type of asynchronous ranging also often referred to as two-way time-of-flight ranging and does not require tight clock synchronization.

2.3 CSS Ranging Standards

In 2007, the IEEE 802.15.4a-2007 [21] standard was introduced to standardize lower network layers of wireless personal area networks with strong focus on low-cost and low-rate communication between devices. This standard includes two physical-layer (PHY) specifications: ultra wideband impulse radio (UWB-IR) and chirp spread spectrum (CSS). ISO/IEC 24730-5:2010 [22] standardizes the use of CSS for ranging systems by defining air interface protocols and an application programming interface (API) for real-time localization systems (RTLS). The defined ranging protocol uses chirp spread spectrum at frequencies from 2.4 GHz to 2.483 GHz. It supports two-way TOF ranging and bidirectional communication between readers and tags of the RTLS.

Nanotron's Ranging Hardware: The NanoLOC transceiver from Nanotron is the only low-cost, low-power CSS-based ranging chip available off the shelf today. It uses BOK modulation and operates in the 2.4 GHz ISM band. Two nominal signal bandwidths are available on the chip: 22 MHz and 80 MHz. The chirp duration is configurable with $T_{chirp} = 1.0, 2.0$ or $4.0\mu s$. The distance range is estimated based on the RTOF measurements. Local clock drifts introduces inaccuracies in the measurements. The system executes a symmetric two-way ranging process referred to as *Symmetric Double-Sided Two-Way Ranging [SDS-TWR]*. The steps involved in the SDS-TWR scheme are illustrated in Figure 3. The first ranging measurement is calculated based on the RTOF from node A to node B and back to node A. A second measurement is determined with B initiating the ranging. In the final step node B shares the measured time values with node A. Node A computes its range estimate and the result is then averaged. This double-sided ranging mechanism mitigates the ranging inaccuracies due to local clock drifts at the nodes.

3. PHYSICAL-LAYER ATTACKS ON CSS RANGING SYSTEMS

In this section we investigate physical-layer distance decreasing attacks on CSS-based ranging systems. We state the system assumptions and discuss two distance decreasing attacks: by the early detection and by the late commit of chirp signals.

3.1 Distance Decreasing Attack by Early Detection and Late Commit

We consider two devices A and B that are able to communicate over a wireless radio link. The devices use the CSS BOK scheme for communication and ranging. We assume device A measures and verifies the distance claimed by device B. Device A is trusted and assumed to be honest. In this setting distance decreasing attacks can be mounted in two ways: (i) by a dishonest device B trying to cheat on its distance to A, referred to as an *internal attack* (ii) by an external attacker who aims to shorten the distance between A and an honest device B, referred to as a "distance-decreasing relay attack".

There are several ways for a dishonest device B to mount an internal attack. For example, device B can cheat on the distance by simply reporting incorrect values of T_2 and T_3 in the two-way ranging scheme as shown in Figure 3. Moreover, device B can reduce its message processing time. The presented techniques in the reminder of this paper can be used by a dishonest device B to decrease its distance to A without any loss of generality. We note that internal attacks can only be prevented by distance bounding techniques which enable very small and fixed processing delays [40, 34].

The distance-decreasing relay attack is performed by an external attacker under the assumption that devices A and B are both honest. To decrease the distance, it is insufficient for an external attacker to simply relay signals between the devices as the round-trip time would still be equivalent to the actual distance between A and B. Instead, a successful attacker must Early Detect (ED) signals from A and Late Commit (LC) those signals to B. Clulow et al. [8] in-

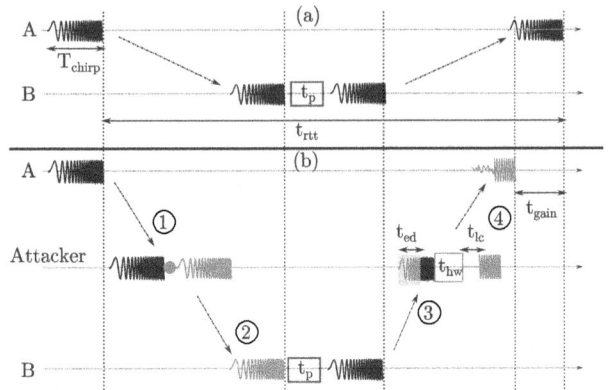

Figure 4: Distance decreasing attack: (a) CSS ranging in a non-adversial setting where t_{rtt} is the estimated RTOF. (b) Attacker reduces the total round-trip time to $t_{rtt}-t_{gain}$ by performing early detect and late commit on node B's response CSS signal while communications from A to B are relayed without any LC or ED.

troduced attacks using ED and LC and their feasibility on RFID was demonstrated in [18]. Here, we study the feasibility of ED and LC attacks on CSS-based ranging. We assume the attacker is able to receive signals over the entire bandwidth necessary and has knowledge of system parameters including the modulation scheme, symbol duration and packet structure.

Figure 4 illustrates how an attacker modifies the distance by means of early detect and late commit of CSS signals. Figure 4(a) shows CSS ranging in a non-adversarial setting, where t_{rtt} denotes the time taken to receive a reply from device B for a ranging signal transmitted by A and t_p is B's processing time. The distance between A and B is computed using the expression $\frac{c \cdot t_{rtt}}{2}$.

Figure 4(b) shows an attack on CSS ranging by ED and LC. We assume that the attacker is closer to A than B is. The attacker first receives the signal transmitted by A, amplifies it and forwards it to B (1). B receives, demodulates, computes the response and transmits the response back after a time delay t_p (2). The attacker now "early detects" the response (3). For early detection, the attacker modifies the receiver circuits to determine the symbol's data earlier than a standard receiver. Let $t_{ed} < T_{chirp}$ be the time required to predict the symbol with a high confidence; T_{chirp} is the time duration of a single chirp signal, i.e., symbol duration. Simultaneously to the early detection phase, the attacker performs a late commit attack. It consists of first transmitting an arbitrary signal (e.g., any signal with zero correlation with the up- or down-chirp) during the early detection phase. Once the symbol is predicted, the attacker stops transmitting the arbitrary signal and switches to transmitting the chirp corresponding to the predicted symbol, i.e., the attacker "commits" to the predicted symbol, commonly known as late commit. Let t_{lc} be the time duration for which the arbitrary signal is transmitted until the correct symbol has been predicted. The early detection of chirps and the late commit signal structure are shown in Figure 5(a) and 5(b) respectively.

The attacker hardware circuitry for performing the early

(a) Signal properties of early detect.

(b) Signal properties of a late committed signal.

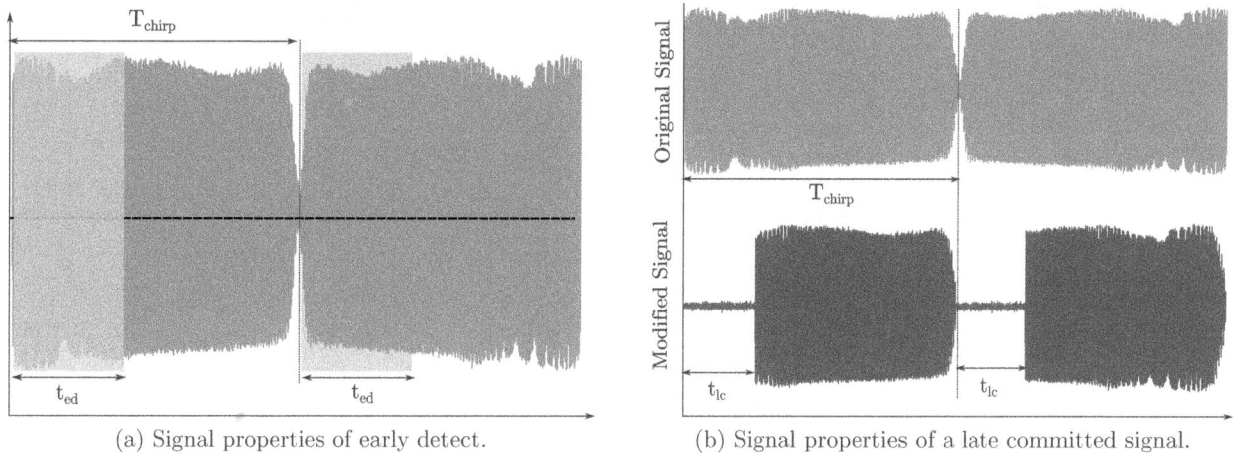

Figure 5: ED and LC signal structure: (a) Early detect: t_{ed} **is the time period over which the CSS signal is observed before predicting the symbol. (b) Late commit: An arbitrary signal (here just channel noise) is transmitted for a time duration** t_{lc} **before committing to the correct symbol.**

detection and late commit introduces an inherent delay t_{hw}. The attacker transmits the chirp corresponding to the predicted symbol which A receives after a total round-trip time $t_{rtt} - t_{gain}$ thereby gaining a distance of $d_{gain} = \frac{c \cdot t_{gain}}{2}$. The effective time gained t_{gain} depends on three factors: (i) the minimum time window t_{ed} required to observe the chirp for early symbol prediction (ii) the maximum time t_{lc} the attacker can delay before committing to the correct symbol without introducing additional bit errors at the receiver (iii) the attacker's hardware delay t_{hw} required for symbol prediction and symbol retransmission. The effective time gain is the sum of all the above factors as follows.

$$t_{gain} = t_{ed} + t_{lc} + t_{hw} \qquad (4)$$

In the following subsections, we discuss how to perform the aforementioned early detection and late commit attacks on CSS based ranging systems. In Section 4.3, we validate these attacks experimentally.

3.2 Early Detection of CSS Signals

We propose two ways of predicting CSS signals without requiring the receiver to receive the entire chirp: (i) zero crossing detection and (ii) early correlation using dispersive delay lines.

Zero crossing detectors detect the transition of a signal waveform through zero level. The basic idea of using zero-crossing detectors to perform early detection is that a low frequency signal has fewer such transitions than a high frequency signal for a fixed time window. As explained in the previous sections, an up-chirp (down-chirp) is a signal whose frequency increases (decreases) with time. Exploiting this property, we observe the signal over a time window much shorter than the chirp duration T_{chirp}. The number of zero crossings is then compared to template chirps and the symbol (bit) value is predicted. Under real-world conditions, channel noise increases signal transitions at the zero mark and thereby reduces prediction accuracy. However, our experiments on signals acquired under real channel fading show that setting a non-zero threshold value improves the symbol prediction accuracy. We were able to early detect by observ-

ing at least 20% of the chirp duration. Further details are provided in Section 4.3.1.

Early correlation with dispersive delay lines Dispersive delay lines are electro-mechanical devices where the delay experienced by the signal in the line is proportional to its frequency. An input signal to the delay line is separated into its frequency components and results in a compressed pulse at the output. Radar systems used Surface Acoustic Wave (SAW) filters for pulse compression. Bulk acoustic wave filters have a higher operation bandwidth with delays in the range of $0.5 - 2.5\mu$ s. It is therefore possible to implement a short-time correlator for the start frequencies of the chirp without the need of digitising the signal. This procedure would "early detect" the chirp structure (up- or down-chirp) by producing an output at the appropriate delay line.

In the digital processing domain, this is analogous to a short-time correlator where we only correlate part of the template chirp signal before predicting the bit. We performed such experiments on signals captured over real channels. Our results indicate that it is possible to predict early by correlating over only 5% of the chirp duration.

3.3 Late Commit of CSS Signals

In a late commit attack, the attacker transmits an arbitrary signal that is constructed based on the receiver's implementation of signal detection and interpretation until the correct bit is available. Since CSS receivers implement matched filters that decode the symbols by cross-correlating the received signal with known template chirps, optimal late commit results are obtained if the attacker does not transmit any signal until the correct symbol is available, i.e., if the attacker's arbitrary signal is a "zero" signal. In order to maximise the effectiveness of the attack, i.e., maximize distance decrease, it is important for the attacker to know its distance from B. Based on this distance, the attacker can time its start of transmissions. Figure 5(b) shows the modified and unmodified signals (2 symbols) as received by the receiver. t_{lc} is the period for which the attacker does not transmit any signal while deciding on the correct chirp signal to be transmitted. We show by simulations in Section 4.3.2

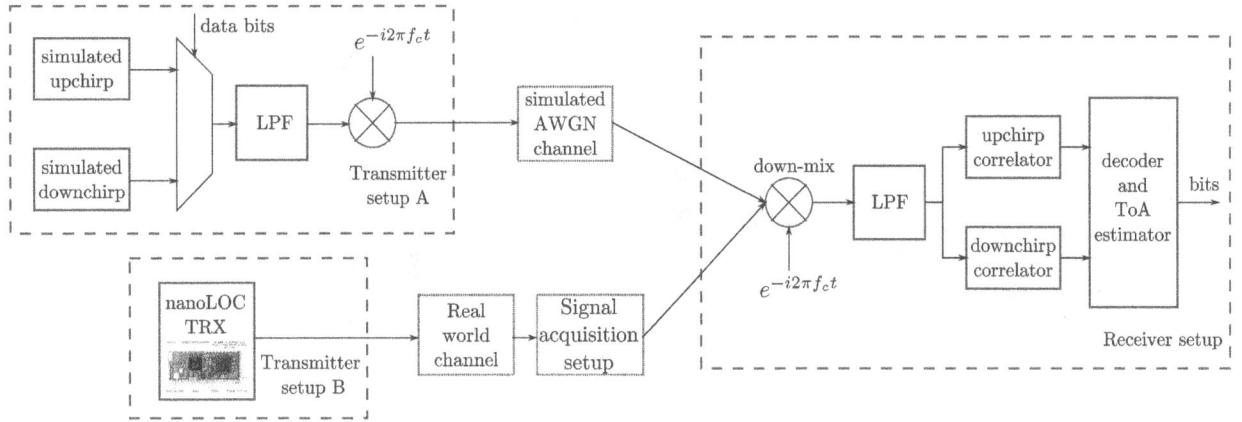

Figure 6: Experimental setup consisting of the simulated chirp transmitter (Transmitter setup A), the NanoLOC transceivers (Transmitter setup B) and the CSS receiver.

that the receiver is still able to decode the modified signal with an acceptable bit error rate.

4. EXPERIMENTAL EVALUATION

In this section we first describe our simulation and experimental setup. We then evaluate the feasibility of ED and LC attacks using simulated and recorded signals from a COTS transceiver in an indoor environment. Finally, we summarize the attacker's distance advantage for several chirp durations.

4.1 Experimental Setup

Our simulation and experimental setup (Figure 6) consists of a simulated chirp transmitter, a COTS chirp-based ranging transceiver and a chirp receiver able to process both simulated and recorded chirp transmissions.

Simulated chirp transmitter: The parameters to simulate the transmitter, i.e., packet structure, data encoding, chirp duration and bandwidth, and carrier frequency were chosen based on the available documentation in the standards and monitoring signals of the NanoLOC transceiver. The transmitter block consists of a chirp generator, a low-pass filter and a mixer. Data bits are encoded using the BOK scheme. One data packet contains 256 bits with 20 bits of alternating 0s and 1s as preamble and a 64 bit sync word. The chosen sync word is same as the one used in the NanoLOC transceiver. The remainder of the data packet consists of a MAC frame, payload and CRC checksums. The chirp duration T_{chirp} (corresponding to one data bit) is varied within the set $T_{chirp} = \{1, 2, 4\}\,\mu s$. The baseband complex chirp signal is quadrature modulated with a 2.441 GHz carrier before transmission. The transmitted CSS signal is subject to additive white gaussian noise with varying signal to noise ratios. Table 1 lists the various system parameters and their corresponding values chosen for the experimental evaluation.

NanoLOC transceiver: In a real-world communication, the wireless channel causes multiple signal impairments that adversely affect the communication and ranging accuracy. We validate our attacks under real-world channels using the NanoLOC transceiver. It is programmed to continuously transmit a known payload data. The receiver later uses this knowledge to estimate the bit errors. The chirp duration T_{chirp} is set to $2\,\mu s$. The NanoLOC is positioned at various locations and at different distances from the receiver setup

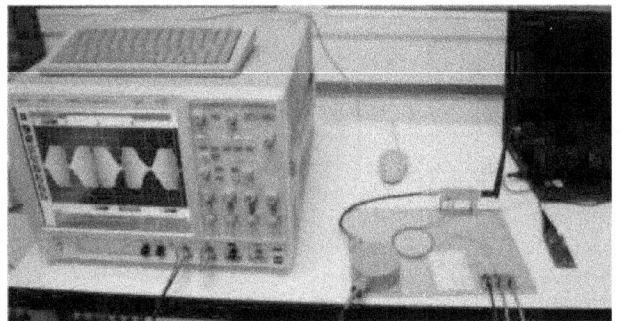

Figure 7: The signal acquisition setup for recording NanoLOC transciever CSS transmissions.

to capture different channel realizations. The captured signal measurements are later used to determine two characteristics under real-world channel effects: (i) an attacker's ability to early detect a chirp (ii) the correctness with which an honest receiver decodes a late-committed CSS signal.

Receiver setup: The receiver consists of a quadrature demodulator, low-pass filter and matched filter blocks implemented in Matlab. The quadrature demodulator converts the received CSS signal to its baseband complex signal. The matched filters correlate this signal with the template up- and down-chirps. The output of the matched filters is compared and the received bit is decoded. To capture the NanoLOC transmissions, we use an additional signal acquisition setup. This setup consists of a horn antenna for better directionality and a 40 dB low-noise amplifier. The received signal is then digitized at RF by an oscilloscope where the data is sampled at 10 GSa/s and stored. Figure 8 shows the received signal under an AWGN channel and real-world channels in comparison to the originally transmitted chirp. In reality, radio signals experience fading as they propagate through the channel to the receiver. Certain frequencies get attenuated more than the others as signals traverse multiple paths to reach the receiver. This effect is observed in the NanoLOC signal recordings at a distance of 2 m as shown in Figure 8.

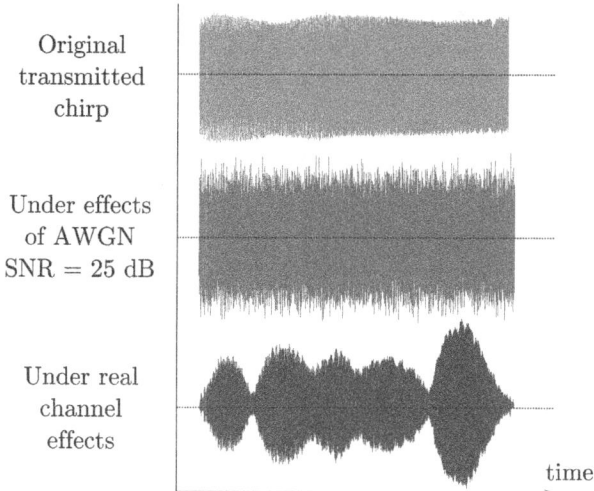

Figure 8: Comparison of the received CSS signal under an AWGN channel and real-world channels with that of the originally transmitted chirp.

Parameter	Value
Simulated Transmitter (A)	
T_{chirp}	$1\mu s, 2\mu s, 4\mu s$
f_c	2.441 GHz
ω_{BW}	80 MHz
Packet length	256 bits
NanoLOC TRX (B)	
T_{chirp}	$2\mu s$
f_c	2.441 GHz
ω_{BW}	80 MHz
$Power_{dBm}$	0 dBm
Packet length	256 bits

Table 1: System parameters used in the analysis.

4.2 Evaluation Metrics

We evaluate the effectiveness of the attacks based on the number of errors introduced at the receiver due to ED and LC modifications of the CSS signal. The decoded bits are compared with the originally transmitted bits and the number of bit errors per packet computed. We indicate the bit error rate as a percentage of the transmitted packet size of 256 bits. In the case of AWGN channel, the evaluations were averaged over 100 different iterations for each SNR value in the set 5, 10, 15, 20, 25 dB. For the experiments performed using the NanoLOC transceiver, the device was positioned at several indoor locations and at varying distances of 1, 2, 3, 5, 10 and 18 meters away from the receiver. We collected 10 sets of traces at every location with each trace containing two 256 bit packets using a digital storage oscilloscope.

4.3 Experimental Results

In this section, we present the results of ED and LC attacks performed on CSS signals. We also evaluate these attacks when error correcting codes are used and summarize the maximum distance decrease gain.

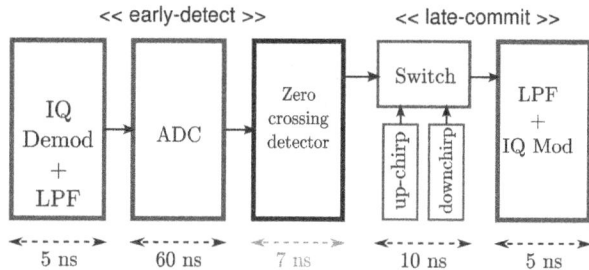

Figure 9: Attacker hardware: The zero crossing detector algorithm tested on a FPGA introduced a delay of 7 ns. Specified time delays of other blocks are based on COTS hardware specifications.

4.3.1 Early detection of chirps

We evaluate the feasibility of early detection using the zero crossing detector and short correlations (Section 3.2).

Our implementation of zero crossing detector-based early detection consists of a counter and comparator. We assume the attacker knows the number of zero crossings that occur in a specified time window for a standard up- or down-chirp. t_{ed} is the time window over which the transmitted signal is observed. The counter contains the number of zero crossings that occurred over the time t_{ed}. The symbol is predicted by comparing the counter value against the expected values for up- and down-chirps over the time t_{ed}. Figure 10(a) shows the number of incorrect predictions for various time window sizes (t_{ed}). We were able to achieve a 100% prediction accuracy when observing every chirp for t_{ed} values from 20% to 80% of T_{chirp} for an SNR of 25 dB under AWGN channel. Under real-world channels, where the CSS signal experiences fading, we were still able to predict with 100% accuracy for t_{ed} values from 20% to 70% of T_{chirp}. This is shown in Figure 10(b). The increase in symbol errors or decrease in prediction accuracy for higher values of t_{ed} is due to the chirp signal property itself. An up-chirp has an increasing frequency sweep while a down-chirp sweeps down the frequencies over the same band. Therefore, the number of zero crossings that occur over the entire duration of a single chirp T_{chirp} is equal for both the chirps. Hence, the number of symbol errors increases as $t_{ed} \rightarrow T_{chirp}$.

The noise introduces randomness in the number of signal transitions at the zero crossing and adversely affects the symbol prediction accuracy. A countermeasure is to use a non-zero value for detecting the transitions. In our implementation, the threshold value is configurable and is not limited to zero. We select the threshold value based on the noise floor level, which is estimated from channel observations in the absence of CSS transmissions.

Dispersive delay lines is an alternative design the attacker can implement to early detect chirp transmissions. As described in Section 3.2, this design is analogous to a short time correlator implemented in a DSP. In our experiments, we correlate the received CSS signal with a fraction of the template chirps, i.e., over a smaller time window (t_{ed}) of the original chirps. Our results indicate that it is possible to achieve 100% symbol prediction accuracy, cross-correlating only 5% of the received chirp even under real-world channels. The results are shown in Figure 10(c). It is important to note that cross-correlation using a DSP introduces a delay of the order of few μs. The exact delays exhibited by dispersive delay lines in a completely analog implementation remain to be explored.

4.3.2 Late commit attack

We evaluated the behaviour of the receiver under a late commit attack. To this extent, an arbitrary signal was transmitted for a time t_{lc} before switching to the appropriate chirp signal. We measure the receiver's ability to decode the symbols for varying t_{lc} and compute the number of symbol errors introduced due to the late-commit chirp signal. Figure 11(a) and Figure 11(b) show the number of symbol errors at the receiver for various hold times before committing the actual chirp, i.e., varying t_{lc}. The results indicate that at high SNR values, the receiver is able to decode all symbols when the attacker takes as long as 70% of T_{chirp} before committing to the correct chirp. We further evaluated the receiver's behaviour under real-world channels. The receiver was able to decode all symbols for t_{lc} values up to 60% of T_{chirp}. In high SNR signal reception, the receiver tolerated t_{lc} values up to 80%. The results under the measured real-world channels are shown in Figure 11(c).

4.3.3 Hardware implementation

The attacker's hardware delay influences the effective distance decrease. Figure 9 shows the building blocks of an attacker's hardware. The received signal is demodulated and sampled before feeding them to the zero crossing detector block for early detection. We implemented the zero crossing detector algorithm in VHDL and tested it on a Xilinx Spartan 3A FPGA board. The time taken for the algorithm (implemented in hardware) to predict the symbol from the moment all required samples from the analog to digital converter is available was 7 ns. The time delays of the demodulator, ADC, switch and the modulator shown in the figure are typical delays based on COTS components. The switch and the IQ modulators form part of the late commit hardware, which also contributes to the total hardware delay ($t_{hw} = 87$ ns). We account for t_{hw} in our effective distance decrease estimates described in Section 4.3.5.

4.3.4 Effect of error correction coding schemes

Errors in wireless communications, e.g., due to channel fading are common. Error correcting codes add reduncdant bits to the message before transmission to improve data communication reliability. The receiver uses this redundant information to detect or correct bit errors that occur during transmission. The NanoLOC transceiver can be configured to enable error correction and implements the $(7,4)$ Hamming code. The linear $(7,4)$ Hamming code [17] encodes 4 data bits into 7 bits by adding 3 parity bits. A scheme implementing the $(7,4)$ Hamming code corrects single bit errors. Therefore a 256 bit packet including redundant bits appended by the data encoder, the receiver would still be able to recover the original message for bit errors up to 14% of the packet. With this information, we conclude from Figure 11(c) that it would be possible for an attacker to commit as late as after 90% of the chirp duration T_{chirp}. For early detection, the attacker could predict 10% of the symbols and yet mount a successful distance decreasing attack. To this extent, from Figure 10(b) it would be sufficient to observe the chirp only for 10% of the chirp.

Common Parameters	T_{chirp}	Distance gained
$t_{ed} = 20\%$ of T_{chirp}	1μs	163 m
$t_{lc} = 80\%$ of T_{chirp}	2μs	313 m
$t_{hw} = 87$ ns	4μs	613 m

Table 2: Effective distance estimates.

4.3.5 Effective distance advantage for an attacker

We summarize the effective distance advantage an attacker gains in executing the ED and LC attacks. We derive our distance decrease estimates based on the experimental results under real-world channels. As described in Section 3.1, the effective distance gained depends on three factors: (i) t_{ed} (ii) t_{lc} and (iii) t_{hw}. From Figure 10(b), the attacker is required to observe at least 20% of the chirp period to predict the symbol with 100% accuracy. Similarly, from Figure 11(c), an attacker can wait no longer than 80% of T_{chirp} for committing to a symbol. The attacker's hardware delay in Section 4.3.3 is 87 ns. The maximum distance decrease possible is calculated using the expression $d_{gain} = \frac{c \cdot t_{gain}}{2}$. The results and the parameters are summarised in Table 2. We conclude that an attacker would be able to successfully mount a distance decrease of more than 150 m for 1μs chirps and up to 600 m for 4μs long chirps. However, the use of error correcting codes increases the above estimates by about 10%.

5. DISCUSSION

Our analysis demonstrates the feasibility of physical-layer distance decreasing attacks on CSS ranging and their security implications. One countermeasure is to estimate the power spectral density (PSD) of the received CSS signal. PSD of a signal indicates the distribution of energy in the various frequency components of the signal. In a late commit attack, the attacker transmits an arbitrary or no signal until the correct symbol is predicted. Since chirp signals are sweep all frequencies in a linear manner, a late commit results in missing frequency bands. The receiver may detect the attack based on the energy voids in the PSD. It is important to note that spectral estimation techniques are computationally intensive and so are unsuitable for ultralow power ranging solutions. An alternative approach is to set a specific threshold on the compressed pulse peak amplitude. The output of the matched filter or the dispersive delay line is a compressed pulse which is an aggregation of the energy present in the received signal's frequency components. Thus, under a late commit attack, the peak amplitude of the compressed pulse would be lower and the receiver could detect this change by setting an appropriate threshold. While low-cost and simple to implement, the major issue with such a countermeasure is to distinguish between actual attacks and channel fading effects. Even in an non-adversarial environment, wireless signals experience fading as they propagate through the channel. Signal frequencies get attenuated which would also affect the peak amplitude. Therefore, setting a threshold needs to take into account the channel uncertainty in order to reduce the false positives, i.e., channels that attenuate the CSS signals in a similar manner as a late commit attack. Further investigation is required to evaluate under what conditions (e.g., SNR) this countermeasure would work in a effective way.

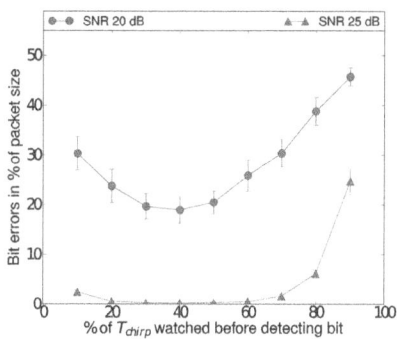

(a) Early detection of chirps on simulated AWGN channel.

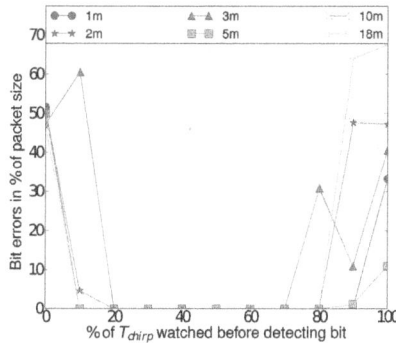

(b) Early detection in real-world channels using zero-crossing detectors.

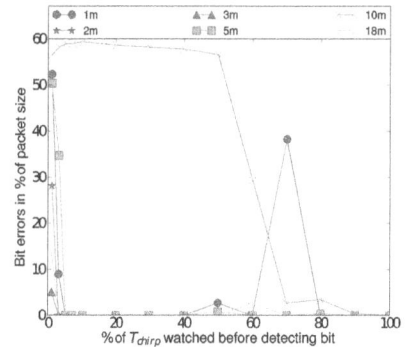

(c) Early detection in real-world channels by early correlation.

Figure 10: Early detection results: (a) Under a high SNR AWGN channel, it was sufficient to observe only 20% of chirp duration to predict the symbol. (b) Similar results for CSS signals received from the NanoLOC transceiver at various positions using zero-crossing detection. (c) Cross-correlating 5% of T_{chirp} is sufficient for predicting the symbol accurately for most channel conditions.

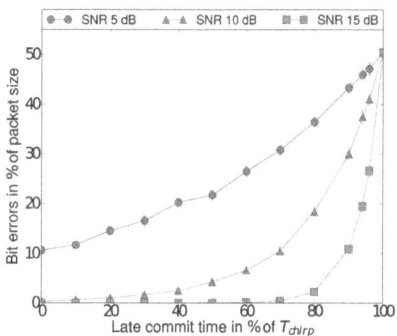

(a) Late commit on chirps with $T_{chirp} = 1\mu s$ and simulated AWGN channel.

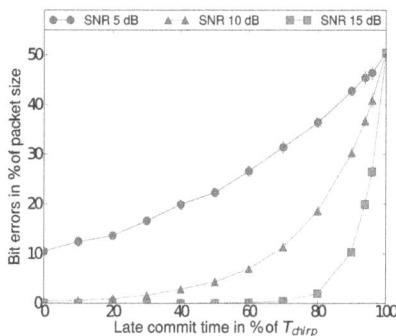

(b) Late commit on chirps with $T_{chirp} = 2\mu s$ and simulated AWGN channel.

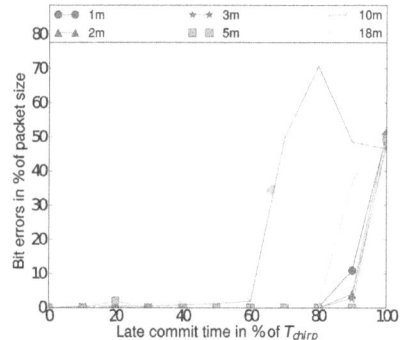

(c) Late commit under real channel effects

Figure 11: Late commit receiver behaviour: (a & b) For high SNR AWGN channels, the attacker can take as long as 70% of T_{chirp} before committing to a symbol. (c) For most of the real-world channels in the experiment, the receiver decoded all symbols for t_{lc} values up to 80% of T_{chirp}.

6. FUTURE WORK

In this work we analyzed CSS ranging systems that modulate data using BOK. The applicability of the ED and LC attacks on ranging systems implementing chirp direct modulation (CDM) needs further investigation. CDM systems primarily use chirps for spreading and modulate data using a m-ary PSK scheme. PSK-based systems encode data in the phase transitions between symbol periods. The time window available to early detect and late commit is therefore smaller than in a BOK scheme and thereby the possibility of distance decreasing attacks would depend on the particular synchronisation and decoding procedures. We intend to consider such techniques in future work.

Physical-layer attacks on ranging systems are highly time-constrained. Existing radio platforms such as USRP have a processing delay of the order of few microseconds (larger than symbol period) before the received signal is decoded; which makes them unsuitable without modification for implementing ED and LC attacks. We intend to realize an end-to-end hardware module with small processing delay

and capable of executing physical-layer attacks in real-time as future work. Such a platform [2] would also enable real-world security analysis of proposed solutions.

7. RELATED WORK

Physical-layer security of wireless systems has gained a lot of interest in the last years. It exploits the physical properties of the radio communication system and are therefore independent of any higher level cryptographic protocols implemented. Several attacks ranging from simply relaying the signal between honest nodes to injecting messages at the physical layer were demonstrated in the past. In this section we discuss relevant related work in physical-layer security of wireless ranging systems beginning with the works closest to ours.

Clulow et al.[8] introduced physical-layer attacks such as early detect and late commit attacks. The feasibility of these attacks on a ISO 14443 RFID was demonstrated in [18]. Flury et al. [12, 32] evaluated the security of IEEE 802.15.4a with impulse radio ultra wide-band PHY layer. The authors demonstrated an effective distance decrease of 140 m for the mandatory modes of the standard. The evaluations were performed using simulations. The inherent hardware delays due to bit detection, antenna and heterodyning circuitry were not considered. Poturalski et al. [31] introduced the Cicada attack on the impulse radio ultra wide-band PHY. In this attack, a malicious transmitter continuously transmits a "1" impulse with power greater than that of an honest transmitter. This degrades the performance of energy detection based receivers resulting in distance reduction and possibly denial of service. Recently, Francillon et al. [13] demonstrated distance decrease attacks on passive keyless entry systems deployed in modern cars by relaying signals at the physical-layer between the key and the car using an USRP [1].

Chirp signals were initially used in radar systems. Due to their resilience towards channel interference, chirp signals were later proposed for use in spread spectrum communications [43, 10]. David Adamy in [4] describes ways to detect, jam, intercept and locate chirped signals and transmitters. The emergence of dispersive delay lines such as the SAW delay lines made it possible to realize less complex wideband pulse generators and detectors [25]. Recent increase in the number of ranging application requirements and the standardization of CSS in the IEEE 802.15.4a as an alternative PHY resulted in a number of CSS-based ranging schemes [27, 23, 5, 35]. Yoon et al. [45], performed an exhaustive experimental analysis of the NanoLOC ranging system under non-adversarial settings in both indoor and outdoor environment and discussed its implications. To the best of our knowledge this work is the first that analyzes the security implications of CSS based ranging systems.

8. CONCLUSIONS

In this paper we described physical-layer attacks on chirp-based ranging systems. More specifically, we focused on distance decreasing attacks based on early detection and late commit of chirp signals. We proposed and evaluated several early detection mechanisms. We also analyzed the receiver's decoding and TOA estimation behavior to late commit attacks on the chirp signals. Our experimental results showed that an attacker can decrease the distance by more than 150 m for 1μs chirps and approximately 600 m for 4μs chirps. Future work needs to investigate the effectiveness of possible countermeasures as well as physical-layer attacks on other CSS-based schemes.

9. ACKNOWLEDGEMENTS

This work was funded by the Swiss National Science Foundation (SNSF) under the grant 200020_129605 and NCCR-MICS. Any opinions, findings, and conclusions or recommendations expressed in this material are those of the authors and do not necessarily reflect the views of SNSF or NCCR-MICS.

10. REFERENCES

[1] Ettus research llc. http://www.ettus.com/.
[2] QuiXilica TRITON VXS-V5 Digitizer. TEK Microsystems, Inc; www.tekmicro.com.
[3] Real Time Location Systems White Paper Version 1.02. Technical report, 2007.
[4] D. Adamy. EW 101: a first course in electronic warfare. Artech House, 2001.
[5] H.-S. Ahn, H. Hur, and W.-S. Choi. One-way ranging technique for CSS-based indoor localization, July 2008.
[6] P. Bahl and V. N. Padmanabhan. RADAR: an in-building RF-based user location and tracking system. In Proceedings of the 19th Annual Joint Conference of the IEEE Computer and Communications Societies, volume 2, pages 775–784, Mar. 2000.
[7] A. J. Berni and W. D. Gregg. On the Utility of Chirp Modulation for Digital Signaling. IEEE Transactions on Communications, 21(6):748–751, June 1973.
[8] J. Clulow, G. Hancke, M. Kuhn, and T. Moore. So Near and Yet So Far: Distance-Bounding Attacks in Wireless Networks. In Proceedings of the 3rd European Workshop on Security and Privacy in Ad-Hoc and Sensor Networks, Lecture Notes in Computer Science, pages 83–97. Springer, Sept. 2006.
[9] C. E. Cook and M. Bernfeld. Radar signals: An introduction to theory and application. Academic Press, New York, 1967.
[10] D. S. Dayton. FM "Chirp" Communications: Multiple Access to Dispersive Channels. IEEE Transactions on Electromagnetic Compatibility, (2):296–297, June 1968.
[11] C. Fischer and H. Gellersen. Location and Navigation Support for Emergency Responders: A Survey. IEEE Pervasive Computing, 9:38–47, Jan. 2010.
[12] M. Flury, M. Poturalski, P. Papadimitratos, J.-P. Hubaux, and J.-Y. L. Boudec. Effectiveness of Distance-Decreasing Attacks Against Impulse Radio Ranging. In Proceedings of the 3rd ACM Conference on Wireless Network Security, pages 117–128. ACM, Mar. 2010.
[13] A. Francillon, B. Danev, and S. Čapkun. Relay Attacks on Passive Keyless Entry and Start Systems in Modern Cars. In Proceedings of the 18th Annual Network and Distributed System Security Symposium. The Internet Society, Feb. 2011.
[14] L. Francis, G. Hancke, K. Mayes, and K. Markantonakis. On the security issues of NFC enabled mobile phones. International Journal of Internet Technology and Secured Transactions, 2, Dec. 2010.
[15] G. Gott and A. Karia. Differential Phase-Shift Keying Applied to Chirp Data Signals. Proceedings of the Institution of Electrical Engineers, 121(9):923–928, Sept. 1974.
[16] S. K. S. Gupta, T. Mukherjee, K. Venkatasubramanian, and T. B. Taylor. Proximity Based Access Control in Smart-Emergency Departments. In Proceedings of the 4th Annual IEEE International Conference on Pervasive Computing and Communications Workshops, pages 512–516, Mar. 2006.
[17] R. W. Hamming. Error Detecting And Error Correcting Codes. Bell System Technical Journal, 29(2):147–160, 1950.
[18] G. P. Hancke and M. G. Kuhn. Attacks on time-of-flight Distance Bounding Channels. In

Proceedings of the 1st ACM Conference on Wireless Network Security, pages 194–202. ACM, Apr. 2008.

[19] M. Hazas, J. Scott, and J. Krumm. Location-aware computing comes of age. *IEEE Computer*, 37(2):95–97, Feb. 2004.

[20] S. Hengstler, D. P. Kasilingam, and A. H. Costa. A Novel Chirp Modulation Spread Spectrum Technique for Multiple Access. In *Proceedings of IEEE Seventh International Symposium on Spread Spectrum Techniques and Applications*, volume 1, pages 73–77, Sept. 2002.

[21] The Institute of Electrical and Electronic Engineers. *IEEE 802.15.4a-2007 Wireless Medium Access Control (MAC) and Physical Layer (PHY) Specifications for Low-Rate Wireless Personal Area Networks (WPANs)*, 2007.

[22] The Institute of Electrical and Electronic Engineers. *ISO/IEC 24730-5 Information technology – Real-time locating systems (RTLS) – Part 5: Chirp spread spectrum (CSS) at 2.4 GHz air interface*, 2010.

[23] J.-E. Kim, J. Kang, D. Kim, Y. Ko, and J. Kim. IEEE 802.15.4a CSS-based localization system for wireless sensor networks. In *Proceedings of the 4th IEEE International Conference on Mobile Adhoc and Sensor Systems*, pages 1–3, Oct. 2007.

[24] H. Liu, H. Darabi, P. Banerjee, and J. Liu. Survey of Wireless Indoor Positioning Techniques and Systems. *IEEE Transactions on Systems, Man, and Cybernetics*, 37(6):1067–1080, Nov. 2007.

[25] H. Matthews. *Surface wave filters: Design, construction, and use*. New York, Wiley-Interscience, 1977.

[26] P. Misra and P. Enge. *Global Positioning System: Signals, Measurements, and Performance*. Ganga-Jamuna Press, 2006.

[27] Y. J. Nam and Y.-G. Park. Efficient Indoor Localization and Navigation with a Combination of Ultrasonic and CSS-based IEEE 802.15.4a. In *Proceedings of the 4th International Conference on Ubiquitous Information Technologies Applications*, pages 1–6, Dec. 2009.

[28] Nanotron Technologies GmbH. *NanoLOC TRX Transceiver (NA5TR1) User Guide Version 2.0*, 2008.

[29] Nanotron Technologies GmbH. *NanoLOC TRX Transceiver (NA5TR1) Datasheet Version 2.3*, 2010.

[30] J. Peck. SONAR–The RADAR of the Deep. In *Popular Science*, volume 147. Nov. 1945.

[31] M. Poturalski, M. Flury, P. Papadimitratos, J.-P. Hubaux, and J.-Y. L. Boudec. The Cicada Attack: Degradation and Denial of Service in IR Ranging. In *Proceedings of 2010 IEEE International Conference on Ultra-Wideband*, volume 2, pages 1–4, Sept. 2010.

[32] M. Poturalski, M. Flury, P. Papadimitratos, J.-P. Hubaux, and J.-Y. L. Boudec. Distance Bounding with IEEE 802.15.4a: Attacks and Countermeasures. *IEEE Transactions on Wireless Communications*, 10(4):1334–1344, Apr. 2011.

[33] K. B. Rasmussen, C. Castelluccia, T. S. Heydt-Benjamin, and S. Čapkun. Proximity-based Access Control for Implantable Medical Devices. In *Proceedings of the 16th ACM conference on Computer and Communications Security*, pages 410–419. ACM, Nov. 2009.

[34] K. B. Rasmussen and S. Čapkun. Realization of RF Distance Bounding. In *Proceedings of the 19th USENIX Security Symposium*, pages 389–402, Aug. 2010.

[35] Z. Sahinoglu and S. Gezici. Ranging in the IEEE 802.15.4a Standard. In *Proceedings of 2006 IEEE Annual Wireless and Microwave Technology Conference*, pages 1–5, Dec. 2006.

[36] Z. Sahinoglu, S. Gezici, and I. Güvenc. *Ultra-wideband Positioning Systems: Theoretical Limits, Ranging Algorithms, and Protocols*. Cambridge University Press, Oct. 2008.

[37] S. Sedighpour, S. Capkun, S. Ganeriwal, and M. B. Srivastava. Distance enlargement and reduction attacks on ultrasound ranging. In *Proceedings of the 3rd ACM Conference on Embedded Networked Sensor Systems*, New York, NY, USA, Nov. 2005. ACM.

[38] A. Springer, W. Gugler, M. Huemer, R. Koller, and R. Weigel. A wireless spread-spectrum communication system using saw chirped delay lines. *IEEE Transactions on Microwave Theory and Techniques*, 49(4):754–760, Apr. 2001.

[39] A. Springer, W. Gugler, M. Huemer, L. Reindl, C. C. W. Ruppel, and R. Weigel. Spread Spectrum Communications Using Chirp Signals. In *EUROCOMM 2000. Information Systems for Enhanced Public Safety and Security. IEEE/AFCEA*, pages 166–170, May 2000.

[40] N. O. Tippenhauer and S. Čapkun. ID-based Secure Distance Bounding and Localization. In *Proceedings of the 14th European Conference on Research in Computer Security*, pages 621–636, Berlin, Heidelberg, Sept. 2009. Springer-Verlag.

[41] Ubisense Technologies. *Ubisense Real-time Location Systems (RTLS)*, 2010.

[42] M. Vossiek, R. Roskosch, and P. Heide. Precise 3-D Object Position Tracking using FMCW Radar. In *Proceedings of the 29th European Microwave Conference*, volume 1, pages 234–237, Oct. 1999.

[43] M. Winkler. Chirp signals for communications. In *WESCON Convention Record*, 1962.

[44] Z. Xiang, S. Song, J. Chen, H. Wang, J. Huang, and X. Gao. A wireless LAN-based indoor positioning technology. *IBM Journal of Research and Development*, 48(5.6):617–626, Sept. 2004.

[45] C. Yoon and H. Cha. Experimental analysis of IEEE 802.15.4a CSS ranging and its implications. *Computer Communications*, 34(11):1361–1374, Feb. 2011.

[46] Zebra Technologies. *Sapphire Dart Ultra-Wideband (UWB) Real Time Locating System*, 2010.

BANA: Body Area Network Authentication Exploiting Channel Characteristics

Lu Shi
Dept. of CS
U. of Arkansas at Little Rock
Little Rock, AR 72211
lxshi@ualr.edu

Ming Li
Dept. of CS
Utah State University
Logan, UT 84322
ming.li@usu.edu

Shucheng Yu
and Jiawei Yuan
Dept. of CS
U. of Arkansas at Little Rock
Little Rock, AR 72211
{sxyu1,jxyuan}@ualr.edu

ABSTRACT

Wireless body area network (BAN) is a promising technology for real-time monitoring of physiological signals to support medical applications. In order to ensure the trustworthy and reliable gathering of patient's critical health information, it is essential to provide node authentication service in a BAN, which prevents an attacker from impersonation and false data/command injection. Although quite fundamental, the authentication in BAN still remains a challenging issue. On one hand, traditional authentication solutions depend on prior trust among nodes whose establishment would require either key pre-distribution or non-intuitive participation by inexperienced users, while they are vulnerable to key compromise. On the other hand, most existing non-cryptographic authentication schemes require advanced hardware capabilities or significant modifications to the system software, which are impractical for BANs.

In this paper, for the first time, we propose a lightweight body area network authentication scheme (BANA) that does not depend on prior-trust among the nodes and can be efficiently realized on commercial off-the-shelf low-end sensor devices. This is achieved by exploiting physical layer characteristics unique to a BAN, namely, the distinct received signal strength (RSS) variation behaviors between an on-body communication channel and an off-body channel. Our main finding is that the latter is more unpredictable over time, especially under various body motion scenarios. This unique channel characteristic naturally arises from the multi-path environment surrounding a BAN, and cannot be easily forged by attackers. We then adopt clustering analysis to differentiate the signals from an attacker and a legitimate node. The effectiveness of BANA is validated through extensive real-world experiments under various scenarios. It is shown that BANA can accurately identify multiple attackers with minimal amount of overhead.

Categories and Subject Descriptors

C.2.0 [**General**]: Security and Protection; C.2.1 [**Network Architecture and Design**]: Wireless Communication

General Terms

Security, Design

Keywords

Wireless Body Area Network, Sensor, Authentication, RSS, Physical Layer

1. INTRODUCTION

Wireless body area network (BAN) or body sensor network (BSN) has been an area of significant research in recent years [24, 46, 7]. A BAN is a wireless network usually formed by lightweight, small-size, ultra-low-power, interoperable and intelligent wearable sensors [7], which are strategically placed on the body surface, around it or implanted inside the human body. To monitor the wearer's health status or motion pattern, these sensors measure, process, and transmit the body's physiological signs to a control unit (CU) without constraining the activities of the wearer. Physicians and caregivers can then access the collected data for real-time diagnosis and trigger treatment procedures in return. For example, upon detecting high blood sugar level from a glucose monitoring device, an insulin pump will receive a command from the CU to inject a required dose of insulin [32]. The BAN technology enables numerous exciting applications, such as ubiquitous health monitoring [17] and emergency medical response (EMS) [25], etc. It has the potential to revolutionize the healthcare delivery in hospitals, operation theaters, and homes.

As BAN applications deal with sensitive patient medical information, they have significant security, privacy and safety implications which may prevent the wide adoption of this technology. There have been wide privacy concerns in the public towards IMDs [1]; however, the data security in a BAN has not drawn enough attention, although the lack of it would lead to fatal consequences [19, 8]. Especially, node authentication is the fundamental step towards a BAN's initial trust establishment (e.g., key generation) and subsequent secure communications. Since IMDs transmit critical health monitor reports to and receive commands from the CU, if an attacker successfully pretends to be a legitimate sensor node or CU and joins the BAN, it can either report wrong patient health status information or inject false commands which may put the patient's safety at risk. In current practices, the interoperable medical devices (IMDs) are not designed with enough security in mind. Over the years, there are a number of reported remote hacking incidents of individual IMDs [42, 14] exploiting the unprotected wireless channel. In a BAN, the situation is even worse if attacker can spoof multiple medical devices simultaneously. Thus, an effective node authentication mechanism is the key to BAN's security and patient safety.

Despite past research efforts on authentication in wireless networks, the same issue in BAN still remains a challenge because of its unique features and stringent application-level requirements. Traditionally, authentication has been relying on pre-distributed secret keys among nodes in a network. For example, there is a lot of literature on key distribution in wireless sensor networks (WSNs) [13, 5, 11, 12, 22, 23, 34]. However, if directly applied to a BAN, this method requires the end-users to basically trust the whole distribution chain which may involve numerous less trustworthy users. In addition, BAN's user is usually unexperienced humans which implies high usability is required, where ideally *"plug-and-play"* is desired. Any key distribution/management process should be minimized, automatic, and transparent to users. Thus, node legitimacy in a BAN should be established *without assuming prior security context* among nodes. Furthermore, as the medical sensors become ubiquitous, they could be compromised and pre-shared secret keys can be stolen. These keys allow attackers to imposter any legitimate node, which renders traditional cryptographic authentication mechanisms ineffective. Therefore, node authentication mechanisms in BAN should have *minimal reliance on cryptography*. Finally, the low-end medical sensor nodes are extremely constrained in resources (including hardware, energy and user interfaces), while existing non-cryptographic authentication mechanisms mostly require advanced hardware such as multiple-antennas [51], or significant modifications to the system software. It is very important to note that, we *should not introduce additional hardware assumptions* to the BAN, not only because that adds cost but also it is not easily compatible with legacy systems.

Identifying these challenges, in this paper, we put forward BANA — a practical node authentication scheme for body area networks that does not depend on prior-trust (or pre-shared secrets) among the nodes. We exploit unique physical layer characteristics within a BAN environment, namely, the distinct received signal strength (RSS) variation behaviors between an on-body and an off-body communication channel. That is, when two legitimate devices are placed on the same user's body, the RSS variation of the channel between them is much more stable than the case when one of the devices is off-the-body, especially when the body as a whole is *in motion*. This channel characteristic arises naturally from the multi-path fading environment surrounding a BAN, thus a legitimate on-body channel's RSS variation profile is very hard to be forged by an off-body attacker, unless it can create a perfect channel[1]. We then design BANA based on this characteristic, and propose to use clustering analysis to differentiate the signals from a legitimate node

and an attacker. We find that BANA works effectively under a wide range of scenarios with low false-positive and false-negative rates, and can correctly identify multiple attackers even when they collude. BANA can be efficiently realized on commercial off-the-shelf low-end sensor devices.

Our Contributions

(1) We identify a new type of channel characteristics in BAN that can be used to increase its security. Namely, the dramatic differences in RSS variations between on-body and off-body channels, especially under artificially induced body motions. We theoretically explain its cause, and validate this characteristic through extensive experimental study under different scenarios.

(2) We propose BANA, a novel non-cryptographic node authentication scheme for BAN based on the new channel characteristics. We perform clustering analysis on the average RSS variation (ARV) to differentiate signals of a legitimate node and an attacker. Our scheme is resource-efficient and does not require additional hardware.

(3) We validate effectiveness and efficiency of BANA through extensive experiments on a body sensor network testbed. In particular, it is shown that our scheme can accurately identify multiple colluding attacker nodes even when their number is up to 5 times of legitimate nodes, while incurring minimal amount of overhead. The time required for authentication can be as short as 12 seconds for a group of six body sensors.

The rest of this paper is organized as follows. We review related work in Section 2. The problem definition, including system model and attack model, will be introduced in Section 3. Section 4 presents our findings on the new channel characteristics, while Sec. 5 gives BANA's main design. In Section 6, we evaluate its security and performance, and discuss its limitations. We conclude the paper in Section 7.

2. RELATED WORK

Related research on authentication in WSNs, especially in BANs can be mainly divided into two categories – cryptographic and non-cryptographic authentication mechanisms. Traditionally, authentication in WSNs and BANs relied on the existence of prior security context [6, 26, 10, 27, 9, 52]. Those mechanisms generally either involve high computational overhead or complex key management. Tan et. al. [41] proposed lightweight crypto-based authentication schemes. However, they still require prior-trust among the nodes or a trusted authority for key distribution, which lowers the usability of a BAN. It is worthy to note that secure device pairing methods are recent alternatives that do not assume pre-shared secrets, while enjoying higher usability (e.g., GDP [21, 20]). However, they assumed the existence of some additional out-of-band (OOB) secure channel that facilitates human-aided verification, which may not be intuitive to use. Thus, in what follows we only survey non-cryptographic authentication techniques related to BAN.

2.1 Biometric-based Authentication

Physiological values are used to assist authentication and key generation by measuring and comparing the physiological signals separately at the sender and the receiver [35, 45, 44, 39, 47, 50, 15], such as electrocardiogram (EEG) and photoplethysmogram (PPG), iris, fingerprint etc. These methods can achieve "plug-and-play" without relying on pre-

---

[1]An attacker equipped with high-gain directional antenna may create a low RSS-variation off-body channel, but this attack involves many difficulties, whose feasibility is discussed in Sec. 6.3.

shared secrets, but it is hard for every body sensor in different positions to measure the same physiological signal with the same accuracy. Others use common accelerometer data extracted from motion of the body [30, 31]. However, they require specialized sensing hardware for every sensor.

2.2 Channel-based Authentication

Zeng et. al. [51] classified non-cryptographic authentication schemes into three different categories: software-based, hardware-based, and channel/location-based. Both software-based and hardware-based solutions are vulnerable to attacks that mimic the characteristics of the signature and impersonation. Channel/location-based solutions leverage the observation that RSS tends to vary over time due to mobility and channel environments.

Recently there have been an increasing interest in RSS-based authentication [43, 18, 4]. Zeng et. al. [51] proposed to use temporal RSS variation lists to deal with identity-based attack, where an intruder T who tries to impersonate another user B that is communicating with A can be detected by A. However, they focused on identification while our work focuses on distinguishing legitimate nodes from false ones (i.e., there is no specific identify to impersonate). The secure device pairing scheme proposed by [4] performed proximity detection based on differential RSS, but requires additional hardware (at least two receiver antennas). Other identification/authentication schemes build a signature for each device's wireless channel, for example, the temporal link signature in [33] uses channel impulse response. However, this method requires a learning phase and also advanced hardware platforms such as GNU radio.

2.3 Proximity-based Authentication

Several schemes are based on co-location detection. Amigo in [43] extends the Diffie-Hellman key exchange with verification of device co-location. Each device monitors the radio environment for a short period of time and generates a signature including its RSS, which is used for similarity detection. In Ensemble [18], with the pairing devices transmitting and the trusted body-worn personal devices receiving, the latter determine proximity by monitoring the transmissions. Similarly, Mathur et. al. [28] proposed a co-location based pairing scheme by exploiting environmental signals. The main drawback of these methods is, the devices need to be within half wavelength distance of each other, which is restrictive for medical sensors deployed in a BAN.

Other works exploit secure ranging techniques to determine a device's proximity [38], such as distance bounding [3]. The general concern with RF distance bounding is it requires specialized/advanced hardware, otherwise high accuracy cannot be achieved. In [37], Rasmussen and Capkun proposed the first design of RF distance bounding that can be realized fully using wireless channel, but that involves multi-radio capabilities and additional hardware.

Our work can be classified as both channel-based and proximity-based authentication, since we exploit the fact that an off-body attacker have quite different RSS variation behavior with an on-body sensor. Different from existing works, BANA does not require any additional hardware, only legitimate sensors need to be placed on/near the body.

3. PROBLEM DEFINITION

3.1 System Model and Assumptions

We consider a wireless body area network composed of n sensors and a CU. The sensors are carried on the body of a patient; they continuously measure and collect physiological data about the patient (e.g., heart rate, blood oxygenation, glucose level, etc.) and send them to the CU. They are limited in energy supply, memory space, and computation capabilities. The CU could be a more powerful hand-held device such as smart phone or PDA; it processes or aggregates the data, and then presents it to physicians/caregivers locally or to remote users. All the devices in a BAN are equipped with a radio interface, which enables them to communicate over wireless channel (e.g., Bluetooth, ZigBee, WiFi, etc.). The devices are also assumed to be within one-hop range of each other. We assume that the CU is not compromised. We do not assume the existence of any additional hardware (e.g., multiple antenna, accelerometer, GPS), or out-of-band communication channel. The CU is placed in close physical proximity of sensors and their distance is normally much smaller than two meters (e.g., holding by the user).

3.2 Attack Model

In this paper, we mainly consider impersonation attacks, where the attacker attempts to join the BAN by disguising either as a legitimate sensor devices or as the CU. The attacker(s) may either be a single device or multiple colluding ones, who may possess advanced hardware. They can forge physical addresses like MAC address, eavesdrop the wireless channel, modify, replay or inject false data, and can transmit packets at varying power levels.

In addition, the attacker may have knowledge about the wireless environment around the BAN. For example, it could survey the location where the BAN will be setup by measuring the channel in advance, and can derive corresponding signal propagation models. Besides, the attacker may make use of the history data collected in previous interactions with the BAN, to predict the path loss of the channel between itself and a legitimate node. The attacker is also aware of the deployed security mechanisms, the transmission technology, and the technical specs of the sensors and CU. Also, the attacker may either locate within either line-of-sight (LOS) or non-line-of-sight (NLOS) with respect to the BAN user and the devices. However, we assume that the attacker's device(s) are away from the body, whose distances are larger than those between legitimate sensors and the CU themselves. If the attacker is physically in close proximity of a user, it would be easily spotted.

Note that, in this paper we do not consider jamming or Denial-of-Service (DoS) attacks. During an authentication process, it is possible that attacker falsely claims to have the ID of a valid sensor, so as to confuse the CU about which one is legitimate, or simply prevent a legitimate sensor from being successfully authenticated. However, this can be regarded as one type of DoS attack.

3.3 Design Requirements

The primary goal is to achieve node authentication, that is, to distinguish a legitimate body sensor/CU from an attacker. This is a fundamental requirement for the security of a BAN. After authentication, a shared secret key can be established between each sensor node and the CU in order to

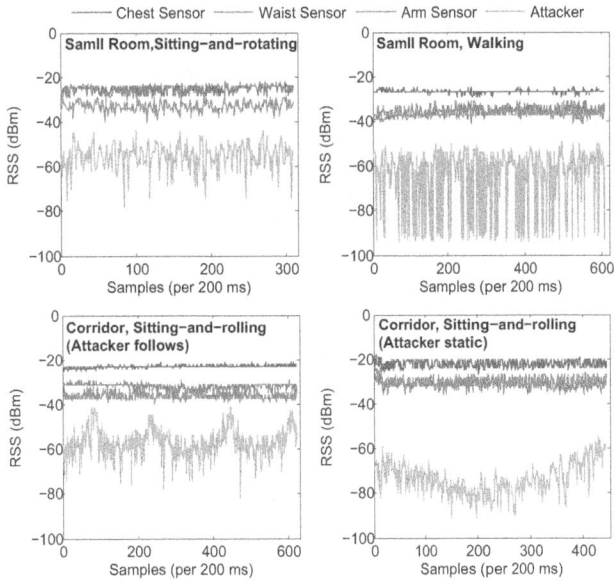

Figure 1: RSS variations in different body motion scenarios.

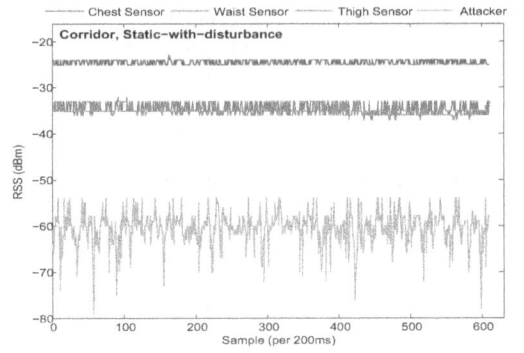

Figure 2: RSS variations under channel disturbance.

protect the sensitive health monitor data. We do not elaborate on shared key establishment in this paper since there are many existing techniques to do so (e.g., Diffie-Hellman)[2].

Moreover, the authentication mechanism shall have the following properties: (1) Usability, since the users of BAN are anticipated to be non-experts like normal patients. "Plug-n-play" is our desired usability goal. (2) Efficiency, resource consumption must be minimized to preserve energy; (3) Speed, since additional latency imposed by security mechanisms may cause a difference between live and death in EMS scenarios; (4) Low-cost: they should rely on commercial off-the-shelf (COTS) hardware and should not require big change to existing platforms. (5) Reliability, which means they should work under various types of scenarios.

4. UNIQUE CHANNEL CHARACTERISTICS OF A BAN

The channel within a BAN can display substantial differences with respect to other types of channels, such as in WLAN and cellular environments. There are some existing research on BAN's channel measurement [40]. Most of them focus on determining the channel model itself for enhancing communication performance; only a few of them studied the characteristics of BAN channel related to security purposes. Recently, Ali et al. observed that the channel between an on-body sensor (OBS) and off-body base station displays both slow and fast fading components [2]. They use it to facilitate secret key extraction from the channel, but it is not clear how can this be applied to BAN authentication.

In what follows, we use on-body channel to refer to the channel where both transceivers are located on the same body or in close vicinity to the body, and use off-body chan-

nel to refer to the situation that one of the transmitters is on-body (on the surface or in close vicinity to body) while the other is off-body (at a distance away). Note that, the off-body channel characteristics analyzed in this section applies to most types of attacker device, except those using a directional antenna to create a pointed, ideal path between the attacker and CU. However, as we will discuss later, although the directional attack seems possible theoretically, in practice it can be hard to carry out mainly due to the body motion in our scheme.

4.1 Distinct RSS Variation Profiles between On-body and Off-Body Channels

In this paper, we observe significant differences between the RSS variation behavior between on-body and off-body channels. That is, the off-body channel displays much severer fading than the on-body channel over time, in terms of both fading amplitude and rate. In particular, we found two classes of scenarios under which this difference is prominent: (1) Body motion, especially when the body parts are relatively static to each other. There are many real-world examples for such motions: slow-walking, sitting in a wheel-chair and pulled by others, rotating, lying on a moving operation table, etc. (2) Channel disturbances. Alternatively, when the body is static, moving objects/people between an off-body link creates a similar effect. For example, in a crowded hospital or emergency room environment.

Experimental Evidences. To testify our claim, we carried out experiments using five Crossbow's TelosB motes (TPR2400). The TelosB platform includes an IEEE 802.15.4 radio with integrated antenna, a low-power MCU with extended memory and an optional sensor suite. We configured three of these devices as body sensors, separately worn on the chest (S_1), strapped to the right waist (S_2), and tied to the left thigh (S_3). For the other two sensors, one works as CU that is tied to a pole carried by the patient (regarded as on-body), and another models an off-body attacker (off-body). The sensor placement and the configuration of small office are shown in Fig. 5. We performed experiments in two scenarios: a small office and a large corridor of a college building. For the small office scenario, the patient either walks randomly, or sits on a chair and spins. The off-body link is non-line-of-sight (NLOS) in this case, and the attacker remains static. For the corridor scenario, the patient sits on a wheelchair and moves back and forth along a straight line with the help of a caregiver; attacker is either static, or follows behind and moves in a similar pattern. In addition, to

---

[2]For example, a possible solution is to split a Diffie-Hellman public key into chunks and carry each of them in an authentication packet in BANA. Then the man-in-the-middle attack will fail, because the middleman's packets' RSS variations cannot pass BANA's check.

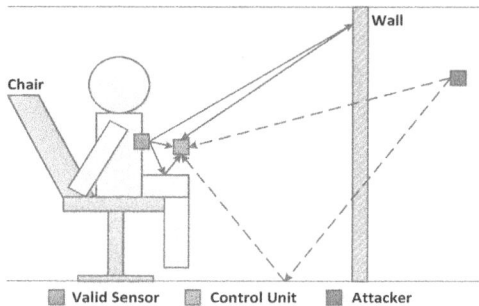

Figure 3: Illustration of wireless channels from the OBS and the attacker, respectively, to the control unit.

simulate channel disturbances, we let the patient be static while there are people walking around the corridor.

We measured the RSSI received from each other sensor by the CU, where the sampling step is 200ms. Results for body motion scenarios are shown in Fig. 1, while those for channel disturbance is shown in Fig. 2. Two prominent characteristics can be observed.

- **On-Body Channel is Much More Stable Even Under Body Motion.** For example, in Fig. 1, the RSS from the attacker is apparently experiencing large variations while RSS from all the OBSes are still stable with small fluctuations. The RSSI variations of OBSs are less than $5 - 10dB$, while for the attacker its RSSI varies much faster with a range of $45dB$. For other scenarios, similar observations can be found.

- **Off-Body Channel is Unpredictable.** The off-body channel's fading is much more random and unpredictable than the on-body channel.

Note that the difference in RSS variation profiles still holds when there is small relative motion between body parts. To validate its universality, we also conducted other sets of experiments in different rooms and on different subjects, and results are consistent. Due to space limitations they are not presented here.

4.2 Theoretical Explanation

Next we will analyze the reasons of above observed phenomenons. As we know, radio wave propagation is greatly affected by direct path loss, multipath, shadowing, and other interference, which are both time and environment specific and difficult to predict. Taking movement into account increases the unpredictability of the radio environment dramatically [18]. However, this has much less effect for an on-body channel than an off-body channel.

On-Body Channel: Although signal propagation over on-body channel suffers from the effect of the human body with its complex shape and different tissues, it is well-known that at very close range, the *direct path* (DP) is the dominant path among all the multi-path components [36]. As depicted in Fig. 3, since the OBS and CU are very close to each other (usually less than 1 meter), the RSS received from reflection off the walls and floors only contributes a small proportion to the overall RSS. Therefore, during body motions, the effects of signal reflection and absorption will not change dramatically as the OBS and the CU keep their

position and distance relatively static. Ideally, the coherence time of the on-body channel goes towards infinity.

Off-Body Channel: For an off-body transceiver, the relative motion between it and CU/OBS results in Doppler shift. In addition, the motion also changes the phases and amplitudes of signals arriving from various multi-paths whereas the DP no long dominates. Thus when the off-body transceiver is at a certain distance away, the superposition of multi-path components lead to large-scale and fast variations in fading amplitude. This effect is particularly conspicuous in NLOS situations, as the signal is subjected to losses caused by penetrating walls, floors, doors and windows. Thus, any change in the environment will result in remarkable RSS variations at the receiver side. For a back-of-the-envelop calculation, assume the body is moving straight at $v = 0.6$m/s. The coherence time of the off-body channel is $T_c = \lambda/2v \approx 0.1$s, where $\lambda = 0.125$m if $f = 2.4$GHz. Note that our sample interval is 0.2s.

5. MAIN DESIGN OF BANA

This section describes the main design of BANA based on the channel characteristics. We first focus on the one-way authentication, that is the CU authenticates other body sensors. Our scheme can be adapted to handle the opposite case, which will be discussed in Sec. 6.

5.1 Overview

Our scheme exploits the fact that the RSS at the CU received from an off-body attacker experiences much larger fluctuations because of the multipath effect and Doppler spread, compared with that of an OBS. We formalize the degree of signal fluctuation as *average RSS variation* (ARV), which indicates the average amplitude of change in path loss between two consecutive time slots of RSS measurement (one time slot is slightly longer than the channel coherence time). In order to prevent the attacker from predicting its channel condition to the CU, we require each sensor to send response messages to the CU, after a time larger than the channel coherence time. After having collected all the RSSes over a short period of time and computed the ARV for each node, the CU uses cluster analysis to classify them into two groups. Due to large differences between the ARVs, the clustering procedure will have high chance of success. Note that, measuring RSS requires no additional hardware and can be fully realized on low-end sensor nodes.

5.2 The BANA Protocol

Our secure authentication protocol assumes that legitimate sensor devices have been attached to the patient's body before the execution of our protocol. One or more off-body attacker nodes may present in vicinity. Our protocol distinguishes legitimate on-body sensors from off-body attacker nodes as follows.

(1) The CU broadcasts a hello message $M = (x, t_0, t)$ using a certain transmission power P_{tx} to nearby devices, asking them to respond after x second(s), where x is a system parameter, e.g., x can be 1. The hello message M sent by the CU requires all the responding devices to send back response messages m repeatedly every t milliseconds after x second(s) and continue for t_0 seconds. The CU will not respond to any sensor device during the t_0 seconds until it finishes the authentication process, providing no oppor-

Stage	The Control Unit (CU)		The ith sensor
(1) Discovering	Broadcasts a hello message; where x is a random number chosen by the CU; t_0 defines total response time; t defines time interval of each response message;	$\xrightarrow{M=(x,t_0,t)}$	Responds after $x + \frac{t_r}{1000}$ seconds where t_r is a random number picked by the sensor;
(2) Responding	Measures the channel;	$\xleftarrow{m_1,m_2,...,m_{NT}}$	Sends response messages every t milliseconds for total time of t_0 seconds, letting $NT = 1000 \times t_0/t$;
(3) Classification	Calculates the average RSS variations ARV_i: $Sum_i = \sum |RSS_k - RSS_{k+1}|$, $ARV_i = Sum_i/NT$; Classifies ARV_1, ARV_2, ... , ARV_n into two groups;		
(4) Decision	Accepts if ARV_i belongs to the group with a smaller average RSS variation value;	$\xrightarrow{Acceptance}$	Ready for data transmission.
	Rejects otherwise.	$\xrightarrow{Rejection}$	Fails in authentication.

Figure 4: Description of the authentication process

tunities to the attacker for measuring the realtime channel between itself and the CU.

(2) Upon receiving the hello message, a sensor device i generates a small random number t_r, e.g., we can have $t_r < t$, and sends it back CU. CU collects the t_r's from all responding devices and make sure there is no duplicated ones to avoids future transmission collision. After the CU has agreed on the random numbers, it notifies the responding devices to repeatedly send messages m to the CU after x seconds plus t_r milliseconds. Specifically, the ith sensor keeps sending response messages $m_1, \ldots, m_{NT}$ every t milliseconds and continue for t_0 seconds, where $NT = 1000 \times t_0/t$. Both t_0 and t are appropriately set system parameters. For t_0, it should be large enough for the CU to collect sufficient signal samples and measure the channel accurately. But if t_0 is too large, a patient will spend too much time on sensor devices authentication which is not affordable to the patient if the data measured by the sensor devices is urgently needed for emergency treatment. For t, generally it must be no less than the coherence time to ensure accurate estimation of channel variation, where the coherence time is defined to be the time duration over which the channel impulse response is considered to be not varying.

(3) After having collected the RSSs for all the responding devices, the CU calculates the average RSS variation for each node i by computing $ARV_i = Sum_i/NT$, where Sum_i is the sum of all the absolute values of RSS variation for every two consecutive time interval t. Finding out values of $ARV_1, ARV_2, ..., ARV_n$ for all the received signals, the CU applies a classification algorithm to partition them into two groups, where one group has a smaller mean of AVR while the other group has a larger one.

(4) Based on the classification result, the CU accepts the sensor devices whose ARV values belong to the cluster with a smaller average of ARV while rejecting the devices in the other group.

5.3 Discussion

1. Deployment: n sensors are put to their designated places on the patient's body. And the CU is attached to an external equipment, which is placed at a relatively constant position and distance to all the worn sensors. All of the OBSes shall have a clear line of sight to the CU. The dis-

tances between each sensor and the CU d_1, d_2, ..., d_n must be larger than half-wavelength. Therefore, no correlation exists between wireless channels to each sensor and those to the CU. In this case, even if the attacker is able to measure the signals sent by the legitimate sensors, it is not able infer the channel to the CU.

2. Average RSS Variation (ARV): to compare and distinguish remote sensors from on-body sensors, measurements of the signal fluctuations are necessary. According to what we observe from Fig.2, the RSS of a remote sensor was experiencing dramatic fluctuations, which changed very fast in a short period of time, while on-body sensors keep relatively stable RSS with small variations over time. So within a small time interval, the RSS variation of a remote sensor is mostly larger than that of a on-body sensor. Then over a period of time, the average RSS variation of the remote sensor will still be larger than that of the on-body sensor. Based on this observation, we utilize average RSS variation to check the degree of signal fluctuations for both remote sensors and on-body sensors. To calculate the average RSS variation, the CU adds up all the absolute values of RSS differences between every time interval for each signal, and divides the sum by the total number of discrete time points for that signal.

3. Classification method: In addition to the obvious differences of the average RSS variations between remote sensors and on-body sensors, we also noticed that the average RSS variation values are closed to each other for remote sensors, so are the on-body sensors themselves. Intuitively, these ARVs will form two distinct groups. In our protocol enables the CU to achieve this by employing a classification method. The sensors whose average RSS variation value belong to the group with a smaller overall average RSS variation, are trusted as valid sensors. Otherwise, they are treated as illegal sensors. As one of the popular classification algorithm, K-means clustering provides a method of cluster analysis aiming to partition n observations into k clusters, in which each observation belongs to the cluster with the nearest mean, and fit well for our scheme. Note that, K-means clustering requires no prior-knowledge about the data distribution, thus there is no training phase.

Test Plan	Location	Movement	Patient	Attacker Placement
1	Small room	sitting-and-rotating	person 1	Attacker #1,2: inside of the room. Attacker #3,4: next door (separated by a wooden wall) Attacker #5,6: more than 5 meters away
2	Small room	walking	person 1	Attacker #1,2: inside of the room. Attacker #3,4: next door (separated by a wooden wall) Attacker #5,6: more than 5 meters away
3	Medium room	sitting-and-rotating	person 3	Attacker #1,2: inside of the room. Attacker #3,4: next door (separated by a wooden wall) Attacker #5,6: more than 5 meters away
4	Corridor	sitting-and-rolling	person 1	Attacker #1: following the patient. Attacker #2-6: static, at different distances
5	Corridor	sitting-and-rolling	person 2	Attacker #1: following the patient. Attacker #2-6: static, at different distances

Figure 6: The Testing Plans

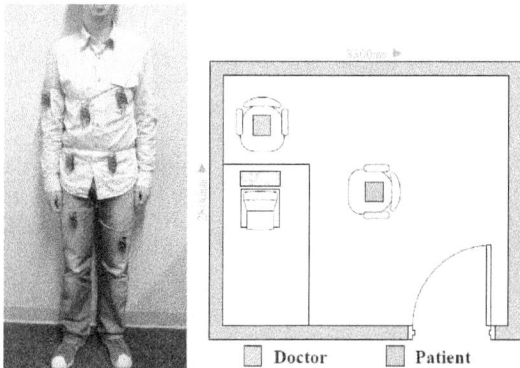

Figure 5: Sensor Placement on the Human Body and the Small Room Layout.

6. EVALUATION

We conducted experiments under different settings to validate our proposed scheme. Specifically, we took into account the effect of the following factors: position of the body sensor, surrounding environment such as room size, type of patient movement, location of the attacker, and difference between individual patients.

6.1 Experimental Setup and Results

In our experiments, we configured seven TelosB motes (numbered from 1 to 7) as OBSes, separately worn on the chest and the arms, strapped to the both sides of waist, and tied to both the left and right thighs. We used a TelosB mote to emulate the controller for simplicity. On receiving the signal from sensors, the controller measures the RSSI and sends it to the computer for analysis. By this we can emulate all the functionalities of a real controller. In each experiment we also put 6 TelosB motes (numbered from 1 to 6) at different locations with different distances to the patient to simulate the attackers. In our experiments, we use these motes mainly to measure the channel properties of body sensors and real attackers. Based on the collected data, we will analyze the probability at which legitimate body sensors are successfully accepted as well as the attackers' strategies and their successful probability of impersonating as authentic body sensors by using the strategies.

To simulate typical real-life scenarios, we choose three lo-cations to conduct the experiments: a small office with a large table and two chairs inside, a medium size room with two large tables and five chairs inside, and the corridor in our university's building. The small room has four walls and its size is 2.8m(width) x 3.3m(length) x 2.7m(height) as shown in Fig. 5. The medium size room has the similar layout but of size 4.5m(width) x 5.5m(length) x 2.7m(height). The size of the corridor is 4.5m(width) x 40m(length) x 3.0m(height).

Our experiments were conducted on three persons to test the difference between individuals - person 1 and person 3 are males with heights of 170cm and 176cm respectively. Person 2 is a female with height of 170cm. During the experiments, we used the following movements which can easily be performed in real life: 1) *sitting-and-rotating*. In this movement, the person acting as the patient sits on a chair (with wheels) with the controller fixed to the front of her/him. Another person helps her/him rotate the chair slowly. This movement is only used in the small room and the medium size room. 2) *sitting-and-rolling*. In this movement, the person acting as the patient sits on a chair (with wheels) with the controller fixed to the front of her/him. Another person pushes the chair from back and walks from one end of the corridor to the other end. 3) *walking*. In this movement, the person acting as the patient stands and walks slowly. This movement will be tested in the small room where there may not be enough space to move the chair. In each movement, we fixed the controller at the distance of about 30cm away from the front side of the "patient".

To validate our proposed scheme we planned several experiment scenarios considering the combinations of the impacting factors. Fig. 6 summarizes out these test plans:

1) *Plan 1, 2:* The experiments were conducted on *Person 1* in the small room. For plan 1, the patient sits on a chair in the middle of the room. The movement used is sitting-and-rotating and the speed of the rotation is about 8 rpm. For plan 2, the person slowly but randomly walks in the room, holding the controller to the front of her/him. In both plans, the 6 "attackers" are strategically placed as follows: #1 and #2 are inside of the room, one on the table and the other hung on the door. Both of them are less than 2 meters away from the patient. #3 and #4 are placed at different places in the room next door, both less than 3 meters away from the patient. The wall between the two rooms is wooden. Both #5 and #6 are placed more than 5 meters away from the patient on the same floor in the building.

33

	Plan 1	Plan 2	Plan 3	Plan 4	Plan 5
OBS1	1.605	0.482	2.012	1.899	1.814
OBS2	2.699	0.932	1.734	2.286	4.870
OBS3	2.463	0.991	1.626	1.923	2.890
OBS4	3.104	1.149	2.142	2.264	2.104
OBS5	3.544	1.181	1.947	2.115	2.395
OBS6	2.133	1.010	1.844	1.910	1.677
OBS7	1.922	0.836	1.709	2.122	2.359
ATK1	5.667	6.182	6.319	4.536	4.447
ATK2	6.346	6.342	5.301	5.971	5.860
ATK3	5.754	7.003	6.005	5.097	4.964
ATK4	5.259	5.936	6.211	5.365	5.359
ATK5	5.835	6.670	5.255	5.173	5.778
ATK6	5.152	4.721	5.438	5.527	5.753

Figure 7: The average RSS variation measurements (in dB) for Test Plan 1-5. On-Body Sensors (OBS) #1-7 are located on middle chest, left waist, right waist, left thug, right thug, left chest, and right arm respectively. Attackers (ATK) are located as described in Fig. 6

2) *Plan 3:* The setting of plan 3 is similar to that of plan 1 and 2. The main difference is that the distances between the attackers and the patient are a bit larger than those in plan 1 and 2 because of a larger room size. In this plan *Person 3* acts as the patient.

3) *Plan 4, 5:* These two experiments were conducted in the corridor in our university's building. In both plans we used the movement of sitting-and-rolling. Plan #4 is conducted on *Person 1* and #5 is on *Person 2*. The placement of the "attackers" are the same in both plans: attacker #1 follows the patient at a fixed distance of 1 meter; attackers #2 - 6 are randomly distributed along the corridor without moving.

We intend to use these experiments to simulate several typical real life scenarios in which the body sensors are authenticated in places such as the hospital testing room, the home room, the hallway of the hospital, etc.

At the beginning of each experiment, the controller broadcasts a hello message to all the nodes. After 1 second, the controller starts to receive messages and measure their RSSIs every 200ms, i.e., $t = 200ms$[3]. Each experiment lasts for 1-2 minutes. After having collected all the RSSIs, for each node i we calculate the the average RSS variation (ARV) between two consecutive 200ms slots. A larger ARV means that the communication channel between the node and the controller undergoes sharp fluctuation during the experiment. To generate sample data for statistics study, we conducted 15 experiments in total, with some of the cases repeatedly tested. Fig. 7 gives a summary of the measured ARVs under different test plans. For brevity, we just show the results of 5 non-repeated experiments. In the following section we will show the statistic data which includes the complete set of results generated in the 15 experiments.

From this table we can observe the following facts: 1) 34 out of the total 35 on-body sensor ARVs are less than 4dB.

---

[3]To make 200 ms greater than the coherence time of the channel between the controller and each individual attacker, in each experiment we assure that the controller moves at a speed greater than 31.25cm per second (Note that the wavelength of IEEE 802.15.4 signal is about 12.5cm).

All of them are less than 5dB. But those of all the "attackers" are greater than 4dB. This verifies our observation that by introducing appropriate movements the off-body nodes (attackers) tend to undergo larger fluctuation in path loss than the on-body sensors. 2) The variance of the ARVs of on-body sensors in each test plan is relatively small (for example in plan 1 it is 0.4609 as compared to 3.0186, the overall variance of all the ARVs in the plan). Intuitively this indicates that the ARVs of on-body sensors tend to converge to a certain (relatively small) value and form a cluster. Correct identification of such a cluster will lead to successful authentication of on-body sensors. 3) Occasionally, few on-body sensors would experience large path loss fluctuation (resulting in a large ARV, e.g., plan 5 OBS2) due to various reasons such as inappropriate placement of the CU, interruption from improper body movement, etc. This will cause rejection of the on-body sensor(s) (i.e., the false positive error). 4) The ARVs of on-body sensors are empirically bounded. In all our 15 test cases, there is no on-body sensor with measured ARV exceeding 5dB. 5) Deploying off-body nodes ("attackers") in vicinity does not necessary results in a relatively similar ARVs. For example, attacker #2 and #3 in plan 1 and 2 are placed about 1 meter away from each other in the same room. But their ARVs differs remarkably as compared to those of other attackers. This can be explained by factors such as different multipath effects as well as distinct Doppler spread if the two nodes are more than half wave length away from each other.

6.2 Evaluation

Based on the experiment results obtained above, we first evaluate the accuracy of our scheme without strategic attackers[4]. In particular, we will study the false positive rate (i.e., rate of failing to accept authentic on-body sensors) and the false negative rate (i.e., rate of failing to reject off-body attackers.). Then, we discuss several possible strategic attacks, their impacts, and our countermeasures. Finally, we evaluate the efficiency of our proposed scheme, including computation/communication costs and authentication time.

6.2.1 *Effectiveness*

To study the statistical property of the scheme we conducted 15 experiments under the five test plans. In addition to the 5 experiments presented in Fig. 7, the other 10 experiments were conducted based on the five plans by slightly but randomly changing some settings such as the speed of movement and the number and/or the position of the on-body sensors. From each experiment, we obtained a set of ARVs on which we ran the classification algorithm to differentiate on-body nodes and off-body nodes (attackers). In particular, we used the *kmeans* function in Matlab with the cluster number set as 2. We study the impacts on the false positive rates and false negative rates by the following factors respectively: the location of the experiment, the type of movements, and the choice of people. For each case, the *false positive rate* is computed as the percentage of total number of rejected on-body sensors out of the total number of on-body sensors, i.e.,

$$\text{false positive rate} = \frac{\sum_{i \in EXP} (\# \text{ of rejected OBSs})}{\sum_{i \in EXP} (\text{total } \# \text{ of OBSs})} \cdot 100\%,$$

where EXP mean the set of all the experiments in the

---

[4]Attackers who employ some strategies to spoof the CU, rather than following the protocol honestly.

	False Positive	False Negative
small	3.7%	0
medium	2.9%	0
corridor	3.3%	0
sitting-and-rotating	2.2%	0
sitting-and-rolling	3.7%	0
walking	4.8%	0
person 1	2.0%	0
person 2	4.8%	0
person 3	2.8%	0
overall	3.3%	0

Figure 8: The false positive rates and false negative rates under different settings with non-strategic off-body attackers.

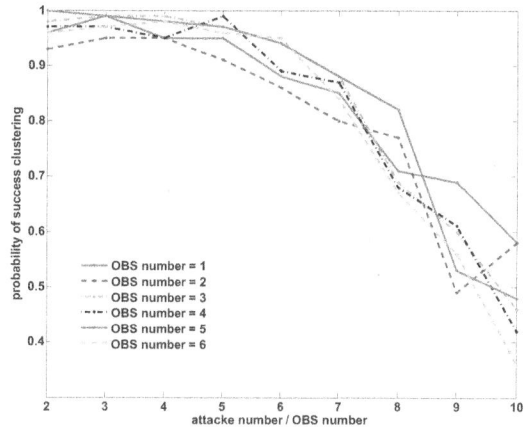

Figure 9: Impact of the attacker node number on our clustering method.

case. Similarly, the *false negative rate* is computed as the percentage of total number of accepted off-body sensors (attackers) out of the total number of off-body sensors (attackers).

Our analysis results are summarized in Fig. 8. From this table we observe that the false negative rate in our experiments is zero. This is mainly due to the fact that the off-body nodes (attackers) did not launch any strategic attack during the experiment. But such a result does indicate that our scheme is effective against non-strategic attacks (in which an off-body device is deployed in the vicinity of the patient hoping to get authenticated as an on-body sensor). The false negative rates are computed for scenarios with different locations and movements as well as different individuals. As is shown the difference among the three locations is no larger than 0.8%, which indicates the less impact from location as long as the environment surrounding the patient is relatively simple, e.g., not many reflecting angles or objects near the patient. The impact of the movement is slightly higher as compared to that of the location. For example, the false positive rate for *walking* almost doubles that for *sitting-and-rotating* (4.8% vs. 2.2%). This is mainly because it is usually harder for individuals, unless well-trained, to control the smoothness of the movement (i.e., keeping the relative location between the CU and on-body sensors stable) while walking. But it will be relatively easier while sitting on a chair. From the results, we also observe a slight difference among individuals. But such a difference is mainly caused by the difference of individuals' controlling of the movements. The overall false positive rate is 3.3% taking all the 15 experiments into accounts.

6.2.2 Security Against Strategic Attackers

A smart attacker may carry out strategic attacks to improve the chance of getting the off-body nodes accepted by the CU. For this purpose the attacker can employ the following two methods: 1) reducing the fluctuation of path loss measured by the CU via varying the transmission power; 2) deviating the clustering method.

Attack Method 1: To reduce the fluctuation of path loss measured by the CU, the attacker needs to accurately measure or predict the communication channel to the CU so as to compensate the path loss via adjusting the transmission power. But as the CU does not transmit any signal after having sent out the request message, the attacker is

not able to measure the realtime channel impulse response. Alternatively, the attacker may resort to measuring the realtime property of the channel to on-body sensors as the estimation of the channel to the CU. However, in our scheme the CU is located at least half wave length away from the on-body sensors, the channel to them are mutually uncorrelated. Another way is to predict the channel based on historical channel measurements. However, the channel coherence time is very short (less than 200ms) due to the movements we introduced.

Attack Method 2: In this method, the attacker attempts to deviate our clustering method through introducing an overwhelming number of off-body attacker nodes. This method may work because for clustering algorithm like k-means the centroid of the clusters tends to locate close to the majority. In the extreme case, if there is just a single on-body sensor but a large number of off-body attacker nodes, the clusters will be centered around the attacker nodes (i.e., their ARVs) with very high probability. To verify the effect of such attack, we did a simulation by varying the number of attacker nodes to make it times more than that of the on-body sensors. Each node is randomly assigned a ARV according to the real distribution measured in our experiments. For any given number of attacker nodes and on-body sensors, we run the classification algorithm 1000 times and measure the probability of successful clustering (i.e., no false positive/negative error). We consider four cases with on-body sensor number of 1, 2, 3, 4, 5, and 6 respectively. The simulation result is shown in Fig. 9. From this figure, it is clear that when the ratio of attacker number to on-body sensor number is less than 6, our clustering scheme always succeeds with a probability greater than 90%.

Although it seems difficult to completely thwart this attack, launching such a powerful attack is not only expensive but also easily detectable due to the large number of attacking devices involved. To keep the cost of such attack high, while clustering the CU can always create a small number of replica nodes for the node with the minimum ARV. This is because the attacker needs to deploy times more nodes to achieve a relatively high success probability.

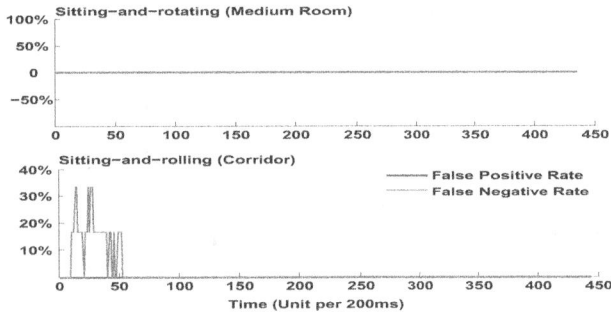

Figure 10: False positive/negative rate at different time.

6.2.3 Efficiency

The efficiency of our proposed scheme can be evaluated by authentication time, computation and communication costs.

Authentication Time: In our experiments, authentication time is set as 1-2 minutes, letting the CU receive sufficient number of sample RSSs for analysis. However, the actual time needed for authenticating a sensor node may not necessarily have to be 2 minutes. To measure the actual time required to authenticate a sensor node, for each $i \leq NT$ we plotted a false positive/negative rate calculated from the subset of sample $[1, \cdots, i]$, where NT is the total number of samples obtained from the experiment and the samples were taken per 200ms. As shown in Fig. 10, for some experiments both false positive rate and false negative rate quickly become stable as 0. This means that for these cases, the on-body sensor nodes and off-body attackers can be immediately differentiated by checking only several samples. For some experiments, the two rates are not stable until some number of samples are examined as shown in the bottom picture in Fig. 10. This is particularly true for some special locations such as large empty hallway with less multi-path effect. This is because the channel between the remote LOS attacker and the CU is less sensitive to certain movement, e.g., slowly rolling toward the attacker, since the affect of Doppler spread is dominant. Interestingly, analysis on these experiment results shows that in each experiment the two error rates become stable after the first 60 samples (i.e., 12s). This means that in all our experiments, the CU just need to measure up to 12 second to obtain the same authentication results as we have had. For cases of small room and medium room, the time can be reduced to less than 1 second.

Computation and Communication Costs: The computational cost for each sensor node is negligible since no time-consuming task is executed on it. On the controller's side, the most computation-intensive task the execution of the clustering algorithm. As the k-means clustering itself is NP-hard, heuristic algorithms are usually employed. The complexity of the algorithm can be $O(n^{dk+1}logn)$ if d and k are fixed[16], where n is the number of $d-$dimension entities to be clustered, and k is the number of clusters. In our scheme, d and k are fixed to 1 and 2 respectively. So the complexity can be $O(n^3logn)$, where n is corresponding to the number of sensor nodes which is a relatively small number. The communication cost for each body sensor is mainly caused by the messages sent to the CU every 200ms, which only needs to include the node's identity.

6.3 Discussion and Future Work

From our experiments, it is clear that our proposed solution is effective, with very high success probability in distinguishing legitimate on-body sensors from off-body nodes, including both non-strategic and strategic attacker nodes. the motions being studied can be easily carried out by any inexperienced patient in typical real life scenarios. They are very effective in creating the difference of RSS variation between on-body and off-body links, which will increase the accuracy of the clustering results.

Realizing two-way authentication: In the above we mainly showed how the CU authenticates body sensor nodes. For the other way round, we can let the CU send response messages to all the sensors after sensors' messages. Note that the real CU in the BAN is assumed to be not compromised (continuously presented). Due to the channel reciprocity, the RSS values received by each sensor from the CU are also more stable over time than those from the attackers. Thus if there exists more than one claimed-to-be CUs, each sensor will pick the node with the smallest ARV as CU.

For the sake of two-way authentication, we are assuming isotropic noise conditions, meaning that the ambient RF energy located at Alice, Bob or Eve are roughly equivalent, and consequently radio links will be approximately symmetric due to channel reciprocity. We note that similar assumptions and limitations were identified in [29]. What is important, though to realize in our work, is that the off-body channel will exhibit significantly higher variance than the on-body channel, thereby facilitating our methods.

We note that there has been further investigation into using the actual channel response, as opposed to RSS, for authentication. We refer the reader to [48, 49] for examples of this complementary work.

Attacks using directional antenna: A possible limitation of BANA is when dealing with attackers provided with a directional antenna. In BANA, the distinction between on- and off-body channels is mainly introduced by the multi-path environment surrounding a BAN. Such a distinction could be eliminated when the attacker uses a directional antenna to create a focused beam to reduce the multi-path effect. While this attack seems to be effective, we believe that it is difficult to launch in practice. In particular, in BANA the patient carries out random motions that we suggested. Such random motions will make it hard for the attacker's directional antenna to accurately direct toward the patient, which is particularly true for NLOS scenarios such as closed rooms. To improve the accuracy of pointing toward the patient, the attacker may want to use an antenna with a wider beam. However, a large beam angle can easily make the multi-path effect eminent. On the other hand, a highly directional antenna with a narrow beam is usually large in size, which would make the attacking device more easily detected in practice. As an interesting future work, we will further study the practicality of attacks using directional antenna.

7. CONCLUSIONS

This paper, for the first time, proposes a lightweight authentication scheme for body area networks – BANA without depending on prior-trust among the nodes. We achieve this by exploiting physical layer characteristics unique to a BAN, namely, the distinct variation behaviors of received signal strength (RSS) between an on-body communication link and an off-body link. Specifically, the latter is much more unstable over time, especially under various artificially induced whole body motions. Our experiment results have validated such an observation and shown that our clustering method is effective in differentiating on-body sensors from off-body nodes. Analysis shows that our scheme is effective even with the presence of a number of strategic attackers. For future work, we will explore a more effective solution that thwarts strategic attackers with an overwhelming number and study the practicality of attacks using directional antenna. In addition, we will explore other implications of BAN's channel characteristics in enhancing its security from physical layer, for example, secret key extraction. Finally, we note that our study has assumed that the radio link is symmetric between Alice and Bob, and the amount to which this assumption is true in general needs to be extensively explored in future work, which we are conducting.

Acknowledgements

We thank the anonymous reviewers, and our shepherd, Prof. Wade Trappe for their helpful comments.

8. REFERENCES

[1] Experts see data breach risks in medical devices on hospital networks. http://www.ihealthbeat.org/articles/2011/5/12/.

[2] S. Ali, V. Sivaraman, and D. Ostry. Secret key generation rate vs. reconciliation cost using wireless channel characteristics in body area networks. In *Embedded and Ubiquitous Computing (EUC), 2010 IEEE/IFIP 8th International Conference on*, pages 644–650. IEEE, 2010.

[3] S. Brands and D. Chaum. Distance-bounding protocols. In *Advances in Cryptology - EUROCRYPT'93*, pages 344–359. Springer, 1994.

[4] L. Cai, K. Zeng, H. Chen, and P. Mohapatra. Good neighbor: Ad hoc pairing of nearby wireless devices by multiple antennas. In *Network and Distributed System Security Symposium*, 2011.

[5] H. Chan, A. Perrig, and D. Song. Random key predistribution schemes for sensor networks. In *IEEE S & P '03*, page 197, 2003.

[6] O. Cheikhrouhou, A. Koubaa, M. Boujelben, and M. Abid. A lightweight user authentication scheme for wireless sensor networks. In *Computer Systems and Applications (AICCSA), 2010 IEEE/ACS International Conference on*, pages 1 –7, may 2010.

[7] M. Chen, S. Gonzalez, A. Vasilakos, H. Cao, and V. C. Leung. Body area networks: A survey. *Mob. Netw. Appl.*, 16:171–193, April 2011.

[8] S. Cherukuri, K. K. Venkatasubramanian, and S. K. S. Gupta. Biosec: A biometric based approach for securing communication in wireless networks of biosensors implanted in the human body. *Parallel Processing Workshops, International Conference on*, 0:432, 2003.

[9] O. Delgado-Mohatar, A. Fuster-Sabater, and J. M. Sierra. A light-weight authentication scheme for wireless sensor networks. *Ad Hoc Networks*, 9(5):727 – 735, 2011.

[10] S. Devi, R. Babu, and B. Rao. A new approach for evolution of end to end security in wireless sensor network. *International Journal on Computer Science and Engineering*, 3:2531–2543, 2011.

[11] R. Di Pietro, L. Mancini, and A. Mei. Random key-assignment for secure wireless sensor networks. In *Proceedings of the 1st ACM workshop on Security of ad hoc and sensor networks*, pages 62–71. ACM, 2003.

[12] W. Du, J. Deng, Y. Han, P. Varshney, J. Katz, and A. Khalili. A pairwise key predistribution scheme for wireless sensor networks. *ACM Transactions on Information and System Security (TISSEC)*, 8(2):228–258, 2005.

[13] L. Eschenauer and V. D. Gligor. A key-management scheme for distributed sensor networks. In *CCS '02*, pages 41–47, 2002.

[14] D. Halperin, T. Heydt-Benjamin, B. Ransford, S. Clark, B. Defend, W. Morgan, K. Fu, T. Kohno, and W. Maisel. Pacemakers and implantable cardiac defibrillators: Software radio attacks and zero-power defenses. In *Security and Privacy, 2008. SP 2008. IEEE Symposium on*, pages 129–142. Ieee, 2008.

[15] X. Hei and X. Du. Biometric-based two-level secure access control for implantable medical devices during emergencies. In *The 30th IEEE International Conference on Computer Communications (INFOCOM 2011)*, pages 346 – 350, Shanghai, P.R.China, April 2011.

[16] M. Inaba, N. Katoh, and H. Imai. Applications of weighted voronoi diagrams and randomization to variance-based k-clustering: (extended abstract). In *Proceedings of the tenth annual symposium on Computational geometry*, SCG '94, pages 332–339, New York, NY, USA, 1994. ACM.

[17] E. Jovanov, A. Milenkovic, C. Otto, and P. C. de Groen. A wireless body area network of intelligent motion sensors for computer assisted physical rehabilitation. *J Neuroengineering Rehabil*, 2(1), March 2005.

[18] A. Kalamandeen, A. Scannell, E. de Lara, A. Sheth, and A. LaMarca. Ensemble: cooperative proximity-based authentication. In *Proceedings of the 8th international conference on Mobile systems, applications, and services*, MobiSys '10, pages 331–344, New York, NY, USA, 2010. ACM.

[19] M. Li, W. Lou, and K. Ren. Data security and privacy in wireless body area networks. *IEEE Wireless Communications Magazine*, Feb. 2010.

[20] M. Li, S. Yu, J. D. Guttman, W. Lou, and K. Ren. Secure ad-hoc trust initialization and key management in wireless body area networks. *ACM Transactions on Sensor Networks (TOSN)*, (To Appear), 2012.

[21] M. Li, S. Yu, W. Lou, and K. Ren. Group device pairing based secure sensor association and key management for body area networks. In *INFOCOM, 2010 Proceedings IEEE*, pages 1 –9, march 2010.

[22] D. Liu and P. Ning. Establishing pairwise keys in distributed sensor networks. In *CCS '03*, pages 52–61, 2003.

[23] D. Liu, P. Ning, and W. Du. Group-based key predistribution for wireless sensor networks. *ACM Transactions on Sensor Networks (TOSN)*, 4(2):1–30, 2008.

[24] K. Lorincz, D. Malan, T. Fulford-Jones, A. Nawoj,

A. Clavel, V. Shnayder, G. Mainland, M. Welsh, and S. Moulton. Sensor networks for emergency response: challenges and opportunities. *IEEE Pervasive Computing*, 3(4):16–23, Oct.-Dec. 2004.

[25] K. Lorincz, D. Malan, T. Fulford-Jones, A. Nawoj, A. Clavel, V. Shnayder, G. Mainland, M. Welsh, and S. Moulton. Sensor networks for emergency response: challenges and opportunities. *IEEE Pervasive Computing*, 3(4):16–23, Oct.-Dec. 2004.

[26] K. Malasri and L. Wang. Addressing security in medical sensor networks. In *HealthNet '07*, pages 7–12, 2007.

[27] M. Mana, M. Feham, and B. A. Bensaber. A light weight protocol to provide location privacy in wireless body area networks. *CoRR*, abs/1103.3308, 2011.

[28] S. Mathur, R. Miller, A. Varshavsky, W. Trappe, and N. Mandayam. Proximate: proximity-based secure pairing using ambient wireless signals. In *Proceedings of the 9th international conference on Mobile systems, applications, and services*, pages 211–224. ACM, 2011.

[29] S. Mathur, W. Trappe, N. Mandayam, C. Ye, and A. Reznik. Radio-telepathy: extracting a secret key from an unauthenticated wireless channel. In *Proceedings of the 14th ACM international conference on Mobile computing and networking*, pages 128–139. ACM, 2008.

[30] R. Mayrhofer and H. Gellersen. Shake well before use: Authentication based on accelerometer data. In A. LaMarca, M. Langheinrich, and K. Truong, editors, *Pervasive Computing*, volume 4480 of *Lecture Notes in Computer Science*, pages 144–161. Springer Berlin / Heidelberg, 2007.

[31] R. Mayrhofer and H. Gellersen. Shake well before use: Intuitive and secure pairing of mobile devices. *IEEE Transactions on Mobile Computing*, 8:792–806, 2009.

[32] M. Patel and J. Wang. Applications, challenges, and prospective in emerging body area networking technologies. *Wireless Communications, IEEE*, 17(1):80 –88, february 2010.

[33] N. Patwari and S. Kasera. Robust location distinction using temporal link signatures. In *Proceedings of the 13th annual ACM international conference on Mobile computing and networking*, pages 111–122. ACM, 2007.

[34] A. Perrig, R. Szewczyk, J. Tygar, V. Wen, and D. Culler. Spins: Security protocols for sensor networks. *Wireless networks*, 8(5):521–534, 2002.

[35] C. Poon, Y.-T. Zhang, and S.-D. Bao. A novel biometrics method to secure wireless body area sensor networks for telemedicine and m-health. *IEEE Communications Magazine*, 44(4):73–81, April 2006.

[36] T. Rappaport and L. Milstein. Effects of radio propagation path loss on ds-cdma cellular frequency reuse efficiency for the reverse channel. *Vehicular Technology, IEEE Transactions on*, 41(3):231 –242, aug 1992.

[37] K. Rasmussen and S. Capkun. Realization of rf distance bounding. In *Proceedings of the USENIX Security Symposium*, 2010.

[38] K. Rasmussen, C. Castelluccia, T. Heydt-Benjamin, and S. Capkun. Proximity-based access control for implantable medical devices. In *Proceedings of the 16th ACM conference on Computer and communications security*, pages 410–419. ACM, 2009.

[39] K. Singh and V. Muthukkumarasamy. Authenticated key establishment protocols for a home health care system. In *ISSNIP '07*, pages 353–358, Dec. 2007.

[40] D. Smith, L. Hanlen, J. Zhang, D. Miniutti, D. Rodda, and B. Gilbert. Characterization of the dynamic narrowband on-body to off-body area channel. In *Communications, 2009. ICC'09. IEEE International Conference on*, pages 1–6. IEEE, 2009.

[41] C. C. Tan, H. Wang, S. Zhong, and Q. Li. Body sensor network security: an identity-based cryptography approach. In *ACM WiSec '08:*, pages 148–153, 2008.

[42] K. Timm. Medical device hacking prompts concern. http://www.cyberprivacynews.com/2011/08/medical-device-hacking-prompts-concern/.

[43] A. Varshavsky, A. Scannell, A. LaMarca, and E. De Lara. Amigo: proximity-based authentication of mobile devices. In *Proceedings of the 9th international conference on Ubiquitous computing*, UbiComp '07, pages 253–270, Berlin, Heidelberg, 2007. Springer-Verlag.

[44] K. Venkatasubramanian, A. Banerjee, and S. Gupta. Pska: Usable and secure key agreement scheme for body area networks. *Information Technology in Biomedicine, IEEE Transactions on*, 14(1):60–68, 2010.

[45] K. Venkatasubramanian and S. Gupta. Physiological value-based efficient usable security solutions for body sensor networks. *ACM Transactions on Sensor Networks (TOSN)*, 6(4):1–36, 2010.

[46] K. Venkatasubramanian, S. Gupta, R. Jetley, and P. Jones. Interoperable medical devices: Communication security issues. *Pulse, IEEE*, 1(2):16–27, 2010.

[47] K. K. Venkatasubramanian and S. K. S. Gupta. Physiological value-based efficient usable security solutions for body sensor networks. *ACM Trans. Sen. Netw.*, 6:31:1–31:36, July 2010.

[48] L. Xiao, L. Greenstein, N. Mandayam, and W. Trappe. Using the physical layer for wireless authentication in time-variant channels. *Wireless Communications, IEEE Transactions on*, 7(7):2571 –2579, july 2008.

[49] L. Xiao, L. J. Greenstein, N. B. Mandayam, and W. Trappe. Channel-based detection of sybil attacks in wireless networks. *Trans. Info. For. Sec.*, 4:492–503, September 2009.

[50] F. Xu, Z. Qin, C. Tan, B. Wang, and Q. Li. Imdguard: Securing implantable medical devices with the external wearable guardian. In *The 30th IEEE International Conference on Computer Communications (INFOCOM 2011)*, pages 1862 – 1870, Shanghai, P.R.China, April 2011.

[51] K. Zeng, K. Govindan, and P. Mohapatra. Non-cryptographic authentication and identification in wireless networks. *Wireless Commun.*, 17:56–62, October 2010.

[52] T. Zia and A. Zomaya. A lightweight security framework for wireless sensor networks. *Journal of Wireless Mobile Networks, Ubiquitous Computing, and Dependable Applications*, 2:53–73, september 2011.

Zero Reconciliation Secret Key Generation for Body-Worn Health Monitoring Devices

Syed Taha Ali
University of New South Wales
Australia
taha@student.unsw.edu.au

Vijay Sivaraman
Unversity of New South Wales
Australia
vijay@unsw.edu.au

Diethelm Ostry
ICT Centre, CSIRO
Australia
diet.ostry@csiro.au

ABSTRACT

Wearable wireless sensor devices are key components in the emerging technology of personalized healthcare monitoring. Medical data collected by these devices must be secured, especially on the wireless link to the gateway equipment. However, it is difficult to manage the required cryptographic keys, as users may lack the awareness or requisite skills for this task. Alternatively, recent work has shown that two communicating devices can generate secret keys derived directly from symmetrical properties of the wireless channel between them. This channel is also strongly dependent on positioning and movement and cannot be inferred in detail by an eavesdropper. Existing schemes, however, yield keys with mismatching bits at the two ends, requiring reconciliation mechanisms with high implementation and energy costs that are unsuitable for resource-poor body-worn devices.

In this work we propose a secret-key generation mechanism which uses signal strength fluctuations caused by incidental motion of body-worn devices to construct shared keys with near-perfect agreement, thereby avoiding reconciliation costs. Our contributions are: (1) we analyse channel measurement asymmetries caused by non-simultaneous probing of the channel by the link end-points, (2) we propose a practical filtering scheme to minimize these asymmetries, dramatically improving signal correlation between the two ends without reducing entropy, and (3) we develop a method to restrict key generation to periods of channel fluctuation, ensuring near-perfect key agreement. To the best of our knowledge, this work is the first to demonstrate the feasibility of generating high quality secret keys with zero reconciliation cost in body-worn networks for healthcare monitoring.

Categories and Subject Descriptors

K.6.5 [**Management of Computing and Information Systems**]: Security and Protection—*physical security, unauthorized access*

General Terms

Experimentation, Performance, Security

Keywords

Body Area Networks, Secret Key Generation

1. INTRODUCTION

Soaring national health expenditures and escalating age-related disabilities are shifting the emphasis from the hospital to the home. Body area networks are at the forefront of emerging technologies in this trend towards personalized healthcare. A body area network typically consists of small sensors mounted on the body to record vital signs and communicate wirelessly with a base-station (a fixed access point or a portable device such as a mobile phone) for real-time analysis and possibly remote diagnosis. Wearable platforms for health monitoring have begun to appear in the market. Apple has recently patented a sensor strip device [1] that interfaces with the iPhone, and IMEC has demonstrated a sensor device [2] which communicates with phones running the Android OS. Fig. 1 illustrates a topology based on the Sensium Digital Plaster [3], a body-worn wireless solution to monitor a subject's ECG, temperature, blood glucose and oxygen levels. A report [4] by ABI forecasts that the market for wearable wireless sensor devices will grow to more than 420 million devices by 2014. Securing these devices is a significant challenge considering their low power and computation capabilities, but it is also critical, since these devices record and handle medical data which comes with stringent privacy and liability concerns.

The high computational cost of asymmetric cryptography precludes its use in the body-worn device for encrypting medical data, leaving symmetric encryption using a shared key as the only viable option. The challenge lies in dynamically sharing a secret key between the body-worn device and the base-station. The secret key cannot be pre-configured at time of manufacture, since the pairing of body-worn device to base-station is done at deployment, and dynamic pairing requires a trusted third-party to store the keys, carrying with it risk of compromise and associated liability. Furthermore, experience has shown [5] that users (such as the elderly) are often unaware of the need, or unable to configure secrets of sufficient strength, or safeguard these secrets adequately. It is far more practical to automatically generate secret keys as needed. Moreover, keys need to be renewed periodically to protect against attack. It is more straightforward to generate shared secret keys using the Diffie-Hellman key exchange but it is expensive to implement and execute on resource-constrained sensor devices [6].

Recent work such as [7, 8] has shown that it is possible to generate a shared secret over an unsecured wireless channel

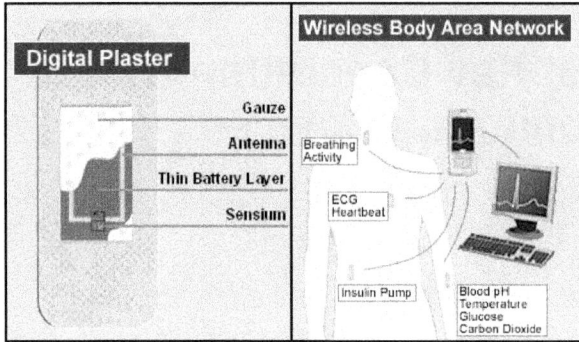

Figure 1: Toumaz Sensium^{TM} Digital Plaster and body area network topology

by exploiting the directional symmetry of the wireless link. Specifically, the multipath propagation characteristics between two communicating parties, Alice and Bob, are symmetric (and hence strongly correlated) at both ends of the link, and yet sufficiently random to allow Alice and Bob to generate shared secret bits. The focus of much of the prior work has been to generate secret bits at a high rate (tens of bits per second), which comes at the cost of more frequent channel probing and greater bit mismatch between the two ends. Even a 2% probability of bit mismatch means that a 128-bit key has only a 7.5% chance of matching perfectly. To resolve mismatch, reconciliation methods such as Cascade [9] are proposed, where the two ends exchange messages to probabilistically identify mismatching bits.

In contrast, we focus on low-data-rate patient monitoring applications that require periodic key renewal. Pairwise temporal keys (or session keys) are advocated in the emerging IEEE 802.15 standard [10] for body area networks. In these applications a high bit generation rate is not essential; for example, if a 128-bit key needs to be renewed every hour, a generation rate of a few bits per minute suffices. This low bit-rate requirement has three benefits for low-complexity key generation schemes. First, the mismatch of key bits generated by the two ends can be avoided to eliminate reconciliation overheads which consume precious computing and communication resources [11]. Second, body-worn devices typically embed their logic in hardware as a single-chip solution (as in the case of the Sensium [3]), and interactive reconciliation protocols requiring real-time communication are too complex to be completely implemented in custom hardware and their flexibility is limited. A third advantage is that the low bit-rate requirement allows the key generation mechanism to piggyback channel sampling on regular data exchanges (typically at rates of the order of 1 packet/s), instead of requiring dedicated channel sounding messages. This significantly reduces radio usage, usually the most expensive operation in small sensor devices.

In this paper, we undertake an experimental study of secret key generation in the specific setting of body-worn devices, and propose a cost-effective scheme to eliminate mismatch between the two ends. Our target is to have at least a 75% chance of generating a fully matching 128-bit secret key, corresponding to bit-agreement probability of at least 99.8%. Our specific contributions are:

1. Our first contribution is a demonstration that the dominant cause of the observed channel mismatch between the two ends of the link during motion is the time delay between measurements by the two ends. We present a theoretical bound on the mismatch, and validate it via experiments with body-worn devices in a representative office environment as well as an anechoic chamber.

2. Our second contribution is a method to reduce this mismatch by filtering the signal using a practical, low-complexity approach that dramatically improves correlation between the two endpoints, without reducing signal randomness.

3. Our third contribution is a mechanism to confine bit generation to periods of high motion-related fluctuation, further reducing disagreement in channel estimation thereby virtually eliminating key-bit mismatch. We show that an activity threshold can be adjusted to yield near-perfect key agreement by trading-off against key generation rate.

For our threat model, we situate passive eavesdroppers at various points in the environment who sample the channel at the same time as the communicating parties and know the key extraction algorithm and its settings. We do not address the issue of authentication in this paper: we believe that establishing initial trust between two parties is a distinct research problem and it is important during the bootstrapping phase, whereas our focus is on key renewal. If we assume a mechanism for bootstrapping initial trust, a basic challenge-response protocol can ensure authenticity of newly generated session keys.

We believe our work is the first to undertake secret-key generation using the wireless channel in the important and unique context of body-worn healthcare devices. Moreover, our scheme dispenses with reconciliation and dedicated channel sampling, while generating high entropy secret bits at a usable rate of approximately 8 bits/min, with 99.8% agreement. At this rate, a usable 128-bit key is generated every 20 minutes. If a session key is renewed over a greater period, say 1 hour, as is recommended for WiFi [12], the probability of generating a perfectly matching key at both endpoints using our mechanism can be up to 99.5%. Our scheme is light-weight, implementable on the current generation of body-wearable devices, and suitable for large-scale deployment in home-based personalized healthcare systems.

The rest of this paper is organized as follows: Section 2 discusses prior work and the key reconciliation process. In Section 3 we identify the cause of mismatch theoretically and experimentally, and in Section 4 describe a filtering technique to minimize it. Section 5 details our region selection and key generation mechanisms, whose performance is then analysed in Section 6. We conclude in Section 7.

2. BACKGROUND

In this section we briefly describe secret key generation and prior contributions, and highlight how our work differs in that it eliminates key reconciliation.

2.1 Secret Key Generation

2.1.1 The Basic Principle

The wireless channel is intrinsically symmetrical by the reciprocity property of electromagnetic propagation. In the absence of interference, noise, and changes in the channel, two communicating parties, Alice and Bob, using identical transceivers and antennas, and transmitting identical signals, will both also receive identical signals. In the complex geometry typical of interior environments, radio signals can propagate via multiple paths, each experiencing a different delay, attenuation, and phase and polarisation distortions which depend on the details of each path. The set of parameters defining the effects of all these paths can be measured by both Alice and Bob and ideally they will agree.

In the time domain, the channel can be represented by the delay spectrum or impulse response, and equivalently by the frequency spectrum in the frequency domain. Measurements of either of these representations can be used by Alice and Bob to construct a shared key, unique to their positions. An eavesdropper, Eve, located outside a distance greater than about one radio wavelength from either Alice or Bob, will measure a different spectrum, and so will be unable to determine their key. This scenario leads to the well-known Jake's uniform scattering model [13] which states that there is rapid decorrelation in the signal over a distance of approximately half a wavelength, and one may assume independent signals for a separation of one to two wavelengths or more.

Measurement of either delay or channel spectra with sufficient resolution to generate long keys requires significant investment in hardware and energy consumption. An approach more suited to energy-constrained devices uses a time series of received signal strengths measured along a trajectory traversed by one or both parties as a source of shared information [7, 8].

In practice, asymmetric components appear in these channel measurements due to transceiver differences, random noise, changes caused by motion, either of the parties or other elements of the environment, and asymmetrically located interference sources. These asymmetries cause discrepancies in the derived keys, requiring additional operations to obtain key agreement.

2.1.2 The Procedure

The process of shared secret key generation described in the literature typically comprises four phases:

1. *Channel sensing:* Alice and Bob each measure some characteristic of the channel. A time series of received signal strengths during node motion is commonly used [7, 8, 14], although other suitable channel characteristics have also been studied [15, 16, 17].

2. *Quantization:* The measurements are converted into a string of key bits. Approaches based on signal extrema [7, 8] and ranking [18] have been described in prior work.

3. *Reconciliation:* Key bit discrepancies at the two ends are discarded or corrected by employing an information reconciliation protocol [19].

4. *Privacy amplification:* The now matching keys are then strengthened by discarding agreed bits or by performing a transformation to increase key entropy and obfuscate any partial information an eavesdropper may have gathered during key reconciliation.

2.1.3 Reconciliation

We now consider the reconciliation phase with a view to showing that it incurs an unjustifiably high cost in body-worn devices, thereby motivating the study in this paper. Information reconciliation mechanisms have been developed mainly in the context of quantum cryptography [19], and key generation schemes for wireless links either borrow these mechanisms or propose non-optimal ad hoc schemes.

To reconcile bitstrings, two parties exchange metadata, (similar in concept to the cyclic redundancy check (CRC)), to identify mismatching bits, whilst simultaneously trying to minimize the potential leakage of information about the bitstring to an eavesdropper. Once mismatching bits are identified, they are either discarded from the bitstring, or else corrected, which may require further message exchanges. Unfortunately, like CRC, reconciliation methods only detect and correct a specific class of errors, with a probability depending on the capabilities of the reconciliation mechanism. If we consider a simple reconciliation scheme which computes a single parity bit over a block, an even number of errors will go undetected. Considering a block of b bits, let q denote the probability that an individual bit differs at both ends. The probability P_q of having mismatching blocks in spite of reconciliation can be expressed as:

$$P_q = \sum_{i=1}^{\lfloor b/2 \rfloor} \binom{b}{2i} (1-q)^{b-2i} q^{2i}$$

Consequently, the probability P, of agreeing on an error-free key of length K is

$$P = (1 - P_q)^{K/b}$$

For example, if there is as little as a 2% chance of a bit mismatching between endpoints, for a block size $b = 8$ there is approximately a 15% chance of uncorrected errors in a key of length $K = 128$, in which case the key will have to be regenerated. And typically, to counter the information leaked to an adversary due to parity bits being exposed, an equal number of bits needs to be dropped from the key, thereby reducing the final key bit rate.

Reconciliation protocols such as Cascade typically perform this parity check multiple times and shuffle the bit sequence in coordination before each test. This incurs significant memory and transmission overheads (as documented in [11]), much more pronounced in the context of a miniature sensor device operating with constrained resources. Furthermore, reconciliation will also add to design complexity, of particular concern since these protocols will typically be implemented in ASICs to provide a single-chip solution for body-worn devices. Our aim, therefore, is to virtually eliminate the need for reconciliation by aiming for a bit agreement ratio of 99.8% or greater, so that a typical 128-bit key has a very good ($> 75\%$) chance of matching perfectly.

2.1.4 Performance Metrics

The following metrics are commonly used to evaluate the performance of secret key generation schemes:

1. *Key Agreement:* the fraction of bits matching at both ends, ideally 100%. Eavesdroppers should match in only about 50% of the bits they generate.

2. *Secret Bit Rate:* the average number of secret key bits extracted from the channel per unit time. This depends on factors such as sampling rate, quantizer parameters, and channel variability.

3. *Entropy:* a measure of the uncertainty (inherent randomness) in the key. A typical measure of entropy of a random variable X, over the set of n symbols $x_1, x_2, ..., x_n$, is

$$H(X) = -\sum_{i=1}^{n} p(x_i) \log_2 p(x_i)$$

where $p(x_i)$ is the probability of occurrence of symbol x_i.

For binary symbols, a value close to 1 indicates high entropy. We use the NIST test suite [20] to estimate entropy.

Ideally a scheme should generate keys with high agreement, at a fast rate, and with high entropy. However, these are conflicting goals and researchers generally focus on one and employ secondary means to improve the others, at additional computational and communication cost. Sampling at a high rate will yield a higher bit rate, but will have greater disagreement, and lower entropy, since the signal variation is lower relative to the sampling rate so that successive bits will be more correlated. Sampling at larger intervals improves key agreement and entropy but reduces bit rate. These tradeoffs are handled in a variety of ways in prior work.

2.2 Prior Work

Prior work in secret key generation for **802.11 WiFi** considers both static and mobile cases. The authors of [7] show that with modified 802.11 hardware able to measure channel impulse response it is possible to obtain keys at a rate of more than 1 bit/s with almost perfect agreement, but use of simple signal strength measurements instead resulted in key disagreements. [8] presents experimental results for several static and mobile scenarios including walking and bicycle-riding. Motion is seen to yield high entropy keys at a high rate and with good key agreement. The authors' emphasis is on high bit generation rates and relatively high bit mismatch is seen (4-30%) making a reconciliation mechanism (Cascade [19]) necessary, along with privacy amplification.

In [21], the authors consider key generation in **ultra wideband channels**, mainly using simulations of static deployments. They use the envelope of the observed channel impulse response, rather than the received signal strength metric. However, successive key values were highly correlated and they use a whitening process employing training data for privacy amplification.

Wireless sensor devices have been specifically considered in some prior work. In [22], the authors measure at a sequence of frequencies to estimate the spectrum and extract keys with agreement of over 97% in static deployments.

In [18], the authors aim for a very high rate key generation of 22 bits per second with 2.2% disagreement, or, alternately 3 bits per second with 0.04% disagreement. The channel is sampled at a rate of 50 probes/s. Extensive processing is done on the data, including interpolation, de-correlation, and multi-bit adaptive quantization. One of the endpoints must be moved continuously in a 'random' manner to induce signal fading fluctuations. This approach is extended in [14] by introducing a ranking mechanism to remove those asymmetries in the received signal strength indicator (RSSI) traces due to differences in hardware characteristics. Experiments with TelosB motes show a key generation rate of 40 bits/s with 4% disagreement.

Body area networks have been considered in only one work in the literature. The authors in [23] simulate a near-body channel to derive an upper bound of 4 bits/s due to inherent limitations on channel entropy but do not describe an actual key generation process.

2.3 Our Focus

Our focus in this paper is on body-worn devices, which have uniquely different constraints and operating conditions. Channel variation is complex and unpredictable in body area networks due to motion, shadowing effects of the human body and multipath propagation [24]. Moreover, due to the limited resources of body-worn devices, key generation has to be done at minimal cost. In contrast to earlier schemes, we forego the high costs of dedicated sampling, reconciliation and privacy amplification. Our scheme samples the channel in the course of routine transmissions, controls the prime source of bit discrepancies using low-complexity filtering, and relies on the user's own motion to create channel entropy which is harnessed for secret key generation.

3. UNDERSTANDING DISAGREEMENT

In this section, we use theoretical and experimental approaches to show that non-simultaneous sampling of the channel contributes significantly to disagreement between the two ends of the link.

3.1 Theoretical Estimation of Disagreement in Measurements of Link Signal Power

Here we carry out a simplified analysis to estimate the effects of motion on the received signal power measured by the nodes at the ends of a link. There are three well-known contributors to changes in signal power caused by node motion [25]: (i) *path loss*, due to geometric signal spreading has an inverse-square law relationship with range, (ii) *shadow* or *large-scale fading*, arising from signal blockage in the environment including the subject's body and from changes in antenna orientation which affect signal strength through the antenna radiation pattern, and (iii) *small-scale fading*, due to signal fluctuations caused by motion induced changes in the multiple propagation paths between the two nodes. At speeds typical of human motion, range (path loss) and orientation (shadow fading) cause only slow variations in signal strength over successive packets. However multipath (small-scale fading) can cause rapid fluctuations in signal strength as a node's position changes. These components are illustrated in Fig. 2.

Consider an environment with appreciable multipath propagation, i.e. where multiple propagation paths exist between the two nodes: suppose at time instant $t = 0$, the stationary node (the base-station (BS)) samples the channel (i.e. hears a transmission from the mobile node), and Δt seconds later the (body-worn) mobile node samples the channel (i.e. hears the transmission from the BS). The difference in channel measurements between the two end-points is equivalent to the change in channel from time $t = 0$ to time Δt as measured by one node (say the mobile node) at the two instants, since the channel is reciprocal at each time. In what follows we estimate this change using a simple model.

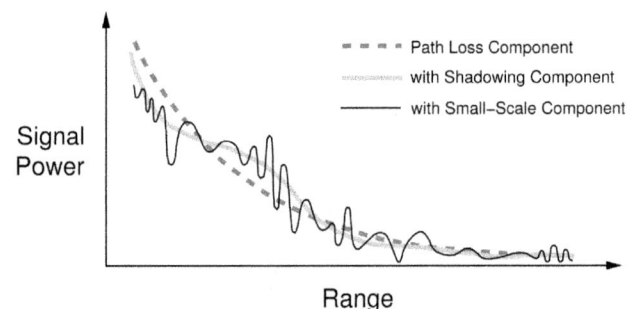

Figure 2: Components of the received signal power

When the BS transmits, signals propagating along the multiple paths combine to form a standing wave pattern in the environment. At places where the signals reinforce due to phase agreement, there is an increase of signal strength, and at places where the signals subtract there is a decrease in signal strength. As the mobile node moves through the environment, the signal strength it observes fluctuates due to these interference effects. Because of the fixed characteristic radio signal wavelength, adjacent locations where the signal is maximum or minimum cannot be separated by less than a distance of the order of half a wavelength [26]. This places an upper bound on the rate at which the received signal power can change as the node moves through the standing wave pattern. If the signal radio wavelength is λ and the receiver moves at velocity v, the maximum frequency at which the observed signal power can change in the receiver is

$$f_{\max} = v \cdot (2/\lambda). \tag{1}$$

This bound limits the worst-case (i.e. highest frequency) signal component that the receiver senses to

$$y(t) = (A/2)\sin 2\pi f_{\max}t. \tag{2}$$

where A is the peak-to-peak amplitude of the signal. The maximum discrepancy in amplitude, Δy between sample points taken Δt apart in time occurs at $t = 0$ and is

$$
\begin{aligned}
\Delta y &\approx dy/dt \cdot \Delta t \\
&= (A/2)\cos(2\pi f_{\max}t)2\pi f_{\max}\Delta t \\
&= A\pi f_{\max}\Delta t, \quad \text{at } t = 0.
\end{aligned} \tag{3}
$$

The fractional discrepancy $\epsilon = \Delta y/A$, namely the change as a fraction of the amplitude, is then

$$
\begin{aligned}
\epsilon &= \pi f_{\max}\Delta t \\
&= 2\pi v\Delta t/\lambda.
\end{aligned} \tag{4}
$$

At an operating frequency of 2.4GHz for example (where $\lambda = 0.125$m) and a node velocity of $v = 1$m/s, a $\Delta t = 20$ms delay between the two ends in sampling the channel leads to a maximum fractional error of $\epsilon \approx 1$, implying that the signal component due to changing multipath (excluding contributions due to variation in range and orientation) may have changed over the entire range from a minimum to a maximum during that interval. Since typical wireless sensor network radios today (e.g. the CC2420 [27]) take 20-40ms to measure the wireless link in two directions, this error can be significant in practice and can lead to mismatch between the two ends, as will be examined experimentally next.

3.2 Experiments in Indoor Environment and Anechoic Chamber

We studied two environments experimentally: a representative indoor office environment, and an RF anechoic chamber with very low reflections. The purpose of the experiments is two-fold: (1) to verify the importance of the small-scale fading component (due to multipath) on channel measurement mismatches between the two ends, and (2) to show the effect of channel sampling delay Δt on measurements at the two ends.

Our experiments used MicaZ motes running TinyOS and operating in the 2.4 GHz band. Their radios output a received signal strength indicator (RSSI), a measure of signal power in logarithmic units, related in a simple way to dBm. Our setup is modeled after a real body area network where

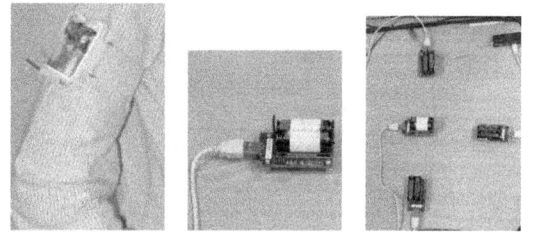

(a) Mobile Mote (b) base-station (c) base-station surrounded by eavesdroppers

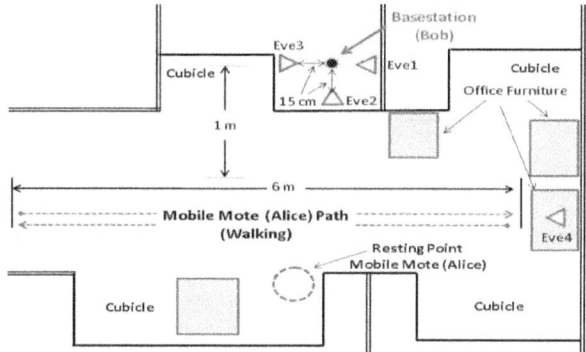

(d) Experimental setup of indoor environment

Figure 3: Mobile node, base-station and experimental layout for indoor environment

(a) RF Anechoic Chamber

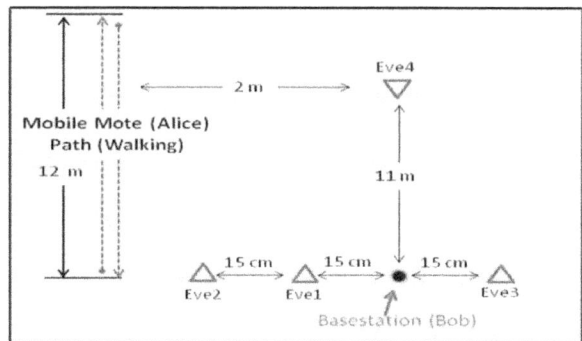

(b) Experimental setup of anechoic chamber

Figure 4: Anechoic chamber and layout

the body-worn node (Alice), shown in Fig. 3(a)), transmits one packet per second, a rate typical for a health monitoring device sending patient physiological information such as heart-rate, ECG, etc. Even though continuous patient monitoring devices may collect medical readings several times per second, they usually process them in-node (e.g. by av-

(a) RSSI trace, indoor

(b) RSSI trace, anechoic chamber

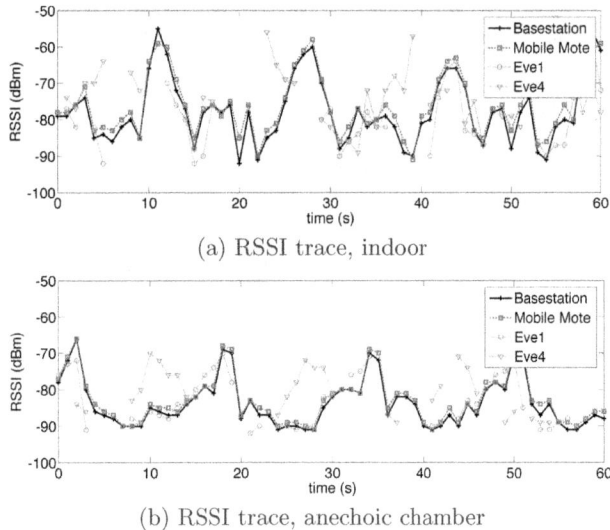

Figure 5: Results for Indoor Office and Anechoic Chamber

Figure 6: Box plot highlighting discrepancy in RSSI for both test environments

eraging or aggregating), and then transmit the result to the base station, thereby reducing radio usage. The base-station (Bob, shown in Fig. 3(b)) responds with an acknowledgement as soon as possible (typically 10-20ms on the MicaZ), and this allows the two ends of the link to probe the channel alternately in quick succession.

Our *indoor environment* experiments have the layout depicted in Fig. 3(d) showing the location of the base-station, the four eavesdroppers labeled Eve1 to Eve4, (as shown in Fig. 3(c)), and the path along which the subject walked back and forth. Multiple WiFi networks were operating at the site, but our results did not show evidence of interference. (It is relevant to mention here that efforts are underway to allocate spectrum specifically to body area network applications, to limit interference from other systems [28]).

The RF anechoic chamber is pictured in Fig. 4(a). All surfaces (floors, ceilings, walls) are covered in material that absorbs electromagnetic energy, thereby minimizing RF reflections and consequently the small-scale fading due to multipath propagation. Our experimental layout is shown in Fig. 4(b). In all experiments the subject walked at a moderate pace of about 1m/s.

For the indoor office environment, we show in Fig. 5(a) the signal strengths measured by the base-station, mobile node, and two eavesdroppers (other eavesdroppers show similar results). We observe that the eavesdroppers are not able to replicate the channel measurements accurately, confirming that the base and mobile can use the RSSI measurements to generate random keys. However, we find that there are discrepancies between the signal strengths measured by the base and mobile. The same experimental procedure repeated in the anechoic chamber (which largely eliminates small-scale fading), gave the RSSI trace shown in Fig. 5(b). The signal strength can be seen to vary more smoothly for the base-station and mobile node as compared to the office environment, and correlates better between the two ends.

We examine the discrepancy (i.e. difference in RSSI between the two ends) more closely in Fig. 6 where a box plot depicts the variance observed by both parties. The central mark is the median, the edges of the box denote the 25th and 75th percentiles, the whiskers extend to the most ex-

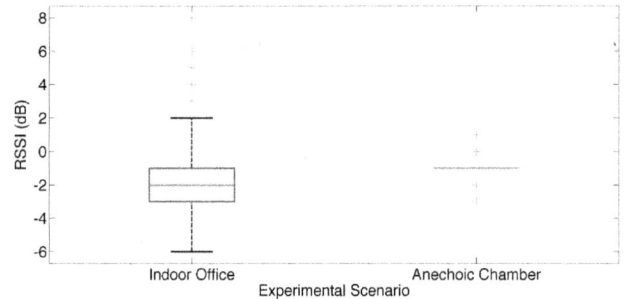

treme datapoints, and the outliers are plotted individually. For the indoor environment, the discrepancy is seen to vary by as much as 12dB (−6dB to 8dB), able to cause significant mismatch in key bits between the two ends. The mismatch is clearly much lower in the anechoic chamber (no more than about 4dB).

This mismatch can be quantified with the Pearson correlation coefficient r:

$$r = \frac{\sum_{i=1}^{n}(X_i - \bar{X})(Y_i - \bar{Y})}{\sqrt{\sum_{i=1}^{n}(X_i - \bar{X})^2} \cdot \sqrt{\sum_{i=1}^{n}(Y_i - \bar{Y})^2}}$$

where X_i and Y_i are the RSSI values of the ith packet of each party and $\bar{X}$ and $\bar{Y}$ are the respective mean RSSI values of a sequence of n packets. The correlation coefficient r returns a value in $[-1, 1]$ where 1 indicates perfect correlation, 0 indicates no correlation, and −1 indicates anti-correlation. This metric has the benefit that it measures variations and not the absolute values, and so is unaffected by offsets in RSSI measurements arising from different receiver sensitivities or transmit powers. For the indoor office environment, the correlation between the RSSI signals at the base-station and the body-worn node over the entire trace (several minutes) is 0.975, while it is higher, at 0.994, in the anechoic chamber. This provides quantitative confirmation that the multipath (i.e. small-scale fading) component, which occurs in the indoor office environment but is largely absent in the anechoic chamber, is a significant contributor to RSSI mismatch (which leads to key disagreements) between the two communicating parties.

We validate experimentally that mismatch increases with increase in probing delay Δt. We configure the mobile node to acknowledge packet reception from a basestation several times at 40ms intervals. The discrepancy between the RSSI of the original packet (from base to mobile) and the RSSI of each subsequent response (acknowledgement from mobile to base) is measured, and plotted in Fig. 7, for both the indoor office environment and the anechoic chamber. Two observations emerge from this plot: (i) the discrepancy is again much lower in the anechoic chamber than in the indoor office environment, and (ii) the RSSI trace of the first acknowledgement shows least fluctuation, while each subsequent response deviates more (i.e. has larger amplitude). The latter visual observation can be quantified with the correlation coefficient, plotted in Fig. 8 as the probing delay Δt between the two ends increases. It clearly demonstrates that the correlation steadily falls (i.e. mismatch increases) as probing delay increases, and that a 40ms probing delay in the indoor environment is equivalent to a 100ms probing

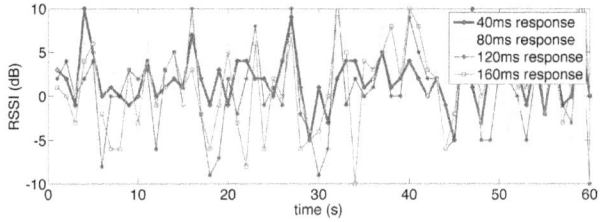

(a) Indoor Environment

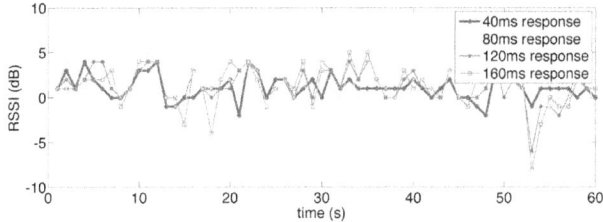

(b) Anechoic Chamber

Figure 7: Mismatch due to probing delay Δt

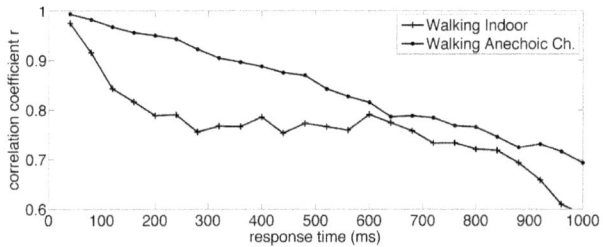

Figure 8: Correlation coefficient r versus sampling delay

delay in the multipath-free anechoic chamber in the sense of yielding a similar correlation of about 0.976.

The theoretical and experimental observations above provide strong evidence that the discrepancy in channel measurement is predominantly due to the lag in sampling by the two ends of the link. In the next section, we develop a novel means of reducing this discrepancy.

We wish to emphasize that other factors such as external interference (which can be asymmetric) and uncorrelated random noise effects (e.g. due to receiver circuitry) also contribute to the discrepancy. To illustrate this, we conducted experiments in which the mobile node is resting at one spot (indicated in Fig. 3(d)), and plot the resulting RSSI in Fig. 9. The channel is relatively static, yet small RSSI discrepancies are visible. Unfortunately these small discrepancies can lead to key mismatch, since the (uncorrelated) noise is amplified by the quantizer to generate key bits. This issue is addressed in Section 5, where we develop a way to eliminate the effects of uncorrelated noise.

4. REDUCING DISAGREEMENT BY FILTERING

In Section 3.1 we developed a simple model showing that the maximum fractional error due to small-scale fading is $\epsilon = \pi f_{max} \Delta t$ where $f_{max} = v \cdot (2/\lambda)$. To reduce this error ϵ, one would ideally like to minimize sampling delay, Δt, but unfortunately the maximum possible reduction is limited by operation in half-duplex mode (although recent proposals for single-channel full-duplex operation [29] may offer a means

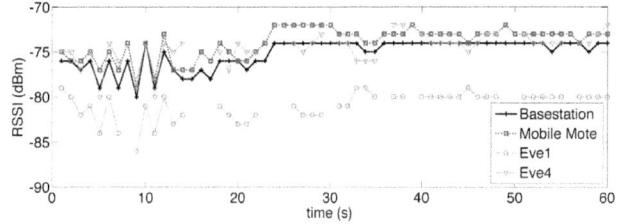

Figure 9: Variation in RSSI for Resting Scenario

of overcoming this in future). The other parameter that can be manipulated is the mobile node velocity v, but that would restrict application to slow-moving mobile nodes.

Instead, we reduce f_{max}, i.e. the maximum frequency of changes in received signal power arising from motion in a small-scale fading environment. By applying a low-pass filter with cutoff frequency $f_c < f_{max}$ at both ends of the link, the maximum fractional error in measuring signal power is reduced to $\hat{\epsilon} = \pi f_c \Delta t = \epsilon f_c / f_{max}$. For the example considered in Section 3.1, where the subject walks at $v = 1\text{m/s}$, the delay in bidirectional probing is $\Delta t = 20\text{ms}$, and operating frequency is 2.4GHz with wavelength $\lambda = 12.5\text{cm}$, we showed that $f_{max} \approx 16\text{Hz}$ and the error can theoretically be as high at $\epsilon \approx 100\%$. To restrict this error to less than a desired bound, say $\hat{\epsilon} \approx 3\%$, we can set the filter cut-off frequency to $f_c = (\hat{\epsilon}/\epsilon) f_{max} \approx 0.48\text{Hz}$.

A low-pass Fourier filter is unsuitable for real-life situations where users' motion causes discontinuities and unpredictable changes in the RSSI trace (and is hence not well-modeled by discrete frequency components). Instead we choose the Savitzky-Golay filter [30] which is better able to match the logarithmic form of signal strength measurements given by the receiver RSSI output data. The Savitzky-Golay filter behaves as a low-pass filter [31], and is able to follow the underlying slow-moving features of the RSSI traces we have observed, while providing a controllable reduction in the bandwidth of fluctuations caused by motion in a multipath environment. Moreover, this filter is a linear algorithm that can be easily implemented in ASIC as part of a body-worn solution.

For our experimental work in this paper we select the parameters of the Savitzky-Golay filter for a cut-off frequency $f_c \approx 0.48Hz$, so that the maximum fractional error $\hat{\epsilon}$ is limited to around 3% (as argued above). The mapping of filter parameters to 3 dB cut-off frequency is based on the approximation derived in [31, Eq. (11)]:

$$f_c \approx \frac{K+1}{1.6F - 3.6}, \qquad (5)$$

where K is the polynomial order used by the Savitzky-Golay filter, and F is the frame (window) size. We chose $K = 5$ (i.e. 5-th order polynomial) and $F = 11$ (for an impulse response half-length of 5), giving a cut-off frequency $f_c \approx 0.43\text{Hz}$, close to the desired value. This filter yielded visually good signals for key generation in all our experiments. Dynamically tuning the filter parameters to adapt to the mobility of the monitored subject is left for future work.

It is important to emphasize that the proposed filtering operation does not reduce the randomness of the signal (and hence of the generated keys). Motion-induced discrepancies occupy a range of frequencies and it is the higher ones, contaminated by the half-duplex delays, which are removed, leaving the lower-frequency components which retain the

(a) Baseline Distribution: Channel Variation

(b) Slow Component

(c) Fast Component

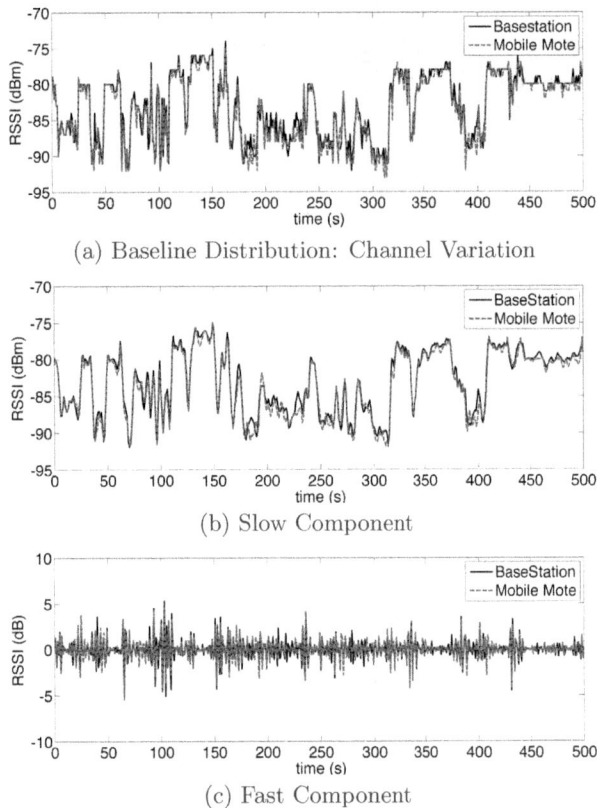

Figure 10: Application of Savitzky-Golay filter

(a) Channel variation (slow component)

(b) Energy of fast component

Figure 11: Region Selection on a trace of routine office activity

information about changes in the multipath with position needed for key generation.

To illustrate the operation of the Savitzky-Golay filter, we show its effect in routine subject activity in the indoor office environment over several hours. Fig. 10(a) shows the original RSSI traces. The output of the Savitzky-Golay filter is shown in Fig. 10(b): we call this the *slow component*, and it is primarily attributable to path loss, shadow fading and filtered small-scale fading. The residual (i.e. original signal less the filter output) is shown in Fig. 10(c). We call this the *fast component*, since it consists of higher frequency small-scale fading components which are primarily responsible for the disagreement between the two ends.

Comparing Fig. 10(b) and 10(a), we see that filtering visibly improves agreement between base-station and mobile node. The correlation coefficient of the original RSSI signal between the two ends is 0.973, whereas after filtering, the correlation (of the slow components at the two ends) improves to 0.986. This is almost comparable to the correlation seen in the anechoic chamber, making near-perfect key agreement feasible.

5. DYNAMIC REGION SELECTION AND SECRET KEY GENERATION

We have shown that correlation between the two ends can be greatly improved by filtering the RSSI signals to attenuate the high-frequency components associated with sampling delay. However, factors such as (asymmetric) interference and (uncorrelated) random noise also contribute to mismatch. Indeed the impact of these effects is amplified when the channel is very quiescent (as we showed for a rest-

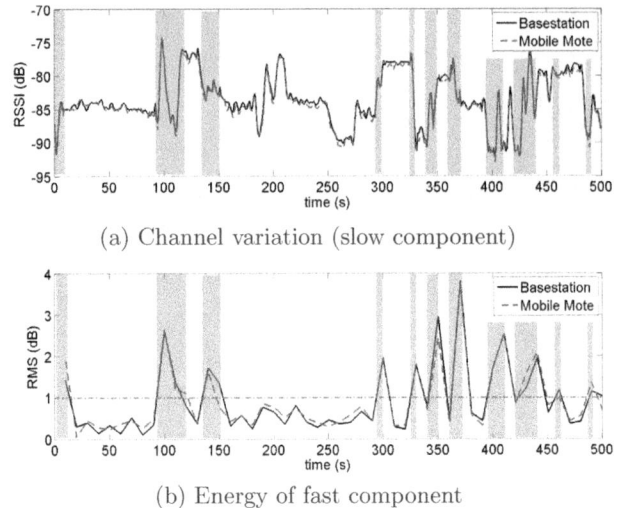

ing subject in Fig. 9), which can lead to an undesirably high rate of secret-key bit-mismatches after quantization. We propose, next, a novel means of dealing with such effects by restricting key-bit generation to periods in which usable signals are available to the quantizer.

5.1 Dynamic Region Selection

When the channel exhibits significant fluctuations (i.e. when the subject is moving rather than resting), the correlated fluctuations in the signal at the two ends have large amplitude and dominate the uncorrelated noise, leading to better agreement (as well as high key entropy). This has been reported in the literature, and indeed some works [14, 8] have explicitly required that the subject should move during key generation. This can place a burden on users, and instead we extend our algorithm to automatically detect time periods (or regions) that are most suitable for secret-key bit generation.

The key observation is that rapid channel variation arises from rapid changes in multipath, and this is strongly expressed in the higher-frequency components of small-scale fading. The latter is already conveniently available to us as the *fast component*, namely the residual between the original and filtered signals. By measuring the RMS energy in the fast component, we can deduce whether there is sufficient activity in the channel for generating high agreement or "good" key-bits at little additional computational cost.

We illustrate this approach in signals obtained in the same office environment as in Section 3 while the subject was engaged in routine office activity. The RSSI (slow component obtained after filtering) is shown in Fig. 11(a), while the RMS energy (in dB, computed using a non-overlapping moving window of $W_{RMS} = 10$ samples) is shown in Fig. 11(b). High energy in the fast component is clearly associated with significant variability in the slow component, and so offers a reliable measure of channel fluctuation. The shaded zones in the figure highlight periods when the fast component energy exceeds a threshold $\theta = 1$dB and dynamically identify regions of high activity during which key bits should be generated from the slow component of the RSSI signal.

5.2 Sampling, Filtering and Quantization

Our threat model considers one or more eavesdroppers (Eve) in the environment who sample the channel at the same time as the legitimate parties, and know the key extraction algorithm and parameters. However, we stipulate that Eve is separated from the two parties by a distance greater than one radio wavelength (~ 12.5 cm for the 2.4GHz band), and thereby restricted to measuring a different multipath channel. We do not consider here the issue of initial trust between base-station and mobile node, nor that of active attackers engaged in jamming and packet injection.

The key generation mechanism runs as a background process to normal device operation, and the process flow is depicted in Fig. 12 identifying the input variables required at every stage. For all experiments, we employ a sampling rate of $\tau = 1$ sample/s, allowing channel sampling through routine data transmissions and also reducing correlation between successive RSSI readings. The channel response profile is passed to the Savitzky-Golay filter (configured with polynomial order $K = 5$ and frame size $F = 11$ as noted earlier) which outputs the "slow component". The "fast component" is obtained by subtracting the slow component from the original distribution, and its RMS energy is computed for region selection. When periods of high activity (i.e. when the energy exceeds a specified threshold θ) are identified, the corresponding segments of the slow component are passed to the quantizer for bit generation.

Our research does not develop a new quantizer. Instead, we use a basic single-bit quantizer, taken from [7] and refined in [8], and operating as follows: the base-station and mobile node define an adaptive moving window of size W_Q, within which they process blocks of consecutive (filtered) RSSI readings. The process is depicted in Fig. 13. For each block, two threshold values are calculated:

$$q+ = \mu + \alpha.\sigma$$
$$q- = \mu - \alpha.\sigma$$

where μ is the mean, σ is the standard deviation, and $\alpha \geq 0$ is an adjustable parameter. If an RSSI reading within a window is greater than $q+$, it is encoded as 1, and if less than $q-$, as 0. The thresholds define an exclusion zone and values falling between them are discarded. Smaller RSSI variations are more likely to disagree at both endpoints and are therefore not considered, in favor of larger excursions. The α parameter allows the operator to adjust quantizer performance to balance between bit generation rate and mismatch. For our purposes, we use a window size of $W_Q = 5$ and $\alpha = 1$, consistent with prior work.

Once both parties generate enough secret bits to form a key, it can be verified using a challenge-response protocol. If the key fails, it is discarded and the process is repeated until keys agree. Results indicate that in typical conditions, this scheme can generate $2 \sim 4$ usable keys per hour.

6. RESULTS AND ANALYSIS

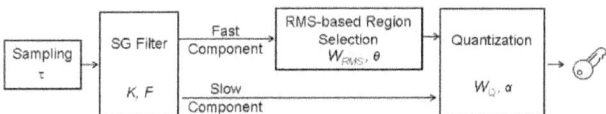

Figure 12: Flow chart of key generation process

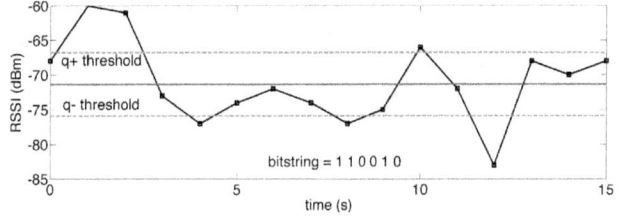

Figure 13: Quantization Process

We tested our key generation mechanism in the office space in Fig. 3(d). The base station is stationary with three eavesdroppers deployed around it at distances of 22cm, 44cm and 100cm. The subject wore the mobile mote on his upper arm. In the first experiment, the subject performed *High Activity*, working, walking and interacting with other people in the room. In the second experiment he performed *Low Activity*, mainly seated at his cubicle working and occasionally getting up to fetch items from other cubicles. Care was taken to ensure the experiments were performed in a realistic manner, as close as possible to an actual deployment of bodyworn sensor devices. Trace data is collected from each experiment for 40 minutes and our key generation scheme is applied offline to assess its performance with different parameter settings.

Table 1 shows, for the *High Activity* scenario, the percentage of key bits that agree for different energy threshold settings. Filtering improved signal correlation between the two ends, but after quantization the key agreement improved only marginally (from 97.27% to 97.91%). This is because the quantizer amplifies uncorrelated random noise during quiescent periods (as explained in Section 4). However, when dynamic region selection is applied to restrict key-bit generation to regions with at least θ dB energy in the fast component, key agreement improves dramatically: a threshold setting of $\theta = 0.5$ dB improves key agreement to over 99%, and at $\theta = 1.5$ dB key bits were found to match with probability over 99.8%.

For *Low Activity*, Table 2 shows that agreement of keys generated from the raw signal is quite low at around 93%. This can be attributed to longer quiescent or low-motion periods during this experiment where the subject just sits at his desk, and uncorrelated noise effects dominate channel variation. Filtering improves this only marginally, but when combined with region selection there is again a dramatic impact. Threshold $\theta = 0.5$ dB improves key agreement to over 98%, while at $\theta = 1.5$ dB key bits were found to match with probability over 99.8%. This demonstrates that filtering and region selection together can effectively improve bit agreement to near-ideal levels.

The high key entropy seen in all cases (> 0.99) (Column 6), and the keys' passing the NIST *approximate entropy* test [20] confirm that the Savitzky-Golay filter retains a sufficient component of the essential randomness arising from motion in a multipath environment.

Filtering and region selection improve bit agreement, but reduce the bit generation rate (Column 2 of the Tables). The Savitzky-Golay filter smooths out the more rapid variations in the raw signal, effectively reducing the number of larger excursions that the quantizer directly maps to key bits. This causes bit generation rate to decrease from 0.33 to 0.24 bits/s (for high activity) and from 0.21 to 0.19 bits/s for low activity. Region selection further reduces bit generation rate, because with increasing threshold, a progressively

Signal quantized	Key Agreement (%)	bit rate (bit/s)	Eve1 Key Agreement (%)	Eve2 Key Agreement (%)	Eve3 Key Agreement (%)	Entropy
unfiltered	97.27	0.33	47.33	47.07	50.42	0.9979
filtered	97.91	0.2435	51.31	51.43	51.20	0.9990
filtered, $\theta = 0.5$	99.08	0.2221	51.68	51.22	51.17	0.9990
filtered, $\theta = 1$	99.74	0.1812	52.03	51.04	51.63	0.9992
filtered, $\theta = 1.5$	99.83	0.1410	51.31	50.66	50.68	0.9992
filtered, $\theta = 2$	99.88	0.1010	50.72	50.74	50.90	0.9995
filtered, $\theta = 2.5$	99.92	0.0647	51.67	52.12	51.27	0.9996
filtered, $\theta = 3$	100	0.0370	51.31	51.18	51.30	0.9997

Table 1: Effect of varying threshold θ on key generation performance metrics for High Activity scenario

Signal quantized	Key Agreement (%)	bit rate (bit/s)	Eve1 Key Agreement (%)	Eve2 Key Agreement (%)	Eve3 Key Agreement (%)	Entropy
unfiltered	93.04	0.2174	49.43	48.89	49.62	0.9970
filtered	93.06	0.1968	49.10	49.04	49.30	0.9993
filtered, $\theta = 0.5$	98.41	0.1323	49.21	48.98	49.43	0.9994
filtered, $\theta = 1$	99.41	0.0861	48.96	48.77	48.24	0.9993
filtered, $\theta = 1.5$	99.80	0.0570	49.51	49.03	50.32	0.9994
filtered, $\theta = 2$	100	0.0365	47.90	49.14	48.54	0.9995

Table 2: Effect of varying threshold θ on key generation performance metrics for Low Activity scenario

smaller proportion of the signal (of high channel activity) is available for quantization. This trade-off is illustrated in Fig. 14, which shows that with increasing threshold θ, the key agreement (left axis) increases while the bit generation rate decreases (right axis), for both high and low activity. A compromise can be chosen by choosing θ appropriately. For the scenarios we considered, a threshold value of $\theta = 1.5$ is sufficient for 99.8% bit agreement, corresponding to a 75% chance of both endpoints' agreeing on a 128-bit secret key. For this threshold setting, our scheme achieves a bit rate of $0.057 \sim 0.141$ bits/s, i.e. it would take $15 \sim 35$ minutes to generate a usable 128-bit key, quickly enough for key renewal purposes. If typical session key lifetime is approximately 1 hour, the chances of having a valid new key perfectly matching at both endpoints varies from $93.5 \sim 99.5\%$ depending on the user's activity.

Tables 1 and 2 also show the percentage of matching bits that each of the eavesdroppers generate by passively listening to the channel. Eavesdropper agreement hovers near 50% for all cases, which is ideal, indicating that their chance

of guessing if a generated bit is correct or not is the same as an unbiased coin toss.

7. CONCLUSION

In this paper we presented a method for generating shared secret keys using motion in body area networks. Our first contribution has been to identify the cause of key mismatch: we presented a theoretical model to account for the mismatch in secret-key agreement, and validated it with experiments in an indoor environment and in an anechoic chamber. Our results showed that disagreement between two endpoints is primarily due to half-duplex measurement delays and random noise. Furthermore, we noted that these discrepancies are concentrated in the rapidly-varying component of the channel RSSI trace. Second, we showed that this component can be removed using the Savitzky-Golay filter to dramatically improve endpoint correlation. Our final contribution demonstrated how this residual fast component can be employed to dynamically identify regions of high channel variability, where near-perfect key agreement occurs. Our mechanism is low-cost, does not require dedicated channel sampling or information reconciliation, and incrementally generates high entropy key bits at a rate suitable for key renewal. We used our key generation solution in a real office environment and showed that it takes $15 \sim 35$ minutes to generate a 128 bit key with a 75% chance of perfect agreement between endpoints. If the typical lifetime of a session key is one hour, depending on the subject's activity, there is a $93.5 \sim 99.5\%$ chance of both parties generating a perfectly matching secret-key.

For future work, we intend to study multi-party key agreement for body area networks, and research safeguards against active attackers.

8. ACKNOWLEDGMENTS

The authors would like to thank Mr. Ken Smart of CSIRO and Mr. Linjia Yao for assistance with experiments in the RF anechoic chamber.

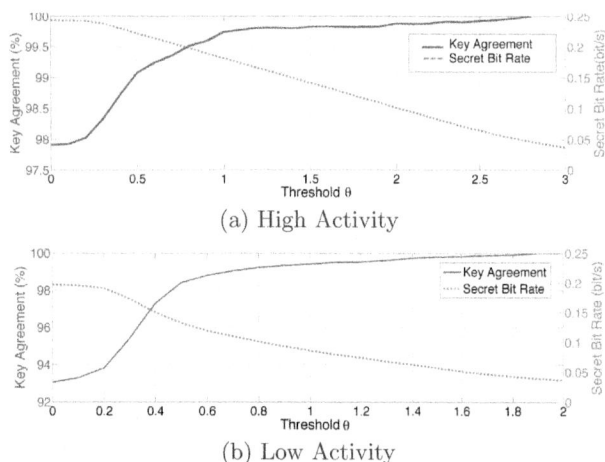

(a) High Activity

(b) Low Activity

Figure 14: Key agreement vs. secret bit rate for varying region selection threshold θ

9. REFERENCES

[1] Apple Inc. *Sensor Strip*.
http://www.patentlyapple.com/patently-apple/2010/03/
body-area-networks-apple-sensor-strips-the-iphone.
html.

[2] D. Graham-Rowe. Body Organs can Send Status Updates to Your Cellphone. New Scientist, October 2010.

[3] Toumaz Technology Ltd. *Sensium Life Platform*.
http://www.toumaz.com/page.php?page=sensium_intro.

[4] ABI Research Service. *Market for Wearable Wireless Sensors to Grow to More than 400 Million Devices by 2014*, 2009. http://www.abiresearch.com.

[5] Bruce Schneier. MySpace Passwords Aren't So Dumb. *WIRED*, December 2006.

[6] E. Blass and M. Zitterbart. Efficient Implementation of Elliptic Curve Cryptography for Wireless Sensor Networks. Technical report, Universität Karlsruhe, 2005.

[7] S. Mathur, W. Trappe, N. Mandayam, C. Ye, and A. Reznik. Radio-telepathy: Extracting a Secret Key from an Unauthenticated Wireless Channel. In *ACM MobiCom*, 2008.

[8] S. Jana, S. N. Premnath, M. Clark, S. Kasera, N. Patwari, and S. Krishnamurthy. On the Effectiveness of Secret Key Extraction Using Wireless Signal Strength in Real Environments. In *ACM MobiCom*, Beijing, 2009.

[9] G. Brassard and L. Salvail. Secret-key Reconciliation by Public Discussion. In *EUROCRYPT*, 1994.

[10] IEEE 802.15 WPAN Task Group 6. *MedWiN MAC and Security Proposal Documentation*, September 2009.

[11] P. Bellot and M. Dang. BB84 Implementation and Computer Reality. In *IEEE RIVF*, 2009.

[12] Tim Moore. IEEE 802.11-01/610r02: 802.1.x and 802.11 Key Interactions. Technical report, Microsoft Research, 2001.

[13] W. C. Jakes. *Microwave Mobile Communications*. Wiley, 1974.

[14] J. Croft, N. Patwari, and S. Kasera. Robust Uncorrelated Bit Extraction Methodologies for Wireless Sensors. In *ACM/IEEE IPSN*, 2010.

[15] B. Azimi-Sadjadi, A. Kiayias, A. Mercado, and B. Yener. Robust Key Generation from Signal Envelopes in Wireless Networks. In *ACM CCS*, 2007.

[16] A. Sayeed and A. Perrig. Secure Wireless Communications: Secret Keys through Multipath. In *IEEE ICASSP*, 2008.

[17] N. Patwari and S. K. Kasera. Temporal Link Signature Measurements for Location Distinction. *IEEE Transactions on Mobile Computing*, 10(3):449–462, March 2011.

[18] N. Patwari, J. Croft, S. Jana, and S. K. Kasera. High Rate Uncorrelated Bit Extraction for Shared Key Generation from Channel Measurements. *IEEE Transactions on Mobile Computing*, 9(1), 2010.

[19] G. Brassard and L. Salvail. Secret-Key Reconciliation by Public Discussion. In *Workshop on the Theory and Application of Cryptographic Techniques (EUROCRYPT)*, 1994.

[20] NIST. *A Statistical Test Suite for Random and Pseudorandom Number Generators for Cryptographic Applications*, 2001.

[21] R. Wilson, D. Tse, and R. A. Scholtz. Channel Identification: Secret Sharing using Reciprocity in Ultrawideband Channels. *IEEE Transactions on Information Forensics and Security*, 2(3), 2007.

[22] M. Wilhelm, I. Martinovic, and J. B. Schmitt. Secret Keys from Entangled Sensor Motes: Implementation and Analysis. In *ACM WiSec*, 2010.

[23] L. W. Hanlen, D. Smith, J. Zhang, and D. Lewis. Key-sharing via Channel Randomness in Narrowband Body Area Networks: Is Everyday Movement Sufficient? In *Bodynets*, 2009.

[24] David Smith, Leif Hanlen, Andrew Zhang, Dino Miniutti, David Rodda, and Ben Gilbert. First and Second-Order Statistical Characterizations of the Dynamic Body-Area Propagation Channel of Various Bandwidths. *Annals of Telecommunications*, 66(3-4):187–203, 2011.

[25] B. Sklar. Rayleigh Fading Channels in Mobile Digital Communication Systems. *IEEE Communications Magazine*, 35(7), 1997.

[26] R.P. Bowman. Quantifying Hazardous Microwave Fields. In *Microwave Bioeffects and Radiation Safety*. University of Alberta, Canada: International Microwave Power Institute, 1978.

[27] ChipCon Products. *2.4 GHz IEEE 802.15.4 / Zigbee-ready RF Transceiver*.

[28] G. Lawton. More Spectrum Sought for Body Sensor Networks. *Computing Now*, Oct. 2009.

[29] J. I. Choi, K. Srinivasan, M. Jain, P. Levis, and S. Katti. Achieving Single Channel, Full Duplex Wireless Communication. In *ACM MobiCom*, 2010.

[30] A. Savitzky and M. J. E. Golay. Smoothing and Differentiation of Data by Simplified Least Squares Procedures. *Analytical Chemistry*, 36:8, 1964.

[31] R. W. Schafer. On the Frequency-Domain Properties of Savitzky-Golay Filters. Technical report, HP Laboratories, HPL-2010-109, September 2010.

Location-Aware and Safer Cards: Enhancing RFID Security and Privacy via Location Sensing

Di Ma[1], Anudath K Prasad[1], Nitesh Saxena[2], and Tuo Xiang[1]
[1]University of Michigan-Dearborn
{dmadma,prasadak,txiang}@umd.umich.edu
[2]University of Alabama, Birmingham
saxena@cis.uab.edu

ABSTRACT

In this paper, we report on a new approach for enhancing security and privacy in certain RFID applications whereby location or location-related information (such as speed) can serve as a legitimate access context. Examples of these applications include access cards, toll cards, credit cards and other payment tokens. We show that location awareness can be used by both tags and back-end servers for defending against unauthorized reading and relay attacks on RFID systems. On the tag side, we design a location-aware selective unlocking mechanism using which tags can selectively respond to reader interrogations rather than doing so promiscuously. On the server side, we design a location-aware secure transaction verification scheme that allows a bank server to decide whether to approve or deny a payment transaction and detect a specific type of relay attack involving malicious readers. The premise of our work is a current technological advancement that can enable RFID tags with low-cost location (GPS) sensing capabilities. Unlike prior research on this subject, our defenses do not rely on auxiliary devices or require any explicit user involvement.

Categories and Subject Descriptors

H.4 [**Information Systems Applications**]: Miscellaneous; C.2.0 [**Computer Systems Organization**]: Computer-Communication Networks—*General, Security and Protection*

General Terms

Security

Keywords

RFID; relay attacks; context recognition; GPS

1. INTRODUCTION

Low cost, small size, and the ability of allowing computerized identification of objects make Radio Frequency IDentification (RFID) systems increasingly ubiquitous in both public and private domains. Prominent RFID applications include supply chain management (inventory management), e-passports, credit cards, driver's licenses, vehicle systems (toll collection or automobile key), access cards (building or parking, public transport), and medical implants.

A typical RFID system consists of tags, readers and/or back-end servers. Tags are miniaturized wireless radio devices that store information about their corresponding subject. Such information is usually sensitive and personally identifiable. For example, a US e-passport stores the name, nationality, date of birth, digital photograph, and (optionally) fingerprint of its owner [21]. Readers broadcast queries to tags in their radio transmission ranges for information contained in tags and tags reply with such information. The queried information is then sent to the server (which may co-exist with the reader) for further processing and the processing result is used to perform proper actions (such as updating inventory, opening gate, charging toll or approving payment).

Due to the inherent weaknesses of underlying wireless radio communication, RFID systems are plagued with a wide variety of security and privacy threats [20]. A large number of these threats are due to the tag's promiscuous response to any reader requests. This renders sensitive tag information easily subject to *unauthorized reading* [18]. Information (might simply be a plain identifier) gleaned from a RFID tag can be used to track the owner of the tag, or be utilized to clone the tag so that an adversary can impersonate the tag's owner [20].

Promiscuous responses also incite different types of *relay attacks*. One class of these attacks is referred to as "ghost-and-leech" [26]. In this attack, an adversary, called a "leech," relays the information surreptitiously read from a legitimate RFID tag to a colluding entity known as a "ghost." The ghost can then relay the received information to a corresponding legitimate reader and vice versa in the other direction. This way a ghost and leech pair can succeed in impersonating a legitimate RFID tag without actually possessing the device.

A more severe form of relay attacks, usually against payment cards, is called "reader-and-ghost"; it involves a malicious reader and an unsuspecting owner intending to make a transaction [12][1]. In this attack, the malicious reader, serving the role of a leech and colluding with the ghost, can fool the owner of the card into approving a transaction which she did not intend to make (e.g., paying for a diamond purchase made by the adversary while the owner only intending to pay for food). We note that addressing this problem requires *transaction verification*, i.e., validation that the tag is indeed authorizing the intended payment amount.

The feasibility of executing relay attacks has been demonstrated on many RFID (or related) deployments, including the Chip-and-PIN credit card system [12], RFID-assisted voting system [31], and keyless entry and start car key system [13].

With the increasingly ubiquitous deployment of RFID applications, there is a pressing need for the development of security primitives and protocols to defeat unauthorized reading and relay attacks. However, providing security and privacy services for RFID tags presents a unique and formidable set of challenges. The inherent difficulty stems partially from the constraints of RFID tags in terms of computation, memory and power, and partially from the unusual usability requirements imposed by RFID applications (originally geared for automation). Consequently, solutions designed for RFID systems need to satisfy the requirements of the underlying RFID applications in terms of not only **efficiency** and **security**, but also **usability**.

1.1 Sensing-Enabled Automated Defenses

Although a variety of security solutions exist, many of them do not meet the constraints and requirements of the underlying RFID applications in terms of (one or more of): efficiency, security and usability. We review related prior work in Section 2.

In an attempt to address these drawbacks, this paper proposes a general research direction – one that utilizes sensing technologies – to address unauthorized reading and relay attacks in RFID systems without necessitating any changes to the traditional RFID usage model, i.e., without incorporating any explicit user involvement beyond what is practiced today. The premise of the proposed work is based on a current technological advancement that enables many RFID tags with low-cost sensing capabilities. Various types of sensors have been incorporated with many RFID tags [36, 19, 37]. Intel's Wireless Identification and Sensing Platform (WISP) [38, 42] is a representative example of a sensor-enabled tag which extends RFID beyond simple identification to in-depth sensing. This new generation of RFID devices can facilitate numerous promising applications for ubiquitous sensing and computation. They also suggest new ways of providing security and privacy services by leveraging the unique properties of the physical environment or physical status of the tag (or its owner). In this paper, we specifically focus on the design of context-aware security primitives and protocols by utilizing sensing technologies so as to provide improved protection against unauthorized reading and relay attacks.

The physical environment offers a rich set of attributes that are unique in space, time, and to individual objects. These attributes – such as temperature, sound, light, location, speed, acceleration, or magnetic field – reflect either

the current condition of a tag's surrounding environment or the condition of the tag (or its owner) itself. A sensor-enabled RFID tag can acquire useful contextual information about its environment (or its owner, or the tag itself), and this information can be utilized for improved RFID security and privacy without undermining usability.

1.2 Our Contributions

In this paper, we report on our work on utilizing *location information* to defend against unauthorized reading and relay attacks in certain applications. We notice that in quite some applications, under normal circumstances, tags only need to communicate with readers at some specific locations or while undergoing a certain speed. For example, an access card to an office building needs to only respond to reader queries when it is near the entrance of the building; a credit card should only work in authorized retail stores; toll cards usually only communicate with toll readers in certain fixed locations (toll booths) or when the car travels at a certain speed. Hence, location or location-specific information can serve as a good means to establish a legitimate usage context.

Specifically, we present two location-aware defense mechanisms for enhanced RFID security and privacy. First, we show that location information can be used to design *selective unlocking* mechanisms so that tags can selectively respond to reader interrogations. That is, rather than responding promiscuously to queries from any readers, a tag can utilize location information and will only communicate when it makes sense to do so, thus raising the bar even for sophisticated adversaries without affecting the RFID usage model. For example, an office building access card can remain locked unless it is aware that it is near the (fixed) entrance of the building. Similarly, a toll card can remain locked unless the car is at the toll booth and/or it is traveling at a speed range regulated by law.

Second, we show that location information can be used as a basis for *secure transaction verification* in order to defend against the reader-and-ghost attacks, a specialized form of relay attacks on payment tokens involving malicious readers. This is based on a straight-forward observation that, under normal scenarios, both the legitimate tag and legitimate reader are in close physical proximity, at roughly the same location. Thus, if the two devices indicate different physically disparate locations, a bank server could detect the presence of a reader-and-ghost attack . For example, the bank server can deny the transaction when it detects the valid tag (RFID credit card) is located in a restaurant, while the valid reader is attack presented in a jewelery shop and prevent the attack presented in [12].

For deriving location information, we make use of the well-known Global Positioning System (GPS). To demonstrate the feasibility of our location-aware defense mechanisms, we first integrate a low-cost GPS receiver with a RFID tag (the Intel's WISP), and then conduct relevant experiments to acquire location and speed information from GPS readings. Our experimental results show that it is possible to measure location and speed with high accuracies even on a constrained GPS-enabled platform, and that our location-aware defenses are quite effective in thwarting many attacks on RFID systems. Besides the traditional RFID tags, our location-aware defenses are also directly applicable to NFC

---

[1]In contrast to the "ghost-and-leech" attack, the owner in the "reader-and-ghost" attack is aware of the interrogation from the (malicious) reader.

(Near Field Communication) enabled phones, which often come readily equipped with GPS receivers.

We note that, in some applications, the proposed approaches may not provide absolute security. However, they still significantly raise the bar even for sophisticated adversaries without affecting the RFID usage model. For example, the selective unlocking mechanism for toll cards, based solely on speed detection, will leave the card vulnerable in other situations where the car is undergoing the same speed designated at the toll booths. However, it still protects the car from being read by an adversary while traveling at other speeds or when stationary. In addition, although the proposed techniques can work in a stand-alone fashion, they can also be used in conjunction with other security mechanisms, such as cryptographic protocols, to provide stronger cross-layer security protection.

1.3 Economic Feasibility

A fundamental question with respect to our sensing-enabled approaches is whether the cost of sensor-enabled tags is acceptable. The cost of an RFID tag is dependent on several factors such as the capabilities of the tag (computation, memory), the packaging of the tag (e.g., encased in plastic or embedded in a label), and the volume of tags produced. High-end RFID tags, such as those available on e-passports or some access cards that are capable of performing certain cryptographic computations, cost around $5; whereas low-end inventory tags that do not support any (cryptographic) computation cost only about $0.20 [45]. (We emphasize that our proposal generally targets high-end RFID tags that open up a wide array of applications and generally require higher level of security and privacy. Inventory tags, at least for the time being, are not within the scope of our research.) The current cost of WISP tags – equipped with a thermometer and an accelerometer – assembled from discrete components is roughly $25 but it is expected that this number will be reduced closer to $1 once the WISPs are mass manufactured [9].

Integrating a GPS sensor with an RFID tag is also quite feasible economically. A few GPS-enabled RFID tags have been reported previously. A tag from Numerex and Savi Technology has been equipped with GPS sensors and has the ability to conduct satellite communications [15]. Researchers in Oak Ridge National Laboratory also worked with RFID system suppliers in developing new intelligent tags by combining GPS and environmental sensors [8]; these tags are designed to track goods anywhere within a global supply chain. We note that usually cost of sensing hardware varies greatly not only between different types of sensors but also between various models of the same kind. GPS receivers, in particular, can be as costly as several hundred dollars [43] or as inexpensive as a couple of dollars when purchased in bulk [3]. The latter cost estimates are certainly acceptable for high-end tags and does not affect their business model. Incorporating sensors on tags – i.e., increasing the capabilities of tags – may raise the price of tags initially. However, in the long run, following Moore's law, advances in process technology and mass production should enable tags with more capabilities (such as sensing, increased computation and memory) at the same cost of today's tags [11].

1.4 Paper Outline

The rest of the paper is organized as follows. In Section 2, we review the most relevant prior work on RFID selective unlocking and transaction verification. Next, we describe our adversary models in Section 3. We present proposed location-aware defense mechanisms and point out applications that could benefit from them in Section 4. In Sections 5 and 6, we discuss the design and implementation of our mechanisms, and present our experimental results, respectively. Finally, we discuss related issues that may rise in practice in Section 7 and Section 8 concludes the paper.

2. PRIOR WORK

Hardware-based Selective Unlocking: These include: Blocker Tag [22], RFID Enhancer Proxy [23], RFID Guardian [35], and Vibrate-to-Unlock [39]. All of these approaches, however, require the users to carry an auxiliary device (a blocker tag in [22], a mobile phone in [39], and a PDA like special-purpose RFID-enabled device in [23, 35]). Such an auxiliary device may not be available at the time of accessing RFID tags, and users may not be willing to always carry these devices. A Faraday cage can also be used to prevent an RFID tag from responding promiscuously by shielding its transmission. However, a special-purpose cage (a foil envelope or a wallet) would be needed and the tag would need to be removed from the cage in order to be read. This greatly decreases the usability of such solutions as users may not be willing to put up with any changes to the traditional usage model. Moreover, building a true Faraday Cage that shields all communication is known to be a significant challenge. For example, a crumpled sleeve is shown to be ineffective for shielding purposes [28].

Cryptographic Protocols: Cryptographic reader-to-tag authentication protocols could also be used to defend against unauthorized reading. However, due to their computational complexity and high bandwidth requirements, many of these protocols are still unworkable even on high-end tags [20]. There has been a growing interest in the research community to design lightweight cryptographic mechanisms (e.g., [24, 7, 25, 14]). However, these protocols usually require shared key(s) between tags and readers, which is not an option in some applications.

Distance Bounding Protocols: These protocols have been used to thwart relay attacks [12, 13]. A distance bounding protocol is a cryptographic challenge-response authentication protocol. Hence, it requires shared key(s) between tags and readers as other cryptographic protocols. Besides authentication, a distance bounding protocol allows the verifier to measure an upper-bound of its distance from the prover [6]. (We stress that normal "non-distance-bounding" cryptographic authentication protocols are completely ineffective in defending against relay attacks.) Using this protocol, a valid RFID reader can verify whether the valid tag is within a close proximity thereby detecting ghost-and-leech and reader-and-ghost relay attacks [12, 13]. The upperbound calculated by an RF distance bounding protocol, however, is very sensitive to processing delay (the time used to generate the response) at the prover side. This is because a slight delay (of the orders of a few nanoseconds) may result in a significant error in distance bounding. Because of this strict delay requirement, even XOR- or comparison-based distance bounding protocols [6, 16] are not suitable for RF distance bounding since simply signal conversion and modulation can lead to significant delays. By eliminating the necessity for signal conversion and modulation, a very recent protocol, based on signal reflection and channel selection, achieves a processing time of less than $1\ ns$ at the prover side [34]. However, it requires specialized hardware at the prover side due to the need for channel selection. This renders existing protocols currently infeasible for even high-end RFID tags.

Context-Aware Selective Unlocking: "Secret Handshakes" is a recently proposed interesting selective unlocking method that is based on context awareness [11]. In order to unlock an *accelerometer-equipped* RFID tag [38, 42] using Secret Handshakes, a user must move or shake the tag (or its container) in a particular pattern. For example, the user might be required to move the tag parallel with the surface of the RFID reader's antenna in a circular manner. A number of unlocking patterns were studied and shown to exhibit low error rates [11]. A central drawback to Secret Handshakes, however, is that a specialized movement pattern is required for the tag to be unlocked. This requires subtle changes to the existing RFID usage model. While a standard, insecure RFID setup only requires users to bring their RFID tags within range of a reader, the Secret Handshakes approach requires that users consciously move the tag in a certain pattern. This clearly undermines the usability of this approach.

"Motion Detection" [40] has been proposed as another selective unlocking scheme. Here a tag would respond only when it is in motion instead of doing so promiscuously. In other words, if the device is still, it remains silent. Although Motion Detection does not require any changes to the traditional usage model and raises the bar required for a few common attacks to succeed, it is not capable of discerning whether the device is in motion due to a particular gesture or because its owner is in motion. Hence, the false unlocking rate of this approach is high.

In our work, we aim to design location-aware secure RFID schemes that (1) have both low *false locking* and *false unlocking* rates, and (2) do not necessitate any changes to the current usage model.

3. ADVERSARIAL MODELS

Our proposed techniques are meant to defend against unauthorized reading, ghost-and-leech, and reader-and-ghost attacks. Adversary models used in the three attack contexts are slightly different. In the following description, we call the tag (reader) under attack as valid tag (reader) and call the tag (reader) controlled by the adversary as malicious tag (reader).

In unauthorized reading, the adversary has direct control over a malicious reader. The malicious reader can be in the communication range of the victim tag without being detected or noticed and thus can surreptitiously interrogate the tag. The goal of the adversary is to obtain tag specific information and (later) use such information to compromise user privacy (through inventory checking), clone the tag (and thus impersonate the user), or track the user.

In ghost-and-leech attack, besides the malicious reader (the leech), the adversary has further control over a malicious tag (the ghost) which communicates with a valid reader. The adversary's goal is to use the malicious tag to impersonate the valid tag by letting the malicious tag respond to interrogations from the valid reader with informa-

tion surreptitiously read from the valid tag by the malicious reader.

In reader-and-ghost attack, the adversary controls a malicious reader and tag pair, just like in the ghost-and-leech attack. However, the malicious reader controlled by the reader-and-ghost adversary is a legitimate reader or believed by the valid tag as a legitimate reader. Hence, the valid tag (or its owner) is aware of and agree with communications with the malicious reader. That is, the interrogation from the malicious reader to the valid tag is not surreptitious as in unauthorized reading and ghost-and-leech attacks. The goal of the adversary is still to impersonate the valid tag.

In all the attack contexts, we assume the adversary does not have direct access to the tag. So tampering or corrupting the tag physically is not possible, or can be easily detected. The adversary is also unable to tamper the tag remotely through injected malicious code. We further assume that the adversary is able to spoof the GPS signal around the victim tag but not around the victim reader. This is because the reader is usually installed in a controlled place (toll booth, office building gate, or retailer store) and thus GPS spoofing around the victim reader can be easily detected. We do not consider loss or theft of tags.

4. LOCATION-AWARE DEFENSES

In this section, we present our location-aware selective unlocking and location-aware transaction verification mechanisms. The former can be used to protect against unauthorized reading and ghost-and-leech attacks, whereas the latter can be used to detect reader-and-ghost attacks.

4.1 Location-Aware Selective Unlocking

Using location-aware selective unlocking, a tag is unlocked only when it is in an appropriate (pre-specified) location. This mechanism is suitable for applications where reader location is fixed and well-known in advance. One example application is RFID-based building access system. An access card to an office building needs to only respond to reader queries when it is near the entrance of the building.

A pre-requisite in a location-aware selective unlocking scheme is that a tag needs to store a list of legitimate locations beforehand. Upon each interrogation from a reader, the tag obtains its current location information from its on-board GPS sensor, and compares it with the list of legitimate locations and decides whether to switch to the unlocked state or not. Due to limited on-board storage (e.g., the WISP has a 8KB of flash memory) of tags, the list of legitimate locations must be short. Otherwise, testing whether the current location is within the legitimate list may cause unbearable delay and affect the performance of the underlying access system. Moreover, the list of legitimate locations should not change frequently because otherwise users will have to do extra work to securely update the list on their tags. Thus, selective unlocking based on pure location information is more suitable for applications where tags only need to talk with one or a few readers, such as building access cards. It may not be suitable for credit card applications as there is a long list of legitimate retailer stores, and store closing and new store opening occur on a frequent basis.

Selective unlocking based on pure location information presents similar problems for toll systems as for the credit card systems because toll cards will need to store a long list of toll booth locations[2]. We notice that vehicles mounted with RFID toll tags are usually required to travel at a certain speed when they approach a toll booth. For example, three out of eight toll lanes on the Port Authority's New Jersey-Staten Island Outer Bridge Crossing permit 25 mph speeds for E-ZPass drivers; the Tappan Zee Bridge toll plaza and New Rochelle plaza, NY has 20mph roll-through speed; Dallas North Toll way has roll-through lanes allowing speeds up to 30 mph. Hence, "speed" can be used as a valid context to design selective unlocking mechanisms for toll cards. That is, a toll card remains in a locked state except when the vehicle is traveling at a designated speed near a toll booth (such as 25-35 mph in the Dallas North Toll Way case). GPS sensors can be used to estimate speed either directly from the instantaneous Doppler-speed or directly from positional data differences and the corresponding time differences [10].

For better protection against attacks, the speed and location can also be used together as a valid context for unlocking of toll cards. Here, the adversary will only be able to unlock the tag if both the valid location and speed criteria are satisfied.

4.2 Location-Aware Transaction Verification

A highly difficult problem arises in situations when the reader, with which the tag (or its user) engages in a transaction, itself is malicious. For example, in the context of an RFID credit card, a malicious reader can fool the user into approving for a transaction whose cost is much more than what she intended to pay. That is, the reader terminal would still display the actual (intended) amount to the user, while the tag will be sent a request for a higher amount. More seriously, such a malicious reader can also collude with a ghost and then succeed in purchasing an item much costlier than what the user intended to buy [12]. As discussed in Section 1, addressing this reader-and-ghost relay attack requires transaction verification, i.e., validation that the tag is indeed authorizing the intended payment amount. Note that selective unlocking is ineffective for this purpose because the tag will anyway be unlocked in the presence of a valid (payment) context.

A display-equipped RFID tag can easily enable transaction verification for detecting reader-and-ghost attacks, as outlined in [30, 27, 12]. This, however, necessitates conscious user involvement because the amount displayed on the tag needs to be validated by the user and any user mistakes in this task may result in an attack. Distance bounding protocols have also been suggested as a countermeasure to the reader-and-ghost attacks [12]. However, these protocols are currently infeasible (as also reviewed in Section 5.1).

In this paper, we set out to explore the design of location-aware automated mechanisms for protecting against reader-and-ghost attacks. We note that under such attacks, the valid tag and the valid reader would usually not be in close proximity (e.g., the tag is at a restaurant, while the reader is at a jewelery shop [12]). This is in contrast to normal circumstances whereby the two entities would be at the same location, physically near to each other. Thus, a difference between the locations of the tag and the reader would imply

the presence of such attacks. In other words, both the valid tag (credit card) and valid reader may transmit their locations to a centralized authority (issuer bank). This authority can then compare the information received from both entities and reject the transaction if the two mismatch. We note that such a solution can be deployed, with minor changes on the side of the issuer bank, under the current payment infrastructure, where cards share individual keys with their issuer banks (as discussed in Section 2.1 of [12]), and all communication takes place over secure channels.

5. DESIGN AND IMPLEMENTATION

5.1 GPS Background

A GPS receiver derives its location by timing the signals sent by GPS satellites high above the Earth. The receiver uses the messages it receives from the satellites to determine the travel time of each message and computes the distance to respective satellite. These distances along with the satellites' own locations are used with the possible aid of trilateration, to compute the position of the receiver.

GPS receivers can relay the gathered location data to a PC or other device using the NMEA 0183 specification [5]. This standard defines electrical signal requirements, data transmission protocol and time, and specific sentence formats for a 4800-baud serial data bus. Our approach is based on location and speed recognition. In order to obtain these two values properly, we need PVT (position, velocity, time) and data uncertainty (needed to establish the consistency of the data). GPGGA and GPRMC, the two most important NMEA sentences, are chosen for our implementation and experiments. GPGGA is an essential fix data which provide 3D location and accuracy (uncertainty) data. GPRMC has its own version of essential GPSPVT (position, velocity, time) data.

There are two methods to obtain the speed of the GPS unit. The first method calculates the speed indirectly from positional data differences and the corresponding time difference. The second method acquires the instantaneous Doppler-speed directly from the GPRMC sentence. For our implementation, we use the Doppler-speed since we can get this information instantaneously once we get a fix. Moreover, the Doppler-speed is very accurate as it matches the readings from the car odometer in our experiments.

5.2 Overview of WISP Tags

To evaluate the effectiveness and performance of the proposed location awareness techniques, we build proof-of-concept prototypes on the WISP tags. WISPs are passively-powered RFID tags that are compliant with the Electronic Product Code (EPC) protocol. Specifically, we utilized the 4.1 version of the WISP hardware, which partially implements Class 1 Generation 2 of the EPC standard. These tags possess an onboard Texas Instruments MSP430F2132 microcontroller and sensors such as a three-axis accelerometer. The 16-bit MCU features an 8 MHz clock rate, 8 kilobytes of flash memory, and 512 bytes of RAM. WISP is chosen as our test platform because: (1) it is the only existing programmable UHF RFID device, and (2) it has an extensible hardware architecture which allows for integration of new sensors.

---

[2]In some countries, toll-collection companies have set up roaming arrangements with each other. This permits the same vehicle to use another operator's toll system, thus reducing set-up costs and allowing even broader use of these systems [1].

5.3 System Overview

GPS Module: As our test module, we have chosen the 66-Channel LS20031 GPS receiver module from LOCOSYS Technologies in our experiments [2]. This module comes with an embedded ceramic patch antenna and GPS receiver circuits which are designed for a broad spectrum OEM applications and outputs the data in more than 6 different NMEA GPS sentences to a TTL-level serial port. It provides us with a variable update rate of 1 to 5 Hz. This module also has a built-in micro battery for rapid satellite acquisition (which it does by preserving data). It also includes a LED indicator to indicate GPS fix or no fix [2].

In our experiments, we have configured the LS20031 to 1Hz update rate, 57600bps serial communication rate and to output GGA and RMC NMEA sentences.

Interfacing the GPS Module with the WISP: The LS20031 (GPS module) communicates via TTL level serial communication (UART) which is interfaced to the A channel communication port (used for UART, SPI and I2C) on the WISP as shown in the block diagram above. The Rx communication on the LS20031 is only used for sending commands to configure it. The Tx port of LS20031 outputs the GPS NMEA sentences. Figures 1 and 2 depict the block diagram as well as a picture from our experimental set-up interfacing the WISP with our GPS module. As observed from Figure 2, LS20031 has a small form factor and the WISP-LS20031 combination can be easily embedded within a traditional access card or toll card.

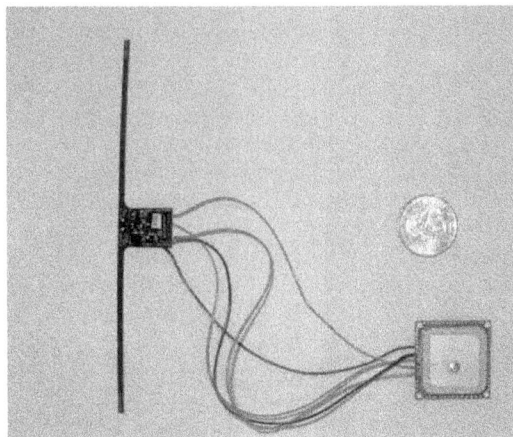

Figure 2: GPS interfaced with the WISP

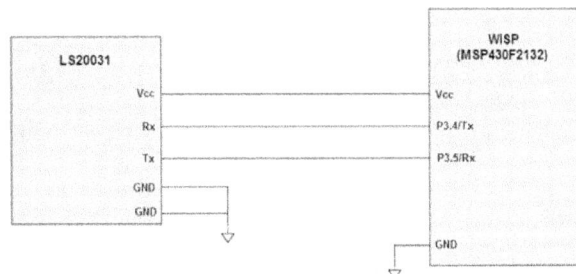

Figure 1: Block Diagram of GPS receiver and WISP interfacing

Storing List of Valid Locations: Since we have limited RAM i.e., only 512 bytes on the WISP controller, we have to store these valid location list on an external memory for the purpose of our selective unlocking mechanism (note that the transaction verification mechanism does not require the tag to store anything). Hence we utilize the onboard EEPROM (8K) present on the WISP for storing the list of valid locations. Since this is an external memory to the controller (though onboard), one consideration we have to take into account is the time taken for the communication to take place between the controller and the EEPROM. This was found to be sufficiently small (about 3 ms) and feasible as we have the GPS output frequency of one sample per second.

We parse out location and the speed data from the GPS NMEA sentences. The latitude, longitude and the speed are obtained from the GPRMC strings. The latitude and longitude data obtained are in degrees and the speed data is in knots. In order to avoid floating point numbers, the data is stored in the form of integers. To eliminate deviation in the GPS and errors, we average 10 such readings for 10 seconds and store these values. The lists of valid locations is then stored on the EEPROM and it serves as our reference to unlock the tag when the tag appears in one of the valid locations in the list.

The EEPROM is non-volatile and so the list of valid location is retained unless it has to be changed or modified as per the requirements of the underlying application.

Location Sensing and Computation: For location sensing, we dynamically obtain the location data from the GPS continuously at the rate of 1 Hz, and compare it with the list of valid locations stored on the tag within a time span.

The issue of error tolerance plays a vital role in location recognition. To check whether an acquired location is a valid location in the location list, we test whether it falls within the square region centered at a valid location. The size of the square space depends on how much error tolerance we can afford. We conduct various experiments to find out the accuracies of location recognition based on different error tolerances. Since the values obtained from the GPS are in degrees, we map the degree error onto meters for easier understanding. We also have to consider the problem of different latitudes. Since the radii vary as we move across different latitudes, the error tolerance also varies. We found that for about 10 degree variation in latitude, the error tolerance varies by less than 1 meter which is reasonably small and is feasible for most of the applications.

6. EXPERIMENTS AND RESULTS

In this section, we present the experiments and associated results corresponding to our location-aware selective unlocking and transaction verification schemes.

6.1 Selective Unlocking Experiments

We conducted three separate experiments to evaluate the performance of our selective unlocking mechanism based on location only, speed only, and both location and speed.

Location Tests: In this experiment, we used location information as a selective control to lock/unlock the tag. We took the reading of 5 locations around the campus and stored them as valid locations where the tag should be in an unlocked state. We performed the test by driving around our university campus around these locations to measure the accuracy in recognition (20 recordings were taken for each error tolerance). A LED was used as an indicator for successful identification. This test was done using different error tolerances and our results were tabulated in Table 1. As an example, ([x] ± 2; [y] ± 2) denotes an error tolerance of 2 meters centered around a valid location ([x], [y]) stored in the list. Referring to this table, we can conclude that we can successfully recognize valid locations under normal usage scenarios.

Test	Error Tolerance (meters)	% Accuracy
1	[x] ± 2; [y] ± 2	100.00% (20/20)
2	[x] ± 5; [y] ± 5	100.00% (20/20)
3	[x] ± 10; [y] ± 10	100.00% (20/20)

Table 1: Location Tests (for 5 different locations)

Speed Tests: We make use of the instantaneous speed of the GPS receiver in our experiments. We found the instantaneous speed from the GPS receiver matches the reading of odometer in the car. We drove around the campus at different speeds (15 mph, 25 mph, and 35 mph) and 5 tests were conducted on each speed with each levels of error tolerance (results under the same error tolerance are clubbed together just to indicate the successful rate). When the speed falls within the pre-defined range, the LED on the WISP is turned on to indicate the tag was unlocked. Experiment results are shown in Table 2. We can conclude, referring to this table, that we can recognize the speed quite accurately.

Test	Error Tolerance (mph)	% Accuracy
1	[v] ± 2	100.00% (15/15)
2	[v] ± 3	100.00% (15/15)
3	[v] ± 5	100.00% (15/15)

Table 2: Speed Tests (for speeds of 15, 25 and 35 mph)

Location and Speed Tests: In this experiment, we used both location as well as speed as contextual parameters together to unlock the tag (as outlined in Section 4.1). This experiment is a combination of the previous two experiments. Here the error tolerance for the location has to be set sufficiently high since the car is moving at a certain speed and the update rate of the GPS is 1 sample per second. Hence we also have to consider the fact that the car moves a certain distance within that span of 1 second. For example, a car moving at 45 mph can travel around 20 meters in 1 second. So, an error tolerance of at least 20 meters has to be provided. This would not affect applications like car toll systems since most of the toll booths are located far away from other places, and hence the recognition area for the toll cards can be large [1]. In other words, using a higher error tolerance for such a system would not affect the system performance. As in prior experiments, an LED indicator was used for successful identification which was later on used for

unlocking the tag. The experimental results are shown in Tables 3 and 4, for two different speeds. We can observe that we were successfully able to unlock the tag based on the location and speed, and our accuracies improved considerably when the location error tolerance was increased.

6.2 Transaction Verification Experiments

We conducted another set of experiments for validating the effectiveness of our location-aware transaction verification scheme. The goal of these experiments was to determine the proximity (or lack thereof) between two devices – a valid tag and a valid reader – based on the location readings reported by their respective GPS receivers. In other words, we wanted to find out as to how accurately GPS sensing can be used to find out whether the two devices are in close proximity (e.g., at most 2 m apart) or are far from each other (e.g., much more than 2 m apart). Please recall that the former case represents a normal usage scenario for a typical payment token in which the user brings her card very close to the reader for processing a transaction. The latter, on the other hand, represents an attack scenario whereby the valid tag is at one location while the valid reader is at a different location [12].

We conducted two experiments to evaluate the proximity detection approach based on location data. By means of the first experiment, we wanted to determine the error tolerance of detecting proximity (within a distance of 2 m). Note that when obtaining the location data from a GPS receiver at one particular location, we are subject to a maximum error around that point in a square region.

We connected a USB GPS sensor (GlobalSat BU-353) to the desktop which was in turn connected to our RFID reader, and set the distance between this receiver and the WISP receiver to be 2 m. We then took 40 different samples from each of the two receivers simultaneously and from that we calculated the distance between the two receivers, and thus found out the range of maximum and minimum values. The minimum value was calculated to be 1.7821 m and the maximum was 6.2093 m. This means that even when the actual distance between the receivers is 2 m, the distance reported by the GPS readings can vary between 1.7821 m to 6.2093 m. Therefore, a maximum error tolerance of 6.2093 m could be used for the purpose of proximity detection.

Using the above error tolerance, we conducted our second experiment. Here, we wanted to determine the accuracy of proximity detection, based on the error tolerance of 6.2093 m, when the distance between the two receivers was varied from 1 m to 50 m. The results of this experiment are reported in Table 5. As we can observe from this table, the accuracies corresponding to a distance of at most 2 m are quite high as desired – this represents the normal use case (i.e., when no attacks occur). As the distance increases, the accuracies go down significantly, reaching a value of 0% for a distance of 20 m or more. This means that if the adversary (illegitimate tag) is located more than 2 m away from the valid tag, the possibility of the transaction being accepted are going to be low; in fact, the adversary does not stand a chance when he is located 20 m or farther. This implies that if an adversary is at physically disparate location (e.g., at a jewelery store, while the valid tag is at a restaurant [12]), he will be easily detected and can not succeed in the reader-and-ghost attack.

Location (meters) →	[x] ± 10; [y] ± 10	[x] ± 20; [y] ± 20
Speed (mph) ↓	% Accuracy	% Accuracy
[v] ± 2	96.67% (29/30)	100.00% (30/30)
[v] ± 3	96.67% (29/30)	100.00% (30/30)
[v] ± 5	100.00% (30/30)	100.00% (30/30)

Table 3: Location and Speed Tests (speed = 25 mph)

Location (meters) →	[x] ± 10; [y] ± 10	[x] ± 20; [y] ± 20
Speed (mph) ↓	% Accuracy	% Accuracy
[v] ± 2	90.00% (27/30)	96.67% (29/30)
[v] ± 3	96.67% (29/30)	100.00% (30/30)
[v] ± 5	100.00% (30/30)	100.00% (30/30)

Table 4: Location and Speed Tests (speed = 35 mph)

Distance (in meters)	% Accuracy
1	100.00% (40/40)
2	92.50% (37/40)
3	85.00% (34/40)
5	67.50% (27/40)
10	10.00% (6/40)
20	0.00% (0/40)
50	0.00% (0/40)

Table 5: Accuracy of proximity detection (error tolerance 6.2093 m).

7. DISCUSSIONS

In this section, we discuss related issues that may arise with respect to the proposed defenses in practice.

7.1 Preventing GPS Spoofing Attacks

Our location-aware defenses rely on the GPS infrastructure and thus may also be prone to the GPS associated vulnerabilities such as spoofing and jamming [46]. Successful spoofing experiments on standard receivers have been reported [33, 17], indicating commercial-off-the-shelf receivers do not detect such attacks. In the context of location-aware selective unlocking, the adversary can falsely unlock the tag if it can spoof the GPS signals coming from the satellites and feed in false location information to the GPS receiver (e.g., corresponding to a toll booth location even though the car/card is at a different location). Similarly, in the context of location-aware transaction verification, the adversary can, for example, fool the valid tag into thinking that it (the tag) is at a jewelery shop even though it is in a restaurant [12]. commercial-off-the-shelf receivers do not detect such attacks.

Of existing GPS spoofing attack countermeasures [41, 29, 32], the one that is most suitable for the RFID setting is the scheme proposed in [32]. This scheme does not require any special hardware and does not rely on any cryptography. Instead, a GPS receiver in this scheme is augmented with inertial sensors (e.g., speedometers or accelerometers). The receiver can measure the discrepancy between its own predicated value (through inertial sensors) and measurements (through received GPS signals) in order to detect spoofing

and replay attacks. The scheme is applicable to any mobile RFID tag setting, such as a toll card.

Since WISP already has an inertial (3-axis accelerometer) sensor onboard, we have the convenience of implementing the idea proposed in [32] against the GPS signal spoofing attack. The flow chart of our GPS detecting algorithm implementation is shown in Figure 3. In our implementation, only two dimensions of the acceleration data have been taken into consideration because we are assuming that the tag is horizontally fixed on vehicle and the vehicle is always running in a horizontal plane. We compare the acceleration derived from the accelerometer data with the one derived using the speed provided by the GPS data over a short interval of time. When the difference between GPS calculated acceleration data and accelerometer data exceed a certain threshold, we consider the former as a possible spoofed data. We repeat this test and if spoofed data is being detected more than 5 times, we consider the tag to be under attack, and thus switch the tag into the locked state. To further reduce computation cost, we have used the square function for difference calculation instead of the square root function since square root is more computationally extensive for the WISP.

By adding inertial detection, we decrease the possibility of performing a successful signal spoofing attack thereby adding another layer of security to our system. However, this approach detects only the inertial abnormalities but not the location abnormalities. Thus, it only applies to situations where GPS receivers are mobile. Recently, a very interesting work on the requirements to successfully mount GPS spoofing attack has been reported [44]. The authors show that it is easy for an attacker to spoof any number of individual receivers. However, the attacker is restricted to only a few transmission locations when spoofing a group of receivers - even when they are stationary - while preserving their constellation (or mutual distances). Moreover, conducting spoofing attack on a group even becomes impossible if the group can hide the exact positioning of at least one GPS receiver from the attacker (e.g., by keeping it mobile on a vehicle) since in such case the attacker cannot adapt to its position [44]. This suggests a cooperative detection scheme where multiple GPS receivers can work together to detect GPS spoofing attacks by also checking their mutual distances. Although it is still hard to foresee this countermeasure can be applied in current RFID application

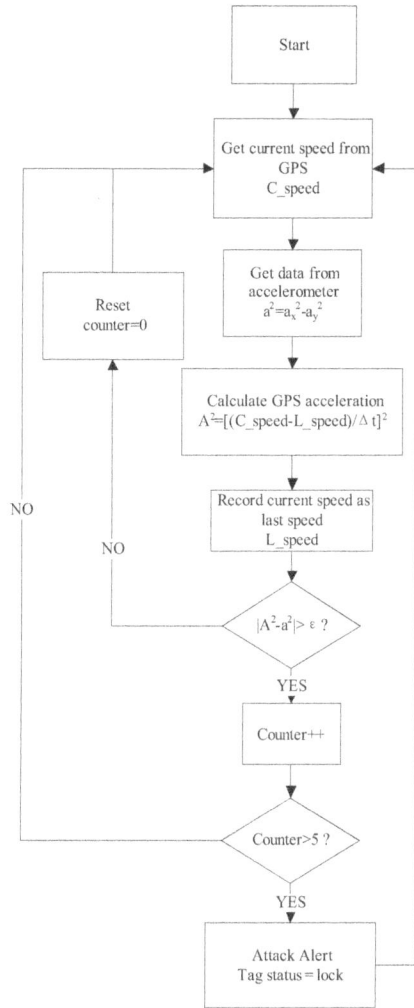

```
                    Start
                      |
                      v
          +----------------------+
    +---->| Get current speed from|<----+
    |     |        GPS            |     |
    |     |      C_speed          |     |
    |     +----------------------+     |
    |               |                  |
    |               v                  |
+--------+  +----------------------+   |
| Reset  |  | Get data from        |   |
|counter=0| | accelerometer        |   |
+--------+  | a²=aₓ²-a_y²          |   |
    ^       +----------------------+   |
    |               |                  |
    |               v                  |
    |     +----------------------+     |
    |     | Calculate GPS        |     |
    |     | acceleration         |     |
    |     | A²=[(C_speed-L_speed)/Δt]²|
    |     +----------------------+     |
    |               |                  |
    |               v                  |
    |     +----------------------+     |
    |     | Record current speed |     |
    |     | as last speed        |     |
    |     | L_speed              |     |
    |     +----------------------+     |
    |               |                  |
    |               v                  |
    |          /|A²-a²|> ε ?\   --NO---+
    |          \           /
    |               | YES
    |               v
    |         +----------+
    |         | Counter++|
    |         +----------+
    |               |
    |               v
    +-NO--- / Counter>5 ? \
                   | YES
                   v
          +----------------+
          | Attack Alert   |
          | Tag status=lock|
          +----------------+
```

Figure 3: Flow chart for detecting GPS spoofing attack

settings, it does state that a network of GPS receivers (or GPS-enabled devices) can be setup on the field to monitor GPS signals when it is necessary and when spoofing attack is a real menace.

7.2 GPS Initialization

A GPS can have either a cold start or hot start. The hot start occurs when the GPS device remembers its last calculated position and the satellites in view, the almanac (i.e., the information about all the satellites in the constellation) used, the UTC Time, and makes an attempt to lock onto the same satellites and calculate a new position based upon the previous information. This is the quickest GPS lock but it only works when the receiver is generally in the same location as it was when the GPS was last turned off. Cold start occurs when the GPS device dumps all the information, attempts to locate satellites and then calculates a GPS lock. This takes the longest because there is no known or pre-existing information [4]. The GPS module used in our experiments can normally acquire a fix from a cold start in

35 seconds, and acquire a hot-start fix in less than 2 seconds [2].

Delay due to GPS initialization, especially cold start, might be unbearable for delay-sensitive applications such as toll cards. However, in the toll card application, delay can be minimized by powering the tag with battery (which is the current power supply of most commercial toll cards) or the vehicle so that the GPS can always keep an updated view of the set of satellites with which it can get a fix immediately. In the building access card application, it is not reasonable to have an always-connected GPS receiver. However, since the receiver is powered up in the same place –e.g., office building entrance– as it was when it shut off last time under normal usage case, we can force the GPS receiver to do a hot start by remembering its last location (storing the location in non-volatile storage). Moreover, the building access card application is more delay tolerant than the toll card application. That is, even the GPS receiver has to have a cold start, 35 seconds (time to have a cold start for the receiver we used in our experiments) might still be tolerable to most users.

7.3 Dealing with Failure Reading in RFID Toll Systems

Our speed-based unlocking scheme for toll cards only works when cars pass by the toll gates at the recommended speed. When a car actually do not pass toll gates at recommended speed, its toll card will be kept in locked state. The toll reader hence cannot read out the card information and the corresponding driver's account thus cannot be successfully charged. So we need to deal with reading failure due to driver's not driving at recommended speed accidentally or intentionally. Actually, there already exists mechanism which deals with failure reading in current RFID toll road system deployments. Current deployments rely on a combination of a camera which takes a picture of the car and a RFID reader which searches for a drivers window/bumper mounted transponder to verify and collect payment. The system sends a notice and fine to cars (identified through either tag information or pictures taken by the camera) that pass through without having an active account or paying a toll. Our speed-based unlocking scheme can work together with the existing camera-based mechanism and drivers are obligated to drive at the recommended speed to avoid fine.

8. CONCLUSIONS

In this paper, we reported a new approach to defend against unauthorized reading and relay attacks in some RFID applications whereby location can be used as a valid context. We argued the feasibility of our approach in terms of both technical and economical aspects. Using location and derived speed information, we designed location-aware selective unlocking mechanisms and a location-aware transaction verification mechanism. For collecting this information, we made use of the GPS infrastructure. To demonstrate the feasibility of our location-aware defense mechanisms, we integrated a low-cost GPS receiver with a RFID tag (the Intel's WISP), and conducted relevant experiments to acquire location and speed information from GPS readings. Our results show that it is possible to measure location and speed with high accuracies even on a constrained GPS-enabled platform, and that our location-aware defenses are quite effective. Moreover, our location-aware defenses, proposed for the traditional RFID tags, are also directly applicable to NFC-enabled phones which often come readily equipped with GPS receivers.

9. REFERENCES

[1] RFID toll collection systems, 2007. Available at: `http://www.securitysa.com/news.aspx?pklnewsid=25591`.

[2] 66-Channel LS20031 GPS Receiver Module, 2011. Available at: `http://www.megachip.ru/pdf/POLOLU/66_CHANNEL.pdf`.

[3] GM-101 Cost Effective GPS Module With Ttl Rs-232 Interface, 2011. Available at: `http://www.alibaba.com/product-gs/435104168/GM_101_Cost_Effective_GPS_Module.html`.

[4] GPS Glossary, 2011. Available at: `http://www.gsmarena.com/glossary.php3?term=gps`.

[5] NMEA 0183 Standard, 2011. Available at: `http://www.nmea.org/content/nmea_standards/nmea_083_v_400.asp`.

[6] S. Brands and D. Chaum. Distance-bounding protocols. In *Advances in Cryptology - EUROCRYPT, International Conference on the Theory and Applications of Cryptographic Techniques*, 1993.

[7] J. Bringer, H. Chabanne, and E. Dottax. HB++: a lightweight authentication protocol secure against some attacks. In *Security, Privacy and Trust in Pervasive and Ubiquitous Computing*, 2006.

[8] M. Buckner, R. Crutcher, M. R. Moore, and S. F. Smith. GPS and sensor-enabled RFID tags. Available online at http://www.ornl.gov/ web-works/cppr/y2001/pres/118169.pdf.

[9] M. Buettner, R. Prasad, M. Philipose, and D. Wetherall. Recognizing Daily Activities with RFID-Based Sensors. In *International Conference on Ubiquitous Computing (UbiComp)*, 2009.

[10] G. Cropsey. Designing a distance and speed algorithm using the global positioning system. Available online at `http://www.egr.msu.edu/classes/ece480/capstone/spring08/group10/documents/Application%20Note-%20Gabe.pdf`, March 2008.

[11] A. Czeskis, K. Koscher, J. Smith, and T. Kohno. RFIDs and secret handshakes: Defending against Ghost-and-Leech attacks and unauthorized reads with context-aware communications. In *ACM Conference on Computer and Communications Security*, 2008.

[12] S. Drimer and S. J. Murdoch. Keep your enemies close:Distance bounding against smartcard relay attacks. In *16th USENIX Security Symposium*, August 2007.

[13] A. Francillon, B. Danev, and S. Capkun. Relay attacks on passive keyless entry and start systems in modern cars. In *18th Annual Network and Distributed System Security Symposium (NDSS)*, 2011.

[14] H. Gilbert, M. Robshaw, and Y. Seurin. HB#: Increasing the security and efficiency of hb+. In *Advances in Cryptology - EUROCRYPT, International Conference on the Theory and Applications of Cryptographic Techniques*, 2008.

[15] Goldiron. Numerex unveils hybrid tag includes active RFID, GPS, satellite and sensors. Available online at http://goldiron.wordpress.com/2009/02/25/numerex-unveils-hybrid-tag-includes-active-rfid-gps-satellite-and-sensors/, February 2009.

[16] G. P. Hancke and M. G. Kuhn. An RFID distance bounding protocol. In *Proceedings of the First International Conference on Security and Privacy for Emerging Areas in Communications Networks*, 2005.

[17] B. Hanlon, B. Ledvina, M. Psiaki, P. K. Jr., and T. E. Humphreys. Assessing the GPS spoofing threat. GPS World, Available online at `http://www.gpsworld.com/defense/security-surveillance/assessing-spoofing-threat-3171?page_id=1`, January 2009.

[18] T. S. Heydt-Benjamin, D. V. Bailey, K. Fu, A. Juels, and T. O'Hare. Vulnerabilities in first-generation RFID-enabled credit cards. In *Financial Cryptography*, 2007.

[19] J. Holleman, D. Yeager, R. Prasad, J. Smith, and B. Otis. NeuralWISP: An energy-harvesting wireless neural interface with 1-m range. In *Biomedical Circuits and Systems Conference (BioCAS)*, 2008.

[20] A. Juels. RFID security and privacy: A research survey. *IEEE Journal on Selected Areas in Communications*, 24(2):381–394, February 2006.

[21] A. Juels, D. Molnar, and D. Wagner. Security and privacy issues in E-passports. In *Security and Privacy for Emerging Areas in Communications Networks (Securecomm)*, 2005.

[22] A. Juels, R. L. Rivest, and M. Szydlo. The blocker tag: selective blocking of RFID tags for consumer privacy. In *ACM Conference on Computer and Communications Security (CCS)*, 2003.

[23] A. Juels, P. F. Syverson, and D. V. Bailey. High-power proxies for enhancing RFID privacy and utility. In *Privacy Enhancing Technologies*, 2005.

[24] A. Juels and S. Weis. Authenticating pervasive devices with human protocols. In *International Cryptology Conference (CRYPTO)*, 2005.

[25] J. Katz and J. Shin. Parallel and concurrent security of the HB and HB+ protocols. In *Advances in Cryptology - EUROCRYPT, International Conference on the Theory and Applications of Cryptographic Techniques*, 2006.

[26] Z. Kfir and A. Wool. Picking virtual pockets using relay attacks on contactless smartcard. In *Security and Privacy for Emerging Areas in Communications Networks (Securecomm)*, 2005.

[27] A. Kobsa, R. Nithyanand, G. Tsudik, and E. Uzun. Usability of display-equipped rfid tags for security purposes. In *European Symposium on Research in Computer Security (ESORICS)*, 2011.

[28] K. Koscher, A. Juels, V. Brajkovic, and T. Kohno. EPC RFID tag security weaknesses and defenses: passport cards, enhanced drivers licenses, and beyond. In *ACM Conference on Computer and Communications Security*, 2009.

[29] M. Kuhn. An asymmetric security mechanism for navigation signals. In *6th Information Hiding Workshop*, 2004.

[30] R. Nithyanand, G. Tsudik, and E. Uzun. Readers behaving badly: Reader revocation in PKI-based

RFID systems. In *European Symposium on Research in Computer Security (ESORICS)*, 2010.

[31] Y. Oren and A. Wool. Relay attacks on RFID-based electronic voting systems. Cryptology ePrint Archive, Report 2009/422, 2009. `http://eprint.iacr.org/2009/422`.

[32] P. Papadimitratos and A. Jovanovic. GNSS-based positioning: Attacks and countermeasures. In *IEEE Military Communications Conference (MILCOM)*, pages 1–7, San Diego, CA, USA, November 16-19 2008.

[33] P. Papadimitratos and A. Jovanovic. Protection and fundamental vulnerability of global navigation satellite systems (GNSS). In *International Workshop on Satellite and Space Communications (IWSSC)*, 2008.

[34] K. B. Rasmussen and S. Čapkun. Realization of RF distance bounding. In *Proceedings of the USENIX Security Symposium*, 2010.

[35] M. R. Rieback, B. Crispo, and A. S. Tanenbaum. RFID guardian: A battery-powered mobile device for RFID privacy management. In *Australasian Conference on Information Security and Privacy (ACISP)*, 2005.

[36] A. Ruhanen and et. al. Sensor-enabled RFID tag handbook. Available online at `http://www.bridge-project.eu/data/File/BRIDGE_WP01_RFID_tag_handbook.pdf`, January 2008.

[37] A. Sample, D. Yeager, and S. J. A capacitive touch interface for passive RFID tags. In *IEEE International Conference on RFID*, 2009.

[38] A. Sample, D. Yeager, P. Powledge, and J. Smith. Design of a passively-powered, programmable sensing platform for UHF RFID systems. In *IEEE International Conference on RFID*, 2007.

[39] N. Saxena, B. Uddin, J. Voris, and N. Asokan. Vibrate-to-Unlock: Mobile Phone Assisted User Authentication to Multiple Personal RFID Tags. In *Pervasive Computing and Communications (PerCom)*, 2011.

[40] N. Saxena and J. Voris. Still and silent: Motion detection for enhanced rfid security and privacy without changing the usage model. In *Workshop on RFID Security (RFIDSec)*, June 2010.

[41] L. Scott. Anti-spoofing and authenticated signal architectures for civil navigation signals. In *16th International Technical Meeting of the Satellite Division of The Institute of Navigation (ION GPS/GNSS)*, pages 1543–1552, 2003.

[42] J. R. Smith, P. S. Powledge, S. Roy, and A. Mamishev. A wirelessly-powered platform for sensing and computation. In *8th International Conference on Ubiquitous Computing (Ubicomp)*, 2006.

[43] sparkfun. 32 Channel San Jose Navigation GPS 5Hz Receiver with Antenna, 2011. Available at: `http://www.sparkfun.com/products/8266`.

[44] N. O. Tippenhauer, C. Popper, K. B.Rasmussen, and S. Capkun. On the requirements for successful GPS spoofing attacks. In *ACM Conference on Computer and Communication Security (CCS'11)*, October 2011.

[45] D. Wagner. Privacy in pervasive computing: What can technologists do? Invited talk, SECURECOMM 2005. Available online at `http://www.cs.berkeley.edu/~daw/talks/SECCOM05.ppt`, September 2005.

[46] J. S. Warner and R. G. Johnston. Think GPS cargo tracking = high security? Technical report, Los Alamos National Laboratory, 2003.

A Privacy-Restoring Mechanism for Offline RFID Systems

Gildas Avoine
Université catholique de
Louvain
ICTEAM/GSI
B-1348, Louvain-la-Neuve,
Belgium
gildas.avoine@uclouvain.be

Iwen Coisel
Université catholique de
Louvain
ICTEAM/Crypto Group
B-1348, Louvain-la-Neuve,
Belgium
iwen.coisel@uclouvain.be

Tania Martin
Université catholique de
Louvain
ICTEAM/GSI
B-1348, Louvain-la-Neuve,
Belgium
tania.martin@uclouvain.be

ABSTRACT

Authentication protocols are usually designed to face an adversary who is able to tamper with the channel, possibly with the prover, but rarely with the verifier. When considering large-scale RFID applications, e.g., mass transportation or ticketing, the last threat is no longer a fiction. A typical case is the loss or theft of a handheld reader. If the protocol is expected to be privacy-friendly, and run by offline readers, there is no solution currently to restore the privacy once the readers are compromised except renewing all the tags, which is definitely impractical.

We introduce a privacy-friendly authentication protocol that is able to maintain the security level in case of compromised readers, but also gradually restores the privacy thanks to the mobility of the customers in the system. We provide a thorough security analysis and a precise performance evaluation of our proposal. The efficiency of our solution is also demonstrated on a real-life case: we analyze the logs of 55 offline readers used during a 3-day sport event in 2010 that involved more than 100 000 tags.

Categories and Subject Descriptors

K.6.5 [**Management of Computing and Information Systems**]: Security and Protection—*Authentication*

General Terms

Security, Design, Theory.

Keywords

Cryptographic Protocols, Privacy, Authentication, RFID, Compromised Readers.

1. MOTIVATIONS

1.1 Scope of the Paper

Privacy.

Ubiquitous contactless technologies recently raised many privacy concerns, including information leakage and malicious traceability [4]. Nowadays, privacy is so important that it is unconceivable to widespread an IT solution without addressing the privacy issues. For example, Ontario Information and Privacy Commissioner Cavoukian promotes the concept of "privacy-by-design" [7] for every large-scale IT application. Privacy Rights Clearinghouse [33], an American non-profit consumer education and advocacy group, also publishes many fact sheets on privacy problems. In 2009 in the European Union, Viviane Reding, Commissioner for Justice, Fundamental Rights and Citizenship, signed a recommendation on the implementation of privacy and data protection in RFID-based applications [35]. Yet, there exists no standardized certification for privacy, although the Common Criteria mention it briefly [20].

Technology.

Contactless technologies such as Radio Frequency IDentification (RFID) are the new trend in many daily-life applications, from logistics to electronic passports. Particularly, public transportation and mass events take advantage of this technology to increase both security and customer flows. Such environments are typically composed of mobile customers, agents, and a back-end server: each customer has an RFID tag, i.e., an integrated circuit coupled with an antenna, which stands for a ticket; the agents hold handheld RFID readers to check the customers' tickets, and the back-end server contains data related to the readers and tags. RFID includes low-resource tags, e.g., EPC-compliant tags [11], but also more advanced contactless smartcards, e.g., [18, 19] that fit applications like access control and ticketing. Powerful batteryless tags that provide public-key cryptography are also available nowadays. An example is the SLE 66 family [16] where one tag costs less than USD 2, yet containing a crypto engine supporting RSA and ECC.

Offline RFID infrastructures.

Today, ad-hoc RFID infrastructures with completely offline readers as the ones deployed for ephemeral events (e.g., culture shows, political conferences, sport events in isolated sites) are more than common. One example is a music festival organized by a city, where the concert areas are split in different districts. In such an event, it is possible to buy a ticket for the concerts, but also for the parking lot or the camping place. Connecting all so spread out places together would not be economically affordable. Instead in such infrastructures, readers are connected only once to the back-end server, during the setup procedure, and then kept off-line.

Authentication in RFID.

In ticketing applications based on RFID systems, a tag (prover) has to convince a reader (verifier) about its identity and/or validity through an authentication protocol. The common way consists in using a challenge/response protocol, based on ISO 9798 [17] for example. Note however that tags are considered to be tamper-resistant to a certain limit only. Indeed, whatever the application (e.g., access control card, credit card, or any other sensitive application), an intrusive attack is doable, e.g., physical attacks such as side-channel, fault injection or reverse engineering. The cost of such an attack should remain higher than the benefit of the attack, which implies that tampering with one tag should not compromise the whole system. We consequently consider that tags should not share any secret data between them for the authentication.

Authentication and privacy in RFID.

Several privacy models have been proposed to evaluate identification / authentication protocols (e.g., [1, 6, 23, 46]). We focus in what follows on the Juels-Weis model [23] which is the most commonly used one. Given that tags should not share common cryptographic material, combining authentication and privacy currently leads to two possible options. The first one is the use of symmetric-key cryptography, but all current protocols require the reader complexity to be at least linear in the number of tags to aspire to the highest privacy degree in the Juels-Weis model. The second one consists in using public-key cryptography, but this approach does not straightforwardly solve the problem, as classical authentication protocols require the prover to send its identifier in the clear to the verifier. Therefore, the current best (in terms of privacy) and known solutions rely on the combination of public key and shared secrets such that the tag sends its secret encrypted to the reader.

1.2 The Problem of Compromised Readers and its Consequences

Compromised readers.

During the last years, several researches have been carried out to improve privacy models of authentication protocols. One step consisted in considering that a reader can also be compromised. This case has been independently introduced in [3] and [12]. Both results rely on the assumption that readers are usually only sporadically connected to the back-end server. But, in a scenario with offline systems, two issues can be raised. First, since readers are offline, they should store the secret keys of all the distributed tags, for example in a Security Authentication Module (SAM). This justifies the use of expensive intrusive attacks to tamper with it. Second, the ubiquity of the readers, usually located in unprotected areas, increases the risk that an adversary steals one of them. Whether or not the adversary gets the keys from the stolen reader, this reader must anyway be considered as "compromised". Up to our knowledge, no solution

exists to maintain or restore both security and privacy of an offline system once a reader is compromised, except physically replacing all the tags. We however discard this solution because (i) it is too costly for the system provider, (ii) if we consider punctual events, the lack of time makes this task not manageable, and (iii) this would alarm the customers and degrade the image of the company.

Case study.

To illustrate that specific problem in offline infrastructures, all along this paper we consider a real-life RFID ticketing system deployed by RFIDea [36] during a 3-day automobile race in 2010. The event area is in the countryside, and stretches over several square kilometers, where deploying wired or wireless networks would not be economically affordable for a single event. Using GSM is neither realistic due to the cost, communication rate, coverage, etc.

In this case study, readers are initialized once by the system administrator and then given to the agents in the field until the end of the event. Those handled readers, which have no means to communicate with the back-end server, must carry the tags secret keys to be able to authenticate all spectators' and employees' badges. Agents are not mobile, while spectators and employees are. Spectators may move inside the area, for example from a Silver zone to a Gold zone according to the rights of their tickets, but they can also leave and return to the event area whenever they want. The RFID system is thus suitable to easily manage the mobility of all the participants to the event.

We highlight that one ticket is typically sold between USD 200 and USD 700. For the event organizer, the factory price of one ticket essentially includes the tag manufacturing process, the customizing of the paper ticket and tag content, and the shipment of the ticket to the customer. The cost of the microcircuit is therefore negligible and can be easily included in the total price of the ticket.

The fear of compromised readers is here realistic: for example, several readers were stolen during the same event in 2009. Spectators and employees were hence traceable, since no adequate solution to handle that problem had been put into place at that time. Also, the ticketing company agrees to spend time dealing with privacy before the event, but certainly not during the D-Day rush.

The association of all above constraints points out the lack of solution to deal with the problem of compromised readers in large-scale offline RFID systems.

1.3 Contributions

We propose an authentication protocol (Section 2) whose aim is threefold: (i) it has to provide security (availability and soundness) (ii) it has to provide forward privacy, and (iii) it has to restore privacy for tags in such a case of compromised readers using an advanced privacy-restoring mechanism based on information spread. Our protocol is the first tentative to design such a mechanism in poorly connected environments, such as offline RFID systems. We then formally analyze the security and privacy of the protocol (Section 3). We practically analyze its efficiency in terms of information spread in our case study of a 3-day sport event (Section 4). Finally, we propose some recommendations about the choice of the algorithms and parameters to use (Section 5), before concluding (Section 6).

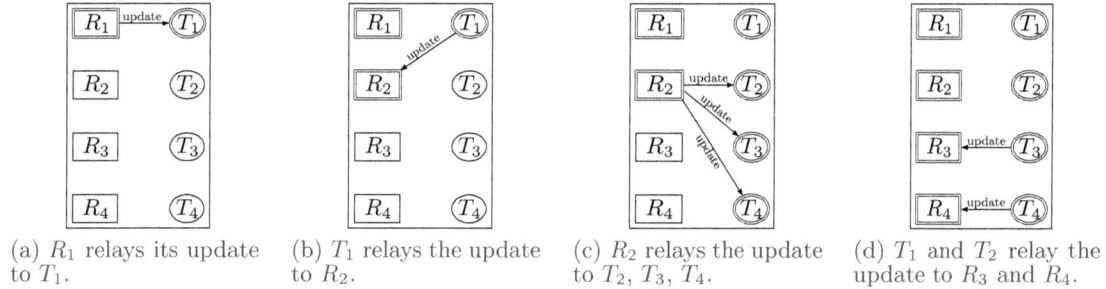

(a) R_1 relays its update to T_1.

(b) T_1 relays the update to R_2.

(c) R_2 relays the update to T_2, T_3, T_4.

(d) T_1 and T_2 relay the update to R_3 and R_4.

Figure 1: A typical example of information propagation with our protocol.

For the interested reader, we survey the studies about information spread in the scientific literature in Appendix A.

2. PROTOCOL

2.1 System Architecture

We consider an RFID system $\mathcal{S}$ composed of a back-end, n tags and m readers. Once initialized by the system administrator, the readers can no longer get connected to the back-end. We assume that the tags are reasonably-costly, implying moderate capabilities in terms of calculation, communication and storage, although capable of verifying electronic signatures and processing symmetric-key cryptography, as explained in Section 5. In addition, tags are tamper-resistant to a certain extent [22]: each tag has a unique secret, so that the cost of a tampering attack is higher than its benefit.

2.2 Security Objectives

We give here the synopsis of the security goals expected for the proposed RFID system. Below, we remind the notions of *availability* (a.k.a. *strong completeness*), *soundness*, and *privacy*, slightly modified from the ones given by Avoine, Coisel, and Martin [2] in the RFID model.

DEFINITION 1 (AVAILABILITY). *An authentication protocol is said to be* available *if, for any adversary, the probability that a legitimate reader successfully authenticates a legitimate tag is overwhelming.*

DEFINITION 2 (SOUNDNESS). *An authentication protocol is said to be* sound *if the probability that an adversary is successfully authenticated as a legitimate tag by a legitimate reader is negligible.*

DEFINITION 3 (PRIVACY). *An authentication protocol is said to be* private *if the probability that an adversary is able to differentiate one legitimate tag from another by interacting/playing with the system is negligible.*

Our protocol has to provide all these security notions, preferably when it faces the strongest adversary. The power classes of an adversary are defined in Section 3.1; they rely on the adversary ability to corrupt readers and/or tags of the system. We prove in Section 3.3 that our protocol remains available and sound when considering the strongest adversary. On the other hand, when an adversary is able to corrupt a reader, she gets all its secret information, and is thus able to successfully authenticate/identify any tag. At

that point, the system privacy is completely lost. Therefore, another objective of the protocol is that it has to restore the system privacy when it faces an adversary whose power is to corrupt readers.

2.3 Privacy-Restoring Mechanism

To restore privacy, the main idea of our solution is to integrate a privacy-restoring mechanism into the authentication protocol. This mechanism spreads the information that a reader has been compromised and repaired/updated to all the tags.

With this mechanism, the protocol is able to face an adversary who can compromise up to α readers ($\alpha \leq m$) where m is the total number of readers in the system. When only one reader is compromised, we can consider w.l.o.g. that it is R_1. We assume that the system administrator is able to detect such a compromised reader because it has been stolen or damaged[1]. In such a case, he is expected to restore the security of R_1 by renewing its secrets and credentials, including replacing the physical device, if needed.

Since all the devices are offline, R_1 repaired/updated information is injected into an arbitrary reader of the system. We consider w.l.o.g. that the information is injected in R_1 itself, after being repaired. Then the repaired R_1 propagates its updated information to all its connecting tags. Thanks to their mobility, these "marked" tags, as mules, carry and propagate R_1 updated information to the readers they meet. These "marked" readers then propagate in turn R_1 updated information. It is possible to point out the parallel with viruses spread between floppy disks and computers (in the early age of computer science). Finally, when all the tags have received R_1 updated information, the system privacy has been fully restored.

The information to spread is related to the fact that a reader has been compromised; but the propagation process can also be used to spread any kind of information (e.g., the new event schedule) whose authenticity must be ensured.

Figure 1 illustrates the behavior of the spread information with four readers and four tags. In the example, R_1 has been compromised and repaired. As caption, a device drawn in a double-box means that this device carries the following information: "R_1 has been compromised and repaired, and here are its new data".

2.4 Protocol Description

We present a challenge/response authentication protocol inspired by a variant of the Needham-Schroeder public-key

---

[1] The detection of such a compromised reader is out of scope in the article.

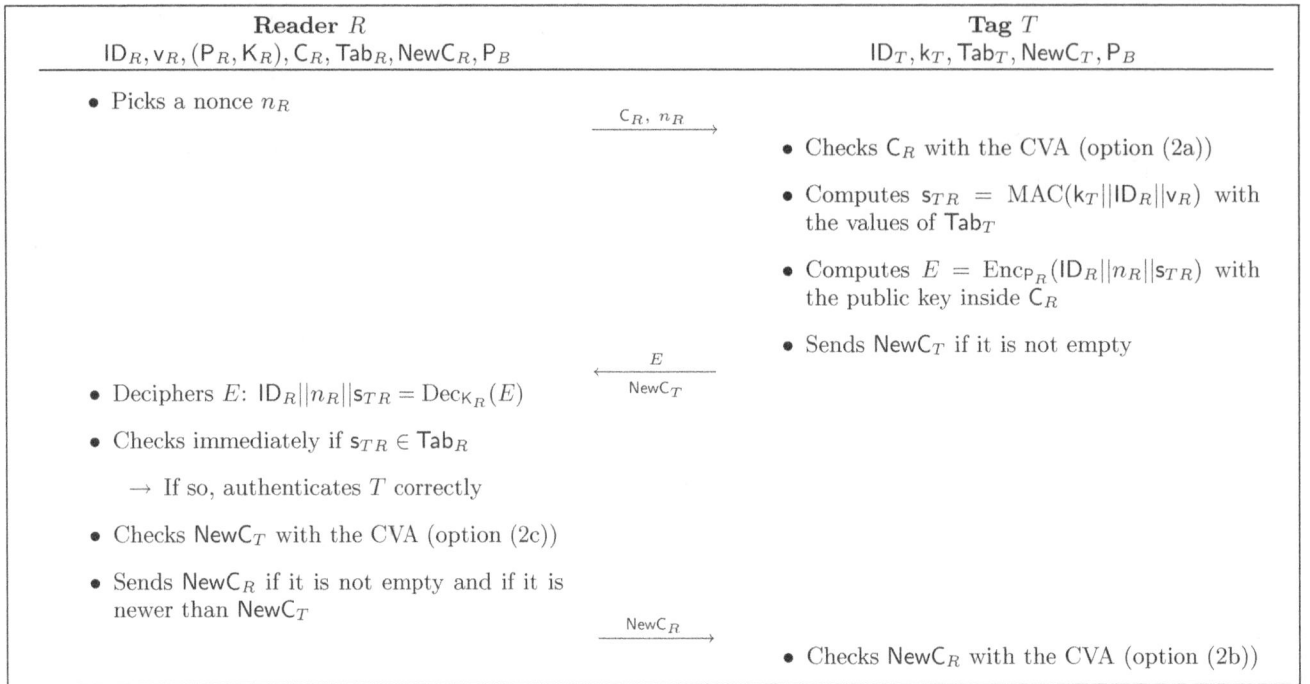

Reader R $ID_R, v_R, (P_R, K_R), C_R, Tab_R, NewC_R, P_B$	**Tag T** $ID_T, k_T, Tab_T, NewC_T, P_B$
• Picks a nonce n_R $\xrightarrow{\;C_R,\; n_R\;}$	• Checks C_R with the CVA (option (2a)) • Computes $s_{TR} = \mathrm{MAC}(k_T\|ID_R\|v_R)$ with the values of Tab_T • Computes $E = \mathrm{Enc}_{P_R}(ID_R\|n_R\|s_{TR})$ with the public key inside C_R • Sends $NewC_T$ if it is not empty

• Deciphers E: $ID_R\|n_R\|s_{TR} = \mathrm{Dec}_{K_R}(E)$
 $\xleftarrow[\; NewC_T\;]{\;E\;}$
 	
 • Checks immediately if $s_{TR} \in Tab_R$
    $\rightarrow$ If so, authenticates T correctly
 	
 • Checks $NewC_T$ with the CVA (option (2c))
 	
 • Sends $NewC_R$ if it is not empty and if it is newer than $NewC_T$
 	
      $\xrightarrow{\; NewC_R\;}$
	• Checks $NewC_R$ with the CVA (option (2b))

Figure 2: Authentication protocol.

protocol [30] where the tag encrypts the data with the reader public key. The main difference is that the secret encrypted by the tag is computed on-the-fly by the tag and is unique for a given couple (*tag, reader*), instead of being a fixed long term identifier associated to the tag.

2.4.1 Cryptographic Building Blocks

We consider a cryptosystem (Enc/Dec), a signature scheme (Sign/Verif), and a MAC function. The cryptosystem is IND-CCA2-secure (see [5, 34] for more details about this scheme). MAC and the signature scheme are EF-CMA [13].

2.4.2 Initialization

Let s be the global security parameter of the system. When the system is set up according to s, the back-end B receives a pair of public/private keys (P_B, K_B). Each tag T is assigned with a unique identifier ID_T, and a long-term secret key k_T. Each reader R is assigned with the following values:

- a unique public identifier ID_R,
- a public version number v_R of R certificate initialized to zero,
- a pair of public/private keys (P_R, K_R),
- its public data $d_R = (ID_R\|v_R\|P_R)$,
- a lightweight certificate of its public data (signed by the back-end B) $C_R = d_R\|t_R\|\mathrm{Sign}_{K_B}(d_R\|t_R)$, where t_R is the creation timestamp of the certificate.

2.4.3 Memory Content

During the system initialization, back-end, readers and tags are loaded with their own values, and additional tables described below.

For every tag T, every reader R stores the couple (ID_T, s_{TR}) in table Tab_R, where s_{TR} is the result of a MAC applied on k_T combined with ID_R and v_R ($s_{TR} = \mathrm{MAC}(k_T\|ID_R\|v_R)$).

This value s_{TR} is a secret computed by the back-end, and shared by R and T only. The reader also has a value $NewC_R$ that is the unique certificate containing all the new data for all the compromised and already repaired readers. At the system setup, $NewC_R$ is empty.

Then for every reader R, every tag T stores the couple (ID_R, v_R) in table Tab_T. Note that T does not store the certificate of every reader. T also has a value $NewC_T$ which has the same definition than $NewC_R$.

Finally, the back-end keeps the values (ID_R, v_R, t_R) of every reader R and (ID_T, k_T) of every tag T.

2.4.4 Authentication

The authentication protocol is a 3-pass protocol as depicted in Figure 2.

2.4.5 The Certificate Verification Algorithm (CVA)

When an entity (tag T or reader R) receives a certificate, then it performs the following.

(1) First, the entity checks if the certificate signature is correct, using "Verif" with P_B. If the verification is wrong, the entity interrupts the protocol.

(2) a. If the entity is a tag T and the certificate is C_R: it compares if v_R is upper than the one stored in its table Tab_T for R. If so, then: (i) T updates v_R in Tab_T, and (ii) T records the certificate in $NewC_T$. If v_R is lower than the one stored in its table Tab_T for R, T interrupts the protocol.

     b. If the entity is a tag T and the certificate is $NewC_R$: it compares if t_{NewC_R} is newer than the one of its stored $NewC_T$. If so, then: (i) T overwrites $NewC_T$ with the new received one (i.e., $NewC_R$), and (ii) T updates v_{R_i} in Tab_T of every compromised and already repaired reader R_i cited in $NewC_R$.

c. If the entity is a reader R and the certificate is NewC_T: it compares if $\mathsf{t}_{\mathsf{NewC}_T}$ is newer than the one of its stored NewC_R. If so, then R overwrites NewC_R with the new received one (i.e., NewC_T).

2.4.6 Update of the System

When the system administrator realizes that the reader R_1 has been compromised, he requires the back-end B to repair R_1 by updating R_1 data. Basically, B computes the following:

- Update $\mathsf{v}_{R_1}^{\mathrm{new}} = \mathsf{v}_{R_1} + 1$
- Update $(\mathsf{P}_{R_1}^{\mathrm{new}}, \mathsf{K}_{R_1}^{\mathrm{new}})$
- Update $\mathsf{d}_{R_1}^{\mathrm{new}} = \mathsf{ID}_{R_1} || \mathsf{v}_{R_1}^{\mathrm{new}} || \mathsf{P}_{R_1}^{\mathrm{new}}$
- Create new certificate
  $\mathsf{C}_{R_1}^{\mathrm{new}} = \mathsf{d}_{R_1}^{\mathrm{new}} || \mathsf{t}_{R_1}^{\mathrm{new}} || \mathrm{Sign}_{\mathsf{K}_B}(\mathsf{d}_{R_1}^{\mathrm{new}} || \mathsf{t}_{R_1}^{\mathrm{new}})$
- Compute the new values of Tab_{R_1}:
  for all T, $\mathsf{s}_{T R_1} = \mathrm{MAC}(\mathsf{k}_T || \mathsf{ID}_{R_1} || \mathsf{v}_{R_1}^{\mathrm{new}})$

R_1 is also reinitialized with a new certificate in NewC_{R_1}. The latter contains in the clear all the couples $(\mathsf{ID}_{R_i} || \mathsf{v}_{R_i})$ for all the compromised and already repaired readers R_i (including R_1), and only one unique signature of all these data: $\mathrm{Sign}_{\mathsf{K}_B}(\{\forall R_i : (\mathsf{ID}_{R_i} || \mathsf{v}_{R_i})\} || \mathsf{t}_{\mathsf{NewC}_{R_1}})$, where $\mathsf{t}_{\mathsf{NewC}_{R_1}}$ is the creation timestamp of this certificate. Finally, the system administrator changes/replaces R_1 with these new values.

3. SECURITY ANALYSIS

In this section, we present the formalization used to analyze our RFID authentication protocol. First, we describe the classes of adversary. Then, we detail the attacks that we take into account to evaluate our protocol. Finally, we analyze our protocol according to this model.

3.1 Adversary Means

We describe three adversary classes that are related to the adversary ability to compromise readers and tags.

The first two classes of adversary against the RFID system $\mathcal{S}$ are the ones given by Juels and Weis in their model [23]. First, the STANDARD adversary is the classical one that can play/interact with all the entities of the system, but that can only compromise the tags, except the two challenge tags. Second, the FORWARD adversary is a STANDARD one without this restriction. Note that relay attacks are not considered here in our adversary classes since our solution is not a distance bounding protocol.

The third class of adversary proposed by Avoine, Lauradoux, and Martin in [3] is formally defined below. Note that this class is orthogonal to the two other ones, and is therefore used as a combination.

DEFINITION 4 (CORRUPT ADVERSARY). *An adversary $\mathcal{A}$ against the RFID system $\mathcal{S}$ is said to be CORRUPT if she can compromise readers.*

3.2 Adversary Goals

An adversary $\mathcal{A}$ is also defined by her objectives. In this paper, we formalize the three security properties by experiments.

Let $\mathcal{S}$ be the RFID system of global security parameter s. Let $\epsilon(.)$ be a negligible function. Note that "entity corruption" does not mean that $\mathcal{A}$ has the control of the entity: she only knows the entity secrets. Note also that, when a reader R is just corrupted (but not repaired yet), it is still

a legitimate reader; once it is repaired, that means that another legitimate reader R' with the same identifier has been put into the system, and R is no longer legitimate.

3.2.1 Availability

$\mathcal{A}$ wants to make a legitimate tag T no longer authenticable by a legitimate reader R. This attack is associated to Definition 1 provided in Section 2.2. The adversary class allowed for this experiment is the strongest one, that is CORRUPT-FORWARD.

Experiment $Exp_{\mathcal{S},\mathcal{A}}^{\mathsf{Avail}}$

1. The challenger $\mathcal{C}$ initializes the RFID system $\mathcal{S}$.
2. $\mathcal{A}$ interacts with the whole system, limited by her class.
3. $\mathcal{A}$ chooses a legitimate tag T and a legitimate reader R.

$\mathcal{A}$ wins if R can no longer successfully authenticate T.

The availability of the system $\mathcal{S}$ is ensured if

$$\Pr(Exp_{\mathcal{S},\mathcal{A}}^{\mathsf{Avail}} \text{ succeeds}) \leq \epsilon(s).$$

3.2.2 Soundness

$\mathcal{A}$ wants to be authenticated successfully as a legitimate non-compromised tag by a legitimate non-compromised reader R. This attack is associated to Definition 2. The adversary class allowed for this experiment is also the strongest one, that is CORRUPT-FORWARD.

Experiment $Exp_{\mathcal{S},\mathcal{A}}^{\mathsf{Sound}}$

1. The challenger $\mathcal{C}$ initializes the RFID system $\mathcal{S}$.
2. $\mathcal{A}$ chooses a legitimate reader R that she will never corrupt.
3. $\mathcal{A}$ interacts with the whole system, limited by her class.
4. $\mathcal{A}$ interacts with R, and outputs an answer to R.

$\mathcal{A}$ wins if R authenticates her as being a legitimate non-compromised tag.

The soundness of the system $\mathcal{S}$ is ensured if

$$\Pr(Exp_{\mathcal{S},\mathcal{A}}^{\mathsf{Sound}} \text{ succeeds}) \leq \epsilon(s).$$

3.2.3 Privacy

$\mathcal{A}$ wants to trace a legitimate tag T and/or gain some information from T. She is able to trace T if she can distinguish it from another legitimate tag T'. This attack is associated to Definition 3. The adversary classes allowed for this experiment are FORWARD or CORRUPT-STANDARD. Note that we only consider privacy at the protocol level (see [4] for more details about privacy in the lower layers of the RFID communication model).

```
┌─────────────────────────────────────────────────┐
│  Experiment $Exp_{\mathcal{S},\mathcal{A}}^{\text{Priv}}$                            │
│                                                   │
│    1. The challenger $\mathcal{C}$ initializes the RFID system $\mathcal{S}$.   │
│    2. $\mathcal{A}$ interacts with the whole system, limited by her class. │
│    3. $\mathcal{A}$ chooses two challenge tags $T$ and $T'$, and gives them │
│       to $\mathcal{C}$.                                          │
│    4. $\mathcal{C}$ chooses a bit $b$ at random. Then $\mathcal{C}$ assigns $T_b = T$ │
│       and $T_{b \oplus 1} = T'$.                                │
│    5. $\mathcal{A}$ interacts with the whole system (including $T_0$ and │
│       $T_1$), limited by her class.                      │
│       If $\mathcal{A}$ is CORRUPT, she cannot corrupt readers anymore. │
│    6. $\mathcal{A}$ outputs a guess bit $b'$.                        │
│                                                   │
│  $\mathcal{A}$ wins if $b = b'$.                                    │
└─────────────────────────────────────────────────┘
```

The privacy of the system $\mathcal{S}$ is ensured if

$$\left|\Pr(Exp_{\mathcal{S},\mathcal{A}}^{\text{Priv}} \text{ succeeds}) - \frac{1}{2}\right| \leq \epsilon(s).$$

In the privacy experiment, four cases Z_1, Z_2, Z_3, and Z_4 appear when $\mathcal{A}$ is CORRUPT-STANDARD. They detail if T_0 and T_1 have been reached by the update of a compromised and already repaired reader.

(Z_1) T_0 and T_1 are updated. If Z_1 occurs, the probability that $\mathcal{A}$ differentiates T_0 from T_1 is $\frac{1}{2} + \epsilon(s)$.

(Z_2) T_0 and T_1 are not updated. If Z_2 occurs, the probability that $\mathcal{A}$ differentiates T_0 from T_1 is 1.

(Z_3) T_0 is updated and T_1 is not updated. If Z_3 occurs, the probability that $\mathcal{A}$ differentiates T_0 from T_1 is 1.

(Z_4) T_0 is not updated and T_1 is updated. If Z_4 occurs, the probability that $\mathcal{A}$ differentiates T_0 from T_1 is 1.

Each tag update contributes to restore the system privacy. The privacy is completely restored when all the tags are updated. Consequently, we define τ as a measurement at time t of the level of privacy restoration for $\mathcal{S}$. τ is a non-increasing function depending on the four cases:

$$\tau(t) = \left(\frac{1}{2} + \epsilon(s)\right)\Pr(Z_1) + \Pr(Z_2) + \Pr(Z_3) + \Pr(Z_4). \quad (1)$$

The four cases to draw T_0 and T_1 follow an hypergeometric distribution. The $u(t)$ function represents the number of tags updated at a given time t. Therefore:

$$\begin{aligned} \tau(t) = & \left(\frac{1}{2} + \epsilon(s)\right)\left(\frac{u(t)}{n}\right)\left(\frac{u(t)-1}{n-1}\right) \quad (2) \\ & + \left(1 - \frac{u(t)}{n}\right)\left(1 - \frac{u(t)}{n-1}\right) + 2\left(\frac{u(t)}{n-1}\right)\left(1 - \frac{u(t)}{n}\right). \end{aligned}$$

The behavior of τ is as follows. When t increases, so does $u(t)$. When $u(t) = 0$, then τ is at its maximum of 1: the privacy restoration has not started yet. When $u(t)$ attains its maximum n (meaning that all the tags have been updated), then τ reaches its lowest value of $\frac{1}{2} + \epsilon(s)$: the privacy restoration has been fully done. Therefore, when $0 < u(t) < n$, τ value measures the current level of privacy restoration of $\mathcal{S}$ at time t.

3.3 Analysis of the Protocol

Now we give the security analysis of our protocol following the classes of adversary defined in Section 3.1 and the security properties experiments given in Section 3.2.

THEOREM 1. *If the public-key cryptosystem used is IND-CCA2-secure, and if the MAC and signature scheme are EF-CMA, then our RFID protocol ensures (i) availability and soundness for a CORRUPT-FORWARD adversary, (ii) FORWARD-privacy, and (iii) CORRUPT-STANDARD-privacy when the challenge tags are in the Z_1 case, and the privacy restoration follows the value of τ given in Eq.(2).*

Sketch of proof (availability).

In this proof, we design an adversary $\mathcal{A}_{\text{EF}}$ taking advantage of $\mathcal{A}$ in order to break the EF-CMA property of the signature scheme. Let T^* and R^* be respectively the tag and reader output by $\mathcal{A}$ at the end of $Exp_{\mathcal{S},\mathcal{A}}^{\text{Avail}}$, and assume that $\mathcal{A}$ wins (i.e., R^* rejects T^*). R^* starts the protocol by sending C_{R^*}. T^* necessarily validates the first step of the CVA as C_{R^*} necessarily contains a valid signature. Then, depending on the option (2a) of the CVA, either T^* outputs E and NewC_T or T^* interrupts the protocol.

In the first case, none of the values involved in E can be modified by the protocol, thus neither by $\mathcal{A}$. The reader R^* retrieves $\text{MAC}(k_{T^*}||\text{ID}_{R^*}||v_{R^*})$ which is in Tab_R, since it cannot be modified. Thus, if T^* responds, it is necessarily accepted by R^*. In the second case, the received v_{R^*} is lower than the one v'_{R^*} stored in $T*$, meaning that it has been previously updated. For this, the tag must have received (either in a previous C_{R^*}, or in a previous $\text{NewC}_{R''}$) a signature on a message containing (at least) the couple $(\text{ID}_{R^*}, v'_{R^*})$. As R^* is legitimate, the back-end cannot have produced this signature, which is thus a forgery. Consequently, we have that $Adv_{\mathcal{A}_{\text{EF}}} = Adv_{\mathcal{A}}$. Since $Adv_{\mathcal{A}_{\text{EF}}}$ is negligible by assumption, so is $Adv_{\mathcal{A}}$.

In the two remaining proofs, we use the game technique as described by Shoup in [42].

Sketch of proof (privacy).

In the case of $\mathcal{A}$ being CORRUPT-STANDARD, we replace the encryptions produced by the two challenge tags, in response to a nonce n_R, by encryption of a nonce, denoted E^*. Then, as the two challenge tags respond identically without using any key, it is infeasible to distinguish them. Consequently, the success probability of the final game is exactly $1/2$. To reach it, q transition games are introduced, where q is the total number of requests to the challenge tags. In each step of this game, we replace one more plaintext by a nonce. This permits to introduce an IND-CCA2 distinguisher for each transition (as detailed in [42]). We finally conclude that:

$$\left|\Pr(Exp_{\mathcal{S},\mathcal{A}}^{\text{Priv}} \text{ succeeds}) - 1/2\right| \leq q.Adv_{\mathcal{A}_{\text{IND-CCA2}}}.$$

Note that this result is only possible if both challenge tags are updated (i.e., in the Z_1 case), otherwise the adversary can decrypt some messages and detect the simulation.

If $\mathcal{A}$ is FORWARD, the messages NewC_R and NewC_T are never sent, and the protocol is a classical challenge/response based on public-key cryptography. It ensures FORWARD-privacy as proved in [6, 46].

Sketch of proof (soundness).

We use the same technique as for privacy, and replace the q' encryptions of tags for the reader R^*. In the last game, the tags never use s_{TR^*}, but $\mathcal{A}$ must use it to be accepted. Thus, $\mathcal{A}$ must produce a forgery of the corresponding MAC. We thus exhibit a reduction between the last game and the existential unforgeability of the MAC. As we do not know which tag will be used, we must do this reduction for each tag of the nb_{tag} uncorrupted tags that $\mathcal{A}$ may want to impersonate. We finally conclude that:

$$\Pr(Exp_{\mathcal{S},\mathcal{A}}^{\text{Sound}} \text{ succeeds}) \leq q'.Adv_{\mathcal{A}_{\text{IND-CCA2}}} + nb_{tag}.Adv_{\mathcal{A}_{\text{EF}}}.$$

4. EFFICIENCY ANALYSIS: PRACTICAL CASE STUDY OF 3-DAY SPORT EVENT

4.1 Experimental Conditions

For this practical study, we consider the 3-day sport event system deployed in 2010 by RFIDea [36]. This system is composed of 55 readers and 102 110 tags. Each tag stands for a badge that allows a person to attend the event. The last day is the most important one: the first two days are the training and qualification days, and the last day is the race. Not all the tags work during all the event: some spectators may only want to see the final competition, while some employees may only work some days. Therefore, tags categories are 1/2/3-day tickets.

We simulate the theoretical propagation of our protocol when one reader has been compromised, using the readers logs of that event. The RFID application managing the event is designed in such a way that the system administrator of the event was only able to supply the last log of every tag for every reader. Hence, if a tag has been authenticated twice by the same reader, then we only know the last authentication. Consequently, our results are a lower bound for the propagation. Holding all the logs would allow us to show better performances.

4.2 Analysis of the Experimental Results

We first analyze the speed of the information spread. We denote R_1 the most used reader of the event. We consider that the update of the system is performed in R_1, and that the time at which the update is put into place is called the ISSP (information spread starting point).

Figure 3 depicts the spread speed of the update when R_1 launches the spread: the plotted data are the number $u(t)$ of tags updated at time t. The stable periods represent the two nights of the event, where the event venue is closed, i.e., the information spread is in stand-by. The propagation increases from one day to another: the more the tags are updated, the better the propagation is. The number of tags updated at the end of the event is 101 637 when the ISSP is at the beginning of the event: this is 99.5% of the total number of tags in the system.

Then, we evaluate the adversary practical advantage to trace one tag when the ISSP is done by R_1. Figure 4 is the plot of the theoretical advantage from Eq.(2), with the practical results of $u(t)$ for the propagation behavior for R_1. The curves represent this advantage at time t, depending on the ISSP. Like τ's behavior, the advantage to trace one tag is a monotonically non-increasing function on $u(t)$. When the ISSP is at the beginning of the event, since almost all the tags are updated at the end, then the advantage to trace one tag is close to 0. The same test of update spread has been run for every reader of the system. The result is that the spread has the same behavior for every reader in average.

In fact, the analysis on the whole three days does not illustrate fairly the spread efficiency because of the 1-day tickets. Actually, if the ISSP is at 6AM the third day, the tags out of circulation during this day will never receive the

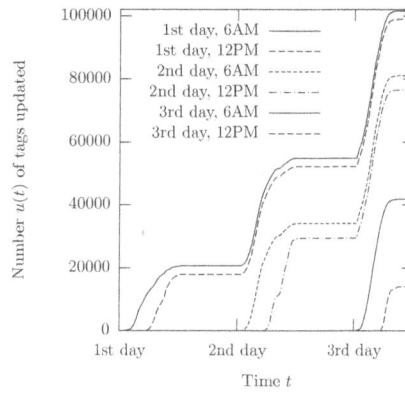

Figure 3: Propagation result at time t, depending on the ISSP, for R_1.

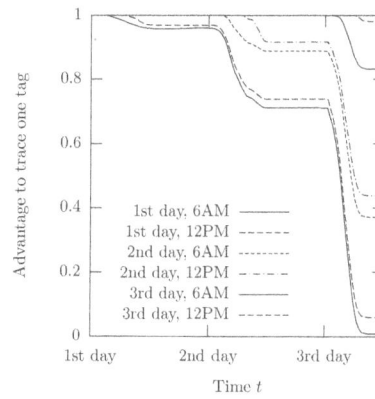

Figure 4: Practical advantage of success to trace one tag knowing $u(t)$ at time t, depending on the ISSP, for R_1.

update, and they will bias the propagation results. The later the ISSP is, the more the set of never-updated tags will increase. For example in Figure 3, the curves related to the ISSP done the third day show that the update does not reach half of the tags. In reality, only 47 694 tags over 102 110 were in circulation during the last day of the event. Consequently, we analyze the information spread done on R_1 only during this last day, and show trustworthy results if we only consider the set S of these 47 694 tags. Figure 5 depicts the advantage to trace one tag knowing the percentage of updated tags of S. If the ISSP is during the morning, the advantage to trace one tag fluctuates between 0.2 and 0.3.

Finally, we study the propagation behavior on the set S during the last day, wherever the ISSP is put into place. First, for every reader R, we measure the percentage x of updated tags of S at the end of the last day, when the ISSP is done at 6AM that day by R. Then, for each percentage x, we count how many readers cause this percentage x, and we plot the results in the histogram of Figure 6. Clearly more than 80% of the readers cause the update of at least 50% of the tags in S; more than one third of the readers cause the update of at least 80% of the tags in S. A side result is that two readers cause the update of only 0.004% and 11% of these tags: these low percentages may result from

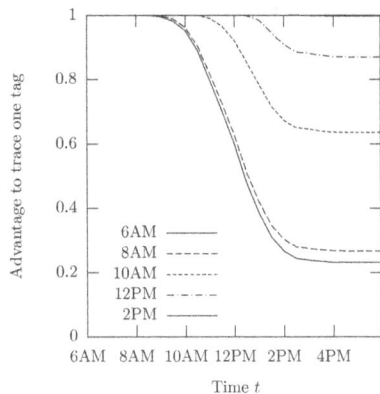

Figure 5: Practical advantage to trace one tag knowing $u(t)$ **in comparison to the number of tags in circulation the last day, at time** t **of the last day, depending on the ISSP, for** R_1**.**

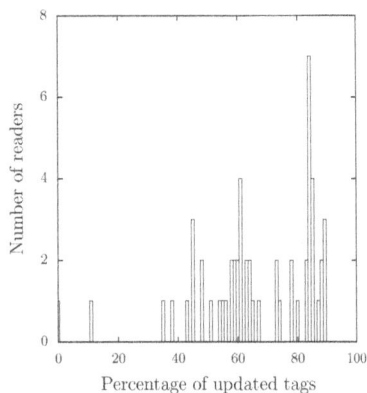

Figure 6: Number of readers that cause the update of $x\%$ **of the tags in circulation the last day, at the end of the last day, when the ISSP is at 6AM the last day.**

either a broken-down reader, or an employees' reader (no so much used). This result shows that the choice of the reader to start the ISSP does not really influence the propagation among the tags in S during the last day.

In conclusion, our results show that the propagation can be efficient in our real-life 3-day sport event. The advantage to trace one tag significantly decreases if the ISSP is at the beginning of the event. If the ISSP is during the second day, around 80% of the tags are reached by the information. Considering only the tags in circulation the last day, the advantage to trace one tag during this day is low. This is a good outcome for this specific scenario. As final remark, do not forget that these results are the lower bound of the propagation: if we had all the logs of the event, the propagation would have still better results.

5. PRACTICAL CONSIDERATIONS

All along this work, we aim to provide a practical and easily deployable protocol. We consequently discuss below the choice of the algorithms and parameters, and demonstrate that our protocol is compliant with real-life constraints. To do so, we consider two off-the-shelf tags, namely SLE 66CLX 360P [16] and NXP JCOP41 [40]. In what follows, the numerical values provided about SLE come from the specification of the device, while the numerical values about JCOP come from our own practical tests applied to a JCOP41 v.2.2.1. We also show in this section how our protocol can be implemented without public-key cryptography (necessarily degrading some other properties) when the available tags are significantly less powerful than the ones mentioned above.

5.1 The Cryptographic Building Blocks

We set the security parameter s as being the pair $(s_{\mathrm{PK}}, s_{\mathrm{SK}})$, where $s_{\mathrm{PK}} = 1024$ bits and $s_{\mathrm{SK}} = 128$ bits. An adequate public-key cryptosystem for our protocol is RSA-OAEP, given that IND-CCA2 property is required. We also suggest RSA-PSS, which is EF-CMA, as signature scheme. Choosing a 1024-bit RSA modulus and a 17-bit exponent appears to be a fair trade-off between security and efficiency in our protocol [28]. Following these choices, Table 1 gives the sizes of the values involved in our protocol.

Table 1: Data sizes in bits of our protocol, with $s_{\mathbf{PK}} = 1024$ **bits and** $s_{\mathbf{SK}} = 128$ **bits.**

Data	$\mathsf{ID}_T, \mathsf{ID}_R, \mathsf{v}_R$	t_R	n_R	k_T	P_R	C_R	E
Size	32	16	64	128	1041	2145	1024

5.2 Tag Memory

Our protocol requires each tag T to store its identifier ID_T, its long term secret k_T, the back-end public key P_B, the table Tab_T containing all the pairs $(\mathsf{ID}_R, \mathsf{v}_R)$ of the m readers. Additionally, each tag may need to store a certificate NewC_T, which contains (i) the pairs $(\mathsf{ID}_R, \mathsf{v}_R)$ of α readers, (ii) the timestamp of this certificate, and (iii) the signature of all these values, where α readers have been compromised.

From Table 1, we deduce that the size of the EEPROM tag must be at least $64(m + \alpha) + 2241$ bits. When $m = 55$ and $\alpha = 10$, which are fairly realistic values, we need a 6401-bit EEPROM, that is about 0.8KB. This widely fits the EEPROMs of the two tags we consider, namely SLE and JCOP, which respectively offer 36KB and 72KB.

REMARK. Two improvements may be added to our solution to decrease the size of the tag memory needed. First, in the setup phase of the protocol, every v_R is initialized to zero, and every tag T stores every pair $(\mathsf{ID}_R, \mathsf{v}_R)$ in Tab_T. If only a few readers are compromised, then one better strategy can be adopted to refine the storage of these values: T may store only one v_R for the non-compromised readers, and may store the complete pairs $(\mathsf{ID}_R, \mathsf{v}_R)$ for the compromised and already repaired ones. Second, if we consider that the readers identifiers are random values, the storage of the pairs $(\mathsf{ID}_R, \mathsf{v}_R)$ on TabID_T is memory-consuming. But if these identifiers are sequential, then T only needs $\lceil \log_2(m) \rceil$ bits of memory to store them. With these two improvements, the required memory is as low as 3851 bits, that is around 0.482KB, using the numerical values provided in Table 1.

5.3 Transmission Time

During one protocol execution, the data exchanged between a reader and a tag are the reader certificate C_R, the reader nonce n_R, the tag answer E, and the values NewC_T, NewC_R, if needed. In the worst case, the number of bits exchanged is hence $64\alpha + 5313$, which equals 5953 bits when

Cryptographic primitives	Adversary	Soundness	Availability	Privacy of any tag
PK Cryptography in $O(1)$	CORRUPT-STANDARD	Yes	Yes	No $\rightarrow$ Yes
	FORWARD	Yes	Yes	Yes
	CORRUPT-FORWARD	Yes	Yes	No
SK Cryptography - in $O(1)$	CORRUPT-STANDARD	Yes	Yes	No $\rightarrow$ Yes
	FORWARD or STANDARD	No	Yes	No
	CORRUPT-FORWARD	No	No	No
- in $O(n)$	FORWARD	Yes	Yes	Yes
	CORRUPT-FORWARD	Yes	No	No

Figure 7: Comparison of the different choices to construct the proposed protocol. The $\rightarrow$ arrow represents the restoration of privacy: the left term is the privacy state at the moment of the attack, and the right term is the privacy state after the privacy-restoring mechanism put into place.

$\alpha = 10$. The average data rate of SLE is 424 bits/ms, yielding a total transmission time equal to 14.04ms. For our JCOP tests, the transmission of 5953 bits takes around 68.04ms.

5.4 Tag Computation Time

A tag has to compute its answer E, and the verification of the two certificates C_R and $NewC_R$ (i.e., the unique update certificate). These computations do not depend on the number of compromised readers. The calculation time at 15MHz for an RSA operation (encryption and signature verification) when $|n| = 1024$ and $|e| = 17$ is 7ms for SLE [16]. Therefore, the expected calculation time is here 21ms. The performances of our JCOP for the same test values $|n|$ and $|e|$ are 104.2ms for signature verification, and 123.3ms for encryption. Thus, the expected calculation time on our JCOP is 331.7ms.

5.5 PK vs. SK Cryptography

Our protocol is based on public-key (PK) cryptography. In some scenarios, we may wish to adapt our protocol to make it using only symmetric-key (SK) cryptography. We explain below how this can be done, implying necessarily to degrade some other properties.

First, the MAC and the PK algorithm are replaced by a unique SK algorithm where the keys are k_T and s_{TR}, but the computation is performed on the same data. The only difference is that the tag puts randomness into its answer along with ID_R and n_R. Second, the certificate of the update is replaced by two SK encryptions. The first one, called N_1 is the encryption of (ID_R, v_R) with a unique master key k_{M_1} shared between the back-end and all the tags. The second one, called N_2 is the encryption of N_1 with a unique master key k_{M_2} shared between the back-end and all the readers. Finally the propagation is done sending $(N_1 || N_2)$ each time: to accept the update, either the tag checks N_1, or the reader checks N_2. In this case, the reader complexity of its database search to authenticate a tag is $O(n)$, since it has to find the right key s_{TR}. But if the tags are tamper-resistant, they can share the same long-term key k_T, and the reader complexity is $O(1)$.

Therefore, three different choices are possible to build this protocol: PK cryptography in $O(1)$, SK cryptography in $O(n)$, or SK cryptography in $O(1)$ with tag tamper-resistance. Figure 7 illustrates the comparison of these choices depending on the power class and goal of an adversary $\mathcal{A}$. We only discuss here the results about the soundness and availability. First, SK cryptography in $O(n)$ may not be so

feasible in practice: if the system has one million tags, the reader search may be too long. Also if $\mathcal{A}$ corrupts both readers and tags (i.e., CORRUPT-FORWARD), the system is no longer available. On the good side, computation time taken by a tag to perform SK cryptography is really fast. In the case of SK cryptography in $O(1)$, the same availability problem happens. Furthermore, even if $\mathcal{A}$ only compromises one tag, she can impersonate any tag: no soundness. This is in contradiction with the requirement pointed out in the introduction (i.e., tampering with one tag should not compromise the whole system). But this choice has all the benefits in terms of computation time and reader complexity. Finally, PK cryptography in $O(1)$ seems the most reasonable option. Whatever $\mathcal{A}$'s goals and means are, the system is sound and available.

6. CONCLUSION

In this paper, we presented a new RFID authentication protocol for offline RFID systems. This protocol is able to face three classes of adversary: STANDARD, FORWARD or CORRUPT. The protocol is designed with a privacy-restoring mechanism that allows the tags of the system to be informed that a reader has been corrupted. For CORRUPT-FORWARD adversaries, we proved that the proposed protocol supplies the required security levels of availability and soundness. Our protocol provides FORWARD-privacy, and CORRUPT-STANDARD-privacy with the use of our privacy-restoring mechanism.

We demonstrated the efficiency of our protocol on a real case study, a 3-day sport event, that used an offline RFID-based ticketing system. We got access to the logs of the 55 readers that authenticated more than 100 000 tags during the event. We showed that our protocol efficiently spreads the information within the RFID system, with an information spread above 99.5% when the attack occurs at the beginning of the event. We emphasize that this result is a lower bound as each reader used during this event only kept the *last* authentication log of every viewed tag in memory.

Lastly, we provided practical guidelines for implementing our protocol and evaluated its performances in terms of tag memory, transmission time, and computation time during an authentication. The results demonstrate that our protocol is deployable with the existing technology.

Up to our knowledge, *restoring* privacy in RFID systems is a new concept introduced in this paper, although the field of RFID security and privacy has already been extensively addressed [26]. We think that the mobility in RFID systems may also be exploited for other features. In this vein, we showed that our protocol can also be used to spread other kinds of information within the system.

Acknowledgements

We thank RFIDea for having furnished the data that allow us to compare our protocol to the practice, and Hugues Libotte for his help on enhancing this work. We also want to thank the reviewers for their thorough comments.

This work is partially funded by the Walloon Region Marshall plans through the SPW DG06 Project TRASILUX and the 816922 Project SEE.

7. REFERENCES

[1] G. Avoine. Adversary Model for Radio Frequency Identification. Technical Report LASEC-REPORT-2005-001, Swiss Federal Institute of Technology (EPFL), 2005.

[2] G. Avoine, I. Coisel, and T. Martin. Time Measurement Threatens Privacy-Friendly RFID Authentication Protocols. In *Workshop on RFID Security – RFIDSec'10*, volume 6370 of *Lecture Notes in Computer Science*, pages 138–157. Springer, 2010.

[3] G. Avoine, C. Lauradoux, and T. Martin. When Compromised Readers Meet RFID. In *Workshop on Information Security Applications – WISA'09*, volume 5932 of *Lecture Notes in Computer Science*, pages 36–50. Springer, 2009.

[4] G. Avoine and P. Oechslin. RFID Traceability: A Multilayer Problem. In *Financial Cryptography – FC'05*, volume 3570 of *Lecture Notes in Computer Science*, pages 125–140. Springer, 2005.

[5] M. Bellare, A. Desai, D. Pointcheval, and P. Rogaway. Relations Among Notions of Security for Public-Key Encryption Schemes. In *Advances in Cryptology –CRYPTO'98*, volume 1462 of *Lecture Notes in Computer Science*, pages 130–141. Springer, 1998.

[6] S. Canard, I. Coisel, J. Etrog, and M. Girault. Privacy-Preserving RFID Systems: Model and Constructions. Cryptology ePrint Archive, Report 2010/405, 2010.

[7] A. Cavoukian. Privacy-by-Design. http://privacybydesign.ca/.

[8] F. Cohen. *Computer Viruses*. PhD thesis, University of Southern California, 1985.

[9] F. Cohen. Computer Viruses: Theory and Experiments. *Journal of Computers and Security*, 6(1):22–35, 1987.

[10] K. Dietz and J. A. P. Heesterbeek. Daniel Bernoulli's Epidemiological Model Revisited. *Mathematical Biosciences*, 180(1-2):1–21, 2002.

[11] EPCglobal. Class-1 Generation 2 UHF Air Interface Protocol Standard Version 1.2.0: Gen 2. http://www.epcglobalinc.org/standards/, 2008.

[12] F. D. Garcia and P. van Rossum. Modeling Privacy for Off-line RFID Systems. In *9th Smart Card Research and Advanced Applications – CARDIS 2010*, volume 6035 of *Lecture Notes in Computer Science*, pages 194–208. Springer, 2010.

[13] S. Goldwasser, S. Micali, and R. Rivest. A "Paradoxical" Solution to the Signature Problem (Extended Abstract). In *25th Annual Symposium on Foundations of Computer Science – FOCS'84*, pages 441–448. IEEE, 1984.

[14] K. A. Harras, K. C. Almeroth, and E. M. Belding-Royer. Delay Tolerant Mobile Networks (DTMNs): Controlled Flooding in Sparse Mobile Networks. In *4th International IFIP-TC6 Networking Conference – Networking'05*, volume 3462 of *Lecture Notes in Computer Science*, pages 1180–1192. Springer, 2005.

[15] H. W. Hethcote. The Mathematics of Infectious Diseases. *SIAM Review*, 42(4):599–653, 2000.

[16] Infineon. Contactless SLE 66 Family. http://www.infineon.com/.

[17] International Organization for Standardization. ISO/IEC 9798: Information technology – Security techniques – Entity authentication, 1991–2010.

[18] International Organization for Standardization. ISO/IEC 15693: Identification cards – Contactless integrated circuit(s) cards – Vicinity cards, 2000–2009.

[19] International Organization for Standardization. ISO/IEC 14443: Identification cards – Contactless integrated circuit cards – Proximity cards, 2001–2008.

[20] International Organization for Standardization. ISO/IEC 15408 (Common Criteria): Information technology — Security techniques — Evaluation criteria for IT security, 2008–2009.

[21] E. P. C. Jones, L. Li, and P. A. S. Ward. Practical Routing in Delay-Tolerant Networks. *IEEE Transactions on Mobile Computing*, 6(8):943–959, 2007.

[22] A. Juels. RFID Security and Privacy: A Research Survey. *IEEE Journal on Selected Areas in Communications*, 24(2):381–394, February 2006.

[23] A. Juels and S. Weis. Defining Strong Privacy for RFID. In *International Conference on Pervasive Computing and Communications – PerCom 2007*, pages 342–347. IEEE, 2007.

[24] J. O. Kephart and S. R. White. Directed-Graph Epidemiological Models of Computer Viruses. In *IEEE Symposium on Security and Privacy – S&P '91*, pages 343–359. IEEE, 1991.

[25] A. Lindgren, A. Doria, and O. Schelén. Probabilistic Routing in Intermittently Connected Networks. In *First International Workshop on Service Assurance with Partial and Intermittent Resources – SAPIR'04*, volume 3126 of *Lecture Notes in Computer Science*, pages 239–254. Springer, 2004.

[26] R. Lounge. http://www.avoine.net/rfid/, 2011.

[27] R. M. May and R. M. Anderson. Transmission Dynamics of HIV Infection. *Nature*, 326:137–142, 1987.

[28] A. Menezes. Evaluation of Security Level of Cryptography: RSA-OAEP, RSA-PSS, RSA Signature. Technical Report 1011, Cryptography Research and Evaluation Committees – CRYPTREC, 2001.

[29] D. Nain, N. Petigara, and H. Balakrishnan. Integrated Routing and Storage for Messaging Applications in Mobile Ad Hoc Networks. *Mobile Networks and Applications*, 9(6):595–604, 2004.

[30] R. M. Needham and M. D. Schroeder. Using

Encryption for Authentication in Large Networks of Computers. *Communications of the ACM*, 21(12):993–999, 1978.

[31] M. E. J. Newman. Spread of Epidemic Disease on Networks. *Physical Review*, 66(1), 2002.

[32] J. Omic, R. Kooij, and P. Van Mieghem. Virus Spread in Complete Bi-partite Graphs. In *2nd International ICST Conference on Bio-Inspired Models of Network, Information and Computing Systems – Bionetics'07*, pages 49–56. ICST, 2007.

[33] Privacy Rights Clearinghouse. Empowering Consumers, Protecting Privacy. https://www.privacyrights.org/.

[34] C. Rackoff and D. R. Simon. Non-Interactive Zero-Knowledge Proof of Knowledge and Chosen Ciphertext Attack. In *Advances in Cryptology –CRYPTO'91*, volume 576 of *Lecture Notes in Computer Science*, pages 433–444. Springer, 1991.

[35] V. Reding. Commission Recommendation of 12.5.2009 - SEC(2009) 585/586, on the Implementation of Privacy and Data Protection Principles in Applications Supported by Radio-Frequency Identification, May 2009.

[36] RFIDea. Engineering & Applications in Electronic Traceability. http://www.rfidea.com/.

[37] M. R. Rieback. *Security and Privacy of Radio Frequency Identification*. PhD thesis, Vrije Universiteit, 2008.

[38] M. R. Rieback, B. Crispo, and A. S. Tanenbaum. Is Your Cat Infected with a Computer Virus? In *Pervasive Computing and Communications*, pages 169–179. IEEE, 2006.

[39] A. Sania, D. Kroesea, and P. Pollett. Stochastic Models for the Spread of HIV in a Mobile Heterosexual Population. *Mathematical Biosciences*, 208(1):98–124, 2007.

[40] N. Semiconductors. JCOP Family. http://www.nxp.com/.

[41] G. Serazzi and S. Zanero. Computer Virus Propagation Models. In *Performance Tools and Applications to Networked Systems*, volume 2965 of *Lecture Notes in Computer Science*, pages 26–50. Springer, 2004.

[42] V. Shoup. Sequences of Games: a Tool for Taming Complexity in Security Proofs. Cryptology ePrint Archive, Report 2004/332, 2004.

[43] T. Small and Z. J. Haas. The Shared Wireless Infostation Model: a New Ad Hoc Networking Paradigm (or Where There is a Whale, There is a Way). In *Proceedings of the 4th ACM International Symposium on Mobile Ad Hoc Networking & Computing – MobiHoc'03*, pages 233–244. ACM, 2003.

[44] T. Spyropoulos, K. Psounis, and C. S. Raghavendra. Single-Copy Routing in Intermittently Connected Mobile Networks. In *First Annual IEEE Communications Society Conference on Sensor and Ad Hoc Communications and Networks – SECON'04*, pages 235–244. IEEE, 2004.

[45] A. Vahdat and D. Becker. Epidemic Routing for Partially-Connected Ad Hoc Networks. Technical report, Duke University, 2000.

[46] S. Vaudenay. On Privacy Models for RFID. In *Advances in Cryptology – Asiacrypt 2007*, volume 4833 of *Lecture Notes in Computer Science*, pages 68–87. Springer, 2007.

[47] Z. Zhang. Routing in Intermittently Connected Mobile Ad Hoc Networks and Delay Tolerant Networks: Overview and Challenges. *IEEE Communications Surveys and Tutorials*, 8(1):24–37, 2006.

APPENDIX

A. INFORMATION SPREAD IN THE LITERATURE

Our protocol relies on the propagation of the information that a reader has been compromised to all the entities of the RFID system. We present here a survey of the information spread in several disciplines. More generally, the data transmission from entities to entities belonging to a group has been analyzed in many domains, from social networks, medicine to computer viruses or networks. As a remark, let us mention that our framework follows a particular model: the RFID system corresponds to a bipartite graph where readers can only communicate with tags, and vice-versa.

The earliest field dealing with information spread is epidemiology in medicine and biology, and more specifically epidemiological models with Bernouilli's precursory works [10]. This research topic aims to create mathematical methods to describe the transmission of contagious diseases through individuals of a population. In such models, it is important to clearly specify several points, such as the structure of the population, the outbreak of the disease and the basic reproduction number. The epidemiological model that is the closest to our RFID system is the one for sexual transmission disease (STD) in an heterosexual population (i.e., bipartite population). The analogy with our protocol is that there are two subgroups in the population (readers and tags), and the STD (the information about compromised readers) that can be spread between two elements of different subgroups, but never between two elements belonging to the same subgroup. Several results have been published for this epidemiological model [15, 27, 31, 39]. But most of them consider that an infected individual eventually dies or cures. This is not the case in our framework, since tags and readers never erase/ignore the information to spread. Therefore, the propagation of the information in our framework is more efficient than a classical contagious disease in medicine.

Another key-domain of data propagation is virus spread in computer systems. In the early age of viruses, the spread was essentially processed via floppy disk exchanges. Therefore, the creation of trustworthy models has always been valuable for information security in order to better understand the spread of new viruses.

In the 1980s, Cohen was the pioneer in defining and describing computer viruses and spreading process [8, 9]. In 1991, Kephart and White proposed in [24] one of the first formalization of virus propagation for computers using mathematical epidemiological models. In 2004, Serazzi and Zanero provided a review of the most popular models about virus and worm spread [41]. Their study does not clearly match our problem though, as the main threat since the last decade has no longer been the viruses but the worms, which do not propagate following a bipartite model. Finally in 2007, Omic, Kooij, and Van Mieghem investigated the propagation of viruses on a complete bipartite graph [32]. Their mathematical model is able to predict the probability of spread accurately. This work is very close to our framework, but the bipartite graph is not complete in our case, since not all the readers and tags communicate with each other. Their results show that the average number of infected nodes is around 85% when the spreading rate is high.

Correlated investigations on virus in RFID have been performed by Rieback, Crispo, and Tanenbaum [38], and by Rieback [37]. They demonstrate that a self-replicating RFID virus carried on an RFID tag may infect the back-end server using SQL injections, but they do not consider the propagation efficiency in their work.

The idea of information spread has also been studied in mobile ad hoc networks and delay tolerant networks. The main motivation comes from the fact that node mobility can be used to forward and disseminate information in the whole system: a given mobile node, which carries some data, transmits them each time it meets another mobile node. This field is strongly connected to RFID systems, since the nodes are mobile, and therefore the propagation of the information can unexpectedly reach several parts of the system. In [47], Zhang proposes a survey of many "store-and-forward" routing protocols.

Two opposed kinds of protocols can be found in the literature. They basically depend on the rate of message redundancy chosen for the spread. On one extreme, there are protocols like Epidemic [45], based on flooding: every node stores and propagates the information to every encountered node, and thus never erases the information. Clearly for such protocols, the success probability in delivering the information to the destination is very high, but it uses all the nodes to reach its goal and thus consumes many network resources (e.g., node memory, bandwidth). On the other extreme, there are protocols like Single-copy [44]: only one copy of the information is in circulation. Here, the consumption of network resources is very low, but the delay to deliver the information to its target can be very long. Between these two opposites, there are many protocols [14, 21, 25, 29, 43]. They are basically a trade-off between statistic profiles, delivery rate, energy consumption to optimize delivery delay.

To summarize, none of the given results is really exploitable in our framework. Indeed, our model does not exactly fit the described ones. A strong deduction is that the information propagation in an environment is clearly specific to the application used and its model.

Private Communication Detection: A Stochastic Approach

Chang-Han Jong
ECE Department
University of Maryland
College Park, Maryland 20742, USA
chjong@umd.edu

Virgil D. Gligor
ECE Department and CyLab
Carnegie Mellon University
Pittsburgh, Pennsylvania 15213, USA
gligor@cmu.edu

ABSTRACT
Private communication detection (PCD) enables an ordinary network user to discover communication patterns (e.g., call time, length, frequency, and initiator) between two or more private parties. Ordinary users have neither eavesdropping capabilities (e.g., the network may employ strong anonymity measures) nor legal authority (e.g., collection of call records—without any voice/data content—requires "national security letters") to collect private-communication records. Analysis of communication patterns between private parties has historically been a powerful tool used by intelligence, military, law-enforcement and business organizations as it can reveal the strength of tie between these parties. In this paper, we show that PCD is possible by ordinary users merely by sending packets to various network end-nodes (e.g., WiFi nodes) and analyzing the timing of their responses. We show that timing side channels, which are caused by distinct resource-contention responses when different applications run in end nodes, enable effective PCD despite network and proxy-generated noise (e.g., jitter, delays). We use a stochastic analysis to demonstrate how PCD exploits indirectly accessible, remote end-node resources, such as WiFi radio channels and computer keyboards in Instant Messaging. Similar analysis enables practical Sybil node detection.

Categories and Subject Descriptors
C.2.0 [**Computer-communication Networks**]: General–*security and protection*.

Keywords
Resource contention; Privacy; Side-channel; Sybil attacks; WiFi; Instant Messaging

1. INTRODUCTION
Ordinary phone call records - even in the absence of voice/data content - have proven to be so useful in discovering relationships between private parties that both law-enforcement and business organizations broke US law to surreptitiously collect them [19][20][28][31]. One does not need to surreptitiously collect over 1.9 trillion call records, as the NSA is reported to have done between 2001 and 2004 [19], to discover communication patterns (e.g., call time, length, frequency, and initiator) revealing the strength of relationships [9] between private parties. A couple of thousand or fewer records, as reported to have been illegally collected by the FBI and by HP's former Chairman of the Board, would suffice [20][28]. The sufficiency of relatively few call records in detecting private relationships is clearly illustrated by

law-enforcement success worldwide; e.g., the discovery of a drug ring in New Zealand, drug smuggling in Minnesota prisons, and pornography groups on Moldova [19][31]. Such success inspired us to ask whether it would be possible for an *ordinary network user*, without any eavesdropping and malware-injection capabilities (or equivalently an ordinary user of a perfectly anonymous network [6][23]) to detect and collect records of private communication between *targeted* network users. In short, we ask whether private communication detection (PCD) is possible without any of the often-assumed capabilities of successful privacy attacks [6][26][29][30][34][35].

Problem. Our network setting, abstractly shown in Figures 1 and 2 below, illustrates the challenge faced by an ordinary user in performing PCD against two targeted network users. Ordinary user Eve sends repeated probe messages to Alice and Bob's nodes and analyzes the timing of their responses to determine whether these nodes communicate with each other, or alternatively whether their nodes are implemented by the same physical network node (as in a Sybil node[1] instance). The type of messages Eve sends does not alert Alice and Bob of Eve's repeated probing. However, Eve faces two PCD challenges. First, the network may have other third-party nodes that communicate with Alice and Bob's nodes separately. As a consequence, the timing of Alice and Bob's node response to Eve's probe messages might be similar to those when Alice and Bob communicate with each other, and Eve must be able to distinguish the former from the latter case. Second, network routers and application-layer proxies[2] located between Eve's node and those of Alice and Bob, respectively, can introduce jitter and delays. Since most interactive WiFi applications require low latencies (e.g., ITU G.114 recommends under 400ms latency for voice communication), the jitter and delay incurred by such networks would not prevent an ordinary user from performing PCD[3].

Our approach. In the simplest form of PCD, ordinary user Eve is presented with two hypotheses, which she must test in the presence of separate third-party communication with Alice and Bob's nodes, and network jitter and delay.

---

[1] Sybil nodes are undesirable because they negatively affect resource allocation, bandwidth utilization and routing [18][24].

[2] Application-layer proxies enable mobility and provide some degree of privacy and security; e.g., a smartphone registering with a server ensures that messages will be forwarded to the phone (mobility) and the phone's IP address is hidden (privacy). Moreover, a phone receives a packet only through a pre-established connection initiated by the phone with server sending it (security). This limitation exists when the node is behind a network address translation router (e.g., AT&T's data plan)

[3] However, we note current low-latency anonymous networks, such as Tor and I2P [6][7][11], cannot be used for real-time WiFi applications since their latency in the order of seconds.

For private communication detection,

H$_0$: Alice and Bob do no communicate with each other
H$_1$: Alice and Bob communicate with each other

For remote Sybil detection,

H$_2$: Alice and Bob are not physically the same node (non-Sybil)
H$_3$: Alice and Bob are physically the same node (Sybil)

During a period of probing, Eve sends packets to Alice and Bob's nodes and receives a (time) series of response times. Given the time series, she can use a classifier to detect which hypothesis (e.g., H$_0$ or H$_1$) is more likely to be true.

The reason why classifying the time series of response times enables the detection of the private communication is that the timing responses caused by resource contention in Alice's, respectively Bob's, node (e.g., back-off in CSMA/CA) are different depending on the type of application running on that node. For example, if Alice and Bob's nodes communicate with each other via a WiFi network in a VoIP application, the WiFi radio channel contention caused by Eve's probe messages would differ from that caused by Alice's or Bob's communication with third parties in web browsing or file transfer applications. Hence, ordinary user Eve can construct two models of timing responses obtained when two remote nodes communicate with each other via a VoIP application and when two remote nodes do not communication with each other via a VoIP application. Then Eve can apply supervised classification to the time series of responses obtained from Alice and Bob's nodes in response to her probes to detect their communication over VoIP, if any. In short, Eve can exploit a *timing side channel* that is caused by different types of resource-contention responses when end nodes run different applications.

Eve can use Markov Chain models for classification and leverage its success in stochastic time series classification of automatic speech recognition [13][14][25]. She can also apply signal-processing techniques to filter out the noise of time series of responses; i.e., we use a high-pass filter to eliminate the noise in certain frequency components. Finding good filters for different time series of device responses is a routine design problem of signal processing, and thus any ordinary user can use standard tools (as illustrated later in this paper) to analyze responses generated from different devices and protocols. In performing such analysis for PCD, ordinary user Eve can merge the time series of probe responses obtained from the targeted nodes into a single time series such that the interactivity between the two targeted nodes can be established in a specific application, such as VoIP.

Limitation. The proposed approach is most effective when the stochastic models chosen to represent the time series of probe responses can accurately model random-access networks (e.g., Markov Chains can model CSMA/CA networks well), and when signal-processing techniques can eliminate much of the noise introduced by the third-party nodes. This is important because high-frequency target probing during the detection period may also cause adversary detection by the targets. Hence, the adversary must strike a delicate balance between detection accuracy and the possibility of attack detection.

Contributions. In this paper we show that ordinary users can perform private communication detection (PCD) by merely sending packets to various WiFi network end-nodes and analyzing the timing of their responses. PCD is enabled by timing side-channels caused by different types of resource contention in end nodes. Exploitation of these timing channels from PCD is effective despite network and proxy-generated noise (e.g., jitter, delays). We use a stochastic analysis to demonstrate how PCD exploits indirectly accessible end-node resources, such as WiFi radio channels and computer keyboards in Instant Messaging. Similar analysis enables practical Sybil node detection.

Roadmap. In the rest of this paper, we show the two applications, starting with the experimental environment and procedure in section 2. Then we illustrate the design of the proposed approach in section 3, followed by evaluation (section 4). We discuss possible countermeasures in section 5, and with environment variations in section 6. The related work is given in section 7 followed by the conclusion (section 8).

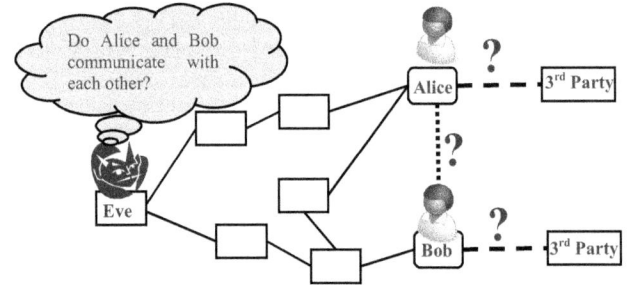

Figure 1. Private communication detection

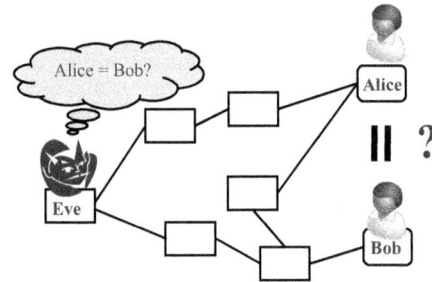

Figure 2. Remote Sybil detection

2. PRACTICAL PCD APPLICATIONS

We will examine two applications for PCD as summarized in Table 1. The first application is WiFi where nodes compete for the radio channel. The second application is Instant Messaging, where the user switches between different chat windows, making the keyboard the resource under contention. The time series of probe responses for WiFi application has strong noise while time series data for Instant Messaging has negligible noise. For each of these two applications, we describe the application, experiment environments, and the procedure of experiments.

Table 1. Two PCD Applications

	WiFi	Instant Messaging
Resource under contention	Radio channel	Keyboard
Noise due to non-targeted nodes	Yes	No*
Noise due to internet and application-layer proxy	Yes	Negligible#

*:For this experimental setting

#: Human actions in Instant Messaging are measured in seconds, while network delay and jitters rarely exceed 1 second

76

2.1 WiFi

WiFi provides multiple access to radio channels through IEEE 802.11 protocol suite as shown in Figure 3. In a radio channel of the selected frequency, nodes compete for channel usage according to CSMA/CA protocol. When a node wants to send a frame, if another node is using the channel or is expected to use the channel (virtual carrier sensing), this node will be back off and try to re-access the channel after a random period; otherwise, the node sends it immediately. In this way, a node's traffic affects other nodes in the same WiFi network.

Because of this structure, if an ordinary user Eve periodically sends probe packets remotely to a targeted node in a WiFi network, the response time will be influenced by the traffic of the WiFi network. If two targeted nodes Alice and Bob in the same WiFi network are communicating with each other under constant-rate traffic (e.g., Voice), the impact on the transmission time is retained during this probing period. Suppose the traffic of other nodes (not Alice nor Bob) in the WiFi network are web browsing, video streaming, or SSH, but not VoIP, the remote ordinary user Eve can distinguish whether VoIP is in session by the time series of the probe responses.

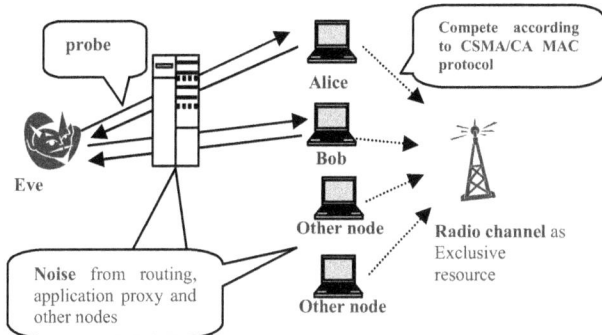

Figure 3. Radio channel is the exclusive resource in WiFi

2.1.1 Experimental Environment

Two nodes Alice and Bob are in the same WiFi network provided by a WiFi Access Point, which is connected to the Internet. Since PCD depends on the stochastic time signals, not the protocols, we would like to know PCD's performance in different network environments. The experiments are performed in two different locations. The university café is in the lobby of a large computer science building where hundreds of WiFi users can access the internet through over about 10 WiFi access points. Hence, the university café is a wireless environment with high dynamics. In the author's apartment, WiFi user dynamics are limited to only one to two WiFi users, in additional to the Alice and Bob.

The configuration for the private communication detection is shown in Figure 4. Nodes Alice and Bob are two laptops, a MacBook Air (Mac OS X version Lion) and a MacBook Pro (Mac OS X version Snow Leopard), respectively. Both have the VoIP client CounterPath X-Lite installed. Eve has the VoIP IDs of node Alice and node Bob, and therefore is able to send probe VoIP packets to the targets through a VoIP proxy and get responses. The VoIP proxy is an OpenSips server running on a Linux server located in a university computer cluster room [21].

The configuration for the remote Sybil detection is shown in Figure 5. The target is a HP laptop which is running Windows 7 and has an Intel WiFi NIC. This Intel NIC supports "My WiFi", a wireless NIC virtualization technology that enables the wireless

NIC to serve as different roles in the same time [5][36]. When "My WiFi" is enabled, an Apple iPhone 4 can access the Internet through the laptop. In this case, the laptop has two virtual identities, fulfilling hypothesis H_3 for remote Sybil detection. One identity connects to the WiFi Access Point and gains Internet access while the other identity acts as a WiFi Access Point, providing WiFi service to iPhone. The laptop is also equipped with VoIP client X-Lite so that Eve can probe the laptop through the VoIP proxy.

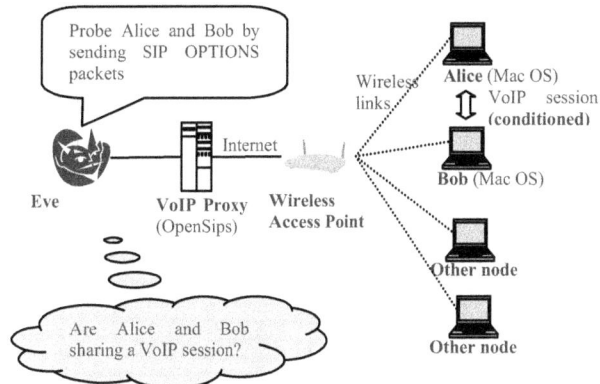

Figure 4. Experimental environment for WiFi private communication detection

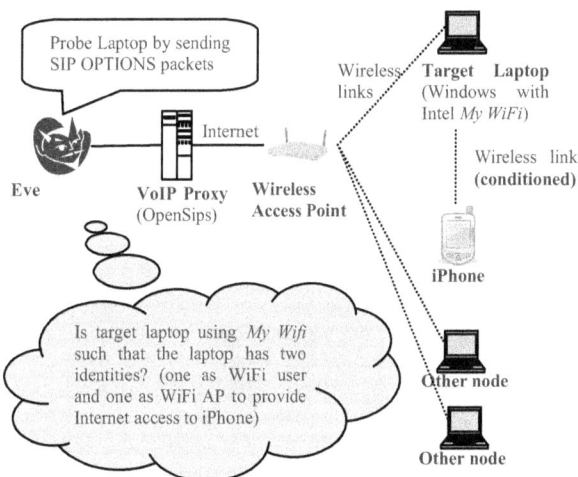

Figure 5. Experimental environment for WiFi remote Sybil detection

2.1.2 Procedure

In both of the settings, Alice or Bob will browse the web and use SSH to connect to remote site as the communication with third parties. For the private communication detection, we condition upon whether Alice and Bob share a VoIP communication (H_0 and H_1). Eve uses a program to probe both Alice and Bob. The program will send SIP OPTIONS requests, VoIP probe packets in the Session Initiation Protocol (SIP), to targeted nodes with a 100ms interval (~10 Hz) [12]. For each condition, the program probes the targeted nodes 120000 times. In section 4.2, we will split the results in each condition to 12 samples.

For the remote Sybil detection, we condition upon whether the laptop enables "My WiFi" and shares the Internet with the iPhone (H_2 and H_3). However, Eve only probes the laptop, not iPhone, due to the fact that the IP address obtained by the iPhone is private and not routable (e.g., 192.168.0.0/16). For each condition, the program probes the targeted nodes for 120000 times as well.

2.2 Instant Messaging

The Instant Messaging (IM) service is an interactive social medium that enables person-to-person real-time text chatting. Common systems include Facebook, AOL AIM, Yahoo Messenger, Microsoft MSN Messenger, Google Talk, and Skype.

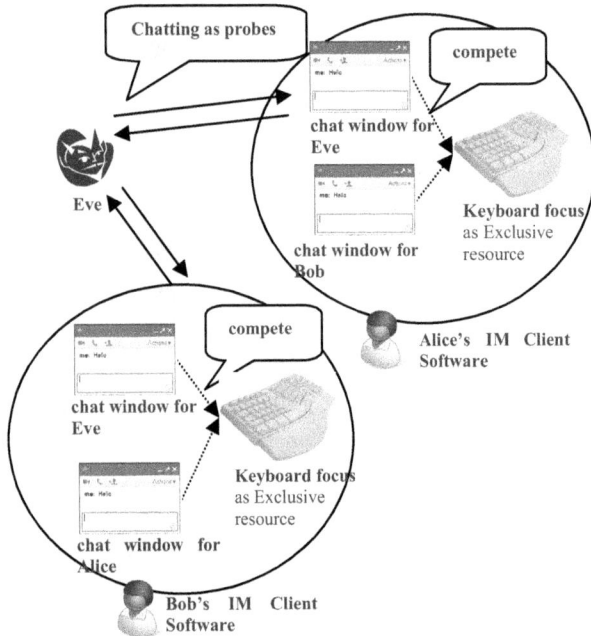

Figure 6. Keyboard is the exclusive resource in Instant Messaging

On the user interface, IM has one contact status window that shows a list of contacts. The IM user can select a contact and begin a one-to-one text chat with the contact via another window. Due to human limitations and the design of the user interface, the IM user can only type in only one window at one time (i.e. only one window gains the keyboard input focus). Therefore, keyboard, or the corresponding end-user attention, is the resource under contention. Chatting with one contact affects chatting with a different contact because the end user needs to switch between chat windows.

Hence, the exclusive keyboard causes side-channels as illustrated in Figure 6. When Eve chats with a targeted user, the timing of the interactions will be affected by the chatting between the targeted user and another user, if one exists. Moreover, besides the regular text messages, all major IM systems support composing notification messages[4], which are sent periodically when the IM user is typing on the keyboard, but has not yet sent the message. Therefore, Eve can use the received regular text messages and composing notification messages to obtain the private information of interest.

---

[4] There are different names for composing notification messages. We use the name composing notification from XMPP, an IETF open standard.

2.2.1 Experimental Environment

Human participants use IM client software named pidgin to chat with their contact [22]. The communications are relayed through an IM server. The pidgin is modified to log received regular text messages and composing notification messages. The investigator (Eve in this case), who also participates in chatting, records the timing of received regular text messages and composing notification messages. In addition, although IM allows conference chatting, we only focus on one-on-one text chatting with one or more contacts.

It is usually a challenge to recruit human subjects for research, and our experiment is no exception. We use the following approaches to ease the recruitment and make maximum use of the data:

1. Virtualization. The participants do not need to come to the designated site. Instead, they use their own computers to connect to the virtual machine where pidgin is installed and investigators' instructions will be displayed. The investigator's computer hosts these virtual machines so that the investigator can monitor whether the participants follow the instructions.

2. Cross-validation: Cross-validation is used to exhaustively utilize the limited number of experiment samples [32]. Given all the samples, a certain number of samples are picked as the training set and the rest are used as the testing set. By iterating combinations of the training vs. sample set, the result utilizes all samples for both training and testing.

2.2.2 Procedure

For private communication detection, we have 5 groups of participants (2 participants/group) who perform 4 sessions of a 5-minutes experiment. In two of the sessions, two participants both chat with the investigator (H_0). In another two sessions, two participants both chat with the investigator as well as chat to each other (H_1). Each session generates a sample of 5-minutes time series and totally 10 samples are available for each hypothesis.

For remote Sybil detection, we can also use the data for private communication detection. In private communication detection, we have 20 existing samples that correspond to H_2 (non-Sybil) data in remote Sybil detection. Therefore, we need only to perform experiments where H_3 (Sybil) is hold. To this end, 5 groups of participants (1 participant/group) perform 4 sessions of experiments where each participant uses two IM accounts to concurrently chat with the investigator. Therefore, we have the samples for H_3 in remote Sybil detection. Combining these 20 samples with the 20 samples obtained in private communication detection as H_2 in remote Sybil detection, we have 20 samples available for both hypotheses for remote Sybil detection.

Before a group of participants begins the experiments, they remotely login to the virtual machine and the investigator gives instructions for how to use the environment. Besides pidgin, there is a program on the virtual machine that displays the investigator's instructions. The investigator gives instructions to the participants for when to chat and whom to chat with.

During the experiments, the pidgin program logs the timing of regular text messages and composing notification messages. The event times are then converted to a time series with the resolution in seconds. Data points in the converted time series indicate whether or not the participant has been busy typing to the investigator at each second. The converting algorithm is described as follows.

The *estimated busy period* is when the contact is busy typing to the investigator. This begins when a composing notification is received, and ends when a regular text message is received. However, the period could be over-estimated in the following scenario. An IM user types something to a contact but does not hit send, but instead switches to chat with another contact. Eventually the user switches back to send the unsent message to the first contact. A simple and effective way is to set an upper bound of the estimated period, say 15 seconds. We assume that 15 seconds is a reasonable period for someone to type and send one message. If the estimated period is larger than 15 seconds, we assume that the estimated busy period is 15 seconds long and ends at the time when the text message is received.

3. STOCHASTIC PCD ANALYSIS

We show the architecture of PCD followed by its components and the design choices we have made.

3.1 Architecture

Notation:

$X[n]$: The input time series or a certain data point of the input time series indexed by n.

$P[n]$ and $Q[n]$: If the input time series is 2-dimensional, then $P[n]$ and $Q[n]$ represent the time series of the first and the second dimension, respectively.

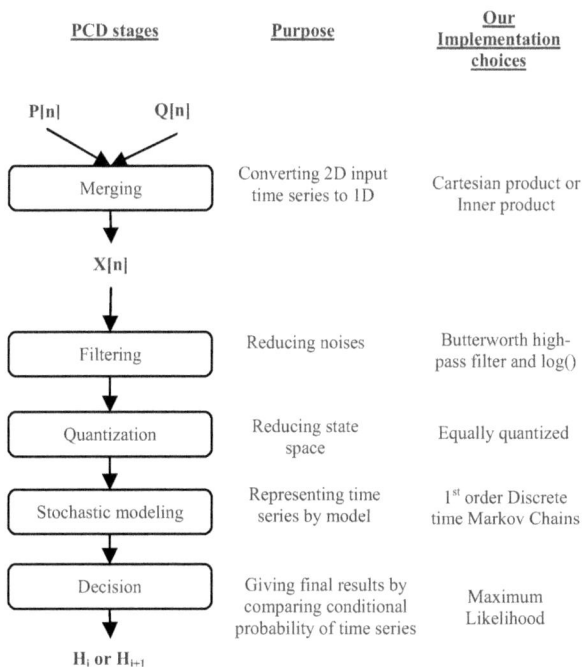

Figure 7. PCD analysis

PCD inputs a time series of response times and outputs which hypothesis is more likely to be true. The input time series is either 1-dimesional or 2-dimensional, is discrete in time, and can be discrete or continuous in value.

As shown in Figure 7, PCD analysis has a 5-stage design, which is partly inspired by Automatic Speech Recognition [13]. The input time series are processed through each applicable stage and the private information of interest is generated in the end.

1. The first stage, *merging,* is only applied when the PCD input time series is 2-dimensional. The merging stage will convert $P[n]$ and $Q[n]$ to a new time series, denoted as $X[n]$ for convenience. This stage reduces dimensionality for ease of classification but retains the information contained in both $P[n]$ and $Q[n]$.

2. The next stage, *filtering,* eliminates the noise contained in series $X[n]$. If $X[n]$ is noisy and this stage is skipped, it is likely Eve cannot gain an information advantage (i.e., accuracy is not much higher than 50%). The filtering stage inputs a time series and outputs another time series. Through filtering, the frequency components where noise resides will be eliminated.

3. The third stage is *quantization*, which reduces the number of possible values of the time series (i.e., size of the sample space). When there are more possible values, a larger the number of parameters will be needed in the next stage.

4. The fourth stage, *stochastic modeling*, which has two stochastic models for the two hypotheses. A stochastic model represents a variable-length time series through a fixed and small set of parameters. Through stochastic models, two operations are available: 1) to estimate the parameters of the stochastic models by given time series and 2) to evaluate the probability of a time series given the model.

5. The final stage, *detection*, is to make the detection decision based on the probability of a time series given the pre-trained models trained.

Assumptions and limitations. PCD assumes that the private information of interest (i.e., whether two targets are communicating; whether nodes Sybil nodes) does not change during the period that PCD probing is performed. This assumption indicates that the time resolution of PCD may be limited and application-dependent. Furthermore, high-frequency target probing may also cause the detection of the attack by the targets. In contrast, in passive probing, such as Instant Messaging, adversary detection is irrelevant since PCD is only applicable when there is an active conversation between the adversary and the targets.

Stochastic PCD can be applied effectively in network protocols where stochastic models capture the time series of probe responses accurately, and when signal processing can eliminate most of the noise introduced by active third-party nodes. The former suggests that stochastic PCD is well suited in random access networks (e.g., CSMA/CA), since Markov Chains can model them properly. In contrast, stochastic PCD is not easily applicable to non-random-access networks such as TDMA. The latter suggests that if the traffic between the target and the third-party nodes (e.g., web browsing, video streaming, and SSH) is different from the traffic between the targets (e.g., VoIP communication), the filtering component of PCD can effectively remove the noise brought by the third-party nodes. However, if the traffic between the targets and third-party nodes is the same with the traffic between the targets, PCD may experience false detection. Despite this, by repeatedly performing PCD, the adversary can still determine the long-term relationship between the targets [9]. Detection confidence increases as the number of communication instances increase.

Optional stages. Some of the stages are optional or unnecessary in certain situations. If the input is 1-dimensional, the merging stage is skipped. If the input time series is not noisy, the filtering stage can be skipped. If the input time series are discrete-valued and the number of distinct values is small enough, the third stage (quantization) can be skipped. If Eve is training models, the last stage is skipped.

3.2 Components

We will describe the choices of each component of PCD. Although our choices are not optimal due to the large design space, our choices do show the achievability of PCD with reasonable accuracy as seen later in the evaluation section. Finding better component implementations, such as trying other filters or stochastic models, would be among the important future work.

3.2.1 Merging Stage

We have two choices, Cartesian and Inner products, to implement the merging stage. The former is suitable for discrete input time series (e.g., IM application) while the latter is suitable for continuous input time series (e.g., WiFi application).

Cartesian Product. If P[n] and Q[n] are discrete in values, the Cartesian product is the simplest way to merge the two time series. For example, if two input time series have sample space (possible values) {0,1}, then the output time series will a sample space {{0,0}, {0,1}, {1,0}, {1,1}} which contains four difference values. The formula of the Cartesian product merging can be written as

$$X[n]=\{P[n], Q[n]\} \text{ for every n.}$$

The size of the new state space is the square of the size of the original state space. However, the Cartesian product has the potential problem of state space explosion, i.e. when the new state space becomes so large that the amount of training data for the stochastic models becomes unwieldy. Therefore, if the input time series is continuous in value, the Cartesian product is inappropriate and the following inner product should be used.

Inner Product. The inner product merge two (continuous-valued or discrete-valued) time series into one, while retaining the information of P[n] and Q[n].

$$X[n]=P[n]Q[n] \text{ for every n}$$

The idea comes from the fact that the inner product is a way to measure the *similarity* between two vectors. For example, the Fourier transform is a function of frequency that converts a time series to the magnitude of a given frequency. The value of a Fourier transform at frequency f is the sum of inner product of the time series and a sine/cosine function. Similarly, then the new X[n] will go up or down when both P[n] and Q[n] go up or down and hence X[n] keeps the information of P[n] and Q[n].

3.2.2 Filtering Stage

The filtering stage uses digital filters to improve the quality of the input time series data to get a better final PCD accuracy. A digital linear filter of input X[n] is a mechanism to process a time series by calculating the difference equation as shown below. The parameters a_i and b_i decide the behavior of a causal filter and N is the order of the filter.

$$Y[n] = \sum_{i=1}^{N} b_i Y[n-i] + \sum_{i=0}^{N} a_i X[n-i]$$

High-Pass Filtering. A high-pass filter is a filter that attenuates the low frequency components of a signal. The frequency components with frequency lower than a given cut-off frequency

will have lowered magnitude. Similarly, a low-pass filter attenuates the high frequency components of a signal. Modern filter design use a prototype filter (e.g., the Butterworth filter) and convert it to be low-pass, high-pass, or an even band-pass filter with different cut-off frequencies. When applying high-pass or low-pass filters on the filtering stage, Eve should choose the type of filter (e.g. Butterworth, Elliptic filters), the order (the value of N), and the cut-off frequency such that the final PCD accuracy is maximized. Our empirical experience on the WiFi application shows that the type and the order of the filter do not have much impact, but the cut-off frequency dominates the performance.

Log. log() can be applied before or after the filtering such that Eve can emphasis the signal change in small values. This is because log() is an increasing and concave function. Other increasing and concave functions, such as the square root, should have a similar effect. Note that if the log transformation is applied before filtering, the inner product of merging stage becomes an addition.

3.2.3 Quantization Stage

If the input time series is continuous or is discrete but the set of possible values (sample space) is large, its value should be converted to a smaller discrete set for efficient stochastic modeling. Stochastic models have parameters which need to be trained before use. In general, a stochastic model with more parameters needs to be trained with a larger set of training data.

We use the simplest quantization scheme which divides the interval between the maximum value and the minimum value into equal size. However, if log() is applied in the previous stage, the equal-quantization can be regarded as log-scale quantization.

3.2.4 Stochastic Modeling Stage

Our choice of stochastic model is 1st order discrete-time Markov Chains due to the fact that it is simple, easy to analyze, and the number of parameters is relatively small. The more parameters included, the more data that is required to train the model. However, it is a common practice in signal processing to model signals by 1st order Markov Chains first and then use more complex stochastic models[5] if necessary.

Markov Chain. A discrete-time Markov Chain is a sequence of random variables $Y_1, Y_2,...$ with the Markov property, that is the state transition from Y_n to Y_{n+1} will not be affected by any of the previous states $Y_{n-1},...,Y_1$. Or we can write as $Pr\{Y_{n+1}|Y_n\}=Pr\{Y_{n+1}|Y_n,Y_{n-1},...,Y_1\}$. We can think of Markov Chains as capturing the relationship between a data point and the next data point in a time series. As a Markov Chain characterizes all pairs of adjacent data points, it characterizes a time series. The parameters of a Markov Chain are the transition probabilities from one state to another state. Therefore, for a state space of size k, a Markov Chain has k^2 parameters, namely a transition matrix.

3.2.5 Detection Stage

Maximum likelihood. The previous stage gives the conditional probability of a time series, given the stochastic models. In this stage, the conditional probabilities will be used to make the final detection result. One of the most popular methods is maximum likelihood (ML), where the detection result belongs to the hypothesis that has larger conditional probability. For the private

---

[5] For example, semi-Markov models and N-order Markov chains are more general and have more parameters (more training data). Hence, it is not practical to deal with the small set of data in the IM application.

communication detection, suppose M_0 and M_1 are models corresponding to H_0 and H_1, the result is

H_i, where i=1$\{Pr\{Y|M_0\}<Pr\{Y|M_1\}\}$

For the remote Sybil detection, suppose M_2 and M_3 are two models corresponding to H_2 and H_3, the result is

H_i, where i=1$\{Pr\{Y|M_2\}<Pr\{Y|M_3\}\}$+2

4. EVALUATION

Table 2. PCD settings in two applications

		WiFi	Instant Messaging
Time series		Continuous-valued; Discrete-time	Binary-valued; Discrete-time
1.Merging stage	private communication detection (2-D)	Inner product	Cartesian product
	remote Sybil detection (1-D)	N/A	N/A
2. Filtering stage		Butterworth high-pass filter with order 10; log() used	N/A
3. Quantization stage		Equally quantized by 12	N/A
4. Stochastic modeling stage		1st order discrete time Markov Chain	1st order discrete time Markov Chain
5. Decision stage		Maximum Likelihood	Maximum Likelihood

First we will show what the time series in both applications looks like. For WiFi application where the signal is noisy, we also show why we would need filtering due to the signal characteristics. We then show the accuracy of both applications as the performance index. The accuracy is defined as the number of correct detections divided by the total number of detections. Since we have half samples in H_0 and another half samples in H_1, a blind guess (50% accuracy) becomes the baseline comparison rate. If the accuracy is much higher than 50%, we can say Eve gains advantages through PCD.

The performance of both applications is evaluated under the settings as shown in Table 2. It is notable that since the time series of IM is a binary-valued (whether a targeted node is busy typing to Eve), we can use the Cartesian product in merging, and skip the filtering and quantization stages.

4.1 Signal characteristics

Two samples of time series for WiFi application for private communication detection are shown in Figure 8. We have two samples of 10000 data points (~1000 seconds) under the hypotheses H_0 and H_1. We can see that values are mostly close to 0ms and around 500ms. The 500ms values are due to the packet lost. Because Eve sends VoIP packets through a VoIP proxy, the proxy will retransmit if the responses are not received in 500ms as defined by Timer E in RFC 3261 [12]. In this figure, it is not easy to visually find the difference of these two signals, except the two spikes in H_0.

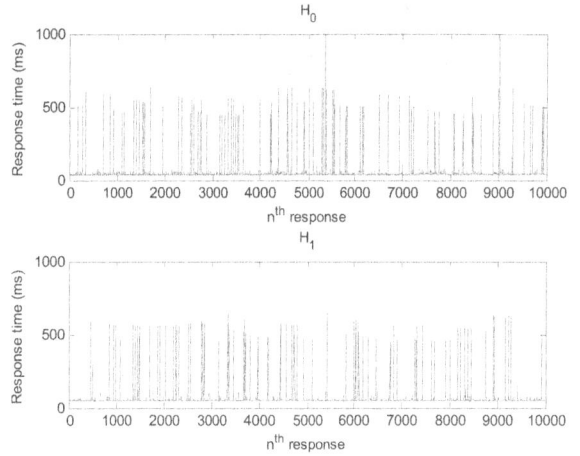

Figure 8. Two examples (H_0 and H_1) of WiFi time series for private communication detection

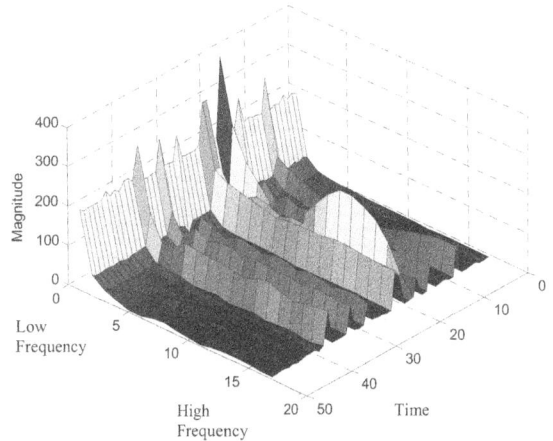

Figure 9. Frequency-time analysis of the H_0 signal in Figure 8 shows strong frequency component in high frequency

Frequency analysis helps to analyze time series in another aspect. A signal can be presented in the time domain as a time series, as well as in the frequency domain. A signal in the time domain is a function of time to show the magnitude at different time. On the other hand, a signal in the frequency domain is a function of frequency to show the magnitude at different frequencies. The Fourier transform can translate a signal from the time to frequency domain. Therefore, by applying the Fourier transform, we can examine a signal in the frequency domain, allowing us to explore the properties that are not easily observed in the time domain. However, the original Fourier transform has the limitation of being a global analysis. For example, if a sine wave appears only in the beginning of the time series, when in the frequency domain, we do not know whether this wave appears in the beginning or in the end of the time series. Such limitation bring us the problem that we will not know if a pattern shown in the frequency domain appears in the whole time series, or just in part of it.

To overcome the drawback of frequency analysis, time-frequency analysis can be used to look at the time and frequency simultaneously. For example, Short Time Fourier Transform (STFT) does Fourier transform on a portion of the signal, repeated many times so that the whole signal is covered. Figure 9 shows the frequency-time analysis of the signals in Figure 8. It is particularly noticeable that the low frequency components remains high at all time. It is easy to say that the low-frequency components are either very important or not wanted at all (noise). From this observation, we tested high-pass and low-pass filters with different cut-off frequency and found that that removing the low-frequency components via high-pass filters helps to improve the performance of PCD in WiFi significantly.

But why are the high-frequency components important and why are the low-frequency components noisy? In Figure 10, we zoom in and see the first 500 data points of the Figure 8 signals. Except for the spikes caused by packet lost, the response time is about 50ms with small fluctuations. The fluctuation is network jitter caused by Internet switching and the WiFi back-off. Since the side-channel we are interested in is the WiFi back-off behavior, the fluctuation of the signals may contain the useful information we are looking for. Since $\log(x)$ is a strictly increasing and concave function when $x>1$, it can emphasis the signals in small values, where the fluctuations are. We applied $\log()$ before and after high-pass filtering (twice), finding that it works.

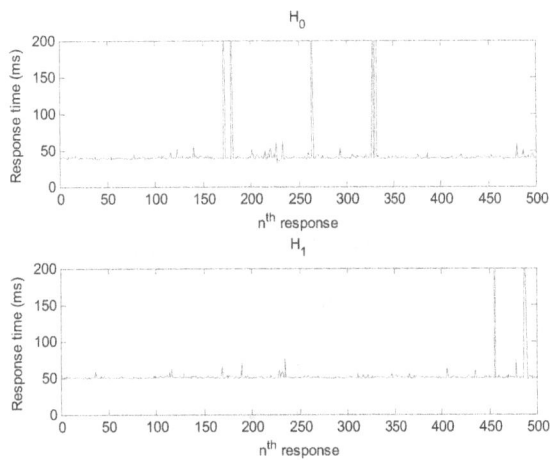

Figure 10. Detail version of Figure 8

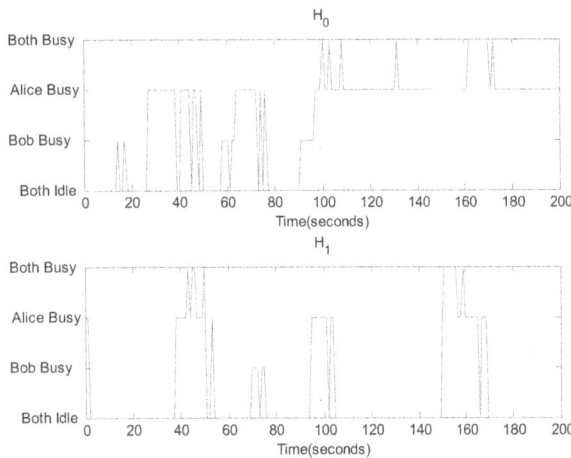

Figure 11. Two examples (H_0 and H_1) of IM time series for private communication detection

We now look at the signals of IM in Figure 11. These are two samples of H_0 (no communication between Alice and Bob) and H_1 (communication between Alice and Bob) in the form of the busy status of Alice and Bob. In the experiments we have samples of

300 seconds, but here we only show the first 200 seconds. Using the Cartesian product to merge the busy status of both targeted nodes, the time series will have four states. These refer to both nodes being busy, only Alice as busy, only Bob as busy and both nodes not busy, as perceived by Eve. Unlike the signals in WiFi which are quite noisy, the signals here seem simpler and there seem to be some patterns.

Through these patterns in the IM time series, we created the first version of PCD which contains only the last two stages. This idea works and then we apply it to WiFi but encounter difficulties because the WiFi signals are very noisy, such that the accuracy is very close to the baseline (50%; blind guess) or even worse than the baseline. To deal with the noise, we brought the first three stages to PCD, finding that it improves the results considerably.

4.2 WiFi

The accuracy of PCD in the WiFi application is shown in Figure 12 for private communication detection and in Figure 13 for remote Sybil detection. The square mark shows the average accuracy using the samples obtained in the university café for training and testing. We use one sample (10000 data points) to train the system and use the other 11 samples for testing. We again use cross-validation so that any one sample used as the training sample will produce an accuracy measure. Thus, averaging of 12 accuracy measures becomes the average accuracy for our results.

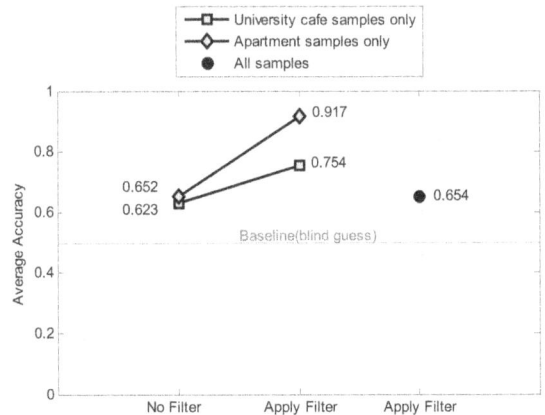

Figure 12. Performance of private communication detection in WiFi (high-pass Butterworth filter with normalized cut-off normalized frequency f=0.3, No log() applied)

The diamond marks show the average accuracy when we use the samples obtained in the apartment setting for training and testing. In both of the figures the average accuracy also rises significantly after applying filtering. In addition, we can see that the performance for the apartment samples is better than the performance for the university café samples. The reason is obvious: the university café environment is noisier (with more WiFi users) than the apartment.

We then consider the case where the system is trained by one sample but is tested on all other samples from both university café and the apartment. This is a way to evaluate the impact of environment variation to the detection. The results are showed by the circle marks in both of the figures. It is not surprising that the performance is lower because the trained models do not fit the testing samples closely. We will discuss about the environment variation in section 6.

We have the following findings:

1. **High-frequency components are useful.** When high-pass filters are applied, the accuracy improves significantly. The reason is that the transmission jitter due to WiFi back-off is subtle in the time scale.

2. **Small values in signals are more important.** It is human nature to notice the spikes (large values) in a time series. However, in this application, small values are more important, as we observed that applying Log() helps to improve accuracy. The reason is that the small fluctuations contain more useful information.

In other words, PCD is successful in this WiFi application because it extracts the useful information from the small time scale (high frequency) and small values from time series. It is different from most signals where high frequency components and visually-recognizable patterns have the most useful information.

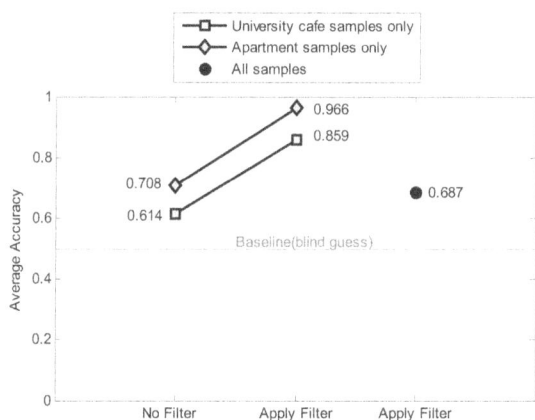

Figure 13. Performance of remote communication Sybil in WiFi (high-pass Butterworth filter with normalized cut-off normalized frequency f=0.3, log() applied before and after high-pass filtering)

4.3 Instant Messaging

The number of samples in the IM condition is extremely limited. Therefore we use a version of cross-validation in which k (k<10 for private communication detection and k<20 for remote Sybil detection) samples are randomly selected to train models and the rest are used to evaluate accuracy. The average accuracy conditioned in the number of training samples is the performance of interest.

Both goals show that average accuracy is above 50% which is the baseline when a blind guess is applied instead of PCD. In addition, both goals also suggest that more samples would give higher average accuracy. For private communication detection, as shown in Figure 14, the average accuracy grows from 65.0% to 70.0% as the number of training samples increases from 1 to 9. Similarly, for remote Sybil detection, as shown in Figure 15, the average accuracy grows from 67.4% to 92.5% as number of training samples increases from 1 to 19.

Therefore we have the following findings for the Instant Messaging application. 1) PCD is achievable in IM since the average accuracy is much better than the baseline. 2) There is a

trend for IM application to gain higher performance when more samples are available.

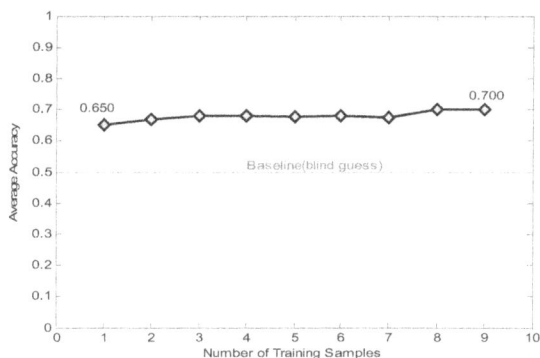

Figure 14. Performance of private communication detection in IM (total 10 samples per hypothesis)

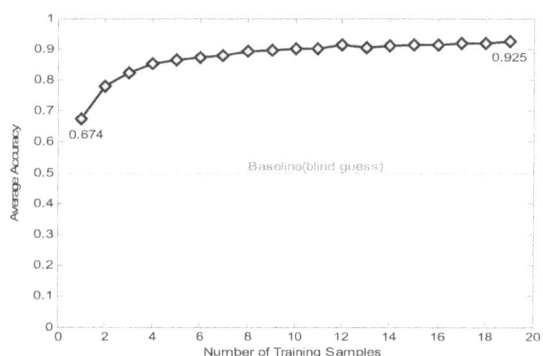

Figure 15. Performance of remote Sybil detection in IM (total 20 samples per hypothesis)

5. COUNTERMEASURES

Three common ways to prevent side-channel attacks are blocking the side-channels, adding noise to the side-channels, and removing the source of side-channels. Firewalls can block the probe packets, such as the ICMP or SIP OPTIONS we used in the WiFi application. However, some packets must pass the firewalls; otherwise applications will not work. Eve may exploit these packets for side-channels. Therefore, blocking suspicious periodic traffic appears to be a better solution than just blocking all packets of certain types.

Adding noise to the side-channels is one possible remedy to this attack, but it requires that we consider where to perform and what noise to add. In the WiFi application, if noise is added in WiFi network, we need to modify the MAC protocol, which is very undesirable. If noise is added in the application proxy, it may be possible but the WiFi user may likely need to convince the application proxy administrator/designers. Adding trivial noise (e.g. a delay randomly chosen from a uniform distribution) may not work because Eve may use another filter to remove the trivial noise, and such added noise is restricted (e.g., the longer the latency is, the worse the quality of network is.). Therefore, this approach needs to be examined through additional experiments.

The third way to defend PCD is removing the source of side-channels, the resource use under contention. In the WiFi application, if CSMA/CA is replaced by TDMA or CDMA, then there is no radio-channel contention. However, replacing a radio technology is often difficult due to non-technical reasons, such as deployment and costs. In the IM application, one trivial countermeasure is to disable or block the composing notification messages. However, this approach may not work, because ordinary messages still provide information about the timing of the messages being sent. Eve can estimate the period that the contact spends typing to the investigator by with a constant value, such as 3 seconds. In addition, adding artificial jitters to messages may break the semantics of Instant Messaging where the goal is that *instant* messaging should be provided.

6. ENVIRONMENTAL VARIATION

The WiFi application shows environment variation reduces the accuracy. In WiFi, both goals have lower accuracy when we use all samples from the university café and apartment for training and testing.

Does it mean that PCD can only work if Eve can obtain many training samples from the place where the targeted nodes reside? From the experiences of speech recognition, from which our architecture is inspired, it may not be true. Speech recognition initially supports only speaker-dependent recognition, meaning that the training and testing samples should come from the same source. However, later speaker-independent recognition is achieved by adjusting the variance, such as using a linear transform of existing models from many speakers [8][13][14]. Therefore, for PCD, once we have enough data from different network environments, similar things can be done to adapt the trained models to the variation of network environment. In other words, training may be achieved from small samples over a variety of situations, rather than just the specific targeted network environment. Also, Eve may use a probe time series to find the optimal way of adjusting trained models.

7. RELATED WORK

PCD is an untraditional side-channel attack. Original side-channel attacks use side-channel information which comes from emitted signals (e.g. power electromagnetic and acoustic signals) from the implementations of systems [1][2][3][4][15][16][33]. However, the side-channels used by PCD are caused by resource contention, not by power, fault or computation complexity. In addition, the methods used to analyze side-channel information are different. Differential power analysis uses averaging or cumulant, which is based on probability moments, to cancel out Gaussian noise in the time domain, while PCD extracts the information from certain frequencies in the frequency domain [16][17]. Moreover, PCD concerns the private information of network nodes, not a single node.

PCD is also an remote traffic analysis. Traditional traffic analysis extracts private information from the secure or anonymous network given the eavesdropping ability. [7][26][29][30][34][35][37]. Remote traffic analysis can obtain the traffic analysis from remote sites through sending requests and analyzing timing of the responses. Gong, Kiyavash, and Borisov suggests that a remote host can ping a DSL router by ICMP packets and use the time series of response time as the fingerprint of the website accessed by a computer served by the router [10]. However, their approach does not deal with noise and randomness. They used Dynamic Time Warping (DTW) distance to match the observed time series and multiple time series of different websites which were recorded previously. Although DTW can identify shifted and stretched signals, it cannot deal with stochastic signals.

In other words, two time series that are realization of the same random process are regarded as different although actually they have the same probability properties. Furthermore, if two computers access the Internet by the same DSL router, the pattern in time series data is likely to be heavily distorted and not recognizable. Moreover, ICMP blocking is a standard function in modern network devices and therefore such attacks can be avoided. In contrast, PCD is designed to be performed in the application layer and pass through application proxies.

In Instant Messaging, John Resig et al. correlate the online/offline status with friendship [27]. If the status of two users shows they become online and offline at almost the same time, these two users are inferred to be friends. However, the information they are dealing with (users' online/offline status) is explicitly provided by users. Although drawing upon their work, PCD will detect the relationship between network nodes with timing information that is not explicitly provided.

There are a number of studies of Sybil detection in wireless, peer-to-peer networks, and other areas. Levine et al. provide a comprehensive survey [18]. They conclude that Sybil attack defenses can be grouped into four categories: trusted certification, resource testing, recurring costs and fees and trusted devices. Our remote Sybil detection is a variation of resource testing, which asks the nodes to access certain exclusive resources (e.g., radio channels) to show they are not Sybil nodes [24]. Unlike other resource testing methods, however, our method does not require the target or its neighbor to perform specific resource testing actions (i.e., that a node send packets to the radio channel at a designated time). In other words, our method can utilize the original networking environments without modifying the nodes or network behavior.

8. CONCLUSION

This paper proposes a problem of communication privacy where an ordinary user with no special ability (e.g. eavesdropping) is able to obtain communication information, even when direct observation is not possible. The solution to the problem is a stochastic attack that extracts non-traditional side-channel information caused by resource contention. As network jitters and delays make the side-channels very noisy, our approach treats the noise with signal processing and other techniques to boost the performance.

Although we discuss countermeasures, whether they will work or not is still unclear. It will be our first priority in future research to prove the effectiveness of countermeasures. Secondly, there are plenty of filters for noise reduction, such as Wiener filters and Wavelet Packet Decomposition. It would be beneficial to test more filters not only for this very problem, but also for bridging signal processing and side-channel attacks.

9. ACKNOWLEDGEMENTS

This research was supported in part by CyLab at Carnegie Mellon under grant DAAD19-02-1-0389 from the US Army Research Office. The first author was also partially supported by the MURI grant W 911 NF 0710287 from the Army Research Office. The views and conclusions contained in this document are those of the authors and should not be interpreted as representing the official policies, either expressed or implied, of any sponsoring institution, the U.S. government, or any other entity. The first author would like to thank Enlu Zhou for helpful discussion on stochastic analysis.

REFERENCES

[1] Agrawal, D., Archambeault, B., Rao, J., Rohatgi, P. 2002. *The EM Side-Channel(s)*. In Proceeding of Workshop on Cryptographic Hardware and Embedded Systems (CHES), 2002

[2] Asnov, D., and Agrawal, R., 2004. *Keyboard Acoustic Emanations*. In Proceeding of the IEEE Symposium on Security and Privacy, 2004

[3] Boneh, D., DeMillo, R. A., and Liptonm, R. J. 1997. *On the Importance of Checking Cryptographic Protocols for Faults*. In Proceeding of EUROCRYPT,1997

[4] Brier, E., Clavier, C., Olivier, F. 2004. *Correlation Power Analysis with a Leakage Model*. In Proceeding of Workshop on Cryptographic Hardware and Embedded Systems (CHES), 2004

[5] Chandra, R., Bahl, P., and Bahl, P. 2004. *MultiNet: Connecting to Multiple IEEE 802.11 Networks Using a Single Wireless Card*. In Proceeding of IEEE Infocom, 2004

[6] Danezis, G. and Diaz, C. 2008. *A survey of anonymous communication channels*. Microsoft Research Technical Report (MSR-TR-2008-35), Jan. 2008

[7] Dingledine, R., Mathewson, N., Syverson, P. 2004. *Tor: The second-generation onion router*. In Proceeding of the 13th USENIX Security Symposium, 2004

[8] Furui, S. 1986. Speaker-Independent Isolated Word Recognition Using Dynamic Features of Speech Spectrum. IEEE Transaction of Acoustics, Speech and Signal Processing, Vol. ASSP-34, No. 1, Feb 1986

[9] Gilbert, E., and Karahalios, K., 2009. *Predicting tie strength with social media*. In Proceeding of the 27th ACM International Conference on Human factors in computing systems (CHI), 2009

[10] Gong, X., Kiyavash, N., and Borisov, N. 2010. *Fingerprinting Websites Using Remote Traffic Analysis*. In Proceeding of ACM CCS, 2010

[11] Herrmann, M., Grothoff, C. 2011. *Privacy-Implications of Performance-Based Peer Selection by Onion-Routers: A Real-World Case Study Using I2P*. In Proceeding of Privacy Enhancing Technologies Symposium (PETS), 2011

[12] RFC 3261, *SIP: Session Initiation Protocol*. IETF

[13] Jurasky, D. and Martin, J. H. 2008. *Speech and Language Processing*. Pearson Prentice Hall, 2nd Edition.

[14] Lee, K.-F. 1988. *On Large-Vocabulary Speaker-Independent Continuous Speech Recognition*. Speech Communication. Elsevier Science Publishers

[15] Kocher, P.C. 1996. *Timing Attacks on Implementations of Diffie-Hellman, RSA, DSS, and Other Systems*. In Proceeding of CRYPTO, 1996.

[16] Kocher, P.C., Jaffe, J., Jun, B. 1999. *Differential Power Analysis*. In Proceeding of CRYPTO, 1999

[17] Le, T.-H., Clédière, J., Servière, and C., Lacoume, J.-L., 2007. *Noise Reduction in Side Channel Attack Using Fourth-Order Cumulant*. IEEE Transaction of Information Forensics and Security, Vol. 2, No. 4, December 2007.

[18] Levine, B. N., Shields, C., and Margolin, N. B. 2000. *A Survey of Solutions to the Sybil Attack*. Tech report 2006-052, University of Massachusetts Amherst, Amherst, MA, October 2006.

[19] Markoff, J. *Taking Spying to a Higher Level*. New York Times, Feb. 2006, http://www.nytimes.com/2006/02/25/technology/25data.htm, (accessed Dec 2, 2011)

[20] McKeay, M. *Taking Corporate Spying to a Higher Level*. Computerworld, 2006, http://blogs.computerworld.com/node/3396 (accessed Dec 2, 2011)

[21] OpenSips software, http://opensips.org

[22] Pidgin software, http://www.pidgin.im

[23] Pfitzmann, A., Pfitzmann, B., Waidner, M. 1991. *ISDN-MIXes: Untraceable Communication with Very Small Bandwidth Overhead*. In Proceeding of Communication in Distributed Systems. Springer-Verlag

[24] Newsome, J., Shi, E., Song, D. and Perrig, A. 2004 *The Sybil Attack in Sensor Networks: Analysis & Defenses*. In Proceeding of the ACM third international symposium on Information processing in sensor networks, 2004.

[25] Rabiner, L. 1989. *A Tutorial on Hidden Markov Models and Selected Applications in Speech Recognition*. In Proceeding of the IEEE, vol. 77, pp. 257–286, Feb 1989.

[26] Raymond, J.-F. 2001. *Traffic analysis: Protocols, attacks, design issues and open problems*. In Proceeding of International Workshop on Design Issues in Anonymity and Unobservability, 2001.

[27] Resig, J., Dawara, S., Homan, C.M., and Teredesai, A. 2004. *Extracting Social Networks from Instant Messaging Populations*. In Proceeding of LinkKDD, 2004

[28] Solomon, J., Johnson, C. *FBI Broke Law for Years in Phone Record Searches*. Washington Post, Jan. 2010

[29] Song, D. X., Wagner, D., Tian, X. 2001. *Timing Analysis of Keystrokes and Timing Attacks on SSH*. In Proceeding of USENIX Security, 2001

[30] Srivatsa, M., Iyengar, A., Liu, L. and Jiang, H. 2011. *Privacy in VoIP Networks: Flow Analysis Attacks and Defense*. IEEE Transaction on Parallel and Distributed Systems, Vol. 22, No. 4, April 2011

[31] Superstructure Group. *SiD Case Study in Drug Intelligence*. rel. 1.1, February 2011, www.superstructuregroup.com/Resources/SiDCaseStudy_DrugIntell.pdf (accessed Aug. 20, 2011)

[32] Tan, P.-N., Kumar, V. 2006. *Introduction to Data Mining*. Addison-Wesley

[33] Messerges, T.S., and Dabbish, E. A. 1999. *Investigations of Power Analysis Attacks on Smartcards*. In Proceeding of USENIX Workshop on Smartcard Technology, 1999

[34] Wang, X., Chen, S., and Jajodia, S. 2005. *Tracking Anonymous Peer-to-Peer VoIP Calls on the Internet*, In Proceeding of the 12th ACM conference on Computer and communications security (CCS), 2005

[35] Wright, C. V., Ballard, L., Coull, S. E., Monrose, F., and Masson, G. M. 2008. *Spot me if you can: Uncovering Spoken Phrases in Encrypted VoIP Conversations*. In Proceeding of IEEE Symposium on Security and Privacy, 2008

[36] Xia, L., Kumar, S., Yang, X., Gopalakrishnan, P., Liu, Y., Schoenberg, S., Guo, X. 2011. *Virtual WiFi: Bring Virtualization from Wired to Wireless.* In Proceeding of ACM International Conference on Virtual Execution Environments (VEE), 2011

[37] Zhang, F., He, W., Liu, X., and Bridges, P. G. 2011. *Inferring Users' Online Activities Through Traffic Analysis.* In Proceeding of ACM WiSec, 2011.

Detection of Malicious Packet Dropping in Wireless Ad Hoc Networks Based on Privacy-Preserving Public Auditing

Tao Shu
Department of Computer Science and
Engineering
Oakland University
Rochester, MI 48309, USA
shu@oakland.edu

Marwan Krunz
Department of Electrical and Computer
Engineering
University of Arizona
Tucson, AZ 85721, USA
krunz@email.arizona.edu

ABSTRACT

In a multi-hop wireless ad hoc network, packet losses are attributed to harsh channel conditions and intentional packet discard by malicious nodes. In this paper, while observing a sequence of packet losses, we are interested in determining whether losses are due to link errors only, or due to the combined effect of link errors and malicious drop. We are especially interested in insider's attacks, whereby a malicious node that is part of the route exploits its knowledge of the communication context to selectively drop a small number of packets that are critical to network performance. Because the packet dropping rate in this case is comparable to the channel error rate, conventional algorithms that are based on detecting the packet loss rate cannot achieve satisfactory detection accuracy. To improve the detection accuracy, we propose to exploit the correlations between lost packets. Furthermore, to ensure truthful calculation of these correlations, we develop a homomorphic linear authenticator (HLA) based public auditing architecture that allows the detector to verify the truthfulness of the packet loss information reported by nodes. This architecture is privacy preserving, collusion proof, and incurs low communication and storage overheads. Through extensive simulations, we verify that the proposed mechanism achieves significantly better detection accuracy than conventional methods such as a maximum-likelihood based detection.

Categories and Subject Descriptors

C.2.0 [**Computer-Communication Networks**]: General—*Security and Protection (e.g., firewalls)*

General Terms

Security, reliability, algorithms, design

Keywords

Denial-of-service, malicious user detection, homomorphic linear authentication, wireless ad hoc networks, security

1. INTRODUCTION

1.1 Motivation

In a multi-hop wireless network, nodes cooperate in relaying/routing traffic. An adversary can exploit this cooperative nature to launch denial-of-service (DoS) attacks. For example, the adversary may first pretend to be a cooperative node in the route discovery process. Once being included in a route, the adversary may start maliciously dropping packets. In the most straightforward form of this attack, the malicious node simply stops forwarding packets received from upstream nodes, completely disrupting the traffic delivery between the source and the destination. Eventually, such severe DoS attacks can paralyze the network by partitioning its topology.

Even though persistent packet dropping can effectively degrade the performance of the network, from the attacker's standpoint performing such an "always-on" attack has its disadvantages in terms of the ease of detection [22]. A malicious node that is part of the route can actually exploit its knowledge of the network protocols and the communication context to launch an *insider's attack*, aiming at achieving the same attack effect but at a much lower risk of being detected. Specifically, the malicious node can identify the importance of various packets and drop a small number of packets that are deemed highly critical to the performance of the network. These important packets are typically control packets. For example, in a frequency-hopping network, these packets may convey frequency hopping sequences; in an ad hoc cognitive radio network, they could be the packets that carry the idle channel lists (i.e., white spaces) that are used to establish a network-wide control channel. By targeting these critical packets, the authors in [18, 21, 22] have shown that a non-persistent insider's attack can cause significant damage to the network performance. In this paper, we are interested in combating such an insider's attack. In particular, we are interested in the problem of detecting the events of selective packet drops and identifying the malicious node(s) responsible for these drops.

Detecting malicious selective packet dropping is extremely challenging in a highly dynamic wireless environment. The difficulty stems from the requirement that we need to not only detect the location (or hop) where the packet drop took place, but also identify whether the drop is intentional or not. Specifically, because of the open nature of the wireless medium, the quality of the channel typically fluctuates due to fading, shadowing, interference, and background noise. As a result, a packet drop in the route could be caused by harsh channel conditions (a.k.a., link errors) or by malicious behavior. In some cases, e.g., a highly mobile environment, link errors are quite significant. So, a malicious node can camouflage its attack under the background of harsh channel conditions by selectively dropping a small number of highly important packets. In this case, observing the packet loss rate is not enough to accurately identify the exact cause of a packet loss, because the packet drop rate by the malicious node is comparable to that of wireless link errors. Clearly, deciding whether a packet drop is intentional or unintentional in such an ambiguous setup is a challenging problem.

The above problem has not been well addressed in the literature. As discussed in Section 2, most of the related works preclude the ambiguity of the environment by assuming that malicious dropping is the only source of packet loss, so that there is no need to account for the impact of link errors. On the other hand, for the small number of works that differentiate between link errors and malicious packet drops, their detection algorithms usually require the number of dropped packets by the attacker to be significantly higher than link errors, in order to provide an acceptable detection accuracy.

1.2 Main Contribution and Paper Organization

In this paper, we develop an accurate algorithm for detecting selective packet drops made by insider malicious nodes. Our algorithm also provides a truthful and publicly verifiable decision statistics as a proof to support the detection decision. The high detection accuracy is achieved by exploiting the correlations between the positions of lost packets, as calculated from the packet-loss bitmap (a bitmap describing the lost/received status of each packet in a sequence of consecutive packet transmissions). The basic idea behind this method is that even though malicious dropping may result in a packet loss rate that is comparable to normal channel losses, the stochastic processes that characterize the two phenomena exhibit different correlation structures (equivalently, different patterns of packet losses). Therefore, by detecting the correlations between lost packets, one can decide whether the packet loss is purely due to regular link errors, or is a combined effect of link error and malicious drop. Our algorithm takes into account the cross-statistics between lost packets to make a more informative decision, and thus is in sharp contrast to the conventional methods that rely only on the distribution of the number of lost packets.

The main challenge in realizing our mechanism lies in how to guarantee that the packet-loss bitmaps reported by individual nodes along the route are truthful, i.e., reflect the actual status of each packet transmission. Such truthfulness is essential for correct calculation of the correlation between lost packets. This challenge is not trivial, because it is natural for an attacker to report false information to the detection algorithm to avoid being detected. For example, the malicious node may understate its packet-loss bitmap, i.e., some packets may have been dropped by the node but the node reports that these packets have been forwarded. Therefore, some auditing mechanism is needed to verify the truthfulness of the reported information. Considering that a typical wireless device is resource-constrained, we also require that a user should be able to delegate the burden of auditing and detection to some public server to save its own resources.

Our solution to the above public-auditing problem is constructed based on the homomorphic linear authenticator (HLA) cryptographic primitive [2][3][24], which is basically a signature scheme widely used in cloud computing and storage server systems to provide a proof of storage from the server to entrusting clients [25]. However, direct application of HLA does not solve our problem well, mainly because in our problem setup, there can be more than one malicious node along the route. These nodes may collude (by exchanging information) during the attack and when being asked to submit their reports. For example, a packet and its associated HLA signature may be dropped at an upstream malicious node, so a downstream malicious node does not receive this packet and the HLA signature from the route. However, this downstream attacker can still open a back-channel to request this information from the upstream malicious node. When being audited, the downstream malicious node can still provide valid proof for the reception of the packet. So packet dropping at the upstream malicious node is not detected. Such collusion is unique to our problem, because in the cloud computing/storage server scenario, a file is uniquely stored at a single server, so there are no other parties for the server to collude with. We show that our new HLA construction is collusion-proof.

Our construction also provides the following new features. First, *privacy-preserving*: the public auditor should not be able to decern the content of a packet delivered along the route through the auditing information submitted by individual hops, no matter how many independent reports of the auditing information are submitted to the auditor. Second, our construction incurs low communication and storage overheads at intermediate nodes. This makes our mechanism applicable to a wide range of wireless devices, including low-cost wireless sensors that have very limited bandwidth and memory capacities. This is also in sharp contrast to the typical storage-server scenario, where bandwidth/storage is not considered an issue.

The remainder of this paper is organized as follows. In Section 2 we review the related work. The system/adversary models and problem statement are described in Section 3. We present the proposed scheme and analyze its security performance and overheads in Section 4. Simulation results are presented in Section 5, and we conclude the paper in Section 6.

2. RELATED WORK

Depending on how much weight a detection algorithm gives to link errors relative to malicious packet drops, the related work can be classified into the following two categories.

The first category aims at high malicious dropping rates, where most (or all) lost packets are caused by malicious dropping. In this case, the impact of link errors is ignored. Most related work falls into this category. Based on the methodology used to identify the attacking nodes, these works can be further classified into four sub-categories. The first sub-category is based on credit systems [7][27]. A credit system provides an incentive for cooperation. A node receives credit by relaying packets for others, and uses its credit to send its own packets. As a result, a maliciously node that continuous to drop packets will eventually deplete its credit, and will not be able to send its own traffic. The second sub-category is based on reputation systems [9][6][11][16][17][8][4]. A reputation system relies on neighbors to monitor and identify misbehaving nodes. A node with a high packet dropping rate is given a bad reputation by its neighbors. This reputation information is propagated periodically throughout the network and is used as an important metric in selecting routes. Consequently, a malicious node will be excluded from any route. The third sub-category of works relies on end-to-end or hop-to-hop acknowledgements to directly locate the hops where packets are lost [15][19][20]. A hop of high packet loss rate will be excluded from the route. The fourth sub-category addresses the problem using cryptographic methods. For example, the work in [14] utilizes Bloom filters to construct proofs for the number of packets that are forwarded at each node. By examining the number of relayed packets at successive hops along a route, one can identify suspicious hops that exhibit high packet loss rates. Similarly, the method in [13] traces the forwarding records of a particular packet at each intermediate node by formulating the tracing problem as a Renyi-Ulam game. The first hop where the packet is no longer forwarded is considered a suspect for misbehaving.

The second category targets the scenario where the number of maliciously dropped packets is significantly higher than that caused by link errors, but the impact of link errors is non-negligible. Certain knowledge of the wireless channel is necessary in this case. The authors in [23] proposed to shape the traffic at the MAC layer of the source node according to a certain statistical distribution, so that intermediate nodes are able to estimate the rate of received traffic by sampling the packet arrival times. By comparing the source traffic rate with the estimated received rate, the detection algorithm decides whether the discrepancy in rates, if any, is within a reasonable range such that the difference can be considered as being caused by normal channel impairments only, or caused by malicious dropping, otherwise. The works in [10] and [26] proposed to detect malicious packet dropping by counting the number of lost packets. If the number of lost packets is significantly larger than the expected packet loss rate made by link errors, then with high probability a malicious node is contributing to packet losses.

All methods mentioned above do not perform well when malicious packet dropping is highly selective. More specifically, for the credit-system-based method, a malicious node may still receive enough credits by forwarding most of the packets it receives from upstream nodes. Similarly, in the reputation-based approach, the malicious node can maintain a reasonably good reputation by forwarding most of the packets to the next hop. As for the acknowledgement-based method, the Bloom-filter scheme, and all the mechanisms in the second category, merely counting the number of lost packets does not give a sufficient ground to detect the real culprit that is causing packet losses. This is because the difference in the number of lost packets between the link-error-only case and the link-error-plus-malicious-dropping case is small when the attacker drops only a few packets. Consequently, the detection accuracy of these algorithms deteriorates when malicious drops become highly selective.

Our study targets the challenging situation where link errors and malicious dropping lead to comparable packet loss rates. The effort in the literature on this problem has been quite preliminary, and there is a few related works. Note that the cryptographic methods proposed in [21] to counter selective packet jamming target a different issue than the detection problem studied in this paper. The methods in [21] delay a jammer from recognizing the significance of a packet after the packet has been successfully transmitted, so that there is no time for the jammer to conduct jamming based on the content/importance of the packet. Instead of trying to detect any malicious behavior, the approach in [21] is proactive, and hence incurs overheads regardless of the presence or absence of attackers.

3. SYSTEM MODELS AND PROBLEM STATEMENT

3.1 Network and Channel Models

Consider an arbitrary path P_{SD} in a multi-hop wireless ad hoc network, as shown in Figure 1. The source node S continuously sends packets to the destination node D through intermediate nodes $n_1, \ldots, n_K$, where n_i is the upstream node of n_{i+1}, for $1 \leq i \leq K-1$. We assume that S is aware of the route P_{SD}, as in Dynamic Source Routing (DSR) [12]. If DSR is not used, S can identify the nodes in P_{SD} by performing a traceroute operation.

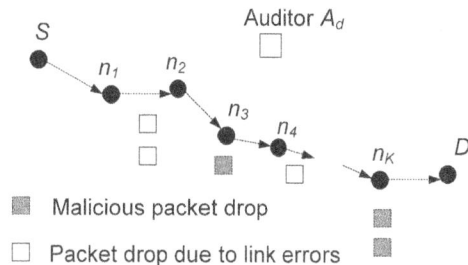

Figure 1: Network and attack model.

We model the wireless channel of each hop along P_{SD} as a random process that alternates between good and bad states. Packets transmitted during the good state are successful, and packets transmitted during the bad state are lost. In contrast to the classical Gilbert-Ellioit (GE) channel model, here we do not assume any Markovian property on the channel behavior. We only require that the sequence of sojourn times for each state follows a stationary distribution, and the autocorrelation function of the channel state, say $f_c(i)$, where i is a discrete time lag measured in packets, is also stationary. The function $f_c(i)$ can be calculated using the probing approach in [1]. In brief, a sequence of M packets are transmitted consecutively over the channel. By observing whether the transmissions are successful or not, the receiver obtains a realization of the channel state $(a_1, \ldots, a_M)$, where $a_j \in \{0, 1\}$ for $j = 1, \ldots, M$. In this sequence, "1" denotes the packet was successfully received, and "0" denotes the packet was dropped. $f_c(i)$ is derived by computing the auto-correlation function of this sample sequence. Such measurement can take place online or offline. A detailed discussion on how $f_c(i)$ is derived is out of the scope of this paper, and we simply assume that this information is given as input to our detection algorithm.

There is an independent auditor A_d in the network. A_d is independent in the sense that it is not associated with any node in P_{SD} and does not have any knowledge of the secrets (e.g., cryptographic keys) held by various nodes. The auditor is responsible for detecting malicious nodes on demand. Specifically, we assume S receives feedback from D when D suspects that the route is under attack. Such a suspicion may be triggered by observing any abnormal events, e.g., a significant performance drop, the loss of multiple packets of a certain type, etc. We assume that the integrity and authenticity of the feedback from D to S can be verified by S using resource-efficient cryptographic methods such as the Elliptic Curve Digital Signature Algorithm (ECDSA). Once being notified of possible attacks, S submits an *attack-detection request* (ADR) to A_d. To facilitate its investigation, A_d needs to collect certain information (elaborated on in the next section) from the nodes on route P_{SD}. We assume that each such node must reply to A_d's inquiry, otherwise the node will be considered as misbehaving. We assume that normal nodes will reply with truthful information, but malicious nodes may cheat. At the same time, for privacy reasons, we require that A_d cannot determine the content of the normal packets delivered over P_{SD} from the information collected during the auditing.

3.2 Adversarial Model

The goal of the adversary is to degrade the network's performance by maliciously dropping packets while remaining undetected. We assume that the malicious node has knowledge of the wireless channel, and is aware of the algorithm used for misbehavior detection. It has the freedom to choose what packets to drop. For example, in the random-drop mode, the malicious node may drop any packet with a small probability p_d. In the selective-mode, the malicious node only drops packets of certain types. A combination of the two modes may be used. We assume that any node on P_{SD} can be a malicious node, except the source and the destination. In particular, there can be multiple malicious nodes on P_{SD}.

We consider the following form of collusion between malicious nodes: A covert communication channel may exist between any two malicious nodes, in addition to the path connecting them on P_{SD}. As a result, malicious nodes can exchange any information without being detected by A_d or any other nodes in P_{SD}. Malicious nodes can take advantage of this covert channel to hide their misbehavior and reduce the chance of being detected. For example, an upstream malicious node may drop a packet on P_{SD}, but may secretly send this packet to a downstream malicious node via the covert channel. When being investigated, the downstream malicious node can provide a proof of the successful reception of the packet. This makes the auditor believe that the packet was successfully forwarded to the downstream nodes, and not know that the packet was actually dropped by an upstream attacker.

3.3 Problem Statement

Under the system and adversary models defined above, we address the problem of identifying the nodes on P_{SD} that drop packets maliciously. We require the detection to be performed by a public auditor that does not have knowledge of the secrets held by the nodes on P_{SD}. When a malicious node is identified, the auditor should be able to construct a publicly verifiable proof of the misbehavior of that node. The construction of such a proof should be privacy preserving, i.e., it does not reveal the original information that is transmitted on P_{SD}. In addition, the detection mechanism should incur low communication and storage overheads, so that it can be applied to a wide variety of wireless networks.

4. PROPOSED DETECTION SCHEME

4.1 Overview

The main idea of our detection algorithm is to compare the autocorrelation function of the observed packet loss process of a link with that of a normal wireless channel (i.e., $f_c(i)$) to accurately identify any possible malicious packet drops. The necessity of exploiting the correlation of lost packets to improve the detection accuracy can be illustrated by examining the insufficiency of the conventional method that relies only on the distribution of the number of lost

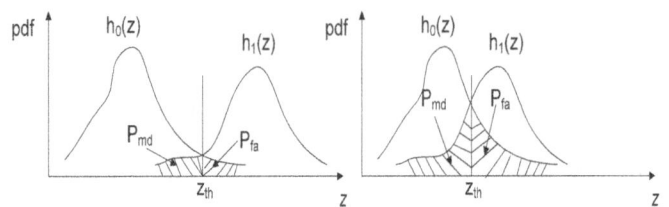

(a) mean of y much greater than mean of x (b) mean of y is comparable to mean of x

Figure 2: Insufficiency of conventional detection algorithms when malicious packet drops are highly selective.

packets. More specifically, under the conventional method, malicious-node detection is modeled as a binary hypothesis test, where H_0 is the hypothesis that there is no malicious node in a given link (all packet losses are due to link errors) and H_1 denotes there is a malicious node in the given link (packet losses are due to both link errors and malicious drops). Let z be the observed number of lost packets on the link during some interval t. Then,

$$z = \begin{cases} x, & \text{under } H_0 \text{ (no malicious nodes)} \\ x + y, & \text{under } H_1 \text{ (there is a malicious node)} \end{cases} \quad (1)$$

where x and y are the numbers of lost packets caused by link errors and by malicious drops, respectively. Both x and y are random variables. Let the probability density functions of z conditioned on H_0 and on H_1 be $h_0(z)$ and $h_1(z)$, respectively, as shown in Figure 2(a). We are interested in the maximum-uncertainty scenario where the *a priori* probabilities are given by $\Pr\{H_0\} = \Pr\{H_1\} = 0.5$, i.e., the auditor has no prior knowledge of the distributions of H_0 and H_1 to make any biased decision regarding the presence of malicious nodes. Let the false-alarm and miss-detection probabilities be P_{fa} and P_{md}, respectively. The optimal decision strategy that minimizes the total detection error $P_{de} \stackrel{\text{def}}{=} 0.5(P_{fa} + P_{md})$ is the maximum-likelihood (ML) algorithm:

$$\begin{cases} \text{if } z \leq z_{th}, & \text{accept } H_0 \\ \text{otherwise}, & \text{accept } H_1 \end{cases} \quad (2)$$

where the threshold z_{th} is the solution to the equation $h_0(z_{th}) = h_1(z_{th})$. Under this strategy, P_{fa} and P_{md} are the areas of the shaded regions shown in Figure 2(a), respectively. The problem with this mechanism is that, when the mean of y is small, $h_1(z)$ and $h_0(z)$ are not sufficiently separated, leading to large P_{fa} and P_{md}, as shown in Figure 2(b). This observation implies that when malicious packet drops are highly selective, counting the number of lost packets is not sufficient to accurately differentiate between malicious drops and link errors. For such a case, we use the correlation between lost packets to form a more solid decision statistic.

To correctly calculate the correlation between lost packets, it is critical to enforce a truthful packet-loss bitmap report by each node. We use HLA cryptographic primitive for this purpose. The basic idea of our method is as follows. An HLA scheme allows the source, which has knowledge of the HLA secret key, to generate HLA signatures $s_1, \ldots, s_M$ for M independent messages $r_1, \ldots, r_M$, respectively. The source sends out the r_i's and s_i's along the route. The HLA signatures are made in such a way that they can be used as the basis to construct a valid HLA signature for any arbitrary linear combination of the messages, $\sum_{i=1}^{M} c_i r_i$, without the use of the HLA secret key, where c_i's are randomly chosen coefficients. A valid HLA signature for $\sum_{i=1}^{M} c_i r_i$ can be constructed by a node that does not have knowledge of the secret HLA key if and only if the node has full knowledge of $s_1, \ldots, s_M$. So, if a node with no knowledge of the HLA secret key provides a valid signature for $\sum_{i=1}^{M} c_i r_i$, it implies that this node must have received all the signatures $s_1, \ldots, s_M$. Our construction ensures that s_i and r_i are sent together along the route, so that knowledge of $s_1, \ldots, s_M$ also proves that the node must have received $r_1, \ldots, r_M$.

Our detection architecture consists of four phases: setup, packet transmission, audit, and detection. We elaborate on these phases in the next section.

4.2 Scheme Details

4.2.1 Setup Phase

This phase takes place right after route P_{SD} is established, but before any data packets are transmitted over the route. In this phase, S decides on a symmetric-key crypto-system $(encrypt_{key}, decrypt_{key})$ and K symmetric keys $key_1, \ldots, key_K$, where $encrypt_{key}$ and $decrypt_{key}$ are the keyed encryption and decryption functions, respectively. S securely distributes $decrypt_{key}$ and a symmetric key key_j to node n_j on P_{SD}, for $j = 1, \ldots, K$. Key distribution may be based on the public-key crypto-system such as RSA: S encrypts key_j using the public key of node n_j and sends the cipher text to n_j. n_j decrypts the cipher text using its private key to obtain key_j. S also announces two hash functions, H_1 and H_{key}^{MAC}, to all nodes in P_{SD}. H_1 is unkeyed while H_{key}^{MAC} is a keyed hash function that will be used for message authentication purposes later on.

Besides symmetric key distribution, S also needs to set up its HLA keys. Let $e : G \times G \to G_T$ be a computable bilinear map with multiplicative cyclic group G and support $\mathbf{Z}_p$, where p is the prime order of G, i.e., for all α, $\beta \in G$ and q_1, $q_2 \in \mathbf{Z}_p$, $e(\alpha^{q_1}, \beta^{q_2}) = e(\alpha, \beta)^{q_1 q_2}$. Let g be a generator of G. $H_2(.)$ is a secure map-to-point hash function: $\{0, 1\}^* \to G$, which maps strings uniformly to G. S chooses a random number $x \in \mathbf{Z}_p$ and computes $v = g^x$. Let u be another generator of G. The secret HLA key is $sk = x$ and the public HLA key is a tuple $pk = (v, g, u)$.

4.2.2 Packet Transmission Phase

After completing the setup phase, S enters the packet transmission phase. S transmits packets to P_{SD} according to the following steps.

Before sending out a packet P_i, where i is a sequence number that uniquely identifies P_i, S computes $r_i = H_1(P_i)$ and generates the HLA signatures of r_i for node n_j, as follows

$$s_{ji} = [H_2(i||j)u^{r_i}]^x, \quad \text{for } j = 1, \ldots, K \quad (3)$$

where $||$ denotes concatenation. These signatures are then sent together with P_i to the route by using a one-way chained encryption that prevents an upstream node from deciphering the signatures intended for downstream nodes. More specifically, after getting s_{ji} for $j = 1, \ldots, K$, S iteratively

computes the following:

$$
\begin{aligned}
\tilde{s}_{Ki} &= encrypt_{key_K}(s_{Ki}) \\
\tau_{Ki} &= \tilde{s}_{Ki} || MAC_{key_K}(\tilde{s}_{Ki}) \\
\tilde{s}_{K-1i} &= encrypt_{key_{K-1}}(s_{K-1i} || \tau_{Ki}) \\
\tau_{K-1i} &= \tilde{s}_{K-1i} || MAC_{key_{K-1}}(\tilde{s}_{K-1i}) \\
&\vdots \\
\tilde{s}_{ji} &= encrypt_{key_j}(s_{ji} || \tau_{j+1i}) \\
\tau_{ji} &= \tilde{s}_{ji} || MAC_{key_j}(\tilde{s}_{ji}) \\
&\vdots \\
\tilde{s}_{1i} &= encrypt_{key_1}(s_{1i} || \tau_{2i}) \\
\tau_{1i} &= \tilde{s}_{1i} || MAC_{key_1}(\tilde{s}_{1i}) \quad (4)
\end{aligned}
$$

where the message authentication code (MAC) in each stage j is computed according to the hash function $H_{key_j}^{MAC}$. After getting τ_{1i}, S puts $P_i || \tau_{1i}$ into one packet and sends it to node n_1.

When node n_1 receives the packet from S, it extracts P_i, $\tilde{s}_{1i}$, and $MAC_{key_1}(\tilde{s}_{1i})$ from the received packet. Then, n_1 verifies the integrity of $\tilde{s}_{1i}$ by testing the following equality:

$$MAC_{key_1}(\tilde{s}_{1i}) = H_{key_1}^{MAC}(\tilde{s}_{1i}). \quad (5)$$

If the test is true, then n_1 decrypts $\tilde{s}_{1i}$ as follows:

$$decrypt_{key_1}(\tilde{s}_{1i}) = s_{1i} || \tau_{2i}. \quad (6)$$

Then, n_1 extracts s_{1i} and τ_{2i} from the decrypted text. It stores $r_i = H_1(P_i)$ and s_{1i} in its proof-of-reception database for future use. This database is maintained at every node on P_{SD}. It can be considered as a FIFO queue of size M, which records the reception status for the most recent M packets sent by S. Finally, n_1 assembles $P_i || \tau_{2i}$ into one packet and relays this packet to node n_2. In case the test in (5) fails, n_1 marks the loss of P_i in its proof-of-reception database and does not relay the packet to n_2.

The above process is repeated at every intermediate node n_j, $j = 1, \ldots, K$. As a result, node n_j obtains r_i and its HLA signature s_{ji} for every packet P_i that the node has received, and it relays $P_i || \tau_{j+1i}$ to the next hop on the route. The last hop, i.e., node n_K, only forwards P_i to the destination D. As proved in Theorem 4 in Section 4.3, the special structure of the one-way chained encryption construction in (4) dictates that an upstream node on the route cannot get a copy of the HLA signature intended for a downstream node, and thus the construction is resilient to the collusion model defined in Section 3.2. Note that here we consider the verification of the integrity of P_i as an orthogonal problem to that of verifying the tag τ_{ji}. If the verification of P_i fails, node n_1 should also stop forwarding the packet and should mark it accordingly in its proof-of-reception database.

4.2.3 Audit Phase

This phase is triggered when the public auditor A_d receives an ADR message from S. The ADR message includes the id of the nodes on P_{SD}, ordered in the downstream direction, i.e., $n_1, \ldots, n_K$, S's HLA public key information $pk = (v, g, u)$, the sequence numbers of the most recent M packets sent by S, and the sequence numbers of the subset of these M packets that were received by D. Recall that we assume the information sent by S and D is truthful, because detecting attacks is in their interest. A_d conducts the auditing process as follows.

91

A_d submits a random challenge vector $\vec{c}_j = (c_{j1}, \ldots, c_{jM})$ to node n_j, $j = 1, \ldots, K$, where the elements c_{ji}'s are randomly chosen from $\mathbf{Z}_p$. Without loss of generality, let the sequence number of the packets recorded in the current proof-of-reception database be $P_1, \ldots, P_M$, with P_M being the most recent packet sent by S. Based on the information in this database, node n_j generates a packet-reception bitmap $\vec{b}_j = (b_{j1}, \ldots, b_{jM})$, where $b_{ji} = 1$ if P_i has been received by n_j, and $b_{ji} = 0$ otherwise. Node n_j then calculates the linear combination $r^{(j)} = \sum_{i=1, b_{ji} \neq 0}^{M} c_{ji} r_i$ and the HLA signature for the combination as follows:

$$s^{(j)} = \prod_{i=1, b_{ji} \neq 0} s_{ji}^{c_{ji}}. \qquad (7)$$

Node n_j submits $\vec{b}_j$, $r^{(j)}$, and $s^{(j)}$ to A_d, as proof of the packets it has received.

A_d checks the validity of $r^{(j)}$ and $s^{(j)}$ by testing the following equality:

$$e(s^{(j)}, g) = e(\prod_{i=1, b_{ji} \neq 0}^{M} H_2(i||j)^{c_{ji}} u^{r^{(j)}}, v). \qquad (8)$$

If the equality holds, then A_d accepts that node n_j received the packets as reflected in $\vec{b}_j$. Otherwise, A_d rejects $\vec{b}_j$ and judges that not all packets claimed in $\vec{b}_j$ are actually received by n_j, so n_j is a malicious node. We prove the correctness of this auditing algorithm in Section 4.3.

Note that the above mechanism only guarantees that a node cannot understate its packet loss, i.e., it cannot claim the reception of a packet that it actually did not receive. This mechanism cannot prevent a node from overly stating its packet loss by claiming that it did not receive a packet that it actually received. This latter case is prevented by another mechanism discussed in the detection phase.

4.2.4 Detection Phase

The public auditor A_d enters the detection phase after receiving and auditing the reply to its challenge from all nodes on P_{SD}. The main tasks of A_d in this phase include the following: detecting any overstatement of packet loss at each node, constructing a packet-loss bitmap for each hop, calculating the autocorrelation function for the packet loss on each hop, and deciding whether malicious behavior is present. More specifically, A_d performs these tasks as follows.

Given the packet-reception bitmap at each node, $\vec{b}_1, \ldots, \vec{b}_K$, A_d first checks the consistency of the bitmaps for any possible overstatement of packet losses. Clearly, if there is no overstatement of packet loss, then the set of packets received at node $j + 1$ should be a subset of the packets received at node j, for $j = 1, \ldots, K - 1$. Because a normal node always truthfully reports its packet reception, the packet-reception bitmap of a malicious node that overstates its packet loss must contradict with the bitmap of a normal downstream node. Note that there is always at least one normal downstream node, i.e., the destination D. So A_d only needs to sequentially scan $\vec{b}_j$'s and the report from D to identify nodes that are overstating their packet losses.

After checking for the consistency of $\vec{b}_j$'s, A_d starts constructing the per-hop packet-loss bitmap $\vec{m}_j$ from $\vec{b}_{j-1}$ and $\vec{b}_j$. This is done sequentially, starting from the first hop from S. In each step, only packets that are lost in the current hop will be accounted for in m_j. The packets that were not received by the upstream node will be marked as "not lost" for the underlying hop. Denoting the "lost" packet by 0 and "not lost" by 1, $\vec{m}_j$ can be easily constructed by conducting a bit-wise complement-XOR operation of $\vec{b}_{j-1}$ and $\vec{b}_j$. For example, consider the following simple case with three intermediate nodes (four hops) on the route and with $M = 10$. Suppose that $\vec{b}_1 = (0, 1, 1, 1, 1, 1, 1, 1, 0, 1)$, $\vec{b}_2 = (0, 1, 1, 1, 1, 1, 1, 1, 0, 1)$, $\vec{b}_3 = (0, 1, 0, 1, 1, 0, 1, 1, 0, 1)$, and the destination D reports that $\vec{b}_D = (0, 1, 0, 1, 1, 0, 1, 1, 0, 1)$. Then the per-hop packet-loss bitmaps are given by $\vec{m}_1 = (0, 1, 1, 1, 1, 1, 1, 1, 0, 1)$, $\vec{m}_2 = (1, 1, 1, 1, 1, 1, 1, 1, 1, 1)$, $\vec{m}_3 = (1, 1, 0, 1, 1, 0, 1, 1, 1, 1)$, and $\vec{m}_4 = (1, 1, 1, 1, 1, 1, 1, 1, 1, 1)$.

The auditor calculates the autocorrelation function γ_j for each sequence $\vec{m}_j = (m_{j1}, \ldots, m_{jM})$, $j = 1, \ldots, K$, as follows

$$\gamma_j(i) = \frac{\sum_{k=1}^{M-i} m_{jk} m_{jk+i}}{M - i}, \quad \text{for } i = 0, \ldots, M-1; j = 1, \ldots, K. \qquad (9)$$

The auditor then calculates the relative difference between γ_j and the ACF of the wireless channel f_c as follows

$$\epsilon_j = \sum_{i=0}^{M-1} \frac{|\gamma_j(i) - f_c(i)|}{f_c(i)}. \qquad (10)$$

The relative difference ϵ_j is then used as the decision statistic to decide whether or not the packet loss over the jth hop is caused by malicious drops. In particular, if $\epsilon_j \geq \epsilon_{th}$, where ϵ_{th} is an error threshold, then A_d decides that there is malicious packet drop over the hop. In this case, both ends of the hop will be considered as suspects, i.e., either the transmitter did not send out the packet or the receiver chose to ignore the received packet. S may choose to exclude both nodes from future packet transmissions, or alternatively, apply a more extensive investigation to refine its detection. For example, this can be done by combining the neighbor-overhearing techniques [9] used in the reputation system. By fusing the testimony from the neighbors of these two nodes, A_d can pin-point the specific node that dropped the packet. Once being detected, the malicious node will be marked and excluded from the route to mitigate its damage.

The above detection process applies to one end-to-end path. The detection for multiple paths can be performed as multiple independent detections, one for each path. Although the optimal error threshold that minimizes the detection error is still an open problem, our simulations show that through trial-and-error, one can easily find a good ϵ_{th} that provides a better detection accuracy than the optimal detection scheme that utilizes only the pdf of the number of lost packets.

Public Verifiability: After each detection, A_d is required to publish the information it received from involved nodes, i.e., $\vec{b}_j$, $r^{(j)}$, $s^{(j)}$, for $j \in P_{SD}$, so that a node can verify all calculation has been performed correctly. Note that no knowledge of the HLA secret key x is required in the verification process. At the same time, because A_d has no knowledge of x, there is no way for it to forge a valid HLA signature for $r^{(j)}$. In other words, A_d cannot claim a misbehaving node to be a normal one. Furthermore, the privacy-preserving property of the scheme (see Theorem 4 in Section 4.3) ensures that publishing the auditing information will not compromise the confidentiality of the communication.

4.3 Security Analysis

We prove that the proposed scheme has the following security properties.

Theorem 1: The verification of $r^{(j)}$ and $s^{(j)}$, as specified in (8), is correct, i.e., (8) must hold for a $(\vec{c}_j, r^{(j)}, s^{(j)})$ tuple that is constructed according to the specification presented in Section 4.2.3.

Proof: The correctness of (8) is shown as follows:

$$
\begin{aligned}
e(s^{(j)}, g) &= e\left(\prod_{i=1, b_{ji} \neq 0}^{M} s_{ji}^{c_{ji}}, g\right) \\
&= e\left(\prod_{i=1, b_{ji} \neq 0}^{M} \{H_2(i||j) u^{r_i}\}^{x c_{ji}}, g\right) \\
&= e\left(\prod_{i=1, b_{ji} \neq 0}^{M} \{H_2(i||j) u^{r_i}\}^{c_{ji}}, g\right)^x \\
&= e\left(\prod_{i=1, b_{ji} \neq 0}^{M} H_2(i||j)^{c_{ji}} u^{c_{ji} r_i}, g\right)^x \\
&= e\left(\prod_{i=1, b_{ji} \neq 0}^{M} H_2(i||j)^{c_{ji}} u^{r^{(j)}}, g^x\right) \\
&= e\left(\prod_{i=1, b_{ji} \neq 0}^{M} H_2(i||j)^{c_{ji}} u^{r^{(j)}}, v\right). \quad (11)
\end{aligned}
$$

So Theorem 1 holds. $\square$

Theorem 2: The construction specified in Section 4.2 is secure under the collusion model defined in Section 3.2, i.e., an adversary that does not receive a packet P_i cannot claim receiving this packet in its $\vec{b}_j$ by forging a HLA signature for a random linear combination of the received packets, even if this adversary colludes with any other malicious node in P_{SD}.

Proof: For a given node n_j, our construction essentially follows the BLS-signature-based HLA construction described in [24]. Under the implicitly assumed condition of no collusion between attackers, the authors in [24] proved that the construction is secure, i.e., no adversary can forge a response to a random challenge if it does not know the HLA signature of each packet in the linear combination. So here, we only need to show that collusion between malicious nodes does not give the attacker more information about the HLA signature of the packets. This can be shown by observing the following novel properties of our HLA construction:

1. For a packet P_i, the signature scheme specified in (3) dictates that its HLA signature s_{ji} is not only tied to the packet sequence number (i), but also related to the node index (j) that is relaying the packet. This means that for the same packet, each hop on P_{SD} is given a different HLA signature. The verification scheme in (8) accounts for both i and j. In the no-collusion case, by treating the concatenation of ($i||j$) as a meta packet sequence number, the security of our construction can be proved in the same way as that in [24].

2. The way that the HLA signatures are distributed to nodes on P_{SD}, as specified in (4), dictates that an upstream node n_j cannot get a copy of the HLA signature $s_{j'i}$ of a downstream node $n_{j'}$, where $j < j' \leq K$, unless the downstream node $n_{j'}$ receives the signature

$s_{j'i}$ *first on* P_{SD} and then sends it through the covert channel to the upstream node n_j. Therefore, there is no way for a downstream malicious node to get any information on its HLA signature if the upstream attacker drops the packet. As a result, the secret information exchange on the covert channel does not help the adversary to get more information on its HLA signature than the scenario where there is no collusion.

Combining the above arguments, Theorem 2 is proved. $\square$

Theorem 3: The proposed scheme ensures that the packet-reception bitmap reported by a node in P_{SD} is truthful.

The validity of Theorem 3 is straightforward, because Theorem 2 guarantees that the node cannot understate its packet loss information. At the same time, from our discussion in Section 4.2.4, it is clear that a malicious node cannot overstate its packet loss either. So a node must report its actual packet reception information truthfully to A_d.

Theorem 4: Our HLA construction is publicly verifiable and privacy preserving, i.e., the auditor A_d does not require the secret key of the HLA scheme to verify a node's response. In addition, A_d cannot determine the content of the packets transmitted over P_{SD} from the information submitted by nodes.

Proof: Public verifiability is clear from the construction of the scheme. The privacy-preserving property is guaranteed by the application of the secure hash function H_1. More specifically, instead of directly computing the HLA signature for a packet P_i, our construction computes the signature for the image of the packet $r_i = H_1(P_i)$. During the auditing phase, A_d can collect a set of linear combinations of r_i's. So it is possible for A_d to calculate r_i's by solving a set of linear equations, if a sufficient number of combinations are collected. Even if A_d can recover r_i, it should not be able to guess P_i because of H_1's resilience to the pre-image attack. $\square$

4.4 Overhead Analysis

The proposed scheme requires relatively high computation capability at the source, but incurs low communication and storage overheads along the route, as explained below.

4.4.1 Computation Requirements

Most of the computation is done at the source node (for generating HLA signatures) and at the public auditor (for conducting the detection process). We consider the public auditor as a dedicated service provider that is not constrained by its computing capacity. So the computational overhead should not be a factor limiting the application of the algorithm at the public auditor. On the other hand, the proposed algorithm requires the source node to generate K HLA signatures for a K-hop path for each data packet. The generation of HLA signatures is computationally expensive, and may limit the applicability of the algorithm. One solution to this problem is to make the signature scalable, e.g., instead of generating a per-packet signature, a per-block signature may be generated, where each block has L packets. Accordingly, the detection will be extended to blocks (a block is defined as lost if a packet in the block is lost). This could significantly reduce the computational overhead at the source. This method will be evaluated in our future work.

4.4.2 Communication Overhead

The communication overhead for the setup phase is a one-time cost, incurred when P_{SD} is established. Here we mainly focus on the recurring cost during the packet transmission and auditing phases (there is no communication overhead in the detection phase). For a transmitted packet P_i, S needs to send one encrypted HLA signature and one MAC to each intermediate node on P_{SD}. Our HLA signature follows the BLS scheme in [5]. So an HLA signature s_{ij} is 160-bit long. If encrypted by DES, the encrypted signature $\tilde{s}_{ij}$ is 192 bits in length (a block in DES is 64-bit long, so the length of the cipher text of DES is multiples of 64 bits). The MAC-related hash function H_{key}^{MAC} can be implemented in SHA-1 and has a length of 160 bits. So for each packet, the per-hop communication overhead incurred by the proposed scheme in the packet transmission phase is $192 + 160 = 352$ bits, or 44 bytes. For a path of K intermediate hops, the total communication overhead for transmitting a packet is $44K$ bytes. For example, when $K = 10$, the overhead is 440 bytes/packet. For an IEEE 802.11 system, this is about 19% of the maximum MSDU (2304 bytes).

In the auditing phase, the auditor A_d sends a random challenge vector $\vec{c}_j$ to each node n_j. Let each element in this vector be a 32-bit integer. The challenge has a length of $4M$ bytes. Based on our simulation in Section 5, $M = 50$ is typically enough to achieve good detection accuracy. So this means each challenge can be delivered in one packet. Node n_j replies to the challenge with $\vec{b}_j$, $r^{(j)}$, and $s^{(j)}$. Among them, $\vec{b}_j$ is an M-bit bitmap. $r^{(j)}$ is the linear combination of the SHA-1 image of the packets, so $r^{(j)}$ also has a length of 160 bits. $s^{(j)}$ is an HLA signature of $r^{(j)}$, so it is also 160-bit long. Overall, the reply from a node to A_d has a length of $320 + M$ bits, which can also be delivered in one packet.

4.4.3 Storage Overhead

During its operation, a node n_j on P_{SD} needs to store the key key_j, the H_1 hash image, and the associated HLA signature for each of the M most recently received packets. Assuming $encrypt_{key}$ and $decrypt_{key}$ are based on DES, key_j has a length of 56 bits. Let the hash function H_1 be based on SHA-1. So the H_1 image of a packet is 160-bit long. The HLA signature is based on BLS (Boneh-Lynn-Shacham) scheme [5] and is 160-bit long. So in total the storage overhead at n_j is $320M + 56$ bits, or $40M + 7$ bytes. This storage overhead is quite low. For example, when $M \leq 50$, the storage overhead at a node is less than 2 KB.

5. PERFORMANCE EVALUATION

5.1 Simulation Setup

In this section, we compare the detection accuracy achieved by the proposed algorithm with the optimal maximum likelihood (ML) algorithm, which only utilizes the distribution of the number of lost packets. For given packet-loss bitmaps, the detection on different hops is conducted separately. So, we only need to simulate the detection of one hop to evaluate the performance of a given algorithm. We assume packets are transmitted continuously over this hop, i.e., a saturated traffic environment. We assume channel fluctuations for this hop follow the Gilbert-Elliot model, with the transition probabilities from good to bad and from bad to good given by P_{GB} and P_{BG}, respectively. We consider two types of malicious packet dropping: random dropping and selec-

tive dropping. In the random dropping attack, a packet is dropped at the malicious node with probability P_M. In the selective dropping attack, the adversary drops packets of certain sequence numbers. In our simulations, this is done by dropping the middle N of the M most recently received packets, i.e., setting the N bits in the middle of the packet-loss bitmap to 0 (if a packet in these positions is dropped due to link errors, then the set of 0's extends to an extra bit in the middle). P_M and N are simulation parameters that describe the selectivity of the attack. In both cases, we let $\epsilon_{th} = 10\%$ for the proposed algorithm.

We are interested in the following three performance metrics: probability of false alarm (P_{fa}), probability of miss-detection (P_{md}), and the overall detection-error probability (P_{error}). We collect these statistics as follows. In each run, we first simulate 1000 independently generated packet-loss bitmaps for the hop, where packet losses are caused by link errors only. We execute our detection algorithm over these packet-loss bitmaps and collect the number of cases where the algorithm decides that an attacker is present. Let this number be I_{fa}. P_{fa} of this run is calculated as $P_{fa} = I_{fa}/1000$. We then simulate another 1000 independently generated packet-loss bitmaps, where losses are now caused by both link errors and malicious drops. Let the number of cases where the detection algorithm rules that an attacker is not present be I_{md}. P_{md} of the underlying run is given by $P_{md} = I_{md}/1000$. P_{error} is given by $P_{error} = (I_{fa} + I_{md})/2000$. The above simulation is repeated 30 times, and the mean and 95% confidence interval are computed for the various performance metrics.

5.2 Results

5.2.1 Random Packet Dropping

The detection accuracy is shown in Figure 3 as a function of the malicious random-drop rate P_M. In each subfigure, there are two sets of curves, representing the proposed algorithm and the optimal ML scheme, respectively. In each set of curves, the one in the middle represents the mean, and the other two represent the 95% confidence interval. In general, the detection accuracy of both algorithms improves with P_M (i.e., the detection error decreases with P_M). This is not surprising, because malicious packet drops become more statistically distinguishable as the attacker starts to drop more packets. In addition, this figure shows that for $\epsilon_{th} = 10\%$, the proposed algorithm provides slightly higher false-alarm rate (subfigure (c)) but significantly lower miss-detection probability (subfigure (b)) than the ML scheme. A low miss-detection probability is very desirable in our context, because it means a malicious node can be detected with a higher probability. The slightly higher false-alarm rate should not be a problem, because a false alarm can be easily recognized and fixed in the post-detection investigation phase. Most importantly, the overall detection-error probability of the proposed scheme is lower than that of the ML scheme (subfigure (a)). We are especially interested in the regime when P_M is comparable to the average packet loss rate due to link errors, given by $\frac{P_{GB}}{P_{GB}+P_{BG}} = \frac{0.01}{0.01+0.5} \approx 0.02$. This regime represents the scenario in which the attacker hides its drops in the background of link errors by mimicking the channel-related loss rate. In this case, the ML scheme cannot correctly differentiate between link errors and malicious drops. For example, when $P_M = 0.01$, the ML scheme results in $P_{md} = 80\%$ and $P_{fa} = 23\%$. This is close to arbitrarily ruling that every packet loss is due to link error only, leading to an overall detection-error rate of 50% (see subfigure (a)). Our proposed algorithm, on the other hand, achieves a much better detection accuracy, because its P_{md} and P_{fa} are both lower than those under the ML scheme. As a result, when $P_M = 0.01$, the total detection-error rate of the proposed algorithm is about 35%. When P_M is increased to 0.04, P_{error} of the proposed scheme reduces to only 20%, which is roughly half of the error rate of the ML scheme at the same P_M. Remembering that the detection-error rate of the ML scheme is the lowest among all detection schemes that only utilize the distribution of the number of lost packets, the lower detection-error rate of the proposed scheme shows that exploiting the correlation between lost packets helps in identifying the real cause of packet drops more accurately. The effect of exploiting the correlation is especially visible when the malicious packet-drop rate is comparable with the link error rate.

In Figure 4, we plot the detection accuracy as a function of the size of the packet-loss bitmap (M). It can be observed that P_{error} for the proposed scheme decreases with M. However, as M becomes sufficiently large, e.g., $M = 30$ in our case, a further increase in the size of the bitmap does not lead to additional improvement in the detection accuracy. This can be explained by noting that the two-state Markovian GE channel model has a short-range dependence, i.e., the correlation between two points of the fluctuation process decays rapidly with the increase in the separation between these points. This short-range dependence is reflected in an exponentially decaying autocorrelation function for the channel. As a result, a good estimation of the autocorrelation function can be derived as long as M is long enough to cover the function's short tail. This phenomenon implies that a node does not need to maintain a large packet-reception database in order to achieve a good detection accuracy under the proposed scheme. It also explains the low storage overhead incurred by our scheme.

The detection accuracy is plotted in Figure 5 as a function of the channel state transition rate P_{GB}. It can be observed from this figure that P_{error} for both algorithms increases with P_{GB}. This is not surprising because at its initial point of $P_{GB} = 0.01$, the expected link error rate is about 0.02, which is much smaller than the malicious packet drop rate of $P_M = 0.1$. So it is relatively easy to differentiate between the case where packet drops are caused by link errors only and the one where such drops are caused by the combined effect of link errors and malicious drops. As P_{GB} increases, the link error probability approaches P_M, making the statistical separation of the two cases harder. As a result, the detection error increases with P_{GB}. For all values of P_{GB} in this figure, the proposed algorithm always achieves significantly lower detection-error probability than the ML scheme.

5.2.2 Selective Packet Dropping

The detection error as a function of the number of maliciously dropped packets is shown in Figure 6. At the low end of the x-axis, maliciously dropped packets account for only $1/50 = 2\%$ of the total packets in the packet-loss bitmap. This is identical to the link error rate of 0.02, assumed in the simulation. Similar performance trends can be observed to the case of the random packet dropping. Fewer detection errors are made by both algorithms when more packets are maliciously dropped. In all the simulated cases, the proposed algorithm can detect the actual cause of the packet drop more accurately than the ML scheme, especially when the number of maliciously dropped packets is small. When

the number of maliciously dropped packets is significantly higher than that caused by link errors (greater than 4 packets in our simulation), the two algorithms achieve comparable detection accuracy. In this scenario, it may be wise to use the conventional ML scheme due to its simplicity (e.g., no need to enforce truthful reports from intermediate nodes, etc).

The detection errors are plotted in Figure 7 as a function of the size of the packet-loss bitmap (M). To conduct a fair comparison, as we increase M, we also increase the number of maliciously dropped packets, so as to maintain a malicious packet-dropping rate of 10%. It can be observed that a small M is enough to achieve good detection accuracy under the proposed scheme, due to the short-range dependence property of the channel.

In Figure 8, the detection errors are plotted as a function of the channel state transition probability P_{GB}. Similar trends are observed to those in the random packet dropping case, i.e., the algorithms make more detection errors when the link error rate approaches the malicious packet-drop rate. Once again, the proposed algorithm consistently outperforms the ML scheme in all the tested cases.

6. CONCLUSIONS

In this paper, we showed that compared with conventional detection algorithms that utilize only the distribution of the number of lost packets, exploiting the correlation between lost packets significantly improves the accuracy in detecting malicious packet drops. Such improvement is especially visible when the number of maliciously dropped packets is comparable with those caused by link errors. To correctly calculate the correlation between lost packets, it is critical to acquire truthful packet-loss information at individual nodes. We developed an HLA-based public auditing architecture that ensures truthful packet-loss reporting by individual nodes. This architecture is collusion proof, requires relatively high computational capacity at the source node, but incurs low communication and storage overheads over the route.

Some open issues remain to be explored. First, the computational overhead at source nodes needs to be reduced. As we pointed out in Section 4.4.1, a block-based HLA signature could be explored. We will evaluate the effect of this method as our next step. Second, in this paper, we mainly focused on showing the feasibility of the proposed mechanism. The decision threshold used in the detection was obtained by trial-and-error. In our future work, we will study the optimization of this threshold. Last but not least, the proposed detection algorithm does not account for topological changes in the network. The impact of dynamic topology remains an issue to be evaluated.

7. ACKNOWLEDGMENTS

This research was supported in part by NSF (under grants CNS-1016943, CNS-0904681, and IIP-0832238), Raytheon, and the ąřConnection Oneąś center. Any opinions, findings, conclusions, or recommendations expressed in this paper are those of the author(s) and do not necessarily reflect the views of the National Science Foundation.

8. REFERENCES

[1] J. N. Arauz. 802.11 Markov channel modeling. *Ph.D. Dissertation, School of Information Science, University of Pittsburgh*, 2004.

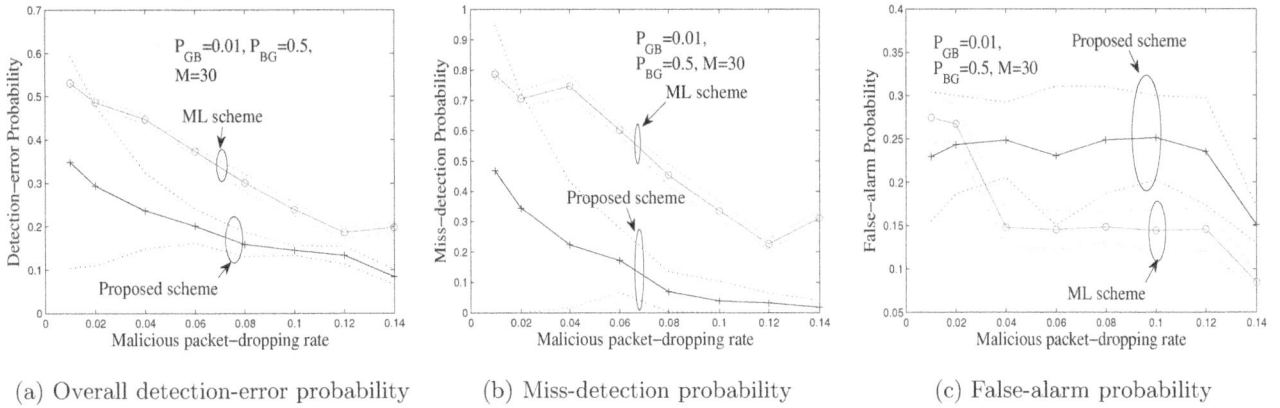

(a) Overall detection-error probability   (b) Miss-detection probability   (c) False-alarm probability

Figure 3: Detection accuracy vs. P_M (random packet-drop case).

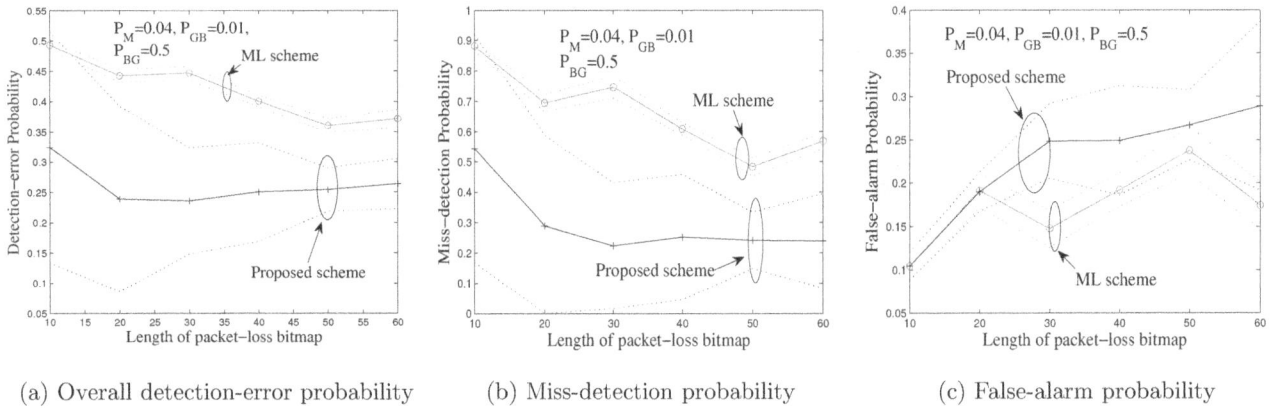

(a) Overall detection-error probability   (b) Miss-detection probability   (c) False-alarm probability

Figure 4: Detection accuracy vs. M (random packet-drop case).

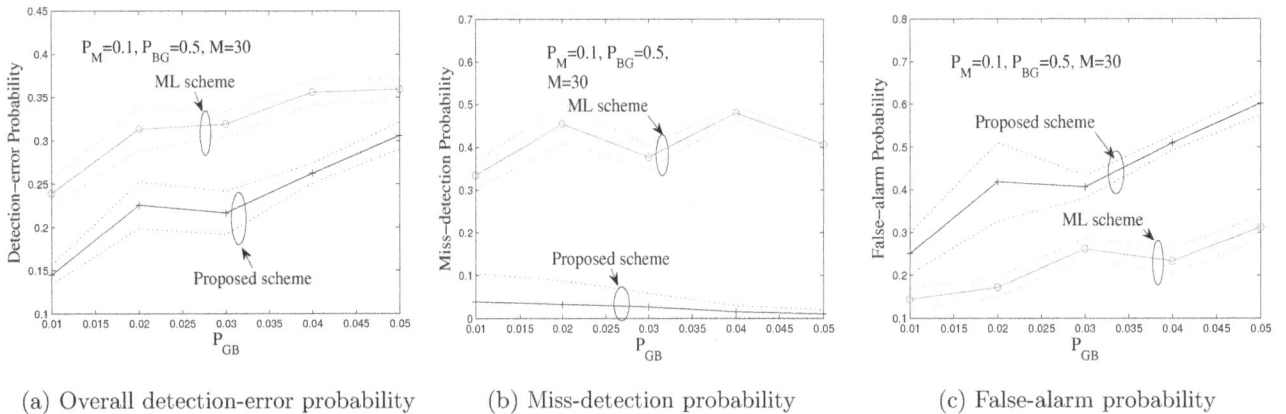

(a) Overall detection-error probability   (b) Miss-detection probability   (c) False-alarm probability

Figure 5: Detection accuracy vs. P_{GB} (random packet-drop case).

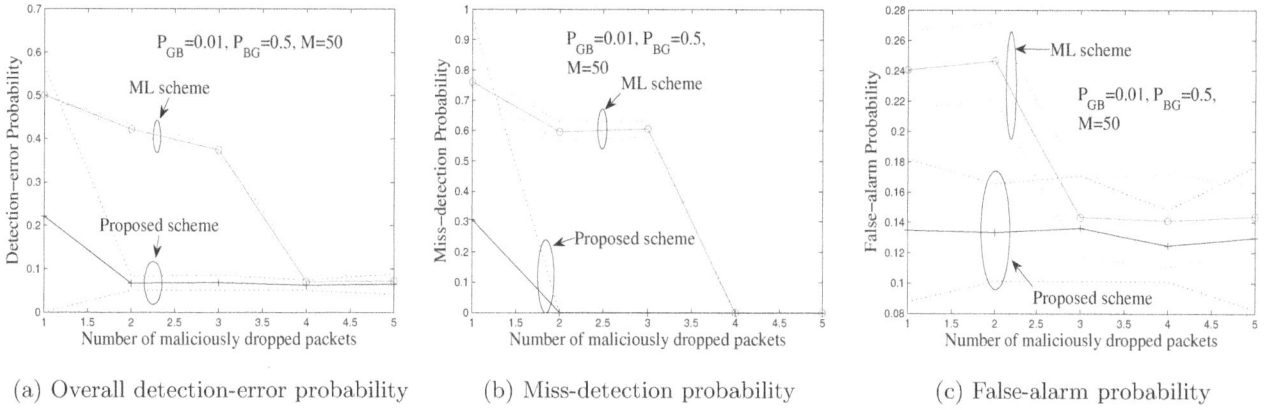

(a) Overall detection-error probability   (b) Miss-detection probability   (c) False-alarm probability

Figure 6: Detection accuracy vs. number of maliciously dropped packets (selective packet-drop case).

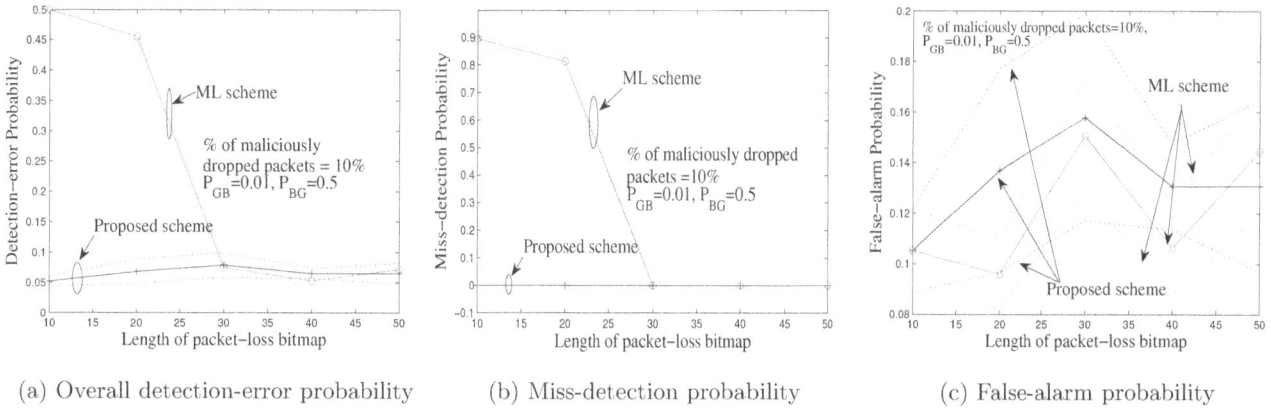

(a) Overall detection-error probability   (b) Miss-detection probability   (c) False-alarm probability

Figure 7: Detection accuracy vs. M (selective packet-drop case).

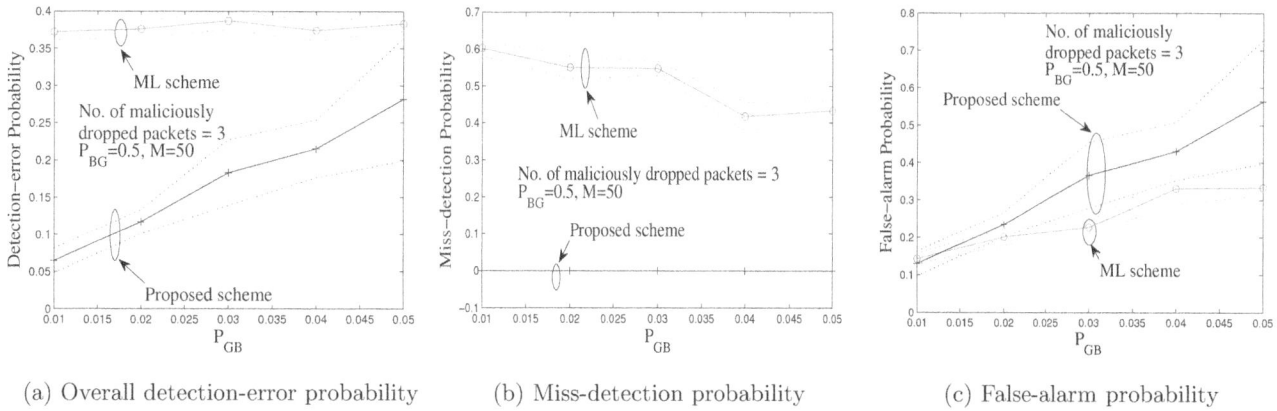

(a) Overall detection-error probability   (b) Miss-detection probability   (c) False-alarm probability

Figure 8: Detection accuracy vs. P_{GB} (selective packet-drop case).

[2] C. Ateniese, R. Burns, R. Curtmola, J. Herring, L. Kissner, Z. Peterson, and D. Song. Provable data possession at untrusted stores. In *Proceedings of the ACM Conference on Computer and Communications Security (CCS)*, pages 598–610, Oct. 2007.

[3] G. Ateniese, S. Kamara, and J. Katz. Proofs of storage from homomorphic identification protocols. In *Proceedings of the International Conference on the Theory and Application of Cryptology and Information Security (ASIACRYPT)*, 2009.

[4] B. Awerbuch, R. Curtmola, D. Holmer, C. Nita-Rotaru, and H. Rubens. ODSBR: an on-demand secure byzantine resilient routing protocol for wireless ad hoc networks. *ACM TISSEC*, 10(4), 2008.

[5] D. Boneh, B. Lynn, and H. Shacham. Short signatures from the weil pairing. *Journal of Cryptology*, 17(4):297–319, Sept. 2004.

[6] S. Buchegger and J. Y. L. Boudec. Performance analysis of the confidant protocol (cooperation of nodes: fairness in dynamic ad-hoc networks). In *Proceedings of the ACM MobiHoc Conference*, 2002.

[7] L. Buttyan and J. P. Hubaux. Stimulating cooperation in self-organizing mobile ad hoc networks. *ACM/Kluwer Mobile Networks and Applications*, 8(5):579–592, Oct. 2003.

[8] J. Eriksson, M. Faloutsos, and S. Krishnamurthy. Routing amid colluding attackers. 2007.

[9] W. Galuba, P. Papadimitratos, M. Poturalski, K. Aberer, Z. Despotovic, and W. Kellerer. Castor: Scalable secure routing for ad hoc networks. In *INFOCOM, 2010 Proceedings IEEE*, pages 1 –9, march 2010.

[10] T. Hayajneh, P. Krishnamurthy, D. Tipper, and T. Kim. Detecting malicious packet dropping in the presence of collisions and channel errors in wireless ad hoc networks. In *Proceedings of the IEEE ICC Conference*, 2009.

[11] Q. He, D. Wu, and P. Khosla. Sori: a secure and objective reputation-based incentive scheme for ad hoc networks. In *Proceedings of the IEEE WCNC Conference*, 2004.

[12] D. B. Johnson, D. A. Maltz, and J. Broch. DSR: the dynamic source routing protocol for multi-hop wireless ad hoc networks. *Chapter 5, Ad Hoc Networking, Addison-Wesley*, pages 139–172, 2001.

[13] W. Kozma Jr. and L. Lazos. Dealing with liars: misbehavior identification via Renyi-Ulam games. In *Proceedings of the International ICST Conference on Security and Privacy in Communication Networks (SecureComm)*, 2009.

[14] W. Kozma Jr. and L. Lazos. REAct: resource-efficient accountability for node misbehavior in ad hoc networks based on random audits. In *Proceedings of the ACM Conference on Wireless Network Security (WiSec)*, 2009.

[15] K. Liu, J. Deng, P. Varshney, and K. Balakrishnan. An acknowledgement-based approach for the detection of routing misbehavior in MANETs. *IEEE Transactions on Mobile Computing*, 6(5):536–550, May 2006.

[16] Y. Liu and Y. R. Yang. Reputation propagation and agreement in mobile ad-hoc networks. In *Proceedings of the IEEE WCNC Conference*, pages 1510–1515, 2003.

[17] S. Marti, T. J. Giuli, K. Lai, and M. Baker. Mitigating routing misbehavior in mobile ad hoc networks. In *Proceedings of the ACM MobiCom Conference*, pages 255–265, 2000.

[18] G. Noubir and G. Lin. Low-power DoS attacks in data wireles lans and countermeasures. *ACM SIGMOBILE Mobile Computing and Communications Review*, 7(3):29–30, July 2003.

[19] V. N. Padmanabhan and D. R. Simon. Secure traceroute to detect faulty or malicious routing. In *Proceedings of the ACM SIGCOMM Conference*, 2003.

[20] P. Papadimitratos and Z. Haas. Secure message transmission in mobile ad hoc networks. *Ad Hoc Networks*, 1(1):193–209, 2003.

[21] A. Proano and L. Lazos. Selective jamming attacks in wireless networks. In *Proceedings of the IEEE ICC Conference*, pages 1–6, 2010.

[22] A. Proano and L. Lazos. Packet-hiding methods for preventing selective jamming attacks. *IEEE Transactions on Dependable and Secure Computing*, 9(1):101–114, 2012.

[23] R. Rao and G. Kesidis. Detecting malicious packet dropping using statistically regular traffic patterns in multihop wireless networks that are not bandwidth limited. In *Proceedings of the IEEE GLOBECOM Conference*, 2003.

[24] H. Shacham and B. Waters. Compact proofs of retrievability. In *Proceedings of the International Conference on the Theory and Application of Cryptology and Information Security (ASIACRYPT)*, Dec. 2008.

[25] C. Wang, Q. Wang, K. Ren, and W. Lou. Privacy-preserving public auditing for data storage security in cloud computing. In *Proceedings of the IEEE INFOCOM Conference*, Mar. 2010.

[26] W. Xu, W. Trappe, Y. Zhang, and T. Wood. The feasibility of launching and detecting jamming attacks in wireless networks. In *Proceedings of the ACM MobiHoc Conference*, pages 46–57, 2005.

[27] S. Zhong, J. Chen, and Y. R. Yang. Sprite: a simple cheat-proof, credit-based system for mobile ad-hoc networks. In *Proceedings of the IEEE INFOCOM Conference*, pages 1987–1997, 2003.

Security for Cyber-physical Systems: Case Studies with Medical Devices, Robots, and Automobiles

Tadayoshi Kohno
Computer Science and Engineering
University of Washington
Seattle, WA, USA
Yoshi@cs.washington.edu

Abstract

Today's and tomorrow's emerging technologies and cyber-physical systems have the potential to greatly improve the quality of our lives. Without the appropriate checks and balances, however, these emerging technologies also have the potential to compromise our digital and physical security and privacy. This talk will explore three case studies in the design and analysis of secure cyber-physical systems: wireless medical devices, robots, and automobiles. We will discuss the discovery of vulnerabilities in leading examples of these technologies, the challenges to securing these technologies and the ecosystem leading to their vulnerabilities, and new directions for security.

Categories & Subject Descriptors: C.2.1 [Computer-Communication Networks]: Network Architecture and Design - Wireless Communication; C.2.m [Computer-Communication Networks]: Miscellaneous - Security; J.3 [Computer Applications]: Life and Medical Sciences – Medical Information Systems

General Terms: Security

Keywords: Security, Cyber-physical systems

Bio

Tadayoshi Kohno is an Associate Professor in the University of Washington Department of Computer Science and Engineering and an Adjunct Associate Professor in the UW Information School. His research focuses on helping protect the security, privacy, and safety of users of current and future generation technologies. Kohno is the recipient of an Alfred P. Sloan Research Fellowship, a U.S. National Science Foundation CAREER Award, and a Technology Review TR-35 Young Innovator Award. Kohno has authored more than a dozen award papers, has presented his research to the U.S. House of Representatives, and is chairing the 2012 USENIX Security Symposium. Kohno received his Ph.D. from the University of California at San Diego.

Unsafe Exposure Analysis of Mobile In-App Advertisements

Michael Grace, Wu Zhou, and
Xuxian Jiang
Department of Computer Science,
North Carolina State University
Raleigh, NC, USA
{mcgrace, wu_zhou,
xuxian_jiang}@ncsu.edu

Ahmad-Reza Sadeghi
Center for Advanced Security Research,
Technical University Darmstadt
Darmstadt, Germany
ahmad.sadeghi@trust.cased.de

ABSTRACT

In recent years, there has been explosive growth in smartphone sales, which is accompanied with the availability of a huge number of smartphone applications (or simply apps). End users or consumers are attracted by the many interesting features offered by these devices and the associated apps. The developers of these apps benefit financially, either by selling their apps directly or by embedding one of the many ad libraries available on smartphone platforms. In this paper, we focus on potential privacy and security risks posed by these embedded or in-app advertisement libraries (henceforth "ad libraries," for brevity). To this end, we study the popular Android platform and collect 100,000 apps from the official Android Market in March-May, 2011. Among these apps, we identify 100 representative in-app ad libraries (embedded in 52.1% of the apps) and further develop a system called AdRisk to systematically identify potential risks. In particular, we first decouple the embedded ad libraries from their host apps and then apply our system to statically examine the ad libraries for risks, ranging from uploading sensitive information to remote (ad) servers to executing untrusted code from Internet sources. Our results show that most existing ad libraries collect private information: some of this data may be used for legitimate targeting purposes (i.e., the user's location) while other data is harder to justify, such as the user's call logs, phone number, browser bookmarks, or even the list of apps installed on the phone. Moreover, some libraries make use of an unsafe mechanism to directly fetch and run code from the Internet, which immediately leads to serious security risks. Our investigation indicates the symbiotic relationship between embedded ad libraries and host apps is one main reason behind these exposed risks. These results clearly show the need for better regulating the way ad libraries are integrated in Android apps.

Categories and Subject Descriptors K.6.5 [**Management of Computing and Information Systems**]: Security and Protection - Invasive Software

General Terms Security

Keywords Smartphone, Privacy, In-App Advertisement

1. INTRODUCTION

Over the past few years, smartphone sales have experienced explosive growth. According to Gartner, sales of these devices increased 74% year-on-year in the second quarter of 2011 [6] and late last year, smartphones already outsold the personal computers for the first time in history [25]. Evidently, the market has embraced these mobile devices due to their convenience and power: these sensor-rich devices are small enough to be carried like a traditional cellphone, yet offer their users a much wider range of functions than simple SMS messages or basic phone calls. Moreover, they are defined by the ability to download and run third-party apps that provide additional useful features. In other words, instead of being restricted to the functions provided by the phone manufacturers, carriers, or limited affiliates, smartphone users can partake of thousands of apps designed for purposes unforeseen by the parties involved in making and distributing the devices. Furthermore, platform vendors (e.g., Google and Apple) also provide centralized app markets where users can simply tap through the process of browsing, searching, purchasing, downloading, and installing these apps.

As part of the mobile eco-system, the app developers, largely motivated by financial incentives, submit their apps to centralized app markets for users to access. Notice that on the Android platform, almost two-thirds of all apps are free to download [5]. To be compensated for their work, many app developers incorporate an advertisement library (also known as an ad library) in their apps. At run-time, the ad library communicates with the ad network's servers to request ads for display and might additionally send analytics information about the users of the app. (For simplicity, we use the term ad libraries to represent both ad libraries and analytics libraries.) The ad network then pays the developer on an ongoing basis, based on metrics that measure how much exposure each individual app gives to the network and its advertisers.

In this paper, we aim to study existing in-app ad libraries and evaluate potential risks from them. Specifically, we focus on the Android platform and determine what risks the popular ad libraries on Android may pose to user's privacy and security. To this end, we collected 100, 000 apps from the official Android Market in a three-month period, i.e., March-May, 2011. Among these apps, we identify and extract 100 representative ad libraries that are used in 52, 067 (or 52.1%) of them. To facilitate our analysis, we further developed a static analysis tool called AdRisk to analyze the extracted ad libraries and report possible risks. In particular, our current analysis mainly focuses on those "dangerous" permissions (Section 2) defined in the standard Android framework, seeking to identify their possible (mis)use by ad libraries.

```
<manifest ... ...
    package="com.rovio.angrybirdsrio" >
    <application
        <activity android:name="com.rovio.ka3d.App">
            <intent-filter>  <action android:name="android.intent.action.MAIN"> </action>
                <category android:name="android.intent.category.LAUNCHER">    </category>
            </intent-filter>
        </activity>
        ... ...
        <meta-data android:name="ADMOB_PUBLISHER_ID" android:value="a14d6f9cc06f96b">
        <meta-data android:name="ADMOB_INTERSTITIAL_PUBLISHER_ID" android:value="a14d6fa2b901034">
        <meta-data android:name="ADMOB_ALLOW_LOCATION_FOR_ADS" android:value="true"> </meta-data>
        <activity android:name="com.admob.android.ads.AdMobActivity"> </activity>
        <receiver android:name="com.admob.android.ads.analytics.InstallReceiver" >
            <intent-filter >
                <action android:name="com.android.vending.INSTALL_REFERRER"></action>
            </intent-filter>
        </receiver>
    </application>
    <uses-permission android:name="android.permission.INTERNET"> </uses-permission>
    <uses-permission android:name="android.permission.ACCESS_NETWORK_STATE"> </uses-permission>
</manifest>
```

Admob Publisher IDs/Settings

Admob Components

Figure 1: The (Abbreviated) *AndroidManifest.xml* File in the Popular Angry Birds Android App (*com.rovio.angrybirdsrio*)

Our analysis revealed a number of privacy and security issues in the 100 representative ad libraries. In particular, most ad libraries collect private information. While some of them may use these information for legitimate purposes (i.e., the user's location for targeted advertising), we noticed a few ad libraries invasively collect information, such as the user's call logs, account information or phone number. Such information can be used to deduce the true identity of the user, enabling more comprehensive tracking of the user's habits – at the cost of all pretense of privacy. One particular popular ad library (used in 4190 apps in out dataset) even allows a variety of personal information to be directly accessible to the advertisers, creating unnecessary additional opportunities for misuse. We also found out that some ad libraries will download additional code at runtime from remote servers and execute it in the context of the running app, opening up the opportunities for exploitation and abuse and making it impossible to ensure its integrity. In fact, we have confirmed one particular case that fetches and loads suspicious payloads. After the finding, we reported those infected apps (7 in our dataset) to Google and all of these apps have now been removed from the official Android Market. These results call for the need for additional mechanisms to regulate the behavior of ad libraries on Android.

The rest of this paper is organized as follows: Section 2 is an overview of the relevant portions of the Android framework. Section 3 explains the system design to assess the threat posed by ad libraries, while Section 4 contains the implementation and evaluation results. Section 5 considers the implications and limitations of our work, which is followed by a survey of related work in Section 6. Lastly, we summarize our paper in Section 7.

2. BACKGROUND

To understand how an ad library is embedded into an Android app, we will consider a popular app, i.e., Rovio's *Angry Birds*, as the example. Initially a paid iPhone app, *Angry Birds* moved to an ad-supported model when Rovio ported it to Android. The game is free to download, but ads are displayed periodically during play and while loading new levels; these ads generate $1 million a month in revenue for Rovio.

Since Rovio is not in the advertising business, the company turned to third-party advertising networks to monetize *Angry Birds* on Android. This is a common arrangement and natural choice for smartphone app developers. After registering some financial information with an ad network, developers receive a developer identifier and a SDK. The SDK's documentation includes instructions on how to use the included ad library. Ad libraries are designed to be embedded in the app that uses them, so the instructions include the necessary permissions required by the ad library; the developer must make sure the ad-supported app requests these permissions by mak-

ing the necessary changes to its manifest file. Similarly, in order to be paid for the ads served by the app, the developer must make sure the ad library is furnished with their developer identifier.

Angry Birds' manifest file (included as Figure 1) provides a representative example of this arrangement. This particular version of *Angry Birds* contains Google's popular AdMob ad library, which pulls some of its control data from the manifest of its host app. Such data includes the crucial publisher identifiers, which are stored as the "ADMOB_PUBLISHER_ID" and "ADMOB_INTERSTITIAL_PUBLISHER_ID" meta-data values. Also in the manifest file, AdMob listens for package installation events by registering the com.admob.android.ads.-analytics.InstallReceiver component, and defines its own Activity (screen) with com.admob.android.ads.AdMobActivity to display full-screen ads.

In general, ad libraries can be classified into three ad-oriented categories: mobile web libraries, rich media libraries, and ad mediators. Mobile web libraries are front-ends to web-based ad networks. Content is requested, delivered and displayed using standard web technologies, with very little interaction with the device's APIs. These libraries typically display only banner or text ads. In our study, we found over half of existing in-app ad libraries are of this type. Rich media libraries have a similar mission, but behave more like powerful platforms. Specifically, they provide feature-rich APIs for both app developers and advertisers. While they can display the simpler ad types, they can also support more advanced kinds such as active content (i.e., JavaScript), video, interstitial ads and the like. Although there are fewer ad libraries as rich media libraries than mobile web libraries, many of the most popular ones, including AdMob, are actually rich media ones. The third category, ad mediators, is different from the previous two by exposing a standard interface through which an app developer can interact with other ad libraries of the other two types. Since ad libraries often request similar information from the app developer in very different ways, these mediator libraries exist to make bundling multiple ad libraries in an app easier.

Our experience indicates that all three kinds of ad libraries tend to share some common characteristics. For example, they have user-interface code (to present their ads) and network code (to request ads from the ad network's servers). They are also designed to be tightly bundled with host apps. In this way, it becomes more difficult to disable the ad functionality or defraud the ad network. To the same end, some ad libraries heavily obfuscate their internal workings in an effort to discourage reverse engineering. AdMob again provides a representative example. Inside the AdMob ad library, only the classes, methods and fields described in the AdMob documentation have meaningful names; everything else has had its name changed to a letter of the alphabet. Moreover, all debugging information is stripped from all the classes in the package.

Protection level	Description
normal	Low-risk permissions granted to any package requesting them
dangerous	High-risk permissions that require user confirmation to grant
signature	Only packages with the same author can request the permission
signatureOrSystem	Both packages with the same author and packages installed in the system image can request the permission

Table 1: Permission Protection Levels in Android

At runtime, the embedded ad libraries execute together with the host app inside the same runtime environment – a Dalvik [4] virtual machine (VM), which is eventually instantiated as a user-level process in Linux. Different apps run in different Dalvik VMs, isolated from each other. The Dalvik VM is derived from Java but has been significantly revised (with its own machine opcodes and semantics) to meet the resource constraints of mobile phones. When an app is installed in Android, it is assigned its own unique user identifier (UID) – as Android relies on the Linux process boundary and this app-specific UID assignment strategy to achieve isolation or prevent a misbehaving or malicious app from disrupting other apps or accessing other apps' files. Unfortunately, this strategy does not separate host apps from the in-app ad libraries they contain, as those libraries inhabit the same Dalvik VM and execute with the same UID. In our example, AdMob could readily send the user's *Angry Birds* scores to Google.

The situation is further complicated by the fact that Android apps are structured differently than programs on most platforms, in that they can contain multiple entry points. These entry points are invoked by the framework in response to inter-process communication (IPC) events; even "running" an app is treated in this way. Technically, each app is composed of one or more different components, each of which can be independently invoked. There are four types of components: *activities*, *services*, *broadcast receivers* and *content providers*. An activity represents part of the visible user interface of an app. A service, much like a Unix daemon, runs in the background for an indefinite period of time, servicing requests. A broadcast receiver receives and reacts to broadcast announcements, while content providers make data available to other apps. Each Android app is deployed in the form of a compressed package (apk). These apk files contain a manifest file (AndroidManifest.xml) that describes various standard properties about the app, such as its name, the entry points (or interfaces) it exposes to the rest of the system, and the permissions it needs to perform privileged actions. The *Angry Birds* manifest (Figure 1) describes two entry points defined by AdMob instead of *Angry Birds*: an activity (com.admob.android.ads.AdMobActivity) and a broadcast receiver (com.admob.android.ads.analytics.InstallReceiver). The activity is designed to be invoked by the code in the app, but the broadcast receiver is interested in com.android.vending.-INSTALL_REFERRER events sent out by the Android Market app. Accordingly, it's possible to invoke the ad library's code directly before any of the host app's code is run.

To better protect personal information and manage system resources, Android defines a permission-based security model [2]. In this model, the principals that have these permissions are apps, not users or libraries. The Android framework contains a predefined set of permissions and also allows developers to define additional permissions as they see fit. Each permission has a protection level [1], which determines how "dangerous" the permission is

and what other apps may request it. Table 1 summarizes the defined protection levels in Android. The signature and signatureOrSystem permission protection levels are reserved to define capabilities that are not meant to be used by apps written by other authors or by apps that are part of the system image. Permissions are checked either through annotating entry points defined in the manifest file or programmatically by the Android framework. Since ad libraries are not principals, they inherit the permissions of the apps they are embedded in. As a result, many ad libraries opportunistically check for and use permissions. Some may allow the host app's author to control their behavior somewhat while most ad libraries simply use what permissions granted to the host apps.

3. SYSTEM DESIGN

The goal of this work is to assess possible privacy and security risks posed by the embedded in-app ad libraries and additionally quantify these risks by measuring their prevalence on Android. Note that the Android's permissions-based security model provides a convenient way to measure the risk inherent in Android APIs, as their documentation typically mentions whether a permission check is required to successfully make the call. However, as mentioned previously, ad libraries are not annotated in any way by the Android framework. Also, the context surrounding each potentially-dangerous Android API call is very important in matters of privacy. For instance, if the user's phone number is retrieved but never sent to the Internet, no privacy violation has occurred. In this work, we opt to crawl and collect available apps from the official Android Market. After that, we systematically identify representative ad libraries from these apps and then develop a system to thoroughly identify possible risks. Figure 2 summarizes the methodology in our study.

3.1 Sampling the Android Market

We crawled the Android Market for apps over three months (March through May, 2011) and chose the first 100,000 downloaded apps as the dataset for our study. With them, we built a database that extracts the features needed to perform our later analysis, i.e., the permissions requested by each app (as defined in its manifest file) as well as the Java class tree hierarchy contained in the app's code.

After that, among the 100,000 apps, we select apps that have the android.permission.INTERNET permission, which is required for communication with the ad network's servers, and organize them into a candidate set. From the candidate set, we randomly select an app and disassemble it. The disassembled bytecode is examined for new ad libraries. Especially, in the search process for new ad libraries, we maintain an ad set, which is initialized to be empty. For each new ad library we identified, we add it to this set. Further, we extract its unique class tree and use it as the pattern to detect the list of host apps that contain this particular ad library. Specifically, we remove those host apps from the candidate set. We repeat the selection process until 100 distinct ad libraries have been selected. By searching the class trees stored by the database for each ad library's package name, we can then determine how many apps within our sample of 100,000 contain the given ad library. Sorting and graphing these figures of the top 20 ad libraries produces the graph in Figure 3. (The list of 100 ad libraries is detailed in Tables 2 and 4 – Section 4.) In total, the 100 ad libraries in our study are present in 52.1% of the collected 100,000 apps.

Among these 100 representative ad libraries, Google's own Ad-Mob, AdSense, and Analytics networks are listed in the top five. We also note that several other networks – Flurry, MillenialMedia, Mobclix, and AdWhirl – appear in a comparatively large number of apps. Given the maturity of these ad networks behind these lead-

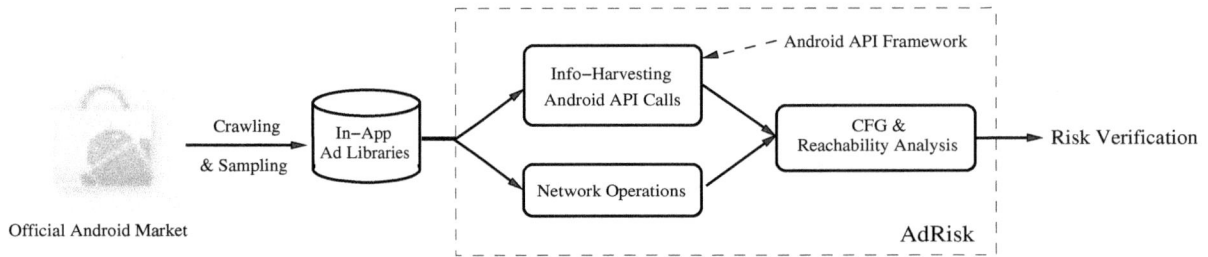

Figure 2: Assessing Possible Risks in Smartphone In-App Advertisements

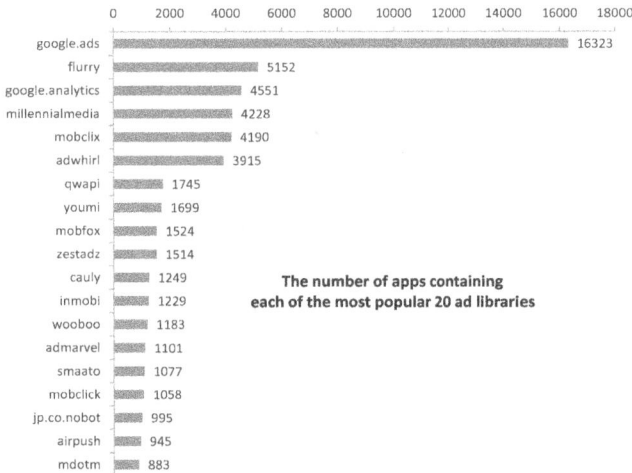

Figure 3: Popularity of the Top 20 Ad Libraries in Our Study

ing libraries, we expect that the libraries themselves offer standard functionality and do not engage in activities frowned upon by the industry as a whole. On the other hand, any potential privacy risks posed by such commonly-deployed libraries would impact many users. Among the remaining libraries, there allegorically appear to be a large number of small ad networks that offer in-app ad libraries on Android. The large number of such libraries, coupled with the relatively small proportion of apps they appear in, make holding their behavior to account more difficult for watchdog organizations inside and outside the ad industry. Analyzing these libraries is therefore important in order to gain perspective on the range of behaviors ad networks will engage in.

3.2 Analyzing Ad Libraries

After identifying the 100 representative ad libraries, we next seek to determine whether a given ad library contains any risks to security or privacy. To do that, we start by considering the permission protection levels [1] defined by the standard Android framework. Note that various standard APIs exposed by the framework require certain permissions to access, which have been annotated by a protection level. Any APIs that require a permission with an elevated protection level (i.e., above "normal") can be considered a risk to security or privacy.

Unfortunately, the relationship between APIs and permissions can be difficult to determine. The Android documentation does not feature an exhaustive list of these relationships, and some permissions are only conditionally checked. For example, Android defines two related permissions that allow access to the user's location data: `android.permission.ACCESS_COARSE_LOCATION` and `android.-permission.ACCESS_FINE_LOCATION`. Both permissions are checked by the methods of the `android.location.LocationManager` class;

however, these methods determine which permission to check by the arguments they are given. For example, calling `LocationManager.-getLastKnownLocation("gps")` requires the `android.permission.-ACCESS_FINE_LOCATION` permission; the same call with the argument of `"wifi"` would instead require the `android.permission.-ACCESS_COARSE_LOCATION` permission.

To address these challenges, we apply and extend Felt et al. [16] to derive a list of API calls that are of interest for our analysis. In particular, we take a similar approach by analyzing the Android documentation, source code and disassembled bytecode to conservatively annotate the standard APIs with the permissions that they require. However, unique to this study, our extensions also include a new set of Android API calls, which do not require any permission (Section 4). In particular, most of them are related to `ClassLoader` and reflection mechanisms. The `ClassLoader` part is responsible for dynamically loading code at runtime. To elaborate, in Dalvik, class references are resolved at run-time. Usually, due to the presence of a verifier looking for undefined references, it is safe to consider a Dalvik app as containing only well-defined static code. When combined with reflection API, it becomes possible to refer to classes using data at run-time, thus invoking the `ClassLoader` functionality *after* the verifier has run. Since the `ClassLoader` is itself just a class, its methods can be overridden to allow developers to pass raw bytecode to the Dalvik VM at run-time. In this fashion, it is possible to download and run arbitrary dynamic code, rendering any static analysis of an app incomplete. Fortunately, the interfaces to the underlying Dalvik VM are well-defined. We treat these interfaces as just another kind of APIs, which not only implicitly marks dynamic code loading as a suspicious behavior, but unifies our analysis framework. In total, our current system considers 76 distinct permissions (34 `dangerous`, 26 `signature`, 11 `signatureOrSystem`, and 5 `normal` – Section 4).

3.3 Identifying Possible Risks

After identifying the set of APIs of interest, we then perform a reachability analysis for each ad library. We are interested in two dimensions of potentially dangerous behaviors, which means we must deal with up to four potential reachability conditions. The first dimension involves the precipitating event for the dangerous behavior; that behavior could come from one of Android's many entry points, or could be in response to a received network packet. Finding a path from either of those start points to an API *could* signal a dangerous situation, but may not necessarily; this is where the second dimension comes into play. Some API calls are dangerous in themselves (such as those that can cost money) while others merely expose personal data that can then be leaked to an external party. In the first case, finding a path from an initiating entry point or network connection is sufficient, but in the second we must further find a dataflow path from the dangerous call to an external sink (e.g., network APIs).

In mechanical terms, our method is as follows: each ad library sample's bytecode is first scanned for the dangerous API calls we previously annotated. For each found API call, we trace backwards through the library source looking for potential entry points and any mitigating circumstances; for example, if such a dangerous API call only occurs if a flag representing the user's consent is set, we note this behavior. Some API calls may not be reachable under any circumstances and therefore may be safely ignored, but all others are recorded if they match these conditions. For those calls that leak information, we then additionally trace forwards through the bytecode looking for a network sink. If one is found, the candidate path from the API call to the network is also recorded[1]. In algorithmic terms, we produce a control-flow graph showing all the possible paths of execution through the library, then determine which of those paths are indeed feasible.

In our prototype, we leverage the existing baksmali Dalvik disassembler [3] to automate some of this process. As part of the greater smali package, this allows us access to a convenient intermediate representation and a limited set of intra-procedural static analysis tools. Using it as the base, we add code to derive the control-flow graph which we will traverse to find the set of feasible paths through the app (and thus the ad library).

Due to a key difference between Android apps and traditional Java programs, traversing the derived control-flow graph poses additional challenges under Android. Specifically, Java programs, like those written in many other languages, start execution at a main method. Android apps have no such method, instead containing a number of entry points based on the components they contain (certain methods in e.g., Service and Receiver objects). In addition to these, the library itself usually exposes some methods to the host app for initialization purposes. The entry points specified by the framework are automatically identified on the basis of the class they belong to, while the library's initialization methods are fed into the system through annotation. We then run the subsequent steps in our analysis over each entry point in turn, finally merging the results.

Our experience indicates that due to the influence of native code and the core classes in Android framework (e.g., the use of threads – a common technique in Android for improved user responsiveness), we observe discontinuities in the generated call graph. To resolve these discontinuities, we elect to load an additional set of class files alongside the library. These files stand-in for core classes and contain simple expressions designed to capture the semantics of each API call. Additionally, these files include the dangerous API calls the system is supposed to identify; each dangerous call contains a sentinel instruction that alerts our analysis code to its nature for the next stage of analysis.

Given this control-flow graph, our algorithm next attempts to find reachable paths from an entry point to a dangerous API call. To do this, we perform the traditional information-flow analysis, where constraints are placed on the variables and checked against by branch instructions. In the resulting feasible control-flow graph, we verify whether each dangerous API call is in a feasible code region. If a call is, execution is traced backwards and the necessary constraints remembered to form an execution path, which is then reported. The paths reported by our system are then verified. The reentrant, multi-threaded nature of Android apps makes points-to analysis difficult, which in turn frustrates efforts to accurately identify only feasible paths through the library. Certain language

features are not fully supported yet in our current prototype. For example, the Java Reflection APIs (i.e., the java.lang.reflect.* package) allow code to be invoked by name, and without perfect dataflow analysis tools this causes an irreconcilable discontinuity in the generated control-flow graph. To accommodate such situations, we take a conservative approach wherever possible, preserving accuracy but necessitating additional manual effort on some occasions. In particular, we report the use of reflection APIs in an ad library to highlight their presence for further investigation (Section 4).

4. PROTOTYPING AND EVALUATION

We base our static analysis tool on the open-source baksmali Dalvik disassembler (version 1.2.6). Implementing the design laid out in the previous section required 2809 new lines of code and four hooks in the original baksmali project. As stated in the design section, our system also required each API of interest to be annotated so that it could be analyzed by the system. Accordingly, we annotated APIs associated with 76 standard Android permissions. As our static analysis approach is rather standard, in the following, we mainly focus on the peculiarities of the Android platform and the new extensions we added for risk analysis.

Specifically, besides reporting potentially-feasible paths, our prototype has been extended to report on five other code patterns of interest: the use of reflection, dynamic code loading, permission probing, JavaScript linkages and reading the list of installed packages. As the presence of one or more of these patterns can color our other findings for a given library, we opt to have our tool automatically report them alongside its feasible-path output.

The first such pattern, the use of reflection, concerns the use of the java.lang.reflect package. As mentioned earlier, this portion of the Java specification allows programmatic invocation of methods and access to fields, which complicates our static analysis. Without it, the static analysis of Dalvik bytecode is reliable and unambiguous. In theory, reflection essentially makes resolving an app's call graph into a dataflow problem. In practice, often reflection appears to involve constant strings, thus introducing no new ambiguity. However, this is not always the case in our collected ad samples. Therefore, our system makes what assumptions it can while flagging the situation for further review.

In a similar vein, Android apps usually are amenable to static analysis techniques because they are designed to be loaded as a whole and statically verified by the framework itself. However, another esoteric Java language feature was carried over into Dalvik: the ClassLoader class. This class is used by the framework to find code resources on demand. Usually, the static verification stage causes practically the entire app to be loaded at once, as the verifier attempts to resolve all the references in the bytecode. However, using reflection, it is possible to cause a class to be loaded that is not directly referenced by any existing code. As the ClassLoader class can be extended by developers, custom versions of this class can be written to load code from non-standard resources. Each such ClassLoader inherits from a parent version of the class, on up to the baseline "system" instance of the class. Since Dalvik, unlike Java, does not permit the "system" ClassLoader to be changed by the developer, dynamic code loading is very explicit: the generic reflection API cannot be used to implicitly reference a class for the first time, so instead the custom ClassLoader must be explicitly queried. Our prototype flags this behavior and raises a serious warning, as its presence negates all existing static analysis efforts and signals suspicious dynamic code loading behavior.

A more common pattern our prototype elects to handle specially is what we call "permission probing." In this pattern, an ad li-

---

[1]Note that we do not ignore calls that do not meet this additional criterion due to the complexities inherent in dataflow analysis. It is possible to introduce dataflow discontinuities using threading, caching, and other behaviors; we elect to involve some additional manual effort in order to ensure the accuracy of our study.

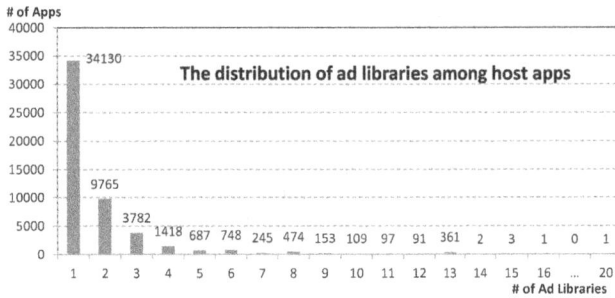

Figure 4: Number of Ad Libraries Contained by Each App

brary contains some API which requires permission to successfully call. Instead of mandating that the developer of the host app requests this permission, the ad library can instead opportunistically attempt to use the API, either by checking that it has the necessary permission beforehand, or by handling the `SecurityException` that is thrown by most APIs when they are called with insufficient permission. These methods of checking permissions are well-defined under Android, and so we can inspect the control-flow graph to detect branches that detour around dangerous API calls.

Similarly, it seems to be common practice for "rich media" ad libraries to offer JavaScript bindings to expose additional functionality to JavaScript ads. We elect to include this practice in our findings for two reasons. Not only is this behavior indicative of "rich media" libraries, it also raises interesting privacy concerns, which we will cover in greater depth in Section 4.2.2.

Lastly, we temper our results by showing one instance of an invasive API that, for whatever reason, requires *no* special permission to access. Some ad libraries we studied collect the list of all apps installed on the device. This information is every bit as personal as the user's browser history, in that it reveals some information about their interests. We include this behavior to demonstrate the guile advertisers have and the incompleteness of the permission-based system.

In the rest of this section, we present our findings from the analysis of 100 representative ad libraries. We first summarize our results in Section 4.1 and then present categorized findings about dangerous behaviors in these ad libraries in Section 4.2. Finally, we evaluate the performance of our prototype in Section 4.3.

4.1 Overall Results

Before tabulating our findings, we stress that our results are for ad libraries rather than apps. Some apps in our sample of 100,000 will contain more than one ad library, while others contain none at all. For the 100 representative ad libraries in our study, we found that they are embedded in 52,067 different host apps in our dataset. As one host app may contain more than one ad library, we show a breakdown of how many libraries each of these apps contain. The result is shown as Figure 4.

From the figure, it seems more than one third of apps (or more precisely, 35,991) contain one ad library and a small fraction of apps (around 3%) include at least five ad libraries for monetization. One particular host app, i.e., com.Dimension4.USFlag, embedded no fewer than 20 ad libraries! However, it is unclear whether the inclusion of more ad libraries necessarily brings more profit to an app's developers.

Our system scans each representative ad library for the use of 76 dangerous APIs. The overall results for the top 50 ad libraries are shown in Table 2, while the results for the remaining 50 are shown in Table 4 (Appendix). In practice many of the Android's dangerous APIs were not used by any ad library, so we choose to omit them for brevity in our results. Specifically, the two tables contain

the 14 dangerous APIs we see used by at least one ad library. In the tables, we also include data on six structural properties of interest, such as the use of obfuscation, conditional API use via permission probing, and dynamic code loading through the `ClassLoader` language feature. Overall, our system reports 318 total API uses and structural patterns. Upon further verification, 19 of them ask permission from the user and our system properly recognizes 15 of these cases, which happen to be all related to text message (SMS) API calls.

Despite all of the reported APIs being marked as "dangerous," our results show that some APIs are commonly used by ad libraries. These include the location APIs and a single "Read Phone Information" API call, both of which are used by at least half of the ad libraries we analyzed. The ad libraries use these APIs for targeting information: the location APIs can be used to serve ad content relevant to the geographic area of the user, while the commonly-used phone information call returns a unique identifier (the phone's IMEI number) that is useful for tracking what content has been served to a particular user. These uses seem plausible, in the context of an ad library; however, we did identify two ad libraries (Mobclix and adserver) that expose this information directly to advertisers, which is harder to justify.

The remaining dangerous APIs either provide some feature, or allow access to more intrusive data maintained by the device. The feature-based APIs appear to be mostly harmless. For example, a number of ad libraries allow ads to place phone calls, send text messages or add an event to the calendar. In all of these cases, these functions are performed only after the user triggers them (i.e., by clicking on an ad) *and* confirms their intentions.

More insidious, however, are requests for information that is not directly useful for ad targeting. Our analysis uncovered a few instances where an ad library accessed information that is only useful when correlated with other facts known about the user. This correlative information is a direct threat to the user's privacy, because it can be used to uncover the user's true identity. For example, it is hard to make a case that the user's call history has any bearing on what ads they will be interested in, yet we discovered one ad library (sosceo) transmitting some of that information to the Internet (to be detailed in Section 4.2.1). In a similar vein, a large number of ad libraries used an API call to retrieve the user's phone number, and another ad library (Mobus) peculiarly reads through the user's SMS messages to determine which text-messaging service center they use. Finally, we identified one particularly worrying use of an otherwise innocent API, where some ad libraries (such as waps) upload a list of all the installed apps on the phone.

Looking beyond privacy concerns, we identified five ad libraries which make use of the `ClassLoader` feature to dynamically load code at runtime. These ad libraries are effectively impossible to statically analyze as a result; at a whim, their code can be changed. A malicious or compromised ad network could command its ad libraries to download a botnet payload or root exploit, for example. Our later investigation indeed captures one suspicious payload, which essentially turns the host app into a remotely-controllable bot (Section 4.2.3).

Moreover, the other structural properties of ad libraries are worth mentioning. Over half of the ad libraries we studied employed obfuscation techniques, presumably to discourage reverse engineering. While not altering the function of the library, these transformations strip human-readable names from methods and classes while optionally muddling the control flow by adding pointless redundancy or by reordering instructions. As an example, we list in Figure 5 the classes contained in one particular ad library, i.e., AirAD. Only a few such classes have names that carry any meaning; all the

Table 2: The Overall Results from the Top 50 Representative Ad Libraries

	Included in Apps	Probes Permissions	Uses Obfuscation	Uses Reflection	Uses JavaScript	Read Installed Packages	Location Data	Place Phone Call	Camera	List Accounts	Read Calendar	Read Contact/Call Logs	Read Browser Bookmarks	Read Phone Information	Read Phone Number	Read SMS	Send SMS	Change Calendar	Change Contacts	Use Vibrator	ClassLoader
admob/android/ads	27235	✓	✓	✓	✓		✓														
google/ads	16323	✓		✓			✓														
flurry	5152	✓	✓		✓		✓														
google/../analytics	4551																				
millennialmedia	4228	✓			✓									✓						✓	
mobclix	4190	✓		✓	✓		✓				✓	✓		✓				✓	✓	✓	
adwhirl	3915	✓		✓			✓							✓							
qwapi	1745	✓					✓							✓	✓						
youmi	1699	✓	✓				✓							✓			✓				
mobfox	1524	✓					✓							✓							
zestadz	1514																				
cauly	1249						✓	✓						✓							
inmobi	1229	✓					✓							✓							
wooboo	1183	✓	✓				✓							✓	✓		✓				
admarvel	1101	✓			✓		✓							✓							
smaato	1077	✓			✓		✓							✓							
mobclick	1058	✓					✓							✓							
jp/co/nobot	995																				
airpush	945	✓	✓				✓							✓			✓				
mdotm/android/ads	883													✓							
vdopia	872		✓		✓									✓							
wiyun	777	✓	✓	✓			✓	✓						✓			✓				
android/adhubs	651				✓		✓							✓	✓						
madhouse	603	✓	✓	✓										✓							
pontiflex	522	✓		✓	✓									✓							
innerActive	497	✓						✓						✓							
adserver/adview	492	✓		✓	✓		✓	✓		✓	✓	✓		✓			✓				
casee	479	✓					✓	✓						✓	✓						
greystripe	440		✓		✓									✓							
omniture	433			✓										✓							
guohead	400	✓		✓	✓	✓	✓														
daum/mobilead	399	✓					✓														
domob	374	✓	✓				✓							✓			✓				
tapjoy	368													✓							
jp/Adlantis	341			✓										✓							
adagogo	339																				
adchina	327						✓	✓						✓	✓		✓				
jumptap	278	✓			✓		✓	✓						✓							
medialets	274	✓	✓	✓	✓		✓													✓	
nowistech	272											✓		✓							
waps	239	✓		✓		✓	✓							✓							
vpon/adon	189						✓							✓			✓				
energysource	160	✓			✓																✓
iconosys	131								✓	✓				✓	✓		✓				
adwo/adsdk	131	✓	✓		✓									✓	✓		✓				
sktelecom/tad	125	✓	✓	✓	✓			✓						✓	✓			✓			✓
kr/uplusad	112																				
smartadserver	102			✓										✓							
mt/airad	89	✓	✓											✓	✓						
emome/hamiapps/sdk	85					✓															
Total	92297	31	14	15	17	3	27	8	1	2	2	3	0	33	9	0	9	2	1	3	2

rest are strings of "l" (lowercase L) and "I" characters. The ad libraries that are noted as using obfuscation in Table 2 all used some scheme to obfuscate their internal classes, and typically also obfuscate the names of fields, methods and the like in a similar fashion. Other obfuscators are known to exist, but all serve the same purpose; for example, the default obfuscator names classes after alphabetical characters, while another uses nonsense dictionary words like "Watermelon" and "Railroad." Applying these techniques to a reasonably large ad library hides the intent behind much of what the library does, while not truly protecting the ad network's trade secrets – as the library can still be unambiguously analyzed, and the network's core functionality resides on its servers regardless, safe from competitors' eyes.

In another common pattern, many ad libraries probe the permissions available to them before attempting to use permission-guarded APIs. Normally, if an Android app calls an API it does not have permission to access, a SecurityException is thrown. If this exception is not caught, the app will crash. In order to prevent this from happening, ad libraries either check their permissions up front or silently catch the thrown exception. It turns out more than half of studied ad libraries (marked in Tables 2 and 4) engage in this sort of behavior. Some of them do log their failed attempts to access

107

AirAD$AdListener   AirAD   MultiAD   IIIIIIIIIIIIIIII
IIIIIIIIIIIIIIII   IIIIIIIIIIIIIIII   IIIIIIIIIIIIIIII   IIIIIIIIIIIIIIII
IIIIIIIIIIIIIIII   IIIIIIIIIIIIIIII   IIIIIIIIIIIIIIII   IIIIIIIIIIIIIIII
IIIIIIIIIIIIIIII   IIIIIIIIIIIIIIII   IIIIIIIIIIIIIIII   IIIIIIIIIIIIIIII
IIIIIIIIIIIIIIII   IIIIIIIIIIIIIIII   IIIIIIIIIIIIIIII   IIIIIIIIIIIIIIII
IIIIIIIIIIIIIIII   IIIIIIIIIIIIIIII   IIIIIIIIIIIIIIII   IIIIIIIIIIIIIIII
IIIIIIIIIIIIIIII   IIIIIIIIIIIIIIII   IIIIIIIIIIIIIIII   IIIIIIIIIIIIIIII
IIIIIIIIIIIIIIII   IIIIIIIIIIIIIIII   IIIIIIIIIIIIIIII

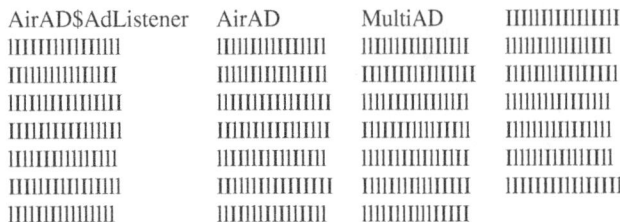

Figure 5: Classes in the Obfuscated com.mt.airad **Package**

these APIs, chastising the host app's developer for not properly requesting the necessary permissions. However, most attempt to do what they can with as many permissions as they can access, again silently. A few libraries, such as AdMob, do permit the host app developer to selectively deny the library permission to use a certain API. This is unfortunately far from the norm, and only Mobclix allows the *user* to disallow access to sensitive APIs – on a case-by-case basis, and with some troubling ramifications, as elaborated in Section 4.2.2.

Lastly, some ad libraries use the Java reflection language feature, which essentially allows programmatic access to methods and fields by their name. Normally, when Dalvik bytecode is loaded, there is a static verification step that ensures all referenced code elements are valid. Reflection sidesteps this mechanism, which allows for the use of dynamic code (discussed at more length in Section 4.2.3), but can also be used to access *any* code that is not guaranteed to resolve correctly on all devices. In this way, it is possible for ad libraries to access "experimental" APIs or vendor-specific APIs. Given the lower maturity of such APIs, their use by ad libraries is suspect.

4.2 Categorized Findings

To provide greater detail about problematic behaviors we came across in our analysis, we organize them into three categories.

4.2.1 Invasively Collecting Personal Information

The first category involves the questionable collection of personal information. Specifically, some ad libraries brazenly request information not directly useful in fulfilling their purpose. Our results show that the larger ad networks typically do not engage in such questionable activities, but smaller ad networks might. Unfortunately, there is no way for the user of an app to know which ad networks it contains.

A representative example of this behavior can be found in the sosceo ad library, one of the least popular libraries studied. Like most ad libraries, sosceo is instantiated by its hosting app making a UI element designed to display an ad, in this case a com.sosceo.android.ads.AdView object. When this object is created, a fairly lengthy set of obfuscated method calls occurs. These method calls ultimately query the device's contact information database for the most recent phone call. This information is duly stored in a field of a data object used by the AdView object; when the AdView object requests an ad from the backing ad network, the information is included as an URL query string under the "dp" key to the ad server.

Other ad libraries engage in similarly strange behaviors; Mobus, for example, reads the SMS (text-message) database looking for administrative information about the user's Short Message Service Center (SMSC). This SMSC is the back-end service provider responsible for routing text messages to and from the user. For some unknown purpose, Mobus transmits this information to its servers.

Similarly, Pontiflex takes an interest in what account credentials the user has on the device. This information is not a direct security risk as the ad library does not have access to the credentials themselves, but it does query the list of accounts the user's phone manages. Somewhat suspiciously, the dangerous API calls in this case are performed via the reflection API, which is a language feature that allows methods to be invoked by means of data strings. It is possible that reflection is being used, in this case, to throw off static analysis of the library.

4.2.2 Permissively Disclosing Data to Running Ads

The second category involves the direct exposure of personal information to running ads. One of the most popular ad libraries, Mobclix, appears at first glance to function like most other ad libraries. To display an ad, Mobclix creates an android.webkit.WebView, which is essentially a miniature web browser. The ad is then rendered by this web browser for display, allowing the advertiser to design their ads using standard web technologies.

However, unlike its principal competitors, Mobclix attempts to gain advantages by offering its advertisers access to certain smartphone features. Since these features do not have standard hooks in HTML or JavaScript, the Mobclix ad library has a class (com.mobclix.android.sdk.MobclixJavascriptInterface) that binds certain Android APIs to JavaScript functions that are then exposed to ads rendered within the WebView. Each API call is wrapped in a method that simply and succinctly exposes it to JavaScript. By doing so, Mobclix exposes a great variety of API calls and allows running ads to most of the sensors and data on the phone. Note that most of these accesses include appropriate user confirmation dialogs. For example, while an ad can call contactsAddContact(...) to add a contact to the user's address book, nothing will happen unless the user gives consent via a dialog box.

Unfortunately, not all functions are safely wrapped in this way. For instance, the gpsStart(...) function allows a JavaScript ad to register a callback function. This function will be called immediately, and again whenever the user's moves more than a defined distance from the last reported position. The user is never asked for their consent, nor are they notified in any way that this feature of their phone is being used by an ad. This particular example sufficiently raises interesting privacy issues. It is reasonable to expect that the Mobclix ad library itself should have access to location information; such information is commonly used to target ads to a certain geographical area. However, this code is not actually using that information for Mobclix's ad-targeting purposes. Instead, the information is being given to a third party advertiser. Indeed, given access to this functionality, the ad itself can be thought of as dynamically-loaded code of unknown provenance (Section 4.2.3).

4.2.3 Unsafely Fetching and Loading Dynamic Code

The third category involves unsafe fetching and loading of dynamic code (possibly from the Internet), which poses an even greater potential threat for two reasons. One is that this dynamically loaded code cannot be reliably analyzed, effectively bypassing existing static analysis efforts. The other is the fact that the downloaded code can be easily changed at any time, seriously undermining the capability of predicting or confining its behavior.

In the 100 representative ad libraries, five of them have this unsafe practice. One particular one will be downloading suspicious payloads, which allows the host app to be remotely controlled. Specifically, the portion of this ad library that is embedded in the host app is very small: a single service, com.plankton.device.android.service.AndroidMDKService. This service contacts a remote server with the list of permissions granted to the host app and the phone's hardware identifier (IMEI); in return, the remote server provides it with the URL to download a .jar file (see Fig-

```
POST /ProtocolGW/installation HTTP/1.1
Content-Length: 1242
Content-Type: application/x-www-form-urlencoded
Host: www.searchwebmobile.com
Connection: Keep-Alive

action=get&applicationId=123456789&developerId=987654321&deviceId=354957034053382
&currentVersion=-1&permissions=android.permission.INTERNET%3Bandroid.permission.
ACCESS_WIFI_STATE%3Bcom.android.browser.permission.WRITE_HISTORY_BOOKMARKS%3B
com.android.browser.permission.READ_HISTORY_BOOKMARKS%3Bcom.android.launcher.
permission.INSTALL_SHORTCUT%3Bcom.android.launcher.permission.UNINSTALL_SHORTCUT%3B
com.android.launcher.permission.READ_SETTINGS%3Bandroid.launcher.permission.
WRITE_SETTINGS%3Bcom.android.htc.launcher.permission.READ_SETTINGS%3Bcom.android.launcher.
permission.READ_SETTINGS%3Bcom.motorola.launcher.permission.WRITE_SETTINGS%3Bcom.
motorola.launcher.permission.INSTALL_SHORTCUT%3Bcom.motorola.launcher.permission.
UNINSTALL_SHORTCUT%3Bcom.motorola.dlauncher.permission.READ_SETTINGS%3Bcom.motorola.
dlauncher.permission.WRITE_SETTINGS%3Bcom.motorola.dlauncher.permission.INSTALL_SHORTCUT
%3Bcom.motorola.dlauncher.permission.UNINSTALL_SHORTCUT%3Bcom.lge.launcher.permission.
READ_SETTINGS%3Bcom.lge.launcher.permission.WRITE_SETTINGS%3Bcom.lge.launcher.permission.
INSTALL_SHORTCUT%3Bcom.lge.launcher.permission.UNINSTALL_SHORTCUT%3Bandroid.permission.
READ_CONTACTS%3Bandroid.permission.READ_PHONE_STATE%3Bandroid.permission.READ_LOGS%3B

HTTP/1.1 200 OK
Date: Sun, 05 Jun 2011 04:30:33 GMT
Server: Apache-Coyote/1.1
Content-Length: 76
Connection: keep-alive

url=http://www.searchwebmobile.com/ProtocolGW/;fileName=plankton_v0.0.4.jar;
```

Figure 6: Handshake Communication between Plankton and its Command-and-Control Server

ure 6). This .jar file contains the vast majority of Plankton's code, which is then dynamically loaded using a dalvik.system.-DexClassLoader object – Dalvik's base implementation of the ClassLoader Java language feature. The downloaded .jar will listen to remote commands and turn the host app into a bot. Based on this discovery, we have reported the seven affected host apps to Google, which promptly removed them from the official Android Market on the same day.

This behavior is interesting because it highlights the dynamically-linked nature of Dalvik. Android apps are distributed as bytecode, which makes app analysis easier due to the clearly-defined semantics of the format. Furthermore, upon loading a class for the first time, a Java-style bytecode verifier makes certain that all references within the class resolve. This verification step seems to preclude adding arbitrary code at runtime. However, via the java.lang.-reflect package, Java (and hence Dalvik) can load classes by name at runtime. Coupling this language feature with the ability to control where Dalvik looks for definitions for such classes – that is, the DexClassLoader class – allows apps to load arbitrary code not contained in the app's package file. In this case, the downloaded .jar file has a predefined entry point, com.plankton.device.android.-AndroidMDKProvider.init(...). DexClassLoader looks for it by name and then invokes the control logic. Within the newly-downloaded code, the bytecode verifier works as usual, since it now uses the modified DexClassLoader to resolve references to unfamiliar classes.

Another four ad libraries make use of this feature, likely as a version-control and content-delivery mechanism. Opening the full expressive power of Dalvik – replete with all the permissions granted by the app – to nebulously downloaded dynamic code has unfortunate privacy implications. Again, given that the code retrieved from the Internet will naturally change, it is impossible to verify that the ad library is only engaging in the behaviors embodied in the library.

4.3 Performance Measurement

Next, we report the performance overhead of our prototype. In our test, we picked up five ad libraries and run our system to analyze each of them ten times. Each analysis run scans the given ad library for all (80) APIs our prototype handles. In each run, we record the processing time and report the average. Our test machine is an AMD Athlon 64 X2 5200+ machine with 2GB of memory and a Hitachi HDP72502 7200 rpm hard drive. We summarize the results in Table 3. The test-case libraries were selected to provide a mix of ad library types and complexities. Each library took, on average, $\sim$ 15.66 seconds to process. Given our tool is designed

Library	Processing Time
AdMob	16.17s
AdWhirl	17.25s
Appmedia	14.58s
Quattro	14.40s
UplusAd	15.91s

Table 3: Processing Time of Analyzed Ad Libraries

to be used in an offline, semi-automated capacity, we believe this performance to be acceptable for our purposes.

5. DISCUSSION

Our study has so far uncovered a number of serious privacy and security risks from existing in-app ad libraries on the popular Android platform.[2] Given this, it is important to examine possible root causes and explore future defenses.

First, due to the fact that ad libraries are incorporated into the host apps that use them, they in essence form an symbiotic relationship. Based on such relationship, an ad library can effectively leverage it and naturally inherit all permissions a user may grant to the host app, thus undermining the app-based privacy and security safeguards. Accordingly, we believe that the exposed risks are fundamentally rooted in the granularity problem in the essential Android's permissions model. Under this model, the smallest entity that can be granted a permission is an app. Even though ad libraries come from a different developer and have different intentions than their hosting apps, they are afforded the same permissions. As we have seen, advertisers themselves are sometimes allowed to execute code within an app, adding yet another untrusted set of principals to the list of parties covered by a single permissions policy. Though an app's requests for access to private information can stem from the app's code, the ad library's code, or both, but the user or rather the Android platform cannot determine at a glance which parties will use the information.

Second, the current situation could also be a product of one central tension: the same solutions that would allow ad libraries to be sandboxed could also be used to disable them, or alternatively, defraud them. Even if Google had provided a separate Advertiser template in the Android framework (i.e., alongside the Services, Receivers, ContentProviders and Activities that exist today), there would be no incentive for ad networks to use it. It is safer to tightly couple ad libraries with their host apps, to keep them from being easily circumvented. Possibly for the same reason, some ad networks take the approach of the worrisome dynamic code loading behavior we observed. In particular, since ad libraries are not their own entity in the framework, they can only be updated alongside their host app. The ad network cannot control the release schedule of all the apps its ad library is bundled with. As a result, any code updates need to be pushed out along side channels. The dynamic code loading apparently becomes the choice at the cost of raising privacy and security concerns to mobile users.

Third, we may also consider ways to design ad libraries that satisfy the needs of advertisers, ad networks and users alike [21, 22, 32]. As in traditional web-based ad libraries, these systems display targeted advertising and report the network impressions, click-throughs, etc. to bill the advertiser. However, they aim to do these things irrefutably yet anonymously. The ultimate aim is to only provide the ad network with the metrics needed for billing, while allowing the user to retain complete and direct ownership of

---

[2]While we only studied one particular platform, due to the similar nature of integrating in-app ads into smartphone apps, we expect similar privacy and security risks will also exist on other platforms.

personally-identifiable information. Unfortunately, each approach proposed so far has required either additional overhead (extra data transfers, extra storage on the device, etc.), an organizational shift (third-party ad "dealers," the direct involvement of wireless providers, etc.), or both. As some ad libraries may not brand the ads that they serve, the user is usually ignorant of the ad networks used by an app. Therefore, these disadvantages may not be offset by competitive advantages for ad networks that operate in a privacy-preserving manner.

From another perspective, our current study is limited to those ad libraries that are simply "piggybacked" into host apps. Particularly, current ad libraries are typically self-contained (as a standalone package) so that they can be readily included by app developers. However, it is possible to have more advanced mechanisms (e.g., collusion [26], re-delegation [18, 20], or indirect channels [31]) that could avoid using dangerous Android APIs being modeled by AdRisk while still accessing various personal information on the phone. Note that there are some ongoing research projects that aim to detect or mitigate these attacks [9, 10, 11, 18]. How to extend AdRisk to seamlessly integrate these systems remains an interesting task for future work.

6. RELATED WORK

Smartphone privacy and security has recently attracted considerable attention. Researchers have employed various techniques to understand or assess these risks. For example, PiOS [12] used program slicing to detect privacy leaks in iOS apps. SCanDroid [19] analyzed Android apps' source code, along with the manifest file included with each app, to produce a data-flow policy specification that describes an app's use of information. Woodpecker [20] uses interprocedural data-flow analysis to detect possible confused-deputy attacks [23] on Android firmware. However, none of them is designed to understand or assess the information leaks and security risks from the embedded ad libraries. In contrast, AdRisk focuses on the risks from these ad libraries in the context of privacy (e.g., information harvesting) and security (e.g., untrusted code downloading and execution). In the case of SCanDroid, its reliance on the Java source code for an app renders it unable to analyze most ad libraries, which typically are only distributed in a compiled form.

TaintDroid [13] takes a different tack to expose and identify privacy leaks in apps as a whole. By using lightweight dynamic taint analysis built into modified Android middleware, the system alerts the user to the presence and nature of the leak. Note it is only concerned about the whole apps, not explicitly the ad libraries they contain. Also, as a dynamic technique, it may be able to precisely pinpoint possible leaks, but it is generally incomplete in not exploring all possible execution paths. Most recently, Enck *et al.* [14] wrote the ded Dalvik decompiler to study around one thousand popular Android apps, and reported a number of findings about them. In this work, we studied one hundred thousand apps, which allowed us to systematically identify and assess a wider variety of ad libraries. For example, none of the libraries that feature dynamic code loading (Section 4.2.3) were included or reported earlier. We believe that such dynamic code loading is dangerous, especially in light of recent Felt *et al.*'s findings [17], which are related to identifying "overprivilege" in Android apps. (An overprivilege occurs when an app requests more permissions than it uses.) In particular, among 940 Android apps being studied, more than one third were found to be overprivileged. Given the permission-probing behavior in existing ad libraries, it is possible that even more apps are requesting unnecessary permissions, which are then opportunistically being used by their embedded ad libraries. Dynamic code loading paints a yet more grim picture, as we found one ad library

uploaded the permissions its host app was granted before downloading the code.

On the defensive side, several related solutions have been proposed and many of them revolve around the permission system. For instance, Kirin [15] checks the manifest of apps that are being installed against a permission-assignment policy, blocking any that request certain potentially unsafe combinations. Saint [28] takes this approach a step further, by allowing app developers to constrain permission assignment at install-time and permission use at run-time. Other systems try to add further expressivity to the permission system, such as Apex [27], which modifies the framework to allow permissions to be selectively granted and revoked at runtime. MockDroid [7] rewrites privacy-sensitive API calls to simulate their failure. TISSA [33] similarly protects user information, but instead does so by modifying the Android framework to support user-defined information disclosure policies; sensitive APIs can return false information under such a scheme instead of simply failing. AppFence [24] further refines this approach by adding taint-tracking, allowing yet more nuanced policies. However, these systems typically treat the apps as a while, without further differentiating the embedded ad libraries from hosting apps.

More generally, researchers have explored ways to deliver targeted ad content without disclosing any private information to the advertiser or ad network. For example, Adnostic [32] addresses the online ads and allows for behavioral web advertising without giving behavioral information to the ad network (by using a dedicated Firefox browser extension to prevent unnecessary information disclosure). MobiAd [22] takes a similar approach by using a broadcast mode available to wireless providers to stream a large amount of tagged ad content that is then filtered by mobile devices. Privad [21] offloads ad selection to the client, but aims to do so in a way that is less disruptive to the existing industry model for ad networks; in particular, much emphasis (including a follow-on work [30]) is placed on preserving the auction mechanism by which advertisers compete for ad slots on the networks. These systems incorporate cryptographic billing to ensure that click-throughs are properly billed to the advertiser without compromising the consumer's privacy, and without encouraging click fraud. Lastly, there are some efforts that specifically aim to address the privacy concerns inherent with location information. PrivStats [29] offers a mechanism so that aggregate location information can be irrefutably collected in a privacy-preserving way. Bindschaedler *et al.* [8] attempts to prevent tracking individual devices' movements by changing their identifiers in crowded regions. While these systems are making progress in mitigating the privacy risks, it is unclear yet whether they can be applied in our context to handle the in-app ad security risks (Section 4.2.3).

7. CONCLUSIONS

In this paper, we systematically examine the security and privacy issues raised by in-app ad libraries. We analyze 100 ad libraries selected from a sample of 100,000 apps collected from the official Android Market, and find that even among some of the most widely-deployed ad libraries, there exist threats to security and privacy. Such threats range from collecting unnecessarily intrusive user information to allowing third-party code of unknown provenance to execute within the hosting app. Since Android's permissions model cannot distinguish between actions performed by an ad library and those performed by its hosting app, the current Android system provides little indication of the existence of these threats within any given app, which necessitates a change in the way existing ad libraries can be integrated into host apps.

8. REFERENCES

[1] Android Permission Protection Levels. http:// developer.android.com/reference/android/ R.styleable.html# AndroidManifestPermission_ protectionLevel.

[2] Android Security and Permissions. http://developer. android.com/guide/topics/security/ security.html.

[3] Baksmali: A Disassembler for Android's Dex Format. http://code.google.com/p/smali/.

[4] Dalvik. http://sites.google.com/site/io/ dalvik-vm-internals/.

[5] Distmo Report: April, 2011 and May, 2011. http://www. distimo.com/publications.

[6] Gartner Says Sales of Mobile Devices in Second Quarter of 2011 Grew 16.5 Percent Year-on-Year. http://www. gartner.com/it/page.jsp?id=1764714.

[7] A. R. Beresford, A. Rice, N. Skehin, and R. Sohan. MockDroid: Trading Privacy for Application Functionality on Smartphones. In *Proceedings of the Twelfth Workshop on Mobile Computing Systems & Applications*, HotMobile '11, May 2011.

[8] L. Bindschaedler, M. Jadliwala, I. Bilogrevic, I. Aad, P. Ginzboorg, V. Niemi, and J.-P. Hubaux. Track Me If You Can: On the Effectiveness of Context-based Identifier Changes in Deployed Mobile Networks. In *Proceedings of the 19th Annual Network and Distributed System Security Symposium*, NDSS '12, February 2012.

[9] S. Bugiel, L. Davi, A. Dmitrienko, T. Fischer, A.-R. Sadeghi, and B. Shastry. Towards Taming Privilege-Escalation Attacks on Android. In *Proceedings of the 19th Annual Network and Distributed System Security Symposium*, NDSS '12, February 2012.

[10] S. Bugiel, L. Davi, A. Dmitrienko, S. Heuser, A.-R. Sadeghi, and B. Shastry. Practical and Lightweight Domain Isolation on Android. In *Proceedings of the 1st Workshop on Security and Privacy in Smartphones and Mobile Devices*, CCS-SPSM'11, 2011.

[11] M. Dietz, S. Shekhar, Y. Pisetsky, A. Shu, and D. S. Wallach. QUIRE: Lightweight Provenance for Smart Phone Operating Systems. In *Proceedings of the 20th USENIX Security Symposium*, August 2011.

[12] M. Egele, C. Kruegel, E. Kirda, and G. Vigna. PiOS: Detecting Privacy Leaks in iOS Applications. In *Proceedings of the 18th Annual Network and Distributed System Security Symposium*, NDSS '11, February 2011.

[13] W. Enck, P. Gilbert, B.-G. Chun, L. P. Cox, J. Jung, P. McDaniel, and A. N. Sheth. TaintDroid: An Information-Flow Tracking System for Realtime Privacy Monitoring on Smartphones. In *Proceedings of the 9th USENIX Symposium on Operating Systems Design and Implementation*, OSDI '10, pages 1–6, February 2010.

[14] W. Enck, D. Octeau, P. McDaniel, and S. Chaudhuri. A Study of Android Application Security. In *Proceedings of the 20th USENIX Security Symposium*, August 2011.

[15] W. Enck, M. Ongtang, and P. McDaniel. On Lightweight Mobile Phone Application Certification. In *Proceedings of the 16th ACM Conference on Computer and Communications Security*, CCS '09, pages 235–245, October 2009.

[16] A. P. Felt, E. Chin, S. Hanna, D. Song, and D. Wagner. Android Permissions Demysti.ed. In *Proceedings of the 18th ACM Conference on Computer and Communications Security*, CCS '11, October 2011.

[17] A. P. Felt, E. Chin, S. Hanna, D. Song, and D. Wagner. Android Permissions Demystified. In *Proceedings of the 18th ACM Conference on Computer and Communications Security (CCS '11)*, October 2011.

[18] A. P. Felt, H. Wang, A. Moschuk, S. Hanna, and E. Chin. Permission Re-Delegation: Attacks and Defenses. In *Proceedings of the 20th USENIX Security Symposium*, August 2011.

[19] A. P. Fuchs, A. Chaudhuri, and J. S. Foster. SCanDroid: Automated Security Certification of Android Applications. http://www.cs.umd.edu/~avik/papers/ scandroidascaa.pdf.

[20] M. Grace, Y. Zhou, Z. Wang, and X. Jiang. Systematic Detection of Capability Leaks in Stock Android Smartphones. In *Proceedings of the 19th Annual Network and Distributed System Security Symposium*, NDSS '12, February 2012.

[21] S. Guha, B. Cheng, and P. Francis. Privad: Practical Privacy in Online Advertising. In *Proceedings of the 8th USENIX Conference on Networked Systems Design and Implementation*, NSDI '11, March 2011.

[22] H. Haddadi, P. Hui, and I. Brown. MobiAd: Private and Scalable Mobile Advertising. In *Proceedings of the 5th ACM International Workshop on Mobility in the Evolving Internet Architecture*, MobiArch '10, pages 33–38, September 2010.

[23] N. Hardy. The Confused Deputy, or Why Capabilities Might Have Been Invented. In *ACM Operating Systems Review*, volume 22, pages 36–38, 1988.

[24] P. Hornyack, S. Han, J. Jung, S. Schechter, and D. Wetherall. "These Aren't the Droids You're Looking For": Retrofitting Android to Protect Data from Imperious Applications. In *Proceedings of the 18th ACM Conference on Computer and Communications Security (CCS '11)*, October 2011.

[25] IDC. Android Rises, Symbian 3 and Windows Phone 7 Launch as Worldwide Smartphone Shipments Increase 87.2% Year Over Year. http://www.idc.com/about/ viewpressrelease.jsp? containerId=prUS22689111.

[26] C. Marforio, F. Aurélien, and S. Čapkun. Application collusion attack on the permission-based security model and its implications for modern smartphone systems. Technical Report 724, ETH Zurich, April 2011.

[27] M. Nauman, S. Khan, and X. Zhang. Apex: Extending Android Permission Model and Enforcement with User-Defined Runtime Constraints. In *Proceedings of the 5th ACM Symposium on Information, Computer and Communications Security*, pages 328–332, April 2010.

[28] M. Ongtang, S. E. McLaughlin, W. Enck, and P. D. McDaniel. Semantically Rich Application-Centric Security in Android. In *Proceedings of the 25th Annual Computer Security Applications Conference*, ACSAC '09, pages 340–349, December 2009.

[29] R. A. Popa, A. J. Blumberg, H. Balakrishnan, and F. H. Li. Privacy and Accountability for Location-Based Aggregate Statistics. In *Proceedings of the 18th ACM Conference on Computer and Communications Security (CCS '11)*, October 2011.

[30] A. Reznichenko, S. Guha, and P. Francis. Auctions in Do-Not-Track Compliant Internet Advertising. In *Proceedings of the 18th ACM Conference on Computer and Communications Security (CCS '11)*, October 2011.

[31] R. Schlegel, K. Zhang, X. Zhou, M. Intwala, A. Kapadia, and X. Wang. Soundcomber: A Stealthy and Context-Aware Sound Trojan for Smartphones. In *Proceedings of the 18th Annual Network and Distributed System Security Symposium*, NDSS '11, pages 17–33, February 2011.

[32] V. Toubiana, H. Nissenbaum, A. Narayanan, S. Barocas, and D. Boneh. Adnostic: Privacy Preserving Targeted Advertising. In *Proceedings of the 17th Annual Network and Distributed System Security Symposium*, NDSS '10, February 2010.

[33] Y. Zhou, X. Zhang, X. Jiang, and V. Freeh. Taming Information-Stealing Smartphone Applications (on Android). In *Proceedings of the 4th International Conference on Trust and Trustworthy Computing*, TRUST '11, June 2011.

APPENDIX

	Included in Apps	Probes Permissions	Uses Obfuscation	Uses Reflection	Uses JavaScript	Read Installed Packages	Location Data	Place Phone Call	Camera	List Accounts	Read Calendar	Read Contact/Call Logs	Read Browser Bookmarks	Read Phone Information	Read Phone Number	Read SMS	Send SMS	Change Calendar	Change Contacts	Use Vibrator	ClassLoader
mopub/mobileads	87	✓		✓			✓														
adfonic	77	✓	✓																		
vdroid	72	✓	✓				✓							✓							
transpera	72	✓												✓							
mobgold	65																				
mobus	64													✓	✓	✓					
hutuchong	63	✓		✓										✓			✓				
mads	56						✓							✓							
everbadge	55				✓									✓							
zetacube/libzc	54																				
livepoint/smartad/sdk	52	✓					✓														
l/adlib_android	45	✓	✓				✓	✓						✓			✓				
eng/trickersticks	45									✓			✓		✓	✓		✓				
ccmedia	36	✓					✓							✓							
sosceo	31		✓				✓	✓					✓		✓	✓		✓		✓		
kr/netsco/Mojiva	29																				
admogo	28	✓		✓			✓							✓	✓						
nexage/android	25	✓		✓			✓							✓							
rhythmnewmedia	23	✓			✓		✓														
mediba/ad/sdk	22	✓												✓							
madvertise	22	✓	✓				✓														
qriously	20	✓					✓														
zumobi/adslib	18													✓							
netmite	15			✓																	
imapp/ads	15		✓																		
cn/yicha/android/ads	14	✓					✓														
oneriot	13		✓				✓														
aduru	11																				
admoda	11	✓																			
jp/co/imobile	10	✓	✓											✓							
moblico	8	✓		✓			✓						✓	✓	✓	✓		✓		✓	✓	
jp/ne/linkshare/android/tgad	8																				
ignitevision	8	✓	✓				✓						✓								
fractalist	8													✓	✓						
plankton	7	✓	✓	✓										✓							✓
cellitads	7													✓							
cn/appmedia/ad	6		✓		✓	✓	✓							✓			✓				
glam/AndroidSDK	5				✓			✓													
adtutu	5		✓											✓	✓						
ru/adfox	4				✓																
netad	4	✓	✓				✓														
freewheel	4	✓		✓										✓							✓
adinside/androidsdk	4						✓														
taobao/ads	3		✓																		
amaze/ad	2							✓						✓							
admozi	2						✓	✓													
wqmobile/sdk	1	✓		✓			✓	✓						✓	✓		✓				
ubermind/ad	1													✓							
innoace/imad	1	✓					✓	✓						✓	✓						✓
AdyxSdk	1						✓														
Total	1239	24	14	9	5	1	22	7	0	1	0	4	1	25	9	1	7	0	2	1	3

Table 4: The Overall Results from the Remaining 50 Ad Libraries

TapLogger: Inferring User Inputs On Smartphone Touchscreens Using On-board Motion Sensors

Zhi Xu
Department of Computer
Science and Engineering
Pennsylvania State University
University Park, PA, USA
zux103@cse.psu.edu

Kun Bai
IBM T.J. Watson Research
Center
Hawthorne, NY, USA
kunbai@us.ibm.com

Sencun Zhu
Department of Computer
Science and Engineering
Pennsylvania State University
University Park, PA, USA
szhu@cse.psu.edu

ABSTRACT

Today's smartphones are shipped with various embedded motion sensors, such as the accelerometer, gyroscope, and orientation sensors. These motion sensors are useful in supporting the mobile UI innovation and motion-based commands. However, they also bring potential risks of leaking user's private information as they allow third party applications to monitor the motion changes of smartphones.

In this paper, we study the feasibility of inferring a user's tap inputs to a smartphone with its integrated motion sensors. Specifically, we utilize an installed trojan application to stealthily monitor the movement and gesture changes of a smartphone using its on-board motion sensors. When the user is interacting with the trojan application, it learns the motion change patterns of tap events. Later, when the user is performing sensitive inputs, such as entering passwords on the touchscreen, the trojan application applies the learnt pattern to infer the occurrence of tap events on the touchscreen as well as the tapped positions on the touchscreen.

For demonstration, we present the design and implementation of *TapLogger*, a trojan application for the Android platform, which stealthily logs the password of screen lock and the numbers entered during a phone call (e.g., credit card and PIN numbers). Statistical results are presented to show the feasibility of such inferences and attacks.

Categories and Subject Descriptors

C.2.m [**Computer-Communication Networks**]: Miscellaneous; C.2.0 [**General**]: Security and protection

General Terms

Security, Design, Experimentation

Keywords

Smartphone, Trojan, Motion Sensor, Accelerometer Sensor, Orientation Sensor, User Inputs Logger, Android

1. INTRODUCTION

Today's smartphones are equipped with various embedded motion sensors, such as the accelerometer, gyroscope, and orientation sensors [40]. These motion sensors are used to gauge the smartphone's status of motion, such as orientation, acceleration, and direction. They are useful in supporting the innovative mobile UI [2], context awareness [31, 19], and motion-based commands(e.g., shuffling songs [1]). Probably due to the assumption that data collected by motion sensors is not sensitive, so far third party applications are allowed to access the readings of embedded accelerometer and orientation sensors without any security permission requirements on all Android [9], iOS [23], and Blackberry [4].

As the use of motion sensors in mobile device has become more widespread, serious concerns have been raised about the potential risks of a user's private information from being leaked through an installed third party application which explores these motion sensors. Recently, Marquardt et al. [28] presented a spying application *(sp)iPhone* which utilizes the vibrations sensed by a smartphone to infer the user inputs on a nearby keyboard. Cai and Chen [5] proposed a motion-based side channel for inferring keystrokes on the smartphone touchscreen. Such security and privacy exposures threaten to stifle the adoption and acceptance of these applications and even the smartphone platforms [39].

In this paper, we explore the feasibility of inferring a user's inputs on the smartphone touchscreen using sensor data collected from motion sensors. Our work is based on the observed correlations between the tap events and the motion change of smartphone. First, during a tap event, the acceleration of smartphone will change caused by the force from finger on the touchscreen. The change of acceleration follows certain patterns that can help the installed trojan application to detect the occurrences of tap events.

Second, tapping different positions on the touchscreen will cause small, but discernable changes of guesture of smartphone by the sensors. For example, tapping on the left side of touchscreen may cause the smartphone to turn left while tapping on the right side may cause the smartphone to turn right. By observing the gesture changes during a tap event, the attacker may roughly infer the tapped position on the touchscreen. The inferred position may not be precise. However, if the attacker knows the context of tap events and the layout of current view on the touchscreen, he may be able to infer the user's inputs (e.g., the pressed number button) with the inferred tap position.

We begin this paper by providing a technical background on this developing threat, and then describe in detail the key contributions of our work, where:

- We show the unique patterns of tap events in terms of changes of acceleration of smartphone. With statistical approaches, such patterns may help the installed trojan application to detect the occurrence of tap events.

- We show the correlation between the tap position and the gesture change during one tap event. With knowledge about the layout of view displayed on touchscreen, we show the feasibility of inferring user inputs with observed readings from the orientation sensor during tap events.

- We present the design and implementation of *TapLogger*, a trojan application that utilizes observed sensor readings to stealthily log the user inputs on touchscreen. For demonstration, we present two types of attacks on Android: stealing the password of screen lock and logging the PIN number entered during a phone conversation.

2. TECHNICAL BACKGROUND

2.1 User Inputs on Touchscreen

The touchscreen is the primary user interface of a touch-capable smartphone, and it presents a target of opportunity for potential hackers and information thieves. When a user taps on the touchscreen, the display and its supporting hardware and firmware will report the coordinates of tap events to the operating system of the smartphone. The coordinates of a tap event together with knowledge of the application view currently displayed on the touchscreen determine the corresponding user input. For example, a tap event with coordinates within the boundary of a button displayed on the touchscreen stands for a tap action on this button. As the layout of many views are public and uniform, such as the layout of screen lock view shown in Figure 6, the coordinates of tap events become extremely sensitive.

To protect user inputs from being eavesdropped, there are rigorous restrictions on the receiver who is allowed to receive the tap events and their coordinate information. For example, on the Android platform, only the *view* that is focused and currently being displayed on the touchscreen will be allowed to receive the coordinate information [10]. Therefore, a third party application running in background (e.g., a *service*) can never receive the coordinate information when the user is tapping the touchscreen to unlock the smartphone with passwords or dial a number during a call.

2.2 Motion Sensors

Motion sensors embedded in smartphones offer the hacker a side channel into a user's mobile device, from which he/she may steal private data. Specifically, we refer to the on-board accelerometer and orientation sensors, which are two of the most commonly equipped motion sensors on commodity smartphones. Up to the most recent version of major platforms, e.g., iOS [23], Android [9], and Blackberry [4], accessing these two sensors requires no security permissions, and enables considerable accesses by a third party application to the underlying resources in the mobile device. As Android is the most popular and most exploited smartphone platform, we adopt the specification and terminology defined on the Android platform in this paper.

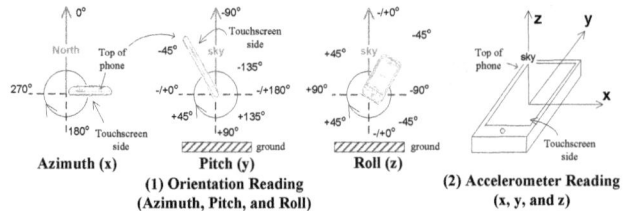

Figure 1: An introduction to accelerometer and orientation readings on the Android platform

2.2.1 Accelerometer Sensor

The accelerometer sensor monitors the current acceleration of a smartphone along three axes: left-right(i.e., lateral or x-axis), forward-backward (i.e., longitudinal or y-axis), and up-down (i.e., vertical or z-axis) [29, 9]. The returned readings of the accelerometer sensor are the rates of change of velocity with time along these three axes in m/s^2.

In Figure 1, we illustrate the mapping of axes in relation to a smartphone that is placed horizontally. As described in this figure, the reading of x-axis acceleration would be positive if the smartphone is moving toward the right side; the reading of y-axis acceleration would be positive if the smartphone is moving in the direction of the top of smartphone; the reading of z-axis acceleration would be positive if the smartphone is being lifted. For instance, when placing the smartphone statically and horizontally on a surface as shown in Figure 1, the reading of x and y-axis will be zero and the reading of z-axis will be the earth gravity (i.e., $9.8m/s^2$) because the surface is supporting the smartphone. When the smartphone is dropping freely, the readings of all axes will be zero.

To facilitate our discussion, we represent the current acceleration A of a smartphone by a vector $\vec{A} = <A_x, A_y, A_z> = A_x\hat{x} + A_y\hat{y} + A_z\hat{z}$, where $\hat{x}, \hat{y}$, and $\hat{z}$ are the unit vectors in the directions of positive x, y, and z axes, respectively.

2.2.2 Orientation Sensor

The orientation sensor tracks the changes of orientation and gesture of smartphone along three dimensions: *Azimuth* (x-axis), *Pitch* (y-axis), and *Roll* (z-axis) [29, 9]. The returned readings of the orientation sensor are the current gesture of the smartphone in these three dimensions. Each reading is measured by degrees. As illustrated in Figure 1, the reading of x-axis is 0° when the smartphone is facing north and the reading changes between 0° and 360°; the reading of y-axis is 0° when the touchscreen side faces to the sky and the reading changes to $-/+180^o$ when facedown; the reading of z-axis represents the sideways tilt between -90° and $+90^o$.

2.2.3 Hardware Specifications

Hardware specifications, such as the sensor sample rate, are important to sensing applications. Different smartphone platforms have different hardware specifications. The brief specifications of three selected smartphone platforms are listed in Table 1. As the orientation sample rate of Motorola Atrix is too low, in this paper, we presents experimental results on HTC Aria and Google Nexus (One).

2.3 Tap-To-Open/Active Interactive Pattern

Many interactive patterns exist for using touchscreens. In this paper, our threat model is based on the "*Tap To Open/Active*" pattern [34] which is almost the simplest but

Table 1: Specifications of selected smartphones

Model	Touch Screen Size (pixels)	Acc. Sample Rate	Ori. Sample Rate	Android
Aria	$W(320) \times H(480)$	$\sim 50Hz$	$\sim 50Hz$	v2.3
Nexus	$W(480) \times H(800)$	$\sim 25Hz$	$\sim 25Hz$	v2.3
Atrix	$W(540) \times H(960)$	$\sim 95Hz$	$\sim 8Hz$	v2.3

most used interactive pattern. With this pattern, a user taps in a specific position of the touchscreen to trigger a feature or to respond, similar to clicking with a mouse. With advanced hardware supports, some latest smartphones may support multi-touch touchscreen and more complex patterns, such as "*Drag To Move*" and "*Slide To Scroll*". However, in this work, our focus is the "*Tap To Open/Active*" pattern because of its extreme popularity as well as simplicity.

The typical scenario we consider here is that *a user holds the smartphone with her left hand and taps the touchscreen using the forefinger of her right hand.* Consider a tap event on the touchscreen that is face up. The motions of smartphone during one tap event can be briefly described as the three consecutive phases: $Action\_Down \rightarrow Hold \rightarrow Action\_Up$: when the user presses down on the touchscreen (i.e., in the $Action\_Down$ phase), the smartphone will be forced to move downward. When the $Action\_Down$ is over; the smartphone will stop (i.e., be in the $Hold$ phase); Then, the user lifts his finger and the hand holding the smartphone will respond by lifting the smartphone back to its original position (i.e., in the $Action\_Up$ phase). The whole tapping action is usually performed in a short time period. According to our measurements, a swift tap event is about $50 \sim 70\ ms$ and an ordinary tap event is about $180 \sim 220\ ms$.

In our discussion, we name the time duration of a tap event as a $SigWin$, representing the time duration when the finger is in touch with the touchscreen (i.e., between $Action\_Down$ and $Action\_Up$).

3. ATTACK OVERVIEW

3.1 Assumptions

On the Android platform, a third party application must explicitly and statically declare the permissions for sensitive resources needed, such as networking and audio recording permissions. As motion sensors are considered as insensitive resource, *TapLogger* does not require any security permission to access the accelerometer and orientation sensors. However, *TapLogging* requires the *networking* permission to send inferred user inputs to a remote attacker, and the *Phone Status* permission for context awareness. Both the *networking* and *Phone Status* permission are very common ones, which are also required by most of popular apps, such as *Angry Bird* [26], *Facebook* [14], and *Kindle* [25]. Therefore, *TapLogger* would have very little chance to draw attention with respect to security permissions.

3.2 Attack Goals

The target in our work is the meaningful user inputs, e.g., the button that is pressed during a tap event, instead of the precise coordinate of a tap event. Inferring the precise coordinate is practically infeasible due to interference factors, such as background noise. However, a button usually covers a zone in the screen and all user's tap events within this zone corresponding to the same user input. Thus, with knowledge about the layout of a target view, e.g., the one in Figure 6, the attacker can infer the user inputs (e.g., the

button that is pressed) instead the precise coordinate of a tap event.

3.3 Attack Workflow

TapLogger works in two modes: *Training Mode* and *Logging Mode*. It switches to the training mode when the user is interacting with the *HostApp*, and switches to the logging mode when the user is performing sensitive inputs. The context related information can be retrieved from the Android operating system. Briefly, we explain the workflow as shown in Figure 2:

Training Mode: In the training mode, when the user is interacting with the *HostApp*, *TapLogger* can legally receive the coordinates of tap events on the touchscreen, and apply the coordinates with the readings of accelerometer and orientation sensors collected during tap events to generate a user's interaction pattern.

Thus, for one tap event detected in the training mode, the *HostApp* records related information including (1) the coordinate (on the screen); (2) the timestamps when it starts and when it ends; and (3) the accelerometer and orientation sensor readings between the start and the end time. The time duration between the start and the end consists a $SigWin$. The number of collected readings in the $SigWin$ depends on the time duration of tap events as well as the sensor sample rate. In addition, we also collect several readings before and after $SigWin$, denoted as $PreWin$ and $AfterWin$, respectively.

Logging Mode: In the logging mode, the $SensorListener$ runs in background and keeps stealthily monitoring the readings of accelerometer and orientation sensors. When the user is performing sensitive inputs, the acquired pattern can be applied to infer the tapped area (i.e., zone) on the touchscreen based on sensor readings collected by the $SensorListener$ service. Then, with the knowledge of the layout of a targeted view, *TapLogger* can then infer the corresponding user inputs. To reduce battery consumption and false positives, the $SensorListener$ service only works in certain sensitive contexts.

3.4 Challenges

To make the proposed attack feasible, several challenges exist, which will be addressed one by one in the following sections.

- How to detect the tap events in the logging mode? An approach is needed for $SensorListener$ to identify the tap events in the logging mode by observing the readings of accelerometer and orientation sensors only in the background.

- How to infer the user inputs on the touchscreen based on observed sensor readings? A tap position classifier is needed to help the attacker to infer the tap positions and their implicated user inputs.

- How to design and implement *TapLogger* that is able to perform the proposed attack stealthily and efficiently? The trojan application should require as few permissions and workload as possible to launch the attack.

4. TAP EVENT DETECTION

In this section, we first introduce the unique change pattern of acceleration readings during tap events, and then show how to build the user's pattern in the training mode and how to apply the pattern in the logging mode.

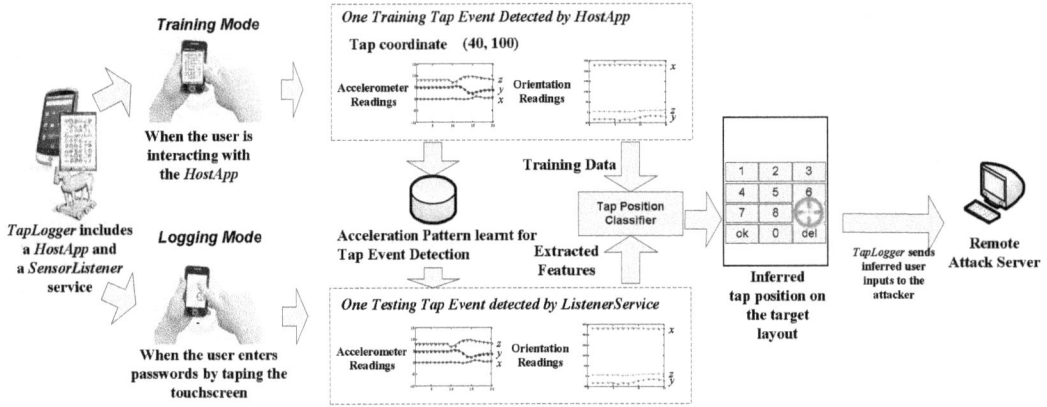

Figure 2: The attack overview

4.1 Observed Pattern of Tap Events

Accelerometers on smartphones have been widely exploited by context-aware applications to infer the current contexts of smartphones, such as transportation mode inference (i.e., inferring if the user is walking or taking vehicles [32, 38]) and activity recognition (i.e., inferring if the user is walking, sitting, or running [36, 37]).

Differently, in our application, our goal is not in context inference but in detecting the occurrences of tap events. These tap events are comparatively small fragments in the sequence of collected readings, thus existing context inference approaches do not work in our case.

To detect the tap events, we utilize the unique change pattern of external force on the smartphone during tap events. To measure the change of the external force F, we use the term $SqSum$ to denote the 2-norm of acceleration vector, i.e., $SqSum=|A|^2 = A_x^2 + A_y^2 + A_z^2$. Obviously, $SqSum$ represents the force on the smartphone and is directly proportional to $|F|^2$. When the smartphone is held statically in one hand, the value of $SqSum$ is equal to the square of gravity, i.e., $G^2 \approx 9.8^2$. When the smartphone is dropping freely, the value of $SqSum$ is 0.

In Figure 3, we show the measured $SqSum$ readings when the user is performing different activities. As shown in this comparison, when the user is tapping buttons shown in the touchscreen, the fluctuation of wave is much smaller. This is reasonable because the user will subconsciously stabilize the smartphone when he taps buttons on the touchscreen.

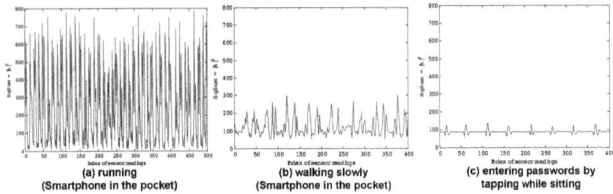

Figure 3: Acceleration readings in different contexts

Admittedly, the tap event detection will be difficult when the background noise is great. Some background noise may also generate acceleration patterns similar to tap event patterns. To lower the interference caused by background noise, *TapLogger* collects data for both training and logging attacks only when the background noise is small. A simple approach to measure the background noise is to calculate the standard deviation of the latest $SqSum$ readings. *TapLogger* collects data when the standard deviation is small. Other activity recognition approaches [36] can also be applied to prevent collecting data in noisy environments. Further, *Ta-pLogger* only starts the *ListenerService* when in sensitive contexts, e.g., during a phone conversation. In this way, we greatly avoid false triggering.

4.2 Proposed Statistic Approach

Based on the observed pattern of tap events, we propose a statistic approach for tap event detection by monitoring the change of force on the smartphone. Specifically, we describe the pattern of tap events by a set of statistic features in terms of $SqSum$ readings. For each feature, *TapLogger* learns its pattern interval through the training data collected by the *HostApp* in the training mode. These learnt pattern intervals are user specific representing a user's pattern of tap events. When *TapLogger* is in the logging mode, the *SensorListener* service monitors the acceleration of smartphone by keeping a monitoring window for a sequence of the latest $SqSum$ readings. If the features extracted from the readings of the monitoring window fall in the learnt pattern intervals, the *SensorListener* will consider a tap event having been detected. The *SigWin* of a detected tap event is within the monitoring window.

4.2.1 Pattern Learning in Training Mode

The unique $\searrow\!\!\nearrow$ pattern of $SqSum$ in the *Action_Down* phase is the key to tap event detection in our case. As shown in the enlarged figure of a tap event in Figure 4(a), the $SqSum$ readings will first go down and then jump up dramatically corresponding to the first *Action_Down* phase in the *Tap-To-Open/Active* interactive pattern. The rest part of tap events represents the motion of smartphone when the user lifts up his finger from touchscreen. The jitter represents the case when the hand holding the smartphone is trying to stabilize the smartphone after the tap event.

To catch the unique patten of tap events, we first identify the start and the end of *SigWin* by the timestamps of received events *Motion.Event.ACTION_DOWN* and *Motion.Event.ACTION_UP*, respectively. Then, we extract five features from the readings of $SqSum$ within the identified *SigWin*:

- P_1: The peak reading of $\searrow\!\!\nearrow$ at the end of *Action_Down* minus the *base*, i.e., $SqSum_{peak} - base$;
- P_2: The trough reading of $\searrow\!\!\nearrow$ of *Action_Down* minus the *base*, i.e., $SqSum_{trough} - base$;
- P_3: Difference between the peak and the trough readings, i.e., $SqSum_{peak}$-$SqSum_{trough}$;
- P_4: Time gap between peak and trough, i.e., $Time_{peak}$-$Time_{trough}$;
- P_5: The standard deviation of the entire *SigWin*, i.e., $Std(SigWin)$;

116

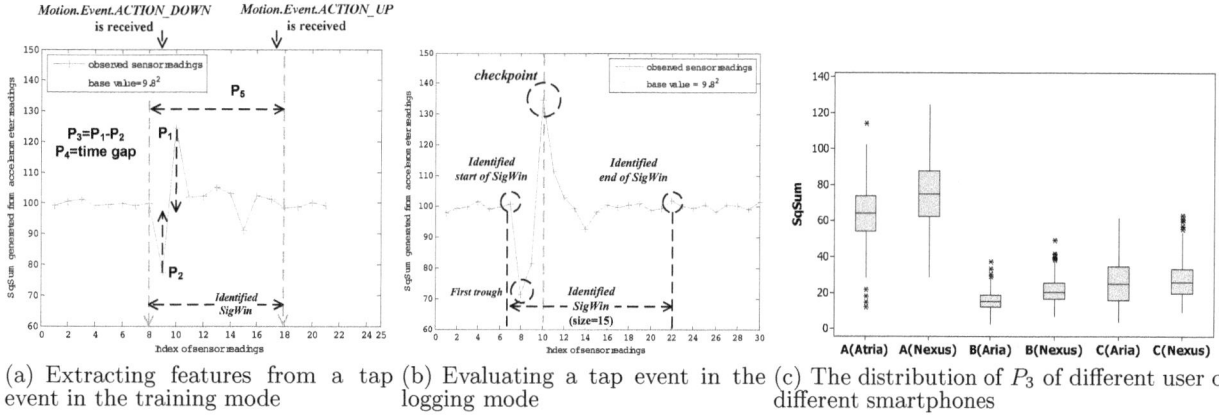

(a) Extracting features from a tap event in the training mode

(b) Evaluating a tap event in the logging mode

(c) The distribution of P_3 of different user on different smartphones

Figure 4: The proposed statistic approach for tap event detection

We briefly explain these measures as follows: $base = G^2$ denotes the $SqSum$ value when the smartphone is placed statically with no external force on it, P_1 measures the magnitude of force when pressing down, P_2 measures the magnitude of force from the hand holding the smartphone when reacting to the tap event, P_3 and P_4 measure the change rate, and P_5 measures the fluctuation. Each tap event is described by these five features in the tap event detection.

With all tap events detected in the training mode, *TapLogger* learns the distributions of these features for the current user on the current smartphone. According to our measurements in experiments, the distributions of these five measures form bell-shaped curves that are close to normal distributions. Thus, with the measurements in our training dataset, we take the range between the *Lower Extreme* and the *Upper Extreme* [33] of each measurement, represented by $[L, U]$, to describe the pattern interval of this measurement. Specifically, $L = Q_1 - 1.5 \times IQR$ and $U = Q_3 + 1.5 \times IQR$, where Q_1 is the *lower quartile*, Q_3 is the *upper quartile*, and $IQR = Q_3 - Q_1$ is the *interquartile range*.

In this way, the pattern for tap event detection can be presented by five sets of boundary values, i.e., $P_S = \{I_1, I_2, I_3, I_4, I_5\}$, where $I_i = \{L_i, U_i\}$. Different people have different tapping patterns.

4.2.2 Tap Event Detection in Logging Mode

When *TapLogger* is in the logging mode, the *SensorListener* service detects tap events by observing the readings of accelerometer. Services running in background (e.g., *SensorListner*) are not allowed to receive touch event information from the touchscreen. Specifically, in the logging mode, the *SensorListner* service keeps a *MonitorWin*, which contains the last K observed $SqSum$ values of acceleration. In our experiments, *TapLogger* calculates the average size of $SigWin$ in the training dataset, and sets K twice the average size. The $SqSum$ readings in the *MonitorWin* are ordered by their generation times. We present an example of *MonitorWin* in Figure 4(b).

Whenever a new $SqSum$ reading is generated, the *SensorListner* service will first update the *MonitorWin* by adding the new $SqSum$ reading, and then check the $SqSum$ reading at a fixed index position named *checkpoint*, e.g., the 10th reading in the *MonitorWin* shown in Figure 4(b). The purpose is to check whether the current $SqSum$ reading at the *checkpoint* is the peak point of the first $\searrow\nearrow$ of a tap event.

Basically, assume that the current *checkpoint* is the peak point of a tap event. The *SensorListner* will try to identify the corresponding trough point in the *MonitorWin*, extract

Table 2: Experimental results of tap event detection

User	Model	Precision	Recall	F-Measure
User A	*Aria*	93.6%	91.8%	92.74%
User B	*Aria*	76.3%	90.0%	82.6%
User C	*Aria*	70.4%	97.4%	81.7%
User A	*Nexus*	99.3%	96.3%	97.8%
User B	*Nexus*	74.67%	95%	83.61%
User C	*Nexus*	83.97%	88.37%	86.12%

features $P_1 \ldots P_5$, and check if the extracted features are within the intervals described in the learnt tap event pattern. The checking scheme is illustrated in Figure 4(b). The detailed checking algorithm is presented in Appendix A.

4.3 Evaluations

In the evaluation, the tester students were first asked to play the *icon-matching game* for 30 rounds, collecting a training dataset of more than 400 tap events. With the collected training dataset, *TapLogger* extracts the proposed five features (i.e., $P_1 \ldots P_5$) from each tap event, and generates a statistic pattern for each dataset. These statistic patterns (i.e., boundaries of parameters) are user specific as well as device specific.

For example, in Figure 4(c), we present the distribution of the P_3 feature collected from training data of different users (i.e. user A, B, and C) on different smartphones. As shown in this comparison, first of all, most of measured P_3 feature falls in the range between the lower extreme and the upper extreme. Secondly, different users have different patterns. The more convergent the distribution of extracted features, the more consistent the pattern. Thirdly, the tap event patterns of the same user are different on different smartphones due to the difference in the hardware, such as the sensor sample rate and weight.

In the testing phase, the tester students were asked to enter a sequence of about 150 numbers in a testbed with UI the same as the number pad layout as shown in Figure 5. During the testing phase, *TapLogger* stealthily monitors the accelerometer readings in the background and used the corresponding statistic patterns to detect the tap events on the touch screen. The experimental results in Table 2 show that the proposed tap event detection approach can achieve high accuracies in identifying the tap events on the touchscreen.

5. TAP POSITION INFERENCE

The goal of tap position inference is to identify the tapped area on the touchscreen. In this section, we first show the

(1. a) when tapping the top left   **(1.b) corresponding orientation sensor**
area of touchscreen   **readings during the tap event**

(2. a) when tapping the top right (2.b) corresponding orientation sensor
area of touchscreen   **readings during the tap event**

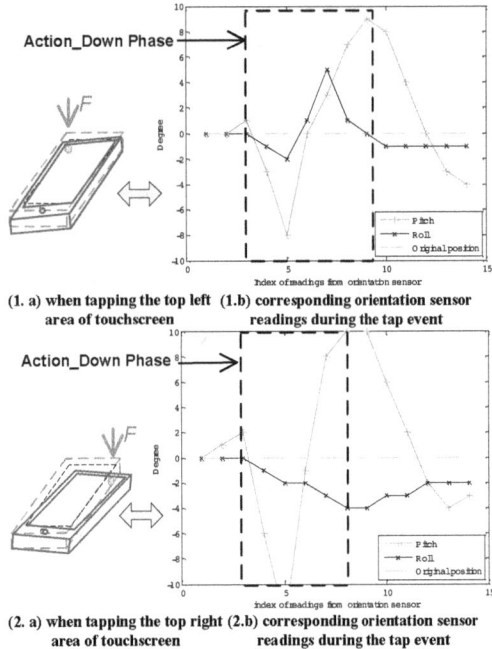

Figure 5: Examples of gesture changes when tapping different areas of the touchscreen

correlation between the position of a tap event and its corresponding gesture changes, measured by the orientation sensor. Then, we present a way of dividing the touchscreen into zones (i.e., tapped area) based on layout of the target view. Finally, with real tap events data collected in our experiments, we show the feasibility of distinguishing tap events in different zones. Limitations and reasons are also presented in the end to show the capacity of inferencing using this correlation.

5.1 Gesture Change Analysis

When a user taps on the touchscreen using his finger, the gesture of smartphone will change caused by the external forces from the finger and the hand holding the smartphone. The way that the gesture changes is related to the position on the touchscreen that has been tapped. Intuitively, when the user taps on the top of touchscreen, the head of smartphone will go down; while the user taps on the right side of touchscreen, the body of smartphone will lean right as well.

TapLogger senses the gesture changes through two types of readings from the orientation sensor: the readings of *Pitch*, measuring turning left or right of smartphone; and the readings of *Roll*, measuring the going down of head or bottom. As shown in Figure 5, when the user taps on the top left of touchscreen, the smartphone will turn left and its head will goes down. Correspondingly, the *Pitch* value goes up because the head goes down, and the *Roll* value goes up because the face of touchscreen turns left. When the tap event is done, the gesture of smartphone will go back to the approximate of its original gesture. For the comparison, we show the gesture change when tapping on top right in Figure 5(2.a). As shown in its corresponding orientation readings, the *Pitch* value goes up because the head goes down, but the *Roll* value now goes down because the face of touchscreen turns right.

Clearly, it would be ideal if one can infer the exact coordinates of tap events based on the observed gesture change of smartphone. However, due to noise and limitation on sensor sample rate, such exact inference is not possible. Instead

of inferencing the exact coordinates, *TapLogger* divides the screen into meaningful zones and infers a zone on the screen that contains the exact coordinates.

5.2 Screen Division

We name the view on which the user is performing sensitive inputs as the *Target View*. In a target view, zones stand for meaningful objects, such as buttons. Therefore, if the attacker can correctly identify the pressed zones, he can get the user inputs on the touchscreen with knowledge about the layout of the target view. In Figure 6, we present the layout of two target views: one is the layout of screen lock view on which the user enters the password by tapping buttons; the other is the layout of number pad view on which the user enters his PIN or credit card number when making calls. As we can see in Figure 6, the layout can easily be divided into meaningful zones by individual buttons. The zones we are interested in are buttons used to enter the password or PIN.

To disguise its purpose, the attacker may also carefully design the user interface of *HostApp*. For example, in Figure 6(1), we present the screen layout of a *icon-matching game* (i.e., the *HostApp*). When playing the *icon-matching game*, the user may not realize that he is contributing training data for the target view in Figure 6(2) .

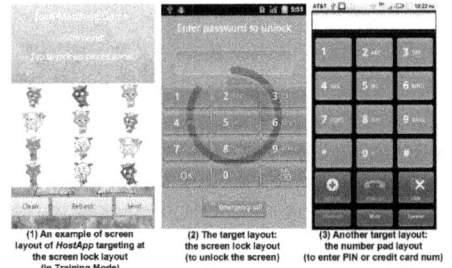

(1) An example of screen   **(2) The target layout:**   **(3) Another target layout:**
layout of *HostApp* targeting at   **the screen lock layout**   **the number pad layout**
the screen lock layout   **(to unlock the screen)**   **(to enter PIN or credit card num)**
(in Training Mode)

Figure 6: An example of *HostApp*'s screen layout and target screen layouts

5.3 Proposed Inference Approach

With the screen division, we convert the tap position inference problem to a classification problem, in which, each class is a labeled zone in the target view. In the training mode, *TapLogger* uses the collected training data to create a tap position classifier following the user's tapping pattern. While in the logging mode, *TapLogger* uses this trained classifier to infer the corresponding class (i.e., the zone or button). For each detected tap event, the output of classification in the logging mode is an estimated zone that contains its real coordinates.

5.3.1 Classifier Generation in Training Mode

Similar to the proposed tap event detection approach, *TapLogger* keeps monitoring the readings of the embedded orientation sensor. When a tap event is observed by the *HostApp*, *TapLogger* first determines the start and end of *SigWin* by events *Motion.Event.ACTION_DOWN* and *Motion.Event.ACTION_UP*, and then, generates the training data for the classifier from the sequence of orientation sensor readings during this *SigWin*.

The training data of an observed tap event consists of a vector $\{L, F_O\}$, where L is the label of zone containing its associated coordinates, and F_O are the set of features extracted from the orientation sensor readings during its *SigWin*. These extracted features measure the gesture changes, and are generated by changes of the orientation sensor readings in *Roll* and *Pitch* during the *Action_Down* phase. Briefly, we list the extracted features as follows:

- F_1: the change of *Roll* in the first monotonic section;
- F_2: the change of *Roll* in the second monotonic section; if *Roll* in the *Action_Down* phase is monotonic as a whole, F_2 is assigned 0.
- F_3: the change of *Roll* from the start to the end of *Action_Down* phase;
- F_4: the change of *Pitch* in the first monotonic section;
- F_5: the change of *Pitch* in the second monotonic section; if *Pitch* the *Action_Down* phase is monotonic as a whole, F_5 is assigned 0;
- F_6: the change of *Pitch* from the start to the end of *Action_Down* phase;

To explain, Features F_1, F_2 and F_3 help to determine if a tap event is on the left side of touchscreen or on the right side; F_4, F_5, and F_6 help determine if a tap event is on the top of touchscreen or on the bottom.

Note that, as shown in Figure 5, the changes of both Roll and Pitch may not be monotonic in the *Action_Down* phase. According to our observation in experiments, the reason is that, when the finger first contacts the touchscreen, two types of movements of the smartphone take place in parallel. One type of movement is that smartphone may move down as a whole, and the other type is the gesture change of smartphone. Thus, we separate the change of readings into two consecutive sections in which the change of readings is monotonic.

5.3.2 Inference in Logging Mode

In the logging mode, *TapLogger* also keeps a *OriMonitor-Win* for the latest orientation sensor readings. When a tap event is detected by the observed *SqSum* readings, its *Sig-Win* will also be determined. With the start and the end of determined *SigWin*, *TapLogger* retrieves the sequence of orientation readings within the *SigWin* from the *OriMonitorWin*, and extracts features F_O from the retrieved orientation sensor readings. These extracted features are supplied to the classifier so as to infer the label of zone that contains the coordinates of this detected tap event.

5.4 Evaluation

The classifier for tap position inference is both user specific and device specific. To show the effectiveness of our selected features in classification, in Figure 7, we show three experimental results of distinguishing tap events at different positions based on extracted features. Specifically, Figure 7(1) and Figure 7(2) compare the experimental results of the same user on different smartphones, i.e., Aria and Nexus; Figure 7(2) and Figure 7(3) compare the experimental results of different users on the same smartphone. In both experiments, we collect about 60 tap events on each of 12 buttons on the number pad layout.

The experimental results in Figure 7 show that the proposed features $\{F_1, F_2, F_3\}$ (i.e., features measuring the change of *Roll*) can help to distinguish tap events on the left side of the touchscreen from those on the right side. Other features $\{F_4, F_5, F_6\}$ (i.e., features measuring the change of *Pitch*) can help to distinguish tap events on the top of the touchscreen from those on the bottom.

Further, by comparing the results of Figure 7(1) and Figure 7(2), we show the hardware factors affecting the accuracy of tap position inference. First of all, the data points in Figure 7(1) are more convergent because the sample rate

of orientation sensor at Aria is about 50 Hz and is much faster than the 25Hz of Nexus. Secondly, despite its lower sample rate, the comparison between Figure 7(1.b) and Figure 7(2.b) shows that it is easier to distinguish buttons in the same column on Nexus. One reason is because the size of Nexus is bigger than the Aria, making the gesture changes in *Pitch* axis more obvious during tap events. Based on the comparison, we see that, besides the user pattern, the inference will be easier on smartphones which are bigger and more sensitive in sensing.

Moreover, Figure 7(2) and Figure 7(3) show the user factors affecting the accuracy of tap position inference. Specifically, Figure 7(2.a) and Figure 7(3.a) show that, although the patterns of different users are different, the tap events by the same user on different side of touchscreen are still distinguishable. However, the distinguishability is different from user to user. Take user B in Figure 7(3) as an example. Figure 7(3.a) shows that it is not difficult to distinguish the tap events of user B in the *Roll* axis. But, in Figure 7(3.b), distinguishing tap events by the *Pitch* axis is difficult. One reason may be that the Arial is small and light, making the gesture change not obvious. Another possible reason is that the way user B holding and tapping the smartphone is different from that of user A.

From the perspective of classification, Figure 7 also shows the difficulty of distinguishing tap events on neighboring buttons. For example, in the target screen lock layout, many tap events on button 9 may be falsely classified as its contiguous buttons, such as button 12 (i.e., the "*Del*" button), 8, and 6. One reason of error is that the number of collected sample readings is not enough to describe the gesture changes because of the limited sample rate. The other reason is that the actual tap position is very close to neighboring nodes, making the inference difficult to distinguish correctly. Therefore, in specific attacks, the attacker may apply additional background knowledge to improve the accuracy of inference. Indeed, in the two attacks shown later, we will use different approaches to improve the inference accuracy.

6. APPLICATIONS ON ANDROID

We have implemented *TapLogger* as an Android application with the attack flow presented in Figure 2. In this section, we show the detailed design of *TapLogger* on the Android platform. Further, two types of attacks with evaluations are also presented to show the effectiveness of *TapLogger* in logging and inferring sensitive user inputs.

6.1 Implementation on Android

TapLogger implements the proposed attack flow presented in Figure 2. The components of *TapLogger* on Android include: a *HostApp* activity, masquerading a benign application (e.g., the *icon-matching game*); a *SensorListener* service, collecting readings from sensors in the background; a *ContextIdentifier* service, starting/stoping the *SensorListener* service based on the context of smartphone; and a *Booter* Broadcast Receiver, starting the *ContextIdentifier* for the context awareness.

6.1.1 Training Mode

The *HostApp* activity starts the *SensorListener* service when it is brought to the foreground. In the training mode, *HostApp* logs coordinate information of tap events and the *SensorListener* service logs the sensor readings during these tap events. Both information are combined at *ContextIden-*

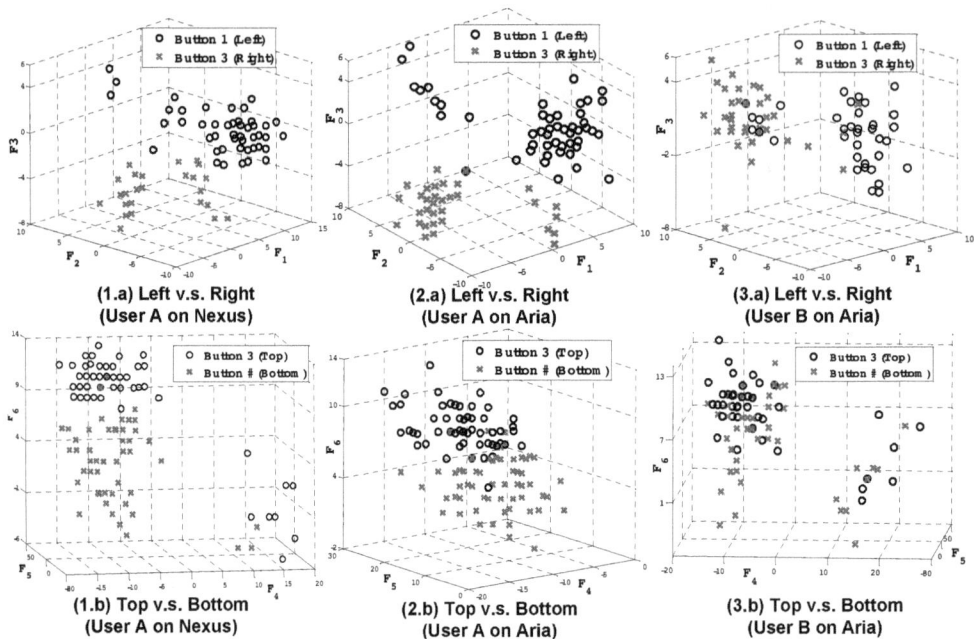

Figure 7: Examples of distinguishing tap events at different positions

tifier and then used as training data for pattern generation in tap event detection and for building the classifier for tap position inference.

6.1.2 Logging Mode

In the logging mode, the *Booter* will be automatically started when receiving the system broadcast (i.e., an Intent) *BOOT_COMPLETED*, indicting that the boot process of smartphone is complete. Thus, even the user has never started *TapLogger* after installation, *TapLogger* can still launch itself when the smartphone is started. Once started, the *Booter* launches the *ContextIdentifier* service which determines the current context of smartphone based on the Intents broadcasted by the Android operating system. By identifying the context, the *ContextIdentifier* services starts the *SensorListener* service only in a sensitive context.

In the end, only the results of inferencing, such as the sequence of labels of pressed buttons, will be sent to a remote attack server. Therefore, the data communication overhead for *TapLogger* is very small.

6.2 Number Pad Logging Attack

6.2.1 Attack Overview

During phone conversations, a user is often asked to enter valuable information on the number pad displayed on the touchscreen. Such valuable information includes the PIN numbers (e.g., requested by IP phone companies), social security numbers (e.g., requested by credit card companies or credit card centers), date of birth (e.g., requested by insurance companies).

In the number logging attack, we apply *TapLogger* to log the user inputs on the number pad during the call. Specifically, in the training mode, the attacker first collects training data by *HostApp* with the layout of number pad (shown in Figure 6), and then builds a classifier for tap position inference. In the logging mode, the *SensorListener* monitors the readings of motion sensors and performs the task of tap event detection and tap position inference. Specifically, the *SensorListener* will be invoked when the phone conversation starts (i.e., upon receiving *CALL_STATE_OFFHOOK* in-

tent) and will be stopped when the phone conversation ends (i.e., upon receiving *CALL_STATE_IDLE* intent).

Figure 8: An example of tap position inference in the number pad logging attack

6.2.2 Tap Position Inference

In the number pad logging attack, we build the classifier by applying k-means clustering to the training data belonging to each label/button. Each label/button will be considered as one class. In the logging mode, given a tap event detected by the *SensorListener* service, we first extract features from the orientation sensor readings, and then measure the distances from this detected tap event to the trained clusters of all labels. Shorter distance means higher similarity to the cluster.

As buttons are close to each other, solely taking the label with shortest distance may cause high inaccuracy. Therefore, in the number logging attack, *TapLogger* may output several top ranked candidate labels for each detected tap event. An example of inference is presented in Figure 8 for demonstration. In this example, the real inputs are 16 numbers entered on the number pad layout shown in Figure 6. For each tap event, *TapLogger* outputs the top 4 candidate labels. The 1st label is the one with the closest distance in the k-means clustering. For example, for the first input "4", the inferred labels are "1, 5, 4, 2" ranked by measured distances. The number pad layout shows that the mistakenly inferred labels "1", "4", and "2" are neighboring buttons around the real input "4". If the attacker only take the top one or top two labels, the true label "4" will not be covered. As shown in the example, for the whole sequence of inputs, the coverage of true inputs with only the 1st label is 0.3125. The coverage will increase as more top ranked candidate labels are taken into consideration. In this example,

Layout of Number Pad		Coverage rate with Top 1 ranked label			Coverage rate with Top 1 & 2 ranked labels		
		0.2759	0.4643	0.5185	0.7931	0.75	0.7037
		0.4138	0.1200	0.3333	0.6897	0.4400	0.6061
1 2 3	4 5 6	0.2069	0.1250	0.2500	0.4483	0.2917	0.6250
7 8 9	* 0 #	0.4348	0.3462	0.8750	0.6087	0.4615	0.9583

Coverage rate with Top 1 & 2 & 3 ranked labels			Coverage rate with Top 1 & 2 & 3 & 4 ranked labels		
0.9310	0.8214	0.9259	0.9310	0.9286	0.9259
0.8621	0.7200	0.9091	0.9655	0.8400	0.9394
0.6897	0.5833	0.8333	0.8966	0.6250	1.0
0.6522	0.6154	0.9583	0.8261	0.7692	1.0

Figure 9: Evaluation of number pad logging attack

the coverage of true inputs will increase to 1.0 when all the top 3 candidate labels are considered.

6.2.3 Evaluations

In the evaluation, we randomly generated 20 sequences of tap inputs with length of 16. Before the testing, the user is asked to play the *HostApp* for about 60 rounds to create the training dataset. We measure the coverage on each button in the number pad layout. The experiments results with different number of top ranked labels are listed in Figure 9.

From the experimental results, several observations attract our attentions. First of all, from the observed coverage, it is easier to distinguish the buttons close to the edge (such as button "#") than the inner buttons (such as button "5" and "8"). Secondly, outputting more top ranked candidate labels can greatly increase the coverage of inference. For example, the average coverage with only the top 1 label is about 0.364, and the average coverage with the top 1&2&3&4 labels is about 0.887. Moreover, taking the top four labels would achieve high coverage rates on all buttons. This is reasonable because the mistakenly inferred labels are mostly neighboring labels of the truly tapped button. Based on these observations, the attacker may achieve a high coverage of the true inputs by slightly increasing the search space.

6.3 Password Stealing Attack

6.3.1 Attack Overview

Passwords (i.e., PINs) based screen lock is the most common way to protect the smartphone from being accessed by unauthorized users. Briefly, when the screen of smartphone is turned on, the user will be asked for entering a sequence of passwords (i.e., PIN numbers) to unlock the screen. Such a sequence of passwords usually consists of a sequence of number from 0 to 9. The length of passwords is 4 on iOS and 4 or more on Android platform. Stealing the password of screen lock provides the attacker the access to the victim smartphone as well as some private information carried by the password itself. For example, people would like to use the same passwords in different occasions.

Before the attack, *TapLogger* first uses the *HostApp* with the layout shown in Figure 6 to collect the pattern of tap events and build the classifier for tap position classifier in the training mode.

To log the screen lock passwords, the *ContextIdentifier* starts the *SensorListener* service when the screen is turned on (i.e., upon receiving *ACTION_SCREEN_ON* intent) and stops the *SensorListener* after a certain period of time (e.g., 10 seconds). Because the user will be asked to enter the passwords whenever the screen is turned on. During this

period of time, if tap events are detected, the *ContextIdentifier* will use the built-in classifier to infer the tap position and further the related button that has been pressed.

6.3.2 Tap Position Inference

To improve the accuracy of inference, we utilize one observation: suppose that the password of screen lock does not change and the user always enters passwords correctly, the user will always enter the same passwords in every round. With this observation, *TapLogger* divides the passwords into a sequence of individual inputs. Each input corresponds to the tap event at a fixed position of this sequence. *TapLogger* builds an *Inference Distribution Table* for each input in this sequence. For example, in Figure 10, the user enters the same passwords "5, 7, 6, 0" for 32 rounds. In each round, the first input is always the same. Thus, for every tap event detected as the first input, *TapLogger* will add one to its inferred label in the table, meaning that the tap event in this round is inferred as this label. In this way, the inference distribution table counts the number of times that a certain label (i.e., button) was inferred as a user input. The more frequently a label is inferred, the more likely this label is the real user input. Note that, if the sample size is small, the true input may not be top ranked in the distribution. As shown in Figure 10, the top ranked label with input # 4 is button *Del* instead of button 0 (the real input).

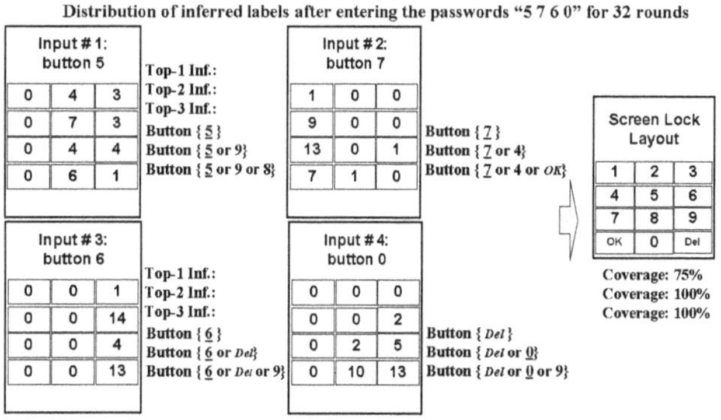

Figure 10: Example of inference distribution table

Thus, *TapLogger* may output several top ranked labels for each input instead of only the toppest one. We name them *Top-1 Inference*, *Top-2 Inference*, and *Top-3 Inference*, representing the number of top ranked label in the inference distribution table. In Figure 10, we show these three types of outputs on the right side. Correspondingly, the *coverage* of an inference is defined as the number of inputs that appear in the inferred labels. In the case of Figure 10, the *Top-1 Coverage* is $3/4 = 75\%$, while the *Top-2 Coverage* and *Top-3 Coverage* are both 100%.

Obviously, *Top-3 Inference* always generates better coverage rate than *Top-1 Inference*. However, it also means a greater search space for identifying the exact true input by the attacker. With the *Top-3 Inference* of a password of length 4, the search space for the attacker to try is $3^4 = 81$, but the search space of a *Top-2 Inference* is only $2^4 = 16$.

6.3.3 Evaluations

Experiments have been done with randomly generated passwords of length 4, 6, and 8. Five passwords are generated for each length. Before the attack, the user is asked to play the *HostApp* for about 60 rounds to build the training dataset. To collect the testing dataset, the user is asked to enter each password 30 rounds with *TapLogger* working

Table 3: The results of screen lock attack

Password Length	4	6	8
Average Top-1 Coverage	0.4	0.266	0.45
Average Top-2 Coverage	0.75	0.6002	0.925
Average Top-3 Coverage	1.0	0.8	0.975

in the logging mode. For tap position inference, we build the classifier using LibSVM [7].

The results of average coverage in our experiments is shown in Table 3. According to the experimental results, with *TapLogger*, the attacker may only need to try the top 3 labels for each input and receive a high probability of hitting the actual password. Note that, in the Table 3, the average coverage with password length 8 is even better than that of length 6. This is because some randomly generated passwords of length 6 contain inner buttons, e.g., Button 5, which causes a low coverage rate.

7. DISCUSSION

7.1 Security Permission Requirements

Note that, as motion sensors are considered as an insensitive resource, *TapLogger* does not require any security permission to access the accelerometer and orientation sensors. In fact, accessing both sensors on other platforms, such as iPhone and Blackberry, do not require security permission either. Due to the space limit, we discuss the feasibility of implementing *TapLogger* on other platforms in Appendix B.

Moreover, as the *ContextIdentifier* service keeps running in the background, the reader may wonder if a curious user may find it suspicious when reviewing the list of running services in *Service Manager*. First of all, we admit that the *ContextIdentifier* service will appear in the list. However, as the smartphone platform and apps are becoming more and more complex, there are usually tens of services, e.g., system's or apps', running in the background. According to our experience on PC, the attacker can easily fool the user by giving the *ContextIdentifier* service a benign name to avoid noticing.

7.2 Overhead Analysis

Computational Overhead: the computational overhead of *TapLogger* on smartphone includes detecting tap events with a *MonitorWin* of sensor readings and training a classifier for tap position inference. The workload of tap event detection is low because the size of *MonitorWin* is fixed and limited (e.g., < 50 readings). Suppose a sensor reading is represented by 4 Bytes. Only 200 Bytes are required in the memory. Also, our tap event detection algorithm relies on heuristic rules and is very lightweight.

For the classifier, both LibSVM and K-means approaches are applied in our attacks. As only six features are applied in the inference, the computational overhead is small. During the experiments, training a classifier with LibSVM with about 800 tap events takes seconds to complete. Thus, the computational overhead is not a problem for *TapLogger*.

Another concern is about the battery consumption caused by continuous sensing with the accelerometer and orientation sensors. According to our measurements on Nexus, the battery can only hold for less than 4 hours if we keep sensing with accelerometer sensors as the highest sample rate. To avoid draining the battery, our *ContextIdentifier* identifies the current context of smartphone and starts the sensing when the touchscreen is on. Therefore, when the touchscreen is off, the sensing will be stopped and *TapLogger* in-

curs no overhead at all. In this way, we avoid draining the battery by continuous sensing.

Communication Overhead Analysis: *TapLogger* sends inferred sensitive user inputs to a remote attack server with labels of zones of a target view. Thus, the generated traffic is very little. To avoid the user from noticing data uploading, *TapLogger* stealthily uploads in two ways. One way is to send the data when the user is interacting with the *HostApp*. For example, *TapLogger* may upload the collected tap events when the user is uploading his local scores to online game center. The other way is to transmits data in background after the touchscreen is turned off. This approach is more timely and the amount of each data transmission will be smaller. It is suggested uploading tap events collected in the logging mode using this approach.

7.3 Countermeasures

The fundamental problem here is that sensing is unmanaged on existing smartphone platforms. People are still unaware of potential risks of unmanaged sensors on smartphones. To prevent such types of attacks, we see an urgent need for sensing management systems on the existing commodity smartphone platforms. For example, we could modify the privacy mode introduced in [43] to place security restrictions on data access to onboard sensors. Sensors, such as accelerometer and orientation sensors, should all be considered as sensitive to user's privacy and need gaining security permissions to access.

Further, even with permission restrictions on the on-board sensors, the attacker may still be able to gain access to sensor readings indirectly, e.g., through the confused deputy attack [17] or the permission re-delegation attacke [15]. In this case, the defense approaches recently proposed in [15] and [11] could be applied on smartphones.

Third, from the perspective of a user, several approaches can all increase the difficulties of attacks launched by *TapLogger*, such as changing the password frequently, choosing password with numbers difficult to infer, and increasing the length of PIN numbers.

8. RELATED WORK

8.1 Logging Attacks on Smartphones

Several logging attacks have been proposed to get user inputs on smartphones. Compromising the operating system [41] or hijacking the touch event with fake user interface [24] are straightforward, but they are complex and easy to be detected. Luring the user to install malicious input method applications is another approach. However, the functionality of input method applications is restricted and the user will be warned before installing such applications [12]. [3] studies the feasibility of identifying the password pattern of screen lock by examining the smudges left on touchscreen after usage. Besides, [27] and [30] propose shoulder surfing attacks which infer user inputs by observing a user's actions on the touchscreen with a camera.

In this work, we utilize the (relatively) insensitive motion sensor readings to infer the sensitive coordinate information of tap events. As shown in Section 6, no specific security permission is required to launch the attack (except the Networking permission required to send the user inputs back to attack server). Moreover, *TapLogger* is automatic in both the training and logging phases. The attacker does not need to be close to the victim user (as in the shoulder surfing attacks) because *TapLogger* will stealthily perform the logging attack and transfer the inferred inputs back to the remote attack server.

8.2 Attacks Relying on Mobile Sensors

The privacy concerns on sensitive mobile sensor data have been raised for some while [22, 8, 6]. Besides the location tracking attacks [16, 18, 21], recent attacks show that the video camera might be controlled by a malware to stealthily record the surrounding when a user enters a building[42] that requires security clearance, credit card and pin numbers can be stolen by a trojan malware which controls the microphone in a smartphone when a user speaks his credit card number to phone menu systems [35]. All these attacks rely on well-known *sensitive sensors*, such as GPS, microphone, and camera. Accessing these sensitive sensors requires security permissions granted by users. Different to existing works, our attack is based on motion sensors that are usually considered insensitive and can be accessed by the background services with no security permissions. Thus, the proposed attack is stealthier and more difficult to detect.

With motion sensors, [20] presented a proof-of-concept of location inference attack that infers the location changes of a vehicle on a city map basing on the accelerometer sensor measurements collected from the driver's smartphone. [28] introduced a spying application, named *(sp)iPhone*, which utilizes the sensed accelerometer readings on a smartphone to infer the user inputs on a nearby keyboard. The work most similar to *TapLogger* are [5] and [13]. [5] observed the correlation between tap event positions and motion changes of smartphone, and validated the observation via a data collection application. [13] divided the touchscreen into zones and studied the feasibility of inferring tapped zones basing on readings collected from accelerometer. However, the differences between *TapLogger* and [5, 13] are significant. First of all, *TapLogger* proposes a new approach for tap event detection which is not discussed in [5, 13]. Secondly, compared to that in [5], *TapLogger* applies different features extracted from orientation sensor readings in the tap position inference. [13] extracted features from accelerometer sensor readings only. Thirdly, we present the complete design and implementation of a trojan which includes a stealthily training phase as well as two practical attacks. Last but not the least, we further showed how the user and device factors impact on the accuracy of logging attacks.

9. CONCLUSION

While the applications relying on mobile sensing are booming, the security and privacy issues related to such applications are not well understood yet. In this paper, we study the feasibility of inferring user inputs on smartphone touchscreen by monitoring readings collected from on-board motion sensors. Specifically, we first present a tap event detection scheme to discover and utilize the user's pattern with statistical measurements on acceleration, and then present an approach of inferring tap position with observed gesture changes. Further, we propose the detailed design of *TapLogger*, a trojan application implementing the proposed two approaches. We show two feasible attacks based on *TapLogger* and use experimental results to show the feasibility of proposed attacks.

9.1 Acknowledgments

We thank the reviewers for the valuable comments. This work was supported in part by NSF CAREER 0643906. The views and conclusions contained in this document are those of the author(s) and should not be interpreted as representing the official policies, either expressed or implied, of NSF or the U.S. Government.

10. REFERENCES

[1] Apple: shuffle songs on iphone, http://www.apple.com/iphone/features/ipod.html

[2] Electronic Arts: Need for speed shift on iphone, http://itunes.apple.com/us/app/need-for-speed-shift/id337641298?mt=8

[3] Aviv, A.J., Gibson, K., Mossop, E., Blaze, M., Smith, J.M.: Smudge attacks on smartphone touch screens. In: Proceedings of the 4th USENIX conference on Offensive technologies. pp. 1–7. WOOT'10 (2010)

[4] BlackBerry: Ui and navigation - development guide - blackberry java sdk - 7.0 beta

[5] Cai, L., Chen, H.: Touchlogger: Inferring keystrokes on touch screen from smartphone motion. In: Proc. of HotSec'11 (2011)

[6] Cai, L., Machiraju, S., Chen, H.: Defending against sensor-sniffing attacks on mobile phones. In: The First ACM SIGCOMM Workshop on Networking, Systems, Applications on Mobile Handhelds (MobiHeld) (2009)

[7] Chang, C.C., Lin, C.J.: Libsvm: A library for support vector machines. ACM Trans. Intell. Syst. Technol. 2, 27:1–27:27 (May 2011)

[8] Das, T., Mohan, P., Padmanabhan, V.N., Ramjee, R., Sharma, A.: PRISM: platform for remote sensing using smartphones. In: Proceedings of the international conf. on Mobile systems, applications, and services (2010)

[9] Android Developers: SensorEvent specification, http://developer.android.com/reference/android/hardware/SensorEvent.html

[10] Developers, A.: Handling UI events, http://developer.android.com/guide/topics/ui/ui-events.html

[11] Dietz, M., Shekhar, S., Pisetsky, Y., Shu, A., Wallach, D.S.: Quire: Lightweight provenance for smart phone operating systems. In: Proc. of Usenix Security'11

[12] Android Dveloper: InputMethodManager, http://developer.android.com/reference/android/view/inputmethod/InputMethodManager.html

[13] Emmanuel Owusu, Jun Han, S.D.A.P.J.Z.: ACCessory: Keystroke Inference using Accelerometers on Smartphones. In: Procceedings of Workshop on Mobile Computing Systems and Applications (HotMobile) (2012)

[14] Facebook: Facebook on android, https://market.android.com/details?id=com.facebook.katana&hl=en

[15] Felt, A.P., Wang, H.J., Moshchuk, A., Hanna, S., Chin, E.: Permission re-delegation: Attacks and defenses. In: Proc. of Usenix Security'11

[16] Golle, P., Partridge, K.: On the anonymity of home/work location pairs. In: Proceedings of the 7th International Conference on Pervasive Computing. pp. 390–397. Pervasive '09, Springer-Verlag, Berlin, Heidelberg (2009)

[17] Hardy, N.: The confused deputy: (or why capabilities might have been invented). SIGOPS Oper. Syst. Rev. 22, 36–38 (October 1988)

[18] Hoh, B., Gruteser, M., Xiong, H., Alrabady, A.: Enhancing security and privacy in traffic-monitoring systems. IEEE Pervasive Computing 5, 38–46 (October 2006)

[19] FitnessKeeper Inc.: RunKeeper application, runkeeper.com

[20] Jun Han, Emmanuel Owusu, T.L.N.A.P.J.Z.: ACComplice: Location Inference using Accelerometers on Smartphones. In: Proceedings of COMSNETS'12 (2012)

[21] Krumm, J.: Inference attacks on location tracks. In: Proceedings of the 5th international conference on Pervasive computing. pp. 127–143. PERVASIVE'07, Springer-Verlag, Berlin, Heidelberg (2007)

[22] Lane, N.D., Miluzzo, E., Lu, H., Peebles, D., Choudhury, T., Campbell, A.T.: A survey of mobile phone sensing. Comm. Mag. 48, 140–150 (September 2010)

[23] Apple iOS Developer Library: Uiaccelerometer class reference, `http://developer.apple.com/library/ios/#documentation/UIKit/Reference/UIAccelerometer_Class/Reference/UIAccelerometer.html`

[24] Lineberry, A.: Android touch-event hijacking (2010), `http://blog.mylookout.com/2010/12/android-touch-event-hijacking/`

[25] LLC, A.: Kindle on android, `https://market.android.com/details?id=com.amazon.kindle&hl=en`

[26] Ltd., R.M.: Angry birds on android, `https://market.android.com/details?id=com.rovio.angrybirds`

[27] Maggi, F., Volpatto, A., Gasparini, S., Boracchi, G., Zanero, S.: Poster: Fast, automatic iphone shoulder surfing. In: Proc. of the 18th Conference on Computer and Communication Security (CCS) (2011)

[28] Marquardt, P., Verma, A., Carter, H., Traynor, P.: (sp)iphone: decoding vibrations from nearby keyboards using mobile phone accelerometers. In: Proceedings of the 18th ACM conference on Computer and communications security. pp. 551–562. CCS '11, ACM (2011)

[29] Meier, R.: Professional Android 2 Application Development. Wiley Publishing, Inc. (2009)

[30] Raguram, R., White, A.M., Goswami, D., Monrose, F., Frahm, J.M.: ispy: automatic reconstruction of typed input from compromising reflections. In: Proceedings of the 18th ACM conference on Computer and communications security. pp. 527–536. CCS '11, ACM (2011)

[31] Ravindranath, L., Newport, C., Balakrishnan, H., Madden, S.: Improving wireless network performance using sensor hints. In: Proceedings of USENIX conference on Networked systems design and implementation (2011)

[32] Reddy, S., Mun, M., Burke, J., Estrin, D., Hansen, M., Srivastava, M.: Using mobile phones to determine transportation modes. ACM Trans. Sen. Netw. 6, 13:1–13:27 (March 2010)

[33] Ross, S.M.: Introduction to Probability and Statistics for Engineers and Scientiests. Academic Press, 2nd edn. (1999)

[34] Saffer, D.: Designing Gestural Interfaces. O'Reilly (2008)

[35] Schlegel, R., Zhang, K., Zhou, X., Intwala, M., Kapadia, A., Wang, X.: Soundminer: A stealthy and context-aware sound trojan for smartphones. In: Proceedings of the 18th Annual Network and Distributed System Security Symposium (NDSS) (2011)

[36] Siewiorek, D., Smailagic, A., Furukawa, J., Krause, A., Moraveji, N., Reiger, K., Shaffer, J., Wong, F.L.: Sensay: A context-aware mobile phone. In: Proceedings of the 7th IEEE International Symposium on Wearable Computers. pp. 248–. ISWC '03, IEEE Computer Society (2003)

[37] Takeuchi, S., Tamura, S., Hayamizu, S.: Human action recognition using acceleration information based on hidden markov model. In: Proc of 2009 APSIAPA Annual Summit and Conference (2009)

[38] Thiagarajan, A., Biagioni, J., Gerlich, T., Eriksson, J.: Cooperative transit tracking using smart-phones. In: Proceedings of the 8th ACM Conference on Embedded Networked Sensor Systems. pp. 85–98. SenSys '10 (2010)

[39] USA Today: Hello, big brother: Digital sensors are watching us, `http://www.usatoday.com/tech/news/2011-01-26-digitalsensors26_CV_N.htm`

[40] wikipedia: Comparison of smartphones, `http://en.wikipedia.org/wiki/Comparison_of_smartphones`

[41] Wikipedia: ios jailbreaking, `http://en.wikipedia.org/wiki/IOS_jailbreaking`

[42] Xu, N., Zhang, F., Luo, Y., Jia, W., Xuan, D., Teng, J.: Stealthy video capturer: a new video-based spyware in 3g smartphones. In: Proceedings of the second ACM conference on Wireless network security (2009)

[43] Zhou, Y., Zhang, X., Jiang, X., Freeh, V.W.: Taming information-stealing smartphoneapplications (on android). In: Proc. of TRUST'11

APPENDIX

A. TAP EVENT DETECTION ALGORITHM

The detailed checking scheme for tap event detection is described in the following Algorithm 1.

---

input : $P_S = \{I_1, I_2, I_3, I_4, I_5\}$, the learnt pattern of tap events, where $I_i = \{L_i, U_i\}$;
MW_S, the sequence of $SqSum$ readings in the current $MonitorWin$;

output: $Indicator$, that returns $TRUE$ if a tap event is detected;
$StartIndex$ and $EndIndex$, that returns the estimated start and end of the detected tap event in the $MonitorWin$, respectively.

1   $base \leftarrow G^2$;
2   **if** $MW_S(checkpoint) - base \notin I_1$ **then**
3     $Indicator \leftarrow FALSE$; Return $Indicator$;
4   **end**
5   $StartIndex \leftarrow$ the first reading that is close enough to $base$ starting from the $checkpoint$ to 0
6   $trough \leftarrow$ the index of minimum reading between $StartIndex$ and $checkpoint$ in the $MonitorWin$;
7   **if** $MW_S(trough) - base \notin I_2$ **then**
8     $Indicator \leftarrow FALSE$; Return $Indicator$;
9   **end**
10 **if** $MW_S(checkpoint) - MW_S(trough) \notin I_3$ **then**
11    $Indicator \leftarrow FALSE$; Return $Indicator$;
12 **end**
13 **if** $checkpoint - trough \notin I_4$ **then**
14    $Indicator \leftarrow FALSE$; Return $Indicator$;
15 **end**
16 $EndIndex \leftarrow StartIndex + AveLength$
17 **if** $std(NW_S[StartIndex, EndIndex]) \notin I_5$ **then**
18    $Indicator \leftarrow FALSE$; Return $Indicator$;
19 **end**
20 Return $Indicator$, $StartIndex$, $EndIndex$;

Algorithm 1: Tap event detection in logging mode

B. ATTACK ON OTHER PLATFORMS

Other smartphones, such as iPhone and BlackBerry, have similar on-board sensors equipped on devices. There are already thousands of iPhone and iPad apps that leverage the accelerometer sensor in gaming, healthcare areas, etc. Similar to the accelerometer usage defined on Android platform, iOS also provides three axes readings: X axis reading for moving left or right, Y axis reading for moving forward or backward, and Z axis reading for moving up or down. We can obtain them by implementing a class specifying the UIAccelerometerDelegate protocol to listen to the accelerometer events. Although iOS 4 does not support true multitasking (except a few services, e.g., streaming etc.,), which means our taplogger cannot reside in background running on iOS devices to keep tracking tap events, it is feasible doing on jailbreaked iOS devices. We do not discuss BlackBerry in this article because touchscreen based BlackBerry devices are rare in the sense of both in BlackBerry family and in smartphone market share. However, our approach will be still valid with careful investigation of the working mechanism of the on-board sensors on BlackBerry. We will address it in our future work.

DroidChecker: Analyzing Android Applications for Capability Leak

Patrick P.F. Chan
The University of Hong Kong
Pokfulam, Hong Kong
pfchan@cs.hku.hk

Lucas C.K. Hui
The University of Hong Kong
Pokfulam, Hong Kong
hui@cs.hku.hk

S.M. Yiu
The University of Hong Kong
Pokfulam, Hong Kong
smyiu@cs.hku.hk

ABSTRACT

While Apple has checked every app available on the App Store, Google takes another approach that allows anyone to publish apps on the Android Market. The openness of the Android Market attracts both benign and malicious developers. The security of the Android platform relies mainly on sandboxing applications and restricting their capabilities such that no application, by default, can perform any operations that would adversely impact other applications, the operating system, or the user. However, a recent research reported that a genuine but vulnerable application may leak its capabilities to other applications. When being leveraged, other applications can gain extra capabilities which they are not granted originally. We present DroidChecker, an Android application analyzing tool which searches for the aforementioned vulnerability in Android applications. DroidChecker uses interprocedural control flow graph searching and static taint checking to detect exploitable data paths in an Android application. We analyzed more than 1100 Android applications using DroidChecker and found 6 previously unknown vulnerable applications including the renowned Adobe Photoshop Express application. We have also developed a malicious application that exploits the previously unknown vulnerability found in the Adobe Photoshop Express application. We show that the malicious application, which is not granted any permissions, can access contacts on the phone with just a few lines of code.

Categories and Subject Descriptors

D.4.6 [**Security and Protection**]: Verification

General Terms

Algorithms, Security, Verification

Keywords

Android, Capability Leaks, Privilege Escalation Attack, Taint Checking, Control Flow Checking

1. INTRODUCTION

Smartphones have evolved rapidly over the last few years. The number of smartphone users is also increasing tremendously. According to figures for 2010 released by Gartner [17], smartphones accounted for 297 million (19%) of the 1.6 billion mobile phones sold that year. That is 72.1% more smartphone sales than in 2009. Another survey conducted by thinkmobile with Google showed that 68% of the participants expressed that they used an app during the week before [40]. This shows that more and more people are using smartphones these days and most of them are using applications on their smartphones.

A recent research from Nielsen shows that Android now owns 29% market share of smartphone users in the US and is pulling ahead of RIM Blackberry (27%) and Apple iOS (27%) [30]. Moreover, the Android Market is the fastest growing mobile application platform. According to a recent report released by mobile security firm Lookout, the Android Market is growing at three times the rate of Apple's App store [25]. However, unlike the Apple's App store, there is no screening process of the apps being published on the Android Market. Occasionally, Google needs to take down some malicious apps from the Android Market after they are found containing malicious code.

Along with the increasing prevalence of smartphones, the security threats to them are also growing. In August this year, an uncovered trojan was found recording phone calls and the recorded calls could be uploaded to a server maintained by the attacker [41]. In June, another trojan, called GGTracker, was uncovered. It sends SMS messages to a premium-rate number and may also steal information from the device [26, 38]. According to a blog entry from lookout [26], after the victims click on a malicious in-app advertisement, they are directed to a malicious website which imitates the Android Market installation screen. The malicious website then lures the victims to download and install a malicious application. The victims are then subject to unpredicted charges.

Android is basically a privilege-separated operating system [2]. Every application runs with a distinct system identity in its own Davik virtual machine. This mechanism isolates applications from each other and from the system. By default, an application is not capable of performing any operations that would adversely impact other applications, the operating system, or the user. In order to obtain extra capabilities, an application needs to declare the permissions that it needs in its *AndroidManifest.xml*. At application installation time, the user decides whether to grant the permissions to the application or not. During the runtime of the application, no further checks with the user are done. The application either was granted a particular permission when installed and can use that feature as desired or the permission was not granted and any attempt to use that feature will fail without prompting the user. For instance, to be able to access the Internet, an application needs to have the *INTERNET* permission.

However, recent research has showed that an application with less permissions (a non-privileged caller) is not restricted to access components of a more privileged application (a privileged callee) [7]. Such attack is called privilege escalation attack or confused deputy attack. It allows a malicious application to indirectly acquire more capabilities leaked from a benign application which fails to guard the permissions granted to it. To prevent this attack, applications must enforce additional checks on permissions to ensure that the callers have the required permissions before doing any dangerous actions. Since most of the application developers are not security experts, delegating the task of performing these checks to them is an error prone approach.

The aim of this research is to develop an automatic analysis system for detecting capability leaks in Android applications and find out how prevalent they are in existing applications. The resulting system is useful for developers to make sure that their applications, while not malicious on their own, do not leak capabilities to other applications. Moreover, Android users can use our system to search for capability leaks in an application before installing it. We propose DroidChecker, an automatic capability leaks detection tool for Android applications.

DroidChecker first parses the *AndroidManifest.xml* file which defines, among other things, the permissions an application uses and the permissions other applications need in order to access the components of that application. Every Android application must include the *AndroidManifest.xml* in its Android package (APK) file as required by the Android system. After that, it identifies components that are potential sources of capability leaks. For each of such components, it looks into its source code and uses interprocedural control flow searching to follow the taint propagation. It then obtains data paths that lead to capability leaks. It raises an alarm whenever such paths are found.

We downloaded 1179 Android applications from the wild and scanned them using DroidChecker. 6 applications were found to have capability leaks with one of them being *Adobe Photoshop Express 1.3.1* (APE). We inspected the source code of APE and found that when it is leveraged, an application with no capability granted can read e-mail addresses of the contacts on the phone by calling a component of it. We illustrate such an attack with a simple application written by us.

The primary contributions of this paper are:

- **Algorithm.** We propose a novel approach to automatically detect capability leaks in Android applications. To the best of our knowledge, we are the first to use interprocedural control flow graph searching coupled with taint checking to detect capability leaks. This significantly increases the granularity and hence the accuracy of the detection. Since any alarms raised by the detection system will likely to be checked manually, a more accurate detection system means less human effort involved and more useable.

- **Evaluation.** We implement a prototype of the proposed approach and use the tool to scan 1179 Android applications from the wild. We demonstrate an attack with a simple application which leverages the capability leak identified by DroidChecker in *Adobe Photoshop Express 1.3.1* to get e-mail addresses from the contacts on the phone. This shows that our system can successfully detect previously unknown capability leak in real-world applications.

- **A Scalable Implementation.** We fully automate every step of the checking tool to make it scalable. It took less than an hour to finish checking all the 1179 Android applications in our testing set. Moreover, we do not achieve such scalability by limiting the method invocations tracing to a certain depth when doing interprocedural checking. Instead, we only avoid running into infinite loop by not checking the same method with argument(s) in the same tainted state twice.

The rest of this paper is organized as follows: Section 2 provides some background information of Android; Section 3 describes the privilege escalation attack on Android; Section 4 provides the details of the design of our system; Section 5 reports the evaluation results; Section 6 illustrates an example attack; Section 7 discusses the limitations and future work. Section 8 surveys related work and compares it with our work; Section 9 concludes the paper.

2. BACKGROUND OF ANDROID

Android is a free, open source mobile platform based on the Linux kernel. Android applications are written in Java and composed of four types of application components: activities, services, content providers, and broadcast receivers. Components can communicate to each other and to components of other applications through an inter component communication (ICC) mechanism called intent messaging. An intent is a passive data structure holding an abstract description of an operation to be performed. To build performance-critical portions of the application in native code, developers can make use of the Android NDK companion tool which provides headers and libraries when programming in C or C++. However, inclusion of C or C++ libraries kicks away the security guarantees provided by the Java programming language. Several different vulnerabilities in native code of the JDK (Java Development Kit) have been identified [39]. In the rest of this section, the various ICC mechanisms for the four types of components will first be discussed. Following that, we will discuss about the four cornerstones of Android security.

2.1 Inter Component Communication

Figure 1 shows the ICC for the four types of components. There are different kinds of intent messages for each of them. For activity components, it can be started by *startActivity* method. The caller can attach some data into the intent message passed to the target activity. However, once the target activity is started, the caller is suspended and cannot interact with it. The control is passed back to the caller once the target activity has finished. In order to get data from the callee, the caller can use the *startActivityForResult* method instead. The difference between it and the *startActivity* method is that, the callee can pass an intent message

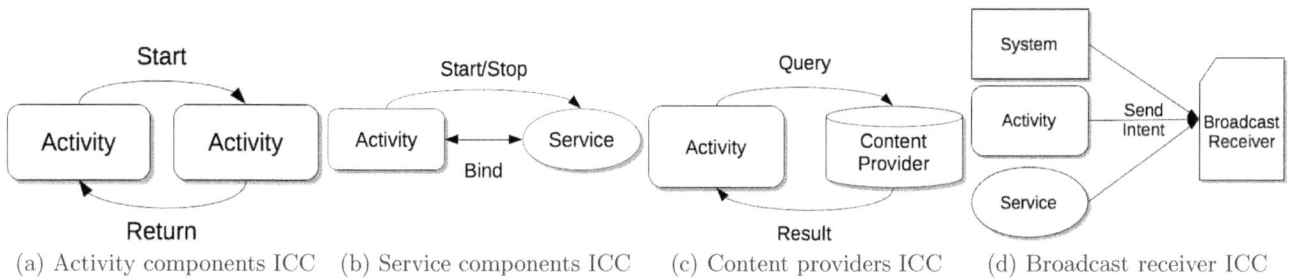

(a) Activity components ICC   (b) Service components ICC   (c) Content providers ICC   (d) Broadcast receiver ICC

Figure 1: The ICC for the four types of components

back to the caller when it has finished. That is the only way the caller can get some data from the callee.

For service components, there are two ways to trigger their executions. The first way is to start the service with the *startService* method. But the service will run in background and the caller has no way to interact with it. The second way is to bind to the service and the caller can interact with it with Remote Procedure Call (RPC). The caller can send commands to the callee and retrieve data from it.

For content providers, it can be treated as a database and an activity component can issue queries to it and get back a result set. This is the only way to share data across applications. There are some content providers shipped with Android which provide convenient access to common data such as contact informations, calendar information, and media files.

Broadcast receivers receive intents sent by *sendBroadcast.* Such intents can be sent by the system or by other applications.

2.2 Cornerstones of Android Security

2.2.1 Sandboxing

Android is a privilege-separated operating system. Each application runs within its own distinct system identity and its own Dalvik virtual machine (DVM). System files are owned by either the "system" or the "root" user. As a result, an application can only access files it owns or files of other applications that are marked as readable / writable /executable for others explicitly. This provides a sandbox for each application which isolates it from other applications and from the system. Applications signed with the same signature can request for being assigned to the same user ID by using the *sharedUserId* attribute in the *AndroidManifest.xml*'s *manifest* tag of each package. Consequently, the two packages are then treated as the same application and can access the same set of files.

2.2.2 Application Signing

Each application must be signed with a certificate and the corresponding private key is held by its developer. The certificate is used solely for distinguishing application authors. It does not need to be signed by a certificate authority. Typically, it is a self-signed certificate. It is used by the Android system to decide whether to grant or deny application access to signature-level permissions and whether to grant or deny an application's request to be given the same Linux identity as another application. The certificate is included in its

APK file such that the signature made by the developer can be validated at installation time.

2.2.3 Permissions

Additional finer-grained security features are provided through a "permission" mechanism that enforces restrictions on the specific operations that a particular process can perform. Also, applications can make use of per-URI permissions to grant ad-hoc access to specific pieces of data. By default, an application has no permission to perform any operations that would adversely impact other applications, the operating system, or the user. To share resources and data with other applications, an application must declare the permissions it needs for additional capabilities not provided by the basic sandbox. The permissions an application requires are declared in the *AndroidManifest.xml* file which is compulsory for all applications. At installation time, the Android system prompts the user for consent. It relies on the user to judge whether he or she permits the application to use all the permissions it requires or refuses to install the application.

2.2.4 Accessibility of Components

Application components can be specified as public or private. A public component can be accessed by other applications. However, it can still perform permission checking to restrict access to only applications that own certain permissions. On the other hand, a private component is only accessible by components within the same application. Making a component private simplifies the security specification. The application developer does not need to assign permission label to it and care about how another application might acquire that label.

3. PRIVILEGE ESCALATION ATTACK ON ANDROID

In this section, we give the details of the privilege escalation attack or confused deputy attack on Android. The attack was first proposed by Lucas Davi et al. in [7]. They stated the problem as follows:

An application with less permissions (a non-privileged caller) is not restricted to access components of a more privileged application (a privileged callee).

Figure 2 illustrates an example of privilege escalation attack on Android. In the figure, there are three applications running in their own DVMs. Application 1 owns no permissions. Since components in application 2 is not guarded by

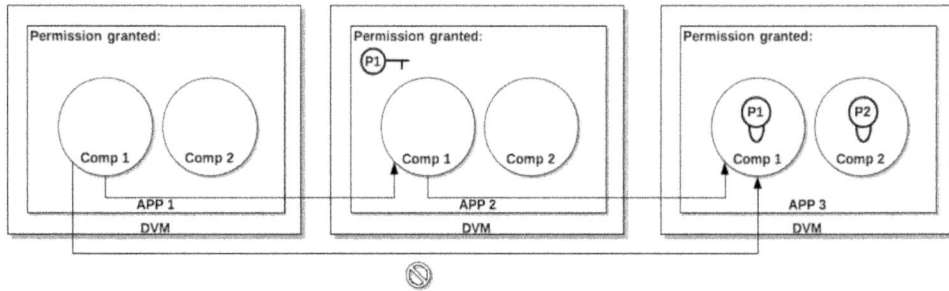

Figure 2: Privilege Escalation Attack

any permissions, they are accessible by components of any other applications. As a result, both components of application 1 can access components 1 in application 2. Application 2 own permission *P1*, Therefore, both components of application 2 can access component 1 of application 3 which is protected by permission *P1*.

We can see that component 1 of application 1 is accessing component 1 of application 2. However, since it does not have permission *P1*, it is not allowed to access component 1 of application 3. On the other hand, application 2 owns permission *P1*. Hence, component 1 of application 2 is allowed to access component 1 of application 3. Therefore, although component 1 of application 1 is not allowed to access component 1 of application 3, component 1 of application 1 can access it via component 1 of application 2. Therefore, the privilege of application 2 is escalated to application 1 in this case.

In order to prevent this attack, component 1 of application 2 should enforce that components accessing it must possess permission *P1*. This can be done at code level using the *checkPermission* API call or by guarding component 1 by permission *P2*. However, most developers are not security experts. They may not be aware of the possibility of leaking capabilities through their applications and the consequences of it. Even if they are aware of it, developers are not motivated to take measures to prevent leaking capabilities as the deputy itself is not harmed in the attack.

The consequences of a capability leak can be serious as Android provides a set of functionality-rich API calls which can get the current location, send text messages, make calls, and reading information on NFC cards. Recently, android applications can also be used to control devices using the Android ADK framework. [19]. Applications granted with permissions to perform such dangerous actions should be carefully protected.

It is obvious that in order to launch such an attack, the existent of application 2 (the deputy) is crucial as it serves as the stepping stone for application 1 to acquire extra capability. More specifically, it leaks to other applications its capability of accessing component 1 of application 3. Our research goal is to identify such capability leaks in applications.

4. SYSTEM DESIGN

4.1 System overview

Figure 3 shows the overview of our system. The APK file of the Android application to be analyzed is first converted into a JAR file. This is done by *dex2jar* which is

a tool for converting Android's *.dex* format to Java's *.class* format [20]. It takes the whole APK file as input and gives a JAR file which contains the *.class* files as output. After that, the manifest file (*AndroidManifest.xml*) is extracted from the JAR file for further inspection. The manifest file defines, among other things, the permissions an application uses and the permissions other applications need in order to access the components of that application. Since the manifest file is in binary XML format, it is first converted back to human-readable XML using another tool called AXML-Printer2 [18]. By looking at the manifest file, we know the answers to the following questions:

1. Is the application asking for additional capabilities by requiring permissions?

2. What are the components that are publicly accessible by other applications?

3. Are those publicly accessible components guarded by permissions?

We then obtain a list of components that have the potential of leaking capabilities. These are the components that have extra capabilities, are publicly accessible, and are not guarded by any permissions. Finally, using interprocedural control flow graph searching and static taint checking, we look for data paths in the source files of these components that will lead to capability leaks. The source files are obtained by decompiling the class files in the JAR archive using Java Decompiler which is the latest Java decompiler [10].

In the rest of this section, we will discuss in details the two key modules, manifest file parsing and capability leak detection.

4.2 Manifest File Parsing

Before going into technical details of the manifest file parsing module, we discuss the structure of the manifest file and briefly explain the various tags found in it. After that, the high-level checking policy is introduced. Finally, we give the low-level details of the manifest file parsing.

4.2.1 The AndroidManifest.xml

Figure 4 shows an abstract of the general structure of the manifest file. The *uses-permission* tag requests a permission that the application must be granted in order for it to operate correctly. The *permission* tag declares a security permission that can be used to limit access to specific components or features. The *android:permission* attribute of the application tag declares the permission that components of

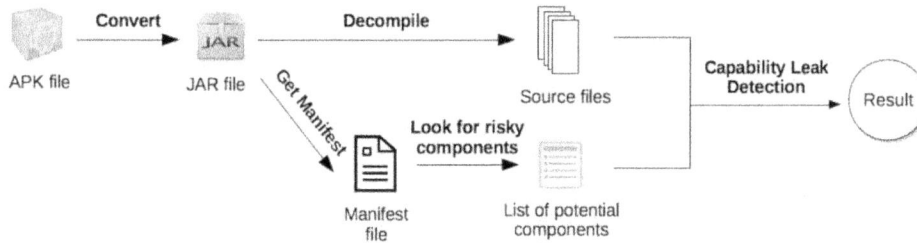

Figure 3: System Overview

```xml
<?xml version="1.0" encoding="utf-8"?>
<manifest>
  <uses-permission />
  <permission />
  <application android:permission="...">
    <activity android:permission="..." android:exported="...">
      <intent-filter> ... </intent-filter>
    </activity>
    <service android:permission="..." android:exported="...">
      <intent-filter> ... </intent-filter>
    </service>
  </application>
</manifest>
```

Figure 4: General structure of AndroidManifest.xml

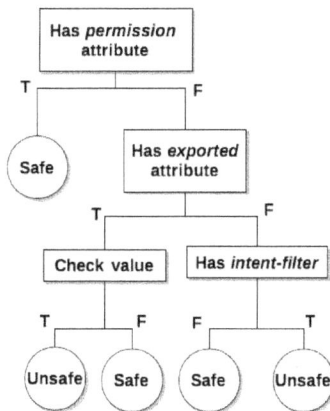

Figure 5: The decision tree of XML parsing

other applications must have in order to interact with the application. Moreover, each component can require extra permission for accessing it. They are declared in the *android:permission* attribute of the tag that declares the component. A component can also be made private by setting the *android:exported* attribute to *false*. Such a component is not accessible by components of other applications. If the *android:exported* attribute is absent, the default value of it depends on whether the component contains intent filters (except for Content Providers, which have the default value being *true*). If there is no intent filters, the default value is *false*. Otherwise, the default value is *true*. An intent filter specifies the types of implicit intents that an activity, service, or broadcast receiver can respond to. However, explicit intents can always target at a specific component no matter

how the intent filters of that component are set. Therefore, intent filters cannot be relied on for security.

4.2.2 The Checking Policy

The checking system parses the *AndroidManifest.xml* to find out if:

1. The application uses at least one permission and;

2. There exists an activity or service component that does not require any permission and is publicly visible

If the above two are both satisfied, components satisfying the second requirement are components that have the potential of capability leak.

We focus on activity and service components as they are the components that can be directly leveraged to launch a privilege escalation attack among the four types of components. The activity component provides a user interface and is what the user will see on the screen. On the other hand, the service component performs long-running operation in the background and does not provide a user interface. Both kinds of components can be protected by permissions.

4.2.3 The Checking Process

The system starts with scanning the *uses-permission* tags to see if there is any permission required by the application. If no, the system terminates. Next, the system parses the *android:permission* attribute of the *application* tag to find out if the application is guarded by any permissions. If yes, the system concludes that the application is safe. Otherwise, it goes on to perform the following checking for each activity or service component.

Figure 5 shows the decision tree for the checking. First, the system checks if there is any permissions declared in the *android:permission* attribute of the tag that declares that component. If yes, the component is safe as it is protected by permission(s). If no, the system checks if the *android:exported* attribute is present. If yes and the value of it is *true*, the component is potentially vulnerable for capability leak and requires further checking. If the *android:exported* attribute is absent, the visibility of the component hinges on the presence of intent filters. If there is no intent filters, the component is not visible to other applications by default, and hence, it is safe. Otherwise, the component is visible to other applications. In that case, it is also potentially vulnerable for capability leak and requires further checking.

129

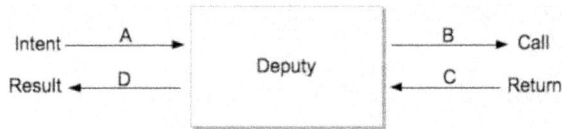

Figure 6: A Deputy Application

4.3 Capability Leak Detection

We build the capability leak detection module based on existing techniques. We look for data paths that lead to capability leaks by following taint propagation [21, 29, 37, 15, 24] in the interprocedural control flow graph [27, 8, 42, 23, 34] built from the source code of an application component. The capability leak detection is performed for each risky component reported by the manifest file parsing module. We will first talk about the nature of the API calls of Android. Then, we will discuss the two kinds of data paths that can be found in a deputy. After that, we will introduce the details of the mechanism we use to search for such data paths.

4.3.1 API Calls of Android

We focus on API calls that are protected by permissions at the dangerous level. They are the API calls that give an application access to private user data or control over the device that can negatively impact the user. Permissions at the dangerous level are not granted to applications automatically even if they request them.

We classify API calls into action calls and data calls. Action calls are API calls that have side effects. Data calls are API calls that will return data to the caller without side effects. For example, the *sendSMS* is an action call that will send an SMS when called but will not return any data. The *managedQuery* is a data call that is used to retrieve records in content providers.

4.3.2 The Two Kinds of Data Paths in a Deputy

Figure 6 shows the bird's-eye view of an application that is acting as a deputy for other applications. Arrow A represents an intent message from another application. Upon receiving the intent message, the deputy invokes an API call represented by arrow B. The API call can be an action call or a data call as explained in previous section. In the case of an action call, the job of the deputy is done. In the case of an data call, the deputy will get the return value of the API call as represented by arrow C. The return value will then be passed back to the application who sent the intent. This is represented by arrow D.

Figure 7a shows an example of a deputy invoking an action call. The *getExtras* method retrieves data from the intent message that triggers this component. At line 20 and line 21, this method is called and the return value is stored in variable *receiver* and *msg*. At line 23, these two variables become the arguments to the *sendTextMessage* method which will send an SMS message to the telephone number stored in *receiver* with the content stored in *msg*. Therefore, even though the application that triggers this component does not have the capability to send SMS, it acquires such capability through this component. It can send an SMS message to whoever it wants with any contents. Therefore, the capability of this component is leaked.

Figure 7b shows an example of a deputy invoking a data

```
20    String receiver = getIntent().getExtras()
        .getString("receiver");
21    String msg = getIntent().getExtras().getString("message");
22    SmsManager sm = SmsManager.getDefault();
23    sm.sendTextMessage(receiver, null, msg, null, null);
```
(a) Deputy for an Action Call

```
30    Location loc =
        getLastKnownLocation(LocationManager.GPS_PROVIDER);
31    String long = loc.getLongitude();
32    String alt = loc.getAltitude();
33    Intent resultIntent = new Intent(null);
34    resultIntent.putExtra("Longitude", long);
35    resultIntent.putExtra("Altitude", alt);
36    setResult(Activity.RESULT_OK, resultIntent);
37    finish();
```
(b) Deputy for a Data Call

Figure 7: Code Example of a Deputy

call. At line 30, the method call *getLastKnownLocation* returns the last known location and the location is stored in the variable *loc*. Eventually, the location is passed to the intent object *resultIntent* which will be returned to the application that started this component. As a result, even that application does not have the capability to get the location information, it can obtain such information from this component. In other words, the capability of getting location information is leaked from this component.

DroidChecker searches for two kinds of data paths corresponding to these two kinds of API calls. The first kind of data paths begin with getting the content of the intent from the sender and end in using it as the input argument(s) to an action call. This corresponds to arrow A followed by arrow B in figure 6. We do not consider dangerous action calls with arguments not coming from the sender of the intent as we consider such applications not working as deputies for other applications. The second kind of data paths begin with getting the return value from a data call and end in passing back the return value to the sender of the intent. This is represented by arrow C followed by arrow D in figure 6. Since application developers can perform dynamic checking on the permissions owned by the sender of an intent message, we consider such checking as a way to prevent capability leak. As a result, a data path is considered safe if such checking is found in the control flow along with the data path.

4.3.3 Path Searching

Each method in the component is represented by a control flow graph (CFG). A node of a control flow graph represents a basic block of code and an edge represents a jump in the control flow. Figure 8 shows two example CFGs which correspond to two methods. We will explain the figure in greater detail later. The system starts with default entry points of the component. For activity components, they are *onCreate*, *onStart*, *onResume*, *onPause*, *onStop*, and *onDestroy* methods. For service components, they are *onCreate*, *onStartCommand*, *onBind*, *onUnbind*, and *onDestroy* methods. There exist some other entry points such as event han-

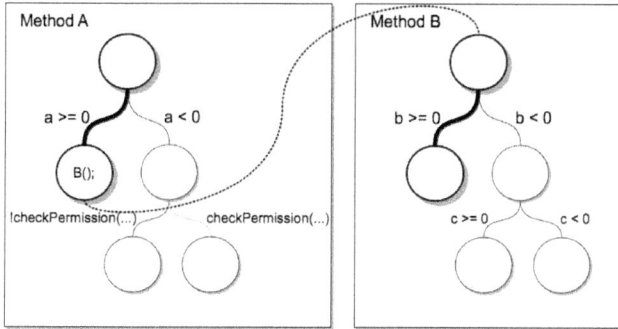

Figure 8: Example CFGs

dlers. Such entry points are also covered in the checking after the default entry methods are checked. After locating the entry methods, the system starts traversing their CFGs.

At anytime, there are two lists of tainted variables. The first list contains variables that are derived from the content of an incoming intent message. The second list contains variables that are derived from the return value of a data call. The system looks for API calls that get content from an intent (e.g. *getExtras*). The return values of such API calls are put into the first list. The system also looks for API calls that are data calls. Their return values are put into the second list. Whenever it comes across an assignment statement or a variable declaration, it checks if any variables on the right-hand side are in the two lists of tainted variables. Any taints of the variables on the right-hand side will be propagated to the variable on the left-hand side.

The are two kinds of sinks for the two kinds of tainted variables. An action call is the sink for those on the first list of tainted variables. The API calls used to attach data to an intent (e.g. *putExtra*) are the sinks for those on the second list of tainted variables. Whenever the system comes across a sink, it checks the two lists of tainted variables to see if the input argument(s) are tainted. If the nature of the taint matches that of the sink, the system raises an alarm for the risky data path found.

To avoid capability leak, application developers can check if the sender of the intent possesses the required permission before invoking an API call. This is done by invoking the *checkPermission* method which checks whether a particular package has been granted a particular permission. If such a checking is found in the control flow, the traversal for graph after the checking is skipped. For example, on Figure 8, the two nodes at the bottom of the CFG of method A are skipped as they are after a conditional check of the return value of the call *checkPermission*.

Most of the time, a method will call another method and the source and sink of a data path may reside in different methods. Therefore, when coming across a method call, the definition of the method is located and the checking moves to that method. Take the path searching shown on Figure 8 as an example. The path searching involves two methods. It starts at method A on the left. It first comes across a conditional check on the value of variable a. It then checks the branch where a is greater than or equal to 0. In that branch, there is a invocation of method B. The checking then goes to the CFG of method B. However, to avoid running into infinite loop in the case of a recursive method call, we

maintain a list of checked methods and checking is skipped if that method has already been checked. A method is identified by its name, the class path of the class in which it is defined, the number of parameters, and the parameters that are tainted. For example, a method has two parameters and the first time when it is checked, the first parameter is tainted but the second is not. Next time, when it is invoked again but with the second parameter being tainted, it needs to be checked again. Therefore, a method with n parameters will be checked at most n times.

5. EVALUATION

5.1 Implementation and Environmental Setup

We implemented a prototype of DroidChecker. The entire system consists of 1013 lines of Java code. Since Java decompiler does not have a command-line interface, we automated the decompiling process by using Sikuli, a visual technology to automate and test graphical user interfaces using images [5]. We made use of ANTLR v3 to build a parser that could generate an abstract syntax tree from Java code [33]. The entire system runs under Ubuntu 11.04.

5.2 Experiment Results

We downloaded 1179 Android applications from Android Freeware[1], an Internet community aimed at collecting and categorizing truly free software, to test our prototype system. Running on a computer with Intel Core2Duo 2.66GHz and 3GB of ram, DroidChecker took about an hour to finish checking all the applications. 711 applications was found potentially risky by the manifest file parsing module. These applications then went through the capability leak detection module. 23 applications were caught for having capability leak problems. We manually checked these 23 applications to find out the data paths that lead to capability leaks. Table 1 summarizes the investigation results of them. For the 8 applications that have real capability leak problems, we confirmed all the data paths found by DroidChecker in their source code and identified capability leaks. However, we found that 2 of them were actually designed that way and their capability leaks are not harmful to the user. For the 15 false alarms, 4 of them are due to nonexistent paths that DroidChecker mistakenly considered. This is caused by reverse engineering problem of the applications. 8 of the false alarms are due to data passed between local application components that DroidChecker mistakenly thought that they were between components from different applications. For the remaining 3 applications, the first one writes data from another application to its logging file. The second one gets data from the caller and prints that to the standard output. This is not harmful but since the *print* method is sensitive, it was caught by DroidChecker. The third one stores some location data in an array and the whole array was tainted by DroidChecker. Eventually, one of the elements in the array is passed to another application. Although DroidChecker was not sure if that element is storing sensitive data, it still raised an alarm under such circumstances to make sure that it did not miss it. This is a generally accepted weakness of static taint checking techniques.

To show how our scheme improves the granularity of the checking, we repeated the experiment but with the second

---

[1]http://www.freewarelovers.com/android

Total no. of Apps	True alarms		False alarms		
	Not intended	Intended	Non-existent path	Leaked to local components	Other reasons
1179	6	2	4	8	3

Table 1: Experiment results

```
27  protected void onCreate(Bundle paramBundle)
28  {
39    Uri localUri = Contacts.ContactMethods.CONTENT_EMAIL_URI;
40    Cursor localCursor1 = localContentResolver.query(localUri,
        arrayOfString1, null, null, "name ASC");
41    mCursor = localCursor1;
58  }
66  protected void onListItemClick(ListView paramListView,
      View paramView, int paramInt, long paramLong)
67  {
68      boolean bool = mCursor.moveToPosition(paramInt);
75      String str = mCursor.getString(i);
76      Intent localIntent3 = localIntent2.putExtra("email", str);
77      setResult(-1, localIntent2);
78      finish();
80  }
```

Figure 9: Excerpt of source code of Adobe Photoshop Express

```
11  public void onCreate(Bundle savedInstanceState) {
23      Intent intent = new Intent();
24      intent.setClassName("com.adobe.psmobile",
          "com.adobe.psmobile.ContactEmailList");
25      intent.setAction("android.intent.action.PICK");
26      intent.addCategory("android.intent.category.DEFAULT");
27      intent.setDataAndType(null, "vnd.android.cursor.dir/email");
28      startActivityForResult(intent, 1);
29  }
31  protected void onActivityResult(int requestCode,
        int resultCode, Intent data) {
34      TextView t = (TextView)findViewById(R.id.textview);
35      t.setText("E-mail address obtained:\n" +
          data.getExtras().getString("email"));
37  }
```

Figure 10: Excerpt of source code of our example attack application

module disabled. This means it scanned the manifest file only and did not perform the interprocedural control flow graph searching and taint checking. We found that module one alone reported 852 applications as vulnerable. In contrast, only 23 alarms were raised when coupled with module 2. This shows that module 2 eliminated 829 false alarms which accounts for 97.3% of the total number of alarms raised.

6. SAMPLE ATTACK

In this section, we demonstrate a sample attack using a tiny Android application developed by us. The application does not have any capability on its own. However, exploiting the capability leak we found on *Adobe Photoshop Express 1.3.1* (APE), it is able to retrieve e-mail addresses of the contacts on the phone. In the rest of this section, we first illustrate the capability leak using the source code we obtained by reverse engineering APE. After that, we show how we can leverage that to obtain extra capability.

6.1 Capability Leak on APE

Figure 9 shows an excerpt from the source code of a component in APE. We extracted the minimum number of lines of code to save space. When the component is started, the *onCreate* function is first executed. At line 40, a query is executed to get the e-mails from the contacts. The *mCursor* reference variable now points to a Cursor object which is positioned before the first entry of the result set. At this point, the program shows the contact e-mails and waits for the user to select an e-mail on the list shown. After a contact e-mail is selected, the *onListItemClick* method is executed. At line 68, the *mCursor* is moved to the entry in the result set representing the contact selected. At line 75, the e-mail is stored in variable *str*. At line 76, the e-mail is put into

the intent object *localIntent3* which is then returned to the application starting this component. Since this component is publicly accessible by other applications, by leveraging it, any applications can acquire access to e-mail addresses of the contacts even though they do not have that capability. Next, we will illustrate such an exploit using a simple Android application developed by us.

6.2 Exploiting the Capability Leak

Our attack application and APE are installed on an emulator running Android 2.3.3 on top of Android SDK Tools revision 11. First, the attack application is launched. After that, it starts the component in APE that has the capability leak. The user is then tricked to select a contact on the contact list. Next, the control is passed back to the attack application. The e-mail address selected is also passed back to the attack application. It can then send it back to a server owned by the attacker. Obtaining valid e-mail addresses is key to successful spamming. We have also tried our attack on a stock Nexus S Android phone running Android 2.3.4 and it worked.

Figure 10 shows an excerpt of the source code of our example attack application. When the application is launched, the method *onCreate* is executed. From line 23 to line 28, an explicit intent message is sent to start the component in APE. After that component has finished, the callback function *onActivityResult* is executed. It then gets the e-mail address from the data returned by APE and shows it on the screen. Note that the attack application does not have any capability originally. This shows that our application has acquired extra capability by exploiting the capability leak in APE.

7. DISCUSSION

7.1 Limitations

Since DroidChecker performs the checking on decompiled source code, it depends on the completeness of the decompilation tool. Designing decompilers for Android applications is an active research area. Dedexer is a disassembler tool for DEX files and decompiles Android applications into an "assembly-like format" [32]. The ded decompiler can decompile Android applications into Java source code [12]. Their work is orthogonal to ours and a better decompiler can help us get a more accurate picture of the Android applications being checked.

Since we use static taint analysis as the underlining technique, we also suffer from the inherent limitations of it. One of them is that it is not able to take into account dynamic features of the Java language like polymorphism. A reference variable may point to an object that inherits it. When a method of that object is invoked, our anaylsis tool will check the method in the superclass but not the one in the subclass. This will harm the soundness and completeness of the checking.

As the *permission* attribute of a component only allows one permission to be set, an application may still be risky even if it has set the *permission* attribute. However, we cannot overcome this limitation as it stems from the design of the Android system. Besides, we currently skip the path searching for code blocks after a conditional check of the return value of a call to *checkPermission*. This is based on the assumption that the presence of *checkPermission* means the developer effectively checks that the caller application has the required permissions for subsequent API calls. However, this may not be the case if the *checkPermission* is not used properly. However, we cannot take into account how it is used as that depends much on the dynamic behavior of the application. It is a balance between false negative and false positive. The assumption we made here is to make the checking more sound. However, it is true that it also makes the checking less complete. We make this as a parameter in our prototype implementation to let the user decide whether the assumption should be made or not.

7.2 Security Guidelines

To make sure that applications do not leak their capabilities to other applications, developers should avoid making the components of their applications accessible by components in other applications. This can be done by either not declaring any intent filters or setting the *android:exported* attributes of components to *false*. In case a component has to be made public, it should be protected by a permission such that other applications have to be privileged in order to access it. Besides, developers should be aware of the explicit intent messages sent to their applications. They should not rely on intent filters to protect a component since other applications can always send an explicit intent message to it. Therefore, a publicly accessible component should not perform security sensitive operations upon receiving an explicit intent message. Before invoking dangerous API calls upon receiving an intent message, developers should check if the sender possesses the required permissions using the *checkPermission()* system call.

7.3 Future Work

Some future work remains. Capability leaks can happen indirectly through content providers. A possible scenario is that an application, which has the required permissions, retrieves private data and stores them in a content provider of its own. Due to certain reasons, it grant the read permission of that content provider to other applications using the URI permissions mechanism. Leakages of this type will not be revealed by our checking tool since it is not able to determine whether a content provider contains private data or not. As a preliminary idea, we can address this by tainting a content provider whenever private data is written into it. Another direction is to make the system run on stock Android phones such that users can check an application for vulnerabilities before installing it.

8. RELATED WORK

The privilege escalation attack on Android was first proposed by Davi et al. [7] in which they demonstrated an example of the attack. They showed that a genuine application exploited at runtime or a malicious application can escalate granted permissions. However, they did not suggest any defense for the attack in the paper.

Some recent work tried to proposal security extensions for Android to remedy the attack. XMandDroid [3] prohibits IPC between applications which own certain combinations of capabilities. For example, an application which can retrieve location information is not allowed to communicate with an application which can access the internet. Permission re-delegation, which is the same as privilege escalation, for web applications and Android applications was studied by Felt et al. in [16]. They proposed IPC Inspector to defend against permission re-delegation. IPC Inspector reduces the permission set of an application after it receives messages from another application which does not own certain permissions the receiver owns. Their mechanism is considered restrictive as applications cannot deliberately receive messages from a less privileged application. Moreover, to avoid multiple reductions of the permission set of an application after communicating with several applications that do not have one or more permissions in its permission set, they create a new instance of an application whenever it encounters in IPC with a new application. This significantly drains the system resources and provides an attack surface for denial of service attack. They also carried out a study to search for vulnerabilities in current Android applications. However, they used call-graph analysis which is coarse-grained and likely to produce false positives for those applications which invoke dangerous calls not under the influence of the intent sender. At about the same time, another group of researchers proposed QUIRE to address the same problem [9]. QUIRE tracks the call chain of on device inter-component communication. When an application receives a message from a less privileged application, it extracts the information about the call chain from the caller. It relies on the application to pass information along the call chain. Provided that application developers are not security experts, it is an error-prone approach to rely on them to carefully pass the information to each receiver of the IPC calls invoked by the application. The advantage of this design is that it allows the developer to choose whether to reduce the set of privileges of the application to that of the sender or to exercise its full privilege set by acting explicitly on its own behalf. This grant applications the freedom to communicate with less privileged applications without being taken away their own privileges. However, their mechanism requires existing applications to be re-compiled in order to enjoy the security service provided. While these work serve the purpose of introducing security measures into the Android system to prevent the attack, our work aims to provide users and developers with a tool to search for vulnerabilities in applications and let them take actions before these security measures are adopted.

There are some work in the literature that use static or dynamic approach to check Android applications for vulnerabilities or malicious behaviors. Chan et al. proposed a static analysis tool of Android applications to determine whether an application can be leveraged to launch privilege escalation attacks [4]. However, their tool looks into the manifest file only. Hence, their tool is more coarse-grained and produces more false positives. Enck et al. proposed a static analysis tool to evaluate the security of Android applications [12]. Their tool makes use of control flow analysis, data flow analysis, structural analysis, and semantic analysis to dangerous functionality and vulnerabilities. Their analysis focuses on a single Android application rather than the interaction between an Android application and other applications. Their work is orthogonal to ours. ComDroid [6] focuses on sniffing, modification, stealing, replacing, and forgery of messages passing between applications. It performs flow-sensitive, intraprocedural static analysis on disassembled assembly-like source code to search for vulnerabilities. Their approach can also be applied to search for capability leaks in applications but would be more coarse-grained and produce more false positives as it looks into the manifest file only. TaintDroid [11] makes use of dynamic taint tracking to keep track of the flow of privacy sensitive data through third-party applications. It monitors in real-time how applications access and manipulate users' personal data. It helps detect when sensitive data leaves the system via untrusted applications. Evaluation of it showed that it incurs significant performance overhead. ScanDroid [1] uses modular data flow analysis to look for data flows in Android applications and make security-relevant decisions automatically based on such flows.

There were some work on security extensions to Android security architecture. Saint [31] is a modification of Android to enable application providers to express the application security polices that regulate the interactions among them. It allows an application to control which applications can be granted the permissions it declares. Moreover, when an application needs to access an component of another application, both parties can assert controls of the communication between them through defining run-time interaction policies. In particular, the caller application selects which application's interfaces it uses and the callee application controls how its interface is used by other applications. Saint policy provides certain protection against privilege escalation attacks as the application can control which applications can access it. However, Saint assumes that access to components is implicitly allowed if no Saint policy exists. This put the burden of enforcing security to application developers which is error prone as most of them are not security experts. Kirin [13] is an application certification service to mitigate malware at installation time. It uses existing security requirements engineering techniques as a reference to identify dangerous application configurations in Android. The rules are a set of combinations of permissions that an application must not be granted at the same time. For example, an application being granted permissions to record audio and access location information may be an voice and location eavesdropping malware. Similar to our approach, their certification process relies on the manifest file in the APK of the application. However, their approach cannot identify applications that can be leveraged to launch privilege escalation attack. Instead, their work is orthogonal to our work and is targeting at a different kind of attack vector.

There are some other work on security of the Android system. Schmidt et al. [35] walked through the smartphone malware evolution. They provided possible techniques for creating Android malware(s). Their approach involves usage of undocumented Android functions enabling them to execute native Linux application even on retail Android devices. They also showed that it is possible to bypass the Android permission system by using native Linux applications. Enck et al. [14] gives a description of the security model of the Android system. Jakobsson et al. [22] proposed a software-based attestation approach to detect any malware that executes or is activated by interrupts. Based on memory-printingof client devices, it makes it impossible for malware to hide inRAM without being detected. Nauman et. al. [28] improved the installation process of Android applications to allow user to selectively grant permissions to applications and impose constraints on the usage of resources. Shabtai et al. [36] makes use of Security-Enhanced Linux (SELinux) to help reduce potential damage on the Android system from a successful attack.

9. CONCLUSION

Android is an open system with some state-of-the-art security measures. Although the idea of privilege-separating the applications can avoid them adversely impacting other applications or the system, it does not prevent applications from leaking capabilities. In this research, we proposed a methodology for detecting capability leaks in Android applications. We utilized interprocedural control flow graph searching and static taint checking technique to identify data paths that will lead to capability leaks. A prototype system was implemented and tested with more than 1000 applications. 6 of applications were found to have capability leaks. We developed a tiny Android application to demonstrate a sample attack. Using one of these 6 applications, our application successfully obtained the extra capability of retrieving e-mail addresses from the contacts on the phone. This showes that our proposed method is effective in identifying the potential risk. As a side product, some security guidelines were provided for Android application developers to avoid capability leaks in their applications.

Acknowledgment

The work described in this paper was partially supported by the General Research Fund from the Research Grants Council of the Hong Kong Special Administrative Region, China (Project No. RGC GRF HKU 713009E), the NSFC/RGC Joint Research Scheme (Project No. N_HKU 722/09), HKU Seed Fundings for Applied Research 201102160014, and HKU Seed Fundings for Basic Research 201011159162 and

200911159149. The authors would like to thank Echo Zhang and anonymous reviewers for their insightful comments.

10. REFERENCES

[1] J. S. F. Adam P. Fuchs, Avik Chaudhuri. Scandroid: Automated security certification of android applications. Technical report, University of Maryland, College Park, 2009.

[2] Android Open Source project. Security and permissions. http://developer.android.com/guide/topics/security/security.html, April 2011.

[3] S. Bugiel, L. Davi, A. Dmitrienko, T. Fischer, and A.-R. Sadeghi. Xmandroid: A new android evolution to mitigate privilege escalation attacks. Technical Report TR-2011-04, Technische Universität Darmstadt, Apr 2011.

[4] P. P. Chan, L. C. Hui, and S. Yiu. A privilege escalation vulnerability checking system for android applications. In *13th IEEE International Conference on Communication Techonologies (ICCT)*, 2011.

[5] S. T.-H. Chang and T. Yeh. Sikuli. http://sikuli.org/.

[6] E. Chin, A. P. Felt, K. Greenwood, and D. Wagner. Analyzing inter-application communication in android. In *Proceedings of the 9th international conference on Mobile systems, applications, and services*, MobiSys '11, pages 239–252, New York, NY, USA, 2011. ACM.

[7] L. Davi, A. Dmitrienko, A.-R. Sadeghi, and M. Winandy. Privilege escalation attacks on android. In *Proceedings of the 13th international conference on Information security*, ISC'10, pages 346–360, Berlin, Heidelberg, 2011. Springer-Verlag.

[8] S. K. Debray and T. A. Proebsting. Interprocedural control flow analysis of first-order programs with tail-call optimization. *ACM Trans. Program. Lang. Syst.*, 19:568–585, July 1997.

[9] M. Dietz, S. Shekhar, Y. Pisetsky, A. Shu, and D. S. Wallach. Quire: lightweight provenance for smart phone operating systems. In *Proceedings of the 20th USENIX conference on Security*, SEC'11, pages 23–23, Berkeley, CA, USA, 2011. USENIX Association.

[10] E. Dupuy. Java decompiler. http://java.decompiler.free.fr/, Aug 2010.

[11] W. Enck, P. Gilbert, B.-G. Chun, L. P. Cox, J. Jung, P. McDaniel, and A. N. Sheth. Taintdroid: an information-flow tracking system for realtime privacy monitoring on smartphones. In *Proceedings of the 9th USENIX conference on Operating systems design and implementation*, OSDI'10, pages 1–6, Berkeley, CA, USA, 2010. USENIX Association.

[12] W. Enck, D. Octeau, P. McDaniel, and S. Chaudhuri. A study of android application security. In *Proceedings of the 20th USENIX conference on Security*, SEC'11, pages 21–21, Berkeley, CA, USA, 2011. USENIX Association.

[13] W. Enck, M. Ongtang, and P. McDaniel. On lightweight mobile phone application certification. In *Proceedings of the 16th ACM conference on Computer and communications security*, CCS '09, pages 235–245, New York, NY, USA, 2009. ACM.

[14] W. Enck, M. Ongtang, and P. McDaniel. Understanding android security. *Security Privacy, IEEE*, 7(1):50 –57, jan.-feb. 2009.

[15] D. Evans and D. Larochelle. Improving security using extensible lightweight static analysis. *IEEE Software*, 19:2002, 2002.

[16] A. P. Felt, H. J. Wang, A. Moshchuk, S. Hanna, and E. Chin. Permission re-delegation: attacks and defenses. In *Proceedings of the 20th USENIX conference on Security*, SEC'11, pages 22–22, Berkeley, CA, USA, 2011. USENIX Association.

[17] Gartner. Gartner says worldwide mobile device sales to end users reached 1.6 billion units in 2010; smartphone sales grew 72 percent in 2010. http://www.gartner.com/it/page.jsp?id=1543014, February 2011.

[18] Google. Axmlprinter2. http://code.google.com/p/android4me/, October 2008.

[19] Google. Android adk. http://developer.android.com/guide/topics/usb/adk.html, December 2011.

[20] Google. dex2jar. http://code.google.com/p/dex2jar/, June 2011.

[21] Y.-W. Huang, F. Yu, C. Hang, C.-H. Tsai, D.-T. Lee, and S.-Y. Kuo. Securing web application code by static analysis and runtime protection. In *Proceedings of the 13th international conference on World Wide Web*, WWW '04, pages 40–52, New York, NY, USA, 2004. ACM.

[22] M. Jakobsson and K.-A. Johansson. Retroactive detection of malware with applications to mobile platforms. In *Proceedings of the 5th USENIX conference on Hot topics in security*, HotSec'10, pages 1–13, Berkeley, CA, USA, 2010. USENIX Association.

[23] T. Jensen, D. Le Metayer, and T. Thorn. Verification of control flow based security properties. In *Security and Privacy, 1999. Proceedings of the 1999 IEEE Symposium on*, pages 89 –103, 1999.

[24] V. B. Livshits and M. S. Lam. Finding security vulnerabilities in java applications with static analysis. In *Proceedings of the 14th conference on USENIX Security Symposium - Volume 14*, pages 18–18, Berkeley, CA, USA, 2005. USENIX Association.

[25] Lookout. App genome report. https://www.mylookout.com/appgenome, February 2011.

[26] Lookout. Security alert: Android trojan ggtracker charges premium rate sms messages. http://blog.mylookout.com/2011/06/security-alert-android-trojan-ggtracker-charges-victims-premium-rate-sms-messages/, June 2011.

[27] J. Midtgaard and T. P. Jensen. Control-flow analysis of function calls and returns by abstract interpretation. In *Proceedings of the 14th ACM SIGPLAN international conference on Functional programming*, ICFP '09, pages 287–298, New York, NY, USA, 2009. ACM.

[28] M. Nauman, S. Khan, and X. Zhang. Apex: extending android permission model and enforcement with user-defined runtime constraints. In *Proceedings of the 5th ACM Symposium on Information, Computer and Communications Security*, ASIACCS '10, pages 328–332, New York, NY, USA, 2010. ACM.

[29] A. Nguyen-tuong, S. Guarnieri, D. Greene, J. Shirley, and D. Evans. Automatically hardening web applications using precise tainting. In *In 20th IFIP International Information Security Conference*, pages 372–382, 2005.

[30] Nielsen. Who is winning the u.s. smartphone battle? `http://blog.nielsen.com/nielsenwire/online_mobile/who-is-winning-the-u-s-smartphone-battle/`, March 2011.

[31] M. Ongtang, S. Mclaughlin, W. Enck, and P. Mcdaniel. Semantically rich application-centric security in android. In *In ACSAC '09: Annual Computer Security Applications Conference*, 2009.

[32] G. Paller. Dedexer. `http://dedexer.sourceforge.net/`, August 2009.

[33] T. Parr. Antlr. `http://www.antlr.org/`.

[34] M. Pistoia, R. Flynn, L. Koved, and V. C. Sreedhar. Interprocedural analysis for privileged code placement and tainted variable detection. In *In Proceedings of the 19th European Conference on Object-Oriented Programming*, pages 362–386. SpringerVerlag, 2005.

[35] A.-D. Schmidt, H.-G. Schmidt, L. Batyuk, J. Clausen, S. Camtepe, S. Albayrak, and C. Yildizli. Smartphone malware evolution revisited: Android next target? In *Malicious and Unwanted Software (MALWARE), 2009 4th International Conference on*, pages 1 –7, oct. 2009.

[36] A. Shabtai, Y. Fledel, and Y. Elovici. Securing android-powered mobile devices using selinux. *Security Privacy, IEEE*, 8(3):36 –44, may-june 2010.

[37] U. Shankar, K. Talwar, J. S. Foster, and D. Wagner. Detecting format string vulnerabilities with type qualifiers. In *Proceedings of the 10th conference on USENIX Security Symposium - Volume 10*, pages 16–16, Berkeley, CA, USA, 2001. USENIX Association.

[38] Symantec. Android.ggtracker. `http://www.symantec.com/security_response/writeup.jsp?docid=2011-062208-5013-99`, June 2011.

[39] G. Tan and J. Croft. An empirical security study of the native code in the jdk. In *Proceedings of the 17th conference on Security symposium*, pages 365–377, Berkeley, CA, USA, 2008. USENIX Association.

[40] thinkmobile with Google. The mobile movement study. `http://www.gstatic.com/ads/research/en/2011_TheMobileMovement.pdf`, April 2011.

[41] D. Venkatesan. A trojan spying on your conversations. `http://totaldefense.com/securityblog/2011/08/26/A-Trojan-spying-on-your-conversations.aspx`, August 2011.

[42] B. Zeng, G. Tan, and G. Morrisett. Combining control-flow integrity and static analysis for efficient and validated data sandboxing. In *Proceedings of the 18th ACM conference on Computer and communications security*, CCS '11, pages 29–40, New York, NY, USA, 2011. ACM.

Design of SMS Commanded-and-Controlled and P2P-Structured Mobile Botnets

Yuanyuan Zeng
Perimeter E-Security
Raleigh, North Carolina
yzeng@perimeterusa.com

Kang G. Shin
University of Michigan
Ann Arbor, Michigan
kgshin@eecs.umich.edu

Xin Hu
IBM Research
Hawthorne, New York
huxin@us.ibm.com

ABSTRACT

Botnets are one of the most serious security threats to the Internet and personal computer (PC) users. Although botnets have not yet caused major outbreaks in the mobile world, with the rapidly-growing popularity of smartphones such as Apple's iPhone and Android-based phones that store more personal data and gain more capabilities than earlier-generation handsets, botnets are expected to become a severe threat to smartphones soon. In this paper, we propose the design of a mobile botnet that makes the most of mobile services and is resilient to disruption. The mobile botnet utilizes SMS messages for C&C and a P2P structure as its topology. Our simulation results demonstrate that a modified Kademlia—a structured architecture—is a better choice for the mobile botnet's topology. In addition, we discuss potential countermeasures to defend against this mobile botnet threat.

Categories and Subject Descriptors

C.2.0 [**Computer-Communication Networks**]: General—*Security and Protection*; D.4.6 [**Operating Systems**]: Security and Protection—*Invasive Software*

General Terms

Security

Keywords

Smartphone Security, Malware, Mobile Botnets

1. INTRODUCTION

Botnets are one of the most serious security threats to the Internet and the personal computer (PC) world, but they are still rare for the mobile world. Recently, with the rapidly-growing popularity of smartphones, such as the iPhone and Android-based phones, attacks on cellular networks and devices have grown in number and sophistication.

A drastic increase in downloading and sharing of third-party applications and user-generated content makes smartphones vulnerable to various types of malware. Smartphone-based banking services have also become popular without protection features comparable to those on PCs, enticing cyber crimes. There are already a number of reports on malicious applications in the Android Market [1]. Although the Android platform requires that applications should be certified before their installation, its control policy is rather loose—allowing developers to sign their own applications—so that attackers can easily get their malware into the Android Market. The iPhone's application store controls its content more tightly, but it fails to contain jailbroken iPhones which can install any application and even run processes in the background. As smartphones are increasingly used to handle more private information with more computing power and capabilities, but without adequate security and privacy protection, attacks targeting mobile devices are becoming more sophisticated. Since the appearance of the first, proof-of-concept mobile worm, Cabir, in 2004, we have witnessed a significant evolution of mobile malware. The early malware performed tasks, such as infecting files, replacing system applications and sending out SMS or MMS messages. One malicious program is usually capable of only one or two functions. Although the number of mobile malware families and their variants has been growing steadily in recent years, their functionalities have remained simple until recently.

SymbOS.Exy.A trojan [2] was discovered in early 2009 and its variant SymbOS.Exy.C resurfaced in July 2009. This mobile worm, which is said to have "botnet-esque" behavior patterns, differs from other mobile malware, because after infection, it connects back to a malicious HTTP server and reports information of the device and its user. The Ikee.B worm [3] that appeared late 2009 targets jailbroken iPhones, and has behavior similar to SymbOS.Exy. Ikee.B also connects to a control server via HTTP, downloads additional components and sends back the user's information. With this remote connection, it is possible for attackers to periodically issue commands to and coordinate the infected devices to launch large-scale attacks. In March 2011, over 50 applications found to contain a type of malware called "DroidDream" were removed from the Android Market. This malware is able to root the infected device and steal sensitive information. It was speculated that the end goal of DroidDream was to create a botnet [4]. In February 2012, RootSmart [5], a malicious application in third party Android markets in China, was reported to create a botnet containing thousands of Android devices. Once started, RootSmart connects to a remote server to send various information of the infected phone and fetches a root exploit from the server to obtain escalated privilege to the phone. The infected phone is configured to send premium SMS messages and use other premium telephony services without users' knowledge, generating profits for the botmaster. Observing the trend of recent mobile malware, we expect that mobile botnets will become a serious threat to smartphones soon.

In this paper, we propose the design of a mobile botnet that makes the most of mobile services and is resilient to disruption. Within this mobile botnet, all C&C communications are done via SMS messages since SMS is available to almost every mobile phone. To hide the identity of the botmaster, there are no central servers dedicated to command dissemination that is easy to be identified and then removed. Instead, we adopt a P2P topology that allows botmasters and bots to publish and search for commands in a P2P fashion, making their detection and disruption much harder. Our contributions are three-fold. First, to the best of our knowledge, we are the first to design mobile botnets with focuses on both C&C protocol and topology by integrating the SMS service and the P2P topology. The main purpose of this work is to shed light on potential botnet threats targeting smartphones. Since current techniques against PC botnets may not be applied directly to mobile botnets, our proposed mobile botnet design makes it possible for security researchers to investigate and develop new countermeasures before mobile botnets become a major threat. Second, we present a method to carefully disguise C&C content in spam-looking SMS messages. Using this approach, the botnet can stealthily transmit C&C messages without being noticed by phone users. Third, we test and compare two P2P architectures that can be used to construct the topology of our mobile botnet on an overlay simulation framework, and finally propose the architecture that best suits mobile botnets.

The remainder of the paper is organized as follows. Section 2 describes the related work. Section 3 details the proof-of-concept design of our mobile botnet. Section 4 presents our simulation and evaluation results. Section 5 discusses potential countermeasures against the mobile botnets. The paper concludes with Section 6.

2. RELATED WORK

The research areas most relevant to our work are P2P-based botnets and botnet C&C evaluation. Wang et al. [6] proposed the design of an advanced hybrid P2P botnet that implemented both push and pull C&C mechanisms and studied its resilience. In [7] they conducted a systematic study on P2P botnets including bot candidate selection and network construction, and focused on index poisoning and Sybil attacks. Overbot [8] is a botnet protocol based on Kademlia. The strength of this protocol lies in its stealth in the communication between the bots and the botmaster, which leverages a public-key model. Davis et al. [9] compared the performance of Overnet with that of Gnutella and other complex network models under three disinfection strategies. Singh et al. [10] evaluated the viability of email communication for botnet C&C. Nappa et al. [11] proposed a botnet model exploiting Skype's overlay network to make botnet traffic undistinguishable with legitimate Skype traffic. All of these dealt with botnets in the PC world, while our work targets mobile botnets, in which C&C channel and network

structure requirements are different, in view of unique services and resource constraints on smartphones. Dagon et al. [12] proposed key metrics to measure botnets' utility for conducting malicious activities and considered the ability of different response techniques to disrupt botnets.

There are numerous efforts on mobile malware focusing on vulnerability analysis and attack measurements. The former investigates ways of exploiting vulnerable mobile services, such as Bluetooth and MMS [13, 14], while the latter characterizes the feasibility and impact of large-scale attacks targeting mobile networks, mostly Denial of Service (DoS) attacks [15]. There are a few recent papers treating the idea of mobile botnets. In [16], the focus is on the attack aspect—whether compromised mobile phones can generate sufficient traffic to launch a DoS attack. Singh et al. [17] investigated using Bluetooth as a C&C to construct mobile botnets without any analysis on their network structure. Hua et al. [18] proposed a SMS-based mobile botnet using a flooding algorithm to propagate commands with the help of an internet server. The use of the central server, however, may lead to single-point-of-failure. Mulliner et al. [19] demonstrated the ways to command and control botnets via SMS or IP-based P2P networks using a tree topology. Under such topology, when a node fails, all of its subnodes will be isolated from the botnet, difficult to get commands. Weidman [20] also considered utilizing SMS messages for botnet C&C and presented a method to conceal malicious SMS messages from users on smartphones. It is worth noting that, different from all these works, our SMS-based botnet is built upon a decentralized P2P topology, without assistance from any central servers. The integration of SMS and P2P makes our botnet stealthy and resilient to disruption.

3. MOBILE BOTNET DESIGN

We now present the detailed design of a proof-of-concept mobile botnet. The botnet design requires three main components: (1) vectors to spread the bot code to smartphones; (2) a channel to issue commands; (3) a topology to organize the botnet. We will briefly overview approaches that can be used to propagate malicious code and then focus on C&C and topology construction.

3.1 Propagation

The main approaches used to propagate malicious code to smartphones are user-involved propagation and vulnerability exploits.

In the first approach, the most popular vector is social engineering. Like their PC counterparts, current smartphones have frequent access to the Internet, becoming targets of malicious attacks. Thus, spam emails and MMS messages with malicious content attachments, or spam emails and SMS messages with embedded links pointing to websites hosting the malicious code, can easily find their way into a mobile phone's inbox. Without enough caution or warning, a mobile phone user is likely to execute the attachments or click those links to download malicious programs. The advantage of such schemes is that they can reach a large number of phones. Nevertheless, as smartphones run on a variety of operating systems, we expect multiple versions of bot code prepared to guarantee its execution. Another user-involved propagation vector can be Bluetooth, which utilizes mobility. Mobile phone users move around so that the compromised phones can use Bluetooth to search for devices nearby and after pairing with them successfully, try to send them malicious files.

Exploiting vulnerabilities to spread malicious code is common in the PC world. However, since there are various mobile platforms and most of them are closed-source, it is relatively difficult to find vulnerabilities in mobile devices. To date, some vulnerabilities have been discovered. For example, the HTC's Bluetooth vulnerability, which allows an attacker to gain access to all files on a phone by connecting to it via Bluetooth, was disclosed by a Spanish security researcher [21]. Mulliner et al. [22] discovered a way of directly manipulating SMS messages on different mobile platforms, without necessarily going through the mobile provider's network. In both cases, OS vendors immediately released patches to the public after the vulnerabilities were publicized, leaving few opportunities for a real exploit in the wild. Once launched in their targets, vulnerability exploits always have a higher success rate than that of user-involved approaches. As mobile platforms open up and mobile applications and services become abundant, vulnerability exploits will play a major role in mobile malware propagation.

3.2 Command and Control

In our mobile botnet, SMS is utilized as the C&C channel, i.e., compromised mobile bots communicate with botmasters and among themselves via SMS messages. Botnets in the PC world mostly rely on IP-based C&C delivery. For example, traditional botnets use centralized IRC or HTTP protocol, whereas newly-emerged botnets take advantage of P2P communication. Unlike their PC counterparts, smartphones can hardly establish and maintain steady IP-based connections with one another. One reason is that they move around frequently. Another reason is that private IPs are normally used when smartphones access networks such as EDGE, 3G and 4G networks, meaning that accepting incoming connections directly from other smartphones is a difficult task. Given this limitation, if a mobile botnet considers an IP-based channel as C&C, it needs to resort to centralized approaches in which bots connect to central servers to obtain commands. Such approaches, however, are vulnerable to disruption because the servers are easy to be identified by defenders. Thus, to construct a mobile botnet in a more resilient manner, a non-IP-based C&C is needed.

There are a few advantages for choosing SMS as a C&C channel. First, SMS is ubiquitous. It is reported that SMS text messaging is the most widely used data application on the planet, with 2.4 billion active users, or 74% of all mobile phone subscribers sending and receiving text messages on their phones [23]. When a mobile phone is turned on, this application always remains active. Second, SMS can accommodate offline bots easily. For example, if a phone is turned off or has poor signal reception in certain areas, its SMS communication messages will be stored in a service center and delivered once the phone is turned back on or the signal becomes available. Third, malicious content in the C&C communication can be hidden in SMS messages. According to a survey in China [24], 88% of the phone users polled reported they had been plagued by SMS spamming. As SMS spamming becomes prevalent, bots can encode commands into spam-looking messages so that users will not suspect. Last but not least, currently there are multiple ways to send and receive free SMS messages directly on smartphones [25, 26] or through some web interfaces. We will describe such

methods in Section 3.2.2. Even when the free texting is unavailable, as many phone users use SMS plans to avoid per-message charge and incoming messages are free of charge in some countries, with the design goal of minimizing the number of SMS messages we expect that using SMS as C&C will not incur considerable costs.

3.2.1 Protocol Design

Our goal is to let a phone that has installed our bot code perform activities according to the commands in SMS messages without being noticed by the user. In our design, every compromised phone has an 8-byte passcode. Only by including this passcode into the SMS messages, can other phones successfully deliver C&C information to this particular phone. Upon receipt of a SMS message, this phone searches for its passcode and pre-defined commands embedded in the message to tell if it is a C&C message. If found, the commands are immediately executed by the phone. Two issues need to be addressed here. First, how are passcodes allocated among compromised phones? Second, how to make C&C SMS messages appear harmless so that users may not notice the malicious content?

In our botnet, passcodes are allocated by botmasters to segment a botnet into sub-botnets, each with a different function. For example, one sub-botnet is responsible for sending out spam messages, while another is in charge of stealing personal data and transferring them to a malicious server. Each sub-botnet will be identified by its unique passcode that is hard-coded into the bot's binary. In other words, all bots within the same sub-botnet share the same passcode so that they can communicate with one another and also with the botmaster. Using a unique passcode for each bot will be more secure than using one passcode for an entire sub-botnet because in the latter case, the passcode will be discovered more easily. However, there is a trade-off: using a unique passcode will add more overhead due to the pairwise passcode exchange before each communication. The additional cost is undesirable since our goal is to minimize the number of SMS messages to be sent.

Not only do we require a passcode included in each SMS communication message, but also we encode commands to make it difficult for a user to figure them out. In fact, on the Android platform, it is possible for an application to send out SMS messages stealthily, to get immediate notification of every incoming SMS message by registering itself as a background service and to read and execute commands or even delete the message before the user sees it. We still want to hide the C&C messages because other mobile platforms are more restricted than Android; they may not allow our bots to both send and receive SMS messages without notifying the user. If malicious messages show contents directly, they will be easily captured and manipulated by defenders. To evade such detection, we want to make a command-embedded SMS message look like a common message such as a spam message. There are benefits of using spam-like messages to transmit C&C. As pointed out in [27], cellular carriers cannot simply block offending SMS messages because the senders have paid for the messages and the carriers fear permanent deletion of legitimate messages when there are no spam folders available. We will present a real-world experiment in Section 4.3. Even if in the future the carriers filter out spam messages and dump them into spam folders, similar to the email filtering, spam messages can still reach

Your paypal account was hijacked (Err msg: NzkxMjAzNDIxODExMDUyM183Mz). Respond to http://www.bhocxx.paypal.com using code Q3MDk2NDUyXzEyMzQ1Njc4

Free ringtones download at www.myringtone.com, using username VIP, password YTJiNGQxMWw to log on

FIND_NODE
7912034218110523 _7347096452
_12345678

SEND_SYSINFO
a2b4d11l

Figure 1: Disguised SMS messages

the target phones by going to the spam directory, which actually helps hide the C&C because users tend to ignore spam.

Considering the fact that each SMS message only contains up to 160 characters, commands in our botnet are concise. For example, "FIND_NODE" instructs a bot to return the phone numbers of certain nodes; "SEND_SYSINFO" asks a bot to reply with system information. To disguise messages, each command is mapped to one spam template. Additional information such as the phone number and the aforementioned passcode are variables in the templates, and they are Base64-encoded. Figure 1 shows two disguised SMS messages. The first one is a "FIND_NODE" message (146 characters) with passcode 12345678 requiring the recipient to locate a bot whose ID is 7912034218110523, and the result should be returned to the bot whose phone number is (734)7096452. NzkxMjAzNDIxODExMDUyM183Mz and Q3MDk2NDUyXzEyMzQ1Njc4—two random strings together —are the Base64-encrypted 7912034218110523_7347096452 _12345678. The entire encoded string is split into two—disguising one as an error message and the other as a code—making it resemble a spam message. The second example is a "SEND_SYSINFO" message (98 characters) with a passcode a2b4d11l. This template is different from that of the "FIND_NODE" message. The passcode is also Base64-encoded and appears as a password in the disguised message. To decode messages, each bot keeps a command-template mapping list. Only tens of commands are needed in our botnet, so this list is not long. To make detection harder, one command message can correspond to different spam templates and the templates can be updated periodically. As just shown, a command along with additional information can be easily embedded into one SMS message which appears to be a spam, familiar to today's phone users, so users are likely to ignore such messages even if they open and read them. If users choose to delete these messages, it will not cause any problem to the botnet because the commands have already been executed upon their receipt.

3.2.2 Sending SMS Through the Internet

Although sending SMS messages through the cellular networks is always possible, the botmasters want to hide their identity and lower costs as much as possible. To achieve this goal, botmasters can use the Internet to disseminate C&C messages to the mobile botnet. There are several ways to do this. Many advertisement-based websites provide free SMS services. Botmasters can type in messages via these websites and have them sent to mobile bots, feasible for low-volume messaging. Using such services does not require the sender's mobile number, an email address is sufficient if a reply is expected. If the botnet is large, botmasters need to create an account with mobile operators or SMS service providers to make high-volume messaging possible at the lowest price. Usually, this can be done by sending and/or receiving SMS messages via email through a SMS gateway connecting directly to a Mobile Operator's SMSC (Short Message Service Center). Currently, smartphone applications such as [25, 26] offer free domestic and international text messaging when the phone is connected to a WiFi and support both one-on-one and group texting. The user only needs to provide a screen name to send and receive messages without revealing its identity. Both the botmasters and bots can take advantage of such a service whenever possible to avoid messaging costs.

To sum up, using SMS messages as the C&C is a viable solution for a mobile botnet. Not only is SMS ubiquitous to every mobile phone, but botmasters and bots are also able to disguise SMS messages, send bulk messages from the Internet at very low cost while hiding their identities. Thus, using SMS is both economical and efficient for the botnet.

3.3 Mobile Botnet Topology

In the previous section we have described the way SMS messages form the C&C communication in our mobile botnet. In what follows, we introduce P2P topologies that may be utilized to organize the botmaster and bots for publishing and retrieving commands, and describe how to leverage existing P2P architectures to meet the need for mobile botnet construction.

3.3.1 Possible Topologies

Similar to botnets in the PC world, a mobile botnet can be structured in a traditional centralized way or in a newly-emerged decentralized P2P fashion. In the first approach, botmasters hard-code into each bot's executable a set of phone numbers that are under their direct control. When a mobile phone is converted to a bot, it contacts those hard-coded phones to request commands or wait for commands to be pushed to them. Such a centralized topology is easy to implement but not resilient to disruption. Obviously, once defenders obtain these phone numbers, they can track down the botmasters and then disable the botnet. To make our botnet robust to defenses, we adopt a P2P structure instead.

Currently, there are several structures for P2P networks; they can be divided into three categories: centralized, decentralized but structured, and unstructured. Centralized P2P networks have a constantly-updated directory hosted at central locations. Peers query the central directory to get the addresses of peers having the desired content. This structure is similar to the traditional centralized botnet architecture and hence vulnerable to the central-point-of failure. Decentralized but structured P2P networks have no central directory and contents are not placed at random nodes but at specific locations. The most common systems in this category are Distributed-Hash-Table (DHT)-based P2P networks, ensuring that any peer can efficiently route a search to some peer with the desired content. One notable implementation is Kademlia [28], used by several current P2P applications, such as eMule and BitTorrent. Decentralized and unstructured P2P networks have neither central directories nor control over content placement. If a peer wants to find certain content in the network in old protocols such as Gnutella, it has to flood its query to the entire network to find peers sharing the data. To address the scalability issues, current unstructured networks adopt different query strategies to avoid flooding. There have also been extensive studies on how to make Gnutella-like systems scalable. One such design is Gia [29].

3.3.2 Design

Both structured and unstructured P2P architectures can be modified to suit our need for the mobile botnet because their decentralized nature hides the botmaster's identity. Since the mobile botnet design should consider not only robustness but also feasibility and efficiency on smartphones, we need to compare these two architectures to see which is more suitable. Specifically, we base our structured and unstructured botnet topology on Kademlia and Gia, respectively, for comparison. Note that in our botnet, bots obtain commands mainly in a *pull* style, i.e., the botmaster publishes commands and bots are designed to actively search for these commands. The other possible mechanism for command transfer is *push*, meaning that bots passively wait for commands. We prefer *pull* to *push* because *push* will get malicious activities exposed easily. That is, under *push* many SMS messages are sent out from one or a few central nodes, whereas *pull* can be implemented in a more distributed fashion. In what follows, we overview each protocol and describe our design.

Kademlia is DHT-based and has a structured overlay topology, in which nodes are identified by node IDs generated randomly and data items are identified by keys generated from a hash function. Node IDs and keys are of the same length (128-bit). Data items are stored in nodes whose IDs are close to data items' keys. The distance between two identifiers, x and y, is calculated by bitwise exclusive or (XOR) operation: $d(x, y) = x \oplus y$. For each $0 \le i < 128$, each node keeps a list for nodes of distance between 2^i and 2^{i+1} from itself. This list is called a k-bucket, and can store up to k elements. There are four types of RPC messages in Kademlia: PING, STORE, FIND_NODE and FIND_VALUE. PING checks whether a node is online. STORE asks a node to store data. FIND_NODE provides an ID as an argument and requests the recipient to return k nodes closest to the ID. FIND_VALUE behaves similarly to FIND_NODE. The only exception is that when a node has the data item associated with the key, it returns the data item. Since there is no central sever, each node has a hard-coded peer list in order to bootstrap into the network.

Considering the differences between smartphones and personal computers as well as the SMS C&C channel we adopt, we modify Kademlia's design to be suitable for our mobile botnet's structured overlay construction. First, we do not use PING messages to query whether a node is alive and should be removed from its k-bucket. One reason for this is that SMS messages transmitting C&C can always reach their recipients even if these phones are not online (messages are stored in the SMSC for later delivery). The other reason is that our design tries to minimize the number of messages sent and received. Removing PING messages effectively reduces C&C traffic and thus, the possibility of being noticed by phone users and defenders. Second, instead of being randomly generated, a node ID is constructed by hashing its phone number, similar to the notion in Chord [30] that a node ID is the hash of its IP address. Doing so can undermine the effectiveness of Sybil attacks in which defenders add nodes to join the botnet to disrupt C&C transmission. Evidently, if node IDs are allowed to be randomly chosen, defenders will take advantage of this by selecting IDs close to command-related keys to ensure a high probability that these sybil nodes are on the route of command search and publish queries. In addition, the absence of an authentication mechanism in Kademlia, meaning that anyone can insert values under specific keys, presents an opportunity for defenders to launch index poisoning attacks by publishing fake values under command-related keys once they know these keys, in order to disrupt C&C. We thus use a public key algorithm to secure the command content. While publishing a command, the publisher (the botmaster) needs to attach a digital signature to that command. The signature is the hash value of the command signed by the botmaster's private key. Its corresponding public key is hard-coded in each bot's binary. In this way, bots that will store the command are able to verify that the command is indeed from the botmaster not anyone else.

Gia improves Gnutella protocol and has an unstructured overlay topology. Since Gnutella has a scaling problem due to the flooding search algorithm, Gia modifies Gnutella's design and improves its scalability significantly. There are four key components in Gia's design: (1) a topology adaptation protocol to put most nodes within short reach of high-capacity (able to handle more queries) nodes by searching and adding high-capacity and high-degree nodes as neighbors; (2) an active flow control scheme to avoid overloaded nodes by assigning flow-control tokens to nodes based on capacity; (3) one-hop replication to maintain pointers to the content offered by immediate neighbors; (4) a search algorithm based on biased random walks directing queries to nodes that are likely to answer the queries.

Our design of unstructured overlay topology is based on Gia as mentioned before. Our design removes the one-hop replication scheme because it requires each node to index the content of its neighbors and to exchange this information periodically. This scheme may help reduce the number of hops for locating a command, but will incur additional storage and computation overheads. Moreover, each SMS message has a limited length so that the exchange of index information cannot be done with a single message but requires multiple messages, increasing the number of messages generated. In our mobile botnet, the drawbacks of using such a scheme will outweigh its benefits, and we thus opt out of this scheme. Three other components are important to our botnet because their combination ensures queries to be directed to high-capacity nodes that can provide useful responses without getting overloaded. This is desirable, especially in a mobile phone network, since smartphones also have different capacities under different situations. For example, in a poor-signal area or when the phone is on a voice call (SMS messages use the same control channel as voice calls for delivery), the phone's capability of handling SMS messages is lowered, so it can only answer fewer queries. Overloading mobile bots is also a concern. If one bot receives/sends a large number of SMS messages during a short period of time, its battery can be drained quickly, and draw the user's attention. Overloading can be prevented using the flow-control scheme in Gia. Another design choice worth mentioning is that similar to the modified Kademila, a digital signature is attached to every command to be published.

4. EVALUATION

4.1 Comparing Two P2P Structures

We now describe our simulation study of structured and unstructured P2P architectures for mobile botnets and compare their performances. In the simulation, all nodes are assumed to have already been infected by the vectors described in Section 3.1. Our evaluation focus is not on how the malicious bot code propagates, but on how the botnet performs under two different P2P structures.

We modified OverSim [31], an open-source overlay network simulation framework, to simulate mobile botnets with the two P2P structures. While comparing P2P structures' performances, logical connections (SMS activities) among mobile nodes matter most, i.e., what we care is the overlay network not the underlying physical network. For example, the fact that mobile bots move around is not important in our simulation because the change of geographic location hardly affects bots' SMS message sending/receiving.

The metrics we use to measure performance are: number of overlay hops needed for a command lookup; total number of SMS messages sent (number of those sent = number of those received) when a botmaster-issued command is acquired by every node; percentage of total number of SMS messages sent by each node during this entire command-lookup; and message delay (from the start of the query until a command is received). These metrics reflect how well each architecture meets the requirement of our mobile botnet, namely, minimizing the number of SMS messages sent and received, load-balancing and locating commands in a timely manner.

The churn (participant turnover) model we adopted in the simulation is the lifetime churn. In this model, on creation of a node, its lifetime will be drawn randomly from a Weibull distribution which is widely used to characterize a node's lifetime. When the lifetime is reached, the node is removed from the network. A new node will be created after a dead time drawn from the same probability distribution function. We set the mean lifetime to 8*3600=28800s, assuming that each phone will stay connected to the botnet for an average of 8 hours. Considering the unavailability of real field data on mobile phones' online behavior, we made this rough estimate. We will later evaluate the effect of different mean lifetimes on the botnet performance.

Besides the aforementioned performance metrics, another important metric is scalability for which we simulated two botnets with 200 and 2000 nodes, respectively. In each bot-

net, a command from the botmaster is published, and every node is designed to locate this command by issuing lookup queries. The simulation ends when all nodes successfully retrieve the command. In the structured botnet case, we ran the modified Kademlia protocol, with k-bucket size $k = 8$ and the number of nodes to ask in parallel $\alpha = 3$. In the unstructured botnet case, we ran the modified Gia protocol, with minimum number of neighbors $min\_nbrs = 3$, maximum number of neighbors $max\_nbrs = 10$ and maximum number of responses $max\_responses = 1$.

Now, we present and discuss the comparison results. For each metric, we first look at the 200-node botnet and then the 2000-node botnet. Figure 2 plots the CDFs of the number of hops needed to retrieve a targeted command. In the 200-node botnet, for the structured architecture, 97% of lookups can be completed within 3 hops. The corresponding number for the unstructured botnet is 5 hops. In the 2000-node botnet, despite the increased network size, 99% of lookups under the structured architecture are fulfilled within 4 hops, but under the unstructured 8 hops are required. Figure 3 shows the CDFs of the total number of SMS messages sent from each node when the command spreads to the entire botnet, which is the total communication overhead. In the 200-node botnet, under the structured architecture, about 80% of nodes generate fewer than 15 messages during the entire period, while under the unstructured architecture 69% of nodes can do so. The average number of messages sent is 11 for the structured and 15 for the unstructured, respectively. In the 2000-node botnet, with more nodes and more lookups, the message overhead unsurprisingly increases. 80% of nodes send fewer than 20 messages (51% of nodes send fewer than 10 messages) for the structured architecture with an average of 22 messages sent by each node. Only 40% of nodes send fewer than 20 messages for the unstructured architecture with an average of 44 messages.

From the above observations, we can see that the structured botnet, in general, requires fewer number of hops to locate a command and incurs a lower message overhead (15 to 20 messages) on each node than the unstructured one does in both 200- and 2000-node cases. Compared to the unstructured botnet, the structured architecture also scales better, considering its slight increases in the number of hops and messages when the botnet becomes large. This is expected because in a structured network, data items are placed at deterministic locations so that fewer hops and query messages are required to locate the targeted data and the network can accommodate a large number of nodes. As mentioned before, on smartphones such as Android-based phones, bots are able to send and receive C&C SMS messages stealthily without notifying users. Users may figure that out while seeing the monthly bills, but by then bots have already performed malicious tasks. Even if users are able to see them on the phone, since the C&C messages are disguised as spam, they cause little suspicion. Even so, one may still wonder: would SMSC observe a surge of messages among infected phones and raise alerts? SMS market statistics show that: "In 2009, U.S. cell phone subscribers sent and received on average 390 text messages per month according to the Mobile Business Statistics [32]." We believe that tens of messages overhead per phone may not draw much attention from the SMSC considering a phone's normal messaging volume. Also, since most attacks such as information steal-

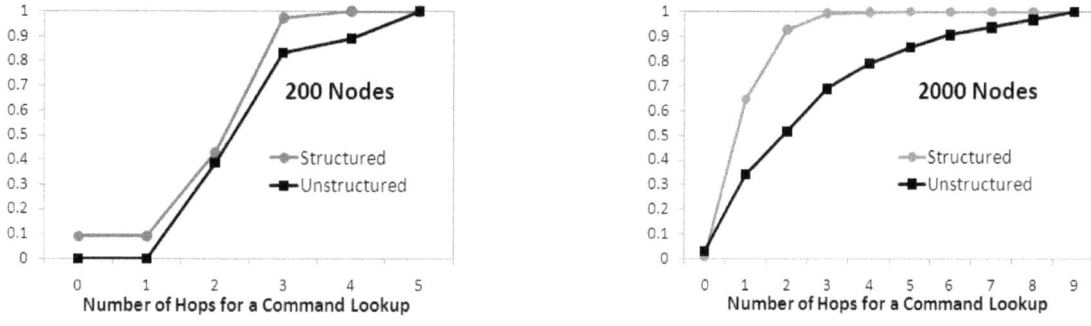

Figure 2: CDFs of the number of hops needed for a command-lookup

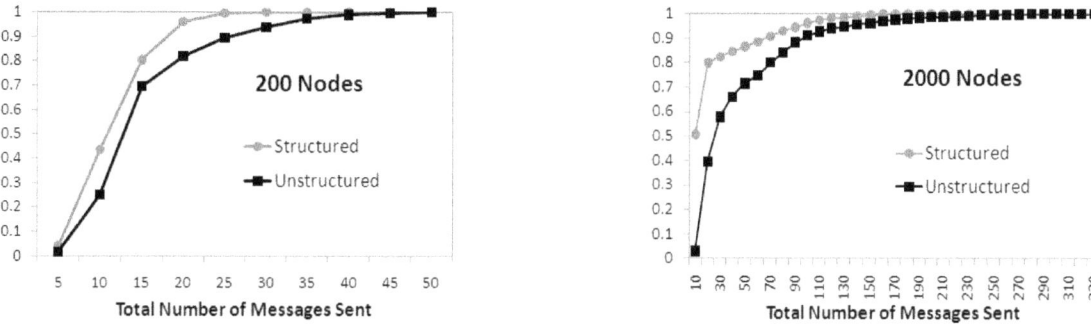

Figure 3: CDFs of the total number of messages sent to perform all lookups

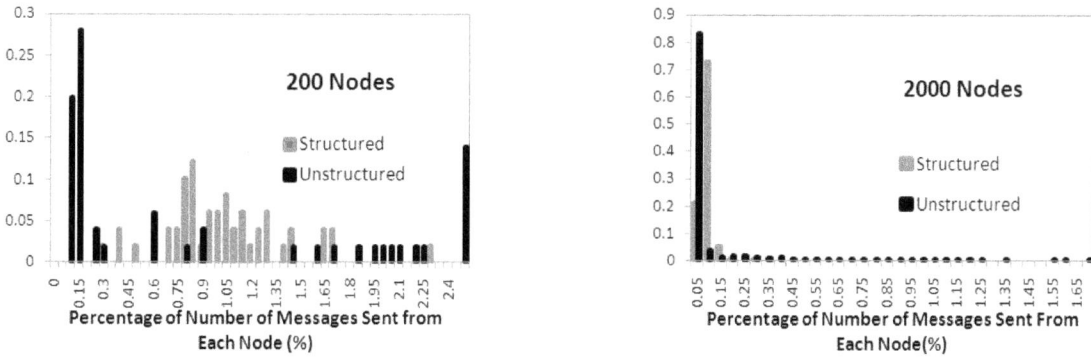

Figure 4: Histograms of the percentage of total messages sent from each node

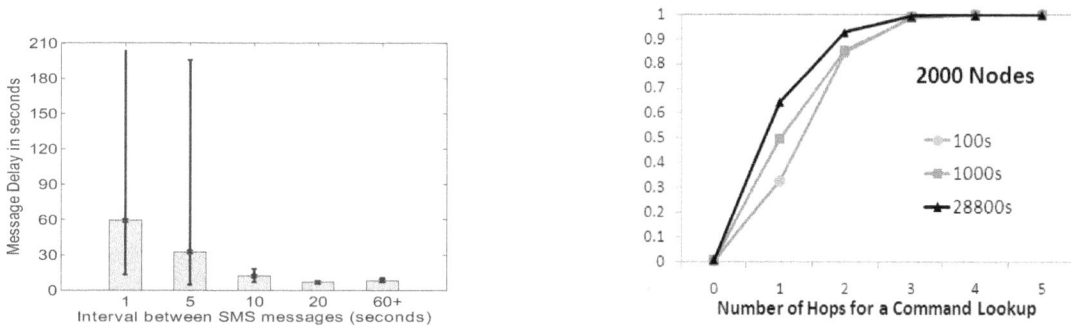

Figure 5: SMS message delays

Figure 6: CDFs of the number of hops for a command lookup under different mean lifetimes (in sec)

ing and spamming are not time-critical, bots do not have to pull commands all at the same time. To further minimize the number of messages sent/received, each bot can be restricted by a threshold. If the number of messages reaches the threshold, the bot will stop sending/receiving messages. The threshold can be customized depending on the usage pattern of SMS on that particular phone. If a bot has frequent normal SMS messaging behavior, its threshold of allowing bot communication could be high since this phone is very likely to use a SMS plan and a few blended malicious messages are less noticeable.

Figure 4 shows the histograms of load distribution on each node, which is the percentage of total messages each node accounts for during the entire simulation. In the 200-node botnet, 76% of nodes in the structured botnet each accounts for 0.75% – 1.25% of total messages sent, whereas in the unstructured one, the percentage values are spread out among different nodes ranging from 0.10% to 6%. The average percentage for the structured one is 1.02% and for the unstructured is 1.01%. To gauge the load-balancing more accurately, we calculated a metric defined as: $\sum_{i=1}^{n} |p_i - \overline{p}|$ $(*)$, where n is the total number of nodes, p_i is the load percentage at node i, and $\overline{p}$ is the average percentage across all nodes. The $(*)$ values for the structured and the unstructured are 13.40% and 55.89%, respectively. In the 2000-node case, all nodes' percentages in the structured botnet range from 0.05% to 0.25% while those in the unstructured botnet are distributed within 0.05% – 1.65%, although the average percentages for both the structured and the unstructured are 0.07%. The metric $(*)$ values for the structured and the unstructured are 23.73% and 145.48%. The unstructured case varies more in load distribution leading to poor load-balancing, probably because Gia uses schemes to direct most queries to a few nodes—forming hub nodes.

To estimate the actual delay of locating a command in our mobile botnet, we measured one-hop latency by sending SMS messages between two smartphones. We implemented a SMS send/receive utility on the Android platform and installed it on two G1 phones: one connected to T-mobile and the other to AT&T. The software continually sent out and received SMS messages between two phones and recorded the exact timestamps. The intervals between two consecutive SMS messages were chosen from 1 second to tens of minutes and the message contents were also randomly generated with various lengths to simulate the realistic SMS usage. During the entire experiment, we sent out a total of 138 SMS messages and collected the corresponding message delays, i.e., the difference between the time sending a message from one phone and the time of receiving that message from the other phone. Figure 5 depicts min/max/average message delays based on different sending intervals (sending rates). We can see that when SMS messages are sent frequently, the message delays vary a lot and have high average values. Take 1 second as an example. Under this interval, delays range from 15 to 205 seconds with an average of 60 seconds. Similar delay patterns occur when the interval is 5 seconds. The general trend is that as intervals become larger, both delay average and variance drop, and that when the interval is greater than 60 seconds, the delays become stable.

Since mobile attacks such as confidential information stealing (especially related to credit card, account number, etc.) are not time-sensitive, bots can send messages at relatively

long intervals to shorten the delay and avoid detection. Using a greater than 1 minute sending interval's delay, we now estimate the total delay for a command-lookup. Under structured Kademlia which uses iterative search, the estimated delay is given by $AverageTotalDelay = 2 \times AverageHops \times AverageOneHopDelay$. When it comes to unstructured Gia which employs recursive search, the equation should be the same. By plugging in the data we obtained, the estimated command-lookup delay is 17 seconds for the structured and 36 seconds for the unstructured in the 2000-node botnet.

The delays seem to be large compared to that of IP-based connections. As briefly mentioned before, our current design does not opt for IP-based C&C or existing IP-based P2P networks for the following reasons. First, some smartphones may not have data plans, not always accessible to the Internet. Second, for smartphones with the Internet access, they can initiate connections to retrieve commands from designated servers but are likely to suffer from a single-point-of-failure. To work in a decentralized P2P fashion, mobile bots should be able to accept incoming connections without any difficulty, which presents a challenge due to private IPs used in most scenarios. A possible solution is to obtain assistance from a third-party such as a mediator server or a rendezvous server, adding complexity to the C&C. Since SMS is ubiquitous across all mobile phones, using SMS as the C&C channel to construct a P2P structure is a feasible and reliable solution for mobile botnets. As future work, we can incorporate IP-based command-transfer into our botnet. For mobile bots without network access, they transmit C&C exclusively via SMS messages. For bots with network access, they can pull commands from an IP-based P2P network. Such a network consisting of PCs can be either constructed by the botmaster or part of an existing P2P network. Doing so may help reduce the message overhead and the delay.

In summary, our simulation results show that the structured architecture outperforms the unstructured one in terms of total number of messages sent, hops needed and delays for a lookup as well as load-balancing, although both the original protocols—Kademlia and Gia—have already been tailored to our mobile botnet's needs through several modifications. Thus, the structured architecture is indeed better suited for our mobile botnet.

4.2 Effect of Churn Rates

Now that we have chosen the structured architecture, we would like to see the effect of different mean lifetimes or churn rates on the number of hops for a command lookup, which directly affects the delay of locating a command. To see the trend, in a 2000-node botnet, we varied the mean lifetimes—100s, 1000s and 28800s. The higher the mean lifetime, the lower the churn rate. Presumably, a large mean lifetime indicates a relatively stable network in which fewer steps are needed to locate a command. This assumption is verified in our simulation. We can see that in Figure 6, differences, though minimal, exist among the three CDFs. With the mean equal to 100s, the average number of hops is 1.8; with the mean equal to 1000s, the average reduces to 1.7; with the mean equal to 28800s, the average decreases further to 1.4. It turns out that a higher churn rate does not degrade much of the lookup performance.

4.3 Can Disguised C&C Messages Go Through?

One concern with our spam-like C&C messages is what if they are filtered and deleted by the service providers without reaching the recipients, which might be the only effective way to mitigate SMS spam (spam-filtering at the end device is not useful as the recipient needs to pay for the messages already). According to some sources [27, 33], mobile carriers do not automatically block SMS spam because there is no spam folder with SMS so that accidental deletion of legitimate messages from the carrier's side cannot be recovered by the users. Also, senders are presumably charged for these messages unlike emails. To confirm this, we ran experiments to see whether carriers will let our spam-like C&C messages pass through. Table 1 shows the spam templates for C&C, which are typical spam messages. The random strings highlighted in grey are variables such as passcodes and node IDs. We tried two methods to send them: web-based and smartphone-based. For the first method, we sent all messages twice to an AT&T phone via free texting service at Text4Free.net and txt2day.com respectively. 100% of them reached the designated phone. For the second method, we wrote an application and installed it on an AT&T Samsung Captivate phone running Android OS 2.2. This application automatically sent the spam messages 5 times at different times of a day to another AT&T phone. The application also kept track of whether a message was sent successfully. Out of the 50 messages, 48 messages were sent and delivered to the target phone and 2 messages failed to be sent due to some generic failure at sender's phone that had nothing to do with the carrier. Although we were not able to thoroughly test every possible spam message on different networks, our experimental results were in line with the aforementioned reports and we believe that as few spam-fighting mechanisms are in place, our disguised C&C messages can safely go through the network.

4.4 How Do SMS C&C and P2P Structure Become One?

Having an impression of how SMS transmits C&C messages and how a structured P2P topology fits our mobile botnet, one may want to know in detail the way we integrate both into the mobile botnet. We now use a simplified example (Figure 7) to illustrate the command publish and search process. For illustration purpose, node IDs and data items' keys are 4-bit long, and SMS messages transmitted are not disguised as spam. In this figure, node 1111 wants to publish certain data—a command—under the key 0111. Note that in Kademlia, data items are stored in nodes whose IDs are close to data items' keys. To locate such nodes, node 1111 first sends SMS messages to nodes in its hard-coded node list; these nodes help to obtain nodes closer to the target from their node lists. The process continues till no closer nodes could be found (this process is omitted in the figure). Finally, node 1111 finds the closest node 0110 ($0110 \oplus 0111 = 0001$), so a publish message containing the command's key (0111), the encrypted command (XXXX) along with a passcode (8888) is sent to node 0110. After verifying the pre-defined passcode and command, node 0110 stores this information so that later any node requests the command associated with key 0111 it is able to return this command. As for the search process, it is similar to the publish process described. Node 0000 looks up a command associated with key 0111 and it has to find the node whose ID is closer to this key. Node 0000 first asks node 0010; node 0010 points it to node 0100; node 0100 provides the closest one, node 0110. Node 0000 contacts node 0110 to request the command.

5. DISCUSSION ON COUNTERMEASURES

Although we have focused on the design of a stealthy and resilient mobile botnet, we would like to discuss potential defensive strategies and challenges in using these techniques.

Similar to the patching mechanism in the PC world, to prevent malicious code from infecting mobile devices by vulnerability exploits, OS vendors and software providers need to push patches to end devices in a timely manner. Certification (only approved applications can be installed) is also an important security measure, but it is far from being perfect as some malware has been able to get around [34] as a disguised harmless application. To nip the mobile malware in the bud, additional protection features are necessary. For example, Kirin [35] is designed for the Android-platform whose certification process is not stringent; it provides application certification at install time using a set of predefined security rules that determine whether the security configuration bundled with an application is safe. With the aid of Kirin, users may be more cautious while installing applications.

Host-based approaches that detect malware at runtime could also serve as a solution. Signature-based detection is effective but cannot handle unknown or polymorphic malware. We prefer use of behavior-based detection. Since our bots send SMS messages stealthily without the user's involvement or awareness, the detector could first characterize the normal process of sending SMS messages by a system-call state-diagram and then keep monitoring the system calls that generate outgoing messages to see if there is any deviation from the normal behavior. To detect incoming C&C messages, the detector needs to know the encoding scheme probably through binary analysis so that it can intercept and delete malicious messages before any application's access. However, the botmaster can apply advanced packing and obfuscation techniques to make the binary analysis harder, and periodically update the spam templates as well as the mapping between them and corresponding commands. In addition, host-level detection is susceptible to compromise by the malware, and consumes much resource.

Deploying detection schemes at the SMSC is another possible solution. Compared to the host-level detection, this centralized approach can acquire a global view of all phones' SMS activities, although the information of each phone might be limited. As mentioned before, simply filtering out spam will not effectively cut off the botnet's C&C. The reason is that even if carriers dump spam-like SMS messages into a spam folder like email service providers do, spam messages will still reach target phones, stay at a less noticeable place—the spam folder and get commands executed. Black-listing and SMS sending/receiving rate-limiting may be difficult because our design attempts to minimize the total number of messages sent/received and to balance the load on each bot. As always, matching signatures extracted from known bots' messages can be bypassed by malicious messages with completely new formats or contents. To differentiate between mobile bots and normal phones, the detector at the SMSC needs to extract more distinctive features from SMS traffic patterns. For example, normal phones may have regularities in whom they send messages to and the sending frequency

Table 1: Spam templates with variable fields in grey

1	Your paypal account was hijacked (Err msg: NzkxMjAzNDIxODExMDUyM183Mz). Respond to http://www.bhocxx.paypal.com using code Q3MDk2NDUyXzEyMzQ1Njc4
2	Free ringtone download at www.myringtone.com, using username VIP, password YTJiNGQxMWw to log on
3	Dear Customer, your order ID dWFuaWRpb3Q is accepted. Please visit: www.xajq.apple.com for more info
4	Your business is greatly appreciated and we would like to award you a free gift. http://www.protending.com/ebay/anVzdDRmdW4
5	To confirm your online bank records, follow the link https://login.personal.wamu.com/logon.asp?id=YWhhaGFoYWg
6	Hey, come on - Purchase G.e.n.e.r.i.c V I A G R A! http://www.WQ9.wesiwhchned.com/default.asp?ID=MTA5MzIxMnc
7	Citi Users: This is an important step in stopping online fraud. Please verify your account at https://www.citi.com.Y2Nzc3Vja3M/verify/
8	Hey alice, I forgot to tell you yesterday that the password to that account(MDkyMzkxMDM0OTgxMjAzN) should be 183MzQyNjIwOTM5XzUxOTQwMTI5
9	Don't miss the chance to win an iPhone 4. Go to www.apple.hak/index.asp?id=OTAxMjc1MjM4OTExMTIzOD, password: QyXzQxNDMyMTg3MzlfNjQ4MTkyMDQ
10	Guess who is tracking your location info? Log on to www.whoistrackingme.com/index.asp?num=YWxqc2hmdy0

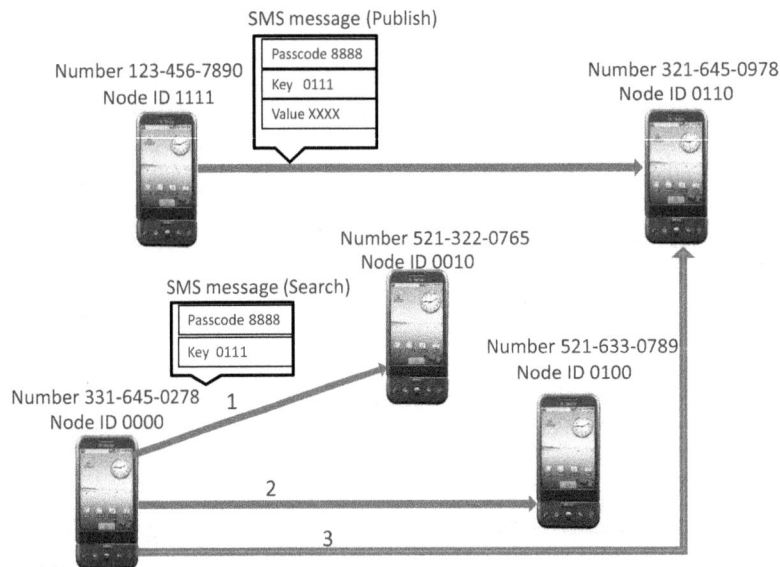

Figure 7: Publish and Search

[36]. The detector can therefore build normal profiles and identify anomalies accordingly. The detector may also adopt a high-level view for detection. As our botnet utilizes a P2P architecture, the resultant network topology stemmed from SMS activities may be different from that formed by benign phones, given the fact that P2P applications are rare in today's mobile phone networks.

6. CONCLUSION

As smartphones are getting more powerful, they become potential targets of profit-driven attacks, especially botnets. In this paper, we presented the design of a mobile botnet that utilizes SMS to transmit C&C messages and a P2P structure to construct its topology. Using simulation, we compared two types of P2P architectures—the structured and the unstructured—based on several metrics critical to the mobile botnet performance. We found that the modified Kademlia—a structured architecture—is more suitable for our botnet in terms of message overhead, delay, and load-balancing. We also investigated possible ways to counter the mobile botnet threat. As future work, we plan to combine SMS-based C&C and IP-based C&C utilizing existing DHT or P2P networks. Since our current work focuses on the aspects of feasibility and efficiency in botnet design, we would also like to measure robustness, i.e., how our botnet performs under different detection and mitigation strategies.

Acknowledgments

The work reported in this paper was supported in part by the US National Science Foundation under Grant No. CNS 1114837.

7. REFERENCES

[1] "Google yanks over 50 infected apps from android market," http://www.computerworld.com/s/article/9212598 /Google_yanks_over_50_infected_apps_from_Android_Market.

[2] SymbOS.Exy.A, http://www.symantec.com/security_response /writeup.jsp?docid=2009-022010-4100-99.

[3] Ikee.B, http://www.symantec.com/security_response /writeup.jsp?docid=2009-112217-4458-99.

[4] "More droiddream details emerge: It was building a mobile botnet," http://www.readwriteweb.com/archives /droiddream_malware_was_going_to_install_more_apps _on_your_phone.php.

[5] RootSmart, http://www.csc.ncsu.edu/faculty/jiang/RootSmart/.

[6] P. Wang, S. Sparks, and C. C. Zou, "An advanced hybrid peer-to-peer botnet," in HotBots'07.

[7] P. Wang, L. Wu, B. Aslam, and C. C. Zou, "A systematic study on peer-to-peer botnets," in ICCCN 2009.

[8] G. Starnberger, C. Kruegel, and E. Kirda, "Overbot - a botnet protocol based on kademlia," in SECURECOMM 2008.

[9] C. R. Davis, S. Neville, J. M. Fernandez, J.-M. Robert, and J. McHugh, "Structured peer-to-peer overlay networks: Ideal botnets command and control infrastructures?" in Proceedings of 13th European Symposium on Research in Computer Security (ESORICS'08).

[10] K. Singh, A. Srivastava, J. Giffin, and W. Lee, "Evaluating email's feasibility for botnet command and control," in Proceedings of 38th Annual IEEE/IFIP International Conference on Dependable Systems and Networks (DSN'08).

[11] A. Nappa, A. Fattori, M. Balduzzi, M. Dell'Amico, and L. Cavallaro, "Take a deep breath: A stealthy, resilient and cost-effective botnet using skype," in Proceedings of 7th International Conference on Detection of Intrusions and Malware, and Vulnerability Assessment (DIMVA'10).

[12] D. Dagon, G. Gu, C. P. Lee, and W. Lee, "A taxonomy of botnet structures," in Proceedings of the 23 Annual Computer Security Applications Conference (ACSAC'07).

[13] A. Bose and K. G.Shin, "On mobile viruses exploiting messaging and bluetooth services," in Proceedings of the 2nd International Conference on Security and Privacy in Communication Networks (SecureComm'06).

[14] R. Racic, D. Ma, and H. Chen, "Exploiting mms vulnerabilities to stealthily exhaust mobile phone's battery," in Proceedings of the 2nd International Conference on Security and Privacy in Communication Networks (SecureComm'06).

[15] W. Enck, P. Traynor, P. McDaniel, and T. L. Porta, "Exploiting open functionality in sms-capable cellular networks," in Proceedings of the 12th ACM Conference on Computer and Communications Security (CCS'05).

[16] P.Traynor, M.Lin, M.Ongtang, V.Rao, T.Jaeger, P.McDaniel, and T.L.Porta, "On cellular botnets: Measuring the impact of malicious devices on a cellular network core," in Proceedings of the 12th ACM Conference on Computer and Communications Security (CCS'09).

[17] K. Singh, S. Sangal, N. Jain, P. Traynor, and W. Lee, "Evaluating bluetooth as a medium for botnet command and control," in Proceedings of the International Conference on Detection of Intrusions and Malware, and Vulnerability Assessment (DIMVA 2010).

[18] J. Hua and K. Sakurai, "A sms-based mobile botnet using flooding algorithm," in The 5th Workshop in Information Security and Privacy (WISTP'11).

[19] C. Mulliner and J.-P. Seifert, "Rise of the ibots: Owning a telco network," in The 5th IEEE International Conference on Malicious and Unwanted Software (Malware), 2010.

[20] G. Weidman, "Transparent botnet command and control for smartphones over sms," in Shmoocon 2011.

[21] "Htc bluetooth vulnerability," http://www.cio.com/article/497146 /HTC_Smartphones_Left_Vulnerable_to_Bluetooth_Attack.

[22] C.Mulliner and C.Miller, "Fuzzing the phone in your phone," in BlackHat Security Conference, 2009.

[23] SMS, http://en.wikipedia.org/wiki/SMS.

[24] "China cracks down on sms spam," http://www.redherring.com/Home/19081.

[25] textPlus, http://www.textplus.com/.

[26] Textfree, http://itunes.apple.com/us/app/textfree-unlimited-send-text/id305925151?mt=8.

[27] "Gsma launches sms spam reporting service," http://www.pcworld.com/businesscenter/article/192469/gsma_launches_sms_spam_reporting_service.html.

[28] P. Maymounkov and D. Mazieres, "Kademlia: A peer-to-peer information system based on the xor metric," in *IPTPS, 2002*.

[29] Y. Chawathe, S. Ratnasamy, L. Breslau, N. Lanham, and S. Shenker, "Making gnutellalike p2p systems scalable," in *ACM SIGCOMM, 2003*.

[30] I. Stoica, R. Morris, D. Karger, M. F. Kaashoek, and H. Balakrishnan, "Chord: A scalable peer-to-peer lookup service for internet applications," in *ACM SIGCOMM 2001*.

[31] OverSim, http://www.oversim.org/.

[32] "Sms market statistics 2009," http://www.massmailsoftware.com/blog/2010/04/sms-market-statistics-2009-know-your-customer/.

[33] "Mobile_phone_spam," http://en.wikipedia.org/wiki/Mobile_phone_spam.

[34] "Researcher says app store open to malware," http://www.iphonealley.com/current/researcher-says-app-store-open-to-malware.

[35] W. Enck, M. Ongtang, and P. McDaniel, "On lightweight mobile phone application certification," in *Proceedings of the 16th ACM conference on Computer and communications security (CCS '09)*.

[36] G. Yan, S. Eidenbenz, and E. Galli, "Sms-watchdog: Profiling social behaviors of sms users for anomaly detection," in *Proceedings of the 12th International Symposium on Recent Advances in Intrusion Detection (RAID'09)*.

Tetherway: A Framework for Tethering Camouflage

Steffen Schulz
Ruhr-University Bochum
Macquarie University
Technische Universität Darmstadt (CASED)
Bochum, Germany
steffen.schulz@rub.de

Ahmad-Reza Sadeghi, Maria Zhdanova
Technische Universität Darmstadt (CASED)
Fraunhofer SIT
Darmstadt, Germany
{ahmad.sadeghi, maria.zhdanova}@cased.de

Hossen A. Mustafa, Wenyuan Xu
University of South Carolina
Columbia, USA
{mustafah, wyxu}@cse.sc.edu

Vijay Varadharajan
Macquarie University
Sydney, Australia
vijay@science.mq.edu.au

ABSTRACT

The rapidly increasing data usage and overload in mobile broadband networks has driven mobile network providers to actively detect and bill customers who *tether* tablets and laptops to their mobile phone for mobile Internet access. However, users may not be willing to pay additional fees only because they use their bandwidth differently, and may consider tethering detection as violation of their privacy. Furthermore, accurate tethering detection is becoming harder for providers as many modern smartphones are under full control of the user, running customized, complex software and applications similar to desktop systems.

In this work, we analyze the network characteristics available to network providers to detect tethering customers. We present and categorize possible detection mechanisms and derive cost factors based on how well the approach scales with large customer bases. For those characteristics that appear most reasonable and practical to deploy by large providers, we present elimination or obfuscation mechanisms and substantiate our design with a prototype Android App.

Categories and Subject Descriptors

C.2.0 [**Security and Protection (e.g., firewalls)**]

Keywords

Mobile Networks, Tethering Detection, Traffic Obfuscation

1. INTRODUCTION

The success of smartphones is having a tremendous impact on the usage and development of mobile phone networks. On the customer side, low prices and the ability to

run sophisticated applications result in a perpetual use of Internet services, such as email, video streaming and social networks. Ubiquitous Internet connectivity enables business professionals to access company resources while traveling, transforming idle time in airports, trains, and hotels into office hours. Since local WiFi connections in hotels or airports are often expensive and sometimes even unavailable, customers are tempted to "tether" their laptops and tablets to the mobile network connection provided by their smartphone. Already, many commodity smartphones such as Android phones or Apple iPhones have integrated mechanisms for sharing the network connection, or can be conveniently modified to do so.

On the provider side, the rapid growth of data usage on devices like tablets and smartphones has incurred large investments to optimize and reduce traffic load on the network infrastructure. Systems and methods are being developed to dynamically optimize hosting locations of content, broadcast data in 3G networks and to adjust the bit rate of content streams based on type and network load. In this setting, unexpected network usage can induce significant network overhead, breaking network optimizations and cost calculations. As such, tethering imposes a significant burden on mobile communication networks, a cost factor that providers like to accommodate in appropriate data plans.

Thus, tethering is usually prohibited for private contracts in most countries, and providers started only recently to offer data plans that explicitly allow tethering at extra cost[1]. In Europe, providers also generally require separate data plans for tethering, and in a few cases providers deployed large-scale tethering detection[2]. However, a limited free riding behavior has been accepted by providers for many years and today, many users do not see why they should pay more

---

[1]For example, the AT&T "unlimited" data plan does not include tethering. Several customers, suspected of tethering, were informed to be switched to a different data plan, unless they report back to AT&T committing to stop their tethering [16]. Similarly, Verizon recently started to detect and redirect tethering users to their website, asking them to switch to a tethering data plan [19].

[2]For instance, O2 was reported to contact tethering customers via phone, to "alert" them to the terms and conditions, and reserve the right to disconnect them [30].

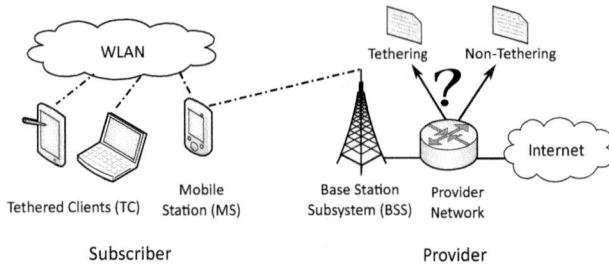

Figure 1: Tethering Detection Scenario

only because they share their paid bandwidth with other devices. Hence, the recent enforcement of contractual agreements through tethering detection is met with resistance, and many users attempt to hide their tethering usage [11].

Regardless of whether tethering should cost extra or not, the fundamental question for customers and providers alike is how to detect tethering, and at what cost. Naturally, there are many possibilities for detecting, e.g., the use of "untypical" web browsers by inspecting application layer content, or performing a generic traffic pattern analysis. However, these mechanisms can be rather costly to apply to large customer bases, and subscribers may apply obfuscation techniques.

To understand the issues associated with tethering, we must identify and analyze the potential mechanisms for the provider to classify traffic as tethering or non-tethering, approximate the costs for these mechanisms and investigate the effort for the subscriber to defeat classification.

Contributions and Outline.

In this work, we provide the first overall analysis on the mechanisms and feasibility of detecting tethering, and investigate how hard it is for the client to hide from such detection mechanism. After introducing the general problem of tethering detection in Section 2, we classify possible detection methods in Section 3 and assign cost factors to them based on the respective associated effort or cost for the provider. In Section 4, we discuss how the vast majority of practical tethering detection mechanisms can be defeated, verifying the feasibility of our approach with an Android-based prototype implementation. After reviewing related work in Section 5 we conclude in Section 6.

2. PROBLEM DESCRIPTION AND MODEL

We consider the tethering detection scenario as illustrated in Figure 1: The subscriber uses a mobile station (MS) to connect to the mobile broadband network of the provider. The MS is a highly customizable smartphone that may be used by the subscriber to connect additional *tethered clients* (TC), to share the mobile network connection. The provider aims to prevent such usage by classifying the network traffic of its subscribers (customer base) into either tethering or non-tethering traffic. The undesired tethering traffic can then be blocked or directly billed according to the provider's policy. On the other hand, the subscriber aims to hide its use of tethering, i.e., to confuse or circumvent the tethering detection of the provider.

Note that there are also other cases of "tethering" where the subscriber shares the mobile connection of the provider not only between own devices but also with third parties. Alternatively, more powerful mobile devices may (soon) be

running virtual machines, creating a "virtual" tethering system. From the perspective of the provider, it is hard to distinguish these types of tethering from each other. However, since all of these approaches result in the same network setup and incur similar load on the mobile provider's network, we assume that they are equally undesirable.

The subscriber could also deploy a VPN tunnel to hide connection details from the provider. However, VPNs introduce configuration and compatibility issues, and increase network delay due to overlay routing. VPNs are also easy to detect, so that a widespread use of VPN to hide tethering may result in a ban of VPNs for cheap data plans.

2.1 Adversary Model

For the purpose of this investigation we treat the mobile provider as the adversary. We assume that the provider has full control over the network connection of the subscriber and may re-route, insert, modify or block transmitted packets. Additionally, the provider is able to read all transmitted data, including application layer information, except in cases where the subscriber uses end-to-end encryption mechanisms like SSL or VPN.

However, the provider is subject to certain practical limitations: The subscriber has full control over the programs running on the mobile station MS and any tethered client TC. Moreover, manipulation of application layer content or active OS fingerprinting may be detected by the subscriber and regarded as an attack, which we consider costly for the provider. Some attacks also require more resources than others, such as application layer inspection or stateful tracking of connections, increasing the cost for tethering detection.

We model these limitations by considering the cost or practicality ("effort") of the attack with regard to the various criteria that may be relevant for the mobile provider. In particular, we rate the effort as "low", "medium", "high" for the following criteria:

Impact Type: We distinguish passive, active and destructive detection methods. Passive methods simply monitor transferred network traffic, such as TCP/IP source and destination header fields, and incur *low* effort. In contrast, active attacks manipulate the data that the provider transfers on behalf of the subscriber or inject custom packets to prompt a reaction from the subscriber. This generally requires more resources due to realtime traffic processing and tracking, which we rate as *medium* effort. Some active attacks can result in noticeable interruption of ongoing network communication for the subscriber and thus are not suitable for large-scale scanning of a provider's customer base. We consider such destructive attacks *impractical*.

Protocol Layer: We distinguish attacks on network layer (*low*), application layer (*medium*) and "behavior layer" (*high*). Application layer attacks are generally more costly than network layer attacks since more complex protocol parsing and interaction is required, while lower layer protocols can be processed by most common hardware. With "behavior layer" attacks we denote the collection of traffic meta-data, which can encompass simple characteristics like timing and size of packets or more complex connection patterns. Due to the required long-term observation of individual customers we rate this as *high* effort attack.

Privacy Violation: We distinguish attacks that are not privacy-critical (*low*) from those that work with privacy-sensitive data (*medium*) (e.g., inspection of application layer data) and attacks that modify or inject application data (*high*). The latter approaches are often problematic with regard to data protection laws, and especially the undesired modification of user data is strictly prohibited in many countries [18].

Pre-condition: We categorize attacks as either unconditional (*low*) or conditional (*medium*). Unconditional attacks can always be launched, e.g., traffic analysis or querying the MS for active fingerprinting. In contrast, conditional attacks such as special HTTP or DNS access patterns depend on the behavior of the targeted subscriber and may be more or less likely to occur. Note that some pre-conditions may be easily met by longer-term passive observation, while others are only realistic if the provider can actively manipulate the MS, such as sending uncommon IP packets for OS fingerprinting. If a pre-condition is unlikely to occur even in active attack scenarios we denote the attack as *impractical*.

Detection Effort: We categorize detection methods based on signatures (*low*), heuristics (*medium*) or profiles (*high*). Heuristic and profile-based methods suffer from increased costs due to the computational efforts required for traffic processing, and profile-based methods are the most expensive as they additionally need traffic profiles to classify collected traffic with high accuracy. For example, network layer fingerprinting uses a simple database lookup ("signature") to classify OS implementations and is generally cheaper than traffic classification with statistical analysis and machine learning.

Using this classification, we derive the overall effort for each attack as the maximum of the efforts for each particular criterion. For example, the effort of evaluating the HTTP *User Agent* header is *medium*: It is a low-impact attack (*low*) but the inspected data is on application layer and may be considered privacy-sensitive (*medium*).

2.2 Communication Architecture

We assume a standard 2G/3G network setup on the provider side and a regular TCP/IP LAN[3] on the subscriber side. The mobile station MS dials into the provider's network and provides multiple interfaces such as wireless LAN, Bluetooth and USB to connect to local devices of the subscriber.

2.2.1 Tethering Technology

The tethering mechanism that connects the subscriber's LAN to the provider's WAN can be implemented in several ways. Most commonly, the MS is used either as a modem or IP gateway. Historically, the modem solution was used as it requires the least resources on the MS. However, the IP gateway solution is preferred on todays smartphones as it allows the simultaneous use of voice and data services. Some applications also offer other tethering techniques like application layer proxies or port-forwarding, however, such

---

[3]Note that we use the term *TCP/IP* in this work to refer to the complete TCP/IP protocol stack with UDP and ICMP.

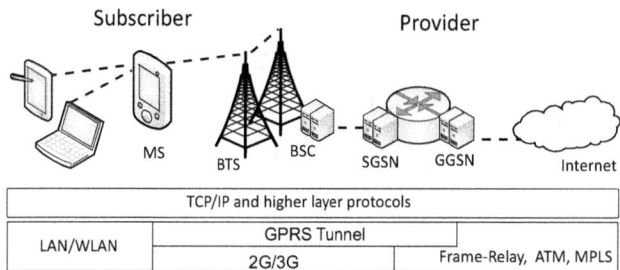

Figure 2: Overview of the 2G/3G communication architecture.

solutions provide only limited connectivity and are not easily deployed in combination with, e.g., VPN or VoIP software. Hence, we focus on the case of tethering where the smartphone acts as an IP router and gateway for the LAN, forwarding IP packets between LAN and WAN.

Technically, IP gateways for tethering on mobile phones are implemented using Network Address Translation (NAT), specifically Network Address Port Translation (NAPT) [33]. In NAT the port numbers and request identifiers of UDP, TCP, ICMP and other protocols are used to multiplex connections from the private LAN IP address space to the single, public IP that is typically issued to the mobile station MS by the provider. The deployment of NAT has three major consequences for tethering detection: (1) NAT transforms forwarded IP traffic, resulting in a modified traffic pattern that may be used to directly detect NAT; (2) a tethered client TC is not directly reachable from the WAN, so that, e.g., active fingerprinting by the provider will always only detect the MS itself but not TC; (3) since NAT is designed to be transparent, TCP and UDP payloads are transmitted unmodified, resulting in several options for tethering detection at application layer.

2.2.2 Mobile Networks Architecture

Figure 2 shows an overview of the 2G/3G mobile communication architecture. On the left, the MS is connected to one or more tethered clients via, e.g., wireless LAN. The mobile station acts as an IP router with NAT for these LAN clients, forwarding their IP packets through the provider's 2G/3G network in a General Packet Radio Service (GPRS) tunnel. The provider's Base Transceiver Stations (BTSs) forwards the GPRS frames on link layer to the Base Station Controller (BSC) and then to the Serving GPRS Support Node (SGSN) [1]. Once in the provider's network, GPRS frames are separated from voice traffic and forwarded to the Gateway GPRS Support Node (GGSN), where they are finally forwarded to the Internet [2].

As can be seen in Figure 2, the lowest protocol layer that is transported all the way from the MS through the provider's network is the topmost IP layer. Any lower layer information in the subscriber's LAN/WLAN is discarded already at MS, where forwarded TCP/IP packets are encapsulated in GPRS frames in the same way as locally generated ("non-tethered") packets, and are thus indistinguishable on link layer. Although the IP layer information can have some effect on lower layers, such as frame length and timing, these characteristics are also extractable at the IP layer. Hence, we reduce our analysis of tethering detection mechanisms to IP and higher layer protocols used by MS and TC.

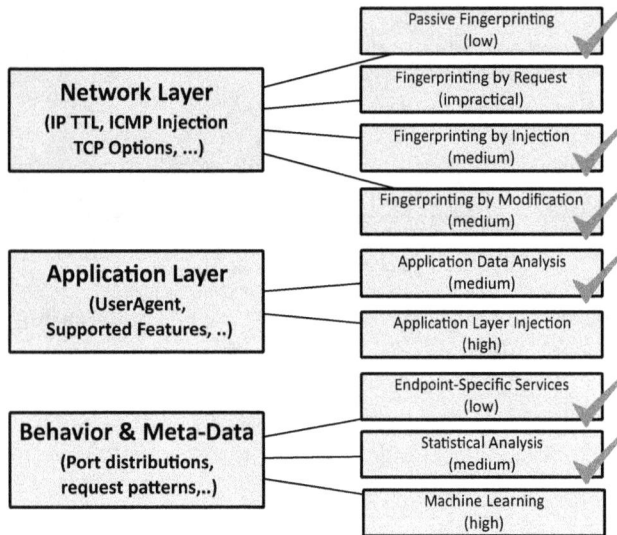

Figure 3: Classification of tethering detection mechanisms. Tetherway includes defenses against all *low* and *medium* effort detection techniques.

3. DETECTING TETHERING

Superficially, tethering detection appears similar to well-known mechanisms from network or OS fingerprinting and analysis of application behavior. However, most common fingerprinting techniques are not actually applicable and more complex attacks like active manipulation or traffic analysis quickly become too costly to be applied to the huge customer base of a mobile provider.

A general overview of the different types of attacks is provided in Figure 3. Abstractly, we can classify the possible tethering detection mechanisms into (1) network layer fingerprinting, (2) application layer inspection and manipulation, and (3) behavior and traffic pattern analysis.

In the following, we discuss each of these approaches in detail and rate their feasibility and practicality by assigning costs based on the adversary model in Section 2.1

3.1 Network Layer Attacks

Tethering detection methods on network layer can be generally described as fingerprinting attacks. However, we must emphasize that tethering detection is different from the well-known OS fingerprinting attacks: In OS fingerprinting, the adversary aims to detect the OS type running on a specific remote machine, while in tethering detection we are interested in identifying *additional* hosts *behind* the MS, or the fact that Network Address Translation (NAT) is enabled at the MS. Hence, many standard attacks are not effective while other and new attacks become useful. In the following we thus distinguish passive attacks and active attacks that are based on (i) requests, (ii) injection, and (iii) manipulation.

3.1.1 Passive Fingerprinting

Passive observation of network and transport layer header fields and traffic flows can be used to distinguish hosts behind NAT or directly detect the use of NAT. In the IP header, the fields for Differentiated Services (DS), Explicit Congestion Notification (ECN), IP Flags and especially Time To Live (TTL) may be used differently depending on

the OS that the packet originates from (e.g., [5, 35, 25]). Similarly, information on the Initial TCP Window Size and Sequence Number, the supported types, values and order of TCP Option fields such as Maximum Segment Size (MSS), Window Scaling and Timestamps can be used to discriminate different TCP/IP implementations behind NAT [7, 37, 9]. We consider such passive network layer attacks as *low* effort, as they are the least invasive and most scalable.

3.1.2 Fingerprinting by Request

Most established OS fingerprinting techniques assume an active adversary to query the target with specially crafted TCP or ICMP requests [32, 4]. However, such requests are usually answered by the mobile station MS itself, and thus can only identify the MS and not the TCs. To the best of our knowledge there are also no active fingerprinting attacks that directly detect the use of NAT by querying the MS. Hence, active fingerprinting attacks based on requests are generally ineffective, as long as they only target the MS itself and cannot detect its use of NAT, so that we denote such attacks as *impractical*.

In the following we discuss two different approaches for active fingerprinting which either inject or manipulate packets of *existing* connections. The NAT at the MS keeps track of such existing connections and will forward injected or manipulated packets as long as they can still be recognized as part of a known ongoing connection[4].

3.1.3 Fingerprinting by Injection

An active fingerprinting attack can traverse the NAT barrier by injecting packets into an existing connection, so that they are recognized and translated by the NAT engine. For the UDP protocol, no such attacks are known in the related work, likely due to its inherent simplicity. TCP packet injection attacks are possible but problematic, as packet injections desynchronize the TCP connection between the original sender and receiver [44]. This requires the provider to constantly manipulate the TCP packet stream until an opportunity for re-synchronization occurs, or until the connection is ended, or otherwise results in a noticeable interruption of the TCP session of the subscriber. We rate the resulting longer-term realtime traffic manipulation as a *high* effort attack.

The remaining network layer protocol that is frequently used today is ICMP. For active fingerprinting of hosts behind NAT, an ICMP error message could be injected from the provider based on an existing UDP or TCP connection. A NAT engine is required to statefully rewrite and forward several types of such messages to ensure transparent IP operation [34]. However, ICMP errors often signal critical faults in the forwarding of IP packets and are thus not designed to generate an observable response. In fact, most ICMP errors will immediately terminate the respective UDP or TCP connection, leading to noticeable interruptions that make such approaches *impractical*.

We have identified only one error message that is (1) regularly forwarded into the LAN behind a NAT gateway, (2) handled by standard TCP/IP implementations, including An-

---

[4]In TCP and UDP, the connection is identified by the source and destination ports and IPs addresses. ICMP packets are recognized by their identifiers or, in case of ICMP error messages, based on the UDP/TCP port and IPs contained in their embedded TCP/UDP fragment [33, 34].

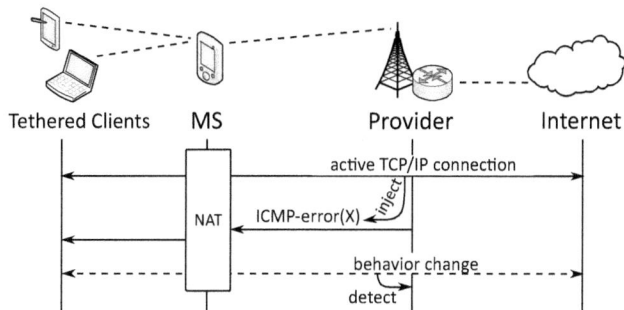

Figure 4: ICMP injection attack for detecting NAT.

droid, and (3) results in changes observable to the provider if handled by a tethering client: the ICMP "fragmentation needed and don't fragment bit was set" error message. As illustrated in Figure 4, the provider may inject such a message as a response to an ongoing TCP/IP connection. The error is forwarded by the NAT gateway, manipulating one of the tethered hosts to believe into a smaller Maximum Transmission Unit (MTU) for this particular *IP route*, i.e., for the IP layer connection between the source and destination of the respective TCP or UDP connection. As a result, the target of the injected ICMP error (TC or MS) will start transmitting smaller packets for that particular IP route, which can be observed by the provider. But since the ICMP error is regularly forwarded to only one of the potentially multiple hosts on subscriber side, the provider can then detect the use of tethering by checking if *all* other connections using the same IP route adopt the same reduced MTU.

The main drawback of this attack is that it only works if multiple IP connections to the same destination hosts are opened at the same time by different tethering hosts, as otherwise no difference in the behavior of any two connections can be observed. While this pre-condition cannot be easily induced by the provider, it is also not very unlikely to occur, especially when considering the high frequency at which email, instant messaging and news aggregation clients connect to popular Internet services today. We classify such ICMP injection as a *medium* effort attack due to its active manipulation of traffic and the required pre-condition.

3.1.4 Fingerprinting by Modification

The adversary may also manipulate IP and TCP headers that are destined for the MS and potential TCs with the goal to create observable changes in the connection state or behavior. The scenario is similar to the ICMP MTU attack illustrated in Figure 4: When manipulating the IP or TCP headers of an ongoing TCP/IP connection, the manipulation propagates through the NAT barrier at the MS. The tethered clients $TC_1, TC_2, \ldots$ may then act differently depending on the included options, creating a client-specific feedback that is observable by the provider.

One example of such an attack is to set the TTL for inbound packets towards the MS to "1". Such packets can be received by the MS, but an additional forwarding to the TCs would decrement the TTL to "0", so that the packet is dropped at the NAT gateway. Similarly, the Flags field or Header Checksum of the IP or TCP header may be manipulated to detect different types of operating systems through their different ways of error handling. However, all these

manipulations involve a high risk to noticeably interrupt ongoing connections, making them *impractical* for scanning of large customer bases.

There are also several less common optional headers in IP and TCP that may be handled and supported differently by different TCP/IP implementations. The provider may exploit the difference in endpoint behavior to detect the existence of multiple hosts at the MS, by injecting TCP options into existing TCP/IP streams and observing the response behavior. Due to their optional nature, the injection or deletion of such options will usually not break the connection, however, they still require an active manipulation and stateful observation of the traffic flow, resulting in *medium* effort attack.

3.2 Application Layer Attacks

A large number of application layer characteristics can be used to differentiate hosts behind a NAT, either explicitly based on meta-data information in protocol headers or implicitly, by exploiting the different features supported by individual applications. However, the line between mobile and desktop "Apps" becomes increasingly blurred by the rapid progress in smartphones and particularly tablets, which are getting as complex and powerful as desktop systems.

3.2.1 Application Data Analysis

The easiest way to identify the number and type of hosts and applications on application layer is passive application layer inspection or Deep Packet Inspection (DPI). Well known examples for application layer data that identify systems and applications behind the MS are the *User Agent* field in the HTTP header and the host identifier strings sent as part of eMail or Instant Messaging (IM) communication [8]. Protocols with more complex negotiation of features and algorithms, such as TLS or IPsec, also often exchange an implementation-characteristic sets of supported features during their negotiation phase, which potentially allow to distinguish multiple hosts behind a NAT gateway even if the actual user data is encrypted.

Passive application layer attacks are highly practical. The required DPI can be done asynchronously and is already available for several policy-enforcement scenarios in the network management. Hence we can rate this approach as *medium* effort.

3.2.2 Application Layer Injection

For active attacks, i.e., the injection of code into transferred websites or the redirection of users to the provider's servers, the attack surface for distinguishing TCs is practically unlimited[5]. However, such active attacks are also rather resource intensive, have a high risk of getting noticed and may be interpreted by the client as intrusion and privacy invasion [19, 30]. According to our cost model, the effort for such attacks is therefore considered to be *high* due to potential privacy violations.

3.3 Traffic Metadata Analysis

The third main category of tethering detection concerns the analysis of traffic meta-data. Similar to application layer attacks, the area of statistical traffic analysis is very large [10]. However, we can single out two approaches that

---

[5]See, e.g., `http://browserspy.dk` and the demonstration at `https://panopticlick.eff.org/`

result in rather efficient detection mechanisms, while the more sophisticated traffic analysis with machine learning is more resource intensive.

We emphasize that the popular packet size and timing analysis usually requires long-term observation and sophisticated machine learning techniques to classify traffic with reasonable accuracy. As such it constitutes a rather *high* effort attack when applied to the large customer base of a mobile phone provider.

3.3.1 Endpoint-Specific Services

Many operating systems and applications can be identified based on the individual Internet services they use. For example, Android phones are unlikely to connect to the Microsoft Windows update servers or to package repositories provided by most large Linux distributions. Instead, they will mainly connect to the Android Market for software update information, and to the configured Google, Exchange or Facebook accounts for synchronization of contact data, etc. Similar considerations apply to individual applications such as anti-virus scanners, office suites, PDF viewers and Java runtime environments that are known to regularly contact the servers of their respective vendors.

A special case of this category are tethering applications provided by the mobile provider itself, which explicitly signal the use of tethering by switching the provider's access point (APN). These applications are regularly shipped with iPhones, but also with many Android phones.

Endpoint-specific tethering detection requires only passive traffic monitoring on network layer, without any particular post-processing of data. While the considered events (preconditions) are usually not easily to trigger by the provider, they are still likely to occur. For example, many systems check for software updates as soon as an Internet connection is established. Hence we rate this kind of attacks as *low* effort.

3.3.2 Statistical Analysis

With this category we denote approaches that use simple frequency or random distribution analysis, i.e., which employ rather simple analysis models [6, 13]. Well-known examples of this category concern the random distribution or range of values in individual network layer header fields, such as the IP ID fields [35, 5] or the clock skew in values of the TCP timestamp header [9]. We also found that the port-multiplexing of NAT leads to distinctive changes in the source port range and distribution. In contrast to previous works [35], we found this characteristic to be highly suitable for tethering detection (cf. Section 4.2.1 and 4.3).

A common property of these attacks is that they concern only lower-layer protocols and require only short to medium observation time, so we consider their overall cost as *medium*.

3.3.3 Machine Learning

Apart from the direct evaluation of header fields and connection states, a major approach in the classification of traffic is the traffic pattern analysis with machine learning. This approach is characterized by collection and model-based analysis of network meta-data such as traffic volume, packet size and timing, as well as more complex patterns like the number of simultaneous TCP connections for given destinations, or with specific higher-layer protocols.

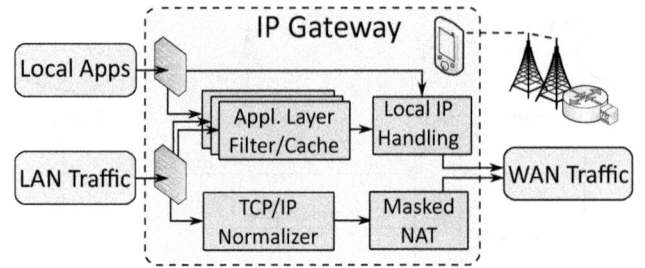

Figure 5: Tethering Normalization Architecture.

An example attack that could be mounted in this way to reveal tethering is the detection of multiple browser caches at the client, which results in different HTTP object request patterns. Alternatively, the provider may attempt to distinguish particular TCP flow control algorithms implemented at the MS, based on how individual TCP connections increase or throttle their packet rates over time.

The data processing phase involves the use of generalized profiles that are created by observing and then either implicitly or explicitly classifying large amounts of data (supervised or unsupervised learning, see [28, 42]). However, supervised learning involves a high effort in the learning phase, and the results of unsupervised learning require similarly high effort to confirm potential matches and filter false positives [20]. In the end, all types of learning-based traffic analysis appear to require long-term observation, careful system analysis and post-processing. Due to the high costs in regard to Detection Effort and Protocol Layer we rate their overall effort as *high*.

4. DEFEATING TETHERING DETECTION

To evaluate the practicality of tethering detection, we have developed a generic architecture for normalization and obfuscation of the tethering characteristics identified in Section 3. In this context, normalization describes the process of modifying the distribution of values for the previously identified characteristics, such that they are close or identical to the distribution of a non-tethering system. We have implemented a prototype to defeat against the most practical (i.e., cheapest) attacks identified above and compare its performance against simple VPN solutions.

4.1 Tethering Normalization Architecture

Figure 5 depicts our approach to normalization and obfuscation of tethering characteristics in network traffic. There are two main components for traffic normalization: (1) the Application Layer Filter and Cache and (2) the TCP/IP Normalizer with Masked NAT. A packet filter is used to assign data streams to the respective components, and after processing all packets are forwarded through the same WAN interface to the provider, as discussed in Section 2.2.

The Application Layer Filters must be developed specifically for each individual application layer protocol, like HTTP, and can thus also normalize application-specific patterns such as the *User Agent* meta-information in HTTP headers. Moreover, they can block, aggregate and cache queries to obfuscate access behavior and traffic patterns or imitate desired patterns. After the application layer payloads are processed, they are forwarded using the local IP handler of the MS, so that no TCP/IP layer normalization is required.

0	7	15	23	31
Version	IHL	DSCP	ECN	Total Length
Identification		Flags	Fragment Offset	
TTL		Protocol	Header Checksum	
Source IP Address				
Destination IP Address				
Options and Padding				

0	7	15	23	31
Source Port		Destination Port		
Length		Checksum		
Data				

Normalized field   Unmodified field

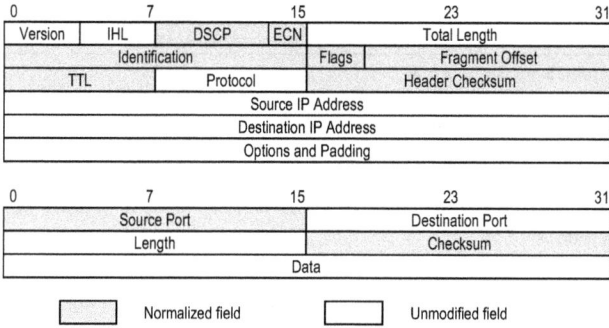

Figure 6: Normalized IP and UDP header fields.

0	7	15	23	31
Source Port		Destination Port		
Sequence Number				
Acknowledgment Number				
Data Offset	reserved	ECN	Control Bits	Window Size
TCP Checksum			Urgent Pointer	
Options: MSS				
Options: SACK OK		Options:Timestamp		
Options: Nop		Options: WScale		
Data				

Normalized field   Unmodified field

Figure 7: Normalized TCP fields and options.

The main disadvantage of this approach is that it must be implemented for each individual application protocol and cannot handle unknown protocols.

Hence, we have added the TCP/IP Normalizer as a generic network layer normalizer in case no Application Layer Filter was defined for a particular data stream. This also includes many protocols where application-layer processing is not possible or not deemed necessary, such as encrypted traffic. As a network layer normalizer, its capabilities are limited to the normalization of header fields and filtering of unusual requests and header options, as detailed in Section 4.2.1. The normalization is followed by the Masked NAT component, which translates the IP address range of the LAN traffic to that of the WAN traffic [33]. The NAT is masked in the sense that the range and distribution of the modified header fields are indistinguishable from that of the local IP stack (cf. Section 4.2.1).

4.2 Tethering with Tetherway

To verify the practicality of network normalization on smartphones, we implemented an Android App for tethering normalization system called *Tetherway*. Tetherway is based on the popular Android App *android-wifi-tether*[6], which can use the ad-hoc wireless network, USB or Bluetooth personal network of the MS to connect to tethered clients, providing a standard IP gateway with DHCP and NAT. In the following we describe the implementation details of the TCP/IP Normalizer, Masked NAT, and two Application Layer Filters for DNS and HTTP. We denote packets that are destined to the Internet or provider network as *outbound* packets, and packets destined for the MS or TCs as *inbound* packets.

4.2.1 TCP/IP Normalization

We have implemented a TCP/IP packet normalization using the *libnetfilter-queue* extension[7] of the Linux firewall subsystem. The extension allows us to program custom packet filters in the Linux userspace, enabling arbitrary rewrite of network packets to simulate non-tethering behavior.

IP Header Normalization.

On IP layer we reset the DS field for outbound packets and enabled ECN. We set the TTL field to 64 and also reset the IP flags and fragment offset to disable fragmentation, as this is the default behavior in Android smartphones.

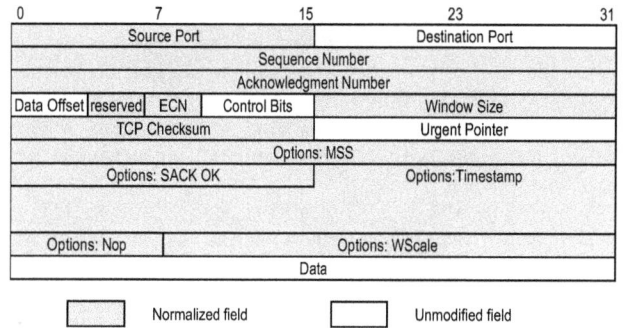

---

[6]http://code.google.com/p/android-wifi-tether/
[7]http://netfilter.org/projects/libnetfilter_queue/

Note that while NAT cannot handle fragments, Linux transparently defragments packets before NAT processing so that they are treated in the same way, regardless of whether they are destined for the MS or TCs.

More involved is the adjustment of the IP ID field to elicit the same random distribution as the IP ID values of a standard Android platform *without* NAT, i.e., a randomized initial value that is incremented with each packet of the same TCP/IP session. To imitate this behavior of modern Linux kernels we have implemented a corresponding stateful rewrite of IP IDs for TCP/IP sessions, using local copies of the respective randomization functions in the Linux kernel. For UDP, no normalization is required since the standard behavior to set the IP ID to zero is the same as it is done by regular NAT in Linux. Only in case of DNS requests, the IP ID may contain a random number to mitigate DNS cache poisoning attacks [21]. However, we have deployed a caching DNS proxy for this case. Finally, our system filters all inbound and outbound IP options as they are usually not used or needed.

ICMP MTU Exceeded Injection.

The ICMP injection attack we proposed in Section 3.1.3 can be partly mitigated by replicating ICMP errors on the NAT gateway: Similar to the approach of IPsec, the gateway can record received ICMP MTU errors from the WAN and distribute them not only to the respective LAN host referenced in the error message, but also to all other hosts that send a packet larger than the reported MTU to the same destination IP. As a result, the provider will not receive any packets larger than the MTU size previously injected. The provider could still wait for the reduced MTU values to time out on the individual TCs, an event that occurs at different times depending on the deployed OS at the TCs. However, this event occurs only after 1-2 minutes, complicating detection as many TCP connections are not sufficiently long-lived.

Hence, while our defense is not perfect, the attack cost is increased by requiring long-term observation and the precondition of multiple long-lived TCP connections is less likely to occur, so we rate the new effort for this attack as *high*.

TCP and UDP Header Normalization.

Figure 6 and 7 give an overview of the normalized fields in the typical TCP/IP headers. For the TCP header, we normalize the Sequence Number field and the ECN and Reserved Flags, as well as several TCP option headers. The Acknowledgment Number, Window Size and Checksum fields are also updated as a consequence of other corrections.

Just like in the IP header, the Explicit Congestion Notification (ECN) flags can be safely reset to always enable ECN support: ECN is supported by all modern hosts, and systems that do not support ECN suffer the resulting performance penalty in any case.

To normalize the TCP (Initial) Sequence Number (ISN), we statefully track TCP connections and use the functions for randomized ISN selection from the Linux kernel to select a new ISN for each TCP connection over NAT. Since the endpoints of a TCP connection rely on the sequence numbering for ordering and acknowledging received TCP segments, we then record the *offset* between the original and newly chosen ISN for each new connection and adjust (1) all subsequent Sequence Numbers on outbound and (2) all Acknowledgment Numbers on inbound packets accordingly. Hence the provider is unable to distinguish ISNs for tethering, and all Sequence Numbers are correctly rewritten regardless of the packet reordering.

TCP Option Headers.

We must normalize the various TCP Option headers to mitigate the problem of fingerprinting by modification (cf. Section 3.1.4). For this purpose, we purge all TCP Options that are not used by Android from inbound as well as outbound packets, i.e., all Option headers except for the Message Segment Size (MSS), Selective ACK (SACK), Timestamp (TS), Window Scale (Wscale) and No Operation (NOP) fields. For outbound packets, we furthermore normalize the order and content of the remaining supported TCP Options.

The MSS Option can be normalized using the iptables *clamp-mss-to-pmtu* option. The SACK and Wscale Options are used only in the initial TCP handshake to signal support for selective acknowledgments and window scaling. The SACK Option does not contain any actual values and thus does not require normalization, except for its location within the TCP header. However, the Wscale Option on mobile stations often advertises the smaller Window Scale factor than the one used for the LAN and WLAN interfaces of desktop systems. To transparently rewrite this value, we statefully track the TCP connection, recording the original Window Scale factor before resetting it to the typical Wscale factor of "1" for Android. For all outbound TCP headers, we recompute (left shift) the Window Size header value to compensate for the smaller Window Scale factor. In the worst case, this modification *reduces* the absolute receive window assumed by the sender, possibly reducing TCP performance. However, this is also the expected behavior for a regular (non-tethering) MS. Finally, the TS Option adds two timestamps to all TCP packets to let endpoints compute the precise Round-Trip Time (RTT) of a connection [17, 9]. To make the TS values indistinguishable from the timestamps of the MS, we simply replace all timestamps inserted by the TCs with values generated by the MS. The resulting change in the computed RTT is negligible, as TC and MS are typically very close.

Apart from the SACK Option, all of the discussed Options could be synthesized on the gateway without breaking the TCP session. However, currently we treat a missing TCP Option as an error and do not currently implement such synthesis.

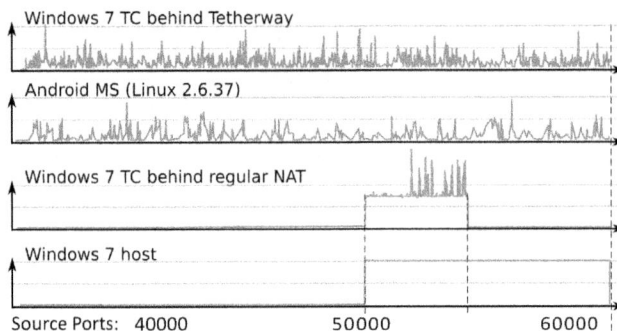

Figure 8: Source port distributions for Android and Windows 7 without NAT, with NAT and with Tetherway.

Masked NAT.

The source port multiplexing by NAT, or more specifically Network Address Port Translation (NAPT), can lead to characteristic source port distributions: Firstly, the standard Linux NAPT implementation uses a different port range than the standard range for ephemeral source ports in outbound connections. Moreover, Linux NAT tries to preserve the original source ports whenever possible, so that source port distributions of different TCs are likely to remain visible regardless of NAT (cf. Figure 8).

Fortunately, the Linux NAPT subsystem also supports two parameters to set the port range and enable port randomization. By source code inspection we confirmed that enabling port randomization disables the preservation of source ports, and that the employed randomization function is the same as the one used in the ephemeral source port selection for local traffic. Hence, we can eliminate differences in the distribution of source port values sent via NAT versus that of local connections by the MS, by enabling randomized port mapping and setting the same range of ports as used by the regular ephemeral port selection of Android.

4.2.2 Application Layer Proxies

We have implemented application layer filtering for the two most used services, DNS and HTTP. In both cases we have deployed standard application layer proxies to implement the filtering and caching required for eluding tethering detection.

For HTTP, we deployed *Privoxy*[8] as a filtering proxy. Privoxy is used to anonymize HTTP traffic for users of *Tor*[9] and provides extensive and well-tested rules for filtering, e.g., user tracking based on cookies and Webbugs, or embedded active content such as Adobe Flash. To obfuscate object request patterns on the behavior layer, the filtering proxy is backed by a caching parent proxy, *Polipo*[10]. As a result of this construction, the HTTP request behavior becomes similar to that of an endpoint with only a single browser cache, as it would be expected from a non-tethering MS.

For DNS, we use *dnsmasq*[11] as a local DNS cache on the MS. We implement a simple DNS filter by returning the local host IP address 127.0.0.1 for blacklisted DNS records.

---

[8] http://www.privoxy.org/
[9] http://www.torproject.org
[10] http://www.pps.jussieu.fr/~jch/software/polipo/
[11] http://thekelleys.org.uk/dnsmasq/doc.html

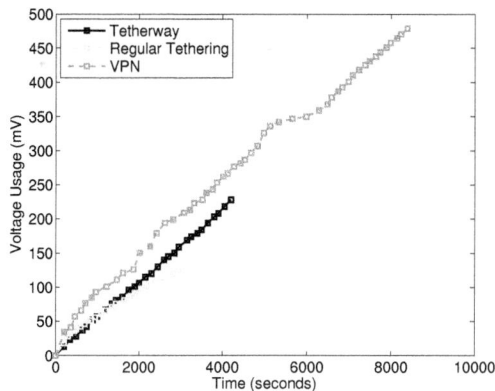

Figure 9: Power consumption for Tetherway compared to regular tethering and VPN.

This can be used to block behavioral patterns like accesses to Windows Update or the standard Windows time synchronization servers.

4.3 Evaluation

We evaluate the efficiency of our normalization engine by comparing the phone's power consumption while downloading 960 objects (50MB total) from 2 websites using (1) regular non-normalizing tethering, (2) a typical VPN software and (3) our Tetherway prototype. In particular, we compared Tetherway against the android-wifi-tether App that it is based on, and against Juniper Junos Pulse VPN for Android. As can be seen in Figure 9, the total energy consumption and the amount of time of Tetherway for completing the same task are close to that of regular tethering and notably below that of a VPN client. This confirms our subjective impression that responsiveness of the VPN connection was notably lower, likely due to the additional hops introduced by the VPN tunnel.

To confirm the proper normalization of header fields, we compare the distributions of critical header fields such as the source ports in Figure 8 and TCP initial sequence numbers in Figure 10. In each case, a clear difference in the distributions of standard Android and a Windows 7 TC can be identified. Specifically, Figure 8 shows a highly predictable port usage for Windows 7 hosts, while Android uses a different port range with randomized source port selection. Similarly, the random distribution of the TCP ISN values shown in Figure 10 is distinctively different for Windows 7 and Linux, with Windows hosts using a larger range of values that are not changed by regular NAT. In contrast, the distribution of the Windows 7 client behind Tetherway is similar to the one expected from a non-tethering Android MS.

We conclude that our normalization is efficient and effective, making tethering detection much harder for the provider. VPN software can also be used to hide all of the identified tethering characteristics, by setting up the MS as a VPN gateway for the TCs. However, VPNs are not designed for this purpose, resulting in noticeable network overhead and increased power consumption. Moreover, with a widespread use of tethering via VPN, mobile providers may be tempted to restrict the use of VPNs to specialized "business" data plans, for exactly the same reasons that they try to restrict the use of tethering today.

4.4 Limitations

Tetherway focuses on the most common and most easily detected tethering characteristics, as illustrated in Figure 3. Several possibilities remain to identify tethering setups. Our HTTP and DNS caches do not enforce a particular packet timing or obfuscate patterns in the network access behavior of email or IM clients. However, such normalization can be added, e.g., using the Linux network emulator *netem*[12].

Furthermore, although HTTP and DNS traffic accounts for a large amount of device mobile traffic, many other protocols such as Simple Mail Transfer Protocol (SMTP), Internet Message Access Protocol (IMAP) or the several Instant Messaging protocols are also in widespread use. However, most modern applications employ encryption based on TLS, hiding any application layer characteristics.

Note that several more complex detection mechanisms, e.g., based on traffic analysis, may still be viable if the provider applies some preliminary filtering to reduce the number of suspects, e.g., based on the amount of traffic usage. However, an in-depth analysis of these approaches is outside the scope of this work.

5. RELATED WORK

To our knowledge, this work is the first to consider the problem of tethering detection, which can be seen as a generalization of the previously considered NAT detection. We systematize tethering detection methods and show that the most cost-effective techniques can be mitigated efficiently.

Vendors like Cisco and Sandvine already provide tethering detection solutions [12, 31]. However, they currently inspect only a rather simple mix of network and application layer headers, indicating that injection or traffic analysis attacks are indeed more costly. Consequently, first tethering Apps also provide correspondingly simple detection countermeasures like resetting the IP TTL field[13] or using proxies[14].

Regarding the general problem of tethering detection, we identify three major categories of related work: (1) Revealing multiple hosts or different operating systems behind an IP gateway, (2) detecting use of NAT and (3) performing general statistical analysis of network traffic.

Direct NAT detection. The use of NAT and the counting of hosts behind NAT was previously considered as a general problem of network mapping and measurement. For example, it was proposed to detect NAT based on analysis of the IP ID field in the IP header and to count "NATed hosts" through reconstruction of IP ID sequences [5]. In another approach, a naive Bayesian classifier was used to detect hosts behind NAT based on IP TTL, DF, initial TCP window size and TCP SYN packet size [7]. Similarly, the authors of [35] propose to combine multiple parameters to increase detection accuracy, using data such as IP ID, TTL and source port distribution.

We consider these attacks among the most practical since they involve only simple statistical analysis on network layer data. We extend on these works by showing that source port distribution is a highly practical tool for detecting NAT, and that countermeasures for all previously presented network layer NAT detection techniques are feasible even on resource-limited devices (cf. Section 4.2.1).

---

[12]See, e.g., `tcn.hypert.net/tcmanual.pdf`
[13]PdaNet 5.01 `http://junefabrics.com/index.php`
[14]`androinica.com/tag/clockwordmod-tether/`

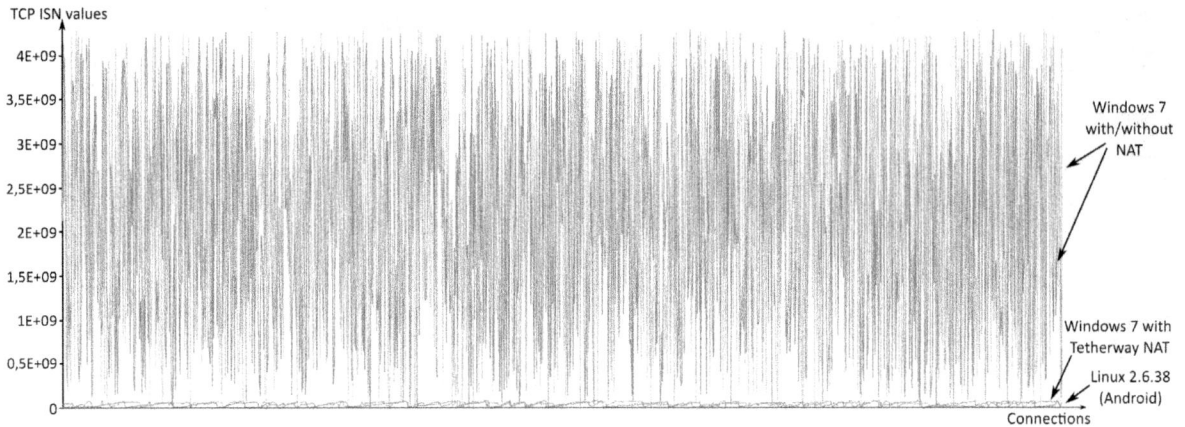

Figure 10: Random distribution of TCP Initial Sequence Number (ISN) values for Windows, Windows behind regular NAT, Linux and Windows behind Tetherway (imitating Linux ISNs)

Fingerprinting and Scrubbing. OS fingerprinting is a general technique to identify remote systems by the difference in their TCP/IP stack implementations [3, 14, 24] and network scanners like Nmap[15] or p0f[16] are widely available.

However, as shown in our analysis, the most common active fingerprinting attacks, which work by sending specially crafted requests to the target, are ineffective in case of tethering detection (cf. Section 3.1). Similarly, most fingerprinting attacks that rely on the modification of header fields often break the affected connection, making them unsuitable for tethering detection by providers.

Multiple works propose normalization or scrubbing of network traffic, such as IP Personality[17], Morph [39] or ipMorph [29]. Network-based normalization has also been proposed to normalize traffic for processing in network intrusion detection systems [26, 15]. The main difference between *Tetherway* and existing solutions is the purpose of normalization, which determines the kind of distributions to imitate and in our case requires, e.g., the use of masked NAT, while defense against active fingerprinting by request is not needed.

Traffic Analysis. Traffic analysis has been used to detect network applications [36], online activities [43], behavior profiles of client systems [42] and properties of the encrypted network, namely routing and flows [13]. Furthermore, it was shown that traffic analysis could yield results even if the transferred packets are encrypted or timing is masked [13, 41, 22, 6]. On the other hand, various countermeasures against traffic analysis have been proposed, ranging from network layer meta-data normalization [38, 40, 27] to efficient application layer obfuscation [23].

We believe that complex traffic analysis attacks are not practical for tethering detection with large customer bases. Instead, we only normalize header fields such as the TCP/IP source ports, which elicit highly characteristic patterns in case of tethering. While we deploy application layer proxies for simple obfuscation of packet timing and connection patterns, we defer a detailed analysis of possible novel attacks and countermeasures for later work.

---

6. CONCLUSION

We have presented the first general analysis and classification of tethering detection techniques. Our analysis indicates that tethering detection is a heuristic, highly fragile process, and many techniques are easily defeated by a modified mobile station.

VPN software can be used as a readily available tool to evade tethering detection, but reduces network performance notably and is easily detected by the mobile provider. In contrast, our Tetherway prototype closely imitates regular non-tethering traffic with modest overhead.

The large amount of potential attacks makes comprehensive precautionary measures impractical. However, given a known specific detection mechanism, additional normalization or obfuscation mechanisms can often be deployed. As a result, we expect that any widespread tethering detection method will quickly be countered through community effort, increasing the development cost at the provider until tethering detection itself is not cost-effective anymore.

For future work, it would be interesting to further investigate the potential and efficiency of traffic analysis in face of basic defenses such as proxies or random packet delays.

7. REFERENCES

[1] 3rd Generation Partnership Project (3GPP). *General Packet Radio Service (GPRS); GPRS Tunnelling Protocol (GTP) across the Gn and Gp interface*, 2011.

[2] 3rd Generation Partnership Project (3GPP). *Mobile Station (MS) - Serving GPRS Support Node (SGSN); Subnetwork Dependent Convergence Protocol (SNDCP)*, 2011.

[3] J. M. Allen. OS and application fingerprinting techniques, 2007.

[4] O. Arkin. ICMP Usage in Scanning. Black Hat Briefings, 2000.

[5] S. M. Bellovin. A technique for counting NATted hosts. In *SIGCOMM Workshop on Internet measurment (IMW)*. ACM, 2002.

[6] L. Bernaille and R. Teixeira. Early Recognition of Encrypted Applications. In *PAM*. Springer, 2007.

[7] R. Beverly. A robust classifier for passive TCP/IP

fingerprinting. In *Passive and Active Network Measurement*. Springer, 2004.

[8] J. Bi, L. Zhao, and M. Zhang. Application presence fingerprinting for NAT-aware router. In *Knowledge-Based Intelligent Information and Engineering Systems*. Springer, 2006.

[9] E. Bursztein. Time has something to tell us about network address translation, 2007.

[10] A. Callado, C. Kamienski, G. Szabo, B. Gero, J. Kelner, S. Fernandes, and D. Sadok. A Survey on Internet Traffic Identification. *Communications Surveys & Tutorials, IEEE*, 11(3):37–52, 2009.

[11] B. X. Chen. AT&T tells free tethering customers it's time to pay up. Wired, 2011.

[12] Cisco Systems. *ASR 5000 Series Enhanced Charging Services Administration Guide Addendum*, 2011.

[13] D. Cousins, C. Partridge, K. Bongiovanni, A. W. Jackson, R. Krishnan, T. Saxena, and W. T. Strayer. Understanding encrypted networks through signal and systems analysis of traffic timing. In *Aerospace Conference*. IEEE, 2003.

[14] F. Gagnon and B. Esfandiari. A hybrid approach to operating system discovery based on diagnosis. *Int. J. Network Mgmt.*, 21(2):106–119, 2011.

[15] M. Handley, V. Paxson, and C. Kreibich. Network intrusion detection: Evasion, traffic normalization, and end-to-end protocol semantics. In *USENIX Security*, 2001.

[16] P. Horowitz. AT&T cracking down on unofficial iPhone tethering & MyWi users. OSXDaily, 2011.

[17] V. Jacobson, R. Braden, and D. Borman. TCP Extensions for High Performance. RFC 1323, 1992.

[18] W. John, S. Tafvelin, and T. Olovsson. Passive Internet Measurement: Overview and Guidelines based on Experiences. *Computer Communications, 33 (5)*, 2010.

[19] C. Johnston. Verizon blocks unlicensed tethering, insists it can charge extra. ArsTechnica, 2011.

[20] H. Kim, K. C. Claffy, M. Fomenkov, D. Barman, M. Faloutsos, and K. Lee. Internet traffic classification demystified: myths, caveats, and the best practices. In *CoNEXT Conference*. ACM, 2008.

[21] A. Klein. OpenBSD DNS cache poisoning and multiple O/S predictable IP ID vulnerability, 2007.

[22] L. Lu, E.-C. Chang, and M. Chan. Website fingerprinting and identification using ordered feature sequences. In *European Symposium on Research in Computer Security (ESORICS)*. Springer, 2010.

[23] X. Luo, P. Zhou, E. W. W. Chan, W. Lee, R. K. C. Chang, and R. Perdisci. HTTPOS: Sealing information leaks with browser-side obfuscation of encrypted flows. In *Network and Distributed Systems Security (NDSS)*. Internet Society, 2011.

[24] G. F. Lyon. Remote os detection via TCP/IP stack fingerprinting. `nmap.org/book/osdetect.html/`, 2011.

[25] G. Maier, F. Schneider, and A. Feldmann. A first look at mobile hand-held device traffic. In *Passive and Active Measurement Conference (PAM 2010)*. Springer, 2010.

[26] G. R. Malan, D. Watson, F. Jahanian, and P. Howell.

Transport and application protocol scrubbing. In *INFOCOM*, 2000.

[27] R. E. Newman, I. S. Moskowitz, P. Syverson, and A. Serjantov. Metrics for traffic analysis prevention. In *Workshop on Privacy Enhancing Technologies (PET)*. Springer, 2003.

[28] T. T. T. Nguyen and G. Armitage. A survey of techniques for internet traffic classification using machine learning. *Communications Surveys & Tutorials, IEEE*, 10(4):56–76, 2008.

[29] G. Prigent, F. Vichot, and F. Harrouet. IpMorph: fingerprinting spoofing unification. *Journal in Computer Virology*, pages 329–342, 2010.

[30] P. Rasmussen. O2 to crack down on iPhone tethering cheats. Fierce Wireless, 2009.

[31] Sandvine. Sandvine tethered device detection solution and service revenue enhancement. Case Study, 2011.

[32] R. Spangler. Analysis of remote active operating system fingerprinting tools. http://www.packetwatch.net, 2003.

[33] P. Srisuresh and K. Egevang. Traditional IP Network Address Translator (Traditional NAT). RFC 3022, 2001.

[34] P. Srisuresh, B. Ford, S. Sivakumar, and S. Guha. NAT Behavioral Requirements for ICMP. RFC 5508, 2009.

[35] K. Straka and G. Manes. Passive detection of nat routers and client counting. In *Advances in Digital Forensics II*. Springer, 2006.

[36] G. Szabo, D. Orincsay, B. P. Gero, S. Gyori, and T. Borsos. Traffic analysis of mobile broadband networks. In *Wireless Internet (WICON)*, 2007.

[37] G. Taleck. Ambiguity resolution via passive OS fingerprinting. In *Recent Advances in Intrusion Detection*. Springer, 2003.

[38] B. R. Venkatraman and R. E. Newman-Wolfe. Transmission schedules to prevent traffic analysis. In *Annual Computer Security Applications Conference (ACSAC)*. IEEE, 1994.

[39] K. Wang. Frustrating OS fingerprinting with Morph. Talk at the fifth HOPE conference, 2004.

[40] C. V. Wright, S. E. Coull, and F. Monrose. Traffic Morphing: An Efficient Defense Against Statistical Traffic Analysis. In *Network and Distributed Systems Security (NDSS)*. Internet Society, 2009.

[41] C. V. Wright, F. Monrose, and G. M. Masson. On Inferring Application Protocol Behaviors in Encrypted Network Traffic. *Journal of Machine Learning Research*, 7:2745–2769, 2006.

[42] K. Xu, Z.-l. Zhang, and S. Bhattacharyya. Profiling internet backbone traffic: Behavior models and applications. In *Applications, technologies, architectures, and protocols for computer communications (SIGCOMM)*. ACM, 2005.

[43] F. Zhang, W. He, X. Liu, and P. G. Bridges. Inferring users' online activities through traffic analysis. In *Wireless network Security (WiSec)*. ACM, 2011.

[44] O. Zheng, J. Poon, and K. Beznosov. Application-based TCP hijacking. In *European Workshop on System Security (EUROSEC)*. ACM, 2009.

Wireless Security Techniques for Coordinated Manufacturing and On-line Hardware Trojan Detection

Sheng Wei   Miodrag Potkonjak
Computer Science Department
University of California, Los Angeles (UCLA)
Los Angeles, CA 90095
{shengwei, miodrag}@cs.ucla.edu

ABSTRACT

This paper addresses the hardware Trojan (HT) attacks that impose severe threats to the security and integrity of wireless networks and systems. We first develop HT attack models by embedding a single HT gate in the target design that triggers advanced malicious attacks. We place the one-gate HT trigger in such a way that it exhibits rare switching activities, consumes ultra-low leakage power, and hides from delay characterizations. Therefore, the HT attack models are capable of bypassing the widely used side channel-based HT detection schemes. Furthermore, based on the HT attack models, we investigate the potential on-line threat models during the system operation and develop an in-field trusted HT detection approach using physical unclonable functions (PUFs). We evaluate the effectiveness of the HT attack and defense models on a set of ISCAS'85, ISCAS'89, and ITC'99 benchmarks.

Categories and Subject Descriptors

K.6.5 [**Management of Computing and Information Systems**]: Security and Protection—*Physical Security*

General Terms

Security

Keywords

Wireless security, hardware Trojan detection, process variation

1. INTRODUCTION

1.1 Motivation

Recently, wireless communication, computation, and sensing devices, such as mobile phones, laptops, and tablets, have been experiencing exceptionally explosive growth. For example, every second more than 30 cell phones are sold

worldwide. In addition, emerging industrial sensor networks are both economically and strategically important. Furthermore, wireless security imposes a technically challenging set of objectives and requirements. For example, side channel and fault induction security attacks [18][19][24][32][41][45] are much more likely on cell phones and, in particular, on sensor nodes that may be deployed in unprotected or even hostile environments. Also, operational conditions and numerous design constraints such as low energy, low power, and low cost impose difficulties on security requirements.

As a consequence, wireless security has emerged as a premier research and development issue. Numerous important aspects have been addressed, such as key management schemes in mobile ad hoc networks [12] and distributed sensor networks [16], secure routing protocols [7] and localization algorithms [26] to prevent wireless sensor attacks, and privacy protection in RFID systems [34]. However, none of these important contributions address the detection of hardware Trojans (HTs) [22][40]. HTs are in a sense the most powerful way to complete compromise the security any wireless or other devices because they enable the attacker to bypass all application and system software defense mechanisms, to access any storage element, change access rights of any program, and abuse (e.g., induce high energy consumption) or destroy any piece of hardware.

1.2 New Types of Security Attacks

Our starting point is the observation that it is exceptionally easy to hide an arbitrary powerful and large HT inside even a small integrated circuit (IC). All what is required is to place the HT circuitry into power down mode that is enabled by rare input activation signals.

There are three main entities that can be measured on an IC: switching energy, leakage energy, and delay. The attacker may create HTs that either do not have impact or have exponentially low probability of impacting any of these three entities. Taking delay measurements as an example, an unresolved difficulty of timing measurements is the inability of individually sensitizing and characterizing each component using the test vectors. This is because of the existence of parallel routes that reconverge to a single point, which make it difficult to map the measured path delay to a specific path for the consideration of Trojans. As shown in a small example in Figure 1, even though we can measure the delay between input x and output y, we are unable to determine whether the measured delay is for path 1 or path 2. Furthermore, the presence of process variation [6][11][14] would further complicate the case, since the delay of path 1 may be smaller than that of path 2 on one chip but could be larger on another.

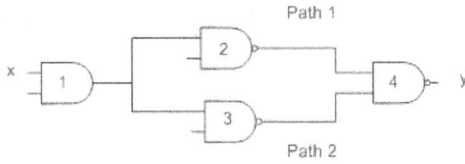

Figure 1: Example of reconvergent path that poses a potential risk for hidden HT attacks.

1.3 Contributions

Our technical contributions include the following.

1. We have invented techniques for creation of new types of exceptionally powerful HTs that are difficult to detect. The key idea is to use power (or clock) gating in such a way that in default mode the HT is placed in power down mode. The HT is activated by a single gate (e.g., an AND gate) that has an output rarely switched to value one (i.e., the activation condition) by anybody except the attacker. The gate is intentionally aged or implemented so to have very high threshold voltage that corresponds to ultra exponentially low leakage energy, which cannot be detected even by the most advanced state-of-the art energy measurement instruments. Therefore, it cannot be detected by any techniques that measures switching and/or energy. Finally, the HT is placed in such a way that it does not have any impact on delays between any two pairs of flip-flops. The HT is activated by an input vector sequence that is known by the attacker but otherwise has exponentially low probability of occurrence.

2. Coordinated manufacturing and in-field testing for HT detection. For the first time it is proposed that results from manufacturing time testing and in-field testing are combined and coordinated. Manufacturing testing provides golden standard measurements for scenarios where there is no HT or it is not activated. Hence, on-line in-field testing for activated HTs can be easily accomplished.

3. Employment of physical unclonable function (PUF) for secure testing. Man-in-the-middle attacks are among the most effective ways to compromise numerous security techniques. We use PUFs combined with random challenges to ensure that the attacker must report measurements that are actually done at the system-under-test at a specified moment.

4. Use of global position signals (GPS) signal to reduce communication and energy cost. To the best of our knowledge this is the first time that GPS is used for testing and HT detection purposes. It is also the first scheme that uses GPS signal to reduce the communications of random challenges.

5. Low energy yet comprehensive HT testing. Privileged information (e.g., passwords) is often data of the highest importance. A sophisticated HT may be enabled and disabled to further complicate their detection. Finally, any wireless security should induce very low energy expenditures. We simultaneously resolve these three requirements, by invoking HT testing only when gates that are associated with storing privileged information are activated and by finding low power HT test vectors.

2. RELATED WORK

In this section, we summarize the related work on hardware Trojan and its detection. We start with introducing the research efforts on process variation, which is considered as the dominant source of challenges for HT detection attempts. Then, we discuss the existing HT detection approaches with emphasis on the major differences in our contributions.

2.1 Process Variation

Process variation (PV) in IC manufacturing is the deviation of IC parameter values from nominal specifications, due to the nature of the manufacturing process [6][11][14] It is observed that PV is caused by the inability to precisely control the fabrication process at small-feature technologies [35]. For example, the lithographic lens aberrations result in systematic errors on transistor sizes, and dopant density fluctuations impose random variations on design parameters. Also, PV has impact on various levels of the IC properties, including wafer-level, die-level, and wafer-die interaction [37]. Consequently, PV is an unavoidable technological phenomenon of all deep submicron and nano IC realization technologies. The main PV ramification is that each device (e.g., gate, transistor, and interconnect) of the same design has different manifestational characteristics (e.g., delay or static power) on different integrated circuits (ICs). These device level characteristics have profound impact on the overall IC characteristics. For example, the operational speed may easily differ by more than 30% from nominal and leakage by factors of 20X [11].

Besides its direct impact on the physical or manifestational properties of ICs, PV is also considered as a major source of risk for hardware-based attacks, because the observable variations caused by the malicious hardware components can be easily attributed to the consequence of PV. It is difficult to identify the source of the variation and determine whether it is from the naturally existed PV or from malicious modifications to the design. Based on these thoughts, several research efforts have been made to characterize and quantify the impact of PV at the gate-level (i.e., gate-level characterization, or GLC) in a non-destructive way [4][5][42][44][43][47] . The scaling factors of the IC key parameters due to PV can be determined by measuring the properties of the entire circuit and solving a set of linear equations.

2.2 Hardware Trojan Detection

Hardware Trojan detection has become an active research area as the increasing trend of IC outsourcing conducted by the IC design companies to increase their revenue. Since DARPA issued its first call for the study of hardware systems security and, in particular, hardware Trojans in 2005, more than a hundred related security techniques have been proposed and evaluated.

Agrawal et al. [2] introduced the hardware Trojan problem and proposed the first HT detection approach using fingerprints generated from IC side channels. Thereafter, a large number of HT detection methods have been proposed, which can be classified into two categories. First, functional test-based HT detection simulates a set of test input vectors and verifies the correctness of the outputs. Researchers have proposed a variety of methods to generate the test input vectors with a goal of maximizing the probability of detection

[8][49]. Second, HT detection techniques using side channel-based analysis have been developed recently. These methods monitor the variations caused by HTs in representative IC properties, such as leakage power [3][42][44][46], switching power [2][9], delay [21][27], or a combination of the properties [23].

Despite the research efforts in various side channel-based HT detection methods, the current HT detection schemes did not consider the cases where the attacker is well aware of the detection techniques. The attacker may tend to minimize the variations in the well known side channels caused by HTs, or attribute them to process variation. We discuss and develop the advanced attack and defense strategies in this paper and showcase their applicability to secure wireless systems.

3. PRELIMINARIES

In this section, we first introduce the power and delay models that are used to quantify the gate-level manifestational properties for HT detection. Then, we discuss the IC aging model that we employ in the design and implementation of our approaches.

3.1 Power Models

Leakage power and switching power have been considered as two major side channels for the observations of HT behaviors. We refer to the leakage power model presented by Markovic et al. [29] for the creation of our leakage power-based HT model. Equation (1) shows the leakage power of a logic gate based on several physical level IC parameters, where W is gate width, L is gate length, V_{th} is threshold voltage, V_{dd} is supply voltage, n is subthreshold slope, μ is mobility, C_{ox} is oxide capacitance, D is clock period, ϕ_t is thermal voltage $\phi_t = kT/q$, and σ is drain induced barrier lowering (DIBL) factor.

$$P_{leakage} = 2 \cdot n \cdot \mu \cdot C_{ox} \cdot \frac{W}{L} \cdot (\frac{kT}{q})^2 \cdot D \cdot V_{dd} \cdot e^{\frac{\sigma \cdot V_{dd} - V_{th}}{n \cdot (kT/q)}} \quad (1)$$

We observe from Equation (1) that the leakage power of a logic gate depends on the threshold voltage (V_{th}) in a non-linear manner. In particular, if one can increase the V_{th}, either in the pre-silicon or post-silicon stage, the leakage power would decrease exponentially. This phenomenon provides attackers with a means of embedding ultra-low power components in the target circuit for HT attacks.

The gate-level switching energy model [29] is described by Equation (2), where α is the switching probability.

$$P_{switching} = \alpha \cdot C_{ox} \cdot W \cdot L \cdot V_{dd}^2 \quad (2)$$

Equation (2) indicates that the total switching power consumed by a logic gate during the IC operation is an accumulated value based on its switching activity. Therefore, one possible way of decreasing the switching power is to limit the number of switches, which can be achieved by controlling the input vectors of the circuit.

3.2 Delay Model

The delay of a single logic gate can be expressed as

$$d = gh + p \quad (3)$$

where g and h are logical effort and electrical effort, respectively; and p is parasitic delay [38]. In particular, we use the delay model in [29] that connects the gate delay to its sizing and operating voltages:

$$Delay = \frac{k_{tp} \cdot k_{fit} \cdot L^2}{2 \cdot n \cdot \mu \cdot \phi_t^2} \cdot \frac{V_{dd}}{(ln(e^{\frac{(1+\sigma)V_{dd} - V_{th}}{2 \cdot n \cdot \phi_t}} + 1))^2} \quad (4)$$
$$\cdot \frac{\gamma_i \cdot W_i + W_{i+1}}{W_i}$$

where subscripts i and $i+1$ represent the the driver and load gates, respectively; γ is the ratio of gate parasitic to input capacitance; and k_{tp} and k_{fit} are fitting parameters.

3.3 IC Aging Model

Phenomena such as hot carrier injection (HCI) and in particular negative-bias temperature instability (NBTI) are causing significant alterations of both delay and leakage characteristics of a gate. For example, aging can increase delay by 10% and leakage energy by several times [1]. For the discussion in this paper, we refer to the NBTI aging model presented by Chakravarthi et al. [13], as shown in the Equation (5):

$$\Delta V_{th} = A \cdot exp(\beta V_G) \cdot exp(-E_\alpha/kT) \cdot t^{0.25} \quad (5)$$

where V_G is the applied gate voltage; A and β are constants; E_α is the measured activation energy of the NBTI process; T is the temperature; and t is the stress time. The aging effect provides a method to increase the threshold voltage of a logic gate in the post-silicon stage regardless of the impact of PV. Considering the leakage power introduced by Equation (1), we consider aging as a convenient means for attackers to create ultra-low leakage HTs that are difficult to detect.

4. HARDWARE TROJAN ARCHITECTURE AND PLACEMENT

4.1 Hardware Trojan Architecture

As the first step toward the wireless security analysis, we design a HT placement model that complicates the detection of embedded HTs in wireless systems. Our observation is that the existing side channel-based HT detection techniques check the exposure of HTs in terms of their manifestational characteristics, such as power and delay. Therefore, in the design of HT attack models, our goal is to minimize the possible variations caused by HTs in all aspects of their manifestational properties. Figure 2 shows the overall architecture of the designed HT model. We use only one single gate as the trigger of the malicious circuitry in order to minimize the observable variations in the original design. The one-gate HT trigger would activate the malicious circuitry only when a rare condition is satisfied, such as a specific combination of input signals. During the normal system operation when the activation condition is not satisfied, the embedded malicious circuitry is under the power off mode, in which it does not consume switching or leakage power nor observable through delay measurements. In this way, we are able to embed a malicious circuitry that is unobservable via all three most widely used manifestational properties, namely switching power, leakage power, and delay. Furthermore, the attacker would induce the wireless system to apply the rare activation condition only once during its life time and activate the security attack.

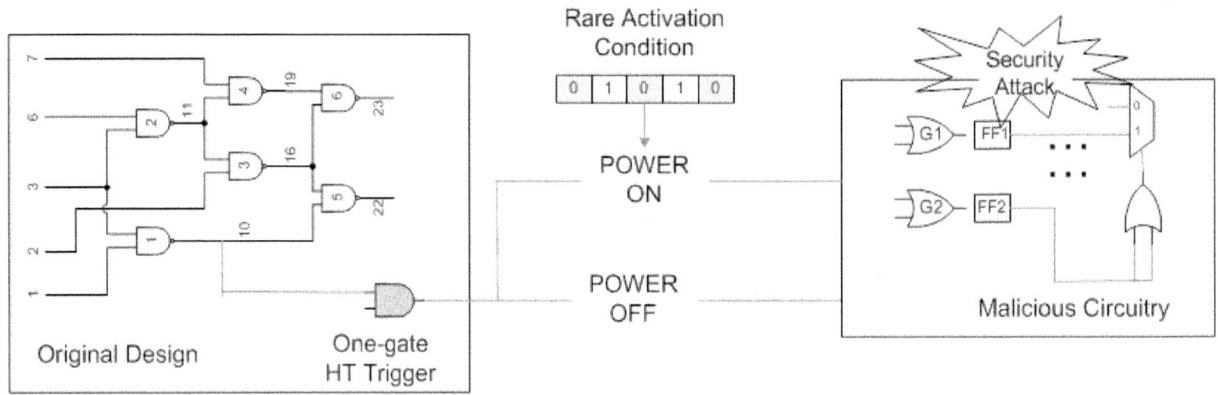

Figure 2: Overall architecture of the hardware Trojan attack.

4.2 Hardware Trojan Placement

The goal in HT placement, from the attacker's perspective, is to hide the HTs in the target IC in terms of the side channels that are commonly monitored in the HT detection schemes. We investigate three widely used IC properties, namely switching power, leakage power, and delay, and develop a HT placement strategy for each case that composes a challenging attack, especially when deployed in a wireless system that operates in an on-line environment. In particular, we have developed the following three HT placement models:

First, based on switching power, we place a HT at a rare switching location in the target design, so that it has an extremely low probability of switching during the normal IC operation. However, the HT can be switched by a certain set of input vector to activate the malicious circuitry.

Second, regarding leakage power, we create ultra-low leakage HTs by intentionally aging the HT to increase the threshold voltage and thus decrease the leakage power exponentially. We determine the input vectors for aging the HT gate using a Boolean satisfiability (SAT)-based approach.

Third, to complicate the timing-based HT detection, we identify the reconvergent paths in the target circuit and intentionally place the HT in one of them. Consequently, even though delay can still be measured, it is difficult for the HT detection method to determine which one of the reconvergent paths is being measured.

4.2.1 Rare Switching HT Placement

In the rare switching-based HT placement, our goal is to find the locations in the design where the gates have the least switching activities during the normal system operation. Meanwhile, those locations for HT placement must be switchable by a certain small set of input vectors, which can be used to activate the malicious circuitry.

In order to find the best location for low switching HTs, our intuition is that the switching activity of a specific gate depends on two factors: (1) the switching probability of its transitive fan-in gates; and (2) the correlation of the switching patterns of its transitive fan-in gates. Here we define correlation as the probability that two or more gates switch at the same time. Therefore, our idea is to create a HT gate and feed it with the outputs of the rare switching and highly correlated gates. We first conduct simulations on the target circuit using a set of random input vectors to find

the least switching gate and add it to a candidate group. Next, we iteratively add to the candidate group one more gate, which is most correlated with the existing gates in the group and has the least switching activity. In particular, the one specific gate that we add in each iteration is determined approximately by the sibling gate of the existing gates in the candidate group that switches the most rarely. Furthermore, in each iteration, we initiate a SAT solving procedure (discussed in details in Section 4.2.2) and ensure that there exists at least one pair of input vectors that can switch the embedded HT and thus trigger the malicious circuitry.

4.2.2 Low Leakage HT Creation

We employ IC aging technique to create a HT gate that consumes ultra low leakage power. In particular, during or after the IC manufacturing process, we intentionally stress the HT gate so that its threshold voltage can be increased and, by following Equation (1), the leakage power would decrease exponentially. In particular, the method we use for aging a set of gates in the circuit is by setting the gates in the stress mode (i.e., signal 1). According to the aging model discussed in Section 3, there is a speed-up in V_{th} increase due to the stress. We use a SAT-based approach to select the input vectors that set the specific set of gates under stress.

SAT is a problem that determines if a set of variables can be assigned to satisfy a boolean formula. In the IC domain, if the netlist of a circuit is known, the signal of each gate can be expressed as a boolean formula with a set of primary input signals as the variables. Therefore, the input vector selection problem that aims to set a specific gate or a set of gates to specific signals can be naturally converted to a SAT problem. By solving the SAT problem, we can provably find the desirable input vectors based on our requirements regarding the gates signals.

SAT has been proved as one of the first known examples of NP-Complete problems. Recently there have been many SAT solvers developed in the SAT community [15] that deliver fast and accurate SAT solutions. In our SAT problem formulation, we use an objective file to specify the signals of a subset of gates that we are obtaining input vectors for. The gates that are not included in the objective file will be assumed as don't-care in the SAT solving process. In particular, the objectives in the SAT problem follow the following format:

$$obj_i = 0|1, i = 1...k \tag{6}$$

where obj_i is corresponding to a gate id in the circuit netlist, and k is the number of gates we expect to specify signal 0 or 1. If the SAT problem is satisfiable, the SAT solver provides a list of input vectors that satisfies the objectives.

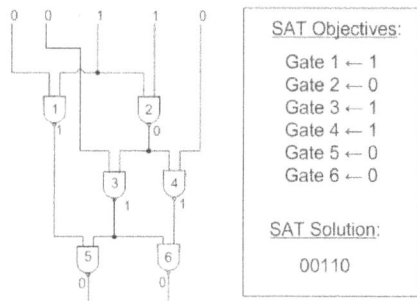

Figure 3: Example of SAT formulation for aging input vector selection. The output from the SAT solver provides the input vectors that satisfy the objectives.

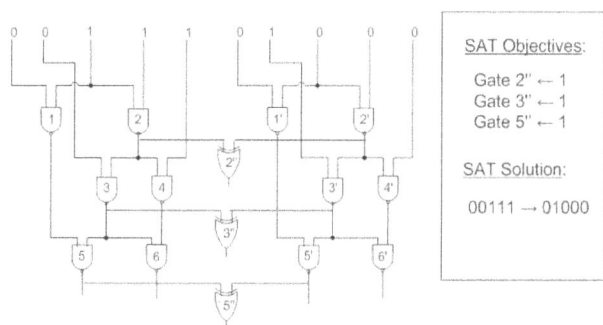

Figure 4: Example of SAT problem formulation for finding input vectors that switch a specific set of gates (e.g., gates 2, 3, and 5).

We demonstrate the SAT problem formulation using a small example in Figure 3. For the clarity of discussion, we consider only a small circuit with 6 NAND gates. In this example, we set gates 2, 5, and 6 to signal 0 and gates 1, 3, and 4 to signal 1, which we specify in the objective file. The SAT solver outputs input vector 00110 that satisfy the specified objectives.

Furthermore, we notice that a variation of the aforementioned SAT formulation method can be used to determine the input vectors that switch a gate in a specific way. In order to accomplish this, we first duplicate the target circuit and generate a "dual-circuit", where every gate in the original design has a duplicated counterpart in the dual section. As shown in Figure 4, each gate i now has a counterpart gate i' in the dual section of the circuit. Then, for each gate i that we want to determine switching input vector for, we add a two-input XOR gate i'' and feed it with the outputs of gates i and i'. The reason why we use a XOR gate is that its output can serve as an indicator of whether gate i switches or not. In other words, if we assume that the original section of the dual circuit represents the status as of clock cycle t, and the dual section represents that of clock cycle $t+1$, we claim that the output signal of the XOR gate i'' is 1 if and only if gate i switches from clock cycle t to $t+1$. There-

fore, by specifying the input signals of the added XOR gates in Equation (6), we have found a method to determine the input vectors for a specific switching pattern.

Pseudocode 1 Backtracking algorithm for reconvergence identification.

Input: Netlist Net; Primary input PI; Primary output PO;
Ouput: A set of Paths P between PI and PO;
1: $curNode \leftarrow PI$;
2: push $curNode$ into stack s;
3: **repeat**
4:    $curNode \leftarrow PI$;
5:    **for** each node in in $curNode's$ inputs **do**
6:       **if** n is not visited **then**
7:          mark in as visited;
8:       **end if**
9:       **if** $in \neq PI$ **then**
10:         continue;
11:       **else**
12:         $curNode \leftarrow in$;
13:         **if** $curNode$ is not a primary input in Net **then**
14:            push $curNode$ to s;
15:            mark $curNode$ as visited;
16:         **else if** $curNode == PI$ **then**
17:            push $curNode$ to s;
18:            mark $curNode$ as visited;
19:            push all the nodes in s to P;
20:            $curNode \leftarrow pop(s)$;
21:            Continue;
22:         **else**
23:            mark $curNode$ as visited;
24:            $curNode \leftarrow top(s)$;
25:         **end if**
26:       **end if**
27:    **end for**
28:    mark $top(s)$ as unvisited;
29:    $pop(s)$;
30:    $curNode \leftarrow top(s)$;
31: **until** s is empty
32: **return** P;

4.2.3 Delay Testing and HT Placement

To prevent the embedded HT from being detected by timing-based approach, an attacker may consider placing the HT in one of the reconvergent paths, with which there are one or more other paths that are in parallel. In this case, it is difficult for the defender to determine which one of the parallel path has been measured and thus malicious modifications to the parallel paths can be well hidden from the delay monitoring.

Assuming that the netlist of the target circuit is a directed graph G, with each pin as an edge $e_i \in E$, and each gate (or input, output) as a node $n_i \in N$, we have the following definition for a reconvergence point on the circuit:

Definition 1. Reconvergence Point. A node $n_i \in N$ in netlist G is a reconvergence point if and only if the in-degree of n_i is larger than 1.

Pseudocode 1 shows the algorithm that we use to find reconvergence points in the target design. We conduct a depth-first search from the specific output PO toward the inputs. During this process, we keep pruning the edges using backtracking to trace all the possible paths toward a specific input PI. If there are more path in between PI and PO, we regard these paths as the possible locations where HT can embedded to bypass the timing-based HT detection.

4.3 Summary

The aforementioned three one-gate HT models greatly complicate the HT detection attempts. If the attacker intentionally places the HT at a location that combines all three types of attack models, an effective detection approach is hardly feasible unless the malicious circuitry that is triggered by the one-gate HT is activated. Therefore, by leveraging the one-gate HT models, an attacker may force the target of HT detection techniques to move from regular post-silicon testing to the system operation period after the IC is released. Therefore, the costs and difficulty level of conducting HT detection is greatly increased due to the one-gate HT models.

5. ON-LINE HARDWARE TROJAN ATTACK AND DEFENSE

During the system operation, the attacker must trigger and power up the malicious circuitry in order to activate the HT attack. Once the malicious circuitry is activated, one can easily detect the abnormality, since the malicious circuitry often contains a large number of gates as well as complicated structures in order to accomplish advanced security attacks, such as leaking confidential information or making the device malfunction. However, it is still possible for the attacker to manipulate the behavior of the wireless system to further bypass the on-line security checks after the activation of malicious circuitry. In this section, we discuss the possible mechanisms that an attacker may leverage to conduct on-line HT attacks and propose the corresponding defense methods.

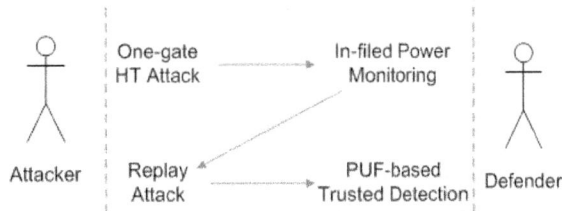

Figure 5: On-line attack and defense model.

5.1 Attack and Defense Models

Figure 5 demonstrates the attack and defense models after the HT-embedded wireless system enters the operation mode. The attacker would activate the malicious circuitry by inducing the system to run an application that satisfies the rare activation condition. Then, as a method of defense, the defender would sample and monitor the power profile of the remote wireless system and observe the variations that may be caused by the activation of the malicious circuitry. However, it is possible for the attacker to conduct a more advanced attack, namely replay attack, that tricks the on-line monitoring scheme with outdated power profiles that do not reflect any variations caused by the malicious circuitry. In order to resolve the replay attack, we develop a

PUF-based trusted HT detection technique that authenticates each sample of power profile with specific time and location information and, therefore, any attempts to report replayed power profiles would be detected.

Pseudocode 2 In-field power monitoring for detecting one-gate HT attack during system operation.

1: Designer implements a test trigger into the design that monitors the activity of the privileged area for security attacks;
2: Attacker embeds the HT gate and the malicious circuitry in the wireless system;
3: The wireless system passes post-silicon test, since the malicious circuitry powered off;
4: The wireless system starts operating;
5: Defender collects power profile during the initialization period as the baseline profile;
6: The wireless system operates normally for a period of time t;
7: Attacker triggers the one-gate HT and activates the malicious circuitry;
8: The test trigger activates the power meter to measure the power profile and reports it to defender;
9: Defender observes abnormal variation in power profile caused by the activated malicious circuitry;
10: Defender terminates the operation of the wireless system that is under HT attack;

5.2 On-line HT Detection by In-field Power Measurements

During the operation mode of the wireless system when the malicious circuitry can be possibly activated, we employ in-field power metering techniques [20][28][36] to keep track of the power profile. The micro power meter that is integrated into the wireless system is capable of measuring the real-time power profiles and reporting to the remote administrator for further assessment. In order to reduce the cost of conducting such power measurements, we employ a test trigger gate to monitor the activity of the privileged area in the design. The test trigger is activated and the power meter starts measuring the power profile only when the privileged area is suspected to be attacked. When this situation occurs, the power profile data is sent to the administrator for further analysis to confirm the existence of HT attacks. Pseudocode 2 describes the detailed procedure of in-field power measurements for HT detection. The power meter in the wireless system first collects a set of power samples at the beginning of the system operation, which can serve as a baseline for the normal power profile. Once the test trigger gate is activated, the administrator would be able to collect instant power profiles from the power meter and determine whether there is any HT attack being conducted. We consider the variation of power profile as an indicator of HT attack, since the activated malicious circuitry would consume a relatively large amount of power and cause a surge in the leakage power profile compared to the baseline.

5.3 On-line Replay Attack

We note that the straightforward HT detection technique via in-field power profiling can still be bypassed by the attacker. For example, it is possible that the attacker conducts replay attack [39], in which a set of normal leakage power profiles are pre-recorded and reported to the monitoring system constantly. Pseudocode 3 illustrates a typical case of replay attack, which results in the failure of detection. Note that the attacker may start or terminate the replay procedure at any time, or vary the power profile considering environmental factors and the workload on the wireless system to generate more trustworthy power reports.

Pseudocode 3 On-line replay attack that bypasses the in-field power sampling approach.

1: Attacker embeds the HT gate and the malicious circuitry in the wireless system;
2: The wireless system passes post-silicon test as the malicious circuitry is powered off;
3: Defender enables the on-line in-field power profiling process;
4: The wireless system starts operating;
5: The wireless system operates normally for a period of time t;
6: Attacker records the power profiles f_t within the time period t;
7: The wireless system starts responding with power profiles f_t anytime when there is a profiling request;
8: Attacker triggers the one-gate HT and activates the malicious circuitry;
9: Defender observes normal power profile f_t constantly;
10: The wireless system is compromised by the activated malicious circuitry;

5.4 Trusted HT Detection Using Physical Unclonable Functions

Considering the possible on-line replay attack, we develop a trusted HT detection approach based on the use of physically unclonable functions (PUFs) [17][30] . A PUF is a specially designed circuitry in which the prediction of output signals from known inputs is computationally infeasible, unless one has access to the netlist of the circuitry and conduct simulations. Figure 6 shows a sample PUF design, where the complexity of determining the output vectors grows exponentially as the increase of the number of levels in the design. Since there is a huge difference between the simulation time (e.g., in the magnitude of nanoseconds) and the prediction time (e.g., in the magnitude of seconds) for obtaining the output signals, PUFs can be used as a security key for identity authentications in many applications [10][31][33][48].

However, a direct use of PUF with randomly generated challenge bits cannot resolve the replay attack, since we must ensure that the collected power profile in the monitoring process are those generated from the specific sensor at the specific time frame. This requires us to associate each sample with both time and location information and take into consideration of the (time, location, power) triplets at the checking time. For the time stamp, we leverage the secure navigation signals that can be received synchronously from integrated GPS systems [25] at both the remote wireless

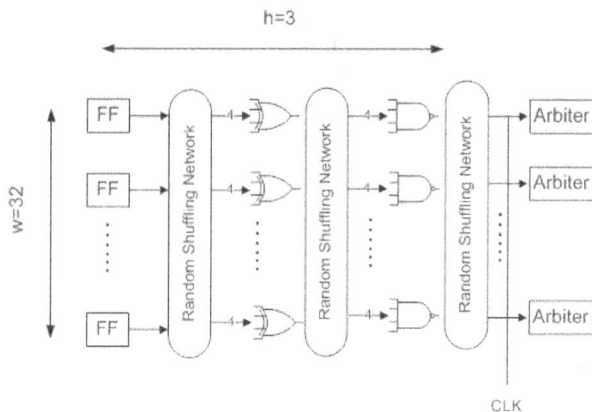

Figure 6: PUF architecture.

system and the local administration site. For the identification of sensors, we leverage the fact that each PUF exhibits different delay characteristics due to process variation. Consequently, the output signals are different for the PUFs on different sensors, since they are highly dependent on the accumulated delay at each level of the design. Figure 7 shows our design of the PUF system for resolving the replay attack toward the remote wireless system.

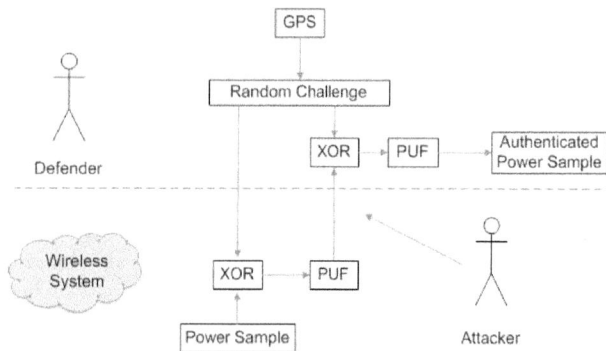

Figure 7: PUF-based trusted HT detection.

6. EXPERIMENTAL RESULTS

We evaluate our HT attack and detection models on a set of ISCAS'85, ISCAS'89, and ITC'99 benchmarks. We model the process variations of the designs following the Gaussian distribution presented in [6] and the quad-tree model presented in [14].

We first examine the effectiveness of the one-gate HT placement by observing the resulting switching activities, leakage power reductions, as well as the number of the delay-unobservable gates due to reconvergent paths. Then, we evaluate the PUF-based trusted HT detection scheme by checking the randomness of the output bits.

6.1 Rare Switching-based HT

Table 1 shows our simulation results regarding rare switching-based HT placement. We select 5 groups of fan-in gates for the one-gate HT (e.g., an AND gate), with up to 10 gates in each group. Our algorithm ensures that the groups of gates, which serve as the fan-in gates of the one-gate HT, would result in rare switching activities of the HT gate. Meanwhile, we ensure that the HT can be switched by a certain set of input vectors to activate the malicious circuitry, which is proved by the solution of the SAT problem. We simulate the switching probability of the HT gate using 5,000 pairs of randomly generated input vectors. The results show that we obtain less than 0.50% switching probabilities of the HT gate in all the benchmark circuits, which is considered very low and difficult to observe by the switching power-based detection. Therefore, our results indicate that the attacker can leverage the rare but non-zero switching activities to activate the HT during the operation of the wireless system, since the one-gate HT is difficult to detect before the actual activation of the malicious circuitry.

6.2 Low Leakage-based HT

Table 2 shows the simulation results of leakage power reduction by intentionally aging the HT gate. For each benchmark circuit, we select three input vectors that would stress the HT gate as well as a minimum number of other gates in the circuit using the SAT-based approach. Then, we apply each input vector to the circuit for a certain amount of time so that the threshold voltages of the stressed gates can be increased by 10% due to aging. We simulate the leakage power reduction of both the HT gate and the entire circuit, by following the leakage power model (i.e., Equation (1)). The results indicate that the selected input vectors can reduce the leakage power of the HT gate by more than 80% in all the tested circuits, while the leakage power reduction of the entire circuit is much less (below 35%). This enables the ultra-low leakage HT to easily hide under measurement errors or process variations.

6.3 Delay Testing and Placement

Figure 8 shows our simulation results on ISCAS'85, IS-CAS'89, and ITC'99 benchmarks regarding the gates that cannot be characterized by using delay as the side channel due to reconvergences. The only possibility to conduct delay characterization is that there is no reconvergence from a specific input to a specific output in the design [1]. We observe that there is a large number of the gates (at least 40%) that are subject to reconvergences and thus are uncharacterizable using non-destructive delay measurements, leaving a large portion of the circuit under the risk of HT insertion. An attacker may easily search in the circuit for reconvergent paths using Pseudocode 1 and embed the one-gate HT in one of the reconvergent paths to bypass security checks.

6.4 PUF-based On-line In-field Detection

In order to evaluate the PUF-based in-field HT detection method, we simulate the implemented PUF design using random challenge bits and observe for the randomness of the output signals. Our idea is that if the output signals are random (i.e., in the optimal case, with 50% probability being 1 and 50% being 0), the prediction attempt within any reasonable amount of time will fail, under the consideration that the complexity of prediction grows exponentially with the number of output pins. Figure 9 shows our simulation

---

[1]Note that the delay characterization is applicable to certain cases of reconvergences, where all paths except the path being tested can be fixed to a certain signal value using SAT. This is out of the scope of this paper.

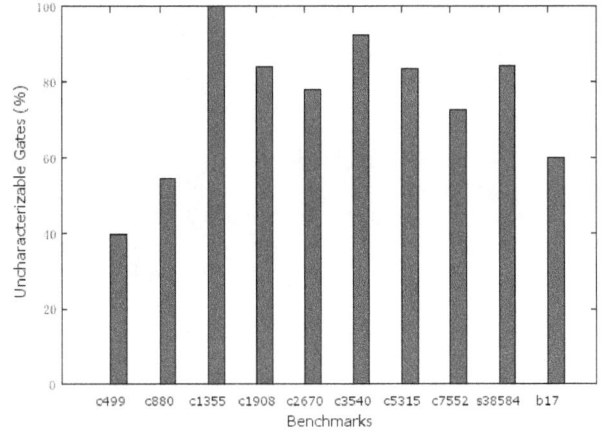

Figure 8: Simulation results regarding delay-uncharacterizable gates due to reconvergences. The high percentage of uncharacterizable gates in each benchmark circuit indicates that there is a large number of candidate locations for embedding the one-gate HT that is difficult to detect using delay-based approaches.

results, where we observe probabilities of signal 1 for all the output pins close to the optimal probability (50%).

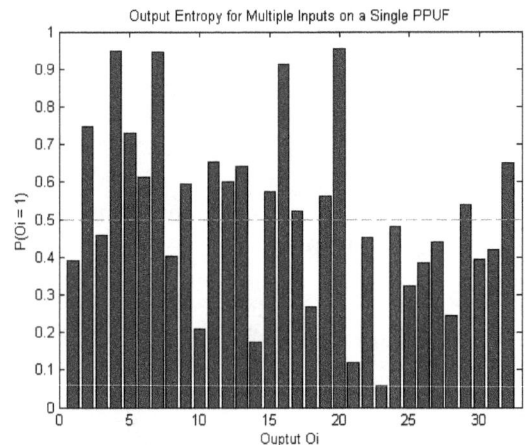

Figure 9: The probability of output bit O_i being 1 in the PUF (w=32, h=3) following the architecture in Figure 6. The probabilities of all output pins are close to the baseline probability (0.5) for a completely random prediction.

7. CONCLUSION

We have developed three one-gate hardware Trojan attack models that can bypass the widely used side channel-based HT detection schemes and pose threats on the security of wireless systems. In particular, the HT models leverage a single HT trigger that exhibits rare switching activities, consumes ultra-low leakage power, and hides from delay characterizations due to reconvergent paths. We showed that the proposed one-gate HT models are capable of compromising

Table 1: Switching probabilities of the embedded HT gate, which are evaluated using simulations with 5000 pairs of random input vectors. For each benchmark, we obtain 5 candidate groups and up to 10 gates in each group that can serve as the transitive fan-in's of the HT gate. Furthermore, the HT gate has been proven by SAT to be switchable by at least one pair of input vectors.

Benchmark	# Gates	# Inputs	# Outputs	Switching Probability of the HT Gate (%)
C499	202	41	32	0.04
C880	383	60	26	0.12
C1355	546	41	32	0.32
C1908	880	33	25	0.20
C2670	1193	233	140	0.04
C3540	1669	50	22	0.12
C5315	2307	178	123	0.32
C6288	2416	32	32	0.04
C7552	3512	207	108	0.28

Table 2: Leakage power reduction of the HT gate and the entire circuit.

Benchmark	# Gates	# Inputs	# Outputs	Leakage Power Reduction of the HT Gate (%)	Leakage Power Reduction of the Entire Circuit (%)
C499	202	41	32	92.2	11.6
C880	383	60	26	95.6	17.2
C1355	546	41	32	97.6	22.9
C1908	880	33	25	93.4	13.5
C2670	1193	233	140	89.7	20.6
C3540	1669	50	22	97.9	32.8
C5315	2307	178	123	98.0	8.8
C6288	2416	32	32	80.3	12.8
C7552	3512	207	108	89.7	21.2

the detection attempts before the activation of the malicious circuitry, forcing effective HT detection to move from post-silicon testing to on-line system operation. Furthermore, we investigated the attack and defense models during the system operation where the malicious circuitry may be triggered by the attacker. We introduced an on-line replay attack model that may be conducted by an attacker, and we developed a PUF-based trusted detection approach to resolve the attack. Simulation results on a set of ISCAS'85, ISCAS'89, and ITC'99 benchmarks verified the effectiveness of the HT attack and detection methods.

8. ACKNOWLEDGEMENTS

This work was supported in part by the NSF under Award CNS-0958369, Award CNS- 1059435, and Award CCF-0926127.

9. REFERENCES

[1] M. Agarwal, B.C. Paul, M. Zhang, and S. Mitra. Circuit failure prediction and its application to transistor aging. In *VLSI Test Symposium (VTS)*, pages 277–286, 2007.

[2] D. Agrawal, S. Baktir, D. Karakoyunlu, P. Rohatgi, and B. Sunar. Trojan detection using IC fingerprinting. In *IEEE Symposium on Security and Privacy (SP)*, pages 296–310, 2007.

[3] Y. Alkabani and F. Koushanfar. Consistency-based characterization for IC Trojan detection. In *International Conference on Computer-Aided Design (ICCAD)*, pages 123–127, 2009.

[4] Y. Alkabani, F. Koushanfar, N. Kiyavash, and M. Potkonjak. Trusted integrated circuits: A nondestructive hidden characteristics extraction approach. In *Information Hiding (IH)*, pages 102–117, 2008.

[5] Y. Alkabani, T. Massey, F. Koushanfar, and M. Potkonjak. Input vector control for post-silicon leakage current minimization in the presence of manufacturing variability. In *Design Automation Conference (DAC)*, pages 606–609, 2008.

[6] A. Asenov. Random dopant induced threshold voltage lowering and fluctuations in sub-0.1 μm MOSFET's: A 3-D "atomistic" simulation study. *IEEE Transactions on Electron Devices*, 45(12):2505–2513, 1998.

[7] B. Awerbuch, D. Holmer, C. Nita-Rotaru, and H. Rubens. An on-demand secure routing protocol resilient to byzantine failures. In *ACM workshop on Wireless security (WiSe)*, pages 21–30, 2002.

[8] M. Banga and M.S. Hsiao. A region based approach for the identification of hardware Trojans. In *IEEE International Workshop on Hardware-Oriented Security and Trust (HOST)*, pages 40–47, 2008.

[9] M. Banga and M.S. Hsiao. VITAMIN: Voltage inversion technique to ascertain malicious insertions in ICs. In *IEEE International Workshop on Hardware-Oriented Security and Trust (HOST)*, pages 104–107, 2009.

[10] N. Beckmann and M. Potkonjak. Hardware-based public-key cryptography with public physically unclonable functions. In *Information Hiding (IH)*, pages 206–220, 2009.

[11] S. Borkar, T. Karnik, S. Narendra, J. Tschanz, A. Keshavarzi, and V. De. Parameter variations and

impact on circuits and microarchitecture. In *Design Automation Conference (DAC)*, pages 338–342, 2003.

[12] S. Capkun, L. Buttyan, and J.-P. Hubaux. Self-organized public-key management for mobile ad hoc networks. *IEEE Transactions on Mobile Computing*, 2(1):52–64, 2003.

[13] S. Chakravarthi, A. Krishnan, V. Reddy, C.F. Machala, and S. Krishnan. A comprehensive framework for predictive modeling of negative bias temperature instability. In *International Reliability Physics Symposium (IRPS)*, pages 273–282, 2004.

[14] B. Cline, K. Chopra, D. Blaauw, and Y. Cao. Analysis and modeling of CD variation for statistical static timing. In *International Conference on Computer-Aided Design (ICCAD)*, pages 60–66, 2006.

[15] N. Een and N. Sorensson. An extensible SAT-solver. In *International Conferences on Theory and Applications of Satisfiability Testing (SAT)*, pages 333–336, 2004.

[16] L. Eschenauer and V. Gligor. A key-management scheme for distributed sensor networks. In *ACM conference on Computer and communications security (CCS)*, pages 41–47, 2002.

[17] B. Gassend, D. Clarke, M. van Dijk, and S. Devadas. Silicon physical random functions. In *ACM Conference on Computer and Communications Security (CCS)*, pages 148–160, 2002.

[18] M. Hicks, M. Finnicum, S. King, M. Martin, and J. Smith. Overcoming an untrusted computing base: Detecting and removing malicious hardware automatically. In *IEEE Symposium on Security and Privacy (SP)*, pages 159–172, 2010.

[19] T. Huffmire, B. Brotherton, G. Wang, T. Sherwood, R. Kastner, T. Levin, T. Nguyen, and C. Irvine. Moats and drawbridges: An isolation primitive for reconfigurable hardware based systems. In *IEEE Symposium on Security and Privacy (SP)*, pages 281–295, 2007.

[20] X. Jiang, P. Dutta, D. Culler, and I. Stoica. Micro power meter for energy monitoring of wireless sensor networks at scale. In *International Conference on Information Processing in Sensor Networks (IPSN)*, pages 186–195, 2007.

[21] Y. Jin and Y. Makris. Hardware Trojan detection using path delay fingerprint. In *IEEE International Workshop on Hardware-Oriented Security and Trust (HOST)*, pages 51–57, 2008.

[22] R. Karri, J. Rajendran, K. Rosenfeld, and M. Tehranipoor. Trustworthy hardware: Identifying and classifying hardware Trojans. *IEEE Computer Magazine*, 43(10):39–46, 2010.

[23] F. Koushanfar and A. Mirhoseini. A unified framework for multimodal submodular integrated circuits Trojan detection. *IEEE Transactions on Information Forensics and Security*, 6(1):162–174, 2011.

[24] F. Koushanfar and M. Potkonjak. CAD-based security, cryptography, and digital rights management. In *Design Automation Conference (DAC)*, pages 268–269, 2007.

[25] M. Kuhn. An asymmetric security mechanism for navigation signals. In *Information Hiding Workshop (IH)*, pages 239–252, 2004.

[26] L. Lazos and R. Poovendran. SeRLoc: secure range-independent localization for wireless sensor networks. In *ACM workshop on Wireless security (WiSe)*, pages 21–30, 2004.

[27] J. Li and J. Lach. At-speed delay characterization for IC authentication and Trojan horse detection. In *IEEE International Workshop on Hardware-Oriented Security and Trust (HOST)*, pages 8–14, 2008.

[28] M. Malinowski, M. Moskwa, M. Feldmeier, M. Laibowitz, and J. Paradiso. CargoNet: a low-cost micropower sensor node exploiting quasi-passive wakeup for adaptive asynchronous monitoring of exceptional events. In *International Conference on Embedded Networked Sensor Systems (SenSys)*, pages 145–159, 2007.

[29] D. Markovic, C.C. Wang, L.P. Alarcon, Tsung-Te Liu, and J.M. Rabaey. Ultralow-power design in near-threshold region. *Proceedings of the IEEE*, 98(2):237–252, 2010.

[30] S. Meguerdichian and M. Potkonjak. Device aging-based physically unclonable functions. In *Design Automation Conference (DAC)*, pages 288–289, 2011.

[31] S. Meguerdichian and M. Potkonjak. Matched public PUF: Ultra low energy security platform. In *International Symposium on Low Power Electronics and Design (ISLPED)*, pages 45–50, 2011.

[32] M. Potkonjak. Synthesis of trustable ICs using untrusted CAD tools. In *Design Automation Conference (DAC)*, pages 633–634, 2010.

[33] M. Potkonjak, S. Meguerdichian, and J.L. Wong. Trusted sensors and remote sensing. In *IEEE Sensors*, pages 1104–1107, 2010.

[34] A. Sadeghi, I. Visconti, and C. Wachsmann. Anonymizer-enabled security and privacy for RFID. In *International Conference on Cryptology and Network Security (CANS)*, pages 134–153, 2009.

[35] S.R. Sarangi, B. Greskamp, R. Teodorescu, J. Nakano, A. Tiwari, and J. Torrellas. VARIUS: A model of process variation and resulting timing errors for microarchitects. *IEEE Transactions on Semiconductor Manufacturing*, 21(1):3–13, 2008.

[36] T. Stathopoulos, D. McIntire, and W.J. Kaiser. The energy endoscope: Real-time detailed energy accounting for wireless sensor nodes. In *International Conference on Information Processing in Sensor Networks (IPSN)*, pages 383–394, 2008.

[37] B.E. Stine, D.S. Boning, and J.E. Chung. Analysis and decomposition of spatial variation in integrated circuit processes and devices. *IEEE Transactions on Semiconductor Manufacturing,*, 10(1):24–41, 1997.

[38] I. Sutherland, B. Sproull, and D. Harris. *Logical effort: designing fast CMOS circuits*. Morgan Kaufmann, 1999.

[39] P. Syverson. A taxonomy of replay attacks. In *Computer Security Foundations Workshop (CSFW)*, pages 187–191, 1994.

[40] M. Tehranipoor and F. Koushanfar. A survey of hardware Trojan taxonomy and detection. *IEEE Design Test of Computers*, 27(1):10–25, 2010.

[41] A. Waksman and S. Sethumadhavan. Silencing hardware backdoors. In *IEEE Symposium on Security and Privacy (SP)*, pages 49–63, 2011.

[42] S. Wei, S. Meguerdichian, and M. Potkonjak. Gate-level characterization: Foundations and hardware security applications. In *Design Automation Conference (DAC)*, pages 222–227, 2010.

[43] S. Wei, S. Meguerdichian, and M. Potkonjak. Malicious circuitry detection using thermal conditioning. *IEEE Transactions on Information Forensics and Security*, 6(3):1136–1145, 2011.

[44] S. Wei and M. Potkonjak. Scalable segmentation-based malicious circuitry detection and diagnosis. In *International Conference on Computer-Aided Design (ICCAD)*, pages 483–486, 2010.

[45] S. Wei and M. Potkonjak. Integrated circuit security techniques using variable supply voltage. In *Design Automation Conference (DAC)*, pages 248–253, 2011.

[46] S. Wei and M. Potkonjak. Scalable consistency-based hardware Trojan detection and diagnosis. In *International Conference on Network and System Security (NSS)*, pages 176–183, 2011.

[47] S. Wei and M. Potkonjak. Scalable hardware Trojan diagnosis. *IEEE Transactions on Very Large Scale Integration (VLSI) Systems*, 2011.

[48] J.B. Wendt and M. Potkonjak. Nanotechnology-based trusted remote sensing. In *IEEE Sensors*, pages 1213–1216, 2011.

[49] F. Wolff, C. Papachristou, S. Bhunia, and R.S. Chakraborty. Towards Trojan-free trusted ICs: Problem analysis and detection scheme. In *Design, Automation and Test in Europe (DATE)*, pages 1362–1365, 2008.

CHECKER: On-site Checking in RFID-based Supply Chains

Kaoutar Elkhiyaoui
EURECOM
2229, route des Cretes
06560 Sophia Antipolis France
elkhiyao@eurecom.fr

Erik-Oliver Blass[*]
College of Computer and
Information Science
Northeastern University
Boston, MA 02115
blass@ccs.neu.edu

Refik Molva
EURECOM
2229, route des Cretes
06560 Sophia Antipolis France
molva@eurecom.fr

ABSTRACT

Counterfeit detection in RFID-based supply chains aims at preventing adversaries from injecting fake products that do not meet quality standards. This paper introduces CHECKER, a new protocol for counterfeit detection in RFID-based supply chains through on-site checking. While RFID-equipped products travel through the supply chain, RFID readers can verify product genuineness by checking the validity of the product's path. CHECKER uses a polynomial-based encoding to represent paths in the supply chain. Each tag T in CHECKER stores an IND-CCA encryption of T's identifier ID and a signature of ID using the polynomial encoding of T's path as secret key. CHECKER is provably secure and privacy preserving. An adversary can neither inject fake products into the supply chain nor trace products. Moreover, RFID tags in CHECKER can be cheap read/write only tags that do not perform any computation. Per tag, only 120 Bytes storage are required.

Categories and Subject Descriptors

H.m [**Information Systems**]: Miscellaneous

General Terms

Security

Keywords

Privacy, RFID, Supply chain management

1. INTRODUCTION

One important application of RFID tags is product tracking and counterfeit detection in supply chains. In such a context, RFID tags are attached to products to enable product tracking along different partners in the supply chain.

In this paper, we propose a solution for genuineness verification based on RFID tags that allows product tracking while protecting the privacy of tags and partners in the supply chain. The main idea is to verify the genuineness of a product by verifying the validity

of the path (sequence of partners) that the product went through in the supply chain as suggested by Blass et al. [4].

However, the solution presented in [4] has two major drawbacks: **1.)** It requires a centralized, trusted party called *"manager"* to carry out the path verification; otherwise, the manager is able to inject fake products into the supply chain. **2.)** The verification can only be performed once the tags arrive at the manager, but not before. This limits the wide deployment of such a solution, especially in a context where partners do not trust each other and demand to be able to verify product genuineness in real-time "on-site".

Contrary to Blass et al. [4], the solution presented in this paper addresses on-site checking by enabling each reader in the supply chain to verify the validity of the path taken by the tag, instead of a global path verification performed by a trusted party that only takes place at the final stage of the supply chain. Though such a solution will allow a faster and a more practical counterfeit detection, it comes with new threats to supply chain security and privacy.

With respect to security, the readers have to be able to verify the genuineness of a product by only reading the tag attached to the product. However, we have to make sure that these readers can by no means succeed in injecting fake products in the supply chain.

Furthermore, a product tracking system must take into account privacy concerns. Any solution that aims at tracking and tracing products is inherently exposed to malicious attacks targeting sensitive information about internal details and strategic relationships in the supply chain. Another requirement is the unlinkability of tags so that a reader in the supply chain must not be able to trace or tell tags apart once they leave its site. Moreover, a reader must not be able to learn any information about the path stored in a tag which has not visited its site.

Also, a secure and privacy preserving RFID-based solution has to be lightweight to allow wide deployment. Ideally, it should be suited to the cheapest RFID tags, i.e., read/write only tags. These tags come only with some re-writable memory and cannot perform any computation, let alone cryptographic operations. Moreover, the path verification at the readers should not be computationally heavy to avoid overloading readers and, thus hindering supply chain performance.

This paper introduces CHECKER, a secure and privacy preserving protocol for on-site genuineness verification and product tracking in supply chains using RFID tags. CHECKER stores in each tag T the tag identifier ID along with a signature of ID. The main idea behind CHECKER is that the secret key used to sign ID is an encoding of the path that T went through, thanks to an original combination of path encoding and signature. By verifying the signature in the tag, each reader thus validates the path taken that far, and by signing the ID the reader updates the path encoding. To protect T's

---

[*]Work done while at EURECOM.

privacy, we encrypt T's ID and ID's signature using elliptic curve Cramer-Shoup encryption [7].

To summarize, CHECKER's main contributions are:

- In contrast to [4], CHECKER does not require a trusted party to perform path verification. Instead, CHECKER allows each reader in the supply chain to individually verify on-site whether a tag went through a valid path or not.

- CHECKER relies only on read/write only tags that are cheap and thus could allow wide deployment of CHECKER. A tag T in CHECKER is not required to perform any computation. T is only required to store its state that will be updated by readers along the supply chain.

- CHECKER is provably secure: an adversary cannot forge new tags. That is, an adversary cannot forge or change a tag T's state to convince a reader in the supply chain that T went through a valid path.

- CHECKER is provably privacy preserving: only readers in the supply chain can verify the validity of paths that tags have taken in the supply chain. Furthermore, an adversary cannot trace or link tags' interactions in the supply chain.

- Finally, CHECKER overcomes some limitations of the formal security and the privacy definitions of [4].

2. BACKGROUND

We use terms and notations in accordance with the ones used by Ouafi and Vaudenay [16] and by Blass et al. [4].

In this paper, the supply chain consists of a set of valid paths: an ordered sequence of steps, i.e., partner sites, that genuine products are allowed to visit.

Now, each read/write only RFID tag is attached to a product and it stores a history of the path that the product has taken. As in [4], each step of the supply chain is equipped with an RFID reader. Each reader reads out the state of tags in its vicinity and checks whether these tags went through a valid path in the supply chain or not. Finally, the reader updates the state of tags accordingly.

2.1 Entities

CHECKER involves the following entities:

Tags T_i: Each tag is attached to a single product or item. Each tag T_i is equipped with a re-writable memory storing T_i's current "state" denoted $s_{T_i}^j$.

Issuer I: The issuer I initializes tags at the beginning of the supply chain. It attaches each tag T_i to a product and writes an initial state $s_{T_i}^0$ into T_i.

Readers R_k: Each reader is associated with a single step in the supply chain. A reader R_k interacts with tags T_i in its range. He reads T_i's current state $s_{T_i}^j$ and based on a set $\mathcal{K}_k^V = \{K_k^1, K_k^2, ..., K_k^{\nu_k}\}$ of ν_k verification keys decides whether T_i went through a valid path or not. Once the verification phase is finished, R_k writes an updated state $s_{T_i}^{j+1}$ into T_i.

2.2 Supply chain

A supply chain is modeled as a digraph $G = (V, E)$, where V is the set of vertexes and E is the set of edges. Each vertex $v_k \in V$ is a step in the supply chain that is uniquely associated with a reader R_k. On the other hand, each edge $e \in E$, $e := \overrightarrow{v_i v_j}$, denotes a valid transition from v_i to v_j. The issuer I is represented in G as being the only vertex with indegree equals to 0 denoted v_0.

A path in a supply chain P is a finite ordered set of steps $P = \{v_0, v_1 ..., v_l\}$, where $\forall i \in \{0, ..., l-1\} : \overrightarrow{v_i v_{i+1}} \in E$, and l is the length of path P.

Naturally, the supply chain contains a set of valid paths P_{valid_i}, which are the set of paths that genuine products are allowed to go through.

Contrary to [4], in this paper we do not assume the existence of a "*manager*" that checks the validity of the path that a product has undertaken. Instead, CHECKER attempts to allow each reader in the supply chain to verify whether the products that it is presented with went through a valid path or not.

2.3 A CHECKER System

A CHECKER system comprises the following:

- A supply chain $G = (V, E)$.

- A set $\mathcal{T}$ of n tags.

- A set of possible states $\mathcal{S}$ that could be stored into tags.

- A set $\mathcal{R}$ of η readers R_k.

- Each reader R_k knows a set $\mathcal{P}_k = \{P_k^1, P_k^2, ..., P_k^{\nu_k}\}$ of ν_k valid paths leading to R_k.

- Also, reader R_k has a set $\mathcal{K}_V^k = \{K_k^1, K_k^2, ..., K_k^{\nu_k}\}$ of ν_k verification keys. Each verification key K_k^j corresponds to a valid path P_k^j.

- Issuer I.

- A set of valid states $\mathcal{S}_{\text{valid}}$. If tag T_i stores a state $s_{T_i}^j \in \mathcal{S}_{\text{valid}}$, then this implies that T_i took a valid path in the supply chain with high probability.

- A function ITERATESUPPLYCHAIN: When called, tags advance by one step in the supply chain and they are read and re-written by readers.

- A function READ : $\mathcal{T} \to \mathcal{S}$ that reads tag T_i and outputs T_i's current state $s_{T_i}^j$.

- A function WRITE: $\mathcal{T} \times \mathcal{S} \to \mathcal{S}$ that writes a new state $s_{T_i}^{j+1}$ into tag T_i.

- A function CHECK: $\mathcal{R} \times \mathcal{T} \to \{0, 1\}$ performed by readers in the supply chain. Based on T_i's current state $s_{T_i}^j$ and the set of verification key $\mathcal{K}_k^V$ of a reader R_k, CHECK decides whether T_i went through a valid path in the supply chain that is leading to R_k or not.

$$\text{CHECK}(R_k, T_i) : \mathcal{S} \to \begin{cases} 1, \text{ if tag } T_i \text{ went through a} \\ \text{valid path } P_k^j \in \mathcal{P}_k \\ \text{or } 0, \text{ if } \nexists\, P_k^j \in \mathcal{P}_k \text{ that matches} \\ T_i\text{'s state.} \end{cases}$$

3. ADVERSARY MODEL

Readers in CHECKER are supposed to read the state stored into tags, check whether the tags took a valid path in the supply chain and then update the tags' states accordingly. We assume that readers' corruption is possible. That is, readers can try tracking tags in order to spy on other readers, as well as injecting fake products in the supply chain.

Moreover, we assume that the issuer I in CHECKER is honest and cannot be corrupt by adversaries. This implies that when tags are initialized at the beginning of the supply chain by I, these tags will definitely meet the supply chain requirements and quality standards. However, these tags may later in the supply chain be corrupt by adversaries.

As CHECKER relies on read/write only tags to implement product tracking, an adversary $\mathcal{A}$ against CHECKER is not only allowed to eavesdrop on tags' communication but to also tamper with tags' internal state. $\mathcal{A}$ can as well have access to the communication between tags and readers and know the steps v_k that a tag T is visiting. He can also monitor a step v_k in the supply chain by eavesdropping on tags going into or leaving the step v_k.

To capture these capabilities in our definitions, an adversary $\mathcal{A}$ has access to the following oracles:

- $\mathcal{O}_{\text{Draw}}(\text{condition})$: When queried with a condition c, $\mathcal{O}_{\text{Draw}}$ randomly selects a tag T from the n tags $\mathcal{T}$ in the supply chain that satisfies the condition c and returns T to $\mathcal{A}$. For example:

  1. To have access to a tag T which just entered the supply chain, i.e., T is at step v_0, $\mathcal{A}$ queries the oracle $\mathcal{O}_{\text{Draw}}$ with condition c = "tag at step v_0".

  2. To have access to a tag T whose identifier is ID, $\mathcal{A}$ calls the oracle $\mathcal{O}_{\text{Draw}}$ with condition c = "tag with identifier ID". $\mathcal{O}_{\text{Draw}}$ returns a tag with identifier ID if there is any.

  3. To have access to a tag T whose next step in the supply chain is step v_k, $\mathcal{A}$ queries the oracle $\mathcal{O}_{\text{Draw}}$ with condition c = "tag's next step is v_k".

  We indicate that adversary $\mathcal{A}$ can query the oracle $\mathcal{O}_{\text{Draw}}$ with any combination of disjunctions or conjunctions of conditions.

- $\mathcal{O}_{\text{Check}}(R_k, T)$: On input of reader R_k and tag T, $\mathcal{O}_{\text{Check}}$ returns the output of the CHECK function performed by reader R_k for tag T.

- $\mathcal{O}_{\text{Step}}(T)$: On input of tag T, the oracle $\mathcal{O}_{\text{Step}}(T)$ returns the *next* step of tag T in the supply chain.

- $\mathcal{O}_{\text{Flip}}(T_0, T_1)$: On input of two tags T_0 and T_1, $\mathcal{O}_{\text{Flip}}$ flips a coin $b \in \{0, 1\}$ and returns tag T_b to $\mathcal{A}$.

- $\mathcal{O}_{\text{Corrupt}}(R_k)$: On input of reader R_k, the oracle $\mathcal{O}_{\text{Corrupt}}$ returns the secret information S_k associated with reader R_k to $\mathcal{A}$. We say that $\mathcal{A}$ corrupted the step v_k associated with reader R_k.

Note that whenever $\mathcal{A}$ is given access to a tag T, $\mathcal{A}$ is allowed to read from T by calling the function READ and to write into T through the function WRITE.

By having access to these oracles, an adversary $\mathcal{A}$ is able **1.)** to corrupt readers, **2.)** to have an arbitrary access to tags, and **3.)** to monitor readers in the supply chain.

3.1 Security

The security goal of CHECKER is to prevent an adversary $\mathcal{A}$ from forging a valid state for a tag T_i that did not go through a valid path in the supply chain. This goal matches the *soundness* property of the CHECK function.

More formally, **if** on input of a of tag T_i and reader R_k, the function $\text{CHECK}(R_k, T_i)$ outputs 1, i.e., there is a path $\mathsf{P}_k^j \in \mathcal{P}_k$ that corresponds to the state s_{T_i} stored into T_i, **then** we conclude that T_i must have gone through P_k^j (with high probability).

It is important to note that when we say that a tag T_i went through path $\mathsf{P} = \overrightarrow{v_0 v_1 ... v_l}$, this means that tag T_i was issued by I and that

the state of T_i has been updated correctly by using the secrets of readers $R_1, R_2, ..., R_l$ in that order. It does not mean that T_i went actually through the steps composing the path P. If we imagine a scenario where an adversary $\mathcal{A}$ knows all the readers' secrets, $\mathcal{A}$ can update the state of any tag T_i and make it look as if T_i went through some path P.

Now, we say that CHECKER is *sound*, if and only if, a reader R_k in the supply chain accepts a tag T_i only when the state of tag T_i has been updated correctly using the secrets of readers in some valid path leading to R_k.

We formalize soundness using an experiment-based definition as in [4]. In this experiment, an adversary $\mathcal{A}$ runs in two phases. First in the learning phase as depicted in Algorithm 1, $\mathcal{A}$ can corrupt up to r readers R_i of his choice by calling the oracle $\mathcal{O}_{\text{Corrupt}}$.

Then, $\mathcal{A}$ is allowed to iterate the supply chain up to ρ times by calling the function ITERATESUPPLYCHAIN. Whenever called, the function ITERATESUPPLYCHAIN advances the tags to their next step.

In each iteration of the supply chain, $\mathcal{A}$ can call the oracle $\mathcal{O}_{\text{Draw}}$ to get up to s tags $T_{(i,j)}$ that satisfy some condition $c_{(i,j)}$ specified by $\mathcal{A}$. $\mathcal{A}$ can read from and write into these tags $T_{(i,j)}$. He can as well query the function CHECK for each tag $T_{(i,j)}$.

---

for $i := 1$ **to** r **do**
   | $S_i \leftarrow \mathcal{O}_{\text{Corrupt}}(R_i)$;
end
for $i := 1$ **to** ρ **do**
   | ITERATESUPPLYCHAIN;
   | **for** $j := 1$ **to** s **do**
   | | $T_{(i,j)} \leftarrow \mathcal{O}_{\text{Draw}}(c_{(i,j)})$;
   | | $s_{T_{(i,j)}}^i := \text{READ}(T_{(i,j)})$;
   | | $\text{WRITE}(T_{(i,j)}, s'^i_{T_{(i,j)}})$;
   | | $b_{T_{(i,j)}} \leftarrow \mathcal{O}_{\text{Check}}(R_{T(i,j)}, T_{(i,j)})$;
   | **end**
end

Algorithm 1: Security learning phase of $\mathcal{A}$

$T_c \leftarrow \mathcal{A}$;
for $i := 1$ **to** η **do**
   | $b_{(i,T_c)} \leftarrow \mathcal{O}_{\text{Check}}(R_i, T_c)$;
end

Algorithm 2: Security challenge phase of $\mathcal{A}$

Finally in the challenge phase, $\mathcal{A}$ selects a challenge tag T_c that he gives to the oracle $\mathcal{O}_{\text{Check}}$, cf., Algorithm 2. $\mathcal{O}_{\text{Check}}$ outputs a set of η bits $b_{(i,T_c)}$ such that $b_{(i,T_c)} = \text{CHECK}(R_i, T_c)$.

$\mathcal{A}$ is said to be successful if and only if:
i.) $\exists R_i$ such that $\text{CHECK}(R_i, T_c) = 1$, i.e., there is a path P_i^j that corresponds to T_c's state; **ii.)** $\exists v \in \mathsf{P}_i^j$ such that step v is not corrupted by $\mathcal{A}$; **iii.)** and finally, T_c did not go through step v.

DEFINITION 1 (SECURITY). CHECKER *provides security* $\Leftrightarrow$ *For adversary* $\mathcal{A}$, *inequality* $Pr[\mathcal{A} \text{ is successful }] \leq \frac{|S_{\text{valid}}|}{S} + \epsilon$ *holds, where ϵ is negligible.*

The adversary $\mathcal{A}$ captured by the definition above is a non narrow strong adversary in the sense of [20]. He can access tags arbitrarily and tamper with their states. He is also allowed to access the output of the protocol and corrupt readers. In the real world, such an adversary corresponds to a partner in the supply chain whose goal is to inject fake products.

Note. As we use read/write only tags, *completeness* of CHECKER cannot be ensured. An adversary $\mathcal{A}$ can always tamper with tags' internal states by writing dummy data into them. Thus, $\mathcal{A}$ can always invalidate the state of T_i leading the CHECK function to output 0.

Cloning. CHECKER targets read/write only tags to perform on-site checking. As a result, any malicious entity can read and rewrite the content of tags, and therewith, it can clone tags. Such an attack cannot be prevented in a setting that relies on read/write only tags which cannot implement any reader authentication.

To mitigate this problem, each partner P_i in the supply chain keeps a database DB_i that contains the identifiers of tags present at P_i's site. Then, time is divided into epochs e_k (typically, the duration of an epoch e_k is one day) and partners are required to update their databases at the beginning of each epoch e_k.

To detect clones, each pair of partners P_i and P_j invoke a protocol for privacy preserving set intersection [8, 9] at the beginning of each epoch e_k, to check whether there is an identifier ID that is present in both of their databases. At the end of the privacy preserving set intersection protocol, both partners obtain a set of identifiers $S_{(i,j)} = DB_i \cap DB_j$ that represent the clones in their sites. If $S_{(i,j)} \neq \emptyset$, then P_i and P_j can discard the clones and investigate where the clones come from.

3.2 Privacy

In line with previous work [4], a privacy preserving verification of product genuineness in the supply chain should meet the two following requirements:

1.) An adversary $\mathcal{A}$ must not be able to distinguish between tags based on their interactions with the readers in the supply chain or based on their interactions with $\mathcal{A}$. This requirement deals with tracking attacks. If the adversary is not able to tell tags apart, he will not be able to track tags along the supply chain. We call this requirement *tag unlinkability* in accordance with [4, 13]. Notice that tag unlinkability is a stronger requirement than tag confidentiality. If an adversary $\mathcal{A}$ is able to jeopardize tag confidentiality, then he is automatically able to tell tags apart. Consequently, if CHECKER ensures tag unlinkability, then it ensures tag confidentiality as well.

2.) An adversary $\mathcal{A}$ must not be able to learn any information about the path of a tag T_i in the supply chain. Such a requirement ensures the privacy of the internal processes of the supply chain. Being unable to disclose any information about the path that tags took, the adversary cannot tell the origin of a tag T_i he is having access to, either the steps that T_i went through or the pallet of tags that T_i belongs to. In [4], this privacy requirement was captured by the notion of *step unlinkability*. More precisely, given two tags T_i and T_j, an adversary $\mathcal{A}$ must not be able to tell whether $P_i \cap P_j = \{v_0\}$ or not, where P_i and P_j denote the paths of tags T_i and T_j respectively. Observe that, all tags are issued by issuer I and thus, they all go through step v_0. For further details on step unlinkability, the interested reader may refer to Appendix A.1.

However, the definitions of tag unlinkability and step unlinkability as presented in [4] have two limitations:

1.) It is assumed that the manager M performing path verification cannot be corrupt. In this paper, path verification is performed by readers along the supply chain and these readers can behave arbitrarily, i.e., can be corrupt.

2.) It is assumed that adversary $\mathcal{A}$ has only a random access to tags in the supply chain. That is, $\mathcal{A}$ cannot choose tags he wants from $\mathcal{T}$. In this work, adversary $\mathcal{A}$ has more freedom in picking tags through the oracle $\mathcal{O}_{Draw}$. We recall that $\mathcal{A}$ can query the oracle $\mathcal{O}_{Draw}$ with a set of conditions c_i, and $\mathcal{O}_{Draw}$ has to return a tag T satisfying these conditions if there is any.

To address these limitations, we extend the privacy definitions of [4] by considering a more realistic adversary $\mathcal{A}$ who is allowed

to corrupt readers and to select tags according to some conditions determined by him through the oracle $\mathcal{O}_{Draw}$.

One result of our modifications to privacy definitions is proving that if CHECKER ensures tag unlinkability, then it will as well ensure step unlinkability, see Appendix A.2 for a thorough analysis. Henceforth, we only focus on tag unlinkability.

Tag unlinkability

Read/write only tags cannot perform any computation. As a result, a tag T_i in CHECKER relies on readers in the supply chain to update its state, i.e., T_i's state does not change in between two protocol executions. Therefore, it is impossible to ensure tag unlinkability against an adversary who monitors all of T_i's interactions. Accordingly, there has to be at least *one unobserved* interaction between T_i and an *honest* reader outside the range of the adversary $\mathcal{A}$. This is in compliance with previous work dealing with read/write only tags, see Ateniese et al. [1], Dimitrou [10], Sadeghi et al. [17] and Blass et al. [4].

However, this assumption alone is not sufficient to ensure tag unlinkability against readers R_k along the supply chain. Notice that the genuineness verification of tags require readers R_k to have access to tags' identifiers or tags' pseudonyms. Although, adversary $\mathcal{A}$ does not observe all of T_i's interaction, he will be always able to link the interactions of tag T_i with corrupt readers.

Thus, we consider that adversary $\mathcal{A}$ is successful in mounting an attack against tag unlinkability if he is able to distinguish between two tags T_0 and T_1 which are not present at corrupt readers, and if T_0 and T_1 had at least one interaction with an honest reader R_i outside the range of $\mathcal{A}$.

We illustrate tag unlinkability by an experiment depicted in Algorithm 3 and Algorithm 4.

In the learning phase, $\mathcal{A}(r, s, \rho, \epsilon)$ can call the oracle $\mathcal{O}_{Corrupt}$ to corrupt up to r readers R_i. $\mathcal{A}$ is provided then with two challenge tags T_0 and T_1 that just entered the supply chain (tags at step v_0) from the oracle $\mathcal{O}_{Draw}$. Adversary $\mathcal{A}$ starts iterating the supply chain up to ρ times.

Before each iteration of the supply chain, $\mathcal{A}$ can read and write into tags T_0, T_1. He can also query the oracle $\mathcal{O}_{Step}$ to get the next steps of tags T_0 and T_1. Moreover, the oracle $\mathcal{O}_{Draw}$ supplies $\mathcal{A}$ with s tags $T_{(i,j)}$ fulfilling some condition $c_{(i,j)}$. $\mathcal{A}$ can read from and write into tags $T_{(i,j)}$. $\mathcal{A}$ is also supplied with the next step of tags $T_{(i,j)}$. $\mathcal{A}$ then iterates the supply chain and reads the state stored into tags $T_{(i,j)}$.

In the challenge phase, cf., Algorithm 4, $\mathcal{A}$ is provided with the next step of tags T_0 and T_1. He is also allowed to read and write into T_0 and T_1 one more time. Then, the supply chain is iterated first outside the range of $\mathcal{A}$. That is, tags T_0 and T_1 has an unobserved interaction with an honest reader outside the range of $\mathcal{A}$.

The oracle $\mathcal{O}_{Flip}$ supplies $\mathcal{A}$ with the tag T_b which $\mathcal{A}$ can read. At the end of the challenge phase, $\mathcal{A}$ is required to output his guess of bit b.

$\mathcal{A}$ is said to be successful if **i.)** his guess of b is correct, **ii.)** the readers associated with steps $v_{T_0}^{k+1}$ and $v_{T_1}^{k'+1}$ are not corrupt, and **iii.)** the reader associated with the next step of tag T_b at the end of the challenge phase is not corrupt by $\mathcal{A}$.

DEFINITION 2 (TAG UNLINKABILITY). CHECKER *provides tag unlinkability* $\Leftrightarrow$ *For adversary $\mathcal{A}$, inequality $Pr(\mathcal{A}$ is successful$) \leq \frac{1}{2} + \epsilon$ holds, where ϵ is negligible.*

In a real world scenario, the adversary $\mathcal{A}$ against the above experiment corresponds to a set of r partners $\{P_1, P_2, ..., P_r\}$ in the supply chain that collude in order to compromise the privacy of another partner P, through eavesdropping and tampering with tags

```
for i := 1 to r do
    S_i ← O_Corrupt(R_i);
end
T_0 ← O_Draw("tag at step "v_0);
T_1 ← O_Draw("tag at step "v_0);
for i := 0 to ρ − 1 do
    v_{T_0}^{i+1} ← O_Step(T_0);
    s_{T_0}^i :=READ(T_0);
    WRITE(T_0, s'^i_{T_0});
    v_{T_1}^{i+1} ← O_Step(T_1);
    s_{T_1}^i :=READ(T_1);
    WRITE(T_1, s'^i_{T_1});
    for j = 1 to s do
        T_{(i,j)} ← O_Draw(c_{(i,j)});
        v_{T_{(i,j)}} ← O_Step(T_{(i,j)});
        s_{T_{(i,j)}} :=READ(T_{(i,j)});
        WRITE(s_{T_{(i,j)}}, s'_{T_{(i,j)}});
    end
    ITERATESUPPLYCHAIN;
    for j = 1 to s do
        READ(T_{(i,j)});
    end
end
```

Algorithm 3: $\mathcal{A}$'s tag unlinkability learning phase

```
v_{T_0}^{k+1} ← O_Step(T_0);
s_{T_0}^k :=READ(T_0);
WRITE(T_0, s'^k_{T_0});
v_{T_1}^{k'+1} ← O_Step(T_1);
s_{T_1}^{k'} :=READ(T_1);
WRITE(T_1, s'^{k'}_{T_1});
ITERATESUPPLYCHAIN; // Outside the range of A
T_b ← O_Flip{T_0, T_1};
s_{T_b} :=READ(T_b);
OUTPUT b;
```

Algorithm 4: $\mathcal{A}$'s tag unlinkability challenge phase

present at P's site.

Note on tag unlinkability. The adversary $\mathcal{A}$ defined above is a narrow adversary as defined by Vaudenay [20]. That is, $\mathcal{A}$ does not have access to the output of the protocol in the challenge phase. In CHECKER's case, this corresponds to not accessing the result of the CHECK function. Note that if we allow $\mathcal{A}$ to have access to the output of the CHECK function, $\mathcal{A}$ can mount a trivial attack where he writes garbage, i.e., "dummy data" into a tag T_i. Tag T_i will not be accepted by any reader in the supply chain with high probability, and thus $\mathcal{A}$ can always distinguish T_i from legitimate tags.

4. PROTOCOL

Protocol overview

In CHECKER, a tag T stores a state s_T^j which consists of the *encryption* of T's identifier ID and the *encryption* of a *path signature* that encodes the sequence of steps that T has visited.

To efficiently encode paths in the supply chain, we rely on a polynomial-based representation as introduced by Blass et al. [4]. That is, each path P in the supply chain will match the evaluation of a unique polynomial Q_P in a fixed value x_0, i.e., a path P in the supply chain is mapped to $Q_P(x_0) \in \mathbb{F}_q$.

A tag T going through a valid path P stores a randomly encrypted state $s_T^j = (\text{Enc}(\text{ID}), \text{Enc}(\sigma_P(\text{ID})))$, such that ID is T's identifier, $\sigma_P(\text{ID}) = H(\text{ID})^{Q_P(x_0)}$, and H is a cryptographic hash function. The state s_T^j could be regarded as a message ID and a signature on this message using the secret key $Q_P(x_0)$.

In CHECKER, the issuer I initializes a tag T by writing an initial encrypted state s_T^0. A reader R_k in CHECKER reads the encrypted state s_T^j stored into T and decrypts it using its secret key sk_k to get the pair $(\text{ID}, \sigma_P(\text{ID}))$. R_k then uses its set of ν_k verification keys $\mathcal{K}_k^V = \{K_k^1, K_k^2, ..., K_k^{\nu_k}\}$ to verify whether T went through a valid path leading to R_k or not. After path verification, reader R_k uses an update function f_k to update the state stored into tag T accordingly. Finally, R_k encrypts the new state of tag T using the public key of T's next step.

Privacy and security overview

To protect *privacy* of tags in the supply chain against readers, tags store an IND-CCA secure encryption of their states. For ease of presentation, we use Cramer-Shoup's scheme (CS for short) [7] as the underlying encryption. As CHECKER takes place in subgroups of elliptic curves that support bilinear pairings, we note that any IND-CCA secure scheme that takes place in DDH-hard groups can be used to encrypt the tag state. Furthermore, readers in the supply chain do not share the same CS pair of keys, instead each reader R_k is equipped with a matching pair of CS public and secret keys $(\text{sk}_k, \text{pk}_k)$.

To ensure security, a tag T in CHECKER stores a signature of its ID using the polynomial-based encoding of the path it took. Without having access to the polynomial-based encoding of valid paths, an adversary cannot forge a valid state; otherwise, we show that there is an adversary who is able to break the bilinear computational Diffie-Hellman (BCDH) assumption.

First, we introduce some of the definitions, notations and assumptions that will be used in the rest of the paper.

4.1 Preliminaries

CHECKER takes place in subgroups of elliptic curves that support bilinear pairings. Similar to related work on elliptic curves supporting bilinear pairings, we use multiplicative group notation [1, 2, 5]. If $\mathbb{G}$ is a subgroup of order q of some elliptic curve $\mathcal{E}$, then for all $g \in \mathbb{G}$ and $x \in \mathbb{Z}_q$, g^x denotes point multiplication of g by x.

4.1.1 Bilinear pairings

Let $\mathbb{G}_1$, $\mathbb{G}_2$ and $\mathbb{G}_T$ be groups, such that $\mathbb{G}_1$ and $\mathbb{G}_T$ have the same order q.

A pairing $e: \mathbb{G}_1 \times \mathbb{G}_2 \to \mathbb{G}_T$ is a bilinear pairing if:

1. e is *bilinear*: $\forall x, y \in \mathbb{Z}_q, g \in \mathbb{G}_1$ and $h \in \mathbb{G}_2, e(g^x, h^y) = e(g, h)^{xy}$;

2. e is *computable*: there is an efficient algorithm to compute $e(g, h)$ for any $(g, h) \in \mathbb{G}_1 \times \mathbb{G}_2$;

3. e is *non-degenerate*: if g is a generator of $\mathbb{G}_1$ and h is a generator of $\mathbb{G}_2$, then $e(g, h)$ is a generator $\mathbb{G}_T$.

CHECKER's security and privacy rely on the Bilinear Computational Diffie-Hellman (BCDH) assumption and the Symmetric External Diffie-Hellman (SXDH) assumption [3, 18].

DEFINITION 3 (BCDH ASSUMPTION). *Let g be a generator of $\mathbb{G}_1$ and h be a generator of $\mathbb{G}_2$. We say that the Bilinear Computational Diffie-Hellman assumption holds if, given $g, g^x, g^y, g^z \in \mathbb{G}_1$ and $h, h^x, h^y \in \mathbb{G}_2$ for random $x, y, z \in \mathbb{F}_q$, the probability to compute $e(g, h)^{xyz}$ is negligible.*

DEFINITION 4 (SXDH ASSUMPTION). *The Symmetric External Diffie-Hellman assumption holds if $\mathbb{G}_1$ and $\mathbb{G}_2$ are two groups with the following properties:*

1. *There exists a bilinear pairing $e : \mathbb{G}_1 \times \mathbb{G}_2 \to \mathbb{G}_T$;*

2. *the decisional Diffie-Hellman problem (DDH) is hard in both $\mathbb{G}_1$ and $\mathbb{G}_2$.*

Hence, CHECKER uses bilinear groups where DDH is hard, see Ateniese et al. [1, 2], Ballard et al. [3], Scott [18]. These groups can be chosen as specific subgroups of non supersingular elliptic curves such as Miyaji-Nakabayashi-Takano (MNT for short) curves [14]. Moreover, results by Galbraith et al. [12] indicate that these elliptic curves are the most efficient setting to implement pairing-based cryptography.

4.1.2 Polynomial-based path encoding

In this section, we briefly recall the polynomial-based path encoding as presented in [4]. In a nutshell, each step v_i, $0 \leq i \leq \eta$, in the supply chain is associated with a unique random number $a_i \in \mathbb{F}_q$, where q is a large prime ($|q| = 160$ bits).

Each path in the supply chain is mapped to a unique polynomial in $\mathbb{F}_q$. The polynomial corresponding to path $P = \overrightarrow{v_0 v_1 ... v_l}$ is defined as:

$$Q_P(x) = a_0 x^l + \sum_{i=1}^{l} a_i x^{l-i} \qquad (1)$$

To have a compact representation of paths, a path P is encoded as the evaluation of Q_P at x_0, where x_0 is a generator of $\mathbb{F}_q^*$. Consequently, providing an efficient encoding of paths that does not depend on the length of the paths.

We point out that when the coefficients a_i are chosen randomly in $\mathbb{F}_q$, then the above encoding has the following property: for any two different paths P and P', $Q_P(x_0) \neq Q_{P'}(x_0)$ with high probability, see [15] for more details.

In the remainder of this paper, we denote $\phi(P) = Q_P(x_0)$ the polynomial-based encoding of path P.

For all paths P and for all steps v_k in the supply chain, the following holds:

$$\phi(\overrightarrow{Pv_k}) = x_0 \cdot \phi(P) + a_k$$

4.1.3 Path signature in CHECKER

Let T be a tag with the unique identifier $ID \in \mathbb{G}_1$ that went through the path $P = \overrightarrow{v_0 v_1 ... v_l}$. In CHECKER we define the *path signature* of tag T as:

$$\sigma_P(ID) = H(ID)^{\phi(P)}$$

where H is a cryptographic hash function $H : \mathbb{G}_1 \to \mathbb{G}_1$. For any $ID \in \mathbb{G}_1$, such a hash function can be computed by using a traditional cryptographic hash function $h : \mathbb{G}_1 \to \mathbb{F}_q$, e.g., SHA-1: first, we compute $r = h(ID)$, then, we output $H(ID) = g^r$, where g is a generator of $\mathbb{G}_1$. In the security analysis, we view H as a random oracle.

Note that $\sigma_P(ID)$ is a signature of ID using the secret key $\phi(P)$. More precisely, it is an aggregate signature using the secret coefficients a_i of readers R_i in path P.

The identifier ID and the path signature $\sigma_P(ID)$ are encrypted and stored into tag T. A reader R_k that is visited by tag T, decrypts T's state, verifies the validity of the state and updates the path signature $\sigma_P(ID)$. Without loss of generality, we assume that T has gone through the path P, and now it arrives at step v_k in the supply chain. T stores the encrypted pair $(ID, \sigma_P(ID))$ and P_k

denotes the path $\overrightarrow{Pv_k}$. To obtain $\sigma_{P_k}(ID)$, reader R_k computes its state update function f_{R_k} defined as:

$$f_{R_k}(x, y) = x^{x_0} H(y)^{a_k} \qquad (2)$$

Thus,

$$\begin{aligned} f_{R_k}(\sigma_P(ID), ID) &= \sigma_P(ID)^{x_0} H(ID)^{a_k} \\ &= H(ID)^{\phi(P) \cdot x_0} H(ID)^{a_k} \\ &= H(ID)^{x_0 \cdot \phi(P) + a_k} \\ &= H(ID)^{\phi(\overrightarrow{Pv_k})} = \sigma_{P_k}(ID) \end{aligned}$$

Therefore, we obtain the path signature of $P_k = \overrightarrow{Pv_k}$ from the path signature of P.

4.1.4 Cramer-Shoup encryption

An elliptic curve Cramer-Shoup encryption consists of the following operations:

- *Setup:* The system outputs an elliptic curve $\mathcal{E}$ over a finite field $\mathbb{F}_p$. Let $\mathbb{G}_1$ be a subgroup of $\mathcal{E}$ of a large prime order q ($|q| = 160$ bits), where DDH is intractable. Let (g_1, g_2) be a pair of generators of the group $\mathbb{G}_1$.

- *Key generation:* The secret key is the random tuple $sk = (x_1, x_2, y_1, y_2, z) \in \mathbb{F}_q^5$. The system computes then $(c, d, f) = (g_1^{x_1} g_2^{x_2}, g_1^{y_1} g_2^{y_2}, g_1^z)$. Let G be a cryptographic hash function. The public key is $pk = (g_1, g_2, c, d, f, G)$.

- *Encryption:* Given a message $m \in \mathbb{G}_1$, the encryption algorithm chooses $r \in \mathbb{F}_q$ at random. Then it computes $u_1 = g_1^r, u_2 = g_2^r, u = mf^r, \alpha = G(u_1, u_2, u), v = c^r d^{r\alpha}$. The encryption algorithm outputs the ciphertext $Enc_{pk}(m) = (u_1, u_2, u, v)$.

- *Decryption:* On input of a ciphertext $C = (u_1, u_2, u, v)$, the decryption algorithm first computes $\alpha = G(u_1, u_2, u)$, and tests if $v = u_1^{x_1 + y_1 \alpha} u_2^{x_2 + y_2 \alpha}$. If this condition does not hold, the decryption algorithm outputs $\perp$; otherwise, it outputs $Dec_{sk}(C) = \frac{u}{u_1^z}$.

4.2 Protocol description

CHECKER consists of an initial setup phase, the initialization of tags by the issuer, and finally the path verification and tag state update by the readers.

4.2.1 Setup

A trusted third party (TTP) outputs $(q, \mathbb{G}_1, \mathbb{G}_2, \mathbb{G}_T, g_1, g_2, h, H, G, e)$, where $\mathbb{G}_1, \mathbb{G}_T$ are subgroups of prime order q. g_1 and g_2 are random generators of $\mathbb{G}_1$. h is a generator of $\mathbb{G}_2$. $H : \mathbb{G}_1 \to \mathbb{G}_1$ is a secure hash function. $G : \mathbb{G}_1^3 \to \mathbb{F}_q$ is a secure hash function, and $e : \mathbb{G}_1 \times \mathbb{G}_2 \to \mathbb{G}_T$ is a bilinear pairing.

The TTP generates $\eta + 1$ pairs of matching public and secret keys for the Cramer-Shoup encryption: $sk_k = (x_{(1,k)}, x_{(2,k)}, y_{(1,k)}, y_{(2,k)}, z_k) \in \mathbb{F}_q^5$ and $pk_k = (g_1, g_2, c_k, d_k, f_k, G)$, $0 \leq k \leq \eta$. The TTP generates as well $\eta + 1$ random coefficients $a_k \in \mathbb{F}_q$. Then, it selects a generator x_0 of $\mathbb{F}_q$.

Through a secure channel, the TTP sends to each reader $R_k, 1 \leq k \leq \eta$, the tuple $(x_0, a_k, sk_k, pk_k, H)$ and sends the tuple $(x_0, a_0, sk_0, pk_0, H)$ to the issuer I.

The TTP computes the verification keys for each reader R_k in the supply chain. Let P_k be a path leading to reader R_k. To obtain the verification key corresponding to path P_k, the TTP computes the path encoding $\phi(P_k)$. Then, the TTP outputs the corresponding verification key $K(P_k) = h^{\phi(P_k)} \in \mathbb{G}_2$.

Once the verification keys are computed, the TTP provides each reader R_k with its set $\mathcal{K}_V^k$ of verification keys.

We assume that the public keys $\text{pk}_k, 0 \leq k \leq \eta$, are known to all parties in the system.

4.2.2   Tag initialization

For each new tag T in the supply chain, I chooses a random identifier $\text{ID} \in \mathbb{G}_1$. The issuer computes the hash $H(\text{ID})$, and using his secret coefficient a_0, he computes $H(\text{ID})^{a_0}$. Provided with the public key of T's next step, the issuer computes a CS encryption of both ID and $\sigma_{v_0}(\text{ID}) = H(\text{ID})^{a_0}$. Without loss of generality, we assume that T's next step is v_1. The public key of step v_1 is $\text{pk}_1 = (g_1, g_2, c_1, d_1, f_1, G)$.

Issuer I draws two random number r_{ID} and r_σ in $\mathbb{F}_q$ and computes the following ciphertexts:

$$
\begin{aligned}
c_{\text{ID}}^0 &= \text{Enc}_{\text{pk}_1}(\text{ID}) = (u_{(1,\text{ID})}, u_{(2,\text{ID})}, u_{\text{ID}}, v_{\text{ID}}) \\
&= (g_1^{r_{\text{ID}}}, g_2^{r_{\text{ID}}}, \text{ID}\, f_1^{r_{\text{ID}}}, c_1^{r_{\text{ID}}} d_1^{r_{\text{ID}} \alpha_{\text{ID}}}) \\
\alpha_{\text{ID}} &= G(u_{(1,\text{ID})}, u_{(2,\text{ID})}, u_{\text{ID}}) \\
c_\sigma^0 &= \text{Enc}_{\text{pk}_1}(\sigma_{v_0}(\text{ID})) = (u_{(1,\sigma)}, u_{(2,\sigma)}, u_\sigma, v_\sigma) \\
&= (g_1^{r_\sigma}, g_2^{r_\sigma}, \sigma_{v_0}(\text{ID})\, f_1^{r_\sigma}, c_1^{r_\sigma} d_1^{r_\sigma \alpha_\sigma}) \\
\alpha_\sigma &= G(u_{(1,\sigma)}, u_{(2,\sigma)}, u_\sigma)
\end{aligned}
$$

Finally, I writes state $s_T^0 = (c_{\text{ID}}^0, c_\sigma^0) \in \mathbb{G}_1^8$ into tag T. T then enters the supply chain.

4.2.3   Path verification by readers

Assume a tag T arrives at steps v_k in the supply chain. The reader R_k associated with step v_k reads the state $s_T^j = (c_{\text{ID}}^j, c_\sigma^j)$ stored in tag T. Without loss of generality, we assume T went through path P. R_k using its secret key sk_k decrypts the CS ciphertexts c_{ID}^j and c_σ^j and gets respectively the pair $(\text{ID}, \sigma_P(\text{ID}))$.

Let $\mathcal{K}_V^k$ denote the set of verification keys $\mathcal{K}_V^k = \{K_k^1, K_k^2, ..., K_k^{\nu_k}\} = \{h^{\phi(P_k^1)}, h^{\phi(P_k^2)}, ..., h^{\phi(P_k^{\nu_k})}\}$ corresponding to the valid paths leading to step v_k.

To verify whether the tag T went through a valid path or not, R_k computes the hash $H(\text{ID})$ and checks whether there exists $i \in \{1, 2, ..., \nu_k\}$, such that:

$$
\begin{aligned}
e(\sigma_P(\text{ID}), h) &= e(H(\text{ID}), K_k^i) \\
&= e(H(\text{ID}), h^{\phi(P_k^i)})
\end{aligned}
$$

If so, this implies that T went through a valid path leading to step v_k. Otherwise, the reader concludes that tag T is illegitimate and rejects T.

4.2.4   Tag state update by readers

If the verification succeeds, the reader R_k in the supply chain is required to update the state of tag T. Using the update function f_{R_k}, the reader computes the new path signature $\sigma_{\overrightarrow{Pv_k}}(\text{ID})$.

$$
\begin{aligned}
f_{R_k}(\sigma_P(\text{ID}), \text{ID}) &= \sigma_P(\text{ID})^{x_0} H(\text{ID})^{a_k} \\
&= H(\text{ID})^{x_0 \phi(P) + a_k} = H(\text{ID})^{\phi(\overrightarrow{Pv_k})} \\
&= \sigma_{\overrightarrow{Pv_k}}(\text{ID})
\end{aligned}
$$

Without loss of generality, we assume that the tag's next step is v_{k+1}. The reader R_k prepares tag T for reader R_{k+1} by encrypting the pair $(\text{ID}, \sigma_{\overrightarrow{Pv_k}}(\text{ID}))$ using the public key $\text{pk}_{k+1} = (g_1, g_2, c_{k+1}, d_{k+1}, f_{k+1}, G)$. Reader R_k obtains therefore, two ciphertexts c_{ID}^{j+1} and c_σ^{j+1}.

Finally, R_k writes the state $s_T^{j+1} = (c_{\text{ID}}^{j+1}, c_\sigma^{j+1})$ into T.

5.   SECURITY AND PRIVACY ANALYSIS

In this section, we state the main theorems regarding CHECK-ER's security and privacy.

5.1   Security analysis

THEOREM 1. CHECKER *is secure under the BCDH assumption in the random oracle model.*

PROOF. Assume there is an adversary $\mathcal{A}$ who breaks the security of CHECKER with a non negligible advantage ϵ, we build an adversary $\mathcal{A}'$ that uses $\mathcal{A}$ as a subroutine to break the BCDH assumption with a non negligible advantage ϵ'.

Let $\mathcal{O}_{\text{BCDH}}$ be an oracle that selects randomly $x, y, z \in \mathbb{F}_q$, and returns $g, g^x, g^y, g^z \in \mathbb{G}_1$, and $h, h^x, h^y \in \mathbb{G}_2$.

Proof overview. If $\mathcal{A}$ has a non negligible advantage in breaking the security of CHECKER, then $\mathcal{A}$ will be able to output a challenge tag T_c that stores a valid encrypted state s_{T_c}, and:

i.) $\exists R_k$ such that $\text{CHECK}(R_k, T_c) = 1$, i.e., there is a path P_k^j that corresponds to T_c'state;

ii.) $\exists v \in P_k^j$ such that step v is not corrupted by $\mathcal{A}$;

iii.) T_c did not go through step v.

To break BCDH, adversary $\mathcal{A}'$ simulates a CHECKER system for $\mathcal{A}$ where he provides a step v_i in the supply chain with the tuple $(x_0, g^x, \text{sk}_i, \text{pk}_i)$ instead of the tuple $(x_0, a_i, \text{sk}_i, \text{pk}_i)$.

Without loss of generality, we assume in the rest of the proof that $v_i = v_0$ and that $\mathcal{A}$ corrupts all readers R_k (but not issuer I) in the supply chain.

Now, $\mathcal{A}'$ must convince $\mathcal{A}$ that v_0 is associated with secret coefficient $a_0 = x$ that corresponds to the pair (g^x, h^x) received from the oracle $\mathcal{O}_{\text{BCDH}}$. Accordingly, $\mathcal{A}'$ has to be able to compute $H(\text{ID})^x$ only by knowing (g^x, h^x). To tackle this issue, $\mathcal{A}'$ simulates a random oracle $\mathcal{H}$ that computes the hash function H.

When $\mathcal{H}$ is queried in the learning phase with identifier ID_j, $\mathcal{A}'$ picks a random number r_j and computes $H(\text{ID}_j) = g^{r_j}$.

Before the challenge phase, $\mathcal{A}$ queries the random oracle $\mathcal{H}$ with an identifier ID_c, where ID_c is the identifier of the challenge tag T_c. Simulating $\mathcal{H}$, $\mathcal{A}'$ picks a random number r_c, computes $H(\text{ID}_c) = g^{zr_c}$, and returns $H(\text{ID}_c)$ to $\mathcal{A}$.

In the challenge phase, $\mathcal{A}$ supplies $\mathcal{A}'$ with the challenge tag T_c.

As adversary $\mathcal{A}$ has a non negligible advantage in the security experiment, the challenge tag T_c stores an encrypted valid state that corresponds to the pair (ID_c, σ_c) such that $\sigma_c = H(\text{ID}_c)^{\phi(P_{\text{valid}})}$, and T_c did not go through step v_0.

Using σ_c, $\mathcal{A}'$ is able to identify the path P_{valid} that corresponds to the state of tag T_c. We assume that $P_{\text{valid}} = \overrightarrow{v_0 P}$, and we denote l the length of path P_{valid}.

By definition, $\phi(P_{\text{valid}}) = a_0 x_0^l + \phi(P) = x x_0^l + \phi(P)$, and given σ_c and the encoding $\phi(P)$ of the sub-path P, $\mathcal{A}'$ computes:

$$
\begin{aligned}
\frac{\sigma_c}{H(\text{ID}_c)^{\phi(P)}} &= \frac{H(\text{ID}_c)^{\phi(P_{\text{valid}})}}{H(\text{ID}_c)^{\phi(P)}} = H(\text{ID}_c)^{x x_0^l} \\
H(\text{ID}_c)^x &= \left(\frac{H(\text{ID}_c)^{\phi(P_{\text{valid}})}}{H(\text{ID}_c)^{\phi(P)}} \right)^{\frac{1}{x_0^l}}
\end{aligned}
$$

$\mathcal{A}'$ thus have access to $H(\text{ID}_c)^x = (g^{zr_c})^x = g^{xzr_c}$, and accordingly, he computes $(g^{xzr_c})^{\frac{1}{r_c}} = g^{xz}$.

Finally, $\mathcal{A}'$ computes $e(g^{xz}, h^y) = e(g, h)^{xyz}$, and this breaks the BCDH assumption which leads to a contradiction.

Simulation of the random oracle $\mathcal{H}$. To respond to the queries to the random oracle $\mathcal{H}$, $\mathcal{A}'$ keeps a table T_H of tuples $(\text{ID}_j, r_j, \text{coin}(\text{ID}_j), h_j)$ as explained below.

On a query $H(\text{ID}_i)$, $\mathcal{A}'$ replies as follows:

1.) If there is a tuple $(\text{ID}_i, r_i, \text{coin}(\text{ID}_i), h_i)$ that corresponds to ID_i, then $\mathcal{A}'$ returns $H(\text{ID}_i) = h_i$.

2.) If ID_i has never been queried before, then $\mathcal{A}'$ picks a random number $r_i \in \mathbb{F}_q$. $\mathcal{A}'$ flips a random coin $\text{coin}(\text{ID}_i) \in \{0, 1\}$ such that: $\text{coin}(\text{ID}_i) = 1$ with probability p, and is equals to 0 with probability $1 - p$. The probability p will be determined later. If $\text{coin}(\text{ID}_i) = 0$, then $\mathcal{A}'$ answers with $H(\text{ID}_i) = g^{r_i}$. Otherwise, $\mathcal{A}'$ answers with $h_i = H(\text{ID}_i) = (g^z)^{r_i}$. Finally, $\mathcal{A}'$ stores the tuple $(\text{ID}_i, r_i, \text{coin}(\text{ID}_i), h_i)$ in table T_H.

Construction. We detail below how $\mathcal{A}'$ breaks the BCDH assumption.

- First, $\mathcal{A}'$ queries $\mathcal{O}_{\text{BCDH}}$ to receive $g, g^x, g^y, g^z \in \mathbb{G}_1$ and $h, h^x, h^y \in \mathbb{G}_2$. Then, $\mathcal{A}'$ simulates a CHECKER system:

  1.) $\mathcal{A}'$ generates $\eta + 1$ pairs of matching CS public and secret keys $(\text{sk}_k, \text{pk}_k)$. Then, he generates η random coefficients a_k.

  2.) $\mathcal{A}'$ provides each reader R_k in CHECKER with the tuple $(x_0, a_k, \text{sk}_k, \text{pk}_k)$.

  3.) $\mathcal{A}'$ provides the issuer I with the tuple $(x_0, g^x, \text{sk}_0, \text{pk}_0)$, as if $a_0 = x$.

  4.) $\mathcal{A}'$ computes the verification keys for each reader R_k in the supply chain. Without loss of generality, a valid path P_{valid} in the supply chain could be represented as $\text{P}_{\text{valid}} = \overrightarrow{\text{v}_0 \text{P}'_{\text{valid}}}$. Thus, the corresponding verification key $K(\text{P}_{\text{valid}})$ is computed as: $K(\text{P}_{\text{valid}}) = (h^x)^{x_0^l} h^{\phi(\text{P}'_{\text{valid}})} = h^{\phi(\text{P}_{\text{valid}})}$, where l is the length of path P_{valid}.

  Once the verification keys are computed for all the readers R_k, $\mathcal{A}$ provides each reader R_k with his set $\mathcal{K}_V^k$ of verification keys.

$\mathcal{A}'$ then calls the adversary $\mathcal{A}$.

- $\mathcal{A}'$ simulates the issuer I and creates n tags T_j of CHECKER.

  $\mathcal{A}'$ selects randomly $\text{ID}_j \in \mathbb{G}_1$. He simulates the oracle $\mathcal{H}$. $\mathcal{A}'$ gets the tuple $(\text{ID}_j, r_j, \text{coin}(\text{ID}_j), h_j)$.

  If $\text{coin}(\text{ID}_j) = 1$, i.e., $h_j = H(\text{ID}_j) = g^{zr_j}$, then $\mathcal{A}'$ cannot compute $H(\text{ID}_j)^x = g^{xzr_j}$ as he does not know both x and z. Consequently, $\mathcal{A}'$ stops the security experiment.

  Otherwise, using r_j $\mathcal{A}'$ computes $H(\text{ID}_j)^x = (g^x)^{r_j}$.

  Finally, $\mathcal{A}'$ encrypts both ID_j and $\sigma_{\text{v}_0}(\text{ID}_j)$ using the public key of the tag T_j's next step. $\mathcal{A}'$ stores the resulting ciphertexts $(c^0_{(\text{ID},j)}, c^0_{(\sigma,j)})$ into tag T_j.

- $\mathcal{A}'$ simulates the oracle $\mathcal{O}_{\text{Corrupt}}$ for $\mathcal{A}$. For ease of understanding, we assume that $\mathcal{A}$ corrupts all readers R_k in the supply chain.

- $\mathcal{A}'$ simulates readers R_k along the supply chain. Let T_j be a tag which went through path P and arrives at step v_k.

  $\mathcal{A}'$ decrypts the tag T_j's state using CS secret key sk_k of reader R_k and gets the pair $(\text{ID}_j, \sigma_{\text{P}}(\text{ID}_j))$. He verifies the path of tag T_j using $\mathcal{K}_k^V$. Then, $\mathcal{A}'$ updates the path of tag T_j using the secret coefficient a_k.

  Then using the public key of T_j's next step, $\mathcal{A}'$ encrypts T_j's identifier and T_j's path signature.

- In the challenge phase, $\mathcal{A}$ outputs a tag T_c.

- $\mathcal{A}'$ simulates all the readers in the supply chain and verifies whether the encrypted state stored into tag T_c matches a valid path in the supply chain. That is, $\mathcal{A}'$ verifies whether there exists a reader R_k in the supply chain that outputs $\text{CHECK}(R_k, \text{T}_c) = 1$ or not.

  Adversary $\mathcal{A}$ has a non negligible advantage in the security experiment, consequently, **i.)** $\exists R_k$ such that $\text{CHECK}(R_k, \text{T}_c) = 1$, and **ii.)** T_c did not go through step v_0.

We assume without loss of generality that T_c's state corresponds to the pair (ID_c, σ_c), and that T_c's path signature σ_c corresponds to path $\text{P}_{\text{valid}} = \overrightarrow{\text{v}_0 \text{P}}$.

- $\mathcal{A}'$ first checks whether $\text{coin}(\text{ID}_c) = 1$ or not.

  If $\text{coin}(\text{ID}_c) = 0$, then $\mathcal{A}'$ stops the experiment. Notice that if $h_c = H(\text{ID}_c) = g^{r_c}$, $\mathcal{A}'$ will not be able to break the BCDH assumption.

  If $\text{coin}(\text{ID}_c) = 1$, i.e., $h_c = H(\text{ID}_c) = g^{zr_c}$, then $\mathcal{A}'$ continues the experiment, and computes $e(g, h)^{xyz}$.

Let l denote the length of path P_{valid}. Accordingly,

$$\phi(\text{P}_{\text{valid}}) = a_0 x_0^l + \phi(\text{P}) = x x_0^l + \phi(\text{P})$$

and,

$$H(\text{ID}_c)^{xx_0^l} = \frac{\sigma_c}{H(\text{ID}_c)^{\phi(\text{P})}} = \frac{H(\text{ID}_c)^{\phi(\text{P}_{\text{valid}})}}{H(\text{ID}_c)^{\phi(\text{P})}}$$

$$H(\text{ID}_c)^x = \left(\frac{H(\text{ID}_c)^{\phi(\text{P}_{\text{valid}})}}{H(\text{ID}_c)^{\phi(\text{P})}} \right)^{\frac{1}{x_0^l}}$$

$$e(H(\text{ID}_c)^x, h^y) = e((g^{zr_c})^x, h^y) = e(g, h)^{xyzr_c}$$

Provided with the random number r_c, $\mathcal{A}'$ finally computes

$$e(g, h)^{xyz} = (e(g, h)^{xyzr_c})^{\frac{1}{r_c}}$$

Here, we compute the advantage of $\mathcal{A}'$.

Notice that $\mathcal{A}'$ succeeds in breaking the BCDH assumption if he does not stop the security experiment.

1.) $\mathcal{A}'$ halts the experiment, if during the initialization phase of the n tags T_j of the CHECKER system, the simulated random oracle $\mathcal{H}$ returns $(\text{ID}_j, r_j, \text{coin}(\text{ID}_j), h_j)$ such that $\text{coin}(\text{ID}_j) = 1$. This event occurs with probability p. Hence, the probability that $\mathcal{A}'$ does not stop the experiment during the learning phase is: $(1 - p)^n$.

2.) $\mathcal{A}'$ stops the experiment during the challenge phase, if $\text{coin}(\text{ID}_c) = 0$. As a result, $\mathcal{A}'$ does not stop the experiment in the challenge phase with probability p.

Let E denote the event: $\mathcal{A}'$ does not abort the security experiment.

Let E_1 denote the event: $\mathcal{A}'$ does not abort security experiment in the learning phase, $Pr(E_1) = (1 - p)^n$.

Let E_2 denote the event: $\mathcal{A}'$ does not abort security experiment in the challenge phase, $Pr(E_2) = p$. Hence,

$$\begin{aligned} \pi &= Pr(E) = Pr(E_1)Pr(E_2) \\ &= p(1 - p)^n \end{aligned}$$

Now, if $\mathcal{A}$ has a non negligible advantage ϵ in breaking the security of CHECKER, then $\mathcal{A}'$ can break the BCDH assumption with advantage $\epsilon' = \pi\epsilon$, leading to a contradiction.

Remark that π is maximal when $p = \frac{1}{n}$ and $\pi_{\text{max}} = \frac{(1-\frac{1}{n})^n}{n} \simeq \frac{1}{en}$. Consequently, the advantage ϵ' in breaking BCDH is in this case $\epsilon' = \frac{\epsilon}{en}$. $\quad\square$

5.2 Privacy analysis

Tag unlinkability

THEOREM 2. CHECKER *provides tag unlinkability under the SXDH assumption.*

PROOF. To prove tag unlinkability, we use the IND-CCA property of Cramer-Shoup encryption ensured under the SXDH assumption.

Before presenting the proof, we introduce the definition of IND-CCA.

Let $\mathcal{O}_{\text{decryption}}$ be the oracle that, on input of a ciphertext c encrypted with public key pk, outputs the underlying plaintext m.

Let $\mathcal{O}_{\text{encryption}}$ be the oracle that, provided with two messages m_0, m_1 and public key pk, randomly chooses $b \in \{0,1\}$, encrypts m_b using public key pk, and returns the challenge ciphertext c_b.

Let $\mathcal{A}\,(r,s,\epsilon)$ be an adversary that is allowed to make r calls to the oracle $\mathcal{O}_{\text{decryption}}$ with arbitrary ciphertexts c_i. Then, $\mathcal{A}$ selects two messages m_0 and m_1 which he provides to the oracle $\mathcal{O}_{\text{encryption}}$. $\mathcal{O}_{\text{encryption}}$ returns the challenge ciphertext c_b. After receiving c_b, $\mathcal{A}$ can still query the decryption oracle $\mathcal{O}_{\text{decryption}}$ with s ciphertexts c_i', with the only restrictions that $c_b \neq c_i'$. Finally, $\mathcal{A}$ is required to output his guess of b. An encryption is IND-CCA secure, if $\mathcal{A}\,(r,s,\epsilon)$ has a negligible advantage ϵ in outputting a correct guess of b.

Assume there is an adversary $\mathcal{A}$ who breaks the security of CHECKER with a non negligible advantage ϵ, we show that there is an adversary $\mathcal{A}'$ that uses $\mathcal{A}$ as a subroutine and breaks the IND-CCA property of Cramer-Shoup encryption with a non-negligible advantage ϵ'.

Proof overview. The idea of the proof is to build a CHECKER system such that there is a step v_i in the supply chain that is associated with the public key pk, where pk is the challenge public key from the IND-CCA security experiment.

In the learning phase, $\mathcal{A}'$ is required to simulate reader R_i. This implies that $\mathcal{A}'$ has to be able decrypt the state of tags arriving at step v_i. Hence the need to a decryption oracle and therewith to an IND-CCA secure encryption. Now, whenever a tag T arrives at step v_i, $\mathcal{A}'$ first calls the decryption oracle for the Cramer-Shoup encryption $\mathcal{O}_{\text{decryption}}$ that returns the underlying plaintexts, i.e., $(\text{ID}, \sigma_P(\text{ID}))$. Then, $\mathcal{A}'$ verifies the validity of the pair and updates the state of T accordingly.

In the challenge phase, $\mathcal{A}$ returns the challenge tags T_0 and T_1 to $\mathcal{A}'$. $\mathcal{A}'$ decrypts the state of tags T_0 and T_1 and gets their identifiers ID_0 and ID_1 respectively. Then, $\mathcal{A}'$ queries the encryption oracle $\mathcal{O}_{\text{encryption}}$ with message ID_0 and ID_1. $\mathcal{O}_{\text{encryption}}$ returns the challenge ciphertext $c_b = \text{Enc}_{\text{pk}}(\text{ID}_b), b \in \{0,1\}$. $\mathcal{A}'$ iterates the supply chain outside the range of $\mathcal{A}$, and simulates $\mathcal{O}_{\text{Flip}}$ by returning T_b which stores the ciphertext c_b along with an encryption of T_b's path signature. As $\mathcal{A}'$ makes a guess for the value of b to update T_b's path signature, this latter will be correct with probability $\frac{1}{2}$.

If $\mathcal{A}$ has a non-negligible advantage ϵ in breaking the tag unlinkability experiment, then he outputs a correct guess for the value of b. If $b = 0$, then this implies that T_b stores an encryption of ID_0 and thus $c_b = \text{Enc}_{\text{pk}}(\text{ID}_0)$; otherwise, $c_b = \text{Enc}_{\text{pk}}(\text{ID}_1)$.

Construction. To break the IND-CCA property of Cramer and Shoup encryption, $\mathcal{A}'$ proceeds as follows:

- $\mathcal{A}'$ creates a supply chain for the CHECKER protocol.

- $\mathcal{A}'$ calls the adversary $\mathcal{A}$. $\mathcal{A}$ queries the oracle $\mathcal{O}_{\text{Corrupt}}$ with the identity of r readers R_k. $\mathcal{A}'$ simulates the oracle $\mathcal{O}_{\text{Corrupt}}$ and assigns to each reader R_k a tuple $(x_0, a_k, \text{sk}_k, \text{pk}_k)$ that he returns to $\mathcal{A}$.

- Now, $\mathcal{A}'$ selects a reader R_i from the set of uncorrupt readers and assigns to R_i the tuple $(x_0, a_i, \text{pk}_i = \text{pk})$. Without loss of generality, we assume that step v_i in the supply chain is associated with reader R_i.

- Simulating $\mathcal{O}_{\text{Draw}}$, $\mathcal{A}'$ supplies $\mathcal{A}$ with two challenge tags T_0 and T_1 that have just been issued by issuer I, i.e., just entered the supply chain.

- $\mathcal{A}$ iterates the supply chain ρ times. Before each iteration j of the supply chain:

  1.) $\mathcal{A}$ reads and writes into tags T_0, T_1.

  2.) Simulating $\mathcal{O}_{\text{Step}}$, $\mathcal{A}'$ provides $\mathcal{A}$ with the next step of tags T_0, T_1.

  3.) $\mathcal{A}$ simulates $\mathcal{O}_{\text{Draw}}$ and supplies $\mathcal{A}$ with s tags $T_{(i,j)}$. $\mathcal{A}$ is also provided with $T_{(i,j)}$'s next step. $\mathcal{A}$ then iterates the supply chain and reads the states stored into tags $T_{(i,j)}$.

- If a tag T in the learning phase arrives at step v_i, then $\mathcal{A}'$ simulates reader R_i as follows:

  1.) $\mathcal{A}'$ reads the state stored into T and gets two CS ciphertexts c_{ID} and c_σ.

  2.) $\mathcal{A}'$ queries the oracle $\mathcal{O}_{\text{decryption}}$ with the ciphertexts c_{ID} and c_σ. The oracle $\mathcal{O}_{\text{decryption}}$ returns the corresponding plaintexts ID and σ.

  3.) $\mathcal{A}'$ checks then if the pair (ID, σ) corresponds to a valid path leading to step v_i.

  4.) Finally, $\mathcal{A}'$ updates the path signature of T accordingly and encrypts both the identifier ID and the path signature using the public key of T's next step.

- In the challenge phase, tags T_0 and T_1 are submitted to $\mathcal{A}'$. $\mathcal{A}'$ decrypts the states stored into T_0 and T_1, and gets ID_0 and ID_1 respectively.

- $\mathcal{A}'$ queries the oracle $\mathcal{O}_{\text{encryption}}$ with messages ID_0 and ID_1. $\mathcal{O}_{\text{encryption}}$ returns $c_{(\text{ID},b)} = \text{Enc}_{\text{pk}}(\text{ID}_b)$.

- $\mathcal{A}'$ prepares the tag T_b for the adversary $\mathcal{A}$:

  1.) $\mathcal{A}'$ updates the path of tags T_0 and T_1 and encrypts the path signature using the public key pk. He obtains two ciphertexts: $c_{(\sigma,0)}$ and $c_{(\sigma,1)}$.

  2.) $\mathcal{A}'$ randomly selects $b' \in \{0,1\}$ and stores the state $s_{\text{T}_b} = (c_{(\text{ID},b)}, c_{(\sigma,b')})$ in T_b. Therefore, T_b's next step is step v_i associated with public key pk.

- Simulating $\mathcal{O}_{\text{Flip}}$, $\mathcal{A}'$ provides $\mathcal{A}$ with the challenge tag T_b. $\mathcal{A}$ is allowed to read from tag T_b.

Notice that if $b = b'$, then the state $s_{\text{T}_b} = (c_{(\text{ID},b)}, c_{(\sigma,b')})$ computed by $\mathcal{A}'$ when simulating CHECKER corresponds to a well formed pair $(\text{ID}_b, \sigma_P(\text{ID}_b))$, and consequently, the simulation of CHECKER by $\mathcal{A}'$ does not differ from an actual CHECKER system. $\mathcal{A}$ can accordingly output his guess for the tag corresponding to the challenge tag T_b with a non-negligible advantage ϵ.

If $\mathcal{A}$ outputs $b = 0$, this means that T_b stores an encryption of ID_0, and $\mathcal{A}'$ outputs 0. If $\mathcal{A}$ outputs $b = 1$, this means that T_b stores an encryption of ID_1, and $\mathcal{A}'$ outputs 1.

If $b \neq b'$, then the probability that $\mathcal{A}'$ breaks the IND-CCA property of CS is at worst a random guess, i.e., $\frac{1}{2}$.

Now, we quantify the advantage of $\mathcal{A}'(q, 0, \epsilon')$, $(q \leq 2(s\rho + 2\rho + 2)$, in breaking the IND-CCA property of CS.

– Let E_1 be the event that $\mathcal{A}'$ breaks the IND-CCA property of CS.

– Let E_2 be the event that $b = b'$.

Since b' is selected randomly, the probability that $b = b'$ is $\frac{1}{2}$. Therefore,

$$
\begin{aligned}
Pr(E_1) &= Pr(E_1|E_2) \cdot Pr(E_2) + Pr(E_1|\overline{E_2}) \cdot Pr(\overline{E_2}) \\
&= \frac{1}{2} Pr(E_1|E_2) + \frac{1}{2} Pr(E_1|\overline{E_2}) \\
&= \frac{1}{2}\left(\frac{1}{2} + \epsilon\right) + \frac{1}{2} Pr(E_1|\overline{E_2}) \\
&\geq \frac{1}{2}\left(\frac{1}{2} + \epsilon + \frac{1}{2}\right) = \frac{1}{2} + \frac{\epsilon}{2}
\end{aligned}
$$

Thus, the advantage of $\mathcal{A}'$ to break the IND-CCA property of CS is at least $\epsilon' = \frac{\epsilon}{2}$. Therefore, if $\mathcal{A}$ has a non-negligible advantage ϵ to break CHECKER, then $\mathcal{A}'(q, 0, \epsilon')$ will have a non-negligible advantage ϵ' to break the IND-CCA property of Cramer and Shoup encryption, which leads to a contradiction. □

6. RELATED WORK

Ouafi and Vaudenay [16] propose a solution that allows product tracking. However, this solution assumes that tags can perform hash functions. We argue that a wide implementation of such tracking systems requires using the cheapest kind of tags which correspond to read/write only tags.

Also Burbridge and Soppera [6] suggest the use of proxy re-signature to allow path segment verification while using read/write only tags. The tag stores a signature of the last trusted party it has visited. To prevent product injection in the supply chain, partners in the supply chain do not have secret keys to sign tags' identifiers, but rather secret proxy keys that only allow partners to transform a valid signature of one partner to their own signature. The paper however does not address the problem of implementing practical proxy re-signatures without trusted third party.

Although these two previous schemes ensure secure product tracking in the supply chain, they fail at providing a privacy preserving solution. We emphasize that any solution dealing with product/tag tracking should preserve tag privacy in order to protect the privacy of the internal processes of partners in the supply chain.

Blass et al. [4] propose a tracking system using read/write only tags that preserve tags' privacy in the supply chain. They use polynomial based path encoding to represent efficiently the paths in the supply chain, and they rely on the use of homomorphic and probabilistic encryption to preserve tag privacy against readers in the supply chain and external adversaries. However, contrary to the work at hand, [4] relies on the assumption that the path verification is carried out by a trusted party called manager M. Thus, it does not permit the readers in the supply chain to perform the path verification which is the main application scenario for CHECKER.

7. EVALUATION

CHECKER targets read/write only tags that do no feature any computational capabilities. A tag in CHECKER is required to store a pair of IND-CCA encryptions of its identifier ID and its path signature $\sigma_{P_{\text{valid}}}(\text{ID}) = H(\text{ID})^{\phi(P_{\text{valid}})}$. In this paper, we use Cramer-Shoup's scheme as the underlying encryption. This results in an overall tag storage of $2 \cdot 4 \cdot 160 = 1280$ bits. We emphasize that any IND-CCA secure encryption in DDH-hard subgroups of elliptic curve is sufficient to implement CHECKER. One possible choice of encryption scheme is CS-lite [7]: a light variant of CS encryption which is IND-CCA secure and costs 480 bits per encryption

instead of 640 bits. Also, there is a variant of Elgamal proposed by Fujisaki and Okamoto [11] which is IND-CCA secure in the random oracle model, and whose storage requirements are comparable to Elgamal's.

We believe that CHECKER can be implemented in current ISO 18000-3 HF tags, such as UPM RFID MiniTrack tags [19] that feature 1 kbit of memory.

Moreover, a reader R_k in the supply chain is required to decrypt the state stored into tags using its secret key sk_k, then to verify the validity of the paths that tags went through, and to update and encrypt the state of tags. This amounts to performing: **1.)** two decryptions in $\mathbb{G}_1$ where $|\mathbb{G}_1| = 160$ bits, **2.)** ν_k bilinear pairings' computation in $\mathbb{G}_T$, where ν_k is the number of verification keys of reader R_k and $|\mathbb{G}_T| = 1024$ bits, **3.)** two exponentiations in $\mathbb{G}_1$ to update the path signature, and finally **4.)** two encryptions in $\mathbb{G}_1$. The costly operation at reader R_k is the verification of the path signature which is linear in the number of valid paths leading to reader R_k. We can further decrease the computation load at the readers by allowing tags to store the verification key that corresponds to the path that they took in the supply chain.

We recall that a verification key of path P_{valid} is $h^{\phi(P_{\text{valid}})} \in \mathbb{G}_2$. Now, instead of storing an encrypted pair $(\text{ID}, H(\text{ID})^{\phi(P_{\text{valid}})})$, a tag T stores the encrypted tuple $(\text{ID}, H(\text{ID})^{\phi(P_{\text{valid}})}, h^{\phi(P_{\text{valid}})})$. When T arrives at step v_k, the reader R_k decrypts T's state and gets a tuple (α, β, γ). First, R_k checks whether γ is in his set of verification keys $\mathcal{K}_V^k$ or not. If so, R_k proceeds in verifying the path signature of tag T. Consequently, the cost of the verification of the path signature at the readers is constant. On the one hand however, readers are required to perform an additional table lookup, one decryption, two exponentiations and one encryption in $\mathbb{G}_2$. On the other hand, tags have to store three encryptions of size 640 bits in the case of Cramer-Shoup, and of size 480 in the case of CS-lite.

8. CONCLUSION

In this paper, we presented CHECKER for a secure and privacy preserving product genuineness verification in supply chains. CHECKER relies solely on read/write RFID tags that do not feature any computational capabilities. CHECKER allows on-site checking by providing the readers with the means to verify the validity of the paths that products took. CHECKER's main idea is to sign the tag's identifier using the encoding of the path that the tag took. Then, each reader in CHECKER is supplied with a set of public keys that correspond to the set of valid paths in the supply chain. This grants readers the ability to verify the genuineness of products, while preventing them from injecting fake products. CHECKER's security and privacy rely on standard assumptions: the BCDH and the DDH assumptions. Finally, CHECKER does not involve a trusted party and therefore, it is well suited for the distributed and heterogeneous setting of supply chains.

Bibliography

[1] G. Ateniese, J. Camenisch, and B. de Medeiros. Untraceable RFID tags via insubvertible encryption. In *CCS '05: Proceedings of the 12th ACM conference on Computer and communications security*, pages 92–101, New York, NY, USA, 2005. ACM. ISBN 1-59593-226-7.

[2] G. Ateniese, J. Kirsch, and M. Blanton. Secret Handshakes with Dynamic and Fuzzy Matching. In *Proceedings of the Network and Distributed System Security Symposium, NDSS*. The Internet Society, 2007.

[3] L. Ballard, M. Green, B. de Medeiros, and F. Monrose. Correlation-Resistant Storage via Keyword-Searchable Encryption. Cryptology ePrint Archive, Report 2005/417, 2005. http://eprint.iacr.org/.

[4] E.-O. Blass, K. Elkhiyaoui, and R. Molva. Tracker: security and privacy for RFID-based supply chains. In *NDSS'11, 18th Annual Network and Distributed System Security Symposium, 6-9 February 2011, San Diego, California, USA, ISBN 1-891562-32-0*, 02 2011.

[5] D. Boneh, B. Lynn, and H. Shacham. Short signatures from the weil pairing. *Journal of Cryptology*, 17:297–319, 2004. ISSN 0933-2790.

[6] T. Burbridge and A. Soppera. Supply chain control using a RFID proxy re-signature scheme. In *RFID, 2010 IEEE International Conference on*, pages 29 –36, april 2010.

[7] R. Cramer and V. Shoup. A practical public key cryptosystem provably secure against adaptive chosen ciphertext attack. In *CRYPTO '98*, pages 13–25. Springer-Verlag, 1998.

[8] E. De Cristofaro and G. Tsudik. Practical private set intersection protocols with linear complexity. In R. Sion, editor, *Financial Cryptography and Data Security*, volume 6052 of *Lecture Notes in Computer Science*, pages 143–159. Springer Berlin / Heidelberg, 2010. ISBN 978-3-642-14576-6.

[9] E. De Cristofaro, J. Kim, and G. Tsudik. Linear-complexity private set intersection protocols secure in malicious model. In M. Abe, editor, *Advances in Cryptology - ASIACRYPT 2010*, volume 6477 of *Lecture Notes in Computer Science*, pages 213–231. Springer Berlin / Heidelberg, 2010. ISBN 978-3-642-17372-1.

[10] T. Dimitrou. rfidDOT: RFID delegation and ownership transfer made simple. In *Proceedings of International Conference on Security and privacy in Communication Networks*, Istanbul, Turkey, 2008. ISBN 978-1-60558-241-2.

[11] E. Fujisaki and T. Okamoto. How to Enhance the Security of Public-Key Encryption at Minimum Cost. In *Proceedings of the Second International Workshop on Practice and Theory in Public Key Cryptography*, PKC '99, pages 53–68, London, UK, 1999. Springer-Verlag. ISBN 3-540-65644-8.

[12] S. D. Galbraith, K. G. Paterson, and N. P. Smart. Pairings for cryptographers. *Discrete Appl. Math.*, 156:3113–3121, September 2008. ISSN 0166-218X.

[13] A. Juels and S. Weis. Defining Strong Privacy for RFID. In *PerCom Workshops*, pages 342–347, White Plains, USA, 2007. ISBN 978-0-7695-2788-8.

[14] A. Miyaji, M. Nakabayashi, and S. Takano. New Explicit Conditions of Elliptic Curve Traces for FR-Reduction. *TIEICE: IEICE Transactions on Communications/Electronics/Information and Systems*, 2001.

[15] G. Noubir, K. Vijayan, and H. J. Nussbaumer. Signature-based method for run-time fault detection in communication protocols. *Computer Communications Journal*, 21(5):405–421, 1998. ISSN 0140-3664.

[16] K. Ouafi and S. Vaudenay. Pathchecker: an RFID Application for Tracing Products in Suply-Chains. In *Workshop on RFID Security – RFIDSec'09*, pages 1–14, Leuven, Belgium, 2009. http://www.cosic.esat.kuleuven.be/rfidsec09/Papers/pathchecker.pdf.

[17] A. Sadeghi, I. Visconti, and C. Wachsmann. Anonymizer-Enabled Security and Privacy for RFID. In *8th International Conference on Cryptology And Network Security – CANS'09*, Kanazawa, Ishikawa, Japan, December 2009. Springer. ISBN 978-3-642-10432-9.

[18] M. Scott. Authenticated ID-based Key Exchange and remote log-in with simple token and PIN number. Cryptology ePrint Archive, Report 2002/164, 2002. http://eprint.iacr.org/.

[19] UPM RFID Technology. UPM Raflatac MiniTrak datasheet, 2011. http://www.upmrfid.com/rfid/images/MiniTrack_SLI_datasheet.pdf/$FILE/MiniTrack_SLI_datasheet.pdf.

[20] S. Vaudenay. On Privacy Models for RFID. In *Proceedings of ASIACRYPT*, pages 68–87, Kuching, Malaysia, 2007. ISBN 978-3-540-76899-9.

APPENDIX

A. STEP UNLINKABILITY

A.1 Definition

As explained in Section 3.2, step unlinkability captures the ability of an adversary $\mathcal{A}$ of telling if the paths of two tags T_0 and T_1 have a step in common besides the step v_0. Notice that step unlinkability as defined hereafter makes sense only when the system comprises at least two tags.

We use an experiment based definition as in Section 3.2. In addition to the oracles presented earlier, $\mathcal{A}$ has access to the oracle $\mathcal{O}_{\text{Path}}$. When $\mathcal{O}_{\text{Path}}$ is queried with a path P, it flips a fair coin $b \in \{0, 1\}$. If $b = 1$, then $\mathcal{O}_{\text{Path}}$ selects randomly a tag T which is going through a step $v \in P \setminus \{v_0\}$ in the next supply chain iteration. Otherwise, $\mathcal{O}_{\text{Path}}$ selects randomly a tag T which is going through a step $v \notin P$. Finally, $\mathcal{O}_{\text{Path}}$ returns the tag T to $\mathcal{A}$.

An adversary $\mathcal{A}(r, s, t, \rho, \epsilon)$ against step unlinkability has access to CHECKER in two phases. In the learning phase as illustrated in Algorithm 5, $\mathcal{A}$ calls the oracle $\mathcal{O}_{\text{corrupt}}$ that furnishes $\mathcal{A}$ with the secret information of r readers R_i of his choice. Now, $\mathcal{A}$ controls steps v_i associated with readers R_i. $\mathcal{A}$ then queries the oracle $\mathcal{O}_{\text{Draw}}$ which supplies $\mathcal{A}$ with a tag T_0 entering the supply chain.

$\mathcal{A}$ is allowed to iterate the supply chain up to ρ times. Before each iteration i of the supply chain, $\mathcal{A}$ can read and re-write the internal state of tag T_0. He also queries the oracle $\mathcal{O}_{\text{Step}}$ that returns the next step $v_{T_0}^{i+1}$ of tag T_0 in the supply chain. $\mathcal{A}$ then calls the oracle $\mathcal{O}_{\text{Draw}}$ which gives $\mathcal{A}$ s tags $T_{(i,j)}$, that are going through $v_{T_0}^{i+1}$ in the next supply chain iteration. Also, $\mathcal{A}$ can query the oracle $\mathcal{O}_{\text{Draw}}$ again to provide him with t other tags $T'_{(i,j)}$, that fulfill some condition $c_{(i,j)}$ specified by $\mathcal{A}$. Now, $\mathcal{A}$ has a full access to these tags, i.e., $\mathcal{A}$ can read from and write into them, he can as well have access to the next step of tags $T'_{(i,j)}$. Finally, $\mathcal{A}$ iterates the supply chain by calling ITERATESUPPLYCHAIN and reads the state stored into the tags $T_{(i,j)}$ and $T'_{(i,j)}$.

Let P_{T_0} denote the path that tag T_0 went through.

In the challenge phase, cf., Algorithm 6, $\mathcal{A}$ queries the oracle $\mathcal{O}_{\text{Path}}$ with path P_{T_0}. $\mathcal{O}_{\text{Path}}$ returns a tag T_1. $\mathcal{A}$ is allowed to read and re-write the state of tag T_1.

$\mathcal{A}$ iterates the supply chain, and reads the state stored into tag T_1.

Let v_{T_1} denote the step that tag T_1 went through during the challenge phase. $\mathcal{A}$'s goal is to decide whether the step $v_{T_1} \in P_{T_0}$ or not. If $v_{T_1} \in P_{T_0}$, then $\mathcal{A}$ outputs $b = 1$; otherwise, $\mathcal{A}$ outputs $b = 0$.

The adversary $\mathcal{A}$ is successful, if **i.)** his guess of bit b is correct, and if **ii.)** the step v_{T_1} is not corrupted by $\mathcal{A}$.

DEFINITION 5 (STEP UNLINKABILITY). CHECKER *provides step unlinkability*⇔ *For adversary $\mathcal{A}$, inequality $Pr(\mathcal{A}$ is successful$) \leq \frac{1}{2} + \epsilon$ holds, where ϵ is negligible.*

A.2 Tag unlinkability and step unlinkability

The following theorem states that if CHECKER ensures tag unlinkability, it will as well ensure step unlinkability.

THEOREM 3. *If CHECKER ensures tag unlinkability, then it also ensures step unlinkability.*

PROOF. Assume there is an adversary $\mathcal{A}$ who breaks the step unlinkability with a non negligible advantage ϵ. We show that there

```
for i := 1 to r do
│  S_i ← O_Corrupt(R_i) ;
end
T_0 ← O_Draw("tag at step "v_0);
for i := 0 to ρ − 1 do
│  v_{T_0}^{i+1} ← O_Step(T_0);
│  s_{T_0}^i := READ(T_0);
│  WRITE(T_0, s'_{T_0}^i);
│  for j := 1 to s do
│  │  T_{(i,j)} ← O_Draw("tag's next step is v_{T_0}^{i+1}"));
│  │  s_{T_{(i,j)}} := READ(T_{(i,j)});
│  │  WRITE(T_{(i,j)}, s'_{T_{(i,j)}});
│  end
│  for j := 1 to t do
│  │  T'_{(i,j)} ← O_Draw(c_{(i,j)});
│  │  v_{T'_{(i,j)}} ← O_Step(T'_{(i,j)});
│  │  s_{T'_{(i,j)}} := READ(T'_{(i,j)});
│  │  WRITE(T'_{(i,j)}, s'_{T'_{(i,j)}});
│  end
│  ITERATESUPPLYCHAIN;
│  for j := 1 to s do
│  │  READ(T_{(i,j)});
│  end
│  for j := 1 to t do
│  │  READ(T'_{(i,j)});
│  end
end
```
Algorithm 5: $\mathcal{A}$'s step unlinkability learning phase

```
T_1 ← O_Path(P_{T_0});
s_{T_1}^k := READ(T_1);
WRITE(T_1, s'_{T_1}^k);
ITERATESUPPLYCHAIN;
s_{T_1}^{k+1} := READ(T_1);
OUTPUT b;
```
Algorithm 6: $\mathcal{A}$'s step unlinkability challenge phase

is an adversary $\mathcal{A}'$ who uses $\mathcal{A}$ to break the tag unlinkability as defined in Section 3.2 with a non negligible advantage ϵ'.

Proof overview. In the proof below, we show that if adversary $\mathcal{A}$ has a non-negligible advantage ϵ in breaking step unlinkability, then $\mathcal{A}'$ can construct a statistical distinguisher that tells tags T_0 and T_1 apart in the tag unlinkability experiment with a non negligible advantage ϵ'.

In a nutshell, adversary $\mathcal{A}'$ supplies adversary $\mathcal{A}$ in the learning phase of step unlinkability with the first challenge tag T_0 that he receives in the tag unlinkability experiment.

Then, at the beginning of the challenge phase of the step unlinkability experiment, $\mathcal{A}'$ provides $\mathcal{A}$ with the second challenge tag T_1 of tag unlinkability.

Finally, at the end of the challenge phase of step unlinkability, $\mathcal{A}'$ replaces tag T_1 by tag T_b that was returned by O_{Flip}.

If $b = 1$, then $\mathcal{A}$ breaks the step unlinkability of CHECKER with a non-negligible advantage ϵ. Otherwise, $\mathcal{A}$'s advantage is negligible in breaking step unlinkability.

Now, the statistical distinguisher works as follows: whenever $\mathcal{A}$ outputs a correct guess for the step unlinkability experiment, then $\mathcal{A}'$ outputs $b = 1$; otherwise, $\mathcal{A}'$ outputs $b = 0$.

Construction. $\mathcal{A}'$ simulates CHECKER to adversary $\mathcal{A}$ whose goal

is to break step unlinkability.

I.) In the learning phase of step unlinkability:

- Whenever $\mathcal{A}$ wants to corrupt a reader R_i, $\mathcal{A}'$ makes a query to the oracle $O_{Corrupt}$ with R_i's identity. $O_{Corrupt}$ returns the secrets of reader R_i to $\mathcal{A}'$, who then returns the same secrets to $\mathcal{A}$.

- When $\mathcal{A}$ queries $\mathcal{A}'$ to get a tag T_0, $\mathcal{A}'$ queries the oracle O_{Draw}. O_{Draw} returns two challenge tags T_0 and T_1 for the tag unlinkability experiment which just entered the supply chain. Then, $\mathcal{A}'$ picks for instance tag T_0 and returns T_0 to $\mathcal{A}$.

- When $\mathcal{A}$ queries $\mathcal{A}'$ to supply him with the next step of tag T_0, $\mathcal{A}'$ queries the oracle O_{step} with tag T_0. O_{step} returns the next step $v_{T_0}^{i+1}$ of tag T_0 to $\mathcal{A}'$, who then returns $v_{T_0}^{i+1}$ to $\mathcal{A}$.

- If $\mathcal{A}$ queries $\mathcal{A}'$ for tags whose next step is $v_{T_0}^{i+1}$, then $\mathcal{A}'$ queries the oracle O_{Draw} with the condition "tag's next step $v_{T_0}^{i+1}$". O_{Draw} supplies $\mathcal{A}'$ with tags $T_{(i,j)}$ satisfying the condition. Finally, $\mathcal{A}'$ gives $\mathcal{A}$ the same set of tags $T_{(i,j)}$.

- If $\mathcal{A}$ queries $\mathcal{A}'$ for tags satisfying some condition $c_{(i,j)}$, then $\mathcal{A}'$ queries the oracle O_{Draw} with $c_{(i,j)}$. O_{Draw} furnishes $\mathcal{A}'$ with tags $T'_{(i,j)}$ fulfilling the condition $c_{(i,j)}$. $\mathcal{A}'$ then returns the tags $T'_{(i,j)}$ to $\mathcal{A}$.

- $\mathcal{A}'$ iterates the supply chain.

- After iterating the supply chain, $\mathcal{A}'$ gives $\mathcal{A}$ the tags $T_{(i,j)}$ and $T'_{(i,j)}$ that $\mathcal{A}$ can read from.

II.) In the challenge phase of step unlinkability:

- $\mathcal{A}'$ simulates the oracle $O_{Path}(P_{T_0})$ and prepares tag T_1 for adversary $\mathcal{A}$.

  1. $\mathcal{A}'$ queries the oracle O_{Step} with the challenge tags T_0 and T_1. $\mathcal{A}'$ gets therefore the next step $v_{T_0}^{k+1}$ and $v_{T_1}^{k'+1}$ of tags T_0 and T_1 respectively.

     Note that if the reader associated with step $v_{T_1}^{k'+1}$ is corrupt by $\mathcal{A}$, and therewith by $\mathcal{A}'$, then $\mathcal{A}'$ stops the experiment as his attack against tag unlinkability is trivial.

  2. $\mathcal{A}'$ reads from tag T_1 and provides $\mathcal{A}$ with T_1.

- $\mathcal{A}$ can read and write into tag T_1. Then, tag T_1 is given back to $\mathcal{A}'$.

- The supply chain is iterated outside the range of $\mathcal{A}'$. The oracle O_{Flip} returns tag T_b, $b \in \{0, 1\}$.

- $\mathcal{A}'$ returns tag T_b to $\mathcal{A}$. Now, $\mathcal{A}$ can read from tag T_b.

- $\mathcal{A}$ then outputs his guess for the bit b' for the step unlinkability experiment, i.e., $b' = 1$, if $v_{T_1}^{k'+1}$ is a step in T_0's path; otherwise $b' = 0$.

If $T_b = T_1$, then $\mathcal{A}'$'s simulation of the CHECKER system is perfect, and $\mathcal{A}$ will have a non-negligible advantage in guessing the value of the bit b'.

If $T_b = T_0$, then $\mathcal{A}$'s view of the step unlinkability experiment is independent of b', and thus $\mathcal{A}$'s advantage is negligible.

This therefore leads to a statistical distinguisher between tags T_0 and T_1. When $\mathcal{A}$ succeeds in the step unlinkability experiment, $\mathcal{A}'$ outputs $b = 1$, otherwise $\mathcal{A}'$ outputs $b = 0$.

Hence, if there is an adversary $\mathcal{A}(r, s, t, \rho, \epsilon)$ who breaks the step unlinkability of CHECKER, then there is an adversary $\mathcal{A}'(r, s + t, \rho, \epsilon)$ who breaks the tag unlinkability of CHECKER. □

Entropy Attacks and Countermeasures in Wireless Network Coding

Andrew Newell
Purdue University
newella@cs.purdue.edu

Reza Curtmola
New Jersey Institute of
Technology
crix@njit.edu

Cristina Nita-Rotaru
Purdue University
crisn@cs.purdue.edu

ABSTRACT

Multihop wireless networks gain higher performance by using network coding. However, using network coding also introduces new attacks such as the well-studied *pollution* attacks and less-studied *entropy* attacks. Unlike in pollution attacks where an attacker injects polluted packets (i.e., packets that are not linear combinations of the packets sent by the source), in entropy attacks an attacker creates non-innovative packets (i.e., packets that contain information already known by the system). In both cases the result is a severe degradation of the system performance. In this paper, we identify two variants of entropy attacks (*local* and *global*) and show that while they share some characteristics with pollution attacks and selective forwarding, none of the techniques proposed to defend against such attacks are applicable to entropy attacks because the packets look legitimate and the packet forwarding is stealthy in nature. We propose and evaluate several defenses that vary in detection capabilities and overhead.

Categories and Subject Descriptors

C.2.1 [**Computer-Communication Networks**]: Network Architecture and Design—*Wireless Communication*; C.2.m [**Computer-Communication Networks**]: Miscellaneous—*Security*

General Terms

Security, Performance

Keywords

Network coding, Wireless, Security, Entropy attacks

1. INTRODUCTION

Traditional, wireless, multi-hop systems consist of forwarders that are constrained to only store and forward packets. Wireless, network coding systems remove this constraint and allow forwarders to use an encoding scheme that creates new packets based on stored packets. Encoding at the forwarders both maximizes the information carried by each packet and reduces the coordination necessary to deliver packets. Theoretical results [4] have shown that network coding can achieve higher network capacity than traditional networks with little coordination [15], and several practical systems [7,9,22,27,37,38] have demonstrated significant performance increases due to network coding.

A node creates *correct* coded packets by computing a random linear combination of packets stored in its *coding buffer*. The coding buffer is the set of coded packets received correctly. A receiver is able to eventually recover the original packets if it obtains n linearly-independent coded packets generated based on original plain packets from the source. A malicious node can deviate from the standard coding procedure and conduct two types of attacks that are specific to network coding systems. The first, well-known attack is called a pollution attack [11, 13] where a node creates an *invalid* coded packet which is not a valid combination of coded packets. The second, less studied attack is called an entropy attack [13,20] where a node creates a *non-innovative* coded packet which is a non-random linear combination of coded packets such that the coded packet is *linearly dependent* with the coded packets stored at a downstream node. A linearly dependent coded packet wastes resources since it adds no useful information to help the receivers decode the original packets. We classify entropy attacks into two categories which require different capabilities from an attacker:

- A *local entropy attack* corresponds to an attacker that produces coded packets that are non-innovative to local neighboring nodes.
- A *global entropy attack* corresponds to a more capable attacker that produces coded packets that are seemingly innovative to local neighboring nodes but are non-innovative to at least one distant downstream node.

Many defenses for pollution attacks were proposed [3,5,8, 10,13,14,19,23,25,26,28,29,33,39], and they are all designed to defend against invalid coded packets but they provide no defense against attacks that use valid, but non-innovative coded packets. Cryptographic-based defenses [3,5,8,10,23, 26,28,29,39] use homomorphic cryptography to detect and drop coded packets that are not valid linear combinations of the source data. Non-innovative packets will pass such verifications since they are valid combinations of the source data. Information theoretic defenses [14, 19, 33] rely on sending additional redundant information to correct invalid coded packets at the receiver. This additional information does not provide any benefit against an attacker that creates non-innovative packets because the added redundancy will only help recover the non-innovative packets. Lastly, existing monitoring defenses for pollution attacks [24, 25] focus on detecting invalid coded packets by comparing the packets received and sent by a node. While such schemes can detect simple types of entropy attacks in which the attacker for example sends the same valid packet repeatedly, they can not detect global entropy attacks.

Previous work [13, 20] showed that receivers waste resources to process non-innovative packets. However, entropy attacks cause more damage to a network than just occupying these resources. An entropy attack disrupts routing the same way selective forwarding attacks [21] disrupt routing in a network. In both cases, the routing algorithm chooses an optimal route or multiple routes to send data on, but the attacking node refuses to participate correctly in the forwarding of packets which prevents information transfer along one or more paths. While the effect of the entropy and selective forwarding attacks are similar, defenses against selective forwarding attacks [21, 30, 35] can not be directly applied to entropy attacks because entropy attackers actually send packets and, in the case of global entropy attacks, the attack can not be locally detected and global information is needed. Multi-path defenses [21] rely on sending redundant information along multiple paths. Network coding routing inherently sends on multiple paths, but performance can still significantly be degraded by entropy attacks since a compromised node can still deny flow on a fraction of the paths. ACK-based defenses [35] are not applicable for entropy attacks since they require nodes to acknowledge that they have received packets and do not provide mechanisms to detect if those packets were innovative or not. Existing monitoring defenses [30] require that watchdog nodes receive a fraction of traffic in and out of a suspected node to make an accurate decision of misbehavior. The approach will not work for entropy attacks since the watchdog must receive all packets that the watched node receives, otherwise it cannot determine if the newly created packets are innovative.

In this paper we study entropy attacks and their impact on wireless network coding systems. Specifically:

- We classify entropy attacks based on attacker's capabilities into *local entropy attacks* and *global entropy attacks*. We introduce a new attack, the *global entropy attack* in which the attacker generates coded packets that seem to be innovative to immediate neighbors, but are non-innovative for nodes that are further downstream. We demonstrate via simulation the negative impact of entropy attacks on network performance.

- We propose a defense scheme against local entropy attacks. The scheme, Non-innovative Link Adjustment (NLA), routes around attackers by adjusting the link quality for each link based on the percentage of non-innovative packets they carry. We show that while NLA works well for local entropy attacks, is not effective for global entropy attacks.

- We propose two defenses to address global entropy attacks. In the first defense, Upstream Buffer Propagation (UBP), downstream nodes share information about received coded packets with upstream nodes such that immediate downstream neighbors of an attacker can detect the attack. In the second defense, Buffer Monitoring (BM), watchdog nodes monitor forwarder nodes to ensure that broadcast coded packets are random linear combinations of all received coded pack-

ets, and the coefficients of this linear combination are chosen according to a publicly known pseudo-random function. BM is essentially different from typical monitoring techniques since watchdogs need to know every packet received by a forwarder. The defenses differ in terms of detection efficacy and overhead cost.

- We analytically compare the security strength of the UBP and BM defense schemes. We are able to quantify the capabilities of an attacker under each global entropy defense.

- We use a real network topology to analyze the applicability of the BM monitoring-based global entropy defense since not every flow in a topology may have sufficient wireless links to monitor traffic. We find that for the real network topology we used the monitoring-based defense can be applied to only 84.7% of flows due to constraints of the topology.

2. RELATED WORK

Entropy attacks. Entropy attacks have been considered for network coding systems, but defenses have been proposed only to mitigate the overhead of transferring non-innovative coded packets [13, 20]. These works do not consider neither the impact on routing nor the possibility of a global entropy attack. In [13], the authors propose additional local coordination in a peer-to-peer network coding system prior to obtaining a coded packet to ensure it is innovative. The authors of [20] are concerned with the additional computation required at a node to determine whether a received coded packet is innovative or not. Their solution is to probabilistically check the linear independence of a coded packet which ensures that non-innovative coded packets are dropped immediately using minor computation.

Selective forwarding attacks. Wireless mesh network security have considered the effects of a Byzantine adversary conducting a selective forwarding attack [21], where a malicious node refuses to forward some packets it receives. Such an attack can cause significant damage to network performance. Monitoring is a suitable solution to detect selective forwarding in a wireless network [30]. Nodes that neighbor an attacker can detect when the attacker has received a packet and not forwarded the packet. One of the defense schemes we propose against global entropy attacks also relies on monitoring. Unlike in defenses against selective forwarding attacks, using monitoring to defend against entropy attacks is more challenging because the attacker in an entropy attack is still forwarding packets, but the neighboring nodes need more information to determine that the attacker is coding non-innovative coded packets.

Wormhole attacks. The global entropy attack that we introduce in this paper may use an out-of-band communication channel between nodes just as in a wormhole attack [16, 17, 34]: An upstream and downstream node collude by using coded packets received at the downstream node to create new coded packets at the upstream node. Existing defenses against wormhole attacks focus on individual packets which cannot be applied to network coding as packets are combined by forwarders. In [17], temporal and geographical leashes are placed on packets to ensure they are correctly forwarded through the network. Such a technique cannot be applied to network coding since packets are coded together and each forwarder creates new packets.

Pollution attacks. Many other works also consider security of network coding systems that contain Byzantine adversaries conducting pollution attacks [3,5,8,19,26,28,33,36, 39]. In a pollution attack, a node creates coded packets that are not valid linear combinations of the source's data. All of the defenses against pollution attacks rely on the fact that an invalid coded packet is not a valid linear combination. Thus, a pollution defense is not helpful against an entropy attack because entropy attackers are still creating coded packets that are valid linear combinations of the source's data.

3. SYSTEM AND ADVERSARIAL MODEL

In this section, we describe intra-flow network coding based on random linear network coding and specifically define entropy attacks in such network coding systems.

3.1 Random Intra-flow Network Coding

A general intra-flow network coding system consists of a *source* and multiple *forwarders* (destinations can be thought of as a special case of a forwarder). The source represents data to be sent as a matrix $\mathbf{B}$ of n linearly independent rows. The matrix $\mathbf{B}$ is created such that any collection of n linear combinations that are linearly independent can be transformed into $\mathbf{B}$ with gaussian elimination. Such a creation of $\mathbf{B}$ is possible by appending coding headers to each row. The source continuously broadcasts *coded packets* $\mathbf{c}(t)$ that are random linear combinations of $\mathbf{B}$:

$$\mathbf{c}(t) = \mathbf{r}(t) * \mathbf{B} \qquad (1)$$

The vector $\mathbf{r}(t)$ is the random vector used to create $\mathbf{c}(t)$ at time t at the source. The source aims to send n coded packets to the destination such that the n coded packets are linearly independent, and this is called a generation.

Each forwarder i has a coding buffer $\mathbf{B}_i(t)$ which is a matrix such that the first rows are the set of all overheard coded packets at node i that are linearly independent when the forwarder i broadcasts a coded packet at time t, and the rest of the rows are zero such that the total number of rows is n. The t component is necessary because the number of non-zero rows in the coding buffer typically grows over time as more coded packets are received. Forwarders have a condition that defines when to forward a packet. E.g., in MORE[7] a forwarder will forward when it has received a sufficient (depending on the topology) number of coded packets. When this condition is met at time t for forwarder i, the forwarder generates broadcasts the coded packet $\mathbf{c}_i(t)$:

$$\mathbf{c}_i(t) = \mathbf{r}_i(t) * \mathbf{B}_i(t) \qquad (2)$$

The vector $\mathbf{r}_i(t)$ is the random vector used to create the coded packet $\mathbf{c}_i(t)$ at time t at node i.

The destinations eventually receive n linearly indendent coded packets. The destinations can decode by performing gaussian elimination on their coding buffers which will result in the original $\mathbf{B}$ matrix from the source.

3.2 Entropy Attacks

We define two classes of entropy attacks, local and global. A global entropy attacker is capable of overhearing traffic on a link that is located several hops downstream. Such overhearing is possible if the attacker has a more advanced antenna for reception or cooperates with another wireless device that is located near the link that must be eavesdropped.

A global entropy attacker requires a much more sophisticated defense to deal with. We will motivate via simulation in Section 6 the need to create sophisticated defenses for detecting the most capable entropy attackers.

Local Entropy Attacks. A local entropy attacker creates coded packets that are non-innovative to neighboring nodes. Such an attacker creates non-innovative coded packets by refusing to code optimally as the optimal is creating a coded packets that is a random linear combinations of all received coded packets. Specifically, we define a local entropy attacker as a forwarder i that deviates from the protocol at some time t by creating a coded packet $\bar{\mathbf{c}}_i(t)$:

$$\bar{\mathbf{c}}_i(t) = \bar{\mathbf{r}}_i(t) * \mathbf{B}_i(t) \qquad (3)$$

The vector $\bar{\mathbf{r}}_i(t)$ is an arbitrary vector chosen by the attacker. A random linear network coding protocol dictates that coded packets are combined randomly, but the attacker deviates by choosing a non-random vector $\bar{\mathbf{r}}_i(t)$. Specifically, a non-random vector is a vector such that at least one element is not chosen randomly, while a random vector has every element chosen randomly.

Global Entropy Attacks. A global entropy attacker uses global information about what coded packets have been sent in the network to create coded packets that are seemingly innovative to local nodes but are non-innovative to some distant downstream node. These coded packets are also created by refusing to create random linear combinations of received coded packets but also by including a combination of coded packets from some other portion of the network to deceptively cause local neighbors to believe the coded packet is innovative. Specifically we define a global entropy attacker as a forwarder i that deviates from the protocol at time t by creating coded packets $\bar{\mathbf{c}}_i(t)$:

$$\bar{\mathbf{c}}_i(t) = \bar{\mathbf{r}}_i(t) * \mathbf{B}_i(t) + \mathbf{d}_i(t) \qquad (4)$$

The vector $\bar{\mathbf{r}}_i(t)$ is not a random vector. The vector $\mathbf{d}_i(t)$ is not an element of the row space of $\mathbf{B}_i(t)$ but is an element of the row space of $\mathbf{B}$. That is, $\mathbf{d}_i(t)$ is a linear combination of some coded packets in the network, but it is not a linear combination of the coded packets that have been received by node i. The $\mathbf{d}_i(t)$ component of $\bar{\mathbf{c}}_i(t)$ is coded information being replayed from some other portion of the network.

4. SIMULATION METHODOLOGY

We aim to motivate the need for defenses against entropy attacks by showing the impact of entropy attacks through simulations. We conduct simulation experiments to measure the performance of a realistic system under various attack and defense scenarios.

We select MORE [7] as our wireless intra-flow network coding protocol that is based on random linear network coding. The source continuously broadcasts coded packets. A node is selected as a forwarder if it lies on a path or multiple paths from the source to destination, and these paths have sufficient link qualities. Based on global link state information, each forwarder is assigned a rebroadcast ratio which determines the number of coded packets received before creating and broadcasting a new coded packet. These ratios reflect how much each node contributes to a flow. Once the destination has received a sufficient number of coded packets for a generation, the destination sends an ACK back to the source. Upon receiving the ACK, the source starts sending a new generation.

Our experiments are conducted using the Glomosim [1] simulator. We use a raw link bandwidth of 5.5 Mbps and 802.11 [18] as the MAC layer protocol. For a realistic network topology and link qualities, we use the link quality measurements from the Roofnet [2] network which is a 38-node 802.11b/g mesh network deployed on MIT campus.

An experiment consists of 200 simulations that each have a random flow. A random flow consists of a randomly chosen source and destination pair. In a given simulation, the source transfers data to the destination for 400 seconds. We measure performance for a simulation and display all 200 simulations as a Cumulative Distribution Function (CDF).

For performance, we measure throughput of the system. Throughput is the rate (in kbps) of data being decoded at the destination. More specifically, throughput is the total amount of data decoded at the destination (r bits) divided by the transfer time (T seconds):

$$Throughput = \frac{r}{1000 * T} \tag{5}$$

We select the network coding parameters to match the default settings for MORE as described in [7]. The number of rows in the matrix $\mathbf{B}$ is $n = 32$, a symbol size of 1 byte $q = 2^8$, and the size of a coded packet is 1500 bytes.

To simulate attackers, we define the specific coding behavior of attackers. Random nodes from the set of forwarders for a flow are selected as attackers, and those attackers follow the specified attack behavior.

5. LOCAL ENTROPY ATTACKS

Using the methodology described in Section 4, we show the impact of a local entropy attack on a typical network, and then we present a defense strategy.

5.1 Threat

The damage caused by a local entropy attack is similar to selective forwarding. A broadcast coded packet that is non-innovative to all neighboring nodes is equivalent to a node not broadcasting a coded packet at all. The local entropy attack does cause some additional damage compared to selective forwarding since bandwidth and computation of neighboring nodes is wasted to receive the non-innovative coded packets and determine that they are non-innovative.

A local entropy attack is effective because the system trusts each node to utilize the link capacities fully to deliver innovative coded packets downstream. Thus, when a local entropy attacker is located at an important position on a path or multiple paths between the source and destination, the system delivers many coded packets to the attacker under the false assumption that new innovative coded packets are delivered further downstream from this node.

To show the effectiveness of a local entropy attack, we conduct an experiment using the simulation methodology from Section 4 with zero, one, and two entropy attackers. These local entropy attackers choose $\bar{\mathbf{r}}_i(t) = \langle r_1, ..., r_{16}, 0, ..., 0 \rangle$, so the first 16 symbols are random while the last 16 symbols are zero. Thus, the attacker codes normally the first 16 received coded packets, but any further coded packets received are never used for coding.

Figure 1(a) shows the results of the local entropy attack. Such a simple attack results in zero throughput for 43% and 70% of flows for one and two attackers, respectively. The zero throughput flows are flows where the attackers happened to cut the topology consisting of the forwarders. Even the throughput in non-zero flows for the attacking scenarios degrade throughput significantly. Roughly 15% of the flows in each case of attackers has non-zero throughput where the throughput is less than the lowest throughput for MORE without an attack. The non-zero flows are affected as well, as the median throughputs are 900, 400, and 0 kbps for 0, 1, and 2 attackers respectively.

5.2 Defense

The ideal defense against a local entropy attacker is to determine which nodes are performing the attack and remove them from the system. This is not straightforward based on local decisions since even honest nodes may unknowingly send some non-innovative coded packets. The reason is because a node knows what it has already sent, but it does not know what downstream nodes may have received from another path, and a downstream node may receive the same information along two upstream paths.

Figure 1(b) shows the proportion of received non-innovative coded packets in each flow for MORE. There is an obvious increase in non-innovative coded packet reception with attackers present, but even for the benign case some flows will contain a significant proportion of non-innovative coded packets. In these benign flows, there are multiple paths to the destination which have high packet reception probabilities, thus there is little diversity in the coded packets downstream when these paths coverage which accounts for the non-innovative coded packet receptions. For 30% of benign flows 10% of received coded packets were non-innovative. This is a total for all nodes in the network, so some links in the flow potentially carry an even larger proportion of non-innovative coded packets.

Non-innovative Link Adjustment (NLA). We propose NLA as a defense against local entropy attacks. Because honest nodes also create some non-innovative packets, we do not adopt a strict node removal strategy. Instead, we punish each link proportionally with the amount of non-innovative coded packets sent on the link. The modified link qualities are obtained by multiplying the original link quality with the proportion of received innovative coded packets to total coded packets on a link. A forwarder notifies the network if it notices a significant change in the modified link qualities. Thus, when a local entropy attacker sends non-innovative coded packets, the routing layer is alerted that specific links are not carrying innovative coded packets. For MORE, nodes recalculate their rebroadcast ratios based on the modified link states which will route data on paths that avoid the attacker node. Performing this securely requires mechanisms that limit the ability of an attacker to falsely accuse other nodes. We assume that such mechanisms are in place and they are out of the scope of this work.

Figure 1(c) demonstrates how the local entropy attack is mitigated by NLA. As a baseline for the defense, we include an ideal defense where the entropy attacker is removed from the network. We removed flows (31 of 200) where the entropy attacker partitions the network from source to destination as there does not exist any set of forwarders that provides positive throughput. Without a defense, 30% of flows result in zero throughput, and these are cases where the entropy attacker partitions the set of forwarders chosen by the routing logic. With NLA, only 5% of flows result in zero throughput because in the majority of cases where the

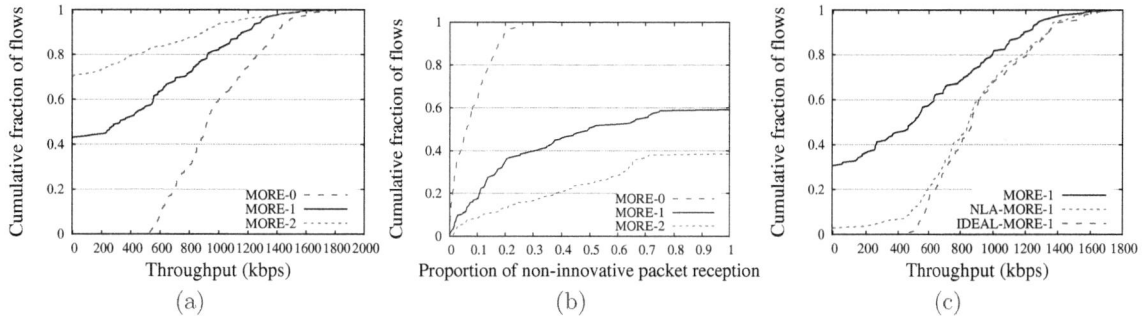

Figure 1: MORE-x is the standard wireless network coding protocol with x local entropy attackers randomly selected on each flow. NLA-MORE-x is MORE-x with the defense NLA. IDEAL-MORE-x is MORE-X with the x local entropy attackers removed from the system which represents the ideal defense against an entropy attack. (a) Throughput CDF of network coding with varying number of entropy attackers. (b) Proportion of non-innovative coded packet reception (summed over all nodes) CDFs for varying numbers of local entropy attackers. (c) Throughput CDF of network coding with one local entropy attacker for no defense, the NLA defense, and the ideal defense.

Table 1: Throughput results of various attack and defense scenarios with the topology in Figure 2

Defense	Throughput (kbps)
None	233
NLA	214
Ideal	345

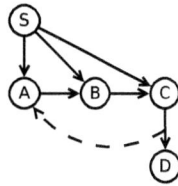

Figure 2: S is the source, D is the destination, A is the global entropy attacker. The solid lines indicate standard wireless links, while the dashed line indicates that node A can overhear the coded packets on the link between C and D.

entropy attacker partitions the initial set of forwarders the NLA defense severely punishes the links outgoing from the malicious node such that the routing logic chooses a new set of forwarders which can route data around the malicious node. With the exception of the lowest performing 20% of flows, the NLA is capable of performing within 50 kbps of the cases where the local entropy attacker is removed.

6. GLOBAL ENTROPY ATTACKS

In this section we first show how a global entropy attack impacts performance and argue that the NLA defense cannot mitigate such an attack. We then propose two defenses that can defend against global entropy attacks.

6.1 Threat

We show in Figure 2 a specific global entropy attack example. A malicious node A is able to perform a global entropy attack that A's downstream neighbor B cannot detect. The malicious node A sets $\bar{\mathbf{r}}_A(t) = \mathbf{0}$ and $\mathbf{d}_A(t) = \mathbf{r}_A(t) * \mathbf{B}_Y(t)$ where $\mathbf{B}_Y(t)$ is a coded buffer created from packets that have been overhead from the link between C and D. With this setting, Equation 4 becomes:

$$\bar{\mathbf{c}}_A(t) = \bar{\mathbf{r}}_A(t) * \mathbf{B}_X(t) + \mathbf{d}_A(t) = \mathbf{r}_A(t) * \mathbf{B}_Y(t)$$

Node A has access to coded packets sent by C to D via some out-of-band channel as shown by the dashed line in the figure, which allows A to create $\mathbf{B}_Y(t)$ (this can be done as simple as overhearing, or by colluding with D). Coded packets broadcast by A are linear combinations of coded packets that are broadcast by C which include coded packets that C received directly from S. B has no knowledge of coded packets that S broadcasts, C receives, and B fails to receive. So, B will receive coded packets that are innovative to B's coding buffer from A, but these coded packets are not innovative to C's coding buffer. Thus, when C receives linearly dependent coded packets from B, C cannot be sure if B or A is the entropy attacker given only local information.

The global entropy attack focuses mainly on being stealthy, but it is still damaging and can reduce throughput signifi-

cantly like the local entropy attack. We performed simulations with the topology from Figure 2 and used high link qualities for edges $(S, A), (A, B), (B, C), (C, D)$, and we used lower link qualities for edges (S, B) and (S, C). Thus, the network assumes many packets are routed through the path S, A, B, C, D. We measured a throughput of 769 kbps when A is honest and 233 kbps when A is a global attacker by replaying combinations of coded packets from link (C, D). Thus, node A harms system performance, and the node still sends coded packets that are innovative to local neighbors but are not innovative to neighbors further downstream.

We apply NLA to the scenario in Figure 2 to show how it fails to prevent the entropy attack. As summarized in Table 1, the throughput is 214 kbps when NLA is applied and 345 kbps when the ideal defense is applied. The ideal defense is the case where the global entropy attacker is removed from the network. NLA actually has lower throughput compared to the case of no defense which has 233 kbps because the modified link quality of (B, C) is lowered to nearly zero and thus the network only utilizes the path S, C, D while the path S, B, C, D still provides some innovative coded packets even under a global entropy attack. This topology illustrates how a global entropy can reduce throughput by roughly 30%, but in other topologies a global entropy attack has the potential to cause greater damage. We conclude that NLA cannot defend against the global entropy attack.

6.2 Global Entropy Defenses Overview

We present two global entropy defenses. In the Upstream Buffer Propagation (UBP) defense, nodes propagate buffer information upstream to pinpoint the origin of the global entropy attack. In the Buffer Monitoring (BM) defense, nodes monitor incoming and outgoing traffic of untrusted, neighbor nodes to immediately detect any coded packets created in a non-random fashion. To contrast these two techniques, UBP is more reactive and thus has lower overhead while BM is more proactive and requires higher overhead and places constraints on the topology. These schemes require the following three wireless communication primitives:

- **Broadcast.** A message is broadcast once and neighboring nodes will receive the message probabilistically.

- **Reliable unicast.** A specific neighboring node is designated and the sender will repeatedly broadcast a message until the receiving node acknowledges the reception of the message. This primitive can be the standard 802.11 unicast.

- **Reliable multicast.** A set of neighboring nodes are designated and the sender will repeatedly broadcast a message until all receiving nodes acknowledge the reception of the message. This primitive does not exist naturally in the 802.11 protocol, but it can be realized efficiently by periodically broadcasting the message until an acknowledgement is received from each of the designated receivers. As this primitive is not standard, we analyze its overhead in Appendix B.

Both defenses propose a mechanism for nodes to make an accurate accusation that another node is a global entropy attacker. A complete solution requires an appropriate response to such an accusation which is not straightforward since an accuser may be malicious. This is a general problem for many security protocols, and it is out of the scope of this work as we can apply approaches from other work that resolve this issue. One approach from a work on a secure wireless multicast protocol [12] proposes to only remove accused nodes temporarily and limit the accusations of a node. Thus, a malicious accusation is not permanently damaging, and a malicious node cannot disrupt the network by accusing many nodes. Another approach is to use a reputation system [6,31] to lower the reputation of nodes that have been accused or have made invalid accusations. With these reputation values, a node with low reputation can be removed from the network and its accusations can be ignored as well.

6.3 Upstream Buffer Propagation

The defense is initiated by the reception of non-innovative coded packets which implies that a global entropy attack is upstream. The entropy attacker may reside along any upstream path. We can determine the entropy attacker by propagating buffer information upstream until it reaches the source of the global entropy attacker. Thus, a legitimate node i, in response to receiving non-innovative coded packets, creates a packet containing its buffer information and sends this packet upstream. When this buffer information reaches the entropy attacker, the entropy attacker has a choice to continue performing the entropy attack and be detected, or to start sending innovative coded packets. Either way, the entropy attack is mitigated.

There are two challenges to reducing the overhead of propagating buffer information upstream to make it practical. The buffer information consists of the coding headers at a node, and as a node receives more coded packets the total size of all coding headers at the node becomes large. Thus, our first challenge is to send a small constant-sized message that conveys to upstream nodes the contents of the buffer, and we do this with a special type of checksum. Our second challenge is to prevent flooding the message upstream and instead choose based on local information at each hop the upstream path that the attack is on.

6.3.1 Null Space Checksums

The buffer checksums utilize the *null space* of the vector space spanned by coding headers which is the space of all vectors that result in a zero when multiplied by a vector from the vector space spanned by the coding headers. We provide background on null spaces and then we explain how to use null spaces to provide a checksum for coding headers which is represented by a *coding header matrix* $\mathbf{V}_i(t)$ which is a matrix of the nonzero coding headers of $\mathbf{B}_i(t)$. We denote these checksums as *null space checksums*.

Consider a vector space A and a null space $N(A)$ of A. Given any two vectors $\mathbf{x}$ and $\mathbf{y}$ such that $\mathbf{x} \in A$ and $\mathbf{y} \in N(A)$, we have:

$$\mathbf{x} * \mathbf{y}^T = 0 \qquad (6)$$

The notation $\mathbf{w}^T$ is the transpose of the matrix or vector $\mathbf{w}$.

For our checksum, we consider A to be the row space of $\mathbf{V}_i(t)$ which has $R(\mathbf{V}_i(t))$ rows (we denote $R(\mathbf{X})$ as a function that returns the number of rows of the matrix $\mathbf{X}$). The vector of the null space is a vector $\mathbf{s}_i(t)^T$ such that:

$$\mathbf{V}_i(t) * \mathbf{s}_i(t)^T = \mathbf{0} \qquad (7)$$

This corresponds to a linear system of $R(\mathbf{V}_i(t))$ equations and n unknowns. To find a valid $\mathbf{s}_i(t)^T$, we simply fill in $n - R(\mathbf{V}_i(t))$ symbols randomly, and we are left with $R(\mathbf{V}_i(t))$ equations and $R(\mathbf{V}_i(t))$ unknowns which is solved to fill in the remaining symbols. Thus, computing this vector is computationally inexpensive.

Given $\mathbf{s}_i(t)^T$ and the coding header matrix of another node j at a time t', $\mathbf{V}_j(t')$, we have the following probability:

$$Pr\left(\mathbf{V}_j(t') * \mathbf{s}_i(t)^T = \mathbf{0}\right) = \left(\frac{1}{q}\right)^d \qquad (8)$$

The variable d is the number of rows of $\mathbf{V}_j(t')$ are linearly independent with all rows of $\mathbf{V}_i(t)$, and the variable q is the cardinality of the field that each symbols lies in (e.g., $q = 256$ for network coding over 1 byte symbols). Any row of $\mathbf{V}_j(t')$ that is linearly dependent with all rows of $\mathbf{V}_i(t)$ results in a zero if multiplied by the vector $\mathbf{s}_i(t)^T$. Any row of $\mathbf{V}_j(t')$ that is linearly independent with all rows of $\mathbf{V}_i(t)$ results in a random symbol when multiplied by the vector $\mathbf{s}_i(t)^T$. Thus, d symbols are random, and the probability that all d symbols are zero is $(\frac{1}{q})^d$.

Thus, a node j that is upstream from node i knows that if $\mathbf{V}_j(t') * \mathbf{s}_i(t) = \mathbf{0}$ then node j at time t' most likely has no innovative packets with respect to node i's coding buffer at time t. Also, if node j finds that $\mathbf{V}_j(t') * \mathbf{s}_i(t) \neq \mathbf{0}$ then j can definitely create coded packets that are innovative with respect to node i's coding buffer. The null space checksums are encapsulated in a Buffer Checksum Packet (BCP) which contains additional information required by the protocol. We show in Appendix A that computational overhead is low to generate and check these BCPs.

6.3.2 Single Path Propagation

Instead of sending the buffer information on all possible paths upstream, it only needs to be sent along one single path. The path can be determined by local decisions while ensuring with high probability that the global entropy attacker will be part of the path. A node attaches a sequence number to every coded packet it creates and forwards, and nodes maintain some state that allows them to determine which upstream neighbor sent the last coded packet that triggered the broadcast of a new coded packet.

To determine a single upstream path for buffer propagation, each node maintains both a sequence number and a Sequence Number Table (SNT). When a node j broadcasts a coded packet, it appends its sequence number u_j to the coded packet and then increments u_j by one. Upon receiving from upstream neighbor i a coded packet that has a sequence number u_i, node j adds an entry $\langle u_i, j, u_j \rangle$ to its SNT and removes any old entries with the same u_i.

A node j receives a BCP because it had broadcast a coded packet that was globally non-innovative which triggered the propagation of this BCP at a downstream node that may be several hops downstream. Based on its SNT, node j knows the upstream neighbor i that sent the last coded packet which was used to create the globally non-innovative coded packet at node j. Thus, the attacker is either node i or some node upstream of node i which caused i to send this packet that is globally non-innovative. The BCP is forwarded upstream to node i along with the sequence number of the coded packet that i created so that, if node i is honest, it can make an accurate decision about which upstream node it should send the BCP on.

6.3.3 Protocol Description

We now describe in Algorithm 1 the UBP defense in detail. These actions are all in addition to normal network coding actions and they are triggered by timer expiration or by packet reception. We assume each node has a public/private key pair, such that any node i can sign a message with its private key K_i which is denoted by $S_{K_i}(\cdot)$ and any other node in the network can verify this signature.

The protocol is initiated when a node receives a non-innovative coded packet and starts the propagation of a BCP upstream (lines 1-3 of receiving a coded packet). Then, an entry is created for the Upstream Accusation Table (UAT), and a timer is started for this entry (lines 4-5 of receiving a coded packet). The purpose of the UAT is to keep track of each upstream neighbor that should send an innovative coded packet since a BCP was sent to that upstream neighbor. The time that an upstream neighbor has to send an innovative coded packet is the estimate of the time taken for the BCP to propagate up to the source and then a coded packet to propagate down to j. Upon UAT expiration, the node accuses the upstream neighbor of being an entropy attacker if the upstream neighbor did not manage to send an innovative coded packet (lines 1-2 of UAT expiration).

A node that receives a BCP will first check the signature and then check whether it has innovative packets with respect to the null space checksum within the BCP (lines 1-2 of receiving a BCP). The actions taken by the node depend on whether it has innovative coded packets. If the node does have innovative coded packets with respect to the null space checksum, then the node will broadcast a coded packet and perform the appropriate updates to the SNT (lines 3-7 of receiving a BCP). Note that these same updates are applied to the SNT for every broadcast of coded packets despite it not being explicitly mentioned. In the other case, the node forwards the BCP upstream by selecting the most likely next hop that sent globally non-innovative coded packets (lines 8-14 of receiving a BCP). The forwarded BCP is modified to include the sequence number of the coded packet that is expected to have been globally non-innovative. This se-

quence number is known since the SNT maintains the sequence number of the coded packet received from an upstream node just before each broadcast.

The propagation of BCPs upstream continues along a path until either a malicious node refuses to keep forwarding it, a node has innovative coded packets and sends them downstream, or the BCP reaches the source. If the BCP reaches the source, then the source always has innovative coded packets and will send an innovative coded packet downstream. Thus, each node has a chance to broadcast and propagate innovative coded packets downstream before the UAT of its downstream neighbor expires. The timers for accusation should be set such that upstream nodes' timers expire first, and only the most upstream node that makes an accusation will count. So, a malicious node will be accused if it refuses to either forward the BCP upstream or forward innovative coded packets downstream.

Algorithm 1 Reactive upstream buffer propagation protocol for node j in addition to normal network coding actions

---

BCP: packet with contents $\langle$originator, null space checksum, sequence number, originator signature$\rangle$
UAT: table with entries $\langle$upstream node, originator, null space checksum$\rangle$
SNT: table with entries $\langle$local sequence number, upstream node, upstream sequence number$\rangle$

Received coded packet $\mathbf{c}$ from upstream neighbor k with sequence number u_k at time t
1: **if** $\mathbf{c}$ is non-innovative **then**
2:      $BCP \leftarrow \langle j, \mathbf{s}_j(t), u_k, S_{K_j}(\mathbf{s}_j(t)) \rangle$
3:      reliable_unicast(k, BCP)
4:      add_entry_to_table$(\langle k, j, \mathbf{s}_j(t) \rangle, UAT)$
5:      start_timer$(\langle k, j, \mathbf{s}_j(t) \rangle)$
6: **else**
7:      remove_entry_from_table$(\langle u_j, *, * \rangle, SNT)$
8:      add_entry_to_table$(\langle u_j, k, u_k \rangle, SNT)$
9:      **if** $\exists \langle k', i, \mathbf{s}_i(t) \rangle \in UAT$ s.t. $k' = k$ **then**
10:          **if** $\mathbf{c}$ is innovative w.r.t. $\mathbf{s}_i(t)$ **then**
11:              remove_entry_from_table$(\langle k, *, * \rangle, UAT)$

Received BCP $\langle i, \mathbf{s}_i(t'), u'_j, S_{K_i}(\mathbf{s}_i(t')) \rangle$ at time t from node l
1: **if** $S_{K_i}(\mathbf{s}_i(t'))$ is correct **then**
2:      **if** $\mathbf{V}_j(t')$ has innovative coded packets w.r.t. $\mathbf{s}_i(t')$ **then**
3:          $c \leftarrow$ create_coded_packet$()$
4:          broadcast$(\langle c, u_j \rangle)$
5:          $\langle u_j, k, u_k \rangle \leftarrow$ get_entry_from_table$(\langle u_j, *, * \rangle, SNT)$
6:          $u_j \leftarrow u_j + 1$
7:          add_entry_to_table$(\langle u_j, k, u_k \rangle, SNT)$
8:      **else**
9:          $\langle u'_j, k, u_k \rangle \leftarrow$ get_entry_from_table$(\langle u'_j, *, * \rangle, SNT)$
10:          $BCP \leftarrow \langle i, \mathbf{s}_i(t'), u_k, S_{K_i}(\mathbf{s}_i(t')) \rangle$
11:          reliable_unicast(k, BCP)
12:          **if** k is not source **then**
13:              add_entry_to_table$(\langle k, i, \mathbf{s}_i(t) \rangle, UAT)$
14:              start_timer$(\langle k, i, \mathbf{s}_i(t) \rangle)$

Expired timer $\langle k, i, \mathbf{s}_i(t) \rangle$ s.t. $\langle k, i, \mathbf{s}_i(t) \rangle \in UAT$
1: **if** no recent accusations with same originator i **then**
2:      accuse(k)

6.4 Buffer Monitoring (BM)

We now present a monitoring-based solution to defend against entropy attacks. Each forwarder is assigned one or more watchdogs. A larger number of watchdogs provides resilience to watchdog failure or misbehavior. The watchdog nodes will ensure that coded packets broadcast by a watched forwarder are random linear combinations of all received coded packets, and the coefficients of this linear combination are chosen according to a publicly known pseudorandom function. This scheme is proactive in nature and thus can immediately detect an attack. However, as any proactive scheme, it has additional overhead for each coded packet broadcast. In addition, there are some network topology constraints that might prevent some flows from having each forwarder assigned the desired number of watchdogs.

For a watchdog to determine whether a coded packet broadcast by a watched forwarder is random linear combinations of all received coded packets by that forwarder, the watchdog must know about all coded packets received by that forwarder for the generation. This poses two challenges. First, the watchdogs must have wireless links to both the watched node and every upstream neighbor of the watched node, which may prohibit BM from being applied to certain topologies. This challenge is a fundamental constraint imposed by the topology, and we analyze in Section 7.2 the feasibility of selecting watchdogs in a realistic wireless network. Second, once a valid set of watchdogs are chosen, we need to send minimal amount of data to the watchdog to ensure accurate detection while not hindering the opportunistic routing of the random network coding system.

6.4.1 Detection at a Watchdog

To determine whether a single coded packet $\mathbf{c}_i(t)$ from a node i at time t is consistent with traffic that entered node i, the watchdog must determine the coefficients $\mathbf{r}_i(t)$ used to create the coded packet from the equation:

$$\mathbf{r}_i(t) * \mathbf{B}_i(t) = \mathbf{c}_i(t) \qquad (9)$$

This is an overconstrained system of $n + m$ equations and n unknowns. Only n equations are needed to determine the relevant elements of $\mathbf{r}_i(t)$. There are some elements of $\mathbf{r}_i(t)$ that correspond to rows of zero vectors in $\mathbf{B}_i(t)$ which cannot be determined, but these are irrelevant elements as they do not affect the coded packet being broadcast.

The impact of this result is that a watchdog only requires the coding headers of the coded packets sent and received by a watched forwarder. A coded packet with typical network coding system parameters has 32 bytes for the coding header while the entire coded packet is 1500 bytes. It is important to only reliably multicast a small portion of the total traffic since random network coding systems gain many advantages by forwarding data opportunistically instead of sending the data reliably each hop. This fundamental characteristic of random network coding systems is still retained with the additional overhead of sending a small portion of a coded packet, the coding header, with reliable multicast. However, simply determining the value $\mathbf{r}_i(t)$ does not completely defend against global entropy attacks as it is difficult to determine whether the values are chosen randomly or to cause a subtle entropy attack.

Instead of attempting to determine whether a $\mathbf{r}_i(t)$ used by a watched forwarder is truly random, we require all nodes to generate the coding coefficients based on a Pseudo-Random Function (PRF). The PRF is keyed with a key known to all nodes in the network (to guarantee the coefficients are pseudo-random, the key only needs to be picked at random and does not need to be secret). The inputs to the PRF are

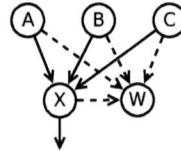

Figure 3: Scenario for monitoring solution. X is the node being monitored, W is the watchdog node, and A, B, C are upstream neighbors of X. Solid lines indicate wireless links of the topology that are used for routing data. Dashed lines indicate wireless links of the topology to send data to the watchdog node.

the node's ID along with a sequence number for the packet. The usage of a PRF makes a watchdog's job simple and deterministic to check whether a set of coefficients used by the watched forwarder is truly random. Also, the inputs to the PRF cannot be controlled by the attacker as a sequence number increases by one with each broadcast coded packet and the node ID does not change. Due to this constraint, the global entropy attacker has no opportunity to guess inputs to the PRF that may produce coefficients that result in an entropy attack. The use of the PRF is computationally inexpensive, and the random coefficients chosen by the PRF are uniformly random which is optimal to satisfy the high decoding probabilities in random network coding systems.

6.4.2 Protocol Description

Figure 3 shows an example of a node with one watchdog and three upstream neighbors. The node X is being watched by a watchdog W. The watchdog must receive all coding headers from the upstream neighbors A, B, and C along the wireless links indicated by the dashed lines. Also, the watchdog must receive the coding headers that are broadcast by node X. With this information, along with knowledge of a global PRF used by each node, the watchdog can deterministically check whether node X is correctly creating coded packets or is performing an entropy attack.

Algorithm 2 describes the specific actions of a node j in a monitoring defense. The node j is a forwarder, a watchdog, or both. We use the notation of two sets that exist for each node (these sets may be empty): $W(i)$ are the watchdogs of node i and $D(i)$ are the downstream neighbors of node i.

To ensure that only a small portion of each coded packet is sent reliably, the coding headers and coded data are sent separately in a Coding Header Packet (CHP) and Coded Data Packet (CDP). The CDP is broadcast unreliably (lines 1-2 of broadcasting a coded packet) and the CHP is reliably multicast to the appropriate set of nodes (lines 3-5 of broadcasting a coded packet). The appropriate set of nodes are the downstream nodes, watchdogs of the downstream nodes, and the watchdog of the broadcasting node (line 4 of broadcasting a coded packet). The watchdogs must receive the CHP to ensure that it has been formed correctly. The downstream nodes must receive the CHP to either reconstruct the coded packet if the downstream node correctly received the CDP (lines 1-2 of receiving CHP from upstream neighbor) or to notify watchdogs that they lost the CDP with a Dropped Data Packet (DDP) (lines 3-5 of receiving a CHP from upstream neighbor). Lastly, watchdogs of downstream neighbors must receive the CHP so that they have a view of the buffer information at the downstream neighbor.

When j is a watchdog and receives a CHP from a node i where $j \in W(i)$, j must create the coding header matrix $\mathbf{V}_i$ of node j (lines 1-3 of received CHP from a watched node), and then check whether the CHP is consistent with $\mathbf{V}_i$ and the random linear combination from the PRF (lines 4-5 of

Algorithm 2 Buffer monitoring protocol for node j in addition to normal network coding actions

---

CHP : packet with contents ⟨source, sequence number, coding header⟩
CDP : packet with contents ⟨source, sequence number, coded data⟩
DDP : packet with contents ⟨node dropping packet, source of packet, sequence number of packet ⟩
WBT : table with entries ⟨ watched node, source, sequence number, coding header ⟩
$W(x)$: set of watchdog nodes for node x
$D(x)$: set of downstream neighbors for node x
$PRF(x, y)$: pseudo-random function which maps $\mathbb{Z}^+ \times \mathbb{Z}^+$ to $\mathbb{F}_q^n$

Received CHP $\langle i, u_i, \mathbf{v} \rangle$ from upstream neighbor i
1: **if** Received CDP $\langle i, u_i, \mathbf{x} \rangle$ **then**
2:    Reconstruct coded packet $\mathbf{c} = \langle \mathbf{v}, \mathbf{x} \rangle$ and store in buffer
3: **else**
4:    $DDP \leftarrow \langle j, i, u_i \rangle$
5:    reliable_multicast($W(j), DDP$)

Broadcasting coded packet $\mathbf{c} = \langle \mathbf{v}, \mathbf{x} \rangle$ created by a random linear combination $PRF(j, u_j)$ of buffered packets
1: $CDP \leftarrow \langle j, u_j, \mathbf{x} \rangle$
2: broadcast(CDP)
3: $S \leftarrow W(j) \cup D(j) \cup \left(\bigcup_{i \in D(j)} W(i) \right)$
4: $CHP \leftarrow \langle j, u_j, \mathbf{v} \rangle$
5: reliable_multicast(S, CHP)

Received CHP $\langle i, u_i, \mathbf{v} \rangle$ from node i s.t. $j \in W(i)$
1: initialize_empty_coding_header_matrix($\mathbf{V}_i$)
2: **for all** $\langle i, *, *, v \rangle$ in WBT **do**
3:    add_coding_header_to_matrix($v, \mathbf{V}_i$)
4: **if** $\mathbf{V}_i * PRF(i, u_i) \neq \mathbf{v}$ **then**
5:    accuse(i)

Received CHP $\langle k, u_k, \mathbf{v} \rangle$ from node k s.t. $i \in D(k)$, $j \in W(i)$
1: add_entry_to_table($\langle i, k, u_k, \mathbf{v} \rangle, WBT$)

Received DDP $\langle i, k, u_k \rangle$ from node i s.t. $i \in D(k)$, $i \in W(j)$
1: **if** $\langle i, k, u_k, * \rangle \in WBT$ **then**
2:    remove_entry_from_table($\langle i, k, u_k, * \rangle, WBT$)
3: **else**
4:    drop_future_receptions($\langle k, u_k, * \rangle$)

---

received CHP from a watched node). The information to perform this check is stored in the Watchdog Buffer Table (WBT) when upstream nodes send coded packets to node i (line 1 of received CHP from upstream neighbor of watched node). The WBT must be correctly modified when a node does not receive a coded packet. This is the purpose of broadcasting the DDP to watchdog nodes of j when j does not receive the corresponding CDP to a CHP. The DDP prompts the watchdogs to either remove the entry or drop a future reception of a CHP that corresponds to the dropped packet (lines 1-5 of receiving a DDP). If an attacker abuses the use of DDPs and claims to drop more coded packets than the the measured link qualities, then the watchdog can inform the routing layer of the change in link qualities which will route data around the attacker much like the modified link qualities in our NLA defense.

7. SECURITY ANALYSIS

We analyze UBP in terms of *attack strength* which denotes

Table 2: Table summarizing notation, each row represents a random variable which include the notation and explanation for the random variable.

$T_{i,j}^{\mathbf{c}}$	Avg. time of a coded packet to propagate downstream from node i to j
$T_{i,j}^B$	Avg. time of a BCP to propagate upstream from node i to j
T_i^S	Avg. time between coded packet sends at node i
T^E	Exoneration time for a hybrid of UBP
$P_{i,j}^R$	Attack strength from node i to j under UBP
$P_{i,j}^H$	Attack strength from node i to j under a hybrid of UBP with an exoneration phase
$N_{i,j}$	Average number of coded packets that can be sent by node i that are globally non-innovative to downstream node j in UBP before i must send an innovative coded packet

the proportion of time which a globally non-innovative coded packet can be sent undetected. The buffer monitoring is much stronger in terms of security since an attacker is not capable of evading detection by a watchdog. However, BM cannot be applied to an arbitrary flow of a topology and has a higher network overhead. So, we analyze the proportion of flows BM can be applied to in the Roofnet topology [2].

7.1 Attack Strength of UBP

We aim to describe the attack strength in terms of the characteristics of the network. Specifically, attack strength represents the proportion of time that coded packets can be sent from an attacker that are globally non-innovative with respect to a victim's coding buffer and the attacker will not be detected as an entropy attacker. In the remainder of the time, the attacker cannot send a globally non-innovative coded packet without being detected. Also, since the sending times of coded packets are fixed by the protocol, the attack strength also represents the proportion of packets sent by the attacker that can be globally non-innovative while not being detected. The attack strength will depend on the network characteristics of the average time taken for both a coded packet (or combinations of the coded packet) to traverse downstream and a BCP to traverse upstream. These averages differ since coded packets are larger and sent opportunistically downstream, while BCPs are smaller and sent reliably upstream immediately at each hop. For this analysis, we use notation from Table 2.

Figure 4 shows the timeline of events that lead to points where an attacker can attack in UBP without detection. The scheme waits until an attack is detected downstream, and then it reacts by sending a BCP upstream along the path that contains the global entropy attacker. The attacker is detected by a timer expiring at the entropy attacker's immediate downstream neighbor which is the time it takes for the BCP to reach the source from the attacker and then an innovative coded packet to traverse downstream to the attacker. During this entire time, the attacker can consecutively send globally non-innovative coded packets and send an innovative coded packet when it knows the immediate downstream neighbor's UAT is about to expire.

We first determine the number of consecutive non-innovative coded packets that can be sent by attacker node i that target victim j without detection as:

$$N_{i,j}^R = 1 + \frac{T_{i,j}^{\mathbf{c}} + T_{j,src}^B + T_{src,i}^{\mathbf{c}}}{T_i^S} \qquad (10)$$

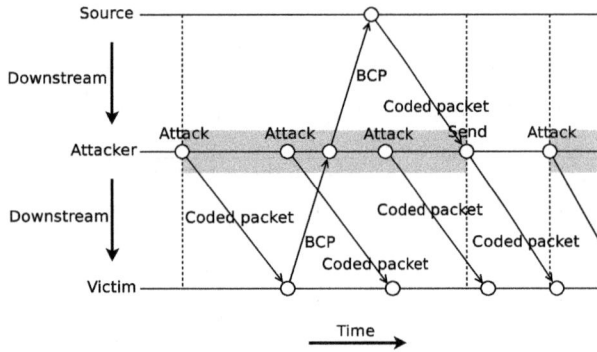

Figure 4: Example timeline for the source, attacker and victim that shows when an attacker can attack without facing detection with the UBP protocol which is denoted by the grey region. Note that there are most likely many hops from source to attacker and attacker to victim, but we assume that we can estimate the time it takes a BCP and coded packet to traverse these hops.

In addition to the one initial attack packet, there are several opportunities for the attacker to send globally non-innovative coded packets. The average number of opportunities is equal to the total time it takes before the attacker must send an innovative coded packet over the average time between coded packet sends of the attacker node.

We can then determine the attack strength from attacker node i to victim node j as:

$$P_{i,j}^R = \frac{N_{i,j}^R}{N_{i,j}^R + 1} \qquad (11)$$

For each consecutive non-innovative coded packet that can be sent by an entropy attacker, the entropy attacker must send one innovative coded packet to remain undetected.

The attack strength $P_{i,j}^R$ is always at least 0.5 which means that at least half of the coded packets can be globally non-innovative. The attack strength increases as the values $T_{src,j}^{\mathbf{c}}$ and $T_{j,src}^B$ become larger compared to T_i^S which happens in larger networks and when the node i does more broadcasting. The large attack strength is due to the exoneration of the attacker given just one innovative coded packet. Thus, the single upstream path found by UBP could enter an exoneration phase for a period of time which requires more overhead but detects a global entropy attack proactively. This results in a hybrid scheme with an attack strength of:

$$P_{i,j}^H = \frac{N_{i,j}}{N_{i,j} + 1 + \frac{T_E}{T_i^S}} \qquad (12)$$

The exoneration period T_E can be varied to obtain various trade-offs between the additional overhead of the proactive detection in the exoneration period and the attack strength possible at the attacker.

An obvious way to enforce an exoneration period for a path is to assign watchdogs as in the BM scheme to these nodes. This would not impose the high overhead of BM throughout the entire network at all times as UBP can reactively determine which path an entropy attacker is on. Alternatively one could design alternate scheme that can provide an accurate proactive defense which can be used in conjunction with UBP in this same manner. We leave this as future work.

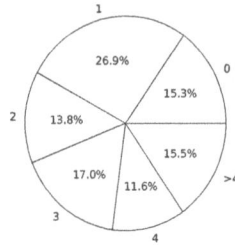

Figure 5: Given flows in the Roofnet topology we show the maximum valid assignment of n watchdogs per forwarder.

7.2 Watchdog Selection Constraints of BM

The buffer monitoring defense has a much higher level of security since it can ensure an attack strength of 0. The watchdog(s) of a forwarder have complete information about the coding headers of the forwarder, and the watchdog can deterministically assess whether the forwarder created a random combination using the entire coding buffer. This scheme cannot be employed for each flow of any topology.

The constraint for using the buffer monitoring defense is:

$$\forall f \in F, \left| \left(L(f) \cap \left(\bigcap_{u \in U(f)} L(u) \right) \right) - f \right| \geq n \qquad (13)$$

F is the set of forwarders for a flow, $L(x)$ is the set of nodes that x has a wireless link to (this includes x itself), $U(x)$ is the set of upstream neighbors of node x, and n is the minimum number of watchdogs assigned to each node. This watchdog assignment allows both the nodes in the flow and nodes outside the flow to act as watchdogs for a forwarder. Furthermore, we allow a forwarders' upstream neighbor to act as its watchdog which will reduce the multicast overhead when the upstream neighbor must reliably multicast coding headers since the upstream neighbor does not need to spend communication overhead sending this coding header to itself.

We use the Roofnet data to represent a typical wireless network topology. There are 38 nodes in the network, so we take all $\binom{38}{2} = 1406$ possible flows. Out of these flows we discard 174 trivial flows that contain no forwarders and present results based on the remaining 1232 flows.

We present information about the maximum watchdog assignment per flow in Figure 5. 15.3% of flows cannot employ a buffer monitoring defense without changing the forwarder nodes that were optimally selected by the routing algorithm. These flows contain some forwarder that does not have a wireless link to any node in the topology that also has a wireless link to each upstream neighbor of the forwarder. At least one watchdog per forwarder is a minimal constraint, a network may aim to protect against an attacker that imposes false accusations. In this scenario, three watchdogs can be assigned to each forwarder to vote on detection, and only 44.1% of flows allow three watchdogs per forwarder.

8. CONCLUSION

We show via simulations the impact of entropy attacks on the overall routing of a wireless network coding system. We propose an effective defense against local entropy attacks and show the difficulties in defending against a global entropy attack. We propose two variations on a global entropy defense which differ in their defense capabilities and overhead. We provide analysis to quantify the defense capabilities of these global defense schemes.

9. REFERENCES

[1] Glomosim.
http://pcl.cs.ucla.edu/projects/glomosim/.

[2] MIT roofnet.
http://pdos.csail.mit.edu/roofnet/doku.php.

[3] S. Agrawal and D. Boneh. Homomorphic macs: Mac-based integrity for network coding. In *Proc. of ACNS*, 2009.

[4] R. Ahlswede, N. Cai, S.-Y. Li, and R. Yeung. Network information flow. *Information Theory, IEEE Transactions on*, 46(4):1204–1216, 2000.

[5] D. Boneh, D. Freeman, J. Katz, and B. Waters. Signing a linear subspace: Signature schemes for network coding. In *Proc. of PKC*, 2009.

[6] S. Buchegger and J. Le Boudec. A robust reputation system for mobile ad-hoc networks. In *Proc. of P2PEcon*, 2004.

[7] S. Chachulski, M. Jennings, S. Katti, and D. Katabi. Trading structure for randomness in wireless opportunistic routing. In *Proc. of SIGCOMM*, 2007.

[8] D. Charles, K. Jain, and K. Lauter. Signatures for network coding. *Proc. of CISS*, 2006.

[9] S. Das, Y. Wu, R. Chandra, and Y. C. Hu. Context-based routing: Technique, applications, and experience. In *Proc. of NSDI*, 2008.

[10] J. Dong, R. Curtmola, and C. Nita-Rotaru. Practical defenses against pollution attacks in intra-flow network coding for wireless mesh networks. In *Proc. of WiSec*, 2009.

[11] J. Dong, R. Curtmola, and C. Nita-Rotaru. Secure network coding for wireless mesh networks: Threats, challenges, and directions. *Computer Communications*, 32(17):1790–1801, 2009.

[12] J. Dong, R. Curtmola, and C. Nita-Rotaru. Secure high-throughput multicast routing in wireless mesh networks. *IEEE Transactions on Mobile Computing*, pages 653–668, 2010.

[13] C. Gkantsidis and P. Rodriguez Rodriguez. Cooperative security for network coding file distribution. 2006.

[14] T. Ho, B. Leong, R. Koetter, M. Medard, M. Eros, and D. R. Karger. Byzantine modification detection in multicast networks using randomized network coding. In *Proc. of ISIT*, 2004.

[15] T. Ho, M. Médard, J. Shi, M. Effros, and D. Karger. On randomized network coding. In *Proc. of Allerton*, 2003.

[16] L. Hu and D. Evans. Using directional antennas to prevent wormhole attacks. In *Proc. of NDSS*, 2004.

[17] Y. Hu, A. Perrig, and D. Johnson. Packet leashes: a defense against wormhole attacks in wireless networks. In *Proc. of INFOCOM*, 2003.

[18] IEEE. *IEEE Std 802.11, 1999 Edition*. 1999. http://standards.ieee.org/catalog/olis/lanman.html.

[19] S. Jaggi, M. Langberg, S. Katti, T. Ho, D. Katabi, and M. Medard. Resilient network coding in the presence of byzantine adversaries. In *Proc. of INFOCOM*, 2007.

[20] Y. Jiang, Y. Fan, X. (Sherman) Shen, and C. Lin. A self-adaptive probabilistic packet filtering scheme against entropy attacks in network coding. *Computer Networks*, 53:3089–3101, December 2009.

[21] C. Karlof and D. Wagner. Secure routing in wireless sensor networks: attacks and countermeasures. *Ad Hoc Networks*, 1(2-3):293 – 315, 2003.

[22] S. Katti, H. Rahul, W. Hu, D. Katabi, M. Médard, and J. Crowcroft. Xors in the air: practical wireless network coding. In *Proc. of SIGCOMM*, 2006.

[23] E. Kehdi and B. Li. Null keys: Limiting malicious attacks via null space properties of network coding. In *Proc. of INFOCOM*, 2009.

[24] M. Kim, M. Médard, a. Barros, Jo and R. Kötter. An algebraic watchdog for wireless network coding. In *Proc. of ISIT*, 2009.

[25] M. Kim, M. Médard, and J. Barros. A multi-hop multi-source algebraic watchdog. *Proc. of CoRR*, 2010.

[26] M. Krohn, M. Freedman, and D. Maziéres. On-the-fly verification of rateless erasure codes for efficient content distribution. In *Proc. of S&P*, 2004.

[27] J. Le, J. C. S. Lui, and D. M. Chiu. DCAR: Distributed coding-aware routing in wireless networks. In *Proc. of ICDCS*, 2008.

[28] Q. Li, D. Chiu, and J. Lui. On the practical and security issues of batch content distribution via network coding. In *Proc. of ICNP*, 2006.

[29] Y. Li, H. Yao, M. Chen, S. Jaggi, and A. Rosen. Ripple authentication for network coding. In *Proc. of INFOCOM*, 2010.

[30] S. Marti, T. Giuli, K. Lai, and M. Baker. Mitigating routing misbehavior in mobile ad hoc networks. In *Proc. of MobiCom*, 2000.

[31] P. Resnick, K. Kuwabara, R. Zeckhauser, and E. Friedman. Reputation systems. *Communications of the ACM*, 43(12):45–48, 2000.

[32] L. Rizzo and L. Vicisano. A reliable multicast data distribution protocol based on software fec techniques. In *Proc. of HPCS*, 1997.

[33] D. Wang, D. Silva, and F. R. Kschischang. Constricting the adversary: A broadcast transformation for network coding. In *Proc. of Allerton*, 2007.

[34] W. Wang, J. Kong, B. Bhargava, and M. Gerla. Visualisation of wormholes in underwater sensor networks: a distributed approach. *International Journal of Security and Networks*, 3(1):10–23, 2008.

[35] B. Yu and B. Xiao. Detecting selective forwarding attacks in wireless sensor networks. In *Proc. of IPDPS*, 2006.

[36] Z. Yu, Y. Wei, B. Ramkumar, and Y. Guan. An efficient signature-based scheme for securing network coding against pollution attacks. In *Proc. of INFOCOM*, 2008.

[37] X. Zhang and B. Li. DICE: a game theoretic framework for wireless multipath network coding. In *Proc. of Mobihoc*, 2008.

[38] X. Zhang and B. Li. Optimized multipath network coding in lossy wireless networks. In *Proc. of ICDCS*, 2008.

[39] F. Zhao, T. Kalker, M. Médard, and K. Han. Signatures of content distribution with network coding. In *Proc. of ISIT*, 2007.

APPENDIX

A. COMPUTATION OVERHEAD

The originator of a BCP in UBP must compute a null space checksum and a signature for the BCP. The following benchmarked time values are performed on general commodity hardware[1]. As noted earlier in Section 6.3.1, creating a null space checksum requires the solution to a system of $R(\mathbf{V}_i(t))$ equations and $R(\mathbf{V}_i(t))$ unknowns where $R(\mathbf{V}_i(t)) < n$. Solving an n by n system of equations requires roughly 0.4 ms (where $n = 32$ and a symbol is 1 byte), which is the largest system of equations that may have to be solved. A single DSA sign requires roughly 1 ms of computation. Thus, overall, the originator of a BCP requires roughly 1.4 ms of computational overhead on general commodity hardware.

Nodes receiving a BCP in UBP must verify the signatures attached to these packets. Verifying a signature requires roughly 1.1 ms of computation. The reception of a BCP message requires a check of the null space checksum that was received which is simply a matrix multiplication. The computational time of a matrix multiplication on the coding headers of a coding buffer is negligible.

B. COMMUNICATION OVERHEAD

The communication overhead in UBP are the BCPs that are sent using reliable unicast due to our strategy of finding the single upstream path that the attacker is on. This communication overhead is quite small as the BCPs are small due to our use of checksums. Thus, we focus on the communication overhead of BM as it relies heavily on reliable multicasts to deliver header information reliably whenever a coded packet broadcast occurs.

Ensuring reliability on the multicast requires overhead in terms of resending the packet until each destination has received the message. Previous work exists on sending large messages with reliable multicast at the link-layer [32]. However, their key contribution is the use of forward error correction codes to break a large message into several small messages. These small messages are easier to receive since the probability of packet delivery is higher for smaller messages. Thus, the recipients just need to receive any number of small messages to reconstruct the original large message.

We reliably multicast much smaller messages that can be easily sent in one small packet (40 bytes). Thus, breaking the small message into even smaller messages will negate any performance improvements since each message has overhead of sending link-layer headers as well as physical layer overhead. Thus, we propose to send the small message multiple times until all receivers obtain the message. We analyze the number of times the message must be broadcast before each receiver obtains the message given the packet delivery probabilities on each link. We do not present analysis on the ACKs that must be sent from each receiver to the sender which would need to be sent in a way to avoid congestion.

We can analyze the number of times a message must be sent given that it is sent to N nodes over links with packet delivery probabilities of $p_1, p_2, ..., p_N$. Let X be a random variable that denotes the fewest number of times a message must be sent such that all N receivers receive the message

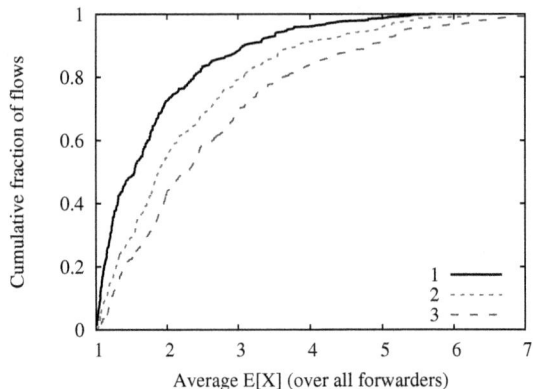

Figure 6: Given flows in the Roofnet topology, we show the communication overhead of reliable multicasts in BM varying the number of watchdogs per node to 1, 2, and 3.

at least once. We aim to calculate $Pr(X = k)$, so we can consider each receiver as an independent geometric random variable Y_i which corresponds to the link state p_i. We can express $Pr(X \le k)$ in terms of the independent geometric random variables as follows:

$$Pr(X \le k) = Pr\left(\bigcap_{i=1}^{N} Y_i \le k\right) = \prod_{i=1}^{N} Pr(Y_i \le k)$$

$$= \prod_{i=1}^{N}\left[\sum_{j=1}^{k} Pr(Y_i = j)\right] = \prod_{i=1}^{N}\left[\sum_{j=1}^{k}(1 - p_i)^{j-1}p_i\right]$$

With $Pr(X \le k)$ we can obtain $Pr(X = k)$ by $Pr(X = k) = Pr(X \le k) - Pr(X \le k - 1)$. The function for $Pr(X = k)$ allows us to compute the expected number of broadcasts of a message such that each receiver obtains the message, $E[X]$. The average overhead for reliably multicasting M bytes of data will be $M * E[X]$.

We use a heuristic for summed link qualities to determine the best watchdog selection out of all possible watchdogs. Each forwarder has each downstream neighbor and the watchdogs of each downstream neighbor as recipients of a DHP. Given the link qualities from the topology and these sets of recipients we can apply the formula for $E[X]$ at each forwarder to obtain an average for a flow.

We use the Roofnet data to show the expected communication overhead when sending DHPs in BM with various number of watchdogs per forwarder. We consider the flows in Roofnet where an assignment of at least 3 watchdogs per nodes is possible (541 flows or 44.1% of non-trival flows). Figure 6 presents a CDF (Cumulative Distribution Function) for $E[X]$ of DHP reliable multicasts in BM. As expected, the overhead increases with more watchdogs being assigned to each node due to more recipients in each wireless multicast.

---

[1] 2.4Ghz processor and OpenSSL library for DSA signature computations

Congestion Lower Bounds for Secure In-network Aggregation

Raghav Bhaskar
Microsoft Research India
Bangalore, India
rbhaskar@microsoft.com

Ragesh Jaiswal
Indian Institute of Technology
New Delhi, India
rjaiswal@cse.iitd.ac.in

Sidharth Telang
Cornell University
Ithaca, USA
sidtelang@cs.cornell.edu

ABSTRACT

In-network aggregation is a technique employed in Wireless Sensor Networks (WSNs) to aggregate information flowing from the sensor nodes towards the base station. It helps in reducing the communication overhead on the nodes in the network and thereby increasing the longevity of the network. We study the problem of maintaing integrity of the aggregate value, when the aggregate function is SUM, in the presence of compromised sensor nodes. We focus on one-round, end-to end, secure aggregation protocols and give a strong, formal security defintion. We show that a worst-case lower bound of $\Omega(n)$ applies on the congestion (maximum size of message between any two nodes) in such protocols, where n is the number of nodes in the network. This is the first such result showing that the most basic protocols are the best one-round in-network aggregation protocols with respect to congestion. We also show that against a weaker adversary (which does not compromise nodes), we can achieve secure in-network aggregation protocols with a congestion of $O(\log_2 n)$.

Categories and Subject Descriptors

C.2.0 [**Computer-Communication Networks**]: General—
Security and protection

General Terms

Security

Keywords

in-network aggregation, security, wireless security

1. INTRODUCTION

In-network aggregation refers to on the fly computations performed on data by the nodes in a network as the data is being sent towards a fixed node called the base station. It is a popular technique, often employed in wireless sensor networks (WSNs), to prolong the longevity of the network. For

	No aggregation	With aggregation
No. of messages	$O(n \log_2 n)$	n
Congestion	$O(n \log_2 R)$	$O(\log_2 nR)$

Table 1: Communication with and without aggregation for a SUM query in a balanced binary tree topology.n denotes the number of nodes in the network, $[0, R-1]$ - message range

example, consider a sensor network where sensors sense the temperature at their location and send it towards the base station. The base station is often interested in knowing the average of the observed readings rather than the individual readings. Thus, while these readings are being transmitted towards the base station, sensor nodes add their reading to the received sum of the readings before forwarding it. Thus, in a single sweep of the network, the base station gets the sum of all the readings and can calculate the average from it. Some of the common aggregate functions are sum, average, histogram, max and min. Not only is the total number of messages that need to be sent are reduced using in-network aggregation, but also the the maximum number of bits communicated over any link (congestion) are reduced. To get an idea of the communication saving made by employing in-network aggregation, consider a network of n nodes in a balanced binary tree topology with the base station at the root and sensors occupying the other nodes. Also, assume the aggregation function is SUM and that each node contributes an integer reading between 0 and $(R-1)$. Then, Table 1 shows the communication costs in the case of no aggregation (when all the messages are sent) and in-network aggregation (when the messages are summed up before sending). Thus, in-network aggregation can reduce both the number of messages sent and congestion significantly for a binary tree topology.

As WSNs are deployed in hostile environments, they are prone to attacks. Attacks can be both from external sources (like other wireless devices, jamming stations) or sensor nodes themselves (which have been compromised by an adversary). While standard cryptographic authentication primitives (like Message Authentication Codes and Digital Signatures [11]) can be used to prevent several kinds of attacks from external sources on the in-network aggregation protocol, more innovative techniques are required to counter attacks from compromised nodes. A compromised node (using its knowledge of keying material of the aggregation protocol) can launch various kinds of attacks without getting detected. For instance, it could drop some received readings, add a huge reading in the current aggregate, not relay any aggregate at all, thereby resulting in incorrect aggregate results. While denial of service attacks (dropping messages etc.) launched by the compromised nodes are beyond the scope of this paper, we define a strong security notion for the SUM aggregate function in the setting where each reading comes from a fixed range $[0, R-1]$. Informally, our security defintion ensures that a compromised node cannot influence the aggregate value by more than $(R-1)$. This insures that even if some nodes report a reading much smaller than $(R-1)$, the compromised node cannot inflate the reading of these nodes to $(R-1)$. Though, a compromised node can always report its reading as $(R-1)$ (or 0), but that is not considered as an attack in our security defintion. Ideally, one would like secure in-network aggregation protocols that impose minimum overhead on existing aggregation protocols. For instance, secure aggregation protocols which continue to work in a single round and do not require the sensor nodes to do much more computation than simply aggregating messages are highly desirable (verification only happens at the end). In this work, we focus on **single round, end-to-end secure** in-network aggregation protocols which meet our strict security definition.

Related Works: A number of prior works have addressed the problem of authentication of aggregate value in sensor networks. Data aggregation in the presence of compromised nodes was first studied by [8]. Hu et al. [8] use delayed aggregation to propose protocols which are secure when at most one node is compromised. [3, 6, 9] consider a single aggregator model in which all nodes report to a single party called the aggregator which aggregates the value and forwards it to the base station. [6] works in this model using 'witness' nodes which serve as additional aggregators. [9] uses threshold signatures and provides security guarantees when a upper bounded fraction of the nodes are compromised. [12] works in a similar setting by dividing the aggregation tree into subtrees each of which aggregate messages and commit to them. Suspect aggregates are later attested using these commitments. Both [4] and [7] achieve strong security against compromised nodes and have a congestion of $O(\log n)$ and $O(\log^2 n)$ respectively, but they require multiple rounds of communication. All of the above protocols involve more than one round of interaction and are basically 'commit and re-check' schemes. In this work, we focus on single round in-network aggregation protocols. [2] talk abouts the impossibility of achieving a straightforward extension of the security goals for Message Authentication Codes to an aggregation setting with compromised nodes. It proposes a weaker notion of security in which nodes that are compromised do not contribute to the aggregate. In our model, each sensor node is both an aggregator and a contributor. [10] proposes a much weaker security notion in which the attacker can inflate the readings of other nodes to the maximum value without violating their security notion. Also, many other works explore the problem of maintaining secrecy of the aggregated value. In this work, we are not worried about the secrecy of the aggregate, in fact, the aggregate could be sent out in the clear in the network and observable by even a *passive* adversary. Our goal is to authenticate the aggregate value, that is, to make sure that illegitimate modifications are not made to the aggregate before it reaches the base station.

Our main result is that any single round, end-to-end secure in-network aggregation protocol (in the sense of our definition) must have a worst-case congestion of $\Omega(n)$, thereby defeating the purpose of aggregation. Note our lower bound is independent of the topology of the network. We then show that for a weaker adversary that does not compromise any sensor node, we can achieve our security definition with a congestion of $O(\log_2 n)$, which is the optimal for a tree topology. The paper is organized as follows: in Section 2 we formally define in-network aggregation. In Section 3, we provide a security definition via a security game to study the security of aggregation protocols against compromised nodes as well as any external adversary. We, then, present two protocols secure against compromised nodes with $O(n)$ congestion. We follow this with a proof which shows $\Omega(n)$ as a congestion lower bound for any protocol secure against compromised nodes. This is a first formal proof to show that strict security definitions may not be achievable with less than $\Omega(n)$ congestion in the internal adversary case. Finally, we propose a protocol secure against an external adversary with a congestion of $O(\log_2 n)$.

2. PROBLEM DEFINITION

We will now introduce our notation and then define an in-network aggregation protocol formally. The security parameter is denoted by k and n denotes the number of nodes in the network. We will assume that n is ploynomial in the security parameter, i.e. $n = poly(k)$. Let $S_1, ..., S_n$ denote the sensor nodes and let V denote the verifier. We assume that each node S_i shares a secret key K_i with the verifier V[1]. The aggregation protocol may be run several times, and each run is referred to as a session and identified by an unique session identifier sid (this may be just the number of the aggregation session). We assume that the start of a new session along with its sid is known to all the sensor nodes. We do not consider that as part of the in-network aggregation protocol. We now define an in-network aggregation protocol for the SUM aggregation function.

2.1 In-network Aggregation

An in-network aggregation protocol consists of the following four functions. All the functions defined below can be computed in time polynomial in the security parameter k and take the session identifier sid inherently as input.

- Setup(1^k, K_i): This function is executed by the sensor nodes at the beginning of each aggregation session. For node S_i, the input to the function is the security parameter, the global secret key K_i, and the session identifier sid. The output of the function for node S_i is the secret key k_i for the session. We call this the session key of the node S_i.

- GenerateTag(m_i, k_i): This algorithm is run by each node S_i to generate an authentication tag for its contributed message m_i. The input to this function is the message m_i and the session key k_i and the output is a tag σ_i that belongs to some tag space $\mathcal{T}$.

- AggregateTag(σ_1, σ_2): This algorithm is run by internal nodes to aggregate authentication tags that it

---

[1]In the public key setting, the key K_i could be derived using a Diffie-Hellman Key exchange protocol between the verifier and the node.

receives from the other sensor nodes. The input to the function are two authentication tags, say $\sigma_1 \in \mathcal{T}$ and $\sigma_2 \in \mathcal{T}$ and the output of the function is the aggregate tag $\sigma_1 \oplus \sigma_2$ obtained by applying some combination operation $\oplus$. Moreover, $(\mathcal{T}, \oplus)$ forms an abelian group such that finding the inverse in the group is computationally efficient.

Node S_i uses this function in the following manner: Once it receives messages and tags from all incoming nodes, it aggregates all these tags along with its own tag and sends the aggregate tag (and sum of all the corresponding messages) along its outgoing edge.

- Verify(M, Σ): This algorithm is run by the verifier V at the end of each aggregation session. The input to this function is the aggregate message M and an aggregate tag Σ. The output of the function is 1 denoting successful authentication and 0 denoting failure.

Given the above functions, the protocol description is very simple. At the beginning of each aggregation session (denoted by session identifier sid), each node executes the Setup to obtain the secret key of the session. The verifier also runs the setup to compute the session keys of all the nodes. Now in a given session, suppose node S_i receives message/tag pairs from nodes S_j, S_k, and S_l and is supposed to send message/tag to node S_p. Suppose S_i intends to contribute m_i and it receives the following message tag pairs (m_j, σ_j), (m_k, σ_k), and (m_l, σ_l). The node S_i does the following: It first uses the function GenerateTag to generate the tag σ_i corresponding to its message m_i. Then it aggregates the tags using the AggregateTag function and send the pair $(m_i + m_j + m_k + m_l, \sigma_i \oplus \sigma_j \oplus \sigma_k \oplus \sigma_l)$ to the node S_p. Finally the verifier on receiving the pair (M, Σ) executes the Verify function and outputs 1 or 0. In the next subsection, we discuss the security definitions for an in-network aggregation protocol.

3. SECURITY DEFINTIONS

We study the security of an in-network aggregation protocol in two different scenarios. In the first scenario, we consider a strong adversary who can not only read and modify messages exchanged between any two nodes in the network, it can also compromise any subset of the sensor nodes or in other words can get access to any of the secret keys of a subset of the nodes. In the second scenario, we consider a weaker adversary who cannot compromise any sensor node. We call the first class of adversary an *insider adversary* and the second one an *outsider adversary*[2]. The message space $\mathcal{M}$ of messages m_i is assumed to be $[0, R-1]$ for some integer R (again polynomial in the security parameter) and we assume that all the n node participate in the protocol.

For completeness, we provide below the standard definition of a pseudorandom family of functions, which we use later.

DEFINITION 1. *A family of functions $H = \{H_k\}_{k \in \mathcal{K}}$ where $H_k : \mathbb{Z}_p \to \mathbb{Z}_p$ is a pseudorandom family of functions if for*

---

[2]For the sake of simplicity, we do not model concurrent executions of the in-network aggregation protocol, in the following security definitions. Against an adversary, which can choose to attack a session after observing many other sessions, our lower bound will continue to hold.

every probabilistic polynomial time algorithm A, $\mathbf{Adv}_H^{prf}(A)$ is negligible in the security parameter, where $\mathbf{Adv}_H^{prf}(A)$ is defined as

$$|Pr[k \leftarrow \mathcal{K} : A^{H_k} = 1] - Pr[RF \leftarrow \mathcal{F} : A^{RF} = 1]|$$

where $\mathcal{F}$ is the set of all functions $f : \mathbb{Z}_p \to \mathbb{Z}_p$

3.1 Security against insider adversaries

Here the adversary gets complete control over a subset of sensor nodes. Since it is not possible for the verifier to distinguish between a compromised node and a non-compromised one, a compromised node may add as large a value that a node is allowed to add. What the verifier can ensure is that a compromised node should not be able to do much more than that. That is, it should not be able to change (increase or decrease) the readings of the non-compromised nodes without being detected by the verifier. This motivates the following security game.

Game $G_A^{insider}$

procedure Initialize
    Let $\mathcal{S} = \{S_1, ..., S_n\}$
    $U \leftarrow \{\}$; $M_h \leftarrow 0$
    Run Setup to fix the session keys $k_1, ..., k_n$

procedure RevealKeys($\mathcal{U}$)
    $U \leftarrow \mathcal{U}$
    return all the session keys of nodes in the subset $\mathcal{U}$.

procedure RevealTags$((m_1, S_{i_1}), ..., (m_k, S_{i_k}))$
    Generate and return tags $\sigma_1, ..., \sigma_k$ for messages
        $m_1, ..., m_k$ corresponding to nodes $S_{i_1}, ..., S_{i_k}$.
    $M_h \leftarrow \sum_{j, S_{i_j} \in \mathcal{S} \setminus U} m_j$

procedure Finalize(M, Δ)
    If $(U = \mathcal{S})$ then return 0
    If $(\text{Verify}(M, \Delta) = 1)$ and
        $((M - M_h > |U| \cdot (R-1))$ or $(M < M_h))$
        then return 1 else return 0

With respect to the above game, we define the advantage of an adversary in breaking a protocol P in the following manner:

$$\mathbf{Adv}_P^{insider}(A) = \mathbf{Pr}[G_P^{insider} \Rightarrow 1]$$

In simpler words, an adversary is allowed to obtain the secret keys of a subset $\mathcal{U}$ of nodes of its choice. The nodes for which the adversary does not have the secret key are called the honest nodes. It may obtain one correctly generated tag for any message of its choice corresponding to the honest nodes. Finally it attacks with a message, tag pair (M, Σ) and it is said to succeed if Verify succeeds for this pair and the message is larger than the sum of messages queried in the RevealTags queries for the honest nodes (M_h) by an additive factor of $(R-1)$ times the number of dishonest nodes or less than it. This captures the case we talked about earlier where we said the the adversary cannot be stopped from tampering the reading of the compromised node but it should not be able to tamper readings of the non-compromised nodes.

DEFINITION 2 (INSIDER SECURITY). *We say a protocol P is insider secure if for every probabilistic polynomial time adversary A, $\mathbf{Adv}_P^{insider}(A)$ is negligible in the security parameter k.*

Now we will first see two protocol constructions that are insider secure but both have linear congestion. Finally, we will argue why any protocol that is insider secure cannot have less than linear amount of congestion.

3.1.1 Aggregate messages, do not aggregate tags

Here we argue that the protocol defined below is insider secure. In order to define the protocol, we just need to define the four functions of Section 2.1. Here is the description of the protocol. We call this protocol P_1:

- Let $MAC_1 : \mathcal{K}_1 \times \mathcal{S} \to \mathcal{K}_2$ and $MAC_2 : \mathcal{K}_2 \times [0, \ldots, R-1] \to \mathcal{U}$ be two message authentication code (MAC) algorithms.

- Setup: The node S_i (and the verifier) applies MAC_1 at K_i and *sid* to compute the session key k_i.

- GenerateTag: The node S_i uses the message authentication code MAC_2 to generate the tag
$$\sigma_i = (0, ..., \underbrace{MAC_2(k_i, m_i)}_{i^{th} \text{ term}}, 0, ..., 0).$$

The tag space is $\mathcal{T} = (\mathcal{U} \cup \{0\}) \times ... \times (\mathcal{U} \cup \{0\})$ where $\mathcal{U}$ denotes the range of MAC_2.

- AggregateTag: Here we define the combination operator $\oplus$ that operates on elements of $\mathcal{T}$. Given $\sigma_1 = (t_1, ..., t_n)$ and $\sigma_2 = (t_1', ..., t_n')$, then $\sigma = (t_1'', ..., t_n'') = \sigma_1 \oplus \sigma_2$ is defined as follows: for all i,

$$t_i'' = \begin{cases} t_i + t_i' & \text{if either } t_i = 0 \text{ or } t_i' = 0; \\ 0 & \text{otherwise.} \end{cases}$$

One can easily verify that $(\oplus, \mathcal{T})$ is a group and finding inverse of any element is simple.

- Verify: Given an input (M, Δ), where $\Delta = (t_1, ..., t_n)$ the verifier does the following: for each i it checks if there exists a message $m_i \in \{0, ..., R-1\}$ such that $MAC(k_i, m_i) = t_i$. If such messages $m_1, ..., m_n$ exist and $\sum_i m_i = M$ then it outputs 1 else it outputs 0. It also returns 0 if any of t_i is 0.

Security.

The security of the above aggregate protocol hinges on the security of the underlying MAC scheme. Given an adversary A with non negligible advantage in $G_P^{insider}$, we can construct an adversary B that can forge the underlying MAC scheme. The following lemma formalizes this.

THEOREM 3. *Let A be an adversary attacking the authenticated aggregation protocol P_1 defined above and having a running time of t. Then there is an adversary B that attacks the message authentication code MAC_2 such that:*

$$\mathbf{Adv}_{MAC_2}^{uf-cma}(B) \geq (1/n) \cdot \mathbf{Adv}_{P_1}^{insider}(A)$$

Furthermore, B makes at most 1 mac generation query and 1 verification query and has a running time of $O(t + n \cdot R)$. [3]

PROOF. We construct the adversary B that attacks MAC_2 using the adversary A that attacks the aggregation protocol P_1. Here is the description of this adversary.

Algorithm B
1. $H \leftarrow [n]$
2. Pick session keys $k_1, ..., k_n$ randomly from the keyspace.
3. Run A
4.   When A asks for session keys for indices in the set $\mathcal{U}$:
5.   return keys $k_{i_1}, ..., k_{i_{|\mathcal{U}|}}$ to A
6.   Let $H = [n] \backslash \mathcal{U}$.
7.   When A asks to reveal tags, i.e., it sends a query $(m_1, S_{i_1}), ..., (m_k, S_{i_k})$:
8.   Pick an index j randomly from the set H.
9.   For each i_r, if $i_r \neq j$, then
            return tag $MAC_2(k_{i_r}, M_r)$ for message m_r.
        else
            make a call to the MAC_2 generation oracle
            for B and use the response of the oracle as
            a tag for message m_r.
10. Suppose A halts and returns $(M, (t_1, ..., t_n))$:
11. For all $i \neq j$, find the message $m_i' \in [0, R-1]$ such that $MAC_2(k_i, m_i') = t_i$.
12. If the above messages are found:
    B sends $((M - \sum_{i \neq j} m_i'), t_j)$ to the
    verification oracle.
    else B sends $(\bot, \bot)$ to the verification oracle.

The analysis of the adversary B that attacks MAC_2 is simple. B executes A. We will assume that A queries tags of chosen messages for *all* the nodes. We can do this since if there is an adversary that makes tag queries for only a subset of nodes, then there is another adversary with higher chance of success that makes tag queries for all nodes. Consider a run of the game G_{P_1} with adversary A in which A wins. Let the set of honest nodes be H and A's final output be $(M, (t_1, ..., t_n))$. Since $\mathsf{Verify}(M, (t_1, ..., t_n)) = 1$, there exist $(m_1', ..., m_n')$ such that $\sum_{i=1}^n m_i' = M$ and for each i, $m_i' \in \{0, ..., R-1\}$ and $t_i = MAC_2(k_i, m_i')$. Let $M_h' = \sum_{i \in H} m_i'$. Since $M_h' \neq M_h$, there exists $p \in H$ such that $m_p \neq m_p'$ where m_p is the message in the tag query for the node p. Conditioned on the success of A's attack, we note that B's attack succeeds if the randomly chosen index j in line (8) is equal to p. The probability that this occurs is at least $(1/n)$. This gives the statement of the theorem. $\square$

3.1.2 Aggregate (XOR) tags, do not aggregate messages

Here we give another protocol that is insider secure but the congestion is linear in the number of nodes in the network. It differs from our protocol in the previous section in that here the length of the aggregate tag is small, whereas the messages are sent without aggregation. Again, we define the the four functions of Section 2.1. Let us call this protocol P_2.

---

[3]The security definitions for message authentication codes above is standard. The reader is requested to refer to notes by Mihir Bellare and Philip Rogaway [1] for this.

- Let $MAC_1 : \mathcal{K}_1 \times \mathcal{S} \to \mathcal{K}_2$ and $H : \mathcal{K}_2 \times [0, \ldots, R-1] \to \{0,1\}^m$ be two message authentication code (MAC) algorithms.

- Setup: The node S_i (and the verifier) applies MAC_1 at K_i and sid to compute the session key k_i.

- GenerateTag: The node S_i uses the message authentication code H to generate the tag $\sigma_i = H_{k_i}(m_i)$. The tag space is $\mathcal{T} = \{0,1\}^m$.

- AggregateTag: Here we define the combination operator $\oplus$ that operates on elements of $\mathcal{T}$. Given $\sigma_1 \in \{0,1\}^m$ and $\sigma_2 \in \{0,1\}^m$, then $\sigma = \sigma_1 \oplus \sigma_2$ is just the bitwise XOR of σ_1 and σ_2.

One can easily verify that $(\oplus, \mathcal{T})$ is a group and finding inverse of any element is simple.

- Verify: The verifier receives the pair (M, Δ), where M in this case is a tuple of messages $M = (m_1, \ldots, m_n)$ and $\Delta \in \{0,1\}^m$. The Verify function is defined in the following manner: Check if $H_{k_1}(m_1) \oplus \ldots \oplus H_{k_n}(m_n) = \Delta$ and $\forall i, 0 \leq m_i \leq R-1$. If both conditions are satisfied, then output 1 else output 0.

Security.

As with the protocol discussed earlier, the security of this protocol hinges on the security of the underlying MAC scheme. Given an adversary A with non negligible advantage in $G_{P_2}^{insider}$, we can construct an adversary B that can forge the underlying MAC scheme, H. The following lemma formalizes this.

THEOREM 4. *Let A be an adversary attacking the authenticated aggregation protocol P_2 defined above and having a running time of t. Then there is an adversary B that attacks the message authentication code H such that:*

$$\mathbf{Adv}_H^{uf-cma}(B) \geq (1/n) \cdot \mathbf{Adv}_{P_2}^{insider}(A)$$

Furthermore, B makes at most 1 mac generation query and 1 verification query and has a running time of $O(n+t)$.

PROOF. As for protocol P_1, we will construct an adversary B that attacks the underlying MAC, H using an adversary A that attacks the protocol P_2. The description of this adversary is very similar to the adversary in the previous subsection.

```
Algorithm B
1.  H ← [n]
2.  Pick session keys k₁, ..., kₙ randomly from the keyspace.
3.  Run A
4.      When A asks for session keys for indices in
           the set U:
5.          return keys k_{i₁}, ..., k_{i_{|U|}} to A
6.          Let H = [n]\U.
7.      When A asks to reveal tags, i.e., it sends a
           query (m₁, S_{i₁}), ..., (m_k, S_{i_k}):
8.          Pick an index j randomly from the set H.
9.          For each i_r, if i_r ≠ j, then
               return tag H_{k_{i_r}}(m_r) for message m_r.
            else
               make a call to the MAC generation oracle
               for B and use the response of the oracle as
               a tag for message m_r.
10. Suppose A halts and returns ((m'₁, ..., m'ₙ), Δ):
11. Compute T = ⊕_{i≠j} H_{k_i}(m'_i) ⊕ Δ
12. B sends (m'_j, T) to the verification oracle.
```

B executes A. We will assume that A queries tags of chosen messages for all the nodes. We can do this since if there is an adversary that makes tag queries for only a subset of nodes, then there is another adversary with higher chance of success that makes tag queries for all nodes. Consider a run of the game $G_{P_2}^{insider}$ with adversary A in which A wins. Let the set of honest nodes be H and A's final output be $((m_1, \ldots, m_n), \Delta)$. Since $\text{Verify}((m_1, \ldots, m_n), \Delta) = 1$, for each i, $m_i \in \{0, \ldots, R-1\}$. Let $M'_h = \sum_{i \in H} m_i$. We have that $\sum_{i=1}^n m_i - M_h$ is either < 0 or $> (n - |H|) \cdot (R-1)$. This implies $M'_h \neq M_h$. Hence there exists $p \in H$ such that $m_p \neq m'_p$ where m_p is the message used in the tag query for node p. Conditioned on the success of A's attack, we note that B's attack succeeds if the randomly chosen index j in line (8) is equal to p. The probability that this occurs is at least $(1/n)$. This gives the statement of the theorem. $\square$

3.2 Congestion lower bound for insider secure protocols

In the previous subsections, we talked about two protocols that are insider secure but there is linear amount of congestion. Here we show that any protocol that is insider secure will necessarily have $\Omega(n)$ congestion.

We will show that if the congestion is less than $(n/2) \cdot \log R$, then there is an adversary that succeeds in attacking the protocol in the sense of Definition 1. The main idea is the following: The verifier receives the aggregate message and an aggregate tag. If the total size of the information that it receives is less than $(n/2) \cdot \log R$, then by simple pigeonhole principle, this means that there are lots of pairs of message tuples $\bar{m} = (m_1, \ldots, m_n)$ and $\bar{m}' = (m'_1, \ldots, m'_n)$ [4] such that the aggregate tag for both these message tuples are the same and the message aggregates for these tuples are also the same. Consider any such pair of tuples. Since the message aggregates are the same, there exists an index $j \in [n]$ such that $m_j > m'_j$. Now, just by knowing the secret key of the jth node and tags of messages $m_1, \ldots, m_{j-1}, m_{j+1}, \ldots, m_n$, an adversary would be able to compute the aggregate tag for the message tuple $(m'_1, \ldots, m'_{j-1}, R-1, m'_{j+1}, \ldots, m'_n)$ without even knowing $m'_1, \ldots, m'_{j-1}, m'_{j+1}, \ldots, m'_n$ (by doing some

---

[4] m_i and m'_i denotes the message of the ith node

simple group operations). Note that the aggregate of this message tuple is just the ((aggregate of $\bar{m}$) - $m'_j + (R-1)$). This is appropriately large for the attack to work. So, an adversary just guesses the index j, $\bar{m}$, and m'_j and mounts an attack. What remains to show is that the probability that this succeeds, is large. This is precisely what we discuss in the remaining section.

THEOREM 5. *Consider any in-network aggregation protocol P. If P is insider secure, then the worst-case congestion of this protocol is $\Omega(n)$.*

PROOF. For the sake of contradiction, assume that the worst case congestion is at most $(\frac{n}{2} \cdot \log R)$. Let $H : \mathcal{K} \times \mathcal{M} \to \mathcal{T}$ be the function that maps the key and message space to the tag space (as specified by the GenerateTag algorithm of P) and $\oplus$ be the aggregation function for tags as specified in AggregateTag. For a fixed value of the session keys $(k_1, ..., k_n)$, consider the mapping f of message tuples to valid (M, Δ) pairs. By valid, it is meant that

$$f(m_1, ..., m_n) = \left(\sum_i m_i, \oplus_i H_{k_i}(m_i) \right)$$

Now since maximum number of bits that the verifier receives is $(n/2) \log R$, the maximum number of distinct (M, Δ) pairs is $R^{n/2}$. Let $f^{-1}(pair)$ denote the set of message tuples that map to $pair$. Let B be the set of bad tuples in the sense that for any tuple $\bar{m} \in B$, $|f^{-1}(f(\bar{m}))| = 1$. Note that $|B| \leq R^{n/2}$. For a randomly chosen message tuple, the probability that it belongs to B is $\leq R^{-n/2}$.

Now conditioned on a message tuple $(m_1, ..., m_n)$ not belonging to B (this happens with probability at least $(1 - R^{-n/2})$), we know that there is another message tuple $(m'_1, .., m'_n)$ such that:

(i) $\sum_i m_i = \sum_i m'_i$

(ii) $\oplus_i H_{k_i}(m_i) = \oplus_i H_{k_i}(m'_i)$

Now because of the first property above we know that there is an index j such that $m'_j < m_j$. We also know that

$$\oplus_{i \neq j} H_{k_i}(m'_i) \oplus H_{k_j}(m'_j) = \oplus_i H_{k_i}(m_i)$$
$$\implies \oplus_{i \neq j} H_{k_i}(m'_i) = \oplus_i H_{k_i}(m_i) \oplus H_{k_j}(m'_j)^{-1}$$
$$\implies \oplus_{i \neq j} H_{k_i}(m'_i) \oplus H_{k_j}(R-1) =$$
$$\oplus_i H_{k_i}(m_i) \oplus H_{k_j}(m'_j)^{-1} \oplus H_{k_j}(R-1) \quad (1)$$

Now given this, we construct the following adversary that attempts to win the game $G_P^{insider}$:

Adversary A

1. Pick j randomly from the set $\{1, ..., n\}$.

2. Pick two distinct messages l_1 and l_2 randomly from $\{0, ..., (R-1)\}$. Let $l_1 < l_2$.

3. Pick $n-1$ messages $m_1, ..., m_{n-1}$ randomly from the set $\{0, ..., (R-1)\}$.

4. Query the procedure RevealKeys with the set $\{S_j\}$ and get back the session key k_j for S_j.

5. Query the procedure RevealTags with input $((m_1, S_1), ..., (m_{j-1}, S_{j-1}),$ $(m_j, S_{j+1}), ..., (m_{n-1}, S_n))$ to obtain tags t_i for every $i \neq j$ and compute the aggregate tag $T = H_{k_j}(l_2) \oplus (\oplus_{i \neq j} t_i)$.

6. Compute $T' = H_{k_j}(l_1)^{-1} \oplus T \oplus H_{k_j}(R-1)$.

7. Output $((\sum_{i=1}^{n-1} m_i + l_2 - l_1 + R - 1), T')$ as an attack for the protocol P

Next, we show that the advantage of the above adversary over the protocol is large.

LEMMA 6. *The following is true for the above adversary A:*

$$\mathbf{Adv}_P^{insider}(A) \geq \frac{1}{n \cdot R} \cdot \left(1 - R^{-n/2} \right)$$
$$\geq \frac{1}{poly(k)}.$$

PROOF. Let $\bar{\alpha} = (\alpha_1, ..., \alpha_n)$ be a randomly chosen message tuple and let $M_{\bar{\alpha}} = \sum_i \alpha_i$ and $\Delta_{\bar{\alpha}} = \oplus_i H_{k_i}(\alpha_i)$. Now if the description size of $(M_{\bar{\alpha}}, \Delta_{\bar{\alpha}})$ is at most $(\frac{n}{2} \cdot \log R)$, then we know that with probability at least $(1 - R^{-n/2})$ there is another tuple of messages $(\beta_1, ..., \beta_n)$ such that for at least one $j \in [n]$, $\beta_j < \alpha_j$. Furthermore, $\sum_i \beta_i = \sum_i \alpha_i$ and $\oplus_i H_{k_i}(\alpha_i) = \oplus_i H_{k_i}(\beta_i)$.

Conditioned on the existence of this tuple, in the case of our adversary, $(m_1, ..., m_{j-1}, l_2, m_j, ..., m_{n-1})$ may be interpreted as $(\alpha_1, ..., \alpha_n)$ above, and l_1 may be interpreted as β_j. Since j and l_1 are chosen randomly, we get that the probability that A gets them correct is at least $\frac{1}{n \cdot R}$. Conditioned on this event happening, we have that the verifier accepts on the input (M, Δ), where

$$M = \left(\sum_{i=1}^{n-1} m_i + l_2 - l_1 + R - 1 \right), \text{and}$$

$$\Delta = \oplus_{i \neq j} H_{k_i}(m_i) \oplus H_{k_j}(l_2) \oplus H_{k_j}(l_1)^{-1} \oplus H_{k_j}(R-1).$$

This is due to equation (1) and that there is only one compromised node and we have

$$M = \sum_{i=1}^{n-1} m_i + l_2 - l_1 + R - 1 > \sum_{i=1}^{n-1} m_i + 1 \cdot (R-1).$$

So, we get that A succeeds with probability at least

$$(1 - R^{-n/2}) \cdot \frac{1}{n \cdot R} \geq \frac{1}{poly(k)}.$$

□

This completes the proof of Theorem 5.

3.3 Security against outsider adversary

The outsider case is similar to the insider case except that here the adversary cannot get access to the session keys of any of the sensor nodes. In terms of the security game, here the adversary does not have access to the **RevealKeys** method and $U = \{\}$. For completeness we give the security game for the outsider case.

Game $G_P^{outsider}$

procedure Initialize
1.   Let $\mathcal{S} = \{S_1, ..., S_n\}$
2. $M_h \leftarrow 0$
3.   Run Setup to fix the session keys $k_1, ..., k_n$

procedure RevealTags$((m_1, S_{i_1}), ..., (m_k, S_{i_k}))$
1.   Generate and return tags $\sigma_1, ..., \sigma_k$ for messages $m_1, ..., m_k$ corresponding to nodes $S_{i_1}, ..., S_{i_k}$.
2. $M_h \leftarrow \sum_{j, S_{i_j} \in \mathcal{S}} m_j$

procedure Finalize(M, Δ)
1.   If (Verify$(M, \Delta) = 1$) and $((M > M_h)$ or $(M < M_h))$ then return true else return false.

3.3.1 An aggregation protocol secure against outsiders

We will now describe an aggregate protocol which is secure against outsider adversaries. The intuition behind the protocol is as follows: Each node shares one long-term key (k_i) with the verifier. The verifier also shares one common key s with all the nodes. A session key is derived from s and the session identifier sid and is the same for all the sensor nodes. The session key is used to aggregate the messages of each node. The protocol is formally defined below. We will call this protocol P_3.

- Let p be a large prime, $H : \mathcal{K}_1 \times \mathcal{S} \to \mathbb{Z}_p$ be a family of pseudorandom functions, and $I : \mathcal{K}_2 \times \mathbb{Z}_p \to \mathbb{Z}_p$ be another such family. Here $\mathcal{K}_1$ is the keyspace of H and $\mathcal{K}_2$ is the keyspace of I. We will assume that the verifier shares the pair of keys (k_i, s) with node S_i. Here $k_i \xleftarrow{\$} \mathcal{K}_1$ and $s \xleftarrow{\$} \mathcal{K}_2$.

- Setup: Each node and the verifier generates common session key k_{sid} by applying the function I on the common shared key s and the session identifier sid (which in this case may be thought of as the aggregation round number). So, $k_{sid} \leftarrow I_s(sid)$.

- GenerateTag: The ith node generates the following tag for its messgae m_i: $\sigma_i \leftarrow m_i \cdot k_{sid} + H_{k_i}(k_{sid})$.

- AggregateTag: The ith node just takes the sum of the all the tags its receives and its own tag.

- Verify: The verifier in this case receives an aggregate message M and an aggregate tag Δ. It checks if

$$\Delta = M \cdot k_{sid} + \sum_i H_{k_i}(k_{sid}).$$

If this check succeeds, it accepts else it rejects.

Security.

For showing that the above protocol is secure from outside adversaries, we will show that an attack on the protocol leads to an attack on the underlying pseudorandom functions. So, as long as we use secure psudorandom functions in our protocol, it will be secure.

For the sake of contradiction, we will start with an adversary that attacks our protocol, i.e,

$$\mathbf{Adv}_{P_3}^{outsider}(A) \geq 1/poly(k).$$

We will assume that the adversary makes **RevealTags** queries for all nodes. This is because if there is an adversary that makes tag queries for only a subset of nodes, then there is another adversary with higher chance of success that makes tag queries for all nodes. The next lemma shows that if any such adversaries exist then there will be an adversary that can compute the value of the session key k_{sid}.

LEMMA 7. *Let A be an adversary for protocol P_3. There is an adversary A' such that A' determines the challenge session key $k_{sid} = I_s(sid)$ with probability at least $\mathbf{Adv}_{P_3}^{outsider}(A)$.*

PROOF. Let (M, Δ) be the forgery by A. Let m_i be the message sent to the ith node in the **RevealTags** query and let y_i be the response (this is the tag for m_i). Given that A succeeds, we have

$$M \neq \Sigma_{i=1}^n m_i.$$

Thus k_{sid} can be determined as follows:

$$\frac{\Delta - \Sigma_{i=1}^n y_i}{M - \Sigma_{i=1}^n m_i} = \frac{k_{sid} \cdot (M - \sum_{i=1}^n m_i)}{M - \sum_{i=1}^n m_i} = k_{sid}$$

$\square$

We will use the following security amplification result from Dodis et. al. [5]. The result says that parallel repetition of pseudorandom functions leads to a stronger psedorandom function.

THEOREM 8   (THEOREM 7, [5]). *If $H : \mathcal{K}_1 \times \mathbb{Z}_p \to \mathbb{Z}_p$ is a secure pseudorandom family of functions then so is $H^n : \mathcal{K}_1^n \times \mathbb{Z}_p \to \mathbb{Z}_p^n$ where*

$$H^n((k_1, k_2...k_n), x) = H_{k_1}(x)|H_{k_2}(x)|...|H_{k_n}(x).^5$$

We use the above result to show that if there is an adversary that attacks P_3, then we can construct an adversary that attacks H^n (in the PRF sense). The next theorem formalizes this.

THEOREM 9. *Let A be an adversary attacking the authenticated aggregation protocol P_3 and having a running time of t. Then there is an adversary B that attacks the pseudorandom function H^n such that:*

$$\mathbf{Adv}_{H^n}^{prf}(B) \geq \mathbf{Adv}_{P_3}^{outsider}(A) - 1/|\mathcal{K}_1|.$$

Furthermore, B makes only one query and has a running time of $O(t)$.

PROOF. We use A to construct an adversary B that distinguishes H^n from a random function f mapping $\mathbb{Z}$ to $\mathbb{Z}_p^n$. We will need the following simple lemma with respect to random functions.

---

[5]here | denotes concatenation.

LEMMA 10. *Let $f : \mathbb{Z}_p \to \mathbb{Z}^n$ be a random function. Consider a variant of game G'_{P_3} in which instead of returning tags $\sigma_i = m_i \cdot k_{sid} + H_{k_i}(k_{sid})$ in the **RevealTags** query, the following tags are returned: $\sigma_i = m_i \cdot k_{sid} + f(k_{sid})[i]$. The probability that A succeeds in computing k_{sid} in such a game $\leq 1/|\mathcal{K}_1|$.*

PROOF. This will be an information theoretic argument. For any fixed value of $m_1, ..., m_n$, and $\sigma_1, ..., \sigma_n$, the distribution

$$(\sigma_1 - m_1 \cdot K)|...|(\sigma_n - m_n \cdot K)$$

for randomly chosen $K \in \mathcal{K}_1$ is a uniform distribution over $\mathbb{Z}_p^n$. This means that for any key $K \in \mathcal{K}_1$, it is as likely to be the challenge session key k_{sid} as any other key. This means that the probability that A can guess the value of the session key is at most $1/|\mathcal{K}_1|$. $\square$

We now give the construction of the adversary B that attacks H^n in the PRF sense.

Algorithm B^g
1. $k_{sid} \leftarrow I_s(sid)$
2. Run A
3.   When A asks to reveal tags, i.e., it sends a
      query $(m_1, S_1), ..., (m_n, S_n)$:
4.   B makes a query to its function oracle g and
         gets back $(y_1, ..., y_n) \leftarrow g(k_{sid})$
5.   Tags $(\sigma_1, ..., \sigma_n)$, where $\sigma_i = m_i \cdot k_{sid} + y_i$
         are returned to A
6. Suppose A halts and returns the key K
7. If $(K = k_{sid})$ then B outputs 1 else B outputs 0.

The analysis of B is simple. When $g = f$ (i.e., random function), then from Lemma 10 we know that

$$\mathbf{Pr}[B^f = 1] \leq 1/|\mathcal{K}_1| \qquad (2)$$

Furthermore, we know that

$$\mathbf{Pr}[B^{H^n} = 1] = \mathbf{Adv}_{P_3}^{outsider}(A) \qquad (3)$$

Finally, combining equations (2) and (3), we get the following:

$$\mathbf{Adv}_{H^n}^{PRF}(B) = |\mathbf{Pr}[B^{H^n} = 1] - \mathbf{Pr}[B^f = 1]|$$
$$\Rightarrow \mathbf{Adv}_{H^n}^{PRF}(B) \geq \mathbf{Adv}_{P_3}^{outsider}(A) - 1/|\mathcal{K}_1|.$$

This concludes the proof of Theorem 9.

4. CONCLUSION

We presented a lower bound of $\Omega(n)$ on congestion in a one-round end-to-end secure in-network aggregation protocol. To prove the lower bound, we formally define an in-network aggregation protocol and a strong security notion to study the security of the protocol against compromised nodes. Our security notion prevents any compromised node from modifying the contributed readings of the honest nodes. We show that for such a strict security notion, we cannot do better in terms of congestion than a trivial protocol which doesn't do any aggregation. The same security notion, though, can be met against a weaker adversary (an adversary that does not compromise nodes) with a better congestion.

In summary, our results can be used to argue that as far as single-round, end-to-end secure in-network aggregation is concerned, the most simple protocols (with linear congestion) are the only solutions. For lower congestion, we have to construct protocols that run in multiple rounds or are not end-to-end.

5. REFERENCES

[1] Mihir Bellare and Philip Rogaway, *Introduction to modern cryptography*, http://cseweb.ucsd.edu/ mihir/cse207/classnotes.html/.

[2] A.C.-F. Chan and C. Castelluccia, *On the (im)possibility of aggregate message authentication codes*, Information Theory, 2008. ISIT 2008. IEEE International Symposium on, july 2008, pp. 235 –239.

[3] Haowen Chan, Adrian Perrig, Bartosz Przydatek, and Dawn Song, *Sia: Secure information aggregation in sensor networks*, J. Comput. Secur. **15** (2007), 69–102.

[4] Haowen Chan, Adrian Perrig, and Dawn Song, *Secure hierarchical in-network aggregation in sensor networks*, Proceedings of the 13th ACM conference on Computer and communications security (New York, NY, USA), CCS '06, ACM, 2006, pp. 278–287.

[5] Yevgeniy Dodis, Russell Impagliazzo, Ragesh Jaiswal, and Valentine Kabanets, *Security amplification for interactive cryptographic primitives*, Lecture Notes in Computer Science, vol. 5444, pp. 128–145, Springer Berlin / Heidelberg, 2009.

[6] W. Du, J. Deng, Y.S. Han, and P.K. Varshney, *A witness-based approach for data fusion assurance in wireless sensor networks*, Global Telecommunications Conference, 2003. GLOBECOM '03. IEEE, vol. 3, 2003, pp. 1435 – 1439 vol.3.

[7] Keith B. Frikken and Joseph A. Dougherty, IV, *An efficient integrity-preserving scheme for hierarchical sensor aggregation*, Proceedings of the first ACM conference on Wireless network security (New York, NY, USA), WiSec '08, ACM, 2008, pp. 68–76.

[8] Lingxuan Hu and David Evans, *Secure aggregation for wireless networks*, In Workshop on Security and Assurance in Ad hoc Networks, IEEE Computer Society, 2003, p. 384.

[9] A. Mahimkar and T.S. Rappaport, *Securedav: a secure data aggregation and verification protocol for sensor networks*, Global Telecommunications Conference, 2004. GLOBECOM '04. IEEE, vol. 4, 2004, pp. 2175 – 2179 Vol.4.

[10] Mark Manulis and Jörg Schwenk, *Security model and framework for information aggregation in sensor networks*, ACM Trans. Sen. Netw. **5** (2009), 13:1–13:28.

[11] Alfred J. Menezes, Paul C. Van Oorschot, Scott A. Vanstone, and R. L. Rivest, *Handbook of applied cryptography*, 1997.

[12] Yi Yang, Xinran Wang, Sencun Zhu, and Guohong Cao, *Sdap: a secure hop-by-hop data aggregation protocol for sensor networks*, Proceedings of the 7th ACM international symposium on Mobile ad hoc networking and computing (New York, NY, USA), MobiHoc '06, ACM, 2006, pp. 356–367.

Author Index